Ivan
Franko
and His
Community

Peter Jacyk Centre

for

Ukrainian Historical Research

Monograph Series

Number eight

UNIVERSITY OF ALBERTA
CANADIAN INSTITUTE
OF UKRAINIAN STUDIES

Ukrainian Research Institute
Harvard University

Ukrainian Studies

Series Editor: Vitaly Chernetsky (University of Kansas)

Ivan Franko
and His
Community

YAROSLAV HRYTSAK

Translated by

MARTA DARIA OLYNYK

Library of Congress Control Number: 2018962515

ISBN 978-1-61811-968-1 (paperback)
ISBN 978-1-61811-969-8 (electronic)

Cover design by Ivan Grave
Book design by Lapiz Digital Services

Published by Canadian Institute of Ukrainian Studies Press, Ukrainian Research Institute
at Harvard University, and Academic Studies Press.

Academic Studies Press
1577 Beacon Street, Brookline, MA 02446
P: (617)782-6290
F: (857)241-3149
press@academicstudiespress.com
www.academicstudiespress.com

Contents

Acknowledgments

This book took many years to write. During that time there emerged a sort of competition between who or what would finish first: either I the book, or it me. In the end a compromise became necessary: instead of Franko's entire biography, the reader would receive only half—a history of his younger years. But even this could not have been achieved without the help of many people and institutions.

The very long list of their names is in the original version of this book, which I wrote in Ukrainian. It was published in Ukraine in 2006 by Krytyka Press with the support from the Harvard Ukrainian Research Institute. Here I would like to thank the persons who helped me with the translation into English. First of all, I express my gratitude to Frank Sysyn, director of the Peter Jacyk Centre for Ukrainian Historical Research (PJC) at the Canadian Institute of Ukrainian Studies, University of Alberta. Without his help and steadfast encouragement this translation would likely never have seen the light of day. I am particularly grateful that it has been published as a volume in the PJC's monograph series. I also thank the Ukrainian Studies Fund, Inc., and its benefactors for supporting this publication.

I am especially beholden to the translator, Marta Daria Olynyk, who not only masterfully transformed it into English but also corrected the mistakes in the Ukrainian original.

I am indebted to those who took care of the book in the process of final editing and publication: Vitaly Chernetsky, editor of the Ukrainian Studies series at Academic Studies Press where it appears, and Oleh Kotsyuba, formerly acquisitions editor for Slavic Studies at Academic Studies Press and now manager of publications at the Harvard Ukrainian Research Institute. Without their energy and persistence in bringing the book to publication it would not have reached its readers. I am also grateful to Marko R. Stech, executive director of the Canadian Institute of Ukrainian Studies Press, for his continuous support of the project. At Academic Studies Press, I am thankful for the care the book was given by Eileen Wolfberg, editorial coordinator, and Ekaterina Yanduganova, acquisitions editor.

A Note on Transliteration

In the main body of the text, personal names and locations are rendered according to a slightly simplified system, following the traditions of English-language common usage, such as rendering the initial *Ia*, *Iu*, and *Ie* as *Ya*, *Yu*, and *Ye* and rendering the *-ii* and *-yi* endings as *-y*. In instances other than place and personal names, as well as in the bibliography and notes, the transliteration from the Cyrillic follows the Library of Congress system (with diacritics and ligatures omitted). In addition, the soft sign is omitted in the body of the text but retained in the notes and bibliography, where it is rendered with a prime.

Abbreviations of Frequently Cited Sources

ZT: Ivan Franko, *Zibrannia tvoriv u piatdesiaty tomakh*. Edited by Ie. P. Kyryliuk et al. Kyiv: Naukova dumka, 1976–86. References to this edition are marked by square brackets enclosing the volume and page(s), e.g., [ZT 19:192]. If a volume consists of several books, the book number will be separated by slash from the volume number, e.g., [ZT 44/1:508–9].

BN WZS: Biblioteka Narodowa w Warszawie, Wydział Zbiorów Specjalnych.

Chaikovs'kyi, *Spohady*: Chaikovs'kyi, Andrii. *Spohady. Lysty. Doslidzhennia*, vol. 3. Lviv: Vyd-vo L'vivs'koho universytetu; NAN Ukrainy; Instytut ukrainoznavstva im. I. Kryp'iakevycha NAN Ukrainy; Nauk. fundatsiia A. Chaikovs'koho, 2002.

DALO: Derzhavnyi arkhiv Lvivs'koi oblasti (State Archive of Lviv Oblast).

HHS: Informationsbüro: Haus-, Hof- und Staatsarchiv, Informationsbüro des k.k. Ministeriums der Äussern, 1960, 1982, 2174, 2262, 3306, 4559 / 70, 1877.

LNV: *Literaturno-naukovyi vistnyk*. Lviv, 1898-1906.

Materialy: Vozniak, Mykhailo, ed. *Materialy dlia kul'turnoi i hromads'koi istorii Zakhidnoi Ukrainy*, vol. 1, *Lystuvannia I. Franka i M. Drahomanova*. Kyiv: Drukarnia Vseukrainskoi Akademii nauk, 1928. [=Vseukrainska Akademiia nauk. Komisiia Zakhidnoi Ukrainy. *Zbirnyk istorychno-filolohichnoho viddilu*.]

Mozaika: Ivan Franko, *Mozaika: Iz tvoriv, shcho ne vviishly do Zibrannia tvoriv u 50 tomakh*. Compiled by Z. T. Franko and M. H. Vasylenko. Lviv: Kameniar, 2001. References to this publication are marked in the text by citations of the given volume and page of the *Mozaika* within square brackets.

TsDAHO Ukrainy: Tsentral'nyi derzhavnyi arkhiv hromads'kykh ob'iednan' Ukrainy (Central State Archive of Civic Associations of Ukraine).

TsDIAL: Tsentral'nyi Derzhavnyi Istorychnyi Arkhiv Ukrainy (Central State Historical Archive of Ukraine), Lviv.

VR IL: Viddil rukopysnykh fondiv i tekstolohii, Instytut literatury im. T. H. Shevchenka Natsional'noi akademii nauk Ukrainy (Department of Manuscript Collections and Textology).

VR LNB: Viddil rukopysiv L'vivs'koi naukovoi biblioteky im. Vasylia Stefanyka NAN Ukrainy (Manuscript Division of the Vasyl Stefanyk Lviv Research Library).

ZNTSh: *Zapysky Naukovoho Tovarystva im. Shevchenka*.

Introduction

The present volume is yet another book about nationalism. However, it differs greatly from other books about the topic, for it is biography by nature and microhistory by genre. Indeed, the genre of microhistory arose from biographies—the life stories of people (peasants, millers, prostitutes, monks, and others) about whom no one would have known, had later researchers not uncovered their life stories in the archives. Still, while the linking of biography and microhistory is not so unusual, the main protagonist of this volume is. Ivan Franko, the hero of this book, was a person of a different caliber. His literary, scientific, and journalistic contributions amount to about 4,000 works. Several of these have been introduced into the curriculum of Ukrainian schools and the canon of Ukrainian literature. They have had massive print runs, both in Ukrainian and in translation. He was famous in his lifetime and glorified after his death; it would be impossible for Ukrainians and their neighbors not to know about him. Figures like Franko deserve great histories like the biographies written about other great authors such as Shakespeare, Voltaire, and Dostoevsky.

Nevertheless, Franko's life can also be told in relation to research about common people. For comparison, we can turn to the hero of one of the most popular microhistories—the French peasant Martin Guerre, or rather the man who pretended to be him.[1] The real Guerre went to war, while for several years an accidental acquaintance of his inserted himself into Guerre's family. Surprisingly, Guerre's parents, relatives, and even his wife claimed not to see through the deception, and who knows how long it would have lasted had not the real Martin Guerre returned from the war.

Franko's life had similarities to the story of Martin Guerre. Franko was, perhaps, the first Ukrainian writer who gave his reader the impression that his heroes were contemporaries: they spoke the same language, discussed the same topics, and reacted in the same manner as Ukrainians or, indeed, Poles, Russians, French, or Germans, of that time. But the world of Franko's heroes had little in common with the actual world contemporary to him. Indeed, critics of his time repeatedly wrote about this. One of them wrote, "The first thing that impresses every reader of his stories is a striking untruth: we hope to see the real world, but we see Franko's world; we hope to see real people, but we see purely Franko's people." In Franko's writings, wrote another, "there is something too fantastic, incommensurate with or even incredible in respect to, the circumstances of Galician life." (For more on this, see chapter 15, "Franko and His Readers.")

Despite what critics wrote, however, contemporary readers believed Franko, just as the false Martin Guerre's new relatives believed him. But while this faith held merely local significance for Guerre's contemporaries, Franko's readers saw in his biography and works a model for creating their own identity. To understand the causes of this mass self-suggestion, we must understand Franko's own story in detail; that is, in the kind of detail that one does not normally see in historical works, where the canvas of the past is often painted with broad brushstrokes.

Therefore, this book examines Franko's life against the background of very small communities: his family, native village, school comrades, the editorial boards of newspapers and journals for which he worked, illegal circles into which he introduced his own propaganda, and other associations. In other words, it attempts to show the interrelations between the individual and society in the creation of modern identities. Franko was born into a region that played a special role in nation-building at the turn of the twentieth century. His native Galicia—an Austrian border province and, over the course of Franko's life (1856–1916), the flashpoint for a fierce struggle between the Habsburgs and the Romanovs—was also the object of particular Ukrainian, Polish, Jewish, and Russian nationalist aspirations. No heavenly portents hinted at the outcome of this contest. Everything was unclear and depended to a great extent upon accidents, as one might expect when it comes to nation-building in borderlands. However, the future geopolitical order of Central and Eastern Europe seemed to depend on the resolution of this contest as it played out in the last third of the nineteenth century.

For anyone interested in the formation of identities in the borderland, biography is an ideal object of research. Franko was an undisputed leader among those who influenced the establishment of a modern Ukrainian identity, as this barely literate, agrarian society was transformed into a literate, industrial one. The difference between these two societies, as Ernest Gellner—one of the most important theorists on nationalism—asserted, is absolutely central to an understanding of the present world.[2] According to Gellner, the appearance of nationalism and modern nations was tightly connected with the newly industrialized world; or, as Benedict Anderson has stated, not without irony, "industrialism was a piece of machinery that demanded the oil of nationalism to function."[3] The history of Austrian Galicia in Franko's time both confirms and undermines Arnold's thesis about the connection between nationalism and modernity. It confirms it because until the mid-nineteenth century—the time of Franko's birth and the beginnings of large-scale modernization—the number of people who thought of themselves as Ukrainians could be counted in the hundreds, if not merely in the dozens. By the time of his death the number had grown so large that it was acceptable to talk about the "Ukrainian conquest of Galicia." Yet, the success of the Ukrainian nation-building project under-mines Gellner's formula, because in this region, only lightly touched by industrialization, nation-building should have been weak, or not occurred at all. However, it did occur—and it was quite strong.[4] Because Franko's biography spans the time of these changes, the study of his life brings us to the very core of the debates about the circumstances of the appearance and development of modern nations.

It is important to note that this story takes us to the halfway point of Franko's life, when he was thirty years old. This cutoff is motivated by several considerations. The first is rather technical: a microhistory is a pains-taking type of investigation, requiring a lot of time. The writing of Franko's whole biography in this genre would have meant several more years before the publication of this book, and the book itself would have been trans-formed into a *Grossbuch*, which might have frightened off readers.

The second consideration is academic in nature. One of the greatest temptations in historical writing is teleology—the reduction of diverse var-iants of the development of events to the single one that became reality. In this case, this would mean writing a biography of Franko exclusively as a national leader who intended to transform a peasant society into the modern Ukrainian nation. Indeed, he truly was this person in the last dec-ades of his life; still, at least to the end of his second decade, he did not yet have the intention to write "for peasants and about peasants" and was not even certain about his own Ukrainian-ness. Even after he had undergone a national conversion, he adhered to the principle "not to curse or slander any other '-isms'" for the sake of nationalism (see chapter 9, "A Journal, All We Need Is a Journal!"). Thus, writing about Franko as merely a Ukrainian nationalist would be only as true as Soviet writings about Franko, which portrayed him exclusively as the predecessor of a communist tendency in Ukrainian intellectual history. The young Franko managed to be a socialist, a feminist, and an atheist, as well as a proponent of free love (see chapters 8, "At the Forefront of the Socialist Movement"; 10, "Franko and His World Perception"; 12, "Franko and His Boryslav"; and 13, "Franko and His Women"), and he created his own formulation of Ukrainian-ness, while also reflecting on the Jewish question (see chapter 14, "Franko and His Jews"). Therefore, Franko cannot be understood by reducing his biography to the person he was in his final years. This biography takes a completely opposite approach: as much as possible, it is written as though Franko had suddenly disappeared in his thirtieth year, as if we did not know what would happen to him thereafter.

Finally, the third reason for choosing this endpoint: the appeal of Franko's Ukrainian ideas is based not only upon his creative works, but also upon certain facets of his biography. In particular, his status as a young poet played an important role and justifies the limitation of our story to his younger years.

This consideration, however, begs the question: how long does a poet's youth last? Of course, youth is not merely a biological idea, but also a social concept—its meaning changes along with societal changes. The nineteenth century brought forth the start of a vast demographic transition. From the time of Christ to that of Napoleon, the average life expectancy remained around twenty-five years, but over the next century it grew to forty-five years.[5] In the nineteenth century, a reader would be completely unsurprised to read in a novel about "an old woman of forty-five years"—in those times, people lived shorter lives, and old age came sooner. Franko at age twenty-eight was already considered an "old bachelor," and with the approach of his fiftieth birthday, the younger generation viewed him as a person of advanced age. Researchers of poetic creativity consider that the youth of a poet in the nineteenth century concluded with the attainment of a stable livelihood—when his level of income allowed him to settle down, have a family and a home.[6] With this in mind, it is completely justifiable to conclude the story about the young Franko with his marriage in 1886.

This book is an academic monograph, but my goal has been to present a text that will appeal to a broader readership not limited to scholars.

To accomplish this, wherever possible, I have dispensed with academic jargon. Furthermore, all the scholarly apparatuses such as footnotes, indexes, and tables have been placed in the end section of the book. In the notes, the reader will also find more detailed argumentation of certain theses and specific subjects. Nonspecialists are not obliged to peruse this part unless the details of the research interest them.

A brief discussion about terms: throughout the book they are used in a strictly neutral sense, irrespective of—as far as possible—any ideological framework that might be associated with the term in public discussions. Let us begin, for example, with the word "nationalism," a term heavily weighted ideologically. In this book it is used similarly to other "-isms": socialism, liberalism, conservatism, feminism—that is, as one of a variety of ideologies and modern political movements. Each "-ism" has a tendency to be turned into an "-asm-" (as in "miasma"). Here, however, we are interested not so much in the evolution of the movements associated with the term with all of their vagaries, as we are in its essence. Following Gellner, I invoke nationalism as an ideology and a political movement, the main organizing principle behind the demand that political and ethnic borders should coincide.[7] This definition brings together all available types of nationalism—liberal, integral, state, nonstate, and so on—leaving to propagandists such adjectives as "militant," "liberational," "bloody," and the like.

Another concept used here is "traditional society." Generally speaking, "tradition" covers the whole cultural inheritance that one generation passes on to another. Its existence is the ultimate condition for the functioning of every society. Hence, each society is, to a certain degree, traditional. In this book, however, "traditional society" refers only to the type of society in which tradition is passed from an older to a younger generation directly, through direct personal contact and oral transmission.[8] This definition allows us to avoid unjustified simplifications, such as the frequent broad identification of traditional society with a particular stratum (for example, the peasantry) or with particular concrete material or spiritual manifestations of traditional culture (such as clothing, songs, and the like). According to this proposed definition, it is not only an illiterate peasant who could be traditional, but also a skilled artisan or a nobleman, or a married priest of the Orthodox Church, as long as he has acquired professional knowledge not through a school, gymnasium, or university, but through the teachings of his father or an experienced master, following the principle "do it as I do."[9] By this same logic, traditions can appear and disappear, and be transformed according to new changes and, as long as the means of transmission of knowledge does not change, such a world remains "traditional."

In the juxtaposition of "traditional" and "modern," the main problem lies not with the first term, but with the second. The term "modern" is highly ambivalent. It has both a temporal meaning (modern as something that took place not long ago) and an ideological one (modern as the superior way to organize social life).[10] Most often the two meanings are combined—as, for example, by the proponents of modernization theories. They reduce modernity to a list of concrete criteria, such as the level of urbanization and industrialization of a society, education, social and geographical mobility, the level of political structuring, and so on. Problems emerge, however, when one applies this categorical apparatus to concrete historical investigations. Firstly, in the past there have always been periods that could be read, according to some of these criteria, as more "modern" than later ones (see chapter 2, "The Riddles of His Birth"). Secondly, there are important reasons not to consider these criteria universal. They reflect the concrete, real conditions of particular countries—generally speaking white, Anglo-Saxon, Protestant countries—where modernization brought the most tangible and rapid results. It is not clear how to apply these criteria to societies with cultural and political environments that differ from those of the countries in which the hallmarks of modernization first appeared.[11]

The way out of this impasse is to move away from an emphasis on objective criteria to what is in fact a subjective perception of the phenomenon called change. If the temporal meaning of the term "modern" is significantly older than the modern world (its appearance dates at least to the sixth century CE), then the positive connotation of the term is relatively recent. From its very first appearances, this word was used overwhelmingly in a pejorative sense, to denote something recognizably worse than, and certainly not ideal in comparison to, the "good old days." The scientific and industrial revolutions of the sixteenth to eighteenth centuries fundamentally changed its meaning. During that period, it became clear that while the poetry of Homer and Virgil remained unsurpassed, the modern discoveries of Copernicus and Newton surpassed the knowledge of Archimedes and Ptolemy.[12] Hence, a modern society can be defined in the broadest sense as not simply a society undergoing rapid changes, but as a society that is conscious of these changes,[13] and (this is most important) a society that views them positively. This definition allows us to explain how it is possible for strong, modern political and intellectual movements to appear in traditional societies, which were under the pressure of transformation. The force of these movements reflected the desire for change, which, in the minds of their leaders and followers, would bring improvement in living conditions. The more backward the society was, the more loudly their battle cries sounded, and the higher they raised their flag. Equally, the proposed definition helps us to understand modernization processes as the sum of more or less autonomous components that were not necessarily interrelated. In particular, I consistently distinguish between "modernization" and "modernity" in this volume: modernity means new political, cultural, and intellectual currents, while modernization denotes social and economic development. Corresponding to this distinction, this book understands Galicia as a historical region, where there was a great deal of modernity but little modernization. By analogy, we could say that at the other end of those Ukrainian lands, in industrial Donbas of the turn of the twentieth century, there was plenty of modernization but only a little modernity.[14]

One could go a step further and present the "traditional–modern society" binary opposition not necessarily as a dichotomy, but as a certain symbiosis, or even as a synthesis. The modern world is best imagined as a palimpsest, where the traditional structures appear distinctly beneath the surface of modern phenomena. This book proposes a perspective that is not so popular in the social sciences and humanities, but is justified in the case of many countries of Central and Eastern Europe—the very recognition that alongside modern political structures, social and economic transformations, and new cultural practices, old ("traditional") religious and cultural differences play a very important role. Moreover, there exists a certain "path dependency" between old and new structures, with the understanding that the former limit the number of possible scenarios for the latter's development, or make some of them more likely than others. Nationalism and national identity, credibly, came historically out of a Christian tradition.[15] Still, the question remains: did they spread with the same force in the Western and Eastern Christian worlds? This book's material leads its author to answer, most likely, in the negative. This thesis remains a working hypothesis, not supported by sufficient argumentation, but it helps us to understand important episodes of Franko's biography.

Identification with one group or another means setting borders— borders to which this group of identities is attributed. Almost always, these borders are imagined—not in the sense that they do not really exist, but in that the only real means of their existence is imagination. Correspondingly, they are not prescribed once and forever, but instead are constructed, changed, and dependent on circumstances. To be Ukrainian in the nineteenth century did not necessarily signify the same set of values as it did in the twentieth century. The absolute majority of Franko's compatriots during his youth called themselves Ruthenians *(Rusyns; rusyny* in Ukrainian), and it was in no way predetermined that Ruthenians would turn into Ukrainians. Such a transformation was the goal of only one cultural and sociopolitical group—the so-called Ukrainophiles. Hence, in this book I use three different terms to refer to three different groups: Ruthenians, Ukrainophiles, and Ukrainians. The relationship between these three can be explained briefly as follows: "Ukrainians" were what Ukrainophiles thought Ruthenians had to become. Analogously, one might distinguish between Jews and Israelis or Masurians and Poles. In each case, the Jews had to become Israelis, and the Masurians had to become Poles in order to accord with the intentions of the corresponding contemporary Jewish and Polish nationalists.

Identities, more often than not, signify a projection of imagined groups onto a certain historical space. The borders upon which this imagining took place were the object of desire of various national and imperial projects. As a result, the majority of regional names and national fatherlands that are employed in this book—Rus, Russia, Poland, Ukraine—were not neutral geographic concepts, and it is not possible to establish them *a priori*. Rather, they are the result of the situational interaction of various actors, and only through this interaction is it possible to define them. Such an approach is becoming widespread in the most recent investigations of the history of national movements in Central and Eastern Europe.[16] The author agrees with this approach and strives to employ it with a few significant amendments. First, researchers of nationalism are often accused (and justifiably so) of having a narrow investigative framework: they fail to place national identities within a broader spectrum of all possible forms of group identification—professional, gender, ideological, religious, and the like.[17] Franko's biography is a convincing example of the falsity of this narrow focus. In the historical theater of Central and Eastern Europe, nationalism was not the only drama. Franko's identity was the result, first of all, of the interaction of various modern political ideologies, among which nationalism was an important one, but not the only one. Thus, the first amendment to this approach adds the requirement for a maximal possible widening of the circle of actors involved.

A second amendment is that the drama itself developed to a great extent on an old stage with old decorations. Therefore, the number of actors that could have influenced Franko's choice cannot be limited to modern ones—bureaucrats, socialists, liberals, conservatives, nationalists, and the like. At least until the First World War, traditional society provided the decorations and the actors. It is important to see how the inclusion of traditional actors (in the first case, peasants and Jews) in the world of modern politics influenced the change of the very field and the rules of play.

The third amendment relates to the very means of investigating this drama. Most importantly, especially after the so-called linguistic turn in historical scholarship, one must analyze the scenario itself—in other words, one must render a discursive analysis. The value of such analysis cannot be denied. Investigations that begin and end with this type of analysis are, however, problematic. Though they are interesting, they create the impression of going through revolving doors but still ending up back where one started.[18] The scenario or script is not the whole of the drama. The very play of the actors and their interaction with the viewers are also important. Franko was precisely one of those authors who actively created new discourses with his texts. However, analysis of the social reception of his works shows that even the most provocative and widely discussed texts had influence only within a small circle of people. Therefore, to ascertain the causes of Franko's popularity—and its limits—we are required to move beyond the discursive fields and to analyze the structures of the life of people who did not have a voice in these discussions, either through illiteracy or indifference.

In any case, the writing of a biography requires one to consider a variety of contexts, and therefore anticipates interdisciplinarity. This book was written at the intersection of history, literature, sociology, and ethnography. Of all these disciplines, I can claim a degree of expertise only in history. In the others, I have been, and remain, a dilettante. The experienced reader will easily tease out the sum of these techniques and methodologies, whether applied with expertise or as a dilettante. Here, I will dwell only on the one that had the most influence upon the general design of the investigation: the theory of fields, advanced by the French social scientist Pierre Bourdieu. Bourdieu introduces the concept of a field of play (*jeu*), the rules of which are not completely clear or codified. The main thing in this play are the stakes (*enjeux*), which mostly arise during competition among the players. The players agree that the game is worth playing and invest their energies in it. Trump cards also exist (economic, social, cultural, and symbolic capital, for instance), the value and hierarchy of which can change in the process of the game itself. In an empirical study, one must determine what the field of the game is, where its boundaries lie, and what types of capital are involved. It is most difficult to determine the borders of the field itself, since they themselves are both the object and the stakes of the game. Game participants—economic firms, fashion designers, writers—constantly strive to distinguish themselves from their closest competitors and to establish their own monopoly over a certain section of the field.[19]

Bourdieu proposes the metaphor and images of a card game (bets, trump cards). In the case of mass political movements, I think it more relevant to compare them with a game in which there are more players, as well as fans, many of whom, although not playing, consider the course of events essentially important for themselves. Soccer is such a game. In developing this metaphor, one could think of the main intrigue of the book as follows: with the downfall of the old regime on the European continent in the nineteenth century, a great tournament began among various ethnic, religious, social, and other groups for the right to enter the twentieth century. Events unfolded in such a way that in Franko's time Galicia became the field where one of the semifinal matches was held. In order to win, one of the outsiders—the Ukrainophile intelligentsia—attempted to master the rules and techniques of the game, to accumulate social and symbolic capital, and to transform the passive inhabitants of their province into a mass group of supporters. All these efforts could have been in vain, however, if the team did not have a good forward, one who could score goals. This history is a story about how Franko became that forward—thanks to circumstances that require separate explanation and are impossible to understand without comprehending the logic of the game itself.

Finally, I will briefly describe the state of another field in which this book aspires to position itself: Franko Studies. The study of the life and creative work of Ivan Franko has a long history and established traditions. The first studies of Franko appeared during his lifetime.[20] The richness of Franko's legacy, combined with relatively well-preserved archives and enduring research traditions, have created a unique situation, one about which the biographers of not every well-known person can boast: in the current state of research, the life of Franko can be noted down all the way to its daily details.

The paradox is that, despite such detailed knowledge, there is still no satisfactory academic biography of Franko. In part, this can be explained by political circumstances. Even during his lifetime, and still more after his death, Franko became the object of struggles between various political currents, each of which strove to establish a monopolistic right to him as its ideological progenitor. Therefore, Franko's life and activities were often described in accordance with ideological schemes that allowed for the deliberate silencing or distortion of certain facts. The most distinguished in this regard was Soviet scholarship, which, in the apt words of Yevhen Sverstiuk, wrote biographies with an apparent obligation to show their heroes' "usefulness for state service."[21] This tendency has remained alive, even after the fall of communism, when Franko Studies has been formally liberated from political pressure and nothing limits researchers' freedom, at least, in principle.

Another obstacle is the general attitude that the pursuit of new facts excludes broad conclusions. This was such a noticeable phenomenon that society paid attention to it and began—mostly in interwar Galician newspapers—a campaign against historians who write about "what" and not about "why."[22] In the overall hierarchy of scholarly values, I place the discovery of new ways of thinking about already known facts above the gathering of new facts. Among the works on Ivan Franko that take this approach, this book is not the first and, of course, will not be the last. Over the past decade, several first-class studies have been published, which are opening the field for new interpretations of his life and creative work. Some of these have appeared outside of Franko Studies, but any serious biography of Ivan Franko must also take into account these studies' results and conclusions. After their publication, to write about Franko has become, if not easier, at least much more interesting than it was at the beginning of the 1990s.[23]

This biography of Franko is also the culmination of my almost twenty years of research. In 1990, I published a small book as a first attempt at a new biography of Franko.[24] Over the twenty-eight years that have since passed, our knowledge about Franko has significantly broadened. However, this has only made it more possible to clearly realize how much we still do not know or understand. Therefore, my credo remains in harmony with the Latin proverb with which I concluded the introduction to that earlier work: "I did what I could; let whoever can do better."

PART 1
Franko and His Times

Chapter 1

Austrian Galicia: Movement without Changes, Changes without Movement

There are places on the world map where a person loses out immediately just by virtue of being born there. In the nineteenth century, Austrian Galicia seemed to be one of those places. The first priority for a Galician who desired wealth and fame, or simply a peaceful and reasonably comfortable life for himself and his family, was to leave. If the Galician forefathers of Karl Marx and Sigmund Freud—to use just these two examples—had remained forever in this land, the world would scarcely have heard about their brilliant heirs.[1]

Galicia was one of those Eastern European lands where neither a large expanse of territory[2] nor natural resources were transformed into social wealth. The largest territory in the Austrian part of the Habsburg monarchy was also the most disadvantaged: in 1880 only 9.2 percent of its industrial enterprises were located on 26.1 percent of its territory, with 26.9 percent of its population.[3] In the late nineteenth century only 8 out of 1,000 people earned a yearly income of 600 guldens or more (compared to 28 people in Bohemia and 99 in Lower Austria).[4] The majority of Galicia's population (nearly 80 percent) earned a living from extensive and low-yield farming, arguably one of the highest percentages in all of Europe. Galicia also lagged in terms of the two most important indicators of civilizational development: mortality (36.4 percent in 1882) and illiteracy (76.8 percent in 1880); this dubious renown was shared with neighboring Bukovyna and the Balkan lands of the Austro-Hungarian Empire).[5]

In 1888 the Polish economist and industrialist Stanisław Szczepanowski published a book whose title, *Galician Misery in Figures*, served as Galicia's calling card throughout Europe. He calculated that the average Galician earned one-quarter of what a European did but consumed one-half.[6] Besides "Galician misery," other expressions also gained currency: "Galician elections," a symbol of political corruption and governmental abuses; "Ternopil-style morality" (Ternopil being a large Galician town),[7] a euphemism for fraud; and "Galician count," a synonym for an impostor. The expression *ein typischer Galizianer* (a typical Galician) was perhaps the most grievous insult that a Western European Jew could fling at an Eastern European Jew: it was believed that Galician Jews were dirty, poorly educated, and overbearing.[8] In the eyes of Vienna and the educated German-speaking public, Galicia was "semi-Asiatic," a "land of bears," and an "Austrian Siberia."[9]

Yet, Galicia was a symbol of backwardness not just for the West but also for the East. Ukrainian socialists in the Russian Empire railed at "Galician barbarism, or, in other words, the civilization that was formed in the homes of Polish footmen and in priests' kitchens."[10] A Pole in Vilnius or Warsaw viewed his Galician fellow nationals—"Galileuszy"—as backward compared to the Poles who lived in Russia or Prussia, and thus deserving of contempt.[11] The intellectual guru of Warsaw Positivism, Aleksander Świętochowski, wrote: "This Galicia of ours is a kind of fatal cliff in the ocean of civilization, against which all its ships smash and on which only birds of prey build their nests."[12]

In the eyes of critics from the West and the East, the embodiment of Galicia's civilizational backwardness was each of the main local socioethnic groups: land-poor and for the most part illiterate Ruthenian-Ukrainian and Polish peasants; equally impoverished and religiously steadfast Galician Jews; Eastern- and Western-rite clergy (Greek Catholic and Roman Catholic, respectively); the petty gentry; and wealthy Polish landowners. Responsibility for the dire state of the province was placed mainly on the latter. The lion's share of economic power and, from the latter third of the nineteenth century, political power, was concentrated in their hands to such an extent that Galicia was called the great "grange of the Polish nobility." In the late 1880s the total area of land in the possession of one great landowner equaled approximately one hundred small farmsteads, and his vote in elections to the parliaments—both the territorial one (*Galicyjsky sejm*) and the imperial parliament (*Reichsrat*)—was worth 180 peasant votes.[13] Vienna sought to undercut the domination of the Polish aristocracy from the very moment that Galicia was annexed to the Habsburg monarchy in 1772. Initially, it abolished the peasants' personal dependence and then, in 1848, the corvée—that is, the right of landowners to freely benefit from peasants' work. However, the aristocracy's other privileges remained in force. The year 1885 saw the formal abolition of the monopoly on manufacturing and selling spirits, the main source of income for landowners and of moral and financial degradation for the rest of Galicians. However, informally this privilege remained in effect until 1910, and the monopoly rights of a landowner to appoint a priest to a parish (right of presentation), possess arms, and hunt and fish remained inviolable until the end of the Habsburg Empire (1918).[14] Politically, Galician landowners were divided into two parties—Western Galician conservatives (*stańczycy*) and Eastern Galician plainsmen (*podolaci*). Malicious tongues claimed that the "plainsmen" were the same as the conservatives, only stupider. The *podolaci* were less amenable to compromises on the rural and Ruthenian questions. For their political slogan, they adopted the words of Kovbasiuk, a Ruthenian peasant delegate to the Galician parliament: "Let it be as it was in the past."[15]

In the age of dynamic socioeconomic and political modernization, the Galician way of life appeared exceptionally anachronistic. It was believed that Austrian Galicia had lost touch with its epoch.[16] It is no surprise that researchers consider it the epitome of a traditional agrarian society.[17] However, it has escaped the attention of many historians that "misery" was not an exclusively Galician feature. Rather, it reflected the state of the entire proto-industrial society of Eastern and Central Europe[18] and, in the broader understanding, of the entire European periphery together with the Balkans, the southern parts of the Apennine and Iberian peninsulas, and Scandinavia. The question of why Austrian Galicia and not Russian-ruled Polissia or Hungarian-ruled Carpathian Ruthenia (present-day Ukraine's Zakarpattia region) came to embody civilizational backwardness requires a separate study.[19] It may be inferred that no other historical region experienced such a dramatic and intensive collision between the forces of modernization and tradition; Galicia's reputation thus became the result of the modernizers' profound exasperation with the vitality of the local traditional world.

Several directions and "small islands" of modernization may be mapped out. The first and earliest one was the so-called "modernization through bureaucratization," in which the main driving force of change was not a banker or an entrepreneur but rather a state functionary.[20] This type of modernization left a vivid mark on Lviv, the capital city and, by definition, a place where administrative bodies and officialdom were concentrated.

Thanks to its status as the capital of the largest Austrian territory, Lviv accumulated a significant portion of state taxes and state investments. The introduction in 1870 of municipal self-government created an opportunity to invest these funds in the development of the city's infrastructure. If, as a criterion of modernity, maximum usage of this infrastructure is applied to the daily needs of urban residents, then in the final decades of the nineteenth century and the early years of the twentieth century Lviv was truly a modern city, perhaps the only modern metropolis in the lands of the former Rzeczpospolita.[21]

One example of industrialization (albeit a very peculiar one with respect to Galician conditions) was the mining industry in Subcarpathia (Prykarpattia). Thanks to this industry, in the early part of the twentieth century Galicia became the third largest oil extraction center in the world.[22] Apart from those "small islands" of modernization, Austrian Galicia was slowly but surely becoming exposed to the pressure of changes that were affecting the way of life of all social strata and people of all confessions. The advent of railways led to the mass importation of goods from the central and industrially developed provinces. These goods were of better quality and, what is most important, cheaper than local products. This led, among other things, to the appearance of previously unseen furniture, fashionable clothing, and new food products (e.g., rice, tea, and coffee) in the homes of landowners and bureaucrats as well as of the families of priests, peasants, and even Jews. Consumerist moods were intensified by the gradual but continuous rise in the education level of the local population; needs were growing not only in the quantitative dimension but also the qualitative one—that is, they were becoming more diversified. In the final decades of the nineteenth century these factors also included the mass labor emigration of peasants, primarily to North America. Many of them sent their wages home, which signified the appearance of free money in natural peasant households; others came back home enriched by new habits, needs, and a new world perception.[23]

Taking place together with the importation of goods and money was the introduction of new ideas and new words: nihilism, materialism, assimilation, socialism, nationalism, liberalism, antisemitism, and decadence.[24] These ideas had ample room in which to become enrooted, thanks to the emergence in the latter third of the nineteenth century of a well-developed public space with its numerous civic institutions, cultural centers, publishing houses, libraries, and reading rooms located in cities as well as in villages.[25]

The growth of public space was the result of political reforms that Austria's military defeats in Italy (1859) and Prussia (1866) had compelled the imperial center to adopt in order to restore its authority. Vienna was forced to expand its citizens' rights. The logic of changes that were introduced in the Russian Empire after its defeat in the Crimean War was similar. However, in Russia the rise of national and revolutionary movements forced the government to scale back its liberal reforms, while in the Habsburg monarchy this reform process never ceased. The landmark changes here were the transformation of the centralized Austrian monarchy into the dual Austria-Hungary (1867), the granting of political autonomy to the territories (1869), and the introduction of general enfranchisement (1905). The political and economic dominance of the landed aristocracy was tottering under the pressure of socialist and nationalist movements. In the final decades of the nineteenth century and the early part of the twentieth century, Galicia was witness to the birth of mass politics complete with political parties, street demonstrations, and acute electoral struggle.[26]

The scale of changes is most noticeable in terms of demographic development, which in the nineteenth century was the sine qua non of socioeconomic transformation. The population of Galicia under Habsburg rule was constantly growing: from 3.3 million in 1785 to 7.9 million in 1910. However, the quantitative turning point occurred in the mid-nineteenth century: whereas between 1785 and 1851 the population grew by 39 percent, between 1851 and 1910 this indicator had already reached 72 percent.[27] This growth was primarily the result of the gradual retreat into the past of Malthusian mechanisms of control over the size of the population: epidemics and famines. The last great period of natural catastrophes—the so-called "difficult years" (the 1840s and 1850s)—which were marked by poor harvests and a cholera epidemic,[28] may be considered a kind of watershed in the history of this land. Although there was still disease and hunger in subsequent years, these events no longer had such painful consequences.[29] The very structure of reproducing the population was changing as a result of the switch from high to low indicators of population replenishment (births and deaths). The main source of growth was becoming the reduction in mortality, thanks to improved sanitary conditions and nutrition and the spread of education, changes that are usually called civilizational.[30]

The demographic boom, combined with the spread of consumerist moods, was leading to inevitable changes in agriculture. The disproportion between the population and its needs, on the one hand, and the possibility of satisfying them, on the other, was chipping away at the old method of extensive farming, forcing it to give way to intensive methods. Historians prefer the term "post-traditional" to describe this new type of rural society, in which tradition coexisted with changes—sometimes competitively, sometimes harmoniously.[31]

One can include the main strata of Galician society during the final decades of the nineteenth century in the camp of "tradition" only with certain reservations, for both the Christian village and the Jewish shtetl were becoming increasingly subject to modernizing influences. It is tempting to accept the theory that the Galicia of the mid-nineteenth century and the Galicia at the turn of the century were two different societies.[32] To many Galicians, the old world appeared to be tottering. In the 1870s and 1880s texts appeared whose authors were writing—some with trepidation, others with joy—about the prospect of the disappearance, within one or two generations, of the main social groups of Galician society: local landowners, Ruthenian peasants, and Galician Jews.[33] Even if these predictions were not correct, they still say much about the state of that society. Torn from their customary ways, masses of Galicians were being forced to master new social roles.

Galicia as a Source of Geopolitical Conflict

Galicians were seeking answers to difficult questions, and geopolitical circumstances were turning those quests into fateful ones for the population of all of Eastern Europe. In the relations between the Austrian / Austro-Hungarian and Russian empires, Galicia acquired particular importance, primarily thanks to its triple borderland status: political, ethnic, and religious. From the perspective of political history, in various periods the lands of Galicia were the borderlands of a number of great states.[34] During the early Middle Ages they formed the western borderland of Kyivan Rus, the northern borderland of the Kingdom of Hungary, and (probably) the eastern borderland of Great Moravia. From the fourteenth century until 1772, Galicia—the "Ruthenian land"—was under Polish crown rule. The borderland status of the Galician lands was interrupted twice: the first time, when it was the heart of the Principality of Galicia during the eleventh to twelfth centuries, and later, in the thirteenth and fourteenth centuries, of the Principality of Galicia-Volhynia, which arose out of the unified western and southern borderlands of Kyivan Rus. The official Austrian name of the land, "Königreich Galizien und Lodomerien," came from the Latin version of the name of the Principality of Galicia-Volhynia. At the peak of its power the rule of the Galician-Volhynian princes reached south to the Black Sea, and for some time they even controlled Kyiv. Local princes intermarried with the Polish and Hungarian kings. Therefore, when the Galician dynasty died out in 1340, Galicia became the object of wars between the former and the latter for the right to rule over it. The victors were the Polish kings.

But the fact that for a short time Galicia belonged to the Hungarian crown of St. Stephen allowed the Habsburgs, as the heirs to this crown, to demand the annexation of Galicia to its domains in 1772. The western part of the Austrian "Kingdom of Galicia and Lodomeria" comprised Little Poland, which was the nucleus of the Kingdom of Poland but never formally a part of the Principality of Galicia-Volhynia. The discrepancy between historical right and the newly established borders was also complicated by the fact that until 1917 Volhynia, the other part of the Principality of Galicia-Volhynia (the mysterious "Lodomeria" in the official title of this land) was under the rule of the Russian emperors after the partitions of the Rzeczpospolita.

For a certain period of time, the fate of the newly annexed lands was uncertain. On the eve of the first partition of Poland (1772), there was a possibility that the country would come under the rule of the Russian Empire. In 1767, Lviv was occupied by Russian troops, and from 1769 there was a Russian garrison permanently stationed in the city. The Russian empress Catherine II opposed Vienna's claims to these lands, believing that because of her title of "autocrat of all Rus lands," she had no less right to them than Empress Maria Theresa of Austria, who initially showed no particular interest in the legacy of the Rzeczpospolita. The interests of the Holy Roman Empire, as the Habsburg monarchy was known at the time, were aimed at the west and the south: the German lands, Italy, and the Balkans. Maria Theresa annexed the future Galicia in the hope that it would be possible to bargain with Frederick II, the king of Prussia, and exchange it for Silesia, which was forfeited in the early part of the eighteenth century. This did not happen. Throughout the entire nineteenth century, however, Habsburg rule over Galicia carried the stigma of temporariness: whenever an international crisis erupted, the specter of Russian reannexation would appear.

The wars with revolutionary France led to a rapprochement among the three monarchies—Austria, Russia, and Prussia—that had participated in the partition of the Rzeczpospolita. During the "Spring of Nations" in 1848–1849, when an anti-Habsburg revolution exploded in Hungary, the Russian tsar Nicholas I provided assistance to the young Franz Josef, and the dispatched troops crossed Galicia. In the second half of the nineteenth century such a situation—the passage of troops of one ally through the territory of another—could not be imagined: even military maneuvers in the adjacent Russian gubernias were taken as a manifestation of hostile intentions. Subsequently, the Habsburgs and the Romanovs managed to normalize their mutual relations, but rather within the framework of a "cold peace" that was characterized by mutual distrust and suspicion.

At the beginning of the twentieth century, Galicia was the second—after the Balkans—source of tensions between Vienna and St. Petersburg. Its problematic geopolitical status was a reverberation of events that had taken place in the Russian Empire. There, the failure of the Polish uprising of 1863–1864 and the wave of anti-Polish repressions stemming from the revolt forced local Polish patriots to move the center of their activities to Austrian Galicia. The relations between the Polish educated classes and Vienna then underwent a clear-cut evolution from conflict to compromise. After a number of anti-Habsburg uprisings took place during the Napoleonic Wars—in 1846 and in the revolution of 1848—in the 1860s the Galician Polish elites declared their loyalty to the Austrian emperor.

The point of reconciliation was the designation of Galicia as an autonomous territory in 1867. Under the conditions of the supremacy of the Polish aristocracy, Galician autonomy automatically meant Polish autonomy. Hereafter, the Poles comprised the majority in the local administrative apparatus, including the highest rungs, and the post of minister of Galicia without portfolio was created in Vienna. In addition, the new Constitution of 1867 guaranteed equal rights to all the officially recognized nations in the empire, in particular the right to use one's native language in schools, state institutions, and public life. In an effort to encourage the empire's subjects to engage in civic activity, the authors of the charter also granted them broad personal freedoms. In these new circumstances, the Polish national movement looked upon Galicia as its "national Piedmont," a territory where, according to the analogy with Italy, the unification of all ethnic Polish lands into a single national state was to commence.[35]

The Ukrainian movement in the Russian Empire imitated these same models. The Russian government perceived Ukrainian nationalism as a "Polish intrigue." As a result, in 1863 and 1876 it issued two special *ukases* that reduced to a minimum the sphere of the public use of the Ukrainian language. These ukases arrested Ukrainian nation building in the Russian Empire for many years; at the same time, they were the reason the center of national life was moved to the "Ukrainian Piedmont" of Austrian Galicia.[36]

The period of autonomy in the history of Galicia (1867–1914) was marked by the founding of Polish and Ukrainian political and cultural organizations, the rise of mass publications in the national language—the burgeoning of everything that was banned or restricted in the Russian Empire. In addition, Galicia's proximity to the Russian territories transformed it into a convenient location for transactions in funds, arms, and the press for Russian revolutionaries. The Russian authorities viewed the events unfolding in Galicia as the malicious nurturing of hostile political movements. Vienna was equally suspicious of the local Russophile movement, in which it perceived Russian perfidy. Tension in the relations between the two empires peaked in the prewar decades. In the atmosphere of mutual suspicion and distrust, St. Petersburg treated even such an innocent matter as the opening of a Ukrainian university in Lviv as a casus belli. It is no wonder, then, that with the onset of the First World War the Russian command chose Galicia as its first target of attack.[37]

The Austro-Russian conflict was exacerbated by the hostility between the local Poles and Ruthenians. Two essential distinctions separated the Ruthenian camp from the Polish one. First of all, the Ruthenians did not have their own aristocracy; therefore, their political influence could not even come close to that wielded by the Galician Poles. Suffice it to say that until the collapse of the Habsburg monarchy, not a single Ruthenian attained a high position in the local administration. Second, in contrast to the Polish elites, educated Ruthenians suffered from a national identity crisis. They were divided into Ukrainophile, Russophile, and Polonophile orientations; the competition among them was an essential part of the history of the national renascence of the Galician Ruthenians in 1830 to 1914.[38] The ultimate victor in this confrontation was the Ukrainian movement. On the eve of the First World War, its political opponents from the Polish national camp were talking about the "Ukrainian conquest" of Galicia and predicting for the Galician Poles the fate of the English in Ireland and the Germans in the Czech lands and Silesia.[39] Consequently, the end of the First World War and the collapse of the Austro-Hungarian Empire marked the beginning of the Polish–Ukrainian War (1918–1919). In 1920, Galicia became one of the main theaters of the Polish–Soviet War, during which the Ukrainian Galician Socialist Republic was established. The Paris Peace Settlement of 1923 decided the fate of this land when it placed it under the control of the restored Polish state.[40]

The example of Galicia as the source of conflicts between opposing imperialisms and nationalisms may serve as an illustration of the enduring historical tendency that related equally to both the eastern borderlands of the Austro-Hungarian Empire and the western borderlands of the Russian Empire and, in a broader sense, to the entire Eurasian space. The geographical particularities of Eurasia—immense territories without clear-cut internal divisions—led to constant debates and confrontation with regard to political and ethnic borders. It has been said that there are few regions in the world where the creation of empires, states, and nations is marked so strongly by ambivalence as here.[41]

Galicia as an Ethnic and Civilizational Borderland

Austrian Galicia was an artificial creation of the Habsburgs, rooted neither in history nor geography. It was not an island or even a peninsula separated from the rest of the world by oceans. That which could be called natural borders—the Vistula, Buh, Prut, and Zbruch rivers—comprised only a small part of its borders. To the south, it was separated from the Pannonian Plain by the Carpathian Mountains—the southern border of Kyivan Rus and of the Principality of Galicia-Volhynia, and later of the Polish Kingdom and the Rzeczpospolita—beyond which stretched the lands of the Crown of St. Stephen. However, these picturesque but low mountains could not serve as a reliable line of defense against invaders. From prehistoric times until the two World Wars, numerous large armies had crossed them. In more peaceful times, traders and smugglers transported their goods over the Carpathian ridges, as well as migrant workers and peasants fleeing hunger.

Historians speak of the existence on the western border of the Principality of Galicia-Volhynia of a belt of unpopulated forestland that served as a natural and stable ethnic boundary between the Western and Eastern Slavs, the later Poles and Ukrainians.[42] The irony is that this line of forests—or at least what remained of it in the nineteenth century—transected the middle of Austrian Galicia. In any case, in the past this forest line could not prevent the mass migration of Poles, Germans, and Jews from the West.

The population of this territory consisted of two larger groups, Poles and Ruthenians (roughly 40–45 percent each), and a Jewish minority (nearly 10–12 percent: see table 1).[43] In the eastern part, Ruthenians (later Ukrainians) comprised a clear majority—65 percent—while the Polish population reached nearly 20 percent and the Jews nearly 10 percent. Ethnic distinctions coincided with social ones. In Eastern Galicia landowners were Poles almost without exception, peasants were mostly Ruthenians, and Jews were the intermediaries between the former and the latter: tavern keepers, traders, and leaseholders. This triangle was supplemented by the figure of a German or German-speaking bureaucrat, who was usually an ethnic Czech.[44] There were also settlements of German colonists scattered throughout Galicia, and Lviv was home to a small Armenian minority that by the nineteenth century had almost completely assimilated into the Polish community.

Of course, the concurrence of ethnic and social distinctions was not absolute. If all of Galicia is considered, not just its eastern part, then peasants comprised the majority of the Polish population. However, they could be regarded as Poles only conditionally: they called themselves "Masurians," and during the Polish uprising of 1846 they took the side of the Habsburg rulers, helping to arrest, and often execute, Polish rebels. There were also many Poles among such urban population groups as tradesmen, merchants, workers, members of the free professions, and bureaucrats. Apart from the peasantry, the Ruthenians included a sizeable stratum comprised of the Greek Catholic clergy. For a lengthy period of time this was the only educated group, which is why the Ruthenians were called a nation of "peasants and priests." This situation began to change in the final decades of the nineteenth century with the appearance of a secular intelligentsia. Burghers formed a small proportion of the Ruthenian population. The fairly sizable petty gentry was a distinctive legacy of the Rzeczpospolita, and in Eastern Galicia many of its members were of Ruthenian background.

The Jewish community quickly became differentiated under the impact of the reforms of the 1860s, which abolished the old feudal restrictions and prohibitions concerning Jews. Most Jews belonged to urban poor, even if they were traders or craftsmen. The upper crust consisted of the families of Orthodox rabbis and Hasidic tzadiks. The wealthier and educated Jews tested out new roles as landowners, entrepreneurs, and members of the free professions. A considerable number of them assimilated into the local German or Polish and, less often, Ruthenian milieus.[45]

Usually, the population was more homogeneous in villages and in the western part of Galicia than in cities and in the eastern part. The most densely settled and diverse part was the territory stretching along the continental trade route from the west to the east through Cracow, Przemysl, and Lviv, all the way to the Austro-Russian border. In medieval and early modern times, this route was the axis around which turned the entire European economic network; during Austrian rule, its Galician branch was transforming into a main trading link connecting the large cities of the Habsburg and Romanov monarchies.[46] Along it huge waves of migrants trekked to Galicia from the west and east. Areas along both sides of this route developed thanks to local human resources. For that reason, the population there was more homogeneous.[47]

There was a much larger Jewish presence in Eastern Galicia: in 1881 Jews comprised 13.4 percent of the population, compared to 8 percent in Western Galicia. In addition, Western Galician Jews were concentrated in counties bordering on the eastern part of Galicia, nearly all of them living in cities, while the Jews of Eastern Galicia were settled in more or less equal proportions in all counties, many living in villages. Another characteristic feature was the predominantly Jewish population in cities in the eastern part of Galicia, for example, Kolomyia or the border city of Brody.[48] The cities and districts of Subcarpathia were the main areas colonized by Germans (the so-called Carpathian Germans). As concerns the autochthonous population, there was a "Mazur colonization of Rus," that is, Eastern Galicia [ZT 44/1:401–3],[49] but there was no Ruthenian colonization of Western Galicia: official statistics indicate the existence in 1881 of several western counties where there lived not a single Ruthenian-speaking Galician and no more than ten Greek Catholics. Meanwhile, in the eastern part, there was not a single county where the number of Polish-speaking Galicians or Roman Catholics was less than a thousand.[50]

Galicia, especially its eastern part, was likened to the Tower of Babel. Until the last third of the nineteenth century the official language was German, knowledge of which was a stepping-stone to a career. In addition, it was considered the language of "high culture," the most suitable one for communication among educated people. In 1869 the official language of the territory became Polish, which began increasingly to penetrate the spheres where German had reigned supreme before. Bureaucrats were required to know a Slavic language in order to communicate with the local population. Therefore, a substantial number of Habsburg functionaries were Czechs, who found it easier to understand the local Poles and Ruthenians. As a result, Galicia "was covered with Czechs, like ants."[51]

Knowledge of French or English was a sign of good manners. With the aid of the French language, particularly in the first decades of Austrian rule, the Polish educated strata shielded themselves from Germanization,[52] while local aristocrats resorted to English whenever they wanted to emphasize their social superiority not only to the German bureaucrat but also to the Polish burgher or petty nobleman. According to the calculations of the Lviv journalist Jan Lam (1838–1886), in addition to the four main languages—German and the three territorial languages (Ruthenian-Ukrainian, Polish, and Yiddish)—Galicians also used linguistic borrowings from twelve other languages: Latin, Romanian, Hungarian, Armenian, French, Czech, Old Church Slavonic, Russian, Italian, English, and even Turkish and Arabic.[53] The local Ruthenian intelligentsia used Russian words whenever there was a need to compensate for the lack of abstract and modern terms in the underdeveloped Ruthenian literary language.[54] This only added to the general confusion. In the 1850s, the son of the famous Ruthenian poet Mykola Ustyianovych asked his father: "Tell me, Dad. What are we really? We think in German, we speak Polish, but how do we write?—in Russian!"[55]

One would think that Galician villages, with their homogeneous Ruthenian-Ukrainian or Polish populations, should have been free of this linguistic mish-mash. However, foreign words were even filtering into the countryside, thanks primarily to soldiers returning from military service who boasted to their fellow villagers about their "tsymbalizatsia" (that is, civilized nature), recounting how they had been summoned to the "befel" (Ger. *Befehl*—order), issued money for "klianigkaity" (Ger. *Kleinigkeit*—trifle), how they had a "roshtok" (Ger. *Rasttag*—day off), how they performed "shalvakh" (Ger. *Schildwache*—sentry duty), and how one "pazdiernik" (Pol.—October) they were served "flaish" with "knokhy" (Ger. *Fleisch mit Knochen*—meat with bones).[56]

Researchers of Galicia as a cultural borderland mostly focus on its linguistic and ethnic wealth. However, they overlook the fact that it was also—and perhaps most of all—a civilizational borderland, if by civilizational limits we mean the divisions among the world's largest religions. Even in medieval times, the border between Poland and Rus played a special role in the divided Europe of that time: this was a border not only between neighboring states but also between Western and Eastern Christianity. In medieval Europe, there were few territories with this kind of structure.[57] The border inscribed these lands in larger religious spaces. One space united Galicia, as well as the neighboring Polish, Czech, and Hungarian lands, with Catholic Europe. Another space led it into the world of Eastern Christianity, whose extreme limits after the fall of the Byzantine Empire moved dynamically eastward and northward together with the territorial expanse of the Grand Duchy of Moscow and the Russian Empire. A feeling of belonging to a huge religious space influenced the identity of the local population. It offered grounds for the population to think about itself in categories that were greater than regional, national, or even imperial identities.

Another consequence of the civilizational borderland was the difference in character and pace of modernization among the various ethnoreligious groups, a factor that merits a separate discussion. Historians of nationalism agree on how important book publishing and the emergence of readers' markets were for the formation of modern identities. The paucity of book production was long a characteristic feature of the Eastern Christian world. The selection of reading matter of an educated Eastern Christian in the sixteenth century was practically the same as three centuries earlier. With its insignificant range, it reproduced the library of an average monastery, sharply contrasting with the rich book production of the Western Christian world.[58] A comparison of the two Christian worlds on the threshold of modern nation building shows that the differences between them were more substantial than a simple disparity in numbers: whereas by the beginning of the seventeenth century nearly 200 million copies of various books had been printed in the West, in the Muscovite tsardom under the most optimal circumstances this indicator could not have exceeded 40,000 to 60,000 copies.[59] In the nineteenth century, the print production situation changed fundamentally. Particularly noteworthy is the dynamic growth of the book and journal market in the Russian Empire during the rule of Alexander II (1855–1881). But even in 1880, Russian book production had not reached the scale that German book publishing had reached before 1848, and in 1870 there were more bookstores in the Netherlands than in the Russian Empire.[60] According to statistics on the number of periodicals per capita in the Russian Empire in 1881, the Russians lagged behind local Swedes, Finns, Germans, and Poles (these statistics did not include Ukrainian and Belarusians, who, because of censorship restrictions, did not have their own national publications, although their educated strata read in Russian).

A considerable part of the responsibility for the backwardness in the publishing industry may be attributed to the Russian government, particularly its harsh censorship policy. However, even in the Austro-Hungarian Empire, where censorship was milder and there were more political freedoms, the publishing activities of the Eastern Christian Ruthenians, Romanians, and Serbs lagged behind the Western Christian Germans, Hungarians, Czechs, Croatians, and Slovenes (this dichotomy was disrupted in the case of the Slovaks, who were closer to the first group[61]; see table 4).

A hindering factor in the development of book printing and a readers' market was the population's low level of literacy. Again, among the Eastern Christian peoples, the literacy level was equally low both in the Russian and Austro-Hungarian empires. In both countries they clearly lagged behind the Protestants, Jews, and Roman Catholics[62] (see tables 2 and 3). In Galicia the number of illiterate people increased going from west to east; the highest level of illiteracy was noted among the Ruthenians. The general tendency was that the larger the proportion of Ruthenians in a certain locale, the higher the level of illiteracy; in certain eastern counties it reached 90 percent.[63]

Differences between Western and Eastern Galicia and between the Polish and Ruthenian populations were also noticeable in the pace of demographic changes. In general, Galician Ruthenians joined the great demographic transformation at a later date; according to many indicators relevant to the traditional approach to population recreation (an extraordinarily low level of unmarried people among the adult population, very high birth and mortality rates), they were closer to the populations of the Balkans, Romania, and the Ukrainian gubernias of the Russian Empire than to Galician Poles.[64]

It is comparatively easy to reveal the "tangible" differences between the Eastern and Western Christian populations on the statistics level. However, it is difficult to explain and conceptualize them.[65] Yet these statistics clearly show the kinds of difficulties that Ruthenian-Ukrainian and other Eastern Christian national patriots encountered during the creation of a modern nation out of poorly educated peasants. Some scholars have confirmed a difference between the Ruthenian and non-Ruthenian population on a level that is no less "tangible" than education or mortality—mentality (this term fits very well here: at the very least, half of all Galician Ruthenians were illiterate and lived in the world of the oral tradition). Based on his twenty-year-long observations, Metropolitan Andrei Sheptytsky, the head of the Ukrainian Greek Catholic Church, wrote the following at the beginning of the twentieth century:

Although it may be difficult to believe this, the mentality of Easterners in general and Ruthenians in particular is "to follow the current." This may be one of the qualities or one of the shortcomings of the race, still too weakly developed and primitive to have its own racial conceptions, practically innate ideas or mentalities, completely individual in their context, entirely different from all others and so widespread among the entire people that among thousands you will not find an individual capable of rising above these ideas; but nevertheless, as I imagine it, this is one of the chief characteristics of peoples that have been formed and developed by the civilizations of the East. There is something passive present in all the forms of these civilizations. Even in their activity the peoples of the East act as a single body, and separate individuals are almost never capable of thinking or acting in a way that is different from that body.[66]

Sheptytsky's words assume even greater importance because they may be qualified as "a witness' testimony against himself": first of all, the head of the Ukrainian Catholic Church treated his flock with sincere sympathy, and second, he traced the Ruthenians' mentality from the ritual practices of the very church that he headed. The thesis about the existence of a separate "Eastern Christian cultural community" is shared by many historians of Eastern Europe. In the nineteenth century, this thesis was most conspicuous among the East Slavic (the later Ukrainian, Belarusian, and Russian) peasants. Their traditional culture was genetically connected with Eastern Christian eschatology. In many respects, it was foreign or even hostile to the modern culture of those East Slavic elites that were experiencing the impact of Westernization.[67] On the mass level, it was manifested in the vitality of the concept of Rus in the imagination of the millions of inhabitants of Central and Eastern Europe—a hazy definition of an East Slavic community whose members used Old Church Slavonic in their church practice, conversed in mutually comprehensible dialects, had a rudimentary historical memory of their common origins, and were conscious of their difference from Western Christians and Jews. Separate national identities began to emerge out of this large space only gradually, submitting to the centripetal influences of important cultural centers, such as Kyiv, Lviv, or Vilnius.[68]

There were several different variants of national identities corresponding to linguistic-cultural similarities and differences: the creation of a single East Slavic nation; the victory of assimilatory projects reinforced by the might of the state (Russian or Polish) apparatus; the consolidation of separate national identities for the larger ethnic groups (Ukrainians, Belarusians, and Russians); or the emergence of mixed identities (for example, a common "Ruthenian" identity for Ukrainians and Belarusians).

On the territory of the immense polyethnic borderlands that comprised the eastern provinces of Austria-Hungary and the western provinces of the Russian Empire, the formation of one nation entailed the destruction of others. This is corroborated, in particular, by the historical experience of the formation of the modern Ukrainian nation, which was simultaneously destroying both the Russian and the Polish national projects.[69] Most researchers overlook the fact that the crucial prerequisite for the formation of modern nations in this region was the destruction of old sacred communities, such as "holy Rus." As an anonymous Ukrainian socialist wrote in 1881, "Besides the three tribes—the Great Russians, Little Russians, Belarusians—there exists a fourth: the all-Ruthenians, something cheerless, a dense stratum that has covered the people's Rus, the national Rus, the tribal Rus."[70]

Like many other borderland regions, Galicia had the special privilege of playing a great role in the articulation of new identities.[71] In opting for one variant or another, it was not a question simply of language or historical memory, the main elements of national identity. The chances for victory of each of the national projects were determined not least of all by the social program that it proposed to the Ruthenian peasantry, the most numerous stratum of the potential nation, in accordance with those new conditions that were formed under the influence of modernizing pressure on the traditional society.

In the final analysis, success would be achieved by the individual who succeeded in overcoming the cultural abyss that separated the mostly semi-literate Eastern Christian population from the secularized and Westernized elite. This was a challenge for those Ruthenian patriots who, in contrast to seekers of an easier and more secure life, did not emigrate but remained in that land—people like Ivan Franko.

Chapter 2

The Riddles of His Birth

Practically every biography of Ivan Franko begins with the fact that he was born into a Ukrainian peasant family on 27 August 1856 in the village of Nahuievychi, in the Sambir district (renamed Drohobych County in 1867).[1] Most of the components of the above statement are subject to various interpretations. It is not that Franko's birth is veiled in secrecy: it is simply that between the date of his birth (1856) and the appearance of his first biographies (the beginning of the twentieth century) lies an abyss between so-called traditional and modern societies.[2] These two societies each have their own cultural codes, and it is sometimes nearly impossible to express traditional concepts by means of contemporary nomenclature: much is lost in translation.

The difference between these two worlds is well illustrated by the Galician-Ruthenian saying, "In the village the stove is the doctor, and the pig is an astronomer." Franko commented on it thus: "The proverb is based on an anecdote about an astronomer who, while spending the night in a peasant's home, saw the latter healing himself by lying with his stomach against the hot stove; and after predicting from the stars that the weather would be nice during the night, ordered his bed to be made outside, although the peasant warned him that 'my pigs are forecasting rain,' and indeed, he was surprised by rain."[3]

If Franko, in the role of a "peasant," had to reply to the "astronomer" about the time and place of his birth, his reply could be approximately the following: "I was born in Sloboda (or on Viitivska Hora),[4] on the summer [feast] of [St.] John, right after the tense years." Such a reply would make sense and would convey some very important highlights of Franko's biography. In order to understand them, one must temporarily reject the astronomer's perspective and switch to the viewpoint of the rural inhabitant of Galician Subcarpathia in 1856.

Between the Village and the City

The "city-village" dichotomy is fundamental to modernization theories. Urban development is treated as the quintessence of the modernizing process, and conversely, the success of the modernizing project is assessed according to how far urbanization has advanced.[5] This opposition between the city and the countryside had little relevance when and where Franko was born. This may be illustrated by the example of such a criterion as population size. In the mid-nineteenth century, this criterion, as the basis for classifying one populated area or another as a city, ranged from 2,000 people in Germany, Austria, France, and Ireland to 20,000 in the Netherlands. The general trend was such that in countries with a traditionally higher level of urbanization this indicator was higher. Until the mid-1850s, agrarian Eastern Europe—just like northern Sweden, Portugal in southwestern Europe, and Serbia in the Balkans—had the lowest level of urbanization, and therefore this criterion was lower there.[6]

Population size was a crucial but inadequate precondition for treating a populated area as a city. For example, near Nahuievychi, the town of Boryslav, which became one of the largest industrial centers of Galicia in the second half of the nineteenth century, with a population of around 10,000–12,000, had the hallmarks of a city, but according to the official nomenclature it was still considered a "village."[7]

Prior to the twentieth century, urbanization cannot be represented as a continuous, ascending movement according to the formula "Up and up and up; On and on and on." It had its highs and lows, which comprised cycles of demographic change and economic development. Extraeconomic factors, such as wars, epidemics, and administrative reforms, also played a role.[8] A particular feature of Eastern European urbanization in the nineteenth century was its weak link with industrialization. Cities developed or emerged, first and foremost, as administrative and trading centers, and rarely as industrial ones. On the other hand, even when peasants were lured to the city by industrial development, they were in no hurry to assimilate into the urban milieu, and thus it was not so much the case of cities "urbanizing" peasants as peasants "ruralizing" cities.[9]

Austrian Galicia was noted for its level of industrialization, which was low even by Central and Eastern European standards. Earlier, some administrative (county) centers did not have municipal rights and privileges, but were simply market settlements, and they were considered cities only because a county court or some other administrative body was located there. Another marker of a city was the numerical strength of the Jewish community: Jews mostly earned a living not from agriculture but from trading and business, and if Jews comprised one-third of the residents of a populated area, then it was considered a city.[10]

However, Galician cities were generally distinguished by their high level of "ruralization." In 1880, the number of rural inhabitants of Drohobych, a city located near Nahuievychi, who were engaged in agriculture stood at 15 percent; in neighboring Stryi 25 percent; and in Sambir as high as 40 percent. Therefore, when speaking about a city, one must specify which part of it is meant: the part that contained stone buildings and a city center paved with sidewalks, or the completely rural-looking suburbs with plots of land and straw-thatched houses.[11]

A consideration of these circumstances provides a better understanding of Nahuievychi's various turning points. At the time of Franko's birth his village was relatively large: in 1850 it had 2,238 residents, almost twice the population of the closest large villages of Popeli (1,307) and Tustanovychi (1,102).[12] In other words, it resembled a city at least in terms of the criterion of numerical strength. The village consisted of three parts: Nyzhni Nahuievychi (1,240 people), Verkhni Nahuievychi (912), and the small hamlet of Sloboda (86), where Franko was actually born. In the seventeenth century, Verkhni Nahuievychi was granted the Magdeburg Law, which was given to cities. It had a reeve—an office that was held for life by a nobleman, just as in large cities. The name of one of the sections of the village—*Bazar*—indicates that there had been permanent marketplaces in this area. Other names—*Valy* and *Vorota*—indicate that access to Nahuievychi had once been protected by fortifications. Documents and various local legends, some of which were recorded by Ivan Franko, also attest to the fact that there was once a fortified castle there. Most likely, Franko's house was located near the castle, traces of which had survived to Franko's day: in the 1870s his stepfather dug up quite a few bricks at the site of the former fortification wall.[13]

In the case of Nahuievychi, several important city-building factors were at work. The first was communication. A city's mission is to connect the population of a certain territory with the surrounding world in order to provide nearby residents with an opportunity to take advantage of all the benefits afforded by the economic specialization of their region.[14] Nahuievychi stood on a beaten track that was part of an old trade route along which the local salt—the main cargo of medieval times—was transported. The village was situated practically in between two historic cities—sixteen kilometers from Drohobych and twenty-four kilometers from Sambir. This is precisely the standard distance between two medieval cities: one day's journey. Peasants from the surrounding villages could make a trip into a city and return home in a day, while burghers or merchants could reach another city by nightfall.[15]

One of the oldest saltworks in all of Subcarpathia was located in Nahuievychi. It may have existed in the times of the Principality of Galicia-Volhynia. As an urbanizing factor, saltworks either intensified industrial-trading activity in ancient towns or led to the founding of new cities. In the case of Nahuievychi, they created a logical chain: freedom of industrial activity was not contemplated beyond the city, and the city was outside Magdeburg Law. Historians believe that Nahuievychi ultimately did not become a city because of opposition from some residents, who objected to the extension of municipal (Magdeburg) rights to the entire village because this would signify the imposition on them of the corvée and other obligations with regard to the reeve. Thus, the authorities were satisfied by the creation of pseudo-Magdeburg Law.[16] By the time the Rzeczpospolita's Ruthenian lands were annexed to the Habsburg monarchy, the local salt industry was in decline, and by 1818 the official excavation of salt-producing sites was completely halted. However, local peasants continued to boil salt illegally for their own needs and to sell it until the Second World War.[17]

At the very moment that the salt-producing industry was going into decline, another type of industry began developing in Nahuievychi: oil extraction. The oil industry became a powerful city-building factor everywhere, and Austrian Galicia was transformed into one of the largest centers of oil extraction in the world.[18] Nahuievychi was known for its oil fields, and by the end of the eighteenth century it had become a center of oil extraction. According to some accounts, a local peasant with the surname of Baitala (first name unknown) discovered a method for distilling oil. However, until the mid-nineteenth century the oil that was extracted and processed here did not command a ready market.[19] Therefore, local oil extraction never turned into large-scale production, and Nahuievychi did not become a city. When the economic situation changed and oil extraction became an extremely lucrative industry, other surrounding villages, like Boryslav, Tustanovychi, and Skhidnytsia, overtook Nahuievychi. Attempts in the 1890s to launch oil extraction in Nahuievychi encountered opposition from the local peasants, who were alarmed by the fate that had befallen the residents of Boryslav: almost everyone lost their lands and became either beggars or oil workers.[20]

In the case of Nahuievychi, neither of the above-mentioned urbanizing factors—geographical advantage or local industries—ever came to fruition. At the time of Franko's birth, memories of Nahuievychi's semiurban status had faded. A geographical description from 1858 lists information about Galicia's most important cities and villages, but Nahuievychi is not even mentioned.[21] The fact that Nahuievychi never became a city was an accident, not the result of "natural" development. What may be regarded as such is the fact that in the 1850s, when Franko was born, a new and unprecedented cycle of urbanization had begun in Galicia and everywhere else in Europe. Proceeding at various rates, it took nearly a whole century— until the mid-1950s—for urbanization to reach the same level in Western and Eastern Europe. In 1910 urban residents of Austrian Galicia comprised 19.8 percent of the population, which corresponded more or less to the urbanization level of most Western countries before the 1850s. One can speak of noteworthy changes only toward the end of the nineteenth century, and even then they concerned such large cities as Lviv and Cracow.[22] Most Galician cities were townlets, which some historians tend to regard as a separate historicocultural type: "This kind of Galician town was still semirural, submerged—and this is important—in the local landscape....That type of local community could not arise without places of public assembly that are offered by a city, but also without contact with the land, its landscape, the local color of the landscape, from which a large and even medium-sized city cuts off its inhabitant."[23]

In Austrian Galicia, the differences between the city and the village did not automatically mean distinctions between modernity and tradition. To a certain extent this concerned even the capital city of Lviv, where during Franko's youth a significant proportion of the population (42.8 percent in 1880)[24] could neither read nor write—that is, it lived in the world of oral tradition, one of the hallmarks of a traditional society.[25] A peasant by birth could move to the city, yet remain within the bounds of the traditional world without radically changing his lifestyle and way of thinking. This hampered social modernization, because the traditional society's resistance to the challenges of the modern world had to be broken not only in villages but also in cities. On the other hand, it changed the character of the modernizing changes, refocusing them from objective processes (of industrialization, almost nonexistent in Galicia, and of urbanization, which was very belated there) to subjective processes: the transformation of mental structures that could be experienced without even leaving the village by virtue of people joining reading rooms, cooperatives, and other rural organizations.

The Son of Peasants?

Ivan Franko was born in a village, but this fact did not make him a peasant.[26] Besides peasants, at least seven other social strata were found in Galician villages: landowners, petty gentry, artisans, Jews, German colonists, state bureaucrats, and priests.[27] The social diversity of the rural world was thoroughly reflected in the folklore that the young Franko collected in Nahuievychi and surrounding areas. Among the depicted characters are members of the nobility (lord, petty noble), officialdom (assignee, reeve, scribe), members of the free professions (lawyer, physician), as well as artisans (blacksmith, shoemaker, painter, miller), priests, Jews, gypsies, rural bandits (*opryshky*: brigands), soldiers, and beggars.[28]

Ivan Franko's father was a blacksmith. Mass consciousness clearly differentiated between a blacksmith and a tiller of the soil. "He who has no plow is not a tiller. He who has no hammer is not a blacksmith," as folk wisdom had it. Another topic that was reflected in proverbs about blacksmiths was their greater financial security. Within a community there could be masters of all trades, who, in a pinch, could perform blacksmithing duties ("And a blacksmith, and a shoemaker, a tailor, and a piper"). But there were specific types of blacksmithing in which no one could supplant the blacksmith—for example, shoeing horses. Only a blacksmith who had completed a special trade school had the right to shoe a horse. ("An ignoramus that shoes horses spoils them.")[29] Franko portrayed his father in many of his works: in one, he mentions that Yakiv—or to be more exact, the principal hero who was endowed with his character traits—had the right to shoe horses [*ZT* 19:192]. In another work he writes that he "served for three years in Drohobych with Moroz, a famous blacksmith and longtime guild master" [*ZT* 22:231].

Thanks to the father's trade, the Franko family was well-to-do.[30] Their property consisted of twenty-four *morgs* (one morg equaled approximately one acre), while the largest land holdings in Nahuievychi rarely reached twenty morgs [*ZT* 44/1:79–80]. The family had several hired servants. The dimensions and appearance of Franko's house indicated the family's affluent status:[31] all those who visited Franko later recalled that it was a large building owned by a wealthy man.[32]

The Franko house was situated in the hamlet of Sloboda, which was founded in 1779 right next to Nahuievychi.[33] The Franko family moved to Sloboda from the neighboring village of Ozymyna in 1824, after buying a house and outbuildings from a local man.[34] Ivan Franko believed that his father's side of the family was descended from Ruthenianized German colonists [*ZT* 31:29], and for that reason he had a "little bit of German" in him [*ZT* 48:370]. This conviction was shared by many of his friends.[35] The recollections of Franko's German background did not fade after his death. Well-wishers associated his German heritage with such traits as free-thinking, punctuality, and his methodical nature, while his detractors pointed out his superior attitude to other Ukrainians and their culture ("That descendant of a German emigrant does not like the Ruthenian race"; he "is not an ordinary Rusyn but a 'höhere deutsche Kultur'!").[36] In one story, Franko writes that his father's great-grandfather was a pure-blooded German, who was brought to Galicia in the early years of Austrian rule [*ZT* 19:193]. If this detail is accepted as confirmation of his German background, then it is very likely that Franko was mistaken at least with regard to the date.[37] Roman Horak, the scrupulous researcher of Franko's genealogy, has confirmed that by the time the Habsburgs began to rule Galicia, Franko's family had already been living there for a long time and considered itself Ruthenian. Birth records for the village of Ozymyna attest to the fact that Teodor (Fed) Franko, Franko's great-grandfather, baptized all his children in a Greek Catholic church, not in a Roman Catholic one, as befitted a German colonist. The Franko family supplied a steady stream of godfathers and godmothers, a clear indication that the members of this family were not cut off from their fellow villagers by religious or cultural barriers.[38]

The Franko surname points to the nonnative origins of his family.[39] The etymology of the Franko surname is not Slavic: it derives from the Latin *Francus*<*Franciscus*, the Roman name for one of the Germanic tribes, which later evolved into "Frantz / Frank,"[40] while the name itself, as often happens, formed the basis of the surname.[41] All the Frankos throughout history (including El Caudillo, as General Francisco Franco of Spain called himself) came from the Roman Catholic space.[42] In Galicia this name was especially common among so-called *latynnyky*—that is, Roman Catholics who had assimilated into the local Ruthenian milieu without abandoning their faith. In adopting the Ruthenian language, they generally did not assume Ruthenian names. Therefore, there were rarely Mykhailos or Ivans among them, but many Frankos, Wojtechs, Cazimirs, and Wladyslaws.[43]

German colonization of Galicia began no earlier than the thirteenth century and continued until the Second World War. Before 1772, the main centers of the German language in Galicia were Lviv and rural Subcarpathia. German colonists usually settled in Galicia in compact groups and lived in considerable isolation from the inhabitants of neighboring villages, creating amid the non-German majority small islands that differed from it not only in terms of language and religion but also in customs. While the German settlers were known as good, hardworking farmers, they were also viewed by their Ruthenian neighbors as lacking in "normal" human traits, such as gaiety, generosity, and hospitality. They called themselves "farmers" or "colonists," but considered the word "peasant" a derogatory term that they applied to Ruthenians and Poles.

At times, mutual alienation led to outbursts of violence. For example, in the vicinity of Drohobych in the 1880s, some German colonists from Neuendorf, armed with cudgels, beat a group of Ruthenian peasants who were going to their houses to sing Christmas carols. However, if the families of the colonists settled among Ruthenian or Polish families, they quickly assimilated, married locals, and adopted their language and customs.[44] So it is not surprising that the Frankos, who comprised a clear minority in Nahuievychi (as they had earlier in Ozymyna) lost all their signs of foreignness, except for their surname. In general, the "medieval" waves of colonization assimilated easily, while the Germans who arrived in Galicia after 1772 often could not assimilate into the Greek Catholic or Roman Catholic milieu because they were Protestants. In addition, they already had a developed network of cultural societies, schools, agricultural associations, and publications—everything that helped them to maintain their German identity.[45]

In any case, the example of Franko's surname contradicts premature conclusions about the purely Ukrainian (Ruthenian) and peasant origins of his family.[46] It was a rural, not peasant, Ruthenian family, but mostly likely not of indigenous background, the product of long-standing assimilation into the Eastern Christian milieu.

The maternal side of Franko's family was not of peasant origin either. It was descended from the Kulchytskys (Kulczyckis), a large, ancient noble family that had produced Yurii Kulchytsky (Jerzy Kulczycki), the hero of the 1683 Siege of Vienna and the founder of one of the first—but not the very first—cafés in Europe.[47] We know much less about Franko's matrilineal family line than about the patrilineal one. Franko's grandfather died before the birth of his grandson. Franko's grandmother was Ludwika Kulczycka from Yasenytsia Silna, a wealthy, widowed noblewoman with six children.[48] The chances of being born into a noble, nonpeasant, family in Galicia were quite high. The Polish Commonwealth was renowned for its excessively high number of nobles, whose proportion of the population hovered between 5 and 10 percent, reaching 16 percent before the partitions (this indicator rarely exceeded 1 or 2 percent in any country). The majority—approximately 75 percent in Austrian Galicia in the mid-nineteenth century—were petty noblemen with little property.[49] The petty nobility was particularly numerous in the Carpathian foothills region, where there were nearly 700 *zahorody*—separate settlements of petty noblemen within the bounds of villages. The main trends in the evolution of this social stratum were economic decline and gradual lowering of class status. Education was frequently an instrument: noble fathers, desiring to ensure a livelihood for their children, provided them with an education, thus paving the way for them to acquire new professions.

However, decline did not signify complete disappearance. As recently as the 1930s, the numerical strength of the Galician nobility stood at nearly half a million people.[50] The local nobility was generally an indigenous one, attested by the surnames of noble families, which were most often linked to the villages where these families resided: Berezhnytsky / Bereżnicki (from Berezhnytsia), Vysochansky / Wysoczański (from Vysotske), Zubrytsky / Zubrycki (from Zubrytsia), Ilnytsky / Ilnicki (from Ilnyk), Korchynsky / Korczyński (from Korchyn), Krushelnytsky / Kruszelnicki (from Krushelnytsia), Chaikovsky / Czajkowski (from Chaikovychi), and so on. Franko's mother's family, the Kulchytskys (Pol. Kulczycki), came from the village of Kulchytsi in the Sambir district. Besides Yurii Kulchytsky, this village was the birthplace of the Ukrainian Cossack hetman, Petro Konashevych-Sahaidachny.[51]

The petty nobility is known by a variety of names: *malozemel´na* (Ukr., owning little land); *chodaczkowa* (the "sandal-nobility," from the Pol. *chodak* (Ukr. *khodak*), the moccasin-style footwear that was frequently worn by poor noblemen); *okoliczna* (local nobility); *zagonowa* (hide nobility); *zagrodowa* (noble smallholders); *zahuminkova* (Ukr., from the word *zahuminok*, meaning "a place beyond the threshing floor"); and *zaściankowa* (neighborhood nobility). Its origins were diverse. Some petty noblemen were the descendants of once-wealthy but now impoverished local (Ruthenian) noble families, while others belonged to the petty Catholic nobility, which, together with the Polish *Drang nach Osten*, had settled in Subcarpathia. Some noble families were descended from peasants who had been granted noble status by Ruthenian and Lithuanian princes and Polish kings for particular services. Others simply purchased this status for themselves or obtained it by legal or nefarious means.[52] The petty nobility enjoyed de jure certain privileges, as well as a nobiliary title that was equivalent to the magnates' ("A nobleman on a farm is the equal of a palatine"). The members of the petty nobility were de facto the clients of wealthy magnates, at whose hands they often endured oppression and abuse. A nobiliary title did not automatically signify wealth: in terms of the size of their properties, the local rural nobility did not differ significantly from the peasantry. In Nahuievychi, there was a proverb about the nobility: "A nobleman says: 'I have three full barns: one contains poppies, the same in the second, and in the third one a mouse got tired out before it found the seed" [*ZT* 26:183].

However, the nobility cultivated the idea that it was distinct from the ordinary peasantry, tracing its origins to the biblical Japheth and those of the peasantry to Ham. At one time this distinction was reflected in terms of the legal status: noblemen did not perform the corvée for a landowner or other obligations. After the abolition of serfdom in 1848, the nobility maintained its otherness through its customs, clothing, and manners at home or in public—even in language: noblemen used Polish words or foreign words borrowed via the Polish language.[53] In Yasenytsia Silna, people recounted the story of a beggar woman named Bachynska (Pol. Baczyńska), who was a widowed noblewoman: she went around begging, covered in rags and tatters. But she did not forgo her noble arrogance. She would enter someone's house, but unlike any other woman, who would say a few words with humility, she would sit down on the bench. And woe betide the housewife who said to her: "What's going on, Mrs. Bachynska?" Well, well, she would give such a tongue-lashing to the housewife that the latter would become totally befuddled. "You, so-and-so! Don't you know who I am? Although I'm dressed in rags, I am a gracious lady!" And never give her, like to another woman, a piece of bread or something—she'll throw it back in your face. But as soon as you place a small dish of some warm food in front of her or put some flour or some kind of grain in her bag, only then will she chat a bit and then leave [*ZT* 26:183].

The difference between the rural nobility and the peasants was particularly revealed in the former's attitude of superiority, or occasionally hostility, to the ordinary peasants. In 1863, the sandal-nobility in Yasenytsia Silna was perturbed by the news of another Polish uprising in the Russian Empire. "Hang on a bit [said one of the Yasenytsia noblemen]. It will not be that quick: the old days will return, once again we will be harnessing peasants for the plowing, peasants and their wives will be harrowing." According to a poem that was making the rounds of the village, the nobility was threatening to take revenge against the peasants for the "Mazurian massacre" of 1846. The last verse of this poem declared: "We will soon be stringing you up by your necks from hooks, and we will light a small lamp for your soul" [ZT 26:182].

It is surprising that Ludwika Kulczycka decided to marry her twenty-year-old daughter Maria to Yakiv Franko, a widowed peasant, who was fifty-three years old. Owing to the difference in their ages and social status, this marriage looked like an obvious "misalliance." As concerns the marriage conduct of the rural nobility, there are two markedly different views. On the basis of his own reminiscences and collected ethnographic materials, Ivan Franko asserted that "there is no division between the nobility and the peasants in matters pertaining to life: peasants marry noblewomen, noblemen (less frequently) marry peasant women" [ZT 26:181]. The opposite view is held by contemporary researchers of the petty nobility: the nobiliary tradition, they claim, strictly forbade marriages with peasant men and women. Such marriages were regarded as a huge disgrace for a nobleman or noblewoman.[54]

The truth lies somewhere in the middle. In general, nobles sought to enter into marriages with each other, and since strict observance of this rule would inevitably require marriages between close relatives, exceptions were permitted but were strictly regulated. This scheme of things is clearly illustrated by the entries recorded in the parish register of Yasenytsia Silna between 1785 and 1855—that is, up to the year in which the marriage between Yakiv Franko and Maria Kulchytska took place. Complete information about the statuses of fiancés and fiancées is listed in 216 entries for these years. In 183 cases these were marriages between peasants; nineteen others were between noblemen and noblewomen. There are only three entries (1830, 1831, and 1845) that record marriages between members of noble and nonnoble families. Out of three noble-peasant marriages, one case concerns the marriage between a nobleman and the daughter of the village reeve; there is no data on the status of the families of the two other peasant women. It may be assumed that there were more cases like this because sometimes the records did not indicate the social status of at least one side. This is precisely the case regarding Yakiv's marriage to Maria: the social status of the fiancée is indicated by the word "noblewoman," yet there is nothing recorded about Yakiv Franko.[55]

The members of the sandal-nobility could marry outside their group, but only with families whose status they considered equal to their own. Equality was not measured in terms of wealth or privileges: among those whose status the nobility considered proximate to its own were people who, thanks to their capabilities, had somehow risen above others. Yakiv Franko was a rich blacksmith, who was known and respected throughout the county; therefore, he was "equal" to the nobility.[56] Obviously, there were enough grounds for Ludwika Kulczycka to select him as her son-in-law.

From the collective portrait of the Ruthenian nobility, researchers single out such traits as staunch individualism, stubbornness, independence, and resistance to external influences.[57] These traits are evident in Franko's character. Those who knew him recalled his spiritual aristocratism, confidence, courage, and sense of self. He seemed to say: "Step aside, here I come." In their opinion, these were the traits of a person that had never experienced the corvée.[58] Franko inherited these traits from his mother. In one of his poems dedicated to her, he wrote that he got his proud soul from her [ZT 2:167].

Many decades after Franko left his birthplace and became famous, members of the local nobility regarded him as "one of them," a nobleman. They felt group pride in his successes and refused to acknowledge him as a "rural poet": "It was the devil who shoved all that stuff into that red head. Eh, if old [Ludwika—Y. H.] would rise up and hear!"[59] There is one more piece of incontrovertible proof of his nonrural origins. After the death of his father (1865) and his mother (1874), the orphaned Ivan, a gifted student, obtained quite a substantial scholarship from the Glowinski Fund,[60] which was awarded to children of the petty nobility; it would never have been given to Franko had he been a peasant.

Franko scholars argue about the nationality of his mother's family. Some claim that the family was Polish, while others note its Ukrainian ("Ruthenian") character.[61] A more detailed study of the history of the Kulczycki / Kulchytsky family militates against easy conclusions. The only thing that may be stated with certainty is that the identity of this family was situational—that is, it depended on circumstances. The members of the Kulchytsky family who remained in the village assimilated into the local Ruthenian milieu. They spoke Ruthenian, sang Ruthenian songs (Franko states this clearly in his reminiscences about his mother), read Ruthenian-Ukrainian publications, became (like Ivan Hvozdetsky, his grandmother's brother) Greek Catholic priests, and the like. The other members of this family identified themselves with the "old" Rzeczpospolita to such an extent that they joined the Polish rebels, like Franko's uncle, Ivan Kulczycki, who died in 1863 at the age of twenty-one, during the Polish uprising against Russia.[62] Other members of the family adopted elements of Polish culture, but without political consequences. Aunt Koszycka, a distant relative of Franko's mother, with whom he lived when he was studying in Drohobych, attended Mass at a Greek Catholic church and a Roman Catholic church, sang Polish and Ruthenian songs, but argued with her husband only in Polish [ZT 21:171–72, 185].

Between the time serfdom was abolished and the First World War, members of the petty nobility filled the ranks of various political and national movements in the Austrian and Russian empires. A certain number identified themselves with Ukrainians. For example, in 1907 the Society of the Ruthenian Nobility in Galicia was founded in Sambir. Its goal was to improve the educational and economic situation of the hide nobility in the region. However, few nobles identified with the Ukrainian nation: the Ukrainian national movement struck them as too "democratic" (peasant), whereas they considered themselves the aristocracy.

Be that as it may, the idea that "Ivan Franko sprang blood and bone, with his ideas and ideals, out of the Ukrainian element" has little in common with real facts. Franko's identity, both social as well as national ("peasant" and "Ukrainian"), was not a product of his surroundings, but of his deliberate choice, which he made after he left Nahuievychi.

Date and Name

The entry in the register recording Franko's birth indicates the date of 27 August 1856. To his school friend Karl Bandrivsky, Franko admitted that in fact he was born two days earlier. He was baptized on 27 August, and this was the date recorded by the priest. It was this date that crept into later official documents and biographies. The confusion around the different dates of his birth is not unusual for a traditional society: until the very end of its existence (roughly the conclusion of the Second World War), the majority of people born in the countryside could only give their approximate age. They did not know the exact day they were born, and often not even the year. This was the case with Franko's father: Yakiv Franko's personal documents list as many as three different birth years—1798, 1802, and 1810. The explanation must be sought in one of the basic elements of the archaic world perception—the supremacy of the concept of cyclical time over linear time. The standard of that period was not the clock or wall calendars, but natural indicators (the sun, stars, change of season, the rooster's crow) or the order of church feast days and fasts. The church calendar was important for marking the time of a person's birth: in the countryside, people celebrated not birthdays but name days, the feast day of one's patron saint. Thus, the date of Franko's baptism is marked as his date of birth.

But this is not the only problem for Franko biographers. In the late 1870s and early 1880s, Franko wrote a series of autobiographical stories in which he depicted himself as a small village boy named Myron [ZT 15: 65–71; 22:35–52]. As is evident from these stories, in the family Franko was called Myron, not Ivan. The custom of giving two names to a child was not uncommon; it had existed in the Eastern Christian tradition since the adoption of Christianity. The names of two different saints were supposed to provide the child with double the protection. However, although the feast day of Myron the Martyr—17 August / 30 August (O.S. / N.S.)—falls very close to the date of Franko's baptism, the entry in the registry of births in Nahuievychi states that Franko was baptized as Ivan, and does not record a second name.[63]

Part of the problem lies in the fact that, according to local tradition, the name Myron was not unusual but not very common. The registry of births in Nahuievychi prior to 1864—that is, the time until which the registry was preserved—contains a notation about only one child that was baptized as Myron: this was the name given in 1844 to the illegitimate son of one Eva Myskyn. In addition, although the choice of this name may have been the result of an understanding between the parents and the priest (who, after receiving a bribe, could have given the illegitimate child a "normal" name, or the reverse: he may have bestowed a rarely used name on a legitimate child if he had quarreled with the parents or not received the expected payment from them),[64] this example illustrates the general rule: a name "marked" a newborn child and indicated its status. The names of the most important Christian saints were given to legitimate children, while illegitimate children were named after lesser known saints. Myron the Martyr was not one of the better known saints, and was thus "designated" for illegitimate children.[65]

How could Franko have acquired this name? There would have been nothing surprising about this had he been an illegitimate child.[66] After all, at the time of Franko's birth pre- and extramarital relations in Galicia were not uncommon. They were forbidden by the church and severely censured by the community, but human nature took its course.[67] Estimates made on the basis of birth registers covering the period from the mid-1840s to the early 1870s show that every tenth to fifteenth child in Nahuievychi was illegitimate. This indicator was significantly higher in large cities: in Lviv's Greek Catholic parishes it hovered between 15 and 45 percent of all children born in this period (see table 7).[68] The idea of Ivan Franko's possible illegitimacy is also suggested by the substantial age difference between his parents—an entire generation: Yakiv Franko was one year older than his deceased father-in-law. There could be various motives behind the practice of marrying off young girls to considerably older husbands, but one of the more frequently encountered was a girl's premarital "despoilment." When Ivan Franko was already a famous writer and social activist, rumors began to circulate in Lviv that he was the illegitimate son of an Orthodox Jew. As proof, gossips pointed to his Judaeophilism and his bright red hair.[69]

Despite the circumstance that the idea of Franko's illegitimacy is bolstered by a few arguments, it should be rejected for several reasons. The first one is biological: Franko was born one year after his parents' marriage, which took place in 1855. After him his two brothers were born, and both of them had the same bright red hair. Second, Franko's reminiscences attest that his father showed him great love and tenderness; that would hardly be the case if Ivan were illegitimate. But even if there were no arguments against his illegitimacy, this supposition must still be rejected because of the presumption of innocence: there is no direct and convincing proof of this idea. The most likely explanation comes from the family's own account: Ivan Franko was named Myron in order to protect him from an early death. Yakiv's first wife and his daughter—the only child of his first marriage—both died. When his first son was born late in his life, he was very frightened of losing him. So the family resorted to a trick that was widespread among Eastern Christians in an attempt to "cheat death": at home, the son was called by a different name than the one recorded in the church register in the belief that when death came to take away the child, it would not be able to find him. The fact that Franko's younger brother Zakhar was called Mykhailo at home may be considered proof that this tradition was alive and well in the Franko home [*ZT* 49:35]. No documented proof of this hypothesis about Ivan Franko has as yet been uncovered. Instead, we have reminiscences pointing to the fact that within the family and in the village he was called by the diminutive pet names of "Ivantsio" and "Ivanchyk" [*ZT* 48:96] or "Yas."[70] These statements do not entirely contradict the "Myron" theory, because they concern Franko at a later age, once the greatest danger of death had passed. But why, then, did the Franko family continue to call Zakhar "Mykhailo" even when he was an adult?[71]

The riddle of Franko's second name will probably never be solved. But what is more important about this story is not so much the motivation of his parents as the decision of the adult Franko to select the name "Myron" as his main literary pseudonym. The choice was a profoundly symbolic one: not ashamed of calling himself by a "bastard's" name, Franko challenged the mores of the traditional society. This was part of his program to modernize Galicia in keeping with the views that he formed after leaving the village—that is, when he stopped thinking like a "peasant" and became an "astronomer."

Chapter 3

Early Childhood

Of all the periods in his life that he described in his reminiscences or auto-biographical works, Franko wrote most frequently about his childhood. He created his very own version of this early period of his life, which numerous Franko specialists later canonized. The first striking thing is the explicit idealization of rural life: Franko never neglected any opportunity to emphasize the superiority of rural relationships and peasant characters over the city and urbanites; he claimed that, in many respects, his childhood years were the happiest, compared to the material hardship and moral rot among which poor children grow up in cities [*Mozaika* 338;[1] *ZT* 39:229].

Partially at work here is the natural tendency of adults to regard their childhood as the happiest time of their lives. However, in Franko's case the influence of his early years on his political and aesthetic views is irrefutable. In depicting his childhood, Franko made use of several ready models; in particular, the model of the "rural poet."[2]

One should also take into account the general context. The civilizational changes of the second half of the nineteenth century were leading to the destruction of traditional society and, accordingly, sparking nostalgia for the disappearing world of the rural idyll. One attempt to preserve that which was being shattered by modernization was the emergence of an entire literary subgenre known as *Dorfgeschichten* (rural stories with a special subgenre called *Gettogeschichten*). This genre was especially popular in modern Ukrainian literature, with its fascination with the language, folklore, and daily life of the village as the chief markers of national life.[3] Franko is associated with the beginnings of a brand new trend—not the idealization of rural life, but the depiction of the oppression, suffering, and other miseries that are part and parcel of the peasants' lot.[4] As it turns out, however, despite the general critical attitude to the idealized depiction of the countryside, Franko is not free of this at least in two cases: when he writes about the poorest, proletarianized peasantry[5] and about his childhood.

It would be unjust, and even naïve, to accuse Franko of deliberately distorting facts. Like any writer, he had the right to *licentia poetica*. To Franko's credit, from time to time he stopped those of his biographers who ventured, in uncritical fashion, to write the history of his childhood based entirely on his literary works [ZT 39:38, 227–31]. However, anyone who undertakes the task of writing about his earliest years must not only have faith in Franko, but must also verify his statements carefully.

Life amidst Nature

Some of the key moments in Franko's accounts of his childhood are the descriptions of the verdant nature in Nahuievychi and its surroundings. Nahuievychi is located in a picturesque valley ringed by the high ridge called Dil. In Franko's imagination, Dil united the terrestrial world and the heavenly world [ZT 22:41]. The village houses on one side of the river seemed to be engulfed in pear and apple orchards, while on the other side the little houses resembled bouquets of flowers scattered on the grass [ZT 22:209]. The surrounding forests, where Franko loved to wander as a small child, were "his church." They awakened in him "those vague feelings, from which religion is born in the human soul" [ZT 22:35]. Evil and injustice in this world come from outside, from beyond the life of the rural community: from the lord's manor, the priest's residence, the Jewish tavern, and the local authorities. Franko consciously leads one to form the impression [ZT 22:204] that, if these factors were nullified, Nahuievychi could then be called "heaven on earth."

What is lacking in these descriptions, however, is recognition of the fact that many village problems derived precisely from "life amidst nature." Preindustrial communities are characterized by their nearly total reliance on natural resources. This dependence was particularly vigorously manifested during poor harvests, epidemics, and other natural disasters that occurred repeatedly, with inflexible regularity.[6] Notations in the margins of the church books in Nahuievychi provide a brief list of the disasters that befell Franko's village: cholera epidemics in 1831 and 1873; bad weather, which destroyed the harvests in 1839, 1848, 1870, 1872, and 1874; cattle plague in 1869; high grain prices in 1854–1855; and the destruction of grain crops by insects ("worms") in 1870. A simple calculation indicates that over a period of forty-four years (1831–1874) various natural cataclysms affected the village eleven times—on average, once every four years.[7]

This list indicates that life in a traditional society is constantly fraught with danger. One of its hallmarks is the banality of death—from malnutrition, the low level of hygiene, the spread of infectious diseases, and the lack of medical care. Death was a constant companion of each family, and its primary victims were children. In order to ensure population growth in such a society, a high mortality rate had to be compensated for by a high birth rate. As long as her health permitted, a woman had to give birth throughout her entire reproductive life—on average, between six and eight times, occasionally reaching the biological maximum of between ten and twelve births. Approximately half of all children survived. Prosperity depended on the size of a family: the larger a family, the greater the chances for a comparatively secure existence, because children were a source of free labor. Under these circumstances, marriage was most often a matter not of love but of calculation. With the rare exception, divorces were forbidden because they destroyed the family homestead. After a husband's or wife's death, the surviving spouse instantly looked for a replacement. The status of widowers and widows was low; thus, the second marriage could join partners a first marriage with whom would be regarded as a misalliance.[8]

The history of the family into which Ivan Franko was born and raised fits into this scheme. No children survived from Yakiv Franko's first marriage, and his second one, contracted rather late in his life, was his last chance to create a family. He remarried two weeks after burying his first wife, who died of cholera in 1855. One year after his marriage, his first son—Ivan, the hero of this account—was born. Maria bore him four more children: two daughters, Tetiana (1858) and Yulianna (1863), and two sons, Zakhar (1859) and Onufrii (1861). Of the five children that were born to Yakiv Franko and Maria Kulchytska, both daughters died in childhood (Tetiana at the age of five, and Yulianna, almost three).

Yakiv Franko lived with Maria for nine years, until his death on 15 April 1865, at the age of sixty-three. Six months after his death, his widow married a villager named Hryhorii (Hryn) Havrylyk, a neighbor of the Kulchytskys, who was six years younger than Maria (at the time of the marriage he was only twenty-three). She bore him three children, only one of whom, a daughter named Yulia, survived. Maria was unable to bear any more children after 1870, when she became ill after her last delivery. The illness made her take to her bed, from which she never rose. Maria Kulchytska died on 1 June 1873 at the age of thirty-eight.

The orphaned Ivan Franko and his brothers were now at the mercy of their stepfather, who did not bother wearing mourning clothing for long; two and a half weeks after burying his wife, on 18 June 1873 he married Maria Terletska, who was also a noblewoman. He lived with her until she died in 1900, and after her death he married a third time, becoming the husband of Yakiv Franko's niece Paraska Franko, who by that time had buried two husbands. Havrylyk died on 22 May 1916, one week before the death of Ivan Franko.[9]

The outlines of the creation and dissolution of families depended to a great degree on the type of farming. The basis of survival was work on the land. A specific feature of Galicia, and all of Eastern Europe, was the predominance of extensive farming, which was based on heavy manual labor. Fertilizers, technology, and crop rotation were unknown or almost nonexistent. In terms of its main features, this was a very conservative type of farming: specialists note that the local agrotechnology had not significantly changed in five millennia, since the advent of Trypillian culture (third millennium BC). On much worse land, where intensive farming was applied, farmers succeeded in growing larger crops: on Czech land in 1890, for example, 17.4 centners (1 centner=a hundredweight) of wheat were harvested from 1 hectare, compared to 12.2 centners in Galicia, 12.5 in Bukovyna, and 8.5 in the mountainous part of the Carpathians. The peasants' assured supply of food somewhat improved in the eighteenth century with the appearance of the potato, which quickly became the chief staple, allowing rural residents to eat their fill for the first time. However, potatoes did not alter the fundamental survival scheme: if the land produced, the peasants had food; if the crops failed, they starved.[10]

Franko's birth and early childhood coincided precisely with the early years during and after the greatest natural catastrophe in Galicia in the nineteenth century. In the people's memory, it was known as the "difficult years" (1840s–1850s). Just like the well-known Irish famine, the Galician catastrophe began with the failure of the potato harvest in 1846, which was repeated in the following years. "At nightfall, many a housewife," as Franko recapitulated the reminiscences of his fellow villagers, "exhausted from a whole day's digging, would gather into her apron everything that had been dug up and, wailing loudly, as though for someone deceased, go back home" [ZT 26:194]. Mykhailo Zubrytsky, a local ethnographer and Franko's friend, has provided another vivid image from those times: "Whenever someone would spot a piece of bread, he would approach it, shaking."[11]

The failure of the potato harvest was only the beginning of a whole range of disasters. After 1850, a cattle plague began, and in 1854 an outbreak of cholera (the cause of death of Yakiv Franko's first wife). The crisis was exacerbated by political events. In connection with the Crimean War (1853–1856), Vienna deployed military units to Galicia, which bordered the Russian Empire. The maintenance of a large army led to a rise in demand for potatoes. The simultaneous closure of the border and the ban on exporting potatoes from Russia, combined with the crop failures, led to a genuine food catastrophe.[12] There were even incidents of cannibalism in some locales. The Galician peasants saved themselves from starvation by fleeing to neighboring lands. Franko's father saved the family from starvation. During the "difficult years," he journeyed to Podillia for wheat, and to Bukovyna for corn, later reselling them at home; he also transported Drohobych salt to Zamostia (Pol. Zamość) and "Lithuania" (the name given to the Belarusian lands that belonged to the Lithuanian part of the former Rzeczpospolita).[13]

All these facts help one to understand how desirable and long awaited the birth of Yakiv and Maria Franko's first son was. In Franko's reminiscences his father appears as a good and generous man. Franko forever retained "lively and unfading" memories of the joy and gaiety that reigned in his father's smithy. They were the "pleasantest and happiest moments of my childhood" [ZT 16:436], he would declare many years later: "at the bottom of my recollections that small but powerful fire still burns" [ZT 21:170]. Ivan would sit in the smithy observing his father's work and listening to the conversations of the peasants from Nahuievychi and neighboring villages. His father always made sure that not a single spark of molten steel fell on him and took care that no conversations on immoral—as he considered—topics took place around his son.

Although Yakiv Franko was illiterate [ZT 31:29], Ivan perceived in him the "starting-point of that rural intelligentsia that already now wanted to turn the course of village matters toward another...order and...in its thoughts was rushing into the future" [ZT 22:221–22]. Yakiv was noted for what today would be called civic activism and selflessness. His motto was "with the people and for the people" [ZT 21:167]. After the abolition of serfdom in 1848, when funds were collected for the church in Nahuievychi, out of the total of 447 gold Austrian florins that were raised by the entire community he donated 189. For this, Yakiv received a mention in the press.[14] In 1849 he was among those Galician peasants in Lviv who solemnly celebrated the first anniversary of the abolition of serfdom [ZT 2:8].

Yakiv Franko's uncommon personality left a mark on his son. Ivan Franko claimed that from his father he inherited the need to work for the benefit of the community [*ZT* 2:468]. Franko also described his father as being gifted with a rich imagination and "colorful manner of expressing his thoughts."[15] Franko's mother also had this talent. Much less is known about her than about Franko's father. A rare mention [*ZT* 42:327] indicates that, despite her noble origins, she was familiar with peasants' work since her girlhood. She was probably beautiful; according to a family story, Yakiv Franko decided to marry her as soon as he met her, so captivated was he by her beauty and youth.[16] Her beauty was destroyed by work and illness: those who saw her ten or fifteen years after her marriage described her as an old and sickly woman (it is worth recalling here that she died when she was thirty-eight years old!).[17] In addition to the gift of picturesque speech, Franko inherited another of his mother's talents. In his formation as a poet and writer, an interest in folklore played a key role (Mykhailo Vozniak even claimed that Franko's activities "began and ended with folklore").[18] As Franko himself admitted, he attributed his love of folklore to his mother [*ZT* 1:74–75]. Among other things, he recorded an entire cycle of wedding songs that she knew, "which I lost, unfortunately, in the whirlwind of my later years."[19]

In contrast, Franko's stepfather, Hryn Havrylyk, was a "practical and realistic character through and through, without a single spark of poetry but, instead, with a healthy dose of skepticism and freethinking, a man of strong will and energy" [*ZT* 49:241]. Franko's father's generosity and hospitality were so great that before his death the household was in debt and was in marked decline. Havrylyk had to take matters into his capable hands and keep a strict eye on the money and all expenses. Like Franko's father, his stepfather had raised himself above the general rural level: he had earned some money from working in Boryslav, he knew how to write, he read a lot, and for five years he held the post of village reeve [*ZT* 49:35]. In adulthood Franko admitted that he had great respect for Havrylyk, "as we usually respect the man who is distinguished by traits that we ourselves have few of." His stepfather reciprocated the feeling [*ZT* 49:35, 241].

On the basis of these words, Franko biographers occasionally describe their relations as being practically idyllic: the stepfather cared for the orphan even after the death of his wife and made sure that Ivan finished school. The Franko family correspondence, however, recreates a different, real—even cruel—world of family relations in Nahuievychi.[20] In this world, quarrels and fisticuffs were not a rarity.[21] Hostility among siblings did not bypass even the family in which Franko grew up. He later admitted to his wife that there was no love lost between him and his younger brothers: the reason for this was their jealousy of Ivan, who was their father's pet.[22]

The available materials do not even hint that there was ever any violence shown toward Ivan in the family. However, Franko was occasionally the target of aggression on the part of his peers. This is connected to certain features that are typical of the socialization of rural children, when a five- or six-year-old child goes outside the bounds of the parental homestead. The child joins a group of children who, in their joint games and other diversions, create what may be called small communities. Such children's communities formed the basis of friendly relations and group solidarity, and as these children became adults, they formed their own families and households. However, not every child easily joins the company of his or her peers: obstacles to this process may come in the form of a physical or intellectual defect, illegitimacy, the parents' bad reputation, or the child's proud behavior or feeling of superiority. Usually, such a child was doomed to solitude and the jibes and anger of his peers; there were even cases where such "outsiders" were murdered.[23]

This was partly Franko's experience. In his stories he refers to himself as a five-year-old boy "amid a whole pack of village boys, just as noisy and merry as I," who play first in his father's yard and then the neighbor's yard [ZT 15:96], running in the nearby fields, woods, and pastureland, climbing trees, like squirrels, searching for birds' nests, and occasionally even scrapping with each other.[24] In this group, the "outsider" was not Franko but a village boy named Mytro, the son of a poor servant woman, who became pregnant and then "got a job as a wet-nurse in the home of a Jew" [ZT 15:97–99]. But Franko was not immune to jibes, either. The gossip about Franko that later circulated in Lviv, to the effect that he was the illegitimate son of an "Orthodox" Jew, was rooted in his childhood days in Nahuievychi. The village children teased Ivan about his red hair.[25] The villagers said that his mother knew how to cast spells and had power over evil spirits.[26] Either of these suggestions was enough to erect a barrier between Franko and his peers, and it is very likely that he felt like an "outsider" in his village. A list of his friends from his childhood days does not contain a single friend from Nahuievychi; all of them come from the neighboring village of Yasenytsia Silna, where, as a six-year-old, he went to live with his grandmother when the time came for him to start elementary school. His Yasenytsia friends remembered the young Franko as a merry and quick child. He often won games, even though he was the smallest. Franko's two greatest passions in life—picking mushrooms and fishing—stem from his childhood. People who met Franko at the peak of his fame recalled that he was unexcelled in both these activities: he fished with his bare hands, with his pants rolled up to the knees or just dressed in a shirt, which often shocked those who were sitting on the riverbank and expected more serious behavior on his part.[27] But even in Yasenytsia Silna he did not have complete peace: as the youngest in his class, he suffered a lot at the hands of his fellow pupils, one of whom used to walk behind him, throwing stones, once nearly killing him.[28]

But the young Franko was not an innocent little child. Even as an adult he was tormented by the image of a baby bird whose neck he had wrung. As he wrote, "everything stupid, pointless, brutal, and bad that I ever did in my life crystallized in the concrete image of that innocent, murdered little bird" [ZT 26:68].[29] The consequences of his other childish pastimes could have been much graver. One time, Franko and two friends of his were jumping from a roof on to straw-covered ground. He jumped first and then quickly took away the straw so that his friend would have to jump onto the bare threshing floor. Only the warning cry of the other boy prevented a tragedy.[30] One day, when he was in school in Yasenytsia Silna, Franko "borrowed" a pencil from a schoolmate, who was punished severely by his father for losing something that had been purchased with his hard-earned money (Franko recounted this incident in the story "Olivets" [The Pencil]).[31] Another time, Franko nearly drowned one of his peers: for a joke he led him into deep water and, declaring, "Here you go, save yourself," he left him there alone. The boy would probably have drowned if an older boy had not appeared and dragged him out of the water.[32]

These episodes from Franko's biography show a real, not idealized, image of rural life and depict Franko as a normal village child. His abnormality lay elsewhere. From time to time he would fall into profound reflection, talk to himself, and ask his elders strange questions or say things that made them just shrug their shoulders. The neighbors claimed that when he was little, Franko "was not the same as other people." But sometimes the little Franko even irritated his own mother. In one of his autobiographical stories he describes the following incident from his childhood. His mother served cabbage for lunch, and everyone was eating in silence. But her oldest son, who was staring fixedly at the picture of the Blessed Virgin Mary on the wall, asked: "Why is the Holy Mother staring and staring, but not eating cabbage?" The family started laughing uproariously, while his mother shouted at him: "Why don't you think before you speak, you dimwit!" [ZT 15:69–70].[33] His elderly father, who had barely managed to see a child of his born, rejoiced in this type of behavior and considered it a sign of high intelligence. At his forge, Yakiv even made his son a bench, on which Ivan tried his hand at blacksmithing. But he was not very good at it, and his father told him: "You won't make a blacksmith; you will be a priest." The same thing was told to Franko by his first teacher, a village deacon named Andrusevych: "You will be a great writer, a very wealthy man, or a great thief."[34]

A bizarre incident took place one summer day, when storm clouds and lightning were clustering above the Dil. Setting out by himself, Ivan went into battle against the weather in order to protect his village and its fields from the rain and hail. Shouting incantations, he forbade the storm to approach Nahuievychi. Having "vanquished" his terrible opponent, Ivan fainted from his profound exaltation and fell into a deep sleep. He lay there sleeping until his mother, worried by his long absence, found him. According to Franko's own words, he allegedly inherited this extraordinary power from his mother.[35]

This incident formed the nucleus of Franko's autobiographical story "Pid oborohom" (Beneath the Hayrick) [ZT 22:35–52]. In the context of the present discussion this story is interesting in that it reveals another characteristic aspect of "life amidst nature," to which contemporary scholars, including Franko biographers, pay hardly any attention. To Franko's contemporaries the external world was populated by unearthly forces. In their imagination, these forces were no less real than nature itself. The villagers, whether they were Ruthenians or Mazurs (Poles), were formally Christian monotheists, but in fact they were pantheists, who believed that the whole world, the sky, the air, and the earth were filled with gods, and that all of nature was alive; and everything in it thought and spoke to people and gods. Belief in these forces provided their intellect with cause-and-effect linkages to the phenomena of their daily lives, which they did not have because of their lack of education. Why did a cow stop giving milk? Because a witch cast a spell, and a witch's main activity is causing a cow to dry up or spoiling its milk. In addition, witches were known to steal stars from the sky, spoil crops and clothing, break up families, cause diseases in people and even death. Only another sorceress—from another village—could undo the harm. How could one recognize a witch? It was simple: on the night before

Easter, when everyone is busy attending the church service, she sits in the corner eating sausage.[36] It was not only witches who could cast spells; Jews also knew how to do this. They were allowed to cast spells on less pious people. Even the souls of deceased engineers could be transformed into an unearthly force. The young Franko's talent for averting storms was the bailiwick of so-called *hradivnyky* (hail stoppers, also known as *hradobury* [cloud drillers] or *khmarnyky* [cloud breakers]). Some village communities had their own hail stoppers and paid them to disperse the clouds.[37]

All this information may amuse the contemporary reader. But in Franko's childhood these beliefs were taken seriously. There was not a single village where at least one woman was taken for a witch—if not several. The slightest pretext was enough to suspect someone of sorcery. This was particularly true during social catastrophes: a poor harvest, famine, an epidemic, and the like. A morbid imagination awakened extraordinary suspicion. Pity the unfortunate person on whom suspicion would fall, unless that individual were protected by his or her social status. One of the last known witch burnings in the entire land took place precisely in Nahuievychi in 1764.[38]

Little Ivan's imagination was captivated by stories of spirits and vampires that he heard on a daily basis from the servant girls or peasants sitting around in the smithy [*ZT* 21:160]. One of the most frightening tales that Ivan ever heard, as a result of which he would cry out or faint at the slightest rustling, was a story about the cholera epidemic in Nahuievychi that took place in 1831, when several peasants, suspected of being vampires who had killed a fellow villager, were burned to death. Rev. Yosafat Kachanovsky, the abbot of the Basilian monastery in Drohobych and the rector of the local school, was regarded as the "oldest vampire" because he was "very red" (his perpetually red face was probably caused by some sort of illness).[39] Aware of the threat to his life because of the peasants' ignorance, for a long time the abbot could not set foot outside the monastery. In 1873 there was another cholera epidemic, and this time a local orphan girl named Zoska was suspected of vampirism. She seemed to have lost her mind: removing most of her clothing, she would wander through the fields dressed only in a shirt, and whenever she encountered people she would wring her hands and begin wailing terribly. Fortunately for her, the girl disappeared from the village, resurfacing once the epidemic had abated. Some of the villagers thought she should be caught and taught a lesson similar to the one their parents once meted out to vampires in 1831 [*ZT* 46/1:565–81].[40]

It may be assumed that if Franko had remained longer in his village, he would have courted disaster through his often strange behavior. In one of his autobiographical stories, he tried to expand upon the fate of strange children like him:

> Everything about them from childhood is not like other people: their gait, and face, and hair, and words, and actions. And when such a child has to live its entire life beneath a cramped peasant thatch, without broader experience, without clearer knowledge, when from its early years its obtuse kinfolk begin to pound into it everything the way "that is customary among people," then they will also succeed in crushing the inborn tendency toward originality; all the child's unused and stunted talents will grow numb and languish from the outset, and little Myron will make a poor householder or, what is worse, the not as yet entirely stunted liveliness and agility of his character will propel him toward evil, unable to develop into goodness—he will become a bully, a fortune-teller who will believe in his own visions and will stupefy people with a sincere heart. [ZT 15:70]

Only education can offer such a child a chance: it may not necessarily improve the child's lot, but at least it will open his or her "eyes to the world," and then the child will get drunk from learning, "like a sick person from fresh air" [ZT 15:71].

In his own way, Franko synthesized the experience of the part of the intelligentsia whose roots lay in the peasantry—"bizarre manifestations," like him. The psychological need for compensation for his "otherness" propelled him toward self-determination through the development of his intellectual talents in school or self-education, learning how to play musical instruments, taking part in religious affairs, and so on.[41] What was needed to bring out the potential hidden in such a child was a favorable set of circumstances that would turn mere chance into a living reality.

Education

In the biography of the little Ivan Franko, there was one detail that made him exceptional: out of all the children produced by the marriages of Yakiv Franko, Maria Kulchytska, and Hryhorii Havrylyk, only he, the eldest, managed to acquire a complete education, from elementary school all the way to university. This accomplishment also marked him out from his peers from the other village families. The first natives of Nahuievychi who managed to complete secondary school and university (including the members of his own family) were thirty to forty years younger than Franko.[42]

In order to understand how and why this happened, it is not enough to cite Franko's exceptional gifts. According to people who knew the family of Yakiv Franko, his son Onufrii was as naturally gifted, if not more so, than his brother Ivan. Onufrii was once apprenticed to a blacksmith in Drohobych, but he spent only two years there: his stepfather Havrylyk took him away because there was no one to herd the horses. The blacksmith's wife said later: "If Onufrii had gone to school, like Ivan, had seen the world, what a talented person he would have been!"[43] The same thing happened to Franko's childhood friend, Ivan Yatsuliak. His parents did not allow him to study because he was the oldest son and had to help his father on the farm. At Franko's urging he even ran away from the village to the school in Drohobych, but his father found him there and brought him back home.[44]

During Franko's lifetime a great change took place in Galician society: a fairly large stratum of peasant-born intellectuals emerged. But, as in the case of his fellow villagers, they were not Franko's contemporaries: they were one or two generations younger. The peasant's realization that education was a tool for the enrichment and success of his children, his desire "to make a human being out of his son" and help him "make something of himself" was a late-nineteenth century phenomenon.[45] This does not mean that the peasants of Franko's childhood had no understanding whatsoever of the practical importance of education. Franko's peer and later friend Mykhailo Zubrytsky recalled that in his native village "people said [that] when a man knows "numbers" [that is, knows how to count and to read—Y. H.], this could often be very helpful in the army in a large city because he would know where to disappear."[46] Some parents were even prepared to hire a village teacher to instruct their sons in reading and writing.[47] Nevertheless, this did not resolve the question of literacy in the countryside, because only wealthier parents could afford to hire a teacher, and furthermore village schoolteachers generally did not have a high level of education.[48]

The key to a career was a gymnasium education (*matura*: matriculation). Peasants who desired this for their children had to ensure that they completed at least a four-year school, which provided knowledge of German or Polish, the languages that were used in gymnasiums. There were few such schools in the countryside,[49] and it was very expensive to send a child to an urban school. But the problem did not lie in just the shortcomings of the state education system. Even after primary school education became mandatory in Galicia (1869), a peasant rarely dared to send his children to school for a longer period of time than the law required. Extensive farming, poor harvests, and the lack of technology made the survival of a rural family dependent on the number of working hands. Children were put to work from an early age. Children between the ages of five and seven had to drive the cattle to pasture: the youngest were in charge of geese, pigs, and calves, while the older ones took care of horses and cows. Boys from the age of eight worked in the fields alongside their fathers, while girls did women's work in the field and the house.[50]

Children's schooling deprived peasant households of crucially needed free labor, and parents had a hard time reconciling themselves to the idea that instead of working on the farm, their children would be spending their time sitting in schools acquiring knowledge that, for the most part, was not required in "practical" life. The peasants used to say: "My dad didn't study, so I don't need to either." Sending peasant children to urban schools was considered unusual because it was mostly the children of priests, forest wardens, and other functionaries who attended them.[51] Peasant-parents, yielding to outside interference, would agree to send their sons to a gymnasium if a local priest, teacher, or landowner, having spotted a gifted child, convinced them of the need for further education.[52] Sometimes a little boy was sent away to school if a genetic or acquired physical defect rendered him incapable of performing agricultural labor.[53]

The negative attitude to education was only partly caused by the onerous conditions of peasant life. It may be explained by certain mental structures that were only indirectly linked to material circumstances. The peasant world perception was based on the veneration of physically exhausting labor, and thus the peasant had a critical and distrustful attitude to the activities, life, and pastimes of the privileged strata.[54] Borys Hrinchenko, the prominent nineteenth-century Ukrainian figure, wrote: "The peasant does not love the lord, he mocks him, but he is also jealous of him. He sees that the lord has greater rights and more wealth and—as it seems to the peasant—he does little because, according to the peasant, intellectual work is not work at all."[55] Heavy physical labor was the essence of peasant identity; the sufferings that they endured silently during its performance were virtuous. Instead, education was offensive to God because it taught people laziness, evil, and atheism.[56] Essentially, education became one of the chief dividing lines between the "peasant" and the "lord": "lords" were not simply one's own landowner or another but the entire educated society in general, and therein lay the fundamental rejection by the peasantry of modern culture and its bearers—educated people.[57]

The extent to which Franko's childhood deviated from the standards of rural life may be inferred from the fact that he was exempted from the work on the homestead. His descriptions of rural work in his autobiographical stories do not go beyond the lowest level of a "peasant's education"—herding geese. Much later, when Franko was an adult and, lacking other means of existence, was forced to resort to performing peasant work, he admitted that "he has no skill at all…for field work" [ZT 48:267].[58] It is possible that the reason for this untypical phenomenon was that Franko's father felt sorry for his long-awaited first-born son,[59] or there was no great need for child labor in his smithy and farm. Even after Yakiv's death, Franko's stepfather allowed him to complete his education so as to exclude him from the children slated to receive a parcel of land. But facts are facts: Franko was not asked to perform the hard physical work that was customarily assigned to his peers.

However, it should be borne in mind that Franko lived with his parents only for the first six years of his life.[60] From 1862 to 1864 he lived with his grandmother Liudvika in Yasenytsia Silna, where he attended primary school. In one of his autobiographies Franko explained that he was sent to his relatives in a neighboring village because the school in Nahuievychi was too far away, it being situated at the upper end of the village. This explanation is not entirely convincing, because after two years of schooling in Yasenytsia, he was sent to a school that was even farther away, in Drohobych.[61]

It would appear that there were plans from the very beginning to provide Franko with a complete education. In contrast to the elementary school in Nahuievychi, the pupils at the Yasenytsia school were taught German and Polish.[62] This assumption looks even more convincing if one considers the fundamental difference between the world perception of the nobility and that of the peasantry. Liudvika Kulchytska's family may be traced back exactly three generations—from her parents to her children—but even during this period of time it is obvious that it was a family tradition to educate the children. Liudvika's brother Ivan was a Greek Catholic priest, who graduated from the Lviv Theological Seminary. It is not known where her sons studied, but there is no doubt that they were educated people: her oldest son was killed during the anti-Russian Polish uprising of 1863, and an uneducated person could hardly have demonstrated such a level of patriotism; and her second oldest son was an officer and later a "liquidator of a cash office,"[63] who died in Lviv. Her third son, Pavlo, never left the village because his mother signed over her estate to him so that she could live with him until the end of her life. But Pavlo, too, was literate: he was the one who taught Ivan Franko how to read when the boy was six years old [ZT 49:241]. Liudvika's youngest son, Ihnatii, was a village schoolteacher.[64] Out of six children, only two daughters (including Franko's mother) did not receive an education, because, after the death of Liudvika's husband in 1840, the widowed mother had to support the family alone. She obtained the money for her children's education by selling off her land, which also indicates a fundamental difference between her attitudes and the world perception of peasants, whereby education, not land, is considered the object of investments in the future of one's children and family.

Franko constantly traveled from Drohobych to spend his holidays with his grandmother, until her death in 1871. People said that he was her favorite. It is significant that she did not ask him to perform any difficult work, although, as the recollections of Pavlo Kulchytsky would indicate, the family worked in the fields, nor did the men shirk women's work in the house [ZT 46/1:578]. Liudvika Kulchytska had an unquestionable influence on her grandson's upbringing. His two younger brothers, who were not under her care, did not receive an education, and they lived and died as ordinary peasants.[65] Their extant letters to Ivan Franko, as well as the stepfather's letters to his stepson, were written when they were adults.[66] It is not only the content of these letters that is important but also the form in which they were written. Onufrii and Zakhar address their brother not only as an older brother but also as a person from a higher social stratum; even Franko's stepfather, who was older than Ivan both in terms of age and family status, occasionally stumbled in his letters to his stepson, switching from the familiar "you" to the deferential plural form of this pronoun. The letters reveal the illiteracy of the Franko brothers and the semiliteracy of their neighbors or children, who wrote to them at the brothers' request: they are printed, not written, there is no punctuation, and they often contain Polish letters, distorted words, or words that are divided according to some incomprehensible rule. But they also reveal the germination of new phenomena: Franko's family members constantly ask for newspapers, journals, popular calendars for reading, and some kind of "interesting books," and, as their letters indicate, their interest was shared by their neighbors and village acquaintances.[67]

The point is not that Franko's brothers were greatly inferior to him in terms of intellect and innate talents: they did not shun books, and Onufrii, for one, showed certain gifts. It is simply that neither of them had a chance in life, like the one that opened up to Ivan Franko, the firstborn son and the favorite of both his parents and his grandmother. Without such a prospect, it is unlikely that even the adult Ivan would have differed much from his brothers. In any case, Franko would never have become Franko had his childhood flowed along the same current as the absolute majority of peasant sons.

Chapter 4

School Years

At the very first opportunity, rural boys who demonstrate an aptitude for learning seek to leave the village and move to the city, a trend well known to historians of education.[1] Franko's stay in the countryside was also not a long one.[2] In early September 1864, Franko's mother took him to the school in Drohobych, where he was immediately registered in second grade [*ZT* 39:38]. He attended this school for a total of eleven years: at first (1864–1868) in the main school, and from fall 1868 to summer 1875 in the gymnasium.[3]

Franko left several autobiographical stories about this period of his life. They make for difficult reading, because they recount the teachers' extraordinary brutality toward the pupils. In the story "Schönschreiben" (Good Handwriting), the victim of this brutality was Franko himself. During the calligraphy class he received a punch in the face from his teacher, a former steward named Valko, for holding his pen incorrectly. Blood poured down the boy's face and he fell unconscious to the floor. Valko became frightened because, at the time, there were ongoing lawsuits in the Drohobych court in connection with the beatings of urban children and children of noble families. But the teacher breathed a sigh of relief when he learned that the boy he had punished was the son of an ordinary peasant from Nahuievychi: "A peasant's son! Bah! Why the devil do those peasants push themselves in here!"

> A weight came off the teacher's heart. He had become alarmed by his misdeed, but a peasant's son meant that you could beat and insult him with impunity because no one would trouble themselves over a peasant's son. Valko was not mistaken in his thinking: no one stood up for the peasant's son. The inhumane conduct of the teacher-steward was easily overlooked, just like his many other misdemeanors. This was a bitter pill to swallow only for the peasant's son, in whose heart the first seeds of indignation, disdain, and eternal enmity toward all manner of subjugation and tyranny took root. [*ZT* 15:90]

There is no telling how much truth or invention there is to this story.[4] At the very least, Franko abides by the truth in the part of the story in which he describes the teachers' brutality. Until 1867 corporal punishment of pupils was normal practice, and even permitted by law. There was a popular joke in Galicia. A teacher asks his pupils: "What does not eat or drink but always goes around and strikes?" The children answered: "A Teacher." (The correct answer was: a clock).[5] Franko's schoolmate, Karlo Bandrivsky, recalled that the teachers took excessive advantage of this rule and beat their pupils with anything at hand: cudgels, canes, a ring of keys, and they would push them to the floor and kick them.[6]

There are doubts concerning the "first seed" of "eternal enmity toward all kinds of subjugation," which was supposedly sown in the heart of the "peasant's son" by a teacher's brutality. This story was written in 1879, a few years after Franko's conversion to socialism, when he became an active promoter of new ideas. It would appear that, in writing the short story "Schönschreiben," he was explaining his current way of thinking about earlier events.[7]

In another short story, "The Priest-Humorist," which was written during his postsocialist period (1903), Franko's response to the brutality of teachers has little in common with a protest against social oppression and injustice. Franko narrates the tragic history of a friend who died from the beatings administered by the Basilian Fathers. The story is a mixture of real events and the author's inventions. The image of the "priest-humorist" is actually a composite portrait of two teachers: a Ruthenian priest named Rev. Telesnytsky and a Pole named Tarczanin, who converted to the Greek Catholic rite and joined a Basilian monastery. Telesnytsky was known for his sadistic tendencies: he beat his pupils with the cudgels that were used to prop windows open in the summer. Tarczanin was responsible for the death of a child—not a peasant's offspring but the son of the nobleman Nowosielski, the senior commissioner of the treasury guards. In Franko's story the narrator shares a desk with this boy, whose name is Voliansky. As the bloodied and severely beaten boy barely manages to return to his desk, the class is laughing uproariously while the narrator is choking on his tears:

> Something was squeezing me by the throat, I felt burning inside, and I was pierced with pain, shame, and grief, as though I myself was guilty of everything that had happened here, as though I had committed a serious crime by gazing calmly on this torture, without screaming for help or not

collapsing from the blows. I bent down surreptitiously and kissed Voliansky's cold hand and wet it with my tears. [*ZT* 21:306]

This description contains much more fundamentally human, spontaneous, and sincere feeling than the idealized reaction to Valko's brutality.[8]

Franko himself clearly indicated that his Drohobych stories add "something superfluous, subsequent that was conveyed by the current of the times" [*ZT* 21:302] to real events, and he cautioned that it is not worth writing a biography of him based on them, especially in dark tones [*ZT* 15:7]. His peers recall that the young Franko was a jolly, healthy, and active child with a friendly nature.[9] The authors of Soviet-era Franko studies, however, viewed "Schönschreiben" and "The Priest-Humorist" as grounds for describing the religious obscurantism that allegedly reigned in the Drohobych school.[10] In fact, the school was far from being the oppressive "vale of tears" evoked in both of these stories. The school was under the supervision of the Greek Catholic monastic order of the Basilian Fathers. The Habsburgs required monastic orders to engage in beneficial social work—for example, to operate educational or health-care institutions; otherwise, monasteries were subject to disbandment. The Basilians were not at risk, because they had been involved in education since before the advent of the Habsburgs. Theirs was an elite and wealthy monastic order; its members were recruited from the ranks of the nobility, and the order was known primarily for its excellent schools.[11]

The fact that the Basilians administered schools did not mean that they catered only to Greek Catholic children: Roman Catholics and Jews also attended them. Austrian school legislation clearly and unambiguously required that education be secular even if monks were in charge of a particular school. At the heart of the imperial educational system was the principle that all pupils, regardless of the crown land in which their school was situated, had to receive the same type of instruction—so that, for example, graduates of any gymnasium would have equal opportunities to compete for the same state positions.[12] Thus, the governmental language in the Drohobych school was German. The Polish and Ruthenian languages were taught as separate subjects, but neither was the language of instruction. When it came to teaching the state language to members of nonstate nations, a tool widely used in schools throughout Europe was applied in the system of instruction: this was a small wooden board that was hung around the neck of the pupil who spoke in his native language. "Anyone who spoke to another person in Polish (at that time no educated people in the city spoke Ruthenian) would get this little board and try to foist it on someone else, and the one who was not able to pass it off to someone else and brought it to school was punished for this. The German language, which I was studying then, specifically German orthography, stayed with me for my entire life," recalled Teofil Hrushkevych, a graduate of the Basilian school in Drohobych and later Franko's teacher.[13]

When Franko began his studies at the Drohobych school, it was still German-speaking (which is why it was called the "German" school). But already at that time, in keeping with the Zeitgeist, the teachers spoke Polish among themselves and to their pupils. The language of instruction for Ruthenian language and religion classes for Greek Catholics was Ruthenian.[14] Besides the Basilian Fathers, the school staff included lay people. The school was under external control. During exam periods, held every six months, a commission consisting of deans, city mayors, and councilors, as well as parents and any other interested individuals, was convened. This ensured a certain degree of impartiality. It suffices to say that twice Franko was sent to the "dunce bench" as punishment for reading a book that he hid in his desk during a lesson. But each time the examining commission, impressed by his knowledge, returned him to the desk at the front of the class. His rural origins mattered little, as is clear from the fact that his mother, dressed like a peasant, was invited to sit in the classroom's place of honor together with her son.[15] Throughout his six semesters at the Basilian school Franko consistently came first or second in his class and received honors.[16]

Schooling in the Habsburg monarchy was structured according to the classical system of education. The Basilian schools in Galicia were also called "Latin" schools because of the vital role assigned to the study of classical languages. When pupils went on to study in gymnasiums, the importance of these languages did not decline, but increased. Learning consisted of memorizing large texts "from here to there" and of lessons interspersed with Latin, Greek, and German expressions, tropes, and figures of speech from the poetry of classical antiquity—everything that mars some of Franko's works, especially his political essays.[17] The memorization of lengthy texts had a threefold aim: to develop and sharpen memory; to offer learners good examples of patriotic love, fortitude, and other virtues of a loyal subject of the empire; and to expose students to the treasures of classical poetry.[18] Some scholars note other goals: the immense quantity of memorized material was supposed to dull the germination of independent thought. "The classics attuned [learners] toward the ideal, romantic literary order, presented life in harmonious colors, but at the same time they led to passivity, engendered feckless characters suitable for competing for government posts, bureaucratic natures unsuited to entrepreneurship, to being able to cope with practical, independent life," wrote one Galician "victim" of a classical education, who studied in the same period as Franko.[19]

Classical education was a two-edged sword. On the one hand, it reduced independent thinking to a minimum. For example, when students analyzed the grammatical structure of Plato's texts in class, they did not discuss their content. On the other hand, even this type of text-learning concealed certain risks because it could spark a fascination with the Greek and Roman republics as opposed to imperial Rome. For that reason, conservatives complained that classical studies led to republicanism and socialism. In the final analysis, during classroom instruction in the traditions of classical antiquity much depended on the teachers and what they emphasized.[20]

In many children, their readings of Homer, Herodotus, Plutarch, and other ancient writers sparked an immediate desire to imitate the heroes of antiquity. This early awakening of ambition is very important in the biographies of such Franko contemporaries as Sigmund Freud or Mykhailo Drahomanov.[21] We find nothing similar in Franko's biography. The absence of this theme is hardly accidental. The young Franko was attracted by the magnificence of Homer, not the heroes of Plutarch. Literature was his greatest passion; he hunted down books like a "fox going after chickens."[22] He read voraciously, even during classes, and to the end of his life he was rarely seen on the street without a book clutched under his arm. The study of classical poetry, which was bolstered by his fascination for folksongs, encouraged Franko to start writing his own verses. Spiritual distress served as an impetus: his father died at the end of his first school year, in the spring of 1865. Franko recalled that his father came to his school a few days before he died. "My father was also present at the exam, which was actually only a big show—I didn't see him, but as soon as I was the first to be called to accept the prize (a book), I heard him burst out crying" [ZT 49:241]. In addition to the acute trauma of becoming semi-orphaned, the young Franko was also affected by the circumstance that his father died during the night between Easter Saturday and Easter Sunday (15–16 April 1865). According to a Ukrainian belief, this meant that the soul of the deceased went straight to heaven. Thus, Franko's very first poem bears the title of "Easter."[23]

Either way, Franko began to write at a very early age—during the first year after his move to the city.[24] The list of what Franko wrote during his school years in Drohobych is already impressive: by the time he completed elementary school and graduated from the gymnasium he had filled several thick copybooks with his poems, dramas, and translations of the writings of the ancient Jewish prophets, the Královédvorský Manuscript, fragments of *The Lay of Ihor's Campaign*, the Songs of the Nibelungs, Sophocles, Homer, Horace, Heine, and others [*ZT* 48:8–9, 11, 16; 49:243]. In the latter years of his life he even began translating and reworking popular plays for the local Ruthenian theater [*ZT* 26:371] and was planning to publish two collections of his works.[25] The body of his work should be much larger, given that from time to time he burned writings that he considered failures. To his first publisher he wrote in a semi-joking vein: "Friend, if I sent you everything that I have scribbled until now, you would become frightened!" [*ZT* 48:15].

The majority of those works were written during his gymnasium days, after he completed his studies at the Basilian school. Franko's high school years were important in many respects. They had a decisive impact on his socialization: entering the gymnasium as a twelve-year-old boy, he graduated as a nineteen-year-old youth. The role of a gymnasium education is difficult to overestimate even in a formal respect, as it opened the way to a career. The document attesting to the completion of the high school exam of maturity (*matura*) divided society into large segments of privileged and unprivileged individuals, similar to the way that, in the old days, the document attesting to one's noble origins divided society into privileged individuals and commoners. The gymnasium, even more than the university, served as the main source of the intelligentsia.[26]

Franko's studies at the gymnasium coincided with the years when Galicia was undergoing several dramatic changes—the introduction of the Constitution and autonomy. These changes also affected Drohobych and the gymnasium, and in a very contradictory way. In 1867 the city's status was raised to administrative center of the newly formed Drohobych County, and Drohobych was included among the so-called "larger cities" (*grössere Stadt*). The granting of this category did not signify recognition of size (although Drohobych was one of the top hundred largest Austrian cities and one of the ten largest cities in Galicia).[27] It was a certain legal status that granted the local population the privilege of electing their parliamentary deputies according to a separate curia (voter category). The three neighboring cities with this type of status were Stryi, Sambir, and Stanyslaviv. Drohobych was distinguished from those three cities by its proximity to the oil and ozocerite extraction industries in neighboring Boryslav. This opened up the possibility, all too rare in Galicia, for Drohobych to become a large industrial center and, together with Boryslav, to create something along the lines of the Eastern European version of the Liverpool-Manchester corridor.

Initially, though, this possibility was not duly exploited. Paradoxically, the proximity of the two cities' industries acted as a braking factor. Boryslav captured the main human and financial resources, leaving Drohobych with remnants. It is striking that the pace of Drohobych's demographic growth in 1857–1900 and the proportion of people engaged in industry, trade, and commerce were lower than in the neighboring cities of Stryi and Stanyslaviv.[28]

If Drohobych benefited at all from its proximity to Boryslav, it was only in that it turned into a consumer center, where large numbers of workers relaxed after their hard week at work: no other city in Galicia generated such huge revenues from the sale of alcoholic beverages than Drohobych, and by its number of taverns (167 in 1875) it outstripped Sambir (52), Stryi (84), and Stanyslaviv (118).[29]

Changes for the better began to appear only in the late 1870s and early 1880s. The most important event was the opening of a railway line connecting Drohobych with Stryi, Sambir, and Boryslav in 1872, Lviv in 1873, and Stanyslaviv in 1875. Now, travelers could take a fast train from Drohobych to Lviv, arriving in less than four hours. The railway transported not just people and goods but also news and certain models for emulation. During the first decade after the opening of the railway link, the headquarters of large companies were established in Drohobych, the city center began to be built up, a whole network of civic societies (firefighters, credit, music, and reading associations) appeared, and two newspapers began publishing: the Jewish *Drohobyczer Zeitung* and the Polish-Ukrainian *Gazeta Naddniestrzańska*. By the end of the nineteenth century, Drohobych had become an industrial city and intellectual center that maintained links with both the provincial and the imperial capitals. David Horowitz, one of the founders of the Zionist youth movement, thus recalled the city in which he spent his childhood:

> Drohobych was, so far as social life in the small towns of Galicia is concerned, an exceptional case. On the surface, it was like all other such

places: melancholy, and a gloomy atmosphere of hopelessness reigned...
And yet it was different...Everything was somehow sharper, more varied,
more conspicuous. It was clear that there was more drive and ferment here.
The oil emerging from the ground in the neighboring small town of Boryslav
created social and economic change unknown elsewhere....This was the
only town in Galicia that attracted international attention.[30]

Horowitz's memoirs are a stark contrast to Franko's reminiscences of
his childhood and youth:

During my gymnasium studies Drohobych was a city that was very rich
in negative features. It would be an awfully long list if you tallied up what
it was missing. There was not a single decent coffeehouse or restaurant,
or a single public library or a single educational society, or a single group
with either a political or educational goal. There was almost nothing that
characterizes at least a semi-European city. There was not even water, aside
from the domestic, salty kind that outsiders could not drink. The majority
of the streets had no sidewalks and lighting, and the extensive suburbs,
particularly Zadvirne, Zavizne, and Viitivska Hora, were just ordinary
villages with thatched roofs, surrounded by fences, with a mode of conduct
of a completely rural character. A railway from Drohobych to Stryi was built
when I was in my seventh year at the gymnasium; until that time Drohobych
was a "free crown city," free, despite its normal school and gymnasium, of
everything that smelled of civilization and a more intensive spiritual life.
[ZT 21:316]

When Franko was going to school, the city had an "urban" look only
in the downtown core; meanwhile, the suburbs were barely distinguishable
from villages. In 1880, the city had a total area of 1,600 morgs, but if you
excluded the land devoted to gardens, fields, and forests, the urban section
barely totaled 300 morgs.[31]

The city air, however, did its work: in Drohobych, Franko acquired
new concepts and habits that are not germane to rural life. His very
first instructors in the wisdom of urban life were trade apprentices,
from whose company he profited while he was living at the home of his
distant relative Koshytska, who owned a carpentry shop in one of the
Drohobych suburbs. The life of the city tradesmen, according to Franko,
was "demarcated according to completely different boundaries, divided
according to a different scale" to what he was used to in the village. From

an apprentice named Yasko Romansky, Franko learned the true value of money:

> In the village I saw how everyone valued money, fretted over it, but what its practical benefit was, how it could serve a person remained a mystery to me. The peasants bought very little with cash: salt, pepper, leather for boots—meaning, things that were of no use to my childish daydreams. The largest proportion of their money went into some sort of incomprehensible abyss called the "shtairant" [a distortion of the Ger. *Steueramt*, taxation office—Y. H.], which the peasants always talked about with a kind of fear, so that I became accustomed to seeing something terrifying and inhumane in it. Sometimes, whenever I had a few kreutzers in the village—usually more well-to-do guests give each of their host's children a kreutzer or two "for a pretzel"—I did not know what to do with them and, after playing with them for a while, I would lose them or give them to my mother. Here, for the first time I learned the value of money as a source of various pleasures. Yasko taught me how to exchange money for candies, apples, nuts, recounted the various ways in which money is earned and spent in the city, described the earnings of beggars, water-carriers, rag-and-bone men, huckstresses, gardeners, and various categories of petty wage earners who populated the industrial section of Drohobych. [*ZT* 21:181–82]

The gymnasium occupied an important place among all the institutions that conferred the look of a city on Drohobych. It also stood out visually, as it was one of only a handful of two-story buildings in the city center, where the majority of the buildings (95 percent) only had one story.[32] The Drohobych Gymnasium could not have been a beacon of enlightenment in a city where, in the early 1880s, 70 percent of the population could not read or write.[33] By the time Franko entered the gymnasium, it had another mission: to Polonize the city. Drohobych was one of the cities in Galicia where Poles comprised a distinct minority (23.5 percent vs. 25.8 percent Ruthenians and 50.4 percent Jews in 1880, if one reckons on the basis of confessional affiliation).[34] The large suburbs were populated by Ruthenians and the downtown area by Jews. Apart from government officials, professors, and tradesmen, there were few Poles.[35] The gymnasium was founded in 1858 by a resolution passed by the municipal bureaucrats, and funded by public money, in order to instill the Polish spirit in young people. The first director of the gymnasium, Bronisław Trzaskowski, who was the grandson of one of Napoleon's officers and a member of the Polish patriotic nobility, succeeded in organizing the curriculum in such a way that, even though there were twice as many Ruthenian students as Poles, out of all the regional languages it was mainly Polish that was taught, while Ruthenian was used only to explain grammatical forms. In addition, all the students had to attend a Roman Catholic church, notwithstanding the protests of the Greek Catholic catechist and the local priest. Trzaskowski was dismissed after the Polish students, in a burst of patriotism, threatened to do bodily harm to the Austrian officers stationed in Drohobych.

The gymnasium followed the old Jesuit tradition of periodic fisticuffs between the older students and Jews. The biggest clash took place in 1863, during which patriotically inclined Polish students, keyed up by news of their peers who were shedding their blood in the Russian Empire, sought an outlet for their emotions. The participants in this pogrom were joined by artisans; even the peasants would have flocked to their side had the army not arrived from Sambir in response to the Drohobych Jews' request for protection. The success of the educational system introduced by Trzaskowski is attested by the fact that some of the attackers were assimilated Jewish students, who were imbued with Polish patriotism.[36]

The introduction in 1867 of Polish as the language of instruction in Galician gymnasiums conferred nearly official status on the policy of assimilating young Ruthenians and Jews. In view of the German language's elevated international status, the level of German belles-lettres and scientific literature, and its crucial necessity for a career, it continued to be one of the main subjects in the curriculum: in terms of the hours of instruction devoted to it in Galician gymnasiums, German was second only to the classical languages.[37] But instruction in all other disciplines had to be in Polish. This reform was implemented in the very years that Franko was in the lower gymnasium grades. It created serious problems for the teachers, most of whom had been educated in German; some barely knew how to speak Polish. There were no Polish textbooks, and Polish terminology was nonexistent. Thus, during their lessons the teachers had to compensate for the lack of books and create new terminology off the cuff. Another negative aspect was the replacement of German teachers by patriotic Polish instructors. "This," Franko wrote in his memoirs, "was a turning point, difficult for the weak but a godsend for the strong, opening up the field to them for their own original work ungoverned by an excess of regulations."[38]

These circumstances explain why the Drohobych Gymnasium had so many weak and strong teachers: the reform seemed to squeeze out average teachers while strengthening the two extremes. A separate role was played by the urban status of the gymnasium: the city could provide teachers with the same salary level that teachers in state gymnasiums enjoyed. Until such time as the gymnasium was switched to state financing (1871), there were few individuals eager to embark on a teaching career. The finest escaped from Drohobych, and in their place came the *suplenty* (younger teachers), most of whom had not completed university.[39] In his reminiscences, Franko wrote that the majority of gymnasium teachers frittered away their time in coffeehouses, neglecting their duties and often returning to class in a state of inebriation. Among those who did not join this fellowship of heavy drinkers were Edward Hückel, the popular botany teacher who spearheaded German-Ruthenian opposition to Polish assimilation;[40] Emeryk Turczyński, another popular teacher, who replaced Hückel;[41] his brother Yulii; Ivan Verkhratsky, Franko's homeroom teacher, who taught history, literature, the Ruthenian language, and algebra; Dr. Mykola Antonevych; and two catechists—the Greek Catholic Rev. Oleksii Toronsky and the Roman Catholic Rev. Andrzej Drążek [*ZT* 21:316].

The reminiscences of Franko's fellow students confirm the fact that there were several exceptional teachers at the Drohobych Gymnasium. They warmly recall the mathematician Edward Michonski, who, with the aid of numerous examples, convinced them that theory without practice is useless;[42] Franciszek Sykora, a Czech, who taught drawing and gymnastics and later became a professor at the Lviv Polytechnic; Ksenofont Okhrymovych, who later became the mayor of Drohobych; and others.[43] Based on these reminiscences, the names of Franko's teachers who were already or eventually became writers, scholars, parliamentary deputies, and directors of gymnasiums in other Galician cities would make for a rather impressive roster.

The same may be said of the students: among Franko's fellow students were the talented painter Maurycy Gottlieb, one of the founders of modern Jewish art; the well-known Vienna-based political essayist, Dr. Henryk Monat; and others. Franko respectfully remembered these talented individuals; he had similarly deferential feelings for Dr. Isaac Tiegerman [*Mozaika* 342], who later became a lawyer in Drohobych, and Leon Sternbach, professor of Cracow University and the eminent classical philologist.[44] A book on the history of the Drohobych Gymnasium, which was published in 1908 on the occasion of the school's fiftieth anniversary, mentions Ivan Franko among the famous graduates of the gymnasium,[45] and whenever the teachers wanted to boast about their school, they would always mention that they had taught him.[46]

The history of the Drohobych Gymnasium in the days when Ivan Franko was a student cannot be limned in one color. Like all other Austrian gymnasiums, its goal was to produce a passive and sterile intelligentsia. The school was governed by a set of strict and petty regulations, from which no one was exempt. It suffices to say that the formal pretext for the dismissal of its first director was the fact that he attended his audience with the minister of education wearing a beard; the ministerial directive of 1852 permitted state functionaries to wear only moustaches and sideburns.[47] The school administration exercised the most captious control over what the students read. Not only was Darwin banned, but so was everything not included in the curriculum. The ban also included newspapers; thus, Franko completed the gymnasium without ever reading any [21:318]. While he was a student, the gymnasium directors expelled the future leader of the Russophile movement, Osyp Markov (1849–1909), for having received by post several issues of the Russian newspaper *Moskovskie vedomosti*.[48] On the other hand, the years Franko spent in the gymnasium also left him with the fondest memories. "The students' social life," he wrote, "was also the kind that provided many innocent pleasures and few real vexations. The teachers' dealings with the students at the gymnasium were usually liberal, although they hardly ever led to closer friendly relations, as occasionally happens in educational institutions" [*ZT* 15:7].

The Drohobych Gymnasium was certainly not on par with Eton. It was not even among the best schools in Galicia.[49] Nevertheless, it provided Franko with the necessary tools to become a Central European intellectual: oral and written fluency in three languages—Ruthenian (Ukrainian), Polish, and German.[50] Granted, the gymnasium could not completely satisfy his interest in learning. Franko the pupil and gymnasium student stood out from his friends by his boots, which had not been polished for several weeks, his dirty shirt, torn frock coat, uncombed hair—and first place in his class [*ZT* 18:179]. He was born with an extraordinary memory: after a lesson he could repeat the teacher's hour-long lecture word for word [*ZT* 49:243]. Capable of writing five completely different assignments for each assigned homework topic, Franko would distribute them among his classmates in exchange for books [*ZT* 39:40]. In his fifth year at the gymnasium (1871–1872), he began to amass his own library, and by the end of his studies in Drohobych his collection numbered nearly 500 volumes. Since his personal library included many books that were not available at the gymnasium, Franko's apartment, including his library, became a meeting place for small groups of gymnasium students. From time to time they would gather there to read and converse. His library also attracted a local bibliophile named Limbach, the father of one of Franko's schoolmates, and Franko thus obtained access to another private collection [ZT 21:316–32].

Franko read completely unsystematically, one book after another: the works of the Polish writers Aleksander Fredro, Józef Dzierzkowski, Jan Zachariasiewicz, Walery Lozinski; the German writers E. T. A. Hoffmann (whose works Franko read avidly), Christoph Wieland, and Heinrich von Kleist; the memoirs of Benvenuto Cellini in Goethe's translation; and the French writers Eugène Sue and Alexandre Dumas. Limbach got Franko interested in Charles Dickens and at the same time put him off French literature [ZT 21:322, 325]. Franko's unsystematic reading reflected the intellectual limitations of the provincial world, which Franko aptly characterized in his ruminations about Limbach. "This was something akin to a whole, the most diverse bits of human knowledge cobbled together with difficulty, which a curious man from a Galician provincial city could cram in those days" [ZT 21:317].

Out of those "bits of human knowledge" the smallest part was comprised of Ruthenian literature. "In Drohobych it is more difficult to obtain a Ruthenian book than it is to get a fern to bloom," wrote Franko the gymnasium student to his friend in 1874 [ZT 48:10].[51] In Franko's library, Ruthenian literature was represented by a single shelf of journals published between 1850 and the 1860s. Some of them he had rescued from being burned or used for wrapping Easter breads; this was precisely the use to which journals were frequently put in the Greek Catholic families that Franko visited [ZT 21:320]. His favorite section in these journals was belles-lettres; political essays and scholarly articles did not interest him. Ivan Verkhratsky, Franko's Ruthenian language teacher, lent him the two most celebrated works of Ruthenian-Ukrainian literature of the time: *Rusalka Dnistrovaia* (The Dnister Nymph) and Taras Shevchenko's *Kobzar* (The Kobza Player). At the time, Franko did not fully understand *Rusalka Dnistrovaia*, just as he did not fully comprehend "either the language or the content" of the first Ukrainian book that he got his hands on: Kostomarov's *Pereiaslavs'ka nich* (The Pereiaslav Night). Shevchenko, however, made a huge impression on him, so much so that he memorized almost all the poems in the *Kobzar* [ZT 49:243].

The sophistication of "high" Ruthenian culture did not eclipse the riches of the local "low" culture. When he was in the lower grades at the gymnasium, Franko developed a passion for collecting examples of folk culture that he recorded from "knowledgeable people"—artisans, traders, burghers, monks, even beggars. Before his graduation, he had two thick copybooks containing 800 entries consisting mostly of *kolomyiky* (Ruthenian-Ukrainian folk ditties) [*ZT* 49:243]. The powerful contrast between the riches of "low" folk culture and the unfilled space of "high" culture encouraged Franko's literary ambitions. What became a clear certainty by the time he was in the upper grades of the gymnasium, but which was only a possibility when he was at the Basilian school and in the lower gymnasium grades, was his conviction that the great poets were the best models worthy of emulation. He began amassing his library after reading Shakespeare and Schiller [*ZT* 21:318]. During the gatherings at his apartment Franko read to his schoolmates from the works of Shevchenko, Mickiewicz, Słowacki, and the celebrated German poets. In general, he loved to talk about famous people and poets.[52]

It is likely that Franko was decisively influenced by one of his teachers, the poet Ivan Verkhratsky,[53] who considered himself the greatest Ukrainian poet, better even than Shevchenko.[54] Every Sunday Verkhratsky invited Ruthenian students to his home to read books. Franko visited him nearly every day; it was in his home that he obtained a copy of Shevchenko's *Kobzar*. Verkhratsky was the first to notice his student's literary talent, but he did not rate him highly—neither then [*ZT* 22:327] nor later.[55] He had greater esteem for the talent of Franko's gymnasium friend Izydor Pasichynsky, who was already publishing his poems in populist periodicals. The public success enjoyed by Pasichynsky and Dmytro Vintskovsky, a senior at the Drohobych Gymnasium and the author of a long but dull poem titled *Popadia* (The Priest's Wife), inspired Franko and bolstered his desire to become a poet [*ZT* 49:242].

In those days writing poems and short stories was something more than a simple literary occupation. Literature was supposed to strengthen national-political aspirations, especially when political practices had still not been formulated and national orientations were vaguely defined. It suffices to say that all of Franko's teachers who taught language and literature were actively engaged in civic-political affairs. Juliusz Turczyński, who taught Polish history and wrote novels, had taken part in the 1863 uprising; Mykhailo Andrukhovych, who taught Old Church Slavonic, became a deputy to the Galician parliament, and Ivan Verkhratsky and Teofil Hrushkevych were activists in the Ukrainian (so-called populist) camp. Literary gatherings of gymnasium students today could become political parties tomorrow. Thus, enlisting young people in literary activity was a struggle for their souls. When Turczyński learned that Ruthenian students were gathering at Verkhratsky's home, he introduced a series of readings for Polish students at his home.

Franko also began writing in Polish and German; according to Turczyński, he wrote better Polish than his Polish students.[56] Still, Franko preferred the Ruthenian language. His choice of national orientation was not an easy one, as might be supposed. In autonomous Galicia it could become the key prerequisite to a successful career for every educated person. The provincial bodies in Lviv made every effort to eradicate all traces of the German system from Galician gymnasiums and replace German and German-speaking teachers with patriotically inclined Poles, often to the detriment of the level of instruction. In the upper classes, Franko thought about forging himself a career as a gymnasium professor, and therefore he would have had to reflect on the consequences of his linguistic-national orientation. Like the German language earlier, the Polish language opened up access to a larger reader market than the language of the Galician Ruthenians: in Galicia, Poles, Jews, and Ruthenians read Polish, but few Poles or Jews knew how to read Ruthenian because of both its low prestige and the Cyrillic alphabet. In addition, Polish nationalism continued to exert an attractive force thanks to its generally democratic character. It suffices to recall that Franko's uncle died in the Polish uprising of 1863.

This kind of choice was faced not just by Ruthenians but also by educated Galician Jews. Franko's peer from the Drohobych Gymnasium, Maurycy Gottlieb, was an advocate of the pro-Polish orientation: he considered himself both a Jew and a Pole and wanted to help bring these two nationalities closer together.[57] Gottlieb's path was taken by many young Jews, whose numbers in Austrian gymnasiums quickly increased after full legal emancipation was granted to the Jews in 1867.[58] Since emancipation often resulted in assimilation into Polish society, the large number of Jewish students conferred a Polish character on the Drohobych Gymnasium. It should also be noted that the Polish language became dominant everywhere in Drohobych due to the speedy assimilation of the Jews: in 1880 Polish was spoken by nearly half of the residents (48.5 percent), although the proportion of Poles (Roman Catholics) was twice as small.[59]

However, in wealthier Jewish families both parents and children preserved their affection for the German language. It is noteworthy that in the 1880s the Drohobych-based newspaper of the local "progressive" Jews was published in German.[60]

It is difficult to establish with any certainty the processes that were taking place among the Ruthenian students. The biographies of Franko's classmates and other well-known Ruthenians who graduated from the Drohobych Gymnasium between the 1870s and 1890s[61] show that quite a few students refused to submit to Polish assimilation.[62] Franko acknowledged that during his years at the gymnasium, Ruthenian-Polish relations had not yet reached the fever pitch of national and confessional antagonisms that eventually emerged.[63] Relations between the Poles and the Ruthenians took the form of more or less passionate discussions about history or literature, into which the Jewish students did not intrude [*Mozaika* 342].

In one case, Franko became the victim of Polish patriotism. During a literature class, the pupils were assigned to comment on a versified epigram by Mickiewicz:

> W słowach tylko chęć widzim, w działaniu potęgę.
> Trudniej dobrze dzień przeżyć, niż napisać księgę.
>
> In words we only see inclination, in action—might.
> It is more difficult to live honestly through one day than to write a book.[64]

Franko mustered the courage to assert that, although Mickiewicz's statement was beautiful, it was not true, because it is more difficult to write a book, and the written word sometimes becomes a great matter. For this, the teacher reprimanded him severely for his disrespect to Mickiewicz. Later, during a teachers' meeting, Franko's conduct was brought up as an example of his flippant disregard for morality, and he was given a low mark for behavior [*ZT* 26:325]. This incident marked the beginning of his struggle against the cult of the greatest Polish poet, one that Franko would wage until the end of his life.

The psychological portrait of Franko the gymnasium student reveals a trait that would clearly emerge in adulthood and which he would convert into a kind of programmatic principle: "To kick against the pricks, to swim against the current" [*ZT* 1:54]. Whenever he felt any pressure directed against him, he resisted, and when there was none, he became indecisive. Franko knew full well that he would never be a Pole, nor would he become a Polish poet. However, he lacked confidence where the choice between a Russophile and a Ukrainophile orientation was concerned. This is most vividly traced in the inconsistent orthography of his early works. Traditionally, Galician-Ruthenian literature was written and printed according to etymological spelling, in which written words did not reflect their contemporary sound but the sound that words had possessed much earlier, in the period when the Old Church Slavonic language was preeminent. In its stead, the Ukrainophile orientation proposed a "phonetic" orthography, the essence of which boiled down to the principle: "Write what you hear, read what you see."

The struggle between the proponents of the two orthographic systems lay at the heart of the disputes taking place in the milieu of the Galician-Ruthenian intelligentsia in the 1860s–1880s. Most Greek Catholic priests championed etymology because they were accustomed to Old Church Slavonic.[65] For nationally aware patriots, what was important was the fact that etymology underscored the antiquity ("historicity") of the Old Church Slavonic culture—and in their eyes this placed it on an equal level with Polish culture. As Rev. Yosyf Levytsky argued in his 1848 lecture at the founding meeting of the Ruthenian Committee in Drohobych, "Our brothers, the Poles, are famous for having many printed books that people do not read, but we Ruthenians do not have so many books. We do not envy them that wealth, and we Ruthenians are satisfied with our books and our literature. We have an entire divine service in the language of ancient Rus, and is that not a beautiful literature?"[66] In their sermons Old Ruthenian priests sought to convince the peasants that as soon as the new orthography was introduced, serfdom would be revived (because the phonetic system was considered a Polish invention). There was a joke circulating throughout Galicia about an Old Ruthenian grandfather who killed his grandson, a gymnasium student, with a staff, after he found him reading books printed phonetically.[67]

Ivan Verkhratsky encouraged his students to write phonetically, but not in their good copybooks. This appeal had an effect on Franko: he wrote most of his literary works in the gymnasium phonetically. Karlo Bandrivsky recalled that in the sixth year of the gymnasium (1872–1873) Franko had frequent arguments with Mykhailo Andrukhovych, the Ruthenian language teacher, which centered on etymology and phonetics, the "iazychie" (the language invented in the nineteenth century by Galician Russophiles) of *Slovo* and the folk language. The discussions took place "so energetically that both of them would usually talk through the entire hour, but the other Ukrainians were indifferent to their conversations."[68] A year later, in 1874, Franko submitted his poems to the Ruthenian students' journal *Druh*, which was published in Lviv. After his first publications he stopped sending his new poems because the previous ones had been so edited to reflect "iazychie" that he barely recognized them.[69] Another friend from the gymnasium recounted the following episode in the life of Franko the student: after compiling several of his translations of Schiller and Goethe, he sent them to a printing house in Kolomyia, owned by a Russophile named Bilous. But he never received a reply, perhaps because most of Franko's translations were written phonetically.[70]

A perusal of Franko's letters from 1874–1875 casts doubt on the veracity of these accounts. It is unlikely that, while he was at the gymnasium, he would have unambiguously opted for phonetics, the folk language and, correspondingly, the Ukrainian orientation. The language of his homework assignments and early works is full of Russophile words, and Verkhratsky did not stop correcting them and replacing them with Ukrainian forms.[71] The editors of *Druh* published poems phonetically if their authors insisted. This is what Franko's colleague, Izydor Pasichynsky, did.[72] For Franko, this question was clearly not a fundamental one. His letters to the editors of *Druh* are written according to the etymological orthography [*ZT* 48:606]. In one of his letters he complains about the lack of Ruthenian literature in Drohobych, but by this literature Franko meant not only Ukrainian ("Little Russian") but also Russian ("Great Russian") literature [*ZT* 48:10].

Franko later admitted that in his last years as a student in Drohobych he was merely an observer of the various parties and shadings of Galician Rus, and that these observations were "not without plentiful disillusionments and mistakes" [*ZT* 15:12–13]. The arguments around language and national orientation were foreign to him and completely incomprehensible. He could not discern any order in them, and for a long time he vacillated between the two sides [*ZT* 49:244]. He sounds like a Russophile when he corresponds with Vasyl Davydiak, a member of the editorial board of *Druh*, and like a Ukrainophile when he writes to Shchasny Selsky, the leader of the Vienna-based Ukrainophile Sich student society [*ZT* 48:17]. In 1875 he writes the poem "Skhid sontsia" (Sunrise), on the occasion of the Russophile popular assembly that was convened in Halych, the ancient capital of Galicia, by the Russophile Mikhail Kachkovsky Society [*ZT* 3:296–99]. But one or two years earlier he had become a member of the Ukrainophile Prosvita Society and was pleased that he belonged to this society, "as though it were the greatest treasure" [*ZT* 49:324].

Had Franko been born earlier or attended a different gymnasium, he might have been able to avoid these vacillations. In the 1860s, when he was still in the lower grades, the "young populists" appeared in the public arena, activists who distinctly and unambiguously declared their Ukrainian identity. They had experienced their conversion to Ukrainianness when they were studying in gymnasiums and universities, and for that reason their activity found expression in the creation of a network of Ukrainophile student communities. In the Drohobych Gymnasium this type of community was founded as early as 1864, but its existence was short-lived.[73] At any rate, it was defunct by the time Franko became a student there. In the 1870s such communities still existed in Berezhany, Ternopil, Lviv, and Stanyslaviv. In Drohobych there was practically no national life among the Ruthenian intelligentsia.[74] In the spring of 1875 the populist student group Druzhnii lykhvar (the Friendly Usurer) asked Franko "to establish a community among the young people in Drohobych, [like the kind] that exist in other places" [*ZT* 48:17]. Nothing came of this proposal. The reasons behind the failure of this project were described in the memoirs of the Galician-Ukrainian writer, Andrii Chaikovsky, who was a student at the Sambir Gymnasium and a member of the local group. During a visit to Drohobych, Chaikovsky and his friends were struck by the lifestyle of the Drohobych students, who drank, caroused, and flirted, some of whom even dallied with the wives of their teachers. When he met Franko, Chaikovsky asked him why it was impossible to organize anything in Drohobych and heard the following reply: "With whom? Don't you know what the local students are like? As long as they have a tavern and a glass [they are content]; but besides that there's nothing."[75] In a letter that Franko wrote to Selsky in April 1875, he said that in the entire Drohobych Gymnasium, there were only three students, including him, who were interested in Ruthenian-Ukrainian affairs [*ZT* 48:17]—too few to form a group.[76]

The young Franko's uncertainty on questions of national identity in Galicia was not an exception from the norm but the norm itself. His personal vacillations reflected the ambiguity and opportunism that characterized his milieu. Many activists in the Ruthenian camp were avoiding having to make a clear-cut national choice. They were active, especially on the grassroots level, both in Russophile and Ukrainophile organizations without making a crucial distinction between the former and the latter.[77] They agreed among themselves that they were not Poles and to a great extent decisively resisted Polish assimilationist pressure, even if they spoke Polish to each other. But they did not know, or did not want to know, whether they were Ukrainians or Russians: both of these national identities fit into the general and rather diluted concept of "Ruthenianness." Furthermore, this concept was convenient in that it did not conflict with one's higher loyalty to the Habsburg monarchy and therefore did not present any threat to one's career.

Several years later, in September 1878, after he had experienced his conversion to Ukrainophilism and socialism, Franko wrote a series of short stories collectively titled *Ruthenians*. In his introduction, Franko sought to characterize Ruthenians "as a social type" whose main traits are "ambiguity, indefiniteness, and half-ness." This type, in Franko's view, came into being as a result of the superimposition of the general European current—the emergence of the bourgeoisie with its bourgeois impulses—over specific Galician conditions [*ZT* 15:13]. Although one can agree with the first part of this description (ambiguity as the Ruthenians' principal trait), it is difficult, however, to accept the second half of Franko's characterization (Ruthenians as a manifestation of bourgeois culture). Franko the newly converted socialist was applying the rigoristic category of Marxist analysis. Ruthenian-ness as a phenomenon was deeply enrooted not in general European bourgeois culture but in the local nobiliary culture. Its roots may be traced to the Habsburgs' enlightenment policy of the late eighteenth century. One of the goals of Maria Theresa and Josef II was to raise the educational level of the Greek Catholic clergy, the only elite in Ruthenian society. However, the policy of enlightenment had an unexpected effect: instead of bringing the Greek Catholic clergy closer to the other strata of Ruthenian society—first and foremost, the peasantry—it led to its assimilation into the ruling nobiliary culture. "Whereas in 1870 a Greek Catholic priest could feel almost at home with peasants in a tavern, in 1830 he sought more refined company.... To rid oneself of one's cultural or social closeness to the peasant meant raising oneself to the status that still had no counterpart in Ukrainian society. Whereas, on the individual level, a move to the city inevitably meant accepting the ruling Polish culture; the same way, advancing up the social ladder led to the Polonization of the entire clerical stratum."[78]

The further development of events turned the Galician Greek Catholic clergy away from Polish assimilation and brought to the fore the Ruthenian national camp. However, the nobiliary culture remained entrenched. Its durability was ensured, among other things, by the fact that Greek Catholic priests were a quasi-nobiliary estate because they were permitted to marry, and their sons frequently chose their fathers' profession. Marriages between the petty nobility and priests' children, and the fact that sons of the nobility often became priests themselves (like the brothers of Franko's grandmother and mother) strengthened this fusion of ecclesiastical tradition with secular nobiliary culture.

In his last years at the gymnasium Franko himself automatically assimilated into this milieu. When he was in the senior classes, during his vacations and religious holidays he spent time as a guest in the families of his high school friends whose fathers were priests. Franko earned money for his upkeep by tutoring two students from the lower grades, Ipolyt Pohoretsky and Yaroslav Roshkevych. (Even though Franko had a tuition waiver owing to his poverty, his stepfather could only afford part of his upkeep in Drohobych.)[79] In the summer of 1874, after completing his pre-graduation class, Franko set out for the first time on a long trip to the Carpathian Mountains in order "to see a bit more of the world and people." The two major stops during his journey were the parish of his uncle (his mother's brother) in the village of Volosianka and the parish headed by the father of his friend, Yaroslav Roshkevych, in the village of Lolyn, Stryi County [ZT 49:244]. In Lolyn, Franko fell in love with Yaroslav's sister Olha, and his long-lasting love affair with this priest's daughter was one of the most memorable events of his youth. Yaroslav and Olha's father, the village priest Rev. Mykhailo Roshkevych, was an Old Ruthenian, who considered Franko a good match for his daughter. Although Franko was poor, his gymnasium education and even greater literary talents gave grounds to expect that, in time, he would attain a respectable and secure position. Reverend Roshkevych had an opportunity to reinforce this conviction when Metropolitan Yosyf Sembratovych visited his parish. Franko ended up in the company of the priests who assembled in Lolyn for this occasion, and, impressed by his erudition, they prophesied a great future for him.[80]

Franko's first visit to the Roshkevych family shocked everyone: he appeared with a bindle tied to a stick held over his shoulder, which held all his belongings; his shabby suit created the impression that he lacked taste and his behavior at the table that he lacked good manners.[81] But he went to considerable effort to meet the expectations and standards of his new social surroundings. Pictured in a photograph with his tutees, Ipolyt Pohoretsky and Yaroslav Roshkevych, he looked like a fashionably dressed dandy:[82] with the help of Pohoretsky and his contacts, Franko managed to get himself a new suit, in which he would not be ashamed to show up at the Roshkevyches' and other priestly families.[83]

Franko's letters to Vasyl Davydiak, one of the members of the editorial board of *Druh*, are very helpful for learning about Franko's personality. They contain very little sincerity and simplicity—the very two traits that in later years he valued most in his friendships. Instead, they are full of affectation, sentimental exaggerations, and ill-disguised flattery. He addresses Davydiak as "my first friend whom I am meeting on the road of life" [*ZT* 48:7], even though, as we have seen, Franko never lacked for friends either in Nahuievychi, or Yasenytsia Silna, or Drohobych. This same tone marks his letters to Olha Roshkevych, and until his acquaintance with her, he writes, "I did not have friends; I did not know anything except my books. To me the world remained unknown, and the great school of friends was closed." It is only now that "the wide world has opened up before my eyes, and it is brighter in front of me. But this change was too abrupt, and my mind worked so much and so intensively that I became completely enervated and felt the seed of death, a presentiment of the grave's cold in my breast. All my views of life from that time onward became utterly different, my entire being changed" [*ZT* 48:18, 20]. There is one distinctive detail: having begun to correspond with Olha in the Ruthenian language, by his second letter (cited immediately above) Franko switched to German, a language that was more appropriate for writing letters. No less telling are passing mentions of the literary models on which Franko was orienting himself: Klara Bauer's novel *Erste Liebe* (First Love), translated by Davydiak, and Mykhailo Vahylevych's novel *Domna Rozanda*. Both of these romance novels, which were published in *Druh*, are steeped in sentimentality and the heady scent of the literary salon, just as the assumed name of the literary beginner, *Dzhedzhalyk*, smacked of a Bohemian atmosphere. Franko was clearly trying to meet the literary tastes of the educated Ruthenian public.

His friend Mykhailo Pavlyk had a completely different experience. Fate brought them together for the duration of their lives after they completed their respective gymnasiums and arrived for their studies at Lviv University. Each of them was born in a village, and for both of them education helped them gain entry to priests' families. But Pavlyk did not know how to integrate into the priestly milieu, nor did he want to. In a letter to Mykhailo Drahomanov (20 April 1876), he writes:

> I have been going around to the priests' homes, as though poisoned, but how could I even contemplate their entertainments when the life in their homes pricked my heart: thus, sitting lost in sadness among the dances and raucous laughter, I sit by myself in a corner and think about what I did not learn in school. And that thought ran through my entire life all the way back to my childhood, where not such a warm heart clasped itself to me like those wax dolls [priests' daughters—Y. H.] who know nothing but how to dress, whiten themselves [powder their faces—Y. H.], jump about, laugh stridently, eat and sleep, and not see anyone in the world besides themselves. They carouse, drink, and even laugh at the motley crew that sometimes peers through the window [watching] the lords banqueting it up with their money. After the banquet that same frolicsome young lady vilifies the peasants and slaps the servants in the face. All that kind of behavior of our nobility [priests' families—Y. H.] toward the working cattle hurts, it hurts a lot, because who can stand it when mud is thrown at one's father and mother![84]

Pavlyk came away with similar impressions of his stay in Lolyn, where Franko would take him as a guest of the Roshkevyches. The Rev. Mykhailo Roshkevych nourished the conviction that the peasants were reptiles. After reading a novel of peasant life that Pavlyk lent him, he became extremely angry with the author: "He must be some kind of pig if he wants to describe such a villainous, wretched life."[85] After returning from Lolyn, Pavlyk advised Franko to tell his beloved to "remove all those rags from her head, from her face, from her heart; and she should incline herself a bit toward the people—if you do not want a doll, then send her to the hundred winds."

Franko's behavior and manners surprised and irritated him: "It's a pity that [Franko] is so chained by the opinions of our intelligentsia: if at least he were a priest's son—but no; so just try and figure out where all this comes from...I would not feel half as sorry if he were from the aristocracy—but it is a bitter thing to see him this way, and I do not know what all this means." Franko gave the following reply to his friend's complaints: "If you spent more time among the intelligentsia, you would not be so ill-disposed toward it."[86]

Pavlyk characterized the Greek Catholic clergy of the time as a "priestly nobility," and he was vexed by the dominance of the nobiliary culture among the Ruthenian students, the most convincing proof of which he considered their superior attitude to "their younger brother," the peasant. "The word 'peasant' amuses [the students—Y. H.], and if you could see that ironic laughter of those future 'spreaders of ignorance' [*proslipyteliv*: Pavlyk's pun on the word "enlighteners," *prosvityteliv*—Trans.]....The academics [students—Y. H.] consider the peasants a nullity, 'oxen,' as they say; in their minds a peasant is lower than a dog," Pavlyk writes in his letters to Drahomanov in 1875–1876.[87] Pavlyk does not say whether Franko, too, was infected by feelings of superiority to the peasants, but in any case it had not occurred to the neophyte writer to write for the peasants. Pavlyk recapitulates Franko's words, uttered in early 1876: "I write for the intelligentsia, and I am not thinking [of writing] for the peasant."[88]

Franko's youthful plans upon completing his studies in Drohobych may be reduced to a few points: he had no intention of returning to the village; he was counting on making himself a career as a gymnasium teacher; and he dreamed about a literary career. Franko was certain that he would not be a Polish poet. But neither did he have any ambitions of becoming a rural poet. His reading public was supposed to be the educated Ruthenian milieu with its specific quasi-nobiliary culture. For the sake of success he was ready to cater to the salon tastes of this milieu; he was not concerned with the prospect of forming new tastes or a new milieu. He would experience the desire to create the former and the latter only as a result of a profound revolution of ideas that took place the first year after he left Drohobych.

Chapter 5

Between the Small and the Large Fatherland

In this chapter, I will digress from Franko's real biography and consider the paths his life might have taken. I will not be discussing here the possible versions of Franko's climb up the social ladder. There are two reasons for this. First, toward the end of his life social circumstances had changed to such a degree that practically all restrictions on upward mobility had disappeared. As the biographies of Franko's contemporaries and fellow Ukrainians attest, a happy coincidence could transform a nonprivileged but educated person from a village into a university professor (for example, Franciszek Bujak, the famous Polish economist and founder of an entire school of economic history), a prime minister (Wincenty Witos), or even a president of a state (Tomáš Garrigue Masaryk). Franko, who did not obtain a professorial chair in the 1890s, died just shortly before likely gaining honors from the newly founded national Ukrainian state, proclaimed in Kyiv in 1917 and in Lviv in 1918. The second reason is that in his lifetime Franko had already achieved the maximum, having attained the symbolic status of a "national prophet" and "Ukrainian Moses."[1] Thus, it makes no sense to discuss other, "inferior," possibilities.

I am interested in something else: in what other communities could Franko have achieved leading positions? This question will be examined by using the example of choice of fatherland. In my view, it is competing images of "fatherland," not "nation" or "class," which most fully recreate the spectrum of alternatives that Franko and his contemporaries faced. A "fatherland" could be a nation, or a community that was larger than a nation (an empire, all of Slavdom) or smaller (an individual territory or other type of land). Furthermore, even the conscious refusal to choose a fatherland enlisted the "refuser" in other modern communities: the international socialists ("The workers have no fatherland") or modernist artists ("Art has no fatherland"). One's attitude to the fatherland presumes the utmost loyalty, for whose sake everything must be sacrificed: personal happiness, property and, if necessary, even life. The construction of a "fatherland" was the joint activity of various groups: politicians and geographers, historians and statisticians, military men and writers. Of all these categories I will focus mainly on the last one, since the role of writers was a special and, in Eastern Europe, even an exceptional one, in a certain sense. It was precisely writers who endowed the image of fatherland with the highest emotional register, something that was lacking in politicians' declarations and geographical or statistical compendia.[2] They created an "imagined fatherland" and transformed all their readers into a "nation of dreamers." It was said of writers that they carry the fatherland with them, and some of them were regarded as its living embodiment.[3]

The following exposition does not pretend to be a systematic discussion of this topic.[4] It touches on it only to the degree that it could have concerned the young Franko, particularly at the time that he was completing his gymnasium studies and preparing to enroll in the university. Hence I focus, above all, on those literary works, individuals, and circumstances that had a direct impact on his formation and to which he referred in his own writings. In this sense, they are part of his biography.

"Sein Vaterland muß größer sein..." (His Fatherland's Not Bounded So!)

In 1904, Franko published a short story titled "Fatherland," in which he recounted certain events from his youth. The main hero of the story is his classmate from the gymnasium, Opanas Morymukha, an invented character, although, one may suppose, not entirely lacking in realistic features. Morymukha is the son of a wealthy peasant from the Drohobych area. When the author of the short story pays a visit to Opanas's village, he realizes that there is something bigger and more abstract behind his friend's stories: "I had never encountered a boy who so passionately loved his own little corner, identified so much with it, and put his entire soul into it, and at the time only one thing mystified me: how could someone become so attached, with one's entire being, to such a miserable, sad, dreary, and thoroughly undistinguished place as his celebrated "fatherland" [*ZT* 21:396].

The years pass. Opanas begins his studies at Lviv University and falls in love with a beautiful young lady, who works in a local café. The male patrons call her "Kitten." The young woman agrees to become Morymukha's mistress in exchange for helping her leave Lviv for the wide world. With this goal in mind, Opanas sells his deceased parents' homestead, and when he is leaving his native village, the peasants throw rocks and mud at him, shouting, "Judas! Judas! You sold the fatherland!"

Morymukha's happiness is short-lived. After Kitten spends all of four days with him in Vienna, she disappears, along with his money. He returns to Galicia and becomes a teacher in a remote Carpathian village, "sowing the seeds of civilization in this dark backwater a little at a time." Years later he is tracked down by the mortally ill Kitten, who has returned to be with her former lover before she dies. The story ends on a moralizing note, with the author commenting on the great numbers of people in Galicia, like Kitten, who have wasted their youth, beauty, and strength of intellect without any benefit to themselves or society. Declaring that there is only one cure for this waste of energy and talent, the narrator sums up: "The 'fatherland' must be kept in one's soul" [ZT 21:423].

In the story of Opanas Morymukha, Franko described the process that millions of his contemporaries had experienced: the displacement of the small fatherland by the large fatherland within the hierarchy of social values. The small fatherlands were the parental home and area in which a person was born, that which was automatically inherited without conscious choice as a result of one's very birth. In contrast, the large fatherland was understood as a community of an ideological nature. It could not be inherited; one had to choose it for oneself, and unconditional loyalty to it was considered the highest virtue.[5] This was not a new idea, having been clearly articulated in antiquity. In his *Odes* Horace wrote, "Dulce et decorum est pro patria mori" (It is sweet and right to die for your country), while Cicero proclaimed, "Patria mihi vita mea carior est" (My country is dearer to me than life). In his *Aeneid* Virgil accorded a place in heaven to those who had died for the fatherland, alongside poets, priests, and prophets.[6] The Western Christian world continued this tradition, endowing the concept of fatherland with two meanings, a narrow one and a broad one (similar to the German *Heimat* and *Vaterland*, respectively). From the late Middle Ages (the twelfth and thirteenth centuries) the second meaning gained greater currency as a symbol of loyalty to a political community. At various times and among various peoples it waned and then reappeared: the actualization of the "ideological fatherland" may be seen during the Crusades, the Hundred Years' War, the Italian Renaissance, and the French Revolution.[7]

The study of old Polish literary texts reveals a trend toward the supplanting of the "small" fatherland by the "large" fatherland in Polish culture, which took place as early as the sixteenth to eighteenth centuries.[8] This trend spread to the eastern ("Ruthenian") borderland of the Rzeczpospolita, a considerable portion of which ended up under Muscovite rule and the later Russian Empire after the Khmelnytsky Uprising (1648–1657). But whereas before the uprising the members of the local Ruthenian elite, together with the Ukrainian Cossack leadership, regarded the Rzeczpospolita as their fatherland, later there emerged a new concept of *otchyzna* (homeland), the newly founded Cossack Hetman State.

The concept of fatherland in the Polish and Ukrainian traditions of the time had a territorial, not national, character. The object of supreme loyalty was territory, not nation. The concept of national affiliation of the people inhabiting a certain territory may have been discussed—in reality, it was—but it did not have any relevant political significance. As well, a territory could signify either a state or a country. For example, the Ukrainian Cossack officers regarded their fatherland both as their own state and the territory that was not included in this state but one over which they sought to establish their control ("Ukraine on both sides of the Dnipro River," including even the later Galicia and the "Ruthenian–Little Russian city of Lviv"). The duality of the fatherland concept transformed it into a very convenient method of political legitimation: as shown by the history of revolts organized by the Polish nobility against the king during the Rzeczpospolita or the Cossack hetman Ivan Mazepa's revolt against Tsar Peter I of Russia, love of fatherland could justify both loyalty to the supreme ruler and a revolt against him. This duality explains why the concepts of "Poland" and "Ukraine" survived even after the Rzeczpospolita and the Hetman state ceased to exist: the disappearance of a state did not signify the disappearance of the land that remained the object of loyalty. Between the seventeenth and eighteenth centuries a third concept of fatherland emerged alongside the Rzeczpospolita and the Hetman State, which competed for loyalty within the milieu of the Eastern Christian intellectuals of the Kyiv-Mohyla Academy, the largest educational center in the Eastern Christian world (until the founding of Moscow University in 1755): the concept of "Rus" / "Ruthenian land" as the ethnic-dynastic unity of Kyiv and Moscow.[9]

Of course, the notions of fatherland in the period between the sixteenth and eighteenth centuries, as well as during the nineteenth century, were not identical even when they were formally called the same way: a good example is the transformations that the concept of "Rus" underwent in imaginary geography. Paramount among the changes that took place in the concept of fatherland during the nineteenth century was the increasingly frequent use of the word "fatherland" as a synonym for the word "nation."[10] But even the very concept of "nation" also underwent a profound change linked to the proliferation of the Jacobin model of the nation based on the idea of a homogeneous cultural community, and which therefore spread to all social strata, not just the privileged elite.[11]

However, one should not overlook elements of a certain continuity—in particular, the role of the tradition of antiquity in the formation of the concept of fatherland. The study of antiquity lay at the heart of gymnasium education in the nineteenth century both in the Austrian (Austro-Hungarian) and Russian empires. Moreover, since this education was the sine qua non of any career, it was difficult to stumble upon an official, officer, teacher, or lawyer who had not been assigned the memorization of the writings of Cicero, Horace, and Virgil on the sanctity of the fatherland. The empire sought to inculcate in their subjects the feeling that their large fatherland was specifically the empire. However, many educated individuals had a more or less conscious awareness that their dreamed-of fatherland did not necessarily coincide with the borders of the empire in which they were fated to be born and reside: to serve it—yes, especially if this promised a paycheck and a pension; but to die for it?

An example of this type of thinking on the part of local intellectuals may be illustrated by the poem "Des Teutschen Vaterland," written by the German poet Ernst Moritz Arndt (1769–1860):

"Was ist des Teutschen Vaterland?
Ist's Preußenland? ist's Schwabenland?
Ist's, wo am Rhein die Rebe blüht?
Ist's, wo am Belt die Möve zieht?"—
O nein, nein, nein!
Sein Vaterland muß größer sein." —

[...]

Was ist des Teutschen Vaterland?
So nenne mir das große Land!

Gewiß, es ist das Östereich,
An Ehren und an Siegen reich?"—
"O nein, nein, nein!
Sein Vaterland muß größer sein."—

"Was ist des Teutschen Vaterland?
So nenne endlich mir das Land!"—
"So weit die deutsche Zunge klingt
Und Gott im Himmel Lieder singt,
Das soll es sein!
Das, wackrer Teutscher, nenne dein!" [...][12]

Which is the German's fatherland?
Is't Prussia's or Swabia's land?
Is't where the Rhine's rich vintage streams?
Or where the Northern sea-gull screams?—
Ah, no, no, no!
His fatherland's not bounded so!

[...]

Which is the German's fatherland?
Come, tell me now the famous land.
Doubtless, it is the Austrian state,
In honors and in triumphs great.—
Ah, no, no, no!
His fatherland's not bounded so!

Which is the German's fatherland?
So tell me now at last the land!—
As far's the German's accent rings
And hymns to God in heaven sings,—
That is the land,—
There, brother, is thy fatherland![13] [...]

Arndt's biography is similar to the life of Franko and of his hero, Opanas Morymukha. Arndt was born into a wealthy peasant family in Lower Pomerania (Vorpommern), at the time ruled by the Swedish kings. In the local inhabitants' perception, Swedish rule was not foreign: the Swedish royal dynasty was related to the Pomeranian line, which had died out several generations earlier. Arndt went from being a loyal Swedish subject to a German patriot. This decisive about-face happened during his studies at the university, where he was a member of the nationalistically inclined German student milieu. His poem "Des Teutschen Vaterland" was written in 1813, on the crest of a wave of German patriotic feeling during the Napoleonic Wars. Arndt dreamed of a single, great Germany as the third largest European state, positioned next to the British and Russian empires. This dream collided with the plans of the Austrian chancellor, Metternich, to restore the French monarchy as a counterweight to Russia. Metternich was prepared to give the new French monarch, Louis XVIII, the lands west of the Rhine, which, in his opinion, formed a natural border between the French and German lands. Arndt's reaction was to write that poem: the only natural border for the German patriot could be the extreme edge of the territory where the German language could be heard.[14]

According to this formal criterion, the "German fatherland" was also supposed to include Austrian Galicia, the easternmost territory where the German language was spoken by Austrian officials, German colonists, and the educated classes (teachers, librarians, newspaper publishers, and the like), who consciously imitated the culture of the central and northern German lands.[15] In addition, the image of Galicia as a German land was bolstered by the presence of a numerically strong Jewish community, whose Yiddish language Austrian legislation and Austrian statistics called a German dialect.

Arndt defined the territory of the German people as the lands stretching "from the North Sea to the Carpathians." The next generation of German nationalists extended the border all the way to the Black Sea coast, while the concept of *Raumgefühl* (the feeling of space) vis-à-vis the East as a land that had neither limits nor borders reigned supreme in the folk culture. German nationalists argued about the way the unification of all the German lands would take place—around the Austrian Habsburgs (the so-called *Grossdeutschland*, or "Great Germany" project) or the Prussian Hohenzollerns' project (*Kleindeutschland*, or "Little Germany"). Both the former and the latter agreed that it was vitally important for the German nation to move eastward (*Drang nach Osten*).[16]

According to each of these criteria, Galicia formally corresponded to the definition of the German fatherland. However, despite the considerable advances of Germanization, during the period of Austrian rule in Galicia or outside its borders not a single poetic text was published that treated Galicia as a part of "Germany" according to Arndt's understanding.[17]

Galicia did not fit the image of a German fatherland either according to the old monarchical principle (because it was never part of the Holy Roman Empire) or by the logic of a modern empire: promoting German nationalism in a state where non-Germans (Hungarians, Poles, Ruthenians, Romanians, and so on) comprised two-thirds of the population would have been suicidal on Vienna's part. The Germans' preeminence in the Habsburg monarchy was derived not from national motives but from their historic-ocultural role: they were true *Staatsvolk* (state people), who dominated state institutions.[18] Where the lands of the former Rzeczpospolita were concerned, there was an additional element, the enduring stereotype of the superiority of German culture over *Polnische Wirtschaft* (Polish economy), which was associated with disorder, anarchy, and, as Arndt claimed, with "the primordial Polish sin—forgetfulness concerning the affairs of the fatherland."[19]

In newly annexed Galicia, Austrian officials perceived a semi-Asiatic land, a symbol of civilizational backwardness. As for the local inhabitants—above all, the Polish nobility, which was regarded as the culpable party behind this backwardness—the Habsburg bureaucrats considered it their mission "to reeducate these Sarmatian beasts into real human beings."[20] Admittance to high German culture was only one instrument, but hardly the primary one, of civilizational reeducation. Consequently, the successes of "Germanization" in the mid-nineteenth century were measured not by linguistic assimilation but by well-paved roads, whose excellence surpassed the old Polish roads and their counterparts in the neighboring Russian Empire. The German character of Lviv ("Lemberg") resided in the cleanliness of its streets; in the feeling which every inhabitant was supposed to have—namely, that the law both afforded protection and reigned supreme; and, last but not least, in the elegant local coffeehouses, whose stylish appearance rivaled the cafés of Dresden and other German cities.[21]

The goal of the government's policy was to create civilized Galicians, not Galician Germans. Austrian Galicia as a civilizational project was formulated to be linguistically and ethnically heterogeneous.[22] It was supposed to recreate the multinational character of the empire, whose natural and cultural diversity was supposed to underscore the unity of the country, just as the history of each ethnic group flowed into the broad river of the "general history of the old fatherland,"—that is, the Habsburg monarchy.[23] But during its existence, the Habsburgs' experiment to create a Galician identity did not produce any conspicuous results.[24] The literature of this period mentions the existence in Galicia of a group of intellectuals who considered themselves Galicians, rather than Poles, Ruthenians, or Jews. However, one should note the scarcity of such mentions as opposed to the number of works whose authors clearly and vigorously discuss Polish, Ruthenian, Ukrainian, Russian, Jewish, and German identities. In addition, in works dating to the 1850s–1880s, "Galicians" figure as "transitional" and "disappearing" types, and in satirical verses they were pitied or mocked by being contrasted to real patriots.[25]

By the end of Habsburg rule, the Galician populace demonstrated a broad spectrum of loyalties, from national apathy to national chauvinism. According to one hypothesis, within this spectrum "Galicianism" could assume a form of conscious opposition to all these competing loyalties[26]—an identity by default, so to speak. Yet, even if the correctness of such a hypothesis were accepted, one must recognize that, in the long run, the "Galician community" had no chance of survival. In the modern world, where, as Ernest Gellner has written, each man "must have a nationality as he must have a nose and two ears,"[27] the Galician, devoid of nationality, was a kind of "man without qualities" (to quote Robert Musil) and thus looked, rather, as bizarre as an antediluvian relic.

"I to wszystko niby moje..." (And all of it seems to be mine...)

In any case, voices of indignation at the Habsburgs' attempts "to bring about the extinction of the nonhistoric Galicians"[28] were occasionally heard among the local educated populace. The main competitor of the Galician fatherland was the concept of a Polish fatherland situated within the old historical borders before 1772. The memory of the Rzeczpospolita was still very fresh, and its bearers, the Polish nobility and Polish burghers, were the only strata in Galicia that, owing to their numerical strength and education, could compete with the Austrian bureaucrats. Until the final third of the nineteenth century local public life was marked by antagonism between the German and Polish cultures. The educated public was divided into two hostile camps: the "Schiller party" and the "Mickiewicz party," named after the most famous poets of the two nations.[29]

The irony is that, as with the majority of Polish patriots, Galicia occupied a secondary place in Mickiewicz's imagination.[30] For him, as for the majority of Polish patriots, the heart of the Polish fatherland beat in the *kresy*, the Belarusian-Lithuanian-Ukrainian borderland of the former

Rzeczpospolita, which had been annexed by the Russian Empire. This borderland was the theater of the two largest Polish uprisings (1830–1831 and 1863–1864) against Russian rule. Mickiewicz, together with the Polish poets of the so-called "Ukrainian school," was instrumental in creating the myth of the *kresy* as a land of social harmony, where Polish landowners fraternized with Ruthenian (read: Belarusian and Ukrainian) peasants, where Jews sang Polish patriotic songs, and where the Ukrainian Cossacks prophesied the restoration of the Rzeczpospolita.[31] The situation changed during the last third of the nineteenth century with the emergence of the concept of Galicia as the Polish "Piedmont." From that point, Galicia shifted into the very center of the imagined Polish fatherland. In the minds of many Poles, Cracow, the capital of Little Poland, the ancient Polish state, transcended "Russified" Warsaw as a symbol of the vitality of Polish state traditions. In Polish literature and political essay writing, the term "Little Poland" gradually grew to embrace all of Galicia, including its eastern, Ruthenian, part.[32]

Polish patriots were aware of the strong regional and linguistic-ethnic differences among the various lands of their fatherland: the "Crown lands," Lithuania, Great Poland, Rus, Podillia, Volhynia, Ukraine, and the Polish Livonia. They believed, however, that all these differences were of secondary importance. In their view, the main "civilizational-cultural" line of differentiation lay between the Polish and German lands in the west and the Polish and Russian lands in the east. Poland's relation to Russia was ostensibly a mirror reflection of Germany's relation to Poland because it was formed within the categories of the West's civilizational superiority over the East—in this case, Poland's over Russia. In extreme cases—for example, the theories of Franciszek Duchiński—the Russians were generally considered as belonging to the non-European ("Turanid") race.[33] The territory up to the Dnipro River, including Kyiv and the local "Ruthenian" (later, Belarusian and Ukrainian) population, was considered to have been ennobled by Polish civilization and was thus part of the Polish cultural and political space.[34]

Confirmation of this view, among others, was the speedy assimilation of the educated strata of Ruthenians, Lithuanians, Jews, and Germans into Polish culture. The example of Wincenty Pol (1807–1873), the famous Polish poet and father of modern Polish geography, may be considered significant. The son of a Habsburg official, Pol took offense whenever he was reminded of his German background. In his view, "historic Poland" was united by the basins of the Vistula, San, Dnister, Dnipro, Oder, Neman, and

Dvina rivers into a single geographic space stretching "from sea to sea." Just as the waters of those rivers flowed into each other, all the peoples inhabiting this territory were also supposed to unite. Pol dressed his geographic vision in poetic forms:

> Byłem w Litwie i w Koronie,
> Byłem w tej i owej stronie,
> Byłem tu i tam;
> Od Beskidów do Pomorza,
> Z Litwy aż do Zaporoża
> Całą Polskę znam.
>
> Znam to całe szczere plemie,
> Polskie morze, polską ziemie,
> I tę polską sól;
> I o wszystkim marzę, roję,
> I to wszystko niby moje,
> Nibym polski król. [...][35]

> I was in Lithuania and in the Crown,
> I was in this and that part, I was here and there;
> From the Beskyds to Pomorze,
> From Lithuania all the way to Zaporizhia
> I know all of Poland.
>
> I know that entire sincere tribe,
> The Polish sea, the Polish land,
> And that Polish salt;
> And I dream of all this,
> And all of it seems to be mine,
> As though I am the Polish king. [...]

This idealized picture became increasingly more divorced from reality as the national movements of local ethnic groups in the *kresy* and Galicia developed and strengthened. At first, Polish patriots underestimated the possibility of national emancipation for the "peasant nations"; and those who did not nevertheless had difficulty understanding the causes and characters of these movements. They considered them to be social movements, not national ones. Władysław, the son of Adam Mickiewicz, criticized the Ruthenian patriots (*rusomany*) as "young people…without property, with distorted minds, and [as] ignoramuses." He considered their works—Shevchenko's *Kobzar* and his long poem *Haidamaky*, the St. Petersburg-based journal *Osnova* and the Lviv newspaper *Slovo*—heavy artillery, which was full of the "ideas of deconstructive communism" and was aimed at the Polish lords.[36] In these movements some perceived an ally in the struggle against Germanization and Russification. A small group was emboldened to join these movements, among them Volodymyr Antonovych and Viacheslav Lypynsky, their leaders and ideologists.[37]

In view of the size of the territory and the large population of Rus, the "Ruthenian question" could have become the key to defining the future borders of the Polish fatherland. Furthermore, from the 1860s the center of the "Ruthenian question" shifted to Galicia, and all crucial discussions took place there. Two distinct lines were drawn between Polish politicians and intellectuals in Galicia with respect to their attitude to the "Ruthenian question": negation of the very existence of the Ruthenians as a separate nation ("There is no Rus, only Poland and Russia"), or the creation of a Polish-Ruthenian alliance ("There is no Poland without Rus, just as there is no Rus without Poland"). In the latter case, the myth of the Rzeczpospolita as a union of Poland, Lithuania, and Rus was to provide ideological legitimization. The transformation of the Rzeczpospolita from a historical union of two (Poland and Lithuania) into a union of three (with the addition of Rus) was one of the largest mutations that the concept of the Polish fatherland underwent in the nineteenth century.

The exponents of the idea of a Polish-Ruthenian union in Galicia were *gente Rutheni, natione Poloni*—educated Ruthenians by birth, Poles by nationality. They cited the authority of Stanisław Orzechowski, the premier writer of the Rzeczpospolita in the sixteenth century. He allegedly devised a formula, according to which *natio* outranks *gens*, while *gens* is synonymous with *natio*.[38] A leading figure among the *gente Rutheni, natione Poloni* was Platon Kostetsky (1832–1908). The son of a Greek Catholic priest from the Sambir area, he graduated from the Sambir Gymnasium but did not complete his studies at Lviv University, having been expelled for his Polish patriotism. Embarking on a journalistic career, he worked for both Ruthenian and Polish periodicals and became the leading personage of one of the first trials in Lviv involving journalists. He had demanded the introduction of the Polish language in Lviv University, and for his efforts he was sentenced to two months' imprisonment in 1861. While serving his sentence, Kostetsky wrote a collection of poems, the most famous of which was "Nasha molytva" (Our Prayer):

Vo im´ia Ottsia i Syna,
To nasha molytva,
Iako Troitsia, tak iedyna
Polshcha, Rus i Lytva. [...]

Iednov my zhyiem nadiiev,
Vspil´naia nam slava,
Vsim zarivno mylyi Kyiv,
Vil´no i Varshava [...][39]

In the name of the Father and the Son,
This is our prayer,
Like the Trinity, so too united
Poland, Rus´, and Lithuania. [...]

We live with one hope,
Common is our glory,
Kyiv, Vilnius, and Warsaw
Are equally dear to all [...].

However, the existence of the *gente Rutheni, natione Poloni* type was short-lived, having already begun gradually to disappear in the 1880s. In the early part of the twentieth century Kostetsky was regarded as the "last of the gente Ruthenus, natione Polonus," and this entire orientation vanished upon his death in 1908.[40]

"And where is my Fatherland?"

For the majority of educated Ruthenians the formula of the "union of Poland and Rus" was nothing more than an invitation to assimilation. Indeed, Polish assimilation of Galician Ruthenians advanced very rapidly, at a faster rate than the Russification of Little Russians (Ukrainians) was proceeding in the Russian Empire.[41] However, its complete success was offset by a number of factors: distinct religious and social differences between the Ruthenian and Polish populations; Vienna's policies, which permitted the institutionalization of these differences in separate political and cultural-educational organizations; and the intensification in the late nineteenth century of a xenophobic trend within Polish nationalism, which narrowed the possibilities for compromise. Although any one of these three realities could not prevent Polish assimilation of the Ruthenian population, taken together they had an insurmountable effect.

There was another weighty factor counteracting assimilation: the vitality of the notion of the Ruthenian fatherland, of which the official name of the land, the Kingdom of Galicia and Lodomeria—the Latinized name for the Principality of Galicia-Volhynia—was ostensibly a reminder. The Habsburg monarchy evolved from a union of historico-political, not ethnic, units. Therefore, historical arguments played an important role in the legitimization of political demands. "Whose Carpathians are these; whose San, Buh, and Dnipro rivers together with the Dnister are these; and the entire space of fertile land between those rivers and their tributaries? What princes were in the capital in Kyiv, in that mother of Rus cities, in Cherven, Volodymyr, Przemyśl, Halych?" was the rhetorical question posed by Antonii Petrushevych, one of the first Galician-Ruthenian historians.[42] From the Revolution of 1848 until the very end of the existence of the Habsburg monarchy, the main political demand of Ruthenian figures was the division of Galicia into two parts, Ruthenian and Polish, along the river San. According to this division, Lviv was to remain on the Ruthenian side, becoming the capital of the Ruthenian land.

Galician Ruthenians believed that, despite everything, "steadfast Rus will survive," and they reiterated with pride that "Mother Rus is great."[43] The problem lay in the fact they could not agree on what "great Rus" actually was and where its borders lay. Historical-geographic "Rus" was demarcated much less distinctly than "historical Poland." In the narrowest sense, these concepts referred to the region lying on the right bank of the Dnipro River; and in the broadest, to the entire East Slavic world.[44] Its derivative names indicated various territories: Chervona (Red) / Subcarpathian / Galician Rus referred to eastern Galicia; Hungarian (Carpathian) Rus, to Transcarpathia; Bila (White) Rus, to contemporary Belarus (and this applied for some time to the Kyiv region and Volyn)[45]; Little Rus and Great Rus—or in the Slavicized Greek version, *Malorosiia* and *Velykorosiia* (Μικρὰ Ῥωσία and Μεγάλη Ῥωσία); Southern and Northern Rus, the terms used to distinguish Ukrainian from Russian ethnic territories; and "all Rus," the term defining the jurisdiction of the Kyiv and, later, the Moscow-based Orthodox Church and the domains of the Muscovite tsar, whose Hellenized form *Rossiia* (Russia) became the official name of the Romanov empire in the eighteenth century.

Each of these terms was customarily used not as the name of a clearly defined territory; instead, they reflected the changeable legal status of the various East Slavic lands and peoples.[46] Therefore, every time the term Rus was used, it was necessary to specify which "Rus" and which "Ruthenians" ("Rusyns," "Rusnaks") were meant: "White," "Southern / Northern," "Great / Little," "Red," "Galician," "Carpathian," "Hungarian," and so on. Galician Ruthenians had several possibilities for defining their fatherland. At the beginning of the nineteenth century there were still occasional attempts to equate it with the "Ruthenian" community of the former Rzeczpospolita (that is, together with the Belarusians and Ukrainians / Little Russians of the Russian Empire).[47] However, as the connection to the Belarusian territories gradually receded into the past, this method of identification became an anachronism. It was simplest and safest to declare oneself a member of the Austro-Ruthenian nation, and such a decision did not question the territorial integrity of the Habsburg monarchy.

Indeed, the very first version of the manifesto issued by the Holovna Ruska Rada (Supreme Ruthenian Council)—the political organ of the Galician Ruthenians, founded during the Revolution of 1848—begins with the words: "We belong to the Galician-Ruthenian people, which numbers 2.5 million." It was only at the decisive urging of one of the council members, Yuliian Lavrivsky, that the final version included a declaration that the Galician Ruthenians are part of the 15-million-strong Little Russian (Ukrainian) people, the majority of whom reside in the Russian Empire.[48] One of the principal reasons behind the unlikelihood of an Austro-Ruthenian solution was that it could not satisfy Ruthenian intellectuals psychologically. They required self-identification with a national community that would at least be equal to or, even better, surpass the imagined Polish nation in terms of size and historical greatness. Two variants could satisfy these demands: the Little Russian variant or the Great Russian one (in contemporary terminology: Ukrainian and Russian). Opting for the Ukrainian variant meant ownership in one the most heroic periods in the history of the Eastern Slavs—the Ukrainian Cossacks. The wave of Cossack uprisings that took place up to and including the Khmelnytsky era rocked the might of the Rzeczpospolita and contributed to its collapse. Where the Great Russian variant is concerned, the Galician-Ruthenian public felt itself involved in the Russian Empire, which had put an end to the existence of the Rzeczpospolita and had crushed two Polish uprisings during the nineteenth century. In addition, a ready-made high culture, which had been evolving dynamically since Pushkin's time and could thus compete with the modern German and Polish cultures, was opening up to the Galician Ruthenians.

Of these two national orientations, the earliest one to be manifested was the Ukrainian. Its early stages are linked to the activities in the 1830s of the "Ruthenian Triad," a group of three young Greek Catholic seminarians, Markiian Shashkevych, Yakiv Holovatsky, and Ivan Vahylevych. The goal of the Ruthenian Triad was to raise the local Ruthenian language and literature to the same level of dignity that was accorded to other Slavic languages and cultures. The group's almanac, *Rusalka Dnistrovaia* (1837), had revolutionary significance, not so much for its content but because of its introduction into literature of the Ruthenian language, which was spoken at this time only by peasants. But Shashkevych and his associates took a further step: in upholding the linguistic criterion, they proclaimed national unity between Austrian Ruthenians and Russian Little Russians as members of a single nation.[49]

The Ukrainian orientation got its second wind during the Revolution of 1848, when, after some vacillations and doubts, it was accepted by the majority of the educated Ruthenian public. The young poet, Ivan Hushalevych, a pupil of Holovatsky, wrote a poem modeled on Arndt's, but with a Ruthenian-Ukrainian reply:

> De iest′ Ruska Otchyna?
> De pshenytsi, iachmina
> I de zhyta iest′ dosyt′
> Kudy holod ne hostyt′
> Na na na na na na
> Oi tam ruska Otchyna!
>
> De Sian, Dnister i Buh reke,
> Porohamy Dnipro triase,
> De shyroki sut′ stepy,
> De huliaiut′ kozaky
> Na na na na na na
> Oi tam ruska Otchyna!
>
> Where is the Ruthenian Fatherland?
> Where there is enough

Wheat, barley, and rye
Where hunger does not visit
There, there, there, there, there
Oh, there is the Ruthenian Fatherland!

Where the San, Dnister, and Buh rivers are,
Where the Dnipro shudders with its rapids
Where the broad steppes are,
Where the Cossacks make merry
There, there, there, there, there,
Oh, there is the Ruthenian Fatherland!

In order to underscore the unity of Galician Rus—"from the shores of the Dnister"—and Ukraine—"from the shores of the Dnipro"—in 1849 Hushalevych coined the term "Ruthenian-Ukrainian" [ZT 35:35–36]. In the late nineteenth century this term was swiftly accepted into the cultural and political lexicon of Galician Ruthenians.[50] However, after the defeat of the revolution Vienna turned its back on the Ruthenians, and the Ukrainophile orientation was extinguished. The subsequent fate of the Ruthenian Triad is the clearest illustration of the precariousness of the Ukrainian choice: Ivan Vahylevych joined the camp of gente Rutheni, natione Poloni; Yakiv Holovatsky eventually took up the banner of Russian nationalism and even moved to the Russian Empire; only Markiian Shashkevych, who died prematurely, remained true to the Ukrainophile orientation.

The revival of the Ruthenian-Ukrainian orientation is connected with an episode that, once again, demonstrates the importance of poets: in 1862, at the request of some local students, the Lviv merchant Mykhailo Dymet (1821–1890) imported copies of Shevchenko's Kobzar from Kyiv. The copies were instantly snapped up, and those who were unable to purchase a copy had to recopy the entire book. The generation born immediately after the Revolution of 1848 shared a common great experience: they were the first to read Shevchenko's Kobzar. Later, almost all of them compared it to a religious conversion. Under the impact of their reading, they turned away from the Polish language, conversing with each other more often in in what they claimed was the "Ruthenian dialect." Shevchenko exerted an influence on young people through his comprehensible language, his depth of feeling, and his passion, which the local Ruthenian poets lacked. The Russophile leader Fylyp Svystun later recalled: "And because the Cossacks were part of the Little Russian people, in their feats young people recognized with pride the knightly feats of their people and fortified their spirit by recalling these deeds, replete with energy."[51]

In the core of his poetry Shevchenko placed Cossack Ukraine as a symbol of freedom and independence. To the poet, Galicia was the same kind of Ukraine as the Little Russian lands under Russian rule. "From the shores of the quiet Don to the siliceous shores of the fast-flowing Dnister," he wrote in 1846, "one soil, one language, one mode of life, one and the same facial features; even the songs are one and the same. Like children of the same mother."[52]

Shevchenko was not disturbed by the fact that the Ruthenian people of Galicia were "Uniates" (Greek Catholics), those "traitors of Orthodoxy," against whom his heroes, the Ukrainian Cossacks, had fought in the seventeenth century.[53] To him, Ukraine was an absolute value, higher even than religious faith or love of God:

> Ia tak ii, ia tak liubliu
> Moiu Ukrainy ubohu,
> Shcho proklenu sviatoho Boha,
> Za nei dushu pohubliu!

> For my indigent Ukraine
> I'll pray to God, because I love her so
> That I would cast a slur on God himself
> For her dear sake, and lose my soul for her.[54]

Owing to Shevchenko's influence, in the 1860s a new generation of Ruthenian patriots proclaimed a return to the ideals of the Ruthenian Triad and the Revolution of 1848. Together with Ukrainian patriots in the Russian Empire, they succeeded in converting the poetic image of Shevchenko's Ukraine into the language of political prose and geography.[55]

Despite apparent successes in creating an image of Ukraine as an immense fatherland, there were serious problems with regard to its consolidation. Some of them were of a technical nature, like the lack of maps and textbooks, which led to semicomic situations where a young person, having read his fill of the works of Shevchenko and Ustyianovych, would commence a search for his "great united Fatherland" in German geographic atlases by using German terminology. In *Erdkunde*, a German book on geography, one young person—the future Ukrainian poet Uliana Kravchenko—found descriptions of the "river *Dniepr* and the *Grassteppe*, where *Distelgewachse* [overgrown thistle] grows; they have *dornige Blütenköpfe* [thorny flower heads]; the flower of these thorny sow-thistles is called *Steppenlicht* [Light of the Steppe]. In autumn the whirlwind carries the dried flowers over the steppes; people are afraid of it, they call it *Steppenhexe* [the witch of the steppes]."[56]

However, it was worse when such a person, upon attaining adulthood and becoming a poet, was confounded by the geography of the "holy fatherland" in the print runs of his or her own works, which numbered in the thousands. In Denys Zubrytsky's poem "Koniushyi" (The Stableman, 1852), for which a great future was portended, the main hero—a Galician—is fleeing from his enemies to Cossack Ukraine. But instead of traveling eastward, he heads for…the northwest! Mykhailo Drahomanov, one of the most principled critics of Galician intellectual life, was correct when he declared: *Rutheni sunt genus gentium, quod de patria sua minime sapit* (The Ruthenians are a nationality that knows the least about its own fatherland).[57]

There was another serious problem that prevented educated Ruthenians from including Galicia unreservedly in Ukraine: the clearly imported character of the Ukrainian fatherland. Galician landscapes did not have the attractions of the Ukrainian steppes, while the local history, in many people's views, was not suited to being the subject of poetic language.[58] A considerable number of Galician Ruthenians, who were enthralled by Taras Shevchenko in their youth, developed a more restrained attitude to the poet once they reached their mature years. Shevchenko continued to be "their own," but in the same sense as Pushkin, Mickiewicz, Kolář, and Karadžić were also "their own" simply because they were Slavic poets.[59] Since the concept of a Ruthenian fatherland was not deeply rooted in people's consciousness and institutions, it changed with every political twist and turn. In August 1866 one of the Ruthenian leaders, Rev. Ivan Naumovych (1826–1891) declared in the newspaper *Slovo*, "in the name of many," that "we have not been Ruthenians since the year 1848, we are true Russians." He claimed that ethnographically, historically, lexically, and ritualistically the Galician, Hungarian, Kyivan, Muscovite, Tobolsk, and other Ruses are parts of one and the same Rus.[60] To a great degree, Naumovych's pronouncement was determined by the Ruthenian leaders' fears of the restoration of Polish dominance in Galicia in the 1860s. These circumstances dictated the following logic: "If we are to drown, we prefer the Russian sea to the Polish swamp."[61] This was both a concealed and overt response to the question once posed by Pushkin:

Slavianskie l' ruch 'i sol 'iutsia v russkom more?
Ono l' issiaknet? Vot vopros.[62]

Will Slavic brooks join in a Russian sea?
Or will it vanish: that's the question.

Naumovych's declaration sounded at the very time that the Ukrainian movement in the Russian Empire was experiencing the brutality of the latest round of repressions. It may be assumed that, if the Russophile orientation had carried the day in Galicia, this victory would have tolled the death knell for the Ukrainian movement both in Galicia and in the Russian Empire. That did not happen, and the reason for this lay above all in the character of the Russophile movement. Opponents of the Galician Russophiles from the Polish and Ukrainophile camps described them as representatives of "Russian irredentism" in the Austro-Hungarian Empire, financed by "Russian rubles." This was also the way Vienna often perceived the Russophile movement. However, this is only partly true. The Russophiles' writings and biographies unmistakably indicate that they sought to be loyal Habsburg subjects. Their activities were restricted to the territory of Galicia, beyond whose borders beckoned Kyiv and Moscow, the spiritual capitals of Eastern Christianity, but not at all cosmopolitan St. Petersburg, which was "corrupted" by Western influences. The Russophiles' perceived fatherland was not the modern Russian empire but the Rus of yore with its Kyivan spiritual scribes. This fatherland's traits were neither political nor ethnic borders but the Byzantine liturgy, Julian calendar, and Cyrillic alphabet with its historical, "etymological," orthography. The term "Russian irredentism" could apply only to a small group (one that made a very late appearance at the end of the nineteenth century) comprising the so-called *novokursnyky* (proponents of what they called the New Direction), who made a clear-cut choice in favor of Russian culture and the Russian Empire.[63]

The opportunity to implement this formula depended on the position of the Russian government and the Russian public. However, for a long time neither showed any particular interest in Galicia. After publishing his survey of Galician-Ruthenian history in Moscow in 1845, Osyp Bodiansky complained about the "dearth of information about our brothers, who are in all respects the same kind of Russians as we are, but inexcusably forgotten by us and our historians, geographers, etc."[64] Prior to 1848 only Slavists knew about the existence of this Slavic people in Galicia. Russian officers, who crossed through Galicia with their regiments in 1849 on their way to crush the Hungarian revolution, got the impression that it was a "German land." They were surprised to hear there was a Slavic people living here, which spoke a language similar to theirs.[65] Seven decades later, in the first weeks of World War One, when Russian troops once again entered Galicia, the situation had changed little. In his introduction to a book published in 1915, aimed at acquainting Russian society with the newly conquered territory, the Russian author Nikolai Yastrebov grumbled that Russian society knew very little about the other Slavic peoples—not only about the Poles but also about "the parts that were torn away for centuries from the body of the Russian people" (for example, the Galician Ruthenians).[66] This applied both to the average Russian and educated individuals who occupied high posts, as well as many intellectuals: they knew considerably more about Germany, France, Italy, Spain, England, and Sweden than about the neighboring Slavs.[67]

On the other hand, Pan-Slavic moods were felt rather strongly among the Slavic peoples of the Austro-Hungarian Empire. Echoes of Pan-Slavism were noticeable in the writings of the Ruthenian Triad, and this movement was not unknown to Galician Russophiles or the members of a marginalized group of Polish patriots. The vision of an all-Slavic fatherland was revived in the late 1860s and early 1870s, during the unification of the German lands around Prussia and the creation of the German Empire, in the face of the feared—and seemingly inevitable—German *Drang nach Osten*. The Lviv-based journal *Słowianin* (1869) shaped this idea in the form of a paraphrase of a poem by Arndt:

Gde iest´ Slovian otechestvo?

Tam iest´ Slovian otechestvo
Gde Slovianska mova hude,
I mater´-Slava vozstaie;
Tam, gde rodynna slava ie,
Zemlia staraia gde zhiie!

Poza Volgu, za Poltavu,
Hen ko Iugu poza Savu
Poza krai nadvyslians´kyi

Poza stepy naddniprians´ki
Ridna mova protsvitaie
K obshchei dole pospishaie.[68]

Where is the fatherland of the Slavs?

The fatherland of the Slavs is
Where the Slavic language hums,
And Mother-Glory rises;
Where the family glory is,
Where the ancient land lives!

Beyond the Volga, past Poltava,
All the way to the South beyond the Sava
Beyond the land above the Vistula
Past the Dnipro steppes
The native language is blossoming
Hastening toward the common fate.

The young Franko and his friends were particularly influenced by the views of the Kyivan historian and political essayist, Mykhailo Drahomanov (1841–1895) who, at the very time the unification of the German lands was taking place, in 1870–1871, was interning in Berlin and Heidelberg, where he had the opportunity to observe firsthand the rise of German chauvinism. Drahomanov's observations led him to write a poem titled "Poklyk do brativ Slavian" (An Appeal to My Slavic Brothers, 1871), which included the following verse:

Z Pivnichnoiu Russiu ne zlomym soiuzu:
My z neiu blyzniata po rodu,
My viky dilyly i radist´ i hore,
I vkupi vstupaiem v svobodu.[69]

We shall not break the alliance with Northern Rus:
We are twins from birth,
Over the ages we shared both joy and misfortune,
And together are advancing to freedom.

Although Drahomanov was a Ukrainian patriot, he mocked the Galician Ukrainophiles' attempts to differentiate between the "Rus people" and the "Russians," appealing to "Little Russian" writers to create a single Russian literature together with their "Great Russian" counterparts.[70]

After a century of Habsburg rule in Galicia, the majority of educated Galician Ruthenians were completely befuddled by ideas and thoughts with regard to their large fatherland. An emblematic example is the Lviv-based student society, "Akademicheskii kruzhok," in whose journal, *Druh*, the young Franko published his first literary works. The leading poet of this milieu, Volodymyr Stebelsky, wrote the following lines in 1872, emulating Arndt:

I gde zh otchyzna iest´ moia?
Razve Galitsii polia?
O net tovaryshy-druzhyna,

Gde Dnestrovs´koiu volnoiu
Mertvetsy situiut´,
Gde Ukrainy getmanskoi
Prezhniaia slava snytsia,
I gde nyvoi velykanskoi
Volga-mat´ struitsia.

And where is my fatherland?
Is it really the Galician fields?
Oh, no, friends and comrades,

It is where the dead lament
On the Dnister's wave,
Where the former glory of
Hetman Ukraine appears in a dream,
And where Mother Volga flows
Through the vast fields.

By the time he wrote the following poem in 1874, Stebelsky's fatherland had shrunk significantly: it now consisted of "All of Halych, Danylo's land fallen into decline" (a reference to the Principality of Galicia-Volhynia during the rule of Danylo Halytsky). In the poem "Do Rusi" (To Rus), written that same year, he further modified the borders of his fatherland:

Prosvishchen´ie vsikh nezriashchykh
To nasha korona,
Shcho rozsypalas´ shcherbamy
Ot Karpat do Dona.[71]

Enlightenment of all the unseeing
That is our crown,

Which has crumbled into pieces
From the Carpathians to the Don.

In these three poems, which were written over a brief period of time, the same author presents three different visions of his fatherland: one extends from the San River to the Zbruch (Galician Rus); the second, from the Carpathian Mountains to the Don River (Ukraine); and the third, from the Dnister River to the Volga (Russia). In order to complete this picture, the only thing that should be added is that Stebelsky ended his career as a Polish poet.[72]

The Workers Have No Fatherland

Misapprehensions and various competing interpretations continued. The penetration in Galicia of Western ideologies in the 1860s and 1870s did not simplify the search for a fatherland; on the contrary, it complicated things. One such ideology was socialism. In their "Manifesto of the Communist Party" (1847), Karl Marx and Friedrich Engels proclaimed that "the workers have no fatherland." According to them, the development of capitalism and a world market was destroying national differences among peoples, and the united effort of the proletariat of various countries was one of the prerequisites of its liberation. Nations were fated to become anachronisms, simply to vanish after the victory of the proletariat. In the meantime, the workers' struggle against the bourgeoisie was a national struggle, not because it was being waged under national flags, but because the proletariat of each country had, first of all, to settle matters with its own bourgeoisie.[73]

This scenario applied only to "civilized" countries. It was not clear, however, what was to be done with the less civilized ones or completely uncivilized lands—for example, Slavic Europe. Discussions around this question flared up in Geneva in 1880, during the meeting held to commemorate the fiftieth anniversary of the 1830 Polish Uprising, as well as at counter-meetings to solemn Polish celebrations that were taking place everywhere, particularly in Galicia, where conditions for holding legal celebrations were better. During his keynote speech in Geneva, the Polish socialist, Ludwik Waryński, declared: "Our fatherland is the entire world....We are fellow countrymen, members of a single great nationality that is even more miserable than Poland—the proletarian nation. The flag of that nation is our flag, its interests are our interests, and its victory will be our victory. And when the moment of our uprising arrives, then we will be greeted not by slogans of 'Long live Poland!' or 'Down with Muscovy!' but by a single slogan common to the entire proletariat: 'Long live the socialist revolution!'"[74]

Waryński's speech garnered passionate support from the Russian socialists (for a splashier effect he gave his speech in Russian), but he disappointed the patriotic wings of the Polish and Ukrainian socialists. Their leaders, Bolesław Limanowski and Mykhailo Drahomanov, respectively, were convinced that without political independence, political freedoms were unattainable, and without political freedoms, all aspirations to socialist changes would remain a pipe dream. Unexpectedly for the organizers, the Geneva meeting was a failure. Marx, from whom the participants were expecting a show of support for the idea of a proletarian nation, sent a letter from London containing words of praise for the Polish Uprising, which concluded thus: "Long live Poland!"[75]

Although these discussions were taking place in faraway Geneva, they had a direct bearing on Galician conditions: Limanowski and Waryński were present at the birth of the socialist movement in Galicia, while Drahomanov had a decisive impact on the young Franko and his friends. At least one of them, Mykhailo Pavlyk, assured Drahomanov that the Galician Ruthenian peasants did not comprehend the slogan "for faith, fatherland, and patriotism," but did understand socialist propaganda.[76]

From this brief survey one may reach the following conclusion: when the real Ivan Franko and the invented Opanas Morymukha left their small fatherland in their youth and set out into the great world, it was no easy task for either of them to figure out which new fatherland they should keep close to their hearts. Arndt and Mickiewicz, Pushkin and Shevchenko, Marx and Drahomanov—to name only the best known and most frequently read authors—offered different answers to this question, and none of them were either decisively superior or entirely convincing.

Chapter 6

Did the Peasants Have a Fatherland?

How did poorly educated people or those without any education whatso-ever—like the parents of Franko and his fictional classmate Morymukha—view things? To what extent did their geographic imagination spur them in their search for a large fatherland? The supreme authority on this ques-tion is still the Polish sociologist, Stanisław Ossowski, who formulated the theory of two fatherlands: "private" and "ideological." He claims that, for a lengthy period of time, the possession of two fatherlands was a class-based privilege of the higher strata. Peasants had their "private fatherland," but they remained outside the bounds of the "ideological Fatherland." They identified themselves mainly with the place where they were born, the reli-gion to which they belonged, and their occupation ("I am from here," "I am a Roman Catholic / Orthodox / Greek Catholic," "I am a peasant").[1] Researchers of traditional peasant culture insist that it did not have any relevant mental tools that would spur rural inhabitants to adopt national identification. The modern concept of fatherland has an ideological char-acter and is built on the opposition between one's own land / one's own people and a foreign land and a foreign people. The traditional image of the world was not ideological but cosmological. Its fundamental trait was not the opposition of "man-man" but "man-cosmos." The main criterion of "kinship" (*sviiskiist´*) is family connections, which are endowed with sacred meaning, the violation of which is considered the greatest sin. Before peas-ants attain a "Fatherland" with a capital "F," prolonged joint work on the part of the state and of intellectuals is required.[2]

This schema is based on both empirical field research (Ossowski's focus of study was the Polish-German borderland) and a twentieth-century analysis of Slavic folklore of the most ancient districts in the

Belarusian-Polish-Russian-Ukrainian borderland (primarily the Polissian region) and the Balkans. In contemporary academic discourses, conclusions stemming from the study of specific regions in a specific period have acquired universality and all but timelessness: they explain the entire rural world from the threshold of Christianity (ninth and tenth centuries) to the Second World War. This pretension to comprehensiveness gives rise to doubts and generates a reappraisal of the concrete material gleaned in another locale and in another period, and particularly at the very moment when the old, traditional perceptions began to erode.

"The Fatherland on One's Lips"

The example of Franko's village and its vicinity is an opportune occasion for this. As mentioned earlier, during his childhood and youth Franko recorded several thousand folksongs, proverbs, and sayings.[3] Familiarity with the tradition of Subcarpathian villages is convincing proof that the imagined world of their inhabitants was not as narrow and parochial as described in the theory of "small" and "large" fatherlands. In folk proverbs and songs one can find references to nearby and distant lands, rivers, and cities. One example records the concept of fatherland in the broader sense: "The Fatherland is on one's lips, but deception is in the heart."[4]

However, what is important is the ability to decipher geographic symbols correctly. Let's take the example of Egypt: in the local folklore this country was not a specific geographic place but a symbol of God's punishment, according to the Old Testament. Depending on the context, it could mean a prison, hard labor, a plague of mice, or a tavern, where peasants drank up their property and ruined their health. This term was not of authentically rural derivation: in his annotations to the proverbs he had collected Franko surmised that at least in one case—Egypt as a tavern—it originated with Greek Catholic priests, who organized sobriety campaigns in villages and chose Jewish taverns as the main target of criticism.[5] As concerns the above-cited proverb about "fatherland," Franko indicated its bookish, literary origins. The very formulation of *otechestvo*, rather than the usual old Ukrainian *otchyzna / otchyna*, or the modern Ukrainian word *bat´kivshchyna*, points to its Old Church Slavonic origins. This is entirely natural, considering the Eastern Christian roots of the Greek Catholic Church.

Ethnographic materials also include borrowings from the Latin literary tradition, which was the foundation of the Catholic culture. For example, the Ukrainian proverb "Piznaty durnoho po smikhu ioho" (A fool is recognized by his laughter) corresponds to the Latin proverb "Per risum multum poteris cognoscere stultum" (Habitual indulgence in laughter betrays a weak mind). The saying "Iedyna lastivka ne robyt vesny" (One swallow does not make spring) is a literal translation of "Una hirundo non facit ver," while "Voda kamin´ tochyt´" (Water wears away a stone) sounds similar to "Gutta cavat lapidem non vi, sed saepe cadendo" (The drop hollows out the stone by frequent dropping, not by force). Of course, it may be assumed that these Ruthenian–Latin parallels do not reflect borrowings from antiquity and neo-Latin sources, but indicate common Indo-European roots. However, in individual cases, Latin influences are indisputable.

One example is a bawdy travesty recorded by Franko in the village of Duliby, Stryi County, of Cicero's famous expression, "Quo usque tandem abutere, Catilina, patientia nostra?" (How long, Catiline, will you abuse our patience?), which was transformed into "Doky ty budesh, Kateryno, khodyty u nashu kukuruzu sr...?" (Kateryna, how long will you go into our cornfield to sh_t?).[6] Another example is the Galician proverb, "Vono by takoho kazusu narobylo, shcho i ne prypovisty" (It would cause such an incident that it would be hard to describe). Franko commented thus: "From the Latin *casus*, especially in the juridical sense."[7]

The incidence of concepts of "bookish derivation" in proverbs demonstrates one of the weaker points of applying the theory of two "fatherlands" to specific examples. This theory is based on the opposition between "low" and "high" culture as two ideal types, a state of affairs that exists, at best, in areas located at great distances from centers of high culture—somewhere in Polissia or here and there in the Balkans. In the majority of cases, both types of culture coexisted, at times in symbiosis. So-called "folk culture" is not an outstandingly spontaneous product of rural inhabitants (or, in the broader context, of a poorly educated or completely uneducated populace). Very often, folklore emerged as a result of high culture's downward filtration to the lower social strata, and this process, in its turn, was balanced out by upward filtration of low culture. Already in a class-based ("feudal," "traditional") society both these processes together could generate a certain community, a universe of national culture, a common fatherland.[8]

The word "could" in the preceding sentence means a possibility that does not necessarily have to be realized. In order to perceive the boundary between possibility and reality, it is worthwhile examining what happened to geographic concepts during the transition from the sphere of "high" culture to the sphere of "low" culture. An example is provided by the term that is central to Ukrainian nation building: "Ukraine" as a symbol of an ideological fatherland. As a geographic concept, "Ukraine" is encountered sporadically in the tradition of chronicle writing, beginning in 1187. There is a clear-cut tendency to use this term in the sense of *okraina* (borderland) rather than of *kraina* (country). In particular, one encounters the term *Ukraina halyts´ka* (Galician Ukraine) as a designation for the southeastern medieval Principality of Halych (the so-called Ponyzzia, the lowlands of Ukraine).[9]

As mentioned earlier, the image of Ukraine as a "large fatherland" arose in the political culture of the eighteenth-century autonomous Cossack State.[10] Folk compilations record the existence of this term in the folk culture of the nineteenth century,[11] and, what is important, its existence in those territories that were not under the control of the Cossack State—in Austrian Galicia. In the foreword to the St. Petersburg edition (1836) of Ukrainian folksongs, the Little Russian patriot Platon Lukashevych insisted that, in order to collect songs about Ukraine, one must travel to Galicia. He claimed that Ukrainian songs had practically disappeared in Little Russia, in the lands of the former Cossack State, having been displaced by soldiers' and coachmen's songs. Meanwhile, even though Galicia had been cut off from its fatherland for several centuries, it still upheld its loyalty to the "promised land": "Who would believe that a Galician shepherd knows many more *dumy* [folk heroic epics of Cossack Ukraine—Trans.] about the heroes of Ukraine and its history than the settled Little Russian Cossack? He takes pride in the Little Russians' deeds as though in his own. He rejoices in their happiness and successes, and in his beautiful songs he mourns "the Cossack adventure."[12]

Lukashevych may have been exaggerating the memory of the Cossacks and Ukraine that had been retained in Galicia. But the very presence of these images in Galician-Ruthenian folklore is indisputable. It is corroborated, in particular, by the songs and the Ukrainian folk ditties called *kolomyiky* that Franko recorded in Nahuievychi. In them, "Ukraine" is associated with a faraway land and freedom, which the Cossacks defend from various enemies (Turks, Tatars, Liakhs / Poles), to where local young men set out and from where news about them reaches their true loves back in the village.[13]

However, the problem is that folk materials do not afford an opportunity to make either a spatial identification of the term "Ukraine" or of the ethnic affiliation of its inhabitants. George S. N. Luckyj analyzed approximately a thousand folksongs that mention Ukraine. In the absolute majority of these songs Ukraine figures not as a historical, geographic, or ethnic concept but rather as a suprahistorical, mythical one.[14] The only identifying detail is the Danube River, which in folksongs frequently separates Ukraine from other territories. In order to reach Ukraine, one must cross the Danube. If we consider the geographic range of these songs (Austrian Galicia and the Ukrainian gubernias of the Russian Empire) and its placement with respect to the Danube (north and east of this river), then we encounter an obvious paradox: Ukraine, as reflected in the song culture, would have to be located not in Cossack Zaporizhia, but in the Pannonian Valley or the Balkans. The solution to this paradox is straightforward if one reflects on the fact that in folk culture all large bodies of water, even floods, are called the Danube. In folk mythology a large river has a sacred meaning: to cross it (including swimming across) means to effect a radical change in one's life, to achieve a qualitatively new state. Similarly, to cross the Danube River means to end up in a distant foreign land and, at the same time, to change oneself; to sever one's ties with the old life; to become free and independent.[15]

"Cossack Ukraine" "on the other side of the Danube" was a transcendental concept, a peasant utopia, a land without "Liakh [Polish] masters, Jews, and the Union [the Greek Catholic Church]."[16] In the folkloric materials that Franko collected, the concept of "a Cossack warrior" ("Cossack Ukraine"), which is linked with Ukraine, is equally extratemporal ("The Cossack kin will never die") and ambivalent: the word *kozak* (Cossack) means a handsome and brave young man, but also a drifter from whom one can expect anything.[17] In loving Cossacks, young girls should be on their guard because they will drive them into madness and deprive them of their chastity. In the image of the Cossack, the sacred is mixed with the profane. Folk icons of the Last Judgment, which are common to the Carpathian region, depict a Cossack among the "peoples [*narody*] seated on the left hand [of God]"—that is, those who are condemned to eternal torment together with peoples of other faiths (Jews, Muslims, Germans).[18] In other words, depending on the context, the word "Cossack" in the consciousness of Galician Ruthenians could mean either "one of us" or, less frequently, "a stranger."

On the other hand, the modern ethnic term "Ukrainian" hardly appears in songs and proverbs, most likely because this term was a rarity in the high culture of the eighteenth century.[19] It does not even appear in Shevchenko's poetry. When Ukrainian patriots in Galicia sought to introduce this term among the peasants, they confronted a wall of incomprehension. Franko's peer, Rev. Fylymon Tarnavsky, recounted the following incident: "In the village where he served as parish priest, a local agitator tried to convince the peasants that they should call themselves Ukrainians. When he entered the home of the old *gazda* [master of the house], Mykhailo Kaluzhka, he told him that he was a Ukrainian. Mykhailo Kaluzhka went to the tavern and asked the tavern-keeper, Shaya Wenglar, what a Ukrainian is. Shaya Wenglar told him: 'A Ukrainian is such a poor fellow that he lives somewhere at the edge of the village, but you, of course, are a householder in the middle of the village; you are not a Ukrainian at all! I would sue him for such a grievous insult.'" Tarnavsky concludes his account with these words: "This proves that the term Ukrainian in those times (1897) was not even known to many people."[20]

The "Ukraine" example demonstrates the ambivalence of folk geography. On the one hand, it features concepts that may be treated as symbols of a "large fatherland." On the other, they are extratemporal and transcendental, and thus do not allow scholars to link this "large fatherland" with a specific locale "here and now."

Homebodies?

At the same time, Galician folklore has many geographic names that reflect local identities—identities associated with a "small fatherland." Even a neighboring village is considered foreign (this was particularly evident in the kolomyiky originating in Nahuievychi, in which the neighboring village of Yasenytsia Silna, where Franko's mother was born, is treated as a foreign village).[21] The saying, "We are homebodies [*petsovi liudy*, people who do not come off their bed-stoves, that is, those who never leave their little corner of the world], not worldly people," serves as additional confirmation of local identities. Franko added the following commentary to this saying: "About themselves the Boiko people say that they are accustomed to spending their entire lives in their village, without ever leaving it."[22] This saying, like the accompanying commentary, should not be taken at face value: the Boikos were known for their trading activities, which led them not only to the larger Galician cities but also to Pest, Vienna, and as far away as Kyiv, Warsaw, Moscow, and Paris.[23]

Folkloric materials indicate that peasants did not stick to their homes. They engaged in travel, and quite regularly at that. People in Nahuievychi were known to say, "It is four miles from Mohyla," which meant the exact distance from the village's Mt. Mohyla to the county city of Sambir. The need to be aware of this may be explained only by the fact that the peasants often had to cover that distance. Kolomyiky explain why people were forced to travel to Sambir: this was the seat of government, and from time to time they had to go there to take care of various matters. The city also had a prison, where fellow villagers languished, serving out their sentences for various crimes.[24] Other cities are similarly mentioned in a very specific context: Kolomyia is famous for its bowls; Brody for its kerchiefs; and Bolekhiv and Stanyslaviv for their bread.[25] Kosiv, Kuty, Stryi, Ternopil, Turka, Chortkiv, Yavoriv, and the rest—there is not a single Eastern Galician city that is not mentioned at least once in the kolomyiky of Nahuievychi. Among Western Galician cities, only Cracow is mentioned.[26] One example that demonstrates, among other things, how quickly folklore reacted to the latest events is the neighboring city of Boryslav, the center of the oil industry from the 1850s onward.[27]

The folk literature of this period also reflected areas outside of Galicia, where local peasants were forced to venture as a result of sundry hazards and needs: Sziget, Olomouc, Vienna, Moravia, the Hungarian lands, and even the borders of Turkey and faraway Italy (called *Hitalia* in the local dialect, it was mentioned frequently in connection with the recent Austro-Italian war, in which many Galician recruits took part).[28]

Naturally, there were lands that the local peasants visited more often than others. Most prominent was, unquestionably, neighboring Podillia, a rich land partly divided by the Austro-Russian border.[29] Peasants traveled to Podillia during the period of the *pereddnivok*, that is, in early spring, once the old harvest had been consumed and there were only a few months left before the new one. In their imagination this was a fairytale land. "In Podillia bread hangs off staves interwoven with sausages," people said, although a more realistic assessment is also found in folklore: "In Podillia fences are not made of sausages."[30] Pursued by hunger or motivated by the desire to obtain earnings, Hutsuls, a local mountain people, came down from the mountains, and *bakuniary* (smugglers) traveled on foot to Hungary for tobacco, but came back with potatoes [*ZT* 26:194, 198].

The example of Franko and his parents' families clearly indicates that the ideal of rural life, which was celebrated in songs—"Where I was born, there I will die"[31]—was occasionally violated. Specialists in medieval Europe urge us to reject the image of traditional peasant society as a nonmobile social order that was little affected by change.[32] In peasant societies, writes Fernand Braudel, *homo stabilis* does not at all mean *homo immobilis*.[33] Scholars infer that the only major reason preventing rural inhabitants from traveling frequently and far afield was the lack of quick and cheap transportation.[34] In Eastern Europe, an additional braking factor was the peasants' forcible attachment to the land. However, this factor was not absolute. First of all, there had always been a stratum of peasants who never lived under serfdom (for example, the family of Franko's father). Second, on less productive lands where the corvée could not generate revenues, landowners forced peasants regularly "to leave" for the cities and engage in trades. Third, from time to time nearly all peasants were compelled to embark on a journey by the need to feed their families during poor harvests or the preharvest period (this is what Franko's father did in order to save his family in the "difficult years"). The memoiristic literature of this period recounts how famine devastated entire villages, their surviving inhabitants abandoning their native places to search for food.[35] Finally, there were always those stalwart few who were prepared to cover a distance of hundreds of kilometers in search of a better and freer life. The origins of the Ukrainian Cossacks best illustrate this: the farthermost points from which these explorers left to assemble beyond the Dnipro Rapids included Scandinavia in the north, Scotland in the west, the Ural region in the east, and the Balkans in the south, although the main "suppliers" were the Rus (later, Ukrainian-Belarusian) lands of the Rzeczpospolita, together with Red Rus, later known as Galicia.[36]

It is logical to assume that once serfdom was abolished in 1848, the geographic mobility of the inhabitants of Galician villages increased. But more precise statements can be made only starting in the late nineteenth century, when systematized data first appeared. They show that the number of Galicians living outside the areas where they were born was constantly on the rise: 10 percent in 1880, 15 percent in 1890, and 20 percent in 1900.[37] However, it should be noted that data gathered in relatively stable periods and "years of plenty" cannot be extrapolated onto periods coinciding with social and natural cataclysms, like poor harvests, famines, and epidemics.

Although geographic mobility was not a defining trait of a traditional society, peasants were in the habit of making short journeys: they traveled to neighboring villages to attend church feast days or to visit relatives, or headed out to the nearest city market. Occasionally, they traveled farther afield—up to a hundred kilometers—setting out on pilgrimages or in search of seasonal labor, and the like. These were the standard types of journeys until the 1890s—that is, before the mass peasant migration to North and South America. Usually, they did not effect great changes in the life of the rural inhabitant, who would always return to his native village, his "small" fatherland. Nevertheless, journeys and encounters with perpetual wanderers—pilgrims, beggars, kobzars (itinerant musicians), gypsies, and Jews—fostered the spread of information about the outside world and sparked self-identification.[38]

In his classic work *Imagined Communities*, Benedict Anderson emphasizes the importance of religious and secular pilgrimages (the latter undertaken in search of work) in the formation of a sense of a protonational community among the inhabitants of South America long before the emergence of nationalism on that continent.[39] A similar conclusion is reached by a Polish scholar, who carried out research on journeys in Eastern Europe, focusing, however, only on the educated classes.[40] The question remains: can this conclusion be extended to ordinary "commoners"? Did the image of a "larger fatherland" emerge in them at the same time?

As in the preceding cases, there are no clear-cut conclusions here. On the one hand, we encounter numerous examples of parochial thinking. In 1822, the peasants of Stanyslaviv County, reacting to their oppression at the hands of a local landowner, requested permission from the Austrian authorities to resettle in another "nation," by which they meant Bukovyna. In the mid-nineteenth century, Galician Ruthenians called it Wallachia, and its inhabitants Wallachians. In their turn, Bukovynian Ruthenians called Galicia "Poland," or *Liadchyna* (Land of the Liakhs; Liakh was an ethnonym meaning "a Pole"). Hungarian Ruthenians generally called Galicia "Rus" and their own land *Uhorshchyna* (Hungary). But whenever there was a need to differentiate themselves from a Magyar, they called him an *uhor* (Ugor) or *uhryn*, themselves *rusyns*, or *rusniaks*, and Catholics *papiezhnyky* (papists). Here is another example of "distorted" geography: Mazurs (Polish peasants from Western Galicia) differentiated themselves from the inhabitants of Eastern Galicia but called that region "Poland." Galician Ruthenians called the neighboring Ukrainian lands of the Russian Empire (Central Ukraine) "Muscovy."[41] The Galician Ruthenian population was divided into *podoliany* (plainsmen) and *horiany* (mountain people); the latter, in turn, were divided into Hutsuls, Boikos, and Lemkos, and were often an object of ridicule among the inhabitants of the Carpathian foothills ("stupid Boiko"; "stupid as a Hutsul").[42]

The Ruthenian Land

There is no doubt whatsoever that in the consciousness of Galician villagers broader identities existed alongside local ones. The kolomyiky collected
by Franko reveal a conspicuous dividing line between a "distant country," a "foreign part,"[43] on the one hand, and the "Ruthenian land" on the
other.[44] However, the concept of "Ruthenianness" is not easily translated
into the language of geography or nationalism. "In general, every person
of the Greek faith in Galicia calls himself a rusyn and his fatherland, Rus,"
Yakiv Holovatsky declared in 1847.[45] What is significant here is the emphasis on the religious character of "Ruthenianness." *Rus* symbolized a sacred
community, which explains why it appeared frequently in folk culture,
accompanied by the epithet "holy." Michael Cherniavsky has demonstrated
that the term "Holy Rus" was never applied to a specific territory. This
was a transcendental, ahistorical Rus, which was identified with Eastern
(Orthodox) Christianity, not with an actual ruler or state. It was foreign to
the Westernized Russian nobility, and neither the Principality of Moscow
nor the Russian Empire called itself by that name. The image of "holy Rus"
was widespread among the peasantry, which monopolized this image as
its own name (reflected in the formula "Ruthenian=Orthodox=peasant").[46]

No single territory could lay claim to being the exclusive embodiment of holy Rus. Neither did this image have clear-cut ethnic coloration.
We encounter it in the epos of the Ukrainian Cossacks;[47] we see it in the
self-definition of Ukrainian and Belarusian peasants, many of whom still
identified themselves as "Ruthenians, Rus people, Rus" until the Second
World War, when it was supplanted by the modern Ukrainian, Belarusian,
Russian, and "Soviet" identities.[48] There is a hypothesis about the "Rusness"
of the Eastern Christian peasants being a relic of medieval high culture,
which was a blend of the Byzantine legacy and heretical Christian movements and which spread orally among the peasants via texts sung by folk
bards (invalids and old men among the Belarusians and Russians), *lirnyky*
(itinerant Ukrainian musicians who performed religious, historical, and
epic songs to the accompaniment of a *lira*, the Ukrainian version of the
hurdy-gurdy), as well as kobzari among the Ukrainians.[49] The itinerary of
these bards covered the entire Eastern Christian world: traversing state
borders in the nineteenth century, they could easily cross over from the
Ukrainian gubernias of the Russian Empire into Galicia and Bukovyna, and
make the return journey.[50]

In the case of Galicia, there were additional factors determining the vitality of the Ruthenian identity. Like Transcarpathia (Hungarian Rus), it was in direct contact with the Western Christian world, and thus the intensity of religious self-identification (the number of cases where it was necessary to assert the distinctiveness of one's faith) was higher there. In the Rzeczpospolita, this land was known as the Ruthenian Voivodeship until it became part of the Habsburg monarchy. On de Beauplan's seventeenth-century map, one of the earliest and most famous maps of Eastern Europe, this land is the one and only Rus. Thus, for Galician Ruthenians "Rus" could be both a "small" and a "large" fatherland.

The dearth of specialized studies militates against determining what Galician peasants understood most often by the term "Ruthenian land"— their own territory or the wider Eastern Christian world. We can only make haphazard suppositions. One noteworthy proverb is "Vid Kyieva do Krakova vsiudy bida odnakova" (From Kyiv to Cracow, misfortune is the same everywhere). Franko comments on it in the national sense, using modern terms not germane to peasant proverbs: "[Misfortune] plagues Ukrainians and Poles alike."[51] This would imply that, for Galician Ruthenians, "our" territory was an immense space, whose center was Kyiv. However, there are proverbs with nearly identical content, in which Kyiv is replaced by Lviv.[52] In another proverb, Kyiv is mentioned as a great city: "Kyiv was not built instantly."[53] It is significant that there are other versions of this proverb, in which Kyiv is replaced by Lviv or Cracow,[54] while the form of this expression is reminiscent of the Latin saying, *Roma die uno non aedificata est* (Rome was not built in a day).

However, Galician-Ruthenian folklore also contains references to Kyiv, a city that cannot be supplanted by any other metropolis. One major reference appears in a Christmas carol recorded by Rev. Mykhailo Zubrytsky in the village of Mshanets in the Stary Sambir area. The carol is about St. Sophia's Cathedral, the holy church in "holy Kyiv." In 1885, Zubrytsky gave the transcription of this carol to Franko, who published it in the journal *Kievskaia starina* [Kyivan Antiquity] in 1889. Franko's publication sparked a lively discussion among ethnographers about the sources and authenticity of this Christmas carol. Franko himself questioned the reference to Kyiv in such a far-off area, "where to this day people barely know anything about Kyiv's existence."[55]

The subsequent discovery, in a completely different part of Galicia, of a legend about the Kyivan Cave Monastery ("Tam v Rosyi ie vylyky take

misto Kyiv i tam ie naivyshcha na tsilyi svit tserkva i nazyvaietsi Lavra":
"In Russia there is a great city known as Kyiv, and the tallest church in
the whole world is there, and it is called the Lavra"[56]) convinced Franko
that his doubts were rather unjustified. It is important to note that both the
Christmas carol from Mshanets and the subsequent legend share a certain
common trope: notions of Kyiv as a city of special Divine favor [ZT 42:259,
261], and thus as the center of "holy Rus."

In the mental geography of Galician folk culture, the easternmost
populated area was Moscow—not the city itself, of course, but the epithet formed from its name ("Muscovite": *moskovs´kyi*) as a synonym of
the Russian state. This image had an unmistakably negative connotation
(*moskovske pozhaluvanie* as a synonym of "severe punishment"), and
penia moskovska, meaning, "all kinds of disasters").[57] The Ruthenian folklore of Galicia, like Ukrainian folk creativity in the Russian Empire, featured numerous anti-Russian stereotypes focused around the image of the
moskal (Muscovite), which in some cases is interpreted as "soldier" and
in others as a "Russian."[58] In other contexts the word means people of a
different religion ("Those Muscovites of today, they are descended from
the Tatars"; the Muscovite tsar only converted to Christianity after he saw
a cross in the sky, and under this sign his army began to gain victory over
all enemies).[59]

One of the proverbs collected by Franko is one that unambiguously
reveals a negative attitude to *katsaps* (a derogatory Ukrainian term for
Russians), that is, those educated Ruthenians who considered themselves
Russians ("Katsap katsapom, pase svyni zahalom, lupyt´ shkiru pazurom";
A katsap is a katsap, he generally herds pigs and scratches his skin with
his nail).[60] Did this mean that the Ruthenian identity of rural inhabitants
could not be transformed into a Russian one?—not at all. This is evident
from the biographies of those village-born people who disseminated the
image of Russia as a fatherland, like Osyp Markov, the peasant son from the
Drohobych area, who studied with Franko at the Drohobych Gymnasium.
The Russophile press offered Markov's life story as a role model to be emu-
lated by all educated peasants: "We, the Russian peasants, can be proud of
such a famous man."[61]

The negative image of the "Muscovite" did not prevent the Ruthenian
peasants from welcoming Russian troops in a rather friendly fashion during their march through Galicia in 1849, and later, during the Russian
occupation in 1914–1915. Galician Ruthenians were particularly impressed

by their "steadfast faith"—the way they prayed piously.[62] Between the 1860s and the 1880s, rumors circulated throughout Ruthenian villages that the Russian tsar would arrive soon in Galicia, chase out the Jews, punish the Poles, take the land away from the lords, and distribute it among the local peasants. Hopes for the speedy arrival of the "White Tsar" were especially raised against the background of the exacerbation of Austro-Russian relations in the 1870s and 1880s. The naïve belief in the Russian tsar had, above all, a social, not national, dimension: similar rumors also circulated among the Czech and Bulgarian peasants. Yet it is difficult to refute their ethnic (anti-Polish and anti-Jewish) coloration. In addition, peasants who labeled themselves Ruthenians called the monarch in St. Petersburg a *rus´kyi tsar* (Ruthenian tsar), without differentiating between the terms *rosiis´kyi* (Russian) and *rus´kyi* (Ruthenian, Rus).[63] They particularly appreciated the fact that "he has a firm faith and conducts himself steadfastly"—meaning, that he strictly upholds all the church fasts.[64]

This latter method of self-identification requires explication. It was based on one of the fundamental features of the traditional world perception of the Eastern European peasantry. As mentioned earlier, the peasants did not identify Holy Rus either with the Russian Empire as a state or with the Russian nobility. They excluded "lords" (by whom they meant the educated classes in general) from Holy Rus because, according to their understanding, they were the personification of the devil and the forces of evil, whose vocation was to live off the exploitation of peasant labor. Only a monarch or God's anointed on earth could protect the peasants from these satanic forces. In the peasants' formula of opposition, of "we" vs. "others," the monarch was on "our" side.[65] Galician peasants were set apart from other Eastern European peasants by the fact that they professed loyalty to two monarchs simultaneously: to Franz Josef, whose cult was extraordinarily popular in Galicia, and to the "White Tsar" of the East. Therefore, in the minds of the inhabitants of the Galician countryside the Romanovs were "Ruthenians," as were the Habsburgs.[66]

It may be assumed that the peasants would be hard put to take sides if war ever broke out between Austria and Russia, a possibility that was frequently predicted throughout the 1860s to 1880s and a matter of great concern to the Galician peasants.[67] Also central to this discussion is the possibility that the identification of "Ruthenianness" with "Russianness" in Galicia endured as long as the monarchial order existed in Russia. After its collapse in 1917 this method of identification lost its raison d'être, something that cannot be said of the image of "Ukraine," which bore the connotation of a free land liberated from all manner of oppression.

A survey of Ruthenian folklore demonstrates that it would have been exceedingly difficult for rural inhabitants to superpose the image of "Rus" onto that of the large Polish fatherland, the goal for which strove more than a few generations of Polish politicians and Polish revolutionaries in Galicia. Formally, there was nothing antihistorical in this superposition, as the Ruthenian Voivodeship had been part of the Rzeczpospolita for a number of centuries. However, there were several concurrent impeding factors: social (Poland was personified by lords and serfdom), religious (Poles were Roman Catholics), and ethnic. Where the latter is concerned, there is a great body of folkloric materials, in which Poles (Liakhs) are presented in a negative light. Hence, the Poles are accursed, demonic, wastrels, stupid, evil, and hateful. Only Galician Jews (*zhydy*) had a worse image.[68] But the Poles were accused specifically of having brought the Jews into Galicia ("Iak pohanyi liakh sprovadyv zhyda, to zhydy staly panamy, a my pishly z torbamy" [When the evil Liakh brought in the Jew, the Jews became lords, and we went off with sacks] is a saying Franko recorded in Drohobych).[69] Certain sayings expressed overt exhortations to rob, beat, and even kill Poles, not infrequently along with Jews ("Vsikh Liakhiv byi kyiem" / Beat all the Liakhs with cudgels; "Tikai liashe, shcho na tobi, to nashe" / Run away, Liakh! What is on you is ours; "Liakha byi i shche inshomu podavai, bo vin til´ky pechenyi dobryi" / Beat the Liakh and dish it out to another, because he is only good roasted; "Kukil´ z pshenytsi vybyraty, zhydiv i liakhiv rizaty" / Pick out the cockles from the wheat, carve up the Jews and the Liakhs; and so on). After analyzing this group of sayings, a scholar of nineteenth-century Ruthenian-Ukrainian folklore concluded that "the ideological basis of the killings in the twentieth century [the Polish-Ukrainian ethnic cleansings in 1919 and 1943 in Galicia and Volhynia—Y. H.] was already in place before the emergence of modern, militant nationalism."[70]

Ethnic stereotypes are, however, ambivalent. There is a small group of sayings, in which Poles are presented neutrally, even positively, and which do not reject the possibility of interethnic solidarity: "Nasha i liasha—ne liuds´ka [dolia]" (Our [fate] and that of the Liakhs is inhuman); "Vid Kyiva do Krakova vsiudy bida odnakova" (From Kyiv to Cracow, misfortune is the same everywhere); "I v Krakovi zlydni odnakovi" (Misery is the same even in Cracow; Franko's commentary: "Misery is the same everywhere"); "Liakhiv hud´mo, ale z Liakhamy bud´mo" (Let's blame the Liakhs, but let's be with the Liakhs).[71] What is missing in Ruthenian folklore is the idea that the Polish king is their own, Rus, monarch. Most likely, the reason for this lies not so much in the king himself as in the image of Poland as an anarchic state ruled by lords: "Nema krilia v Pol´shchi" (There is no king in Poland); "Liashky sia buntuiut´, bo korolia v Pol´shchi ne chuiut´" (The Liakhs are rebelling because they do not hear the king in Poland). The Rzeczpospolita is a symbol of disorder: "Oho, zrazu vydno, shcho tu nema krili v Polshi!" (O-ho, it is instantly clear that there is no king in Poland); "Iakoi Polshi vy meni tut narobyly" (What kind of Poland have you fashioned for me here? Franko comments: "What kind of disorder, trouble").[72] A Pole is a synonym of "rebel" (specifically, a rebel against Russia: "What kind of Pole am I? I did not fight against the Muscovites!").[73]

The folklore collected by Franko contains only one example of a positive attitude to the Rzeczpospolita, and, what is noteworthy, a negative attitude to the Habsburgs. In Yasenytsia Silna he heard the saying "Iak Polshcha znovu nastane, tohdy Maria Tereza z pekla vyide" (When Poland is restored once again, Maria Theresa will then come out of hell). The implication is obvious: Maria Theresa committed a great sin when she agreed to involve herself in the partitions of Poland. This saying was not recorded from the peasants: it reflected the beliefs of the local petty gentry.[74] It may be assumed that if Franko had adopted this nobiliary tradition, his personal integration into the large Polish Fatherland would not have posed any special difficulties. However, it is highly doubtful that the majority of his peers of nonnoble origins and upbringing could have followed this path.

In order to gain some idea of the identity of the Ruthenians living in Galician Subcarpathia, it is important to examine a group of proverbs that instantly positions them vis-à-vis several groups and reflects the genre of *descriptio gentium*, which was prevalent in the "high culture" during the sixteenth to eighteenth centuries:[75] "Po nimetsky netsko, po pol´s´ky koryto, po rus´ky valiv" (*Netsko* [trough] in German, *koryto* in Polish, *valiv* in Ruthenian); "Pol´s´kyi mist, nimets´kyi pist, turets´ke nabozhenstvo, to vse blazenstvo" (A Polish bridge, a German fast, Turkish piety, it's all buffoonery); "…a zhydivs´ke hi…—to vsio iedno" (Jewish sh_t is all the same); "Liuters´kyi pist, nimetske hi…—vshytko iedno" (Lutheran fast, German sh_t—it's all the same).[76] This "humorous comparison of absurd things" (Franko's term) accurately indicates who the Ruthenians are not: Poles, Germans, Turks, Jews, Protestants.[77]

However, it leaves unanswered the question of who they are—that is, to which larger community outside the borders of their small fatherland do they belong? It is precisely this type of identification (knowing who we are not, before we know who we are) that distinguishes ethnic identity from national identity: an ethnic group can define itself vis-à-vis others, but a nation must define itself vis-à-vis itself.[78] This group of proverbs reveals another trait of the identity of "commoners." A comparison of diverse misfortunes demonstrates that ethnic definitions coexist with local, professional definitions, and the like: "Sokhrany Bozhe vid pol's'koho mosta, vid kalus'koho batoha, i vid halyts'koi spravy!" (May God preserve [us] from the Polish bridge, from the Kalush whip, and from the Galician cause!); "…vid skalats'koho bolota, vid pans'koi karnosty i vid liuds'koi nenavysty" (…from the mud of Skalat, from the lords' punishment, and from people's hatred). (Polish bridges were known for their state of disrepair; Kalush and Skalat are towns in Galicia.)[79]

With regard to the question of ethnic identity in a traditional society, the situation was approximately the same as that of geographic mobility: it was an important feature of daily life, but not a key one.[80] However, social identities could play the exact same role. As the anonymous reviewer of the first collection of Ruthenian folk proverbs compiled by Hryhorii Ilkevych (1841) noted, "No less strikingly does that diversity of classes and their extremes break through: the priest, the peasant, the Liakh, the Jew, and the German."[81] The clearest and most ostentatious cases were those where ethnic differences coincided with social and religious ones (a "Pole" as a symbol of a lord, a Catholic, and a non-Ruthenian). However, in other circumstances ethnic or religious closeness could not guarantee a sense of "closeness" where social distance was concerned, which is indicated, among other things, by the existence of a sizeable group of Galician-Ruthenian proverbs about Greek Catholic priests (*popy*) as negative personages.

The self-definition of a rural dweller in Galicia may be presented as a certain continuum, the furthermost point of which was represented by the Pole and the Jew ("Liakh, zhyd i sobaka, to vira odnaka" [The Liakh, the Jew, and the dog, that is one and the same faith]),[82] while the closest point is represented by the members of his family (within the family unit itself a distinction is made between one's own, legally sired, children and stepchildren or bastards). Where the dividing line lay between "us" and "them" or "outsiders" depended on concrete circumstances. Sometimes this line could divide the inhabitants of two neighboring villages, two corners of the same village, or even two neighbors. In the case of the peasantry, the most frequent criterion was physical labor and its accompanying attributes. In the eyes of the Galician peasant a "lord" was anyone dressed in city clothing, while a noblewoman was any woman wearing a hat.[83] It could also happen that Ruthenians from a rural area closed ranks, drawing in even individuals with a different social status but common faith and ethnic background (nation of "peasants and priests"). This method of identification could be activated in crisis conditions, when the inhabitants of a village had to define their attitudes toward the state or the powers that be.

Here, the example of the revolution of 1848 is significant: that year, the peasants signed a mass petition about the division of Galicia into Eastern ("Ruthenian") and Western ("Polish") parts, enlisted in the Ruthenian People's Guard, and collected money for the "sacrificial altar of the fatherland"[84] (as in the case of Franko's father). In individual cases, peasants could support the idea of forming a separate "Ruthenian Gubernia" and their own "Ruthenian government," but they refused to affix their signatures, fearing "that serfdom would return or that there could be a betrayal."[85]

The "our own / outsider" continuum was not restricted to lords, Liakhs, and Jews as the personification of evil. Once again, beyond the furthermost point of "outsiderness," began the zone of "kinship" with the anointed monarch. His role lay in maintaining a balance between "good peasants" and "bad lords" because, otherwise, the "godless and idle" lords would reinstate serfdom. In any event, as Franciszek Bujak noted on the basis of his observations, rural inhabitants in the 1880s were at a stage where they still needed personification of the concept of "fatherland," and the image of the "good monarch" served this goal well.[86]

A survey of Galician-Ruthenian folklore allows scholars to reach two conclusions. Both are very preliminary ones; however, they allow for the introduction of correctives to the theory of a "private" and an "ideological" fatherland. The first confirms the fact that before the peasants began moving to a new, national, fatherland, their identity was not merely local. They had a sense of belonging to a community that was greater than their village. The daily circumstances of their lives propelled them toward this: the need to leave their homes from time to time, as well as to spend time in a world filled with religious beliefs and symbols. These concepts of a fatherland embraced the "Ruthenian land" (Rus) and Ukraine. Neither had national meaning—that is, they did not signify an ethnic territory that, in accord with the basic principle of nationalism, should attain separate political status. These "prenational" concepts were distinguished not so much by the breadth of the space represented in them ("small fatherland"—"large fatherland") as by the method of that representation: geographically, they were weakly defined and vague; they had a transcendental meaning.

The second conclusion boils down to the fact that the peasants' change of identification did not mean unilinear growth from small to large fatherland. There were several visions of large fatherlands, both "old" and "new," which vied in order to capture the imagination and consciousness of rural inhabitants. It would appear that in the case of Galicia, it is not Ossowski's scheme that is more adequate but the interpretation proposed by Peter Sahlins in his research on the Franco-Spanish borderland in the Pyrenees. He contrasts the model of the identity that resembled several concentric circles of different sizes (ranging from smaller to larger fatherland, inscribed within each other) with the model of counter-identities, which are not fixed in a constant hierarchy but, rather, exist on various levels and in interaction with each other: in championing the interests of their fatherland, the inhabitants of one village could be in opposition to a neighboring one. The same could be said of the inhabitants of a neighboring county or region, yet they could all unite with each other in certain cases, whenever the need arose.[87] The historical development of national identities in the borderland lay precisely in the competition of alternative conceptions. One of the key conditions of success was the amplification of projects "from above" by means of visions "from below," which somewhat narrowed down the choice, but did not eliminate it entirely.

Chapter 7

The Turning Point

The Modern Metropolis

After graduating from the gymnasium in the fall of 1875, Franko arrived in Lviv, where he enrolled in the Faculty of Philosophy at the local university. Apart from incidental mentions, no detailed descriptions of the circumstances surrounding his move to Lviv exist. In a letter that he wrote to Olha Roshkevych immediately after registering for university, he confessed that he was "afraid of Lviv" and admitted that his fears were borne out during his first weeks in the city: he was destitute and had already experienced several bouts of disillusionment [ZT 48:39]. However, these confessions may be treated as rhetorical exaggerations calculated to tug at his beloved's heartstrings, because, as Franko writes in this same letter, not having received a single "word of comfort" about his sufferings and myriad experiences, "My life here is a kind of unyielding, uninterrupted trance because I have lost my mainstay, I have lost hope!" [Ibid.].

The lack of data leaves the field open to speculation. The Ukrainian Franko specialist Rostyslav Chopyk insists that Franko's first impressions of Lviv were incredibly gloomy:

> His reception of [Lviv's—Y. H.] "fauna," the setting in which he found himself in the 1870s, is almost wholly embraced by the "Galapagos" metaphor (according to Charles Darwin and Kurt Vonnegut). An archipelago of "tortoise islands" isolated from the mainland by 1,000 kilometers of ocean; the time-space continuum, which led to evolution, having preserved, during one of the early stages, a plethora of "petrifactions," "premature maturations," and "rigidifications" hermetically sealed in a carapace of armor. An exceptional, even grotesque, conservatism—a key trait of the majority of the subcultures that he encountered on the dry shore of the "Galapagos."[1]

Everything in this statement is upside down. Metaphorically speaking, Lviv in those days should be likened not to Darwin's Galapagos Islands but to a little island of modernity amid an ocean of obsolescence. Meanwhile, the young Franko, who had just arrived from the provincial town of Drohobych, was himself a representative of a world of "petrifactions," "premature maturations," and "rigidifications." His transformation into "one of the most ardent spokesmen of progress in our land," "a well known demoralizer of Rus," "Myron" (son of peasants), and "Moses" (national prophet) occurred later, in great measure because of those unique opportunities and challenges that Lviv offered to newcomers like him.

The move to Lviv must have been a very important event in Franko's life. In the imagination of the newly graduated gymnasium student from the provinces, Lviv, the capital city of the largest Austrian land, "lay somewhere in the mythical distance" [ZT 21:184]. By his own admission, he had come there "full of small-town fantasies and small-town sensitivity" [ZT 15:15].

The memoirs that were written by newcomers to Lviv during the Habsburg era all have a single, unifying theme: amazement at the large city. Everything their eyes beheld was fantastically strange: the tall, stone buildings; many imposing Roman Catholic and Eastern-rite churches; and masses of people on the streets, like ants bustling around an anthill—among whom were large numbers of Jews.[2] This theme is characteristic not only of Galician provincials but also the newcomers who were flocking in from other Austrian or German lands: they never expected to see anything like it so far east.[3] What's more, the awe with which Lviv was regarded is also recorded in many earlier Ruthenian, Armenian, and Catalan documents dating to the fourteenth century, and German documents of the sixteenth century.[4]

The history of Lviv followed the general European pattern according to which the majority of large cities were founded before 1300.[5] It owed its status as a metropolis to a combination of three factors. The first was Lviv's advantageous location on the great overland trade route connecting the West and the East, around which, according to Fernand Braudel, revolved the entire European economic system.[6] The other two factors were Lviv's capital city status (it became the seat of the Ruthenian princes in the thirteenth century) and municipal self-government, as embodied in Magdeburg Law, which permitted the accumulation of a considerable amount of revenues from trade and their investment into building up the city. It was a given that Lviv rarely benefited from all three factors, and during its most difficult periods—for example, in the eighteenth century—it did not enjoy any of them. During the existence of the Rzeczpospolita, the city's importance was downgraded as a result of becoming an administrative center of the small Ruthenian palatinate and the sharp decline in trade owing to protracted wars. In addition, the political dominance of the nobility negated the benefits accruing from municipal self-government.[7]

Thus, when the Habsburgs annexed Galicia in 1772, they found the city in a pitiful state: reports written by the first Austrian bureaucrats describe the exceptionally poor state of roads and buildings, many of which were standing in ruins or simply abandoned. Habsburg rule restored Lviv's past grandeur, bestowing on it the status of capital city of the Kingdom of Galicia and Lodomeria, the largest province of the Habsburg monarchy. This status was the main source of its wealth, which flowed there from the entire breadth of the immense land.[8] Thanks to its new standing, Lviv obtained a university in 1784. This, in turn, led to a paradox: two out of the six universities in the Habsburg monarchy were located in its "most backward" land (the other was the ancient Jagiellonian University in Cracow). Together with bureaucrats, university lecturers and their students comprised one of the most numerous new social groups in the city. During the period of Austrian rule, in addition to the university there were five institutions of higher learning in Lviv, including a polytechnic institute, several gymnasiums and a couple of dozen public and private schools.[9]

The Austrian administration did everything to bestow a modern look on the Galician capital. Between 1772 and 1825, all the ancient fortifications were demolished and wide streets and avenues were laid in their place. This reconstruction was a characteristic feature of urban planning policies throughout the monarchy. In Lviv, however, it took place significantly earlier than in Vienna (1857) or Prague (1870).[10] During the decades of Habsburg rule, the role of Lviv as a large trading center devolved to the borderland town of Brody. However, Lviv became a large transportation hub after the opening, in 1861–1871, of two railways linking Lviv with Vienna and the Russian border, respectively. This railway link marked the beginning of the intensive movement of passengers and goods between Austro-Hungary and the Russian Empire. For the citizens of Austro-Hungary and Russia who were visiting the spas in Karlovy Vary or the theaters and museums of Vienna and Prague, leaving for their studies in Geneva, and fleeing to the West in order to evade government repressions or anti-Jewish pogroms (1881)—or for those who, in a reverse move, were transporting illegal publications and weapons from the West to the East—Lviv gradually became a mandatory transit point and, frequently, a stopping place for a longer sojourn or even permanent residence.

The Habsburg reforms led to the restoration in 1870 of municipal self-government, the last historical factor that helped transform this city into a metropolis. During the latter third of the nineteenth century another factor emerged, one that was connected with Galicia's "Piedmontese calling": the capital of the largest territory in the Austro-Hungarian Empire also became the "hidden capital" of nationally aware Ukrainians and Poles. Here they created a network of national institutions and publications that could never exist in the Russian Empire—or, where the Poles were concerned, in the German Empire. As early as the first decades of the nineteenth century Lviv ranked third, after Warsaw and Vilnius, in the number of Polish-language publications, and by the end of the century it had attained the same ranking as those two cities.[11] In Ukrainian-language publishing, Lviv was unequaled, until the abolition in 1905 of the restrictions against the Ukrainian printed word in the Russian Empire.[12] In the early 1880s, the total number of periodical publications appearing in various languages per capita in Lviv significantly surpassed Moscow. Had Galicia then become part of the Russian Empire—and in the late 1870s the threat of an Austro-Russian war resulting in the occupation of Galicia was quite real—Lviv's publishing output would have been surpassed only by St. Petersburg and Warsaw.[13]

It is not surprising that the period of Lviv's most intensive growth took place during the final decades of Habsburg rule. Demographics bear this out: between 1880 and 1910 the city's population nearly doubled—from 103,000 to 196,000—mainly thanks to newcomers like Franko. The closest cities that were approximately the same size as Lviv were Vilnius and Kyiv in the Russian Empire, and Trieste in the Austro-Hungarian Empire. In Galicia, the next largest city was Cracow, whose population was nearly two times smaller (between 50,000 and 60,000 in the 1870s–1880s). If a circle with a radius of 300 km were to be drawn with Lviv in its center, there would be no other city of like size within its limits.[14]

Nevertheless, Lviv's focused development differed from that of other large cities in the Austro-Hungarian and Russian Empires.[15] The changes that were taking place in Lviv were more qualitative in nature than quantitative, owing to the advantages that accrued to its residents from capital city status. During Austrian rule Lviv never became a large industrial center. In 1880, 1.8 percent of the total population of Galicia lived in the city, compared to bureaucrats (13 percent) and the members of the free professions (18 percent). Yet only 7 percent of the population and 3.5 percent of all workers were engaged in industry in Lviv.[16] The majority of people who flocked to Lviv from neighboring towns and villages because of the lack of factories and plants found employment in tradesmen's workshops or on construction sites and railway depots, or they hired themselves out as domestic servants. Labor migration was negligible and did not burden the urban infrastructures, as it typically did in large industrial centers like Warsaw, Łódź, Yuzivka, or Baku. Mass labor migration was also held back by the fact that Lviv was a wealthy city in a poor province, and not everyone was able to afford to live there. The latest Viennese fashions that flooded Lviv, the planning of luxurious buildings, including the third largest theater in Europe, and the bohemian culture, as typified by numerous coffeehouses and restaurants—all of which led the city to be dubbed the "Vienna of the East"—meant, among other things, that the cost of housing, goods, and services was relatively high.

In any event, between the time of Franko's arrival in Lviv in 1875 and his death in 1916, the Galician capital came to symbolize changes, thanks to which its political and cultural influence radiated to a large chunk of territory, thereby turning Lviv into a political and cultural metropolis. But its rays spread much farther afield. First and foremost, the city transformed its newcomers. After Franko arrived in Lviv, he could not have failed to note the large number of scaffolds on practically every corner: his own suburban apartment was located on a puddle-filled street surrounded by construction sites.[17] From that time onward until 1902, when he moved into his own villa, Franko frequently changed apartments. Crisscrossing the city, he breathed in the atmosphere surrounding the construction of buildings and railways, the unveiling of monuments and pavilions, and the paving of streets. Serving as an illustration of the social progress that was taking place according to a concerted plan and efforts, this atmosphere of urban growth and development would leave a vivid mark on his individual literary works, such as "Kameniari" (The Stone-Cutters) and "Muliar" (The Stone-Mason) as well as his general world perception.

University

During the last third of the nineteenth century, German Lemberg was being transformed all over again—this time into Polish Lwów. The Polish character of the city was manifested on various levels and in diverse ways: from the predominance of Poles in the local administration to the renaming of streets in honor of Polish heroes.[18] A clear picture of the course of Polonization emerges from the reminiscences of two of Franko's friends who, like him, arrived in Lviv in the 1870s. The first was the Polish revolutionary Bolesław Limanowski, who found refuge in Galicia (1870) after he completed his term of imprisonment in Siberia. The newcomer was struck by the German character of the capital city:

> Lviv gave the impression of being a strongly Germanized city. This was a time when roasted chestnuts appeared on the streets, with Jews shouting: "Heisse Maronen! Heisse Maronen!" Small shops were called "graizleriany" (*Greisslerei*). There were many German signs. In restaurants the German language was heard more often than Polish. For a while I ate lunch at a restaurant located near the theater. I would often encounter practically the same group of people at a certain table. Everyone spoke German, and the salutation "panie dobrodzieju" [Honorable Sir] was frequently interwoven into their language. I realized later that they were Polish-speaking Lviv burghers….In theaters German plays were performed more often than Polish ones. At the Jesuits' church the Sunday sermon was delivered in German. In the government and schools the German language still had not been supplanted by Polish. Public lectures held at City Hall were mostly given in German. Vienna was the model for Lviv in terms of food and drink, entertainment and fashion. Gradually, however, Polishness squeezed out Germanness. And by the time I left Lviv in 1878 it had the look of a Polish city.[19]

The same year Limanowski left Lviv, Yevhen Olesnytsky, Franko's friend, enrolled at Lviv University. In his estimation, Lviv was almost an exclusively Polish city:

> All government offices are Polish, schools and universities are Polish, the theater is Polish, signs everywhere are Polish, trade is in the hands of Poles, and Jews who, in the national sense, have proclaimed themselves as Poles. Everywhere the language was Polish—people spoke Polish in shops, restaurants, and cafés. It took great courage to speak to a waiter or merchant in Ukrainian, and everyone looked upon such a person as someone extraordinary. The numerically small Ukrainian population that was in the city was hidden away somewhere in secluded nooks, but it was not seen on the surface: the numerically largest Ukrainian element was in the lowest workers' strata, between domestic servants and building caretakers.

The public that filled the churches on Sundays and feast days was recruited mainly from those spheres.[20]

Ivan Franko began his studies at Lviv University at the very moment when this largest center of German culture was losing its German character. On 4 July 1871, the Vienna government abolished the mandatory use of the German language in the university's faculties of law and of philosophy. The only professors with the right to lecture were those who knew at least one of the regional languages. A three-year transition period was instituted. In 1874 German-language lecturers who had not learned Ruthenian or Polish were obliged to leave the university. A directive issued in 1871 led to a mass exodus of German professors, and Lviv University was struck off the list of German universities. Its role was eventually taken over by the University of Chernivtsi, which was founded in 1875 with the goal of "[carrying] the German light to the East."[21] In connection with this, the Austrian parliamentary deputy and professor at the University of Vienna, Eduard Suess, proposed that Lviv University be closed because it was declining and generally superfluous; after all, he declared, Galicia still had another university—the one in Cracow. In his book on Austrian universities, Armand Dumreicher, another Viennese academic, categorically refused to discuss the state of affairs in Cracow and Lviv because he was convinced that, after the introduction of the Polish language, scholarship had disappeared from both these universities, and to educated Germans they had become institutions that were as alien as French and English universities.[22]

A local professor named Xaver Liske (1838–1891), one of the founders of modern Polish historical studies, rose to the defense of Polish scholarship and Lviv University. In 1876, in response to Edward Suess's critical remarks, he wrote a brochure titled *On the Apparent Decline of Lviv University*. As his main argument he cited statistics pointing to the increase in the number of both scholarly publications and students at Lviv University following the introduction of the Polish language. His argumentation is not free of national megalomania: he claims that no other nation in the world has penned as many scholarly works in foreign languages as the Poles.

He was right about one thing, though: de-Germanization had not generally lowered, but rather had raised, the teaching level. In this connection, German professors were divided into two groups: the first, consisting of mediocrities, regarded their positions at Lviv University as a sinecure, while the professors in the second group, who were more talented and ambitious, dreamed of achieving scholarly success as quickly as possible in order to obtain invitations to teach at the central German universities.[23]

The Polonization of Lviv University took place less because of the reduction in its German population than the drop in Ruthenian numbers. On the eve of the reforms Ruthenians were the most populous ethnic group at the university, comprising nearly half of the student population (45.6 percent in 1857). By 1883, however, they formed barely a third (34.8 percent).[24] There is no firsthand evidence of Franko's reception of these changes. His acquaintances advised him to take up his studies at the universities in Vienna or Chernivtsi, where the language of instruction was German. However, he did not act on their advice. But it was not as though he welcomed Polonization: the poems that he wrote in his first years at the university are full of strongly worded anti-Polish sentiments. It may be assumed that the main reason behind his desire to remain in Lviv is that it was a large cultural center of the Galician Ruthenians.

If Franko nurtured any hopes of obtaining a good education in Lviv, they were probably dispelled rather quickly. In one of his autobiographies he recalls:

At that time Lviv University was not a light in the kingdom of the spirit; what is more, one could compare it to an institution of cultural barrenness *in spiritualibus*. Even today I get the chills whenever I recall the pedantic, absurd lessons of Wenclewski, Czerkawski, [and] Ohonovsky, the arduous remastication of dead scholasticism, this slavish adherence to published models and literary formulae. After he retired, one of the most gifted teachers of the day, F. Zrodlowski, was in the habit of introducing himself to new people in the following manner: "I am that Zrodlowski who, over a period of thirty years, made young people dizzy from Roman law, and when things finally became clear to me, they did not consider me a criminal, only a madman." Other, more inane gentlemen, did not lose their minds, but calmly and with sacred dignity remasticated their cud until their blessed demise.

It should be added that neither philosophy nor psychology nor Slavic or Romance studies were taught at Lviv University in those days. But psychology, philosophy, and pedagogy were in the hands of one professor, Yevsebii Cherkavsky, a Ukrainian by birth, a Polish chauvinist by conviction, and a politician by profession.[25] Being a deputy, he was left with little time for the university, and when he was there he had the habit of lecturing in a horrible, sepulchral voice, reading all kinds of drivel from old notebooks, which had neither a beginning nor an end—this was probably a course that he had dragged out not for an entire semester, but a whole five-year period.

I craved knowledge with a passion, but I got only dead goods that you had to swallow if you wanted to obtain an imperial-royal position. To study for a crust of bread and not scholarship—this was the slogan of Lviv University at the time, the sole exception being, perhaps, the historian, Prof. Liske, but I did not attend his lectures.

I became disillusioned; I felt disgust and began to seek knowledge outside the university. [ZT 34:371–72]

The university lectures did not engage me at all and did not offer me anything—neither methods nor scholarly achievements. I attended the late Wenclewski's classical philology lectures and yawned; I listened to Dr. Ohonovsky's lectures on Ruthenian grammar and literature. [ZT 49:245]

According to a line of thought in contemporary Polish historiography, this negative assessment was determined by Franko's nationalistic views: he was allegedly bitterly upset by the cutbacks in educational opportunities for Ukrainians at the university; it is hinted that Franko was "known for his dislike of the Polish nation."[26] It is difficult to agree with this statement. Disregarding for the moment the general question of Franko's opinion of Poles, let us focus on his positive attitude toward the Polish professors at Lviv University—Xaver Liske, Julian Ochorowicz, and Leon Biliński— and his extraordinarily critical attitude toward the Ukrainian professor, Omelian Ohonovsky.

Franko could be very biased in his opinions, which could also change, depending on the circumstances or time: in another context (which, however, has nothing in common with Polish–Ukrainian antagonism) he made very critical comments about Liske and his historical school [ZT 48:257]. Therefore, we should not accept them at face value, but rather juxtapose them with other people's opinions. From this perspective it is instructive to read about the polemic that Franko's erstwhile professor, Omelian Ohonovsky, waged with him much later, in the early 1890s. By that time Franko's autobiography, a fragment of which is cited above, had already been published, and Ohonovsky was aware of Franko's critical evaluation of his courses. In the following passage Ohonovsky expresses his disagreements with Franko by referring to himself in the third person:

It is strange that Franko is complaining that he could not learn anything good at the university. After all, the late Wenclewski was clever, and later his teaching produced quite a few able lecturers of classical philology; and perhaps one [could] learn something even from Omelian Ohonovsky, considering that in 1878–1879 his most diligent student was Oleksandr Brykner [Brückner— Y. H.], who is now a professor at the University of Berlin.[27]

Ohonovsky introduces another argument: in his opinion Franko liked sociology, but one could hardly expect professors of philology to be conversant in this subject.[28] This argument sounds anachronistic in the context of their discussion: Franko was not instantly captivated by sociology, and in his first year of studies he registered for courses on philology, particularly Ohonovsky's. On the other hand, Franko's extremely critical attitude toward Ohonovsky was shared by Mykhailo Drahomanov, the former Kyivan professor. During his brief stay in Lviv, Drahomanov visited the university, where he sat in on a lecture on Ruthenian literature. He later told a group of young people that "having spent much time in Russia and Europe, he had never heard such stupid lectures as in Lviv."[29]

A similar view was held by Mykhailo Pavlyk, with whom Franko had shared an apartment for one year. About Ohonovsky, Pavlyk wrote: "Whoever has heard him one year has nothing more to hear the second year."[30] Pavlyk described the general state of university studies by paraphrasing the well known Latin adage, *Non scholae sed vitae discimus* (We learn not for school, but for life). According to him, the reverse was true of Lviv University: everything for school, nothing for life. He therefore declared, "I would rather smash rocks than study."[31]

It is very likely that both Franko and Pavlyk, with his harsh assessments of university education, were strongly influenced by their later acquaintance with Russian revolutionary literature, which placed self-learning on a higher plane than formal university education.[32] Numerous traces of this influence may be found in Pavlyk's letters. In private conversations later he allegedly declared that, after reading Belinsky, Dobroliubov, and Chernyshevsky, "[he] had the impression that [he] had been released from an Austrian prison into the wide steppe."[33]

There was one objective reason for these reactions, however: the provinciality of Lviv's intellectual life in general, and particularly at Lviv University. The following words are attributed to Emperor Franz I, the founder of the university: "I don't want scholars; I want bureaucrats." Accordingly, Lviv

University was established in order to serve a dual goal: the training of government functionaries and of priests (who were also state officials); thus, its two main departments were law and theology. The program of the third faculty, philosophy, was set up according to the "residual principle": courses in the humanities were taught there, as well as some natural sciences courses that were not included in the curriculum of the law and theology faculties (this universal character of the philosophy faculty has been preserved at certain contemporary German, Austrian, and Swiss universities). Occasionally there were some colorful characters among the lecturers, such as Jozef Mauss, the Swabian-born professor of history, who had been the tutor of Ferdinand of Austria. His former status gave him a sense of freedom, allowing him to proclaim his liberal views without the need to look over his shoulder. But Mauss was an exception; furthermore, he was no longer teaching at the university when Franko enrolled there. In general, professorial influence did not extend past the university walls: they "shone but did not cast their rays." The absence of organized life at the university inevitably left its mark on the city. As a provincial capital, until the last third of the nineteenth century Lviv did not have the necessary means to become a beacon of science and literature.[34] In 1861 Yakiv Holovatsky, Omelian Ohonovsky's predecessor at Lviv University, gave the following response to the Russian consul in Vienna, Mikhail Raevsky, who had requested local news articles on a weekly basis: "Nevertheless, Lviv is a provincial city; there are so few important events that so many materials, enough [for me] to be able to send a constant stream of articles every week, can scarcely be accumulated."[35]

The provincial status of Lviv University stemmed from the cultural-geographical fact that, until the final quarter of the nineteenth century, it was the easternmost outpost of German culture. It could not boast of a brilliant faculty: scholarly talents were lured by the "central" universities of Berlin, Vienna, Leipzig, Heidelberg, and Tübingen. The Polonization of Lviv University fundamentally changed its status in the configuration of relations between the "center" and the "periphery." In 1831, after the Russian government closed Vilnius University, and both Kyiv University—formed in part from the core of Vilnius University in 1834—and the newly founded University of Warsaw (1882) became tools of Russification in the Russian Empire's western borderlands,[36] the now Polonized Lviv University was acquiring a symbolic role as the largest Polish university in the lands of the former Rzeczpospolita. From a former provincial German university it turned into an institution of higher education situated in the "hidden" Polish capital. Such a reputation served to attract the attention of Polish academics from Russia and Prussia, who took advantage of the local liberal regime and began erecting a beacon of Polish scholarship with patriotic zeal.

Objectively speaking, the Polonization of Lviv University exerted a positive influence on Franko's life. This is particularly noticeable after his first arrest and imprisonment (12 June 1877–15 March 1878), after being convicted of disseminating illegal socialist propaganda. This experience changed Franko's life in a fundamental way: these two events, among others, led both him and Pavlyk onto the path of sociopolitical activity. As Franko later wrote, prior to engaging in this type of activity both of them lacked a theoretical-academic background. Although they still had a lot to learn, a handful of young people had already begun flocking to their side [ZT 49:246]. Convinced that university studies were to no avail, Pavlyk quit school, urging Franko to do the same because neither he nor Franko would ever obtain a government position. Fortunately, Franko did not listen to Pavlyk. During the winter semester of 1878–1879 Franko registered for three courses with Prof. Ochorowicz (Philosophy of Physics, Practical Philosophical Studies, and a psychology seminar) and one economics course taught by Prof. Biliński. Both professors were luminaries of Polish academic life, who, like Xaver Liske, had moved to Lviv when the university began to be Polonized.

Julian Ochorowicz (1850–1917) was one of the founders of psychology, as well as a philosopher, writer, and inventor. His formation as a scholar took place at the universities of Warsaw and Leipzig. In Warsaw, he was famously known as one of the initiators of the journalistic campaign waged under the slogan of the "struggle of the young press against the old" (1868–1875). Together with Aleksander Świętochowski, he was one of the leaders of the Warsaw Positivists, and their main theoretician. In 1875, after obtaining his doctorate in Leipzig, he established contact with Lviv University, which offered him the position of private docent of courses in psychology and the philosophy of nature. Ochorowicz's classes were always popular, and he was much loved by his students.[37] He influenced Franko's ideological formation at the very moment when he saw the need to boost his theoretical knowledge. According to Franko's own admission, in the last years of his university studies he benefited mainly from Ochorowicz's lectures [ZT 48:213; 49:246].

Ochorowicz introduced Franko to the philosophy of positivism. For a two-week period in the summer of 1879, arguments about socialism and

Darwinism raged during his classes (with Franko taking part in them). The university administration also looked askance at Ochorowicz's extracurricular activities. His contemporaries claimed that he did not prepare for his lectures, believing that his passion alone would suffice; hence his lectures were superficial. This was noted by the students, and the hostile members of the teaching faculty used this as an argument in order to deny him a permanent position.[38] Ochorowicz did not receive the promised promotion to the rank of professor, and in 1882 he was forced to leave Lviv University, and the city.

In contrast, Leon Biliński (1846–1923) was the embodiment of conscientiousness and respectability. A well-known economist, he obtained tenure owing to his work on Malthusian and Ricardian theory. Biliński was a proponent of the school of economics that the Germans dubbed "socialists ex cathedra": he was a member of an organization of German economists, founded in Eisenach in 1873, who sought the implementation of social reforms.[39] The phenomenon whereby Franko rose swiftly to the position of chief theoretician of Galician socialism in the late 1870s and early 1880s cannot be completely understood without considering Biliński's influence. In his later political essays on economic topics, Franko attested to his esteem and respectful attitude to Biliński's works [ZT 44/1:338; 44/2:432].

Franko continued his studies during the winter semester of 1879–1880, and once again Ochorowicz was his favorite professor, teaching three out of the five courses for which he registered.[40] Before he managed to complete the semester, Franko was rearrested in early March. His new prison sentence, this time for three months, did not dampen his desire to finish his education, and in the fall of 1880 he registered for university studies for the last time. However, there are no records of his winter semester, 1880–1881. What is clear is that he never finished his studies at Lviv University. He was destined to complete his university education ten years later, in 1890, but in Chernivtsi, not Lviv. He did this in order to obtain the right to begin his doctorate at the University of Vienna.

One of the greatest ironies of Franko's biography and his posthumous fame is the fact that his name was given to the very university from which he never graduated and where he was never permitted to teach. Franko's main university was prison. Although it did not provide him with a formal education, his imprisonment turned him into a truly free and independent human being, and confirmed his moral authority among several generations of Ruthenian-Ukrainian intellectuals.

The Birth of Myron

Franko realized his main ambitions outside the university. He dreamed of becoming a "Ruthenian writer." By the time he had arrived in Lviv, he was already famous among the local Ruthenian students, who regarded him as a distinguished young writer.[41] He wrote about this to his sweetheart after several months of living in the city:

> Here in Lviv I am starting to become some kind of curiosity or celebrity, I don't know. Many a time so-and-so comes to the circle:
> "With whom do I have the pleasure of speaking?"
> "Ivan Franko!"
> And someone at the back adds his two cents:
> "Vulgo *Dzhedzhalyk.*"[42]
> And that Christian stands there with his eyes bulging out! [*ZT* 48:47]

As a young writer, Franko had to define his national orientation. To a great extent, the content of his works and their success among readers depended on this. During the period of Galician autonomy, Lviv was a "nationalizing city": discussions of identity reached their peak intensity here and few people remained on the sidelines.[43] After the somnolence of public life in provincial Drohobych, this experience was a completely novel one for the young Franko. He later admitted: in Lviv, "I suddenly found myself in the middle of linguistic and national disputes, which until that time had been almost totally alien and incomprehensible to me; so, clearly, I could not find any rhyme or reason in them, and for a long time I vacillated between one side and the other" [*ZT* 49:244].

After arriving in Lviv, Franko joined the Russophile society *Akademicheskii kruzhok* (Academic Circle). Later he claimed that his ties to Russophilism were random, and that he did not share any ideas with it. He explained his decision to join the society by his desire to be published on the pages of *Druh* and to gain access to its library.[44] But his acquaintances from those years tell another story: there was a "trace of Russophilism" in Franko at the time.[45] This is confirmed by several minor but telling details: the minutes of meetings at the Academic Circle reveal that Franko added the patronymic "Yakovlevych," in the Russophile manner, next to his first name;[46] in one of his reviews he titled the name of the reviewed author with the Russian word *gospodin* (Mister) [*ZT* 26:29]; and voting ballots from the year 1876 indicate that out of fifty-six students, only seven used the phonetic orthography, and Franko was not one of them.[47]

Most Ruthenian students had a Russophile orientation. Franko's friend, the ardent "etymologist" Mykhailo Pavlyk, and another "fresh" literary force, Volodymyr Levytsky, were both Russophiles. Levytsky had left the provinces to come to Lviv at the same time as Franko, and joined the editorial board of *Druh*.[48] Russophilism was then the leading trend in the Ruthenian camp. This was reflected in the superior financial and material status of the Academic Circle compared to that of the populist society, the Friendly Usurer. The former received subsidies from Russophile societies and institutions that were significantly better-off than the populist associations because they had more members, among whom were people from the top ranks of Ruthenian society.[49] The Russophile society occupied three large rooms in the *Narodnyi dim* (People's Home), the main Ruthenian institution in Lviv. It had a reading room and a library, and members could obtain loans and stipends as well as discounted tickets to the theater. In contrast, the populist society had neither accommodations nor a library of its own, and—what was most important to Franko—it did not have a publication comparable to *Druh*. *Pravda*, the journal published by the populists, had more of a political than a literary orientation, and it came out irregularly to boot. The possibility for *Pravda* of being published on a regular basis was remote because, according to Austrian legislation, this would require a financial pledge, which the populists could ill afford. The activities of their Prosvita Society were very lackluster, consisting mainly of twice-yearly meetings: a general meeting to deal with administrative questions, and a commemorative evening held in early March in honor of Taras Shevchenko (even then it was necessary to rent a hall from strangers and engage non-Ukrainian talent—for example, a choir and soloists from a Polish society).[50]

Any discussion of the young Franko's national orientation must also take into consideration the fact that the Academic Circle and the Friendly Usurer were not in a state of permanent conflict. Rather, both of these societies were two different directions *within* a single current: the national movement of the Galician Ruthenians, before it became crystallized.[51] Even the composition of the Academic Circle was not homogeneous. Among its members was a small group of students—"hard-line Ruthenians" (that is, convinced Russophiles)—who were led by Stepan Labash. At the other end of the spectrum were the so-called *uhodovtsi*, who were in favor of establishing a compromise with the populists. Their leaders were Antin Dolnytsky, Mykhailo Pavlyk, and Volodymyr Levytsky. Franko belonged to the center, which consisted of those who were uncertain about which side they should align with.[52]

It cannot be said that Franko was ambivalent and indefinite in all things. Occasionally, the tone of his published works was decisive. In the poem "Napered!" (Forward!, written in the fall of 1875) Franko appealed to the Ruthenians to engage in the "terrible struggle" that "awaits us," not with swords of steel but with the truth of knowledge. In "Dzhedzhalyk's" view, the main enemy was Poland. With regard to the struggle against it, Franko strikes a heroic note here: "Nai sam Mitskevych zryt´ / Dnes´ Pol´shchu roz-valym!" (Let Mickiewicz himself behold / Today we will destroy Poland!")[53] Another of his poems is written in the name of the "God of liberty." The poet appeals to all the fraternal Slavic nations (of course, Poles were not part of this group) to engage in a "holy struggle" in order "to topple the tyrant from the heights"—the Ottoman Empire.

> "On ne opresia nam,—on khoryi! / V Evropi vstane den novyi:
> Herzegovyna i Chornohora / Nai bude klyk nash boievyi!"
>
> [He will not resist us—he is sick! / A new day will rise in Europe:
> Herzegovina and Montenegro / Will be our battle cry!][54]

The two enemies of the young Franko were both external ones. It should be noted that the Russian Empire is not one of them: On the contrary, his enemies are Russia's "historical" adversaries. Therefore, Franko's Russophilism did not rule out a Russian orientation, at least implicitly. This is confirmed by his understanding of Ruthenian literature as being common to both Little Russians and Great Russians [ZT 48:10]. This perception echoed the appeals of other authors whose works appeared in Druh, who urged that these two cultural currents not be separated: "There is only one Russian people in history; in culture generally there is only one development in literature….And Shevchenko, and Pushkin, and Gogol, and Fedkovych, and others are the expression of the multifaceted, brilliantly shining Russian spirit."[55]

The ideal espoused by the young Franko is "holy Rus." It is difficult to make any definite claims about his religiosity during this period of his life, but he deemed it necessary at the very least to proclaim it publicly in his poems. One of them is titled "Bozheskost´ liuds´koho dukha" (The Divine Nature of the Human Spirit), while another has an even more imposing title: "Stykh v chest´ ho V[ysoko]p[r]e[vosshenstva] Kyr Iosyfa

Sembratovycha Mytropolyta…v narochytyi den´ tezoimeniia 26 dekemvriia 1875 (7.1.1876) v chuvstvi iskrennei blahodarnosty i izriadnoho pochytania Pytomtsamy hr. k. hen. Semynarii L´vovskoi predlozhennyi 'Khresta my znamenem khrestylys´'" (1875) (A Verse Titled "We Crossed Ourselves with the Sign of the Cross" Proposed in Honor of His Beatitude Kyr Yosyf Sembratovych, Metropolitan, on the Planned Day of his Name Day, 26 December 1875 (1 January 1876) with a Feeling of Sincere Gratitude and Considerable Esteem from the Alumni of the Gr[eek] C[atholic] M[ain] Lviv Seminary).[56] At approximately the same time Franko was writing his "verse in honor" of Metropolitan Sembratovych, he gave a public lecture at the Academic Circle on "The State of Poetry in Our Times," in which he declared that "poetry is the discovery of the spark of divinity in reality."[57]

There is also no clear indicator of the link between the young Franko's religiosity and his patriotic feelings. In order to safeguard the integrity of "Rus," which was split between the Orthodox and the Greek Catholic churches, it was necessary to rise above religious feelings. During a private conversation with Sylvester Sembratovych, the editor of the church newspaper, *Russkii Sion*, Franko argued that *narodnist´* (nation, the people) must stand above faith,[58] but in all likelihood this discussion took place later, in 1875. In any case, Franko rises to the defense of "Rus" with no less determination than when he calls for a struggle against Poland and Turkey. He condemned the young Ukrainophile poet, Kornylo Ustyianovych, for daring, in one of his poetry collections, "to pour hatred for the term[s] of Rus, Ruthenian, into us" [*ZT* 26:18].[59] "Our personal feeling simply rebels against the former," Franko wrote. "History has sanctified the term Rus. Our ancestors fought under this name and laid down their lives; it was that name and faith in its sanctity that safeguarded us from national and moral perdition" [*ZT* 26:18].

Franko's criticism of the younger Ustyianovych deserves special attention for two reasons. First, this is a discussion about which social values and reference points all national Ruthenian poets should proclaim. This was the specific angle from which Franko viewed Ustyianovych and, it may be assumed, that was how he saw himself in the future. Second, Franko's criticism allows scholars to position him with respect to the division of Ruthenian patriots not only into Ukrainophiles and Russophiles but also into conservatives and democrats. Specialists on the Galician student movement of the 1870s maintain that the second line of demarcation was, perhaps, more important than the first. The members of various societies

were divided not so much into Russophiles and Ukrainophiles as into supporters of "greater or lesser conservatism, [and] greater or lesser sympathy
toward the people," although even these concepts are too obvious for them
"to be applied to any of the warring sides."[60]

Franko's critique of Ustyianovych positions the former closer to the
Russophiles and conservatives, and the latter closer to the Ukrainophiles
and democrats. What is fascinating about this disagreement is the fact
that Ustyianovych, a few years earlier, had himself been the same kind of
"pan-Russian" as Franko. He hated Poland the same way, roused the "spirit
of the Slav" in himself, glorified "victorious Moscow" in the Balkans, and
was a "defender of Rus." Ustyianovych, nevertheless, became a Ukrainophile
after his two visits to the Russian Empire in 1867 and 1872. There, among
other things, he developed a fascination for the Ukrainophile movement,
but more for its democratic nature than its nationalism, its desire "to get
closer to the people, to uplift that people to our level."[61]

Within the space of a single year, between 1875 and 1876, a considerable number of Ruthenian students, including Franko, experienced the same
kind of inner revolution as Ustyianovych—without, however, embarking on
any journeys. The one who triggered these changes was the Ukrainophile
and associate professor of Kyiv University Mykhailo Drahomanov, who
had set himself the task of establishing close contacts with the Ruthenian
students in Lviv. It is impossible to grasp Franko's ideological evolution in
1875–1876 without a brief excursus into the history of the Ukrainophile
orientation. This orientation is usually examined within the context of
Ukrainian nationalism, and is seen at best as on par with other alternative
national orientations, within the force field between Polish nationalism and
the imperial governments of Vienna and St. Petersburg.[62] However, most
researchers overlook the fact that Ukrainophilism not only concerned
national orientation, but also proposed certain sociopolitical preferences
in the system of coordinates of "left-right," "conservative-progressivist,"
and the like. It is not always easy to determine which was more important:
social or national motives. But to gain an adequate understanding of the
nature of Ukrainophilism one cannot separate the two.

This is clear from the example of the Cyril and Methodius Brotherhood
(1845–1847), the first organization to distinguish Ukrainian identity from
the common Rus current. Like other nationalistic organizations that had
sprung up at this time (Young Italy, Young Germany, Young Ireland, among
others), it sought to unite national slogans with the idea of democracy. The

aspirations of the "Brothers" may be boiled down to a few points: emancipation of the peasantry, enlightenment of the common people, and the creation of a Slavic federation on a democratic-republican basis (there was absolutely no mention of Ukraine's separation from Russia). The ideological cornerstone of modern Ukraine became the catchword of the most distinguished member of the Cyril and Methodius Brotherhood, Taras Shevchenko, who called for simultaneous national and social liberation.[63]

The Kyiv Hromada—the Ukrainian organization that emerged later, in 1859, to which Drahomanov belonged—carried on this line, but with a modification in favor of a different, more radical, *Zeitgeist*. The authors of tsarist government reports describe the Hromada members as a "community of communists," who are disseminating "harmful ideas and thoughts" among the people,[64] and who carry the writings of "father Taras" (Shevchenko) in one pocket and Karl Marx's *Das Kapital* in the other.[65] It was Mykhailo Drahomanov who came up with the formula of merging national and social motives, which became the moral imperative for several generations of Ukrainian national activists until the Revolution of 1917. He believed that for the Ukrainian nation as a "plebeian" people, in which the basic mass comprised land-starved peasants while the ruling classes were Polish, Russian, German, or Jewish, the tasks of social and national liberation coincide. In Drahomanov's view, "consistent with Ukraine's circumstances, it is a bad Ukrainian who has not become a radical [a socialist—Y. H.] and it is a bad radical who has not become a Ukrainian."[66]

The Kyiv Hromada was not homogeneous. Drahomanov was the leader of the left wing, whose members came from various classes (*raznochintsy*: people of non-noble birth) in Left-Bank Ukraine (Little Russia), where memories of the Cossack Host and the Cossack State were still fresh. Relying on Western ideologies and young people's fascination with Russian progressive literature, this memory created an atmosphere of radical sentiment.[67] The more moderate wing consisted mostly, but not exclusively, of Polonized landlords from Right-Bank Ukraine. But their choice of Ukrainian orientation was also dictated not so much by national as social motives. Many of them had passed through the Polish revolutionary movement, but at a certain point they had severed links with it and crossed over to the side of the Ukrainian peasantry so as not to feel like "spongers and parasites."[68] The right-wing members of the Hromada had been raised in the Polish and French cultures, which were dominant in Right-Bank Ukraine, and they had a superior attitude to Russians, considering them an uncultured nation. The leader of the "European Right-Bankers," Volodymyr Antonovych, regarded the influence of Russian culture on Ukraine as excessive and therefore harmful.[69]

The differences between the "right" and "left" wings of the Kyiv Hromada reflected two different models on which the Ukrainian nation was supposed to be constructed. Both acknowledged the key role of the Ukrainian peasantry. But in the Left-Bank version, the Ukrainian nation was to be restricted mainly to the peasantry. An exception was made for the local laboring masses and leading intellectuals—"all those who conduct work that is beneficial to the community" (Drahomanov).[70] Meanwhile, the right-wingers were in favor of an expanded understanding of nation, for including other classes in it so that a Ukrainian could be "a priest, and a landowner, and a merchant, and a judge, and a functionary, and a police-man, and a political essayist, and a socialist, and a radical, and a conserva-tive, and a liberal, and a legitimist, and a bourgeois."[71]

Until the mid-1880s the (insignificant) differences between the two wings of the Kyiv Hromada yielded to compromise. A clear indicator of this is the close cooperation between Volodymyr Antonovych and Mykhailo Drahomanov, the two acknowledged leaders of the Hromada.[72] With the exception of their shared views of *khlopomanstvo* (the name given to the Hromada's populism by their opponents in the Polish and Russian camps), both wings were united around the idea of the "indissoluble unity of Little Russia and Great Russia."[73] They were convinced that Ukrainians ought to share a common destiny with Russia in the hope that, sooner or later, that empire would embark on a different path, the path of political liberty and the broad development of the individual.[74]

At first, the Russian government did not express excessive hostility toward the organized Ukrainian movement. In the same way that it used Marxism to fight its main political opponent—Russian populism—the tsarist government perceived the development of Ukrainian culture as a shield against the Polish national movement, the only nationalism in the Southwestern Krai that caused serious anxiety in St. Petersburg.[75] The Ukrainian (Little Russian) and Belarusian cultures were regarded as parts of the single great Rus (but not Great Russian!) culture that was supposed to resist Polish cultural and national influences in the western borderlands of the Russian Empire.

This modus operandi foundered in the early 1860s. The Polish Uprising of 1863 had momentous significance; it was a turning point. Like the preceding uprising, which took place in 1831, it questioned the civic model of loyalty to the empire. Now, the loyalty of the monarchy's subjects alone was not sufficient; also required was loyalty to the culture, language, and religion of the people / nation whose name was carried by the empire itself. The Russian Empire had only just begun to master the logic of nationalism, and liberal reforms had not been rejected yet. But their implementation became dependent upon the successes of Russification in the various regions of the empire.[76]

The Ukrainian movement became one of the first victims of the changes in the official policy. The 1863 uprising sparked the unjustified suspicion that the Ukrainian movement was a Polish intrigue. The Russian government was now beginning to grasp the threat to the integrality of the empire that was emanating from the Ukrainian national project. This resulted in the 1863 prohibition against the use of the Ukrainian language in education and mass publications. Tsarist policy toward the Ukrainian movement was not characterized by consistency; thus, periods of repression alternated with interludes of relative tolerance. In the early 1870s, the Hromada members succeeded in resuming their activities. They acquired a certain number of votes during the municipal elections in Kyiv, began publishing the newspaper *Kievskii telegraf*, and took over the local department of the Imperial Geographic Society, whose goal was to collect and publish ethnographic materials. The Hromada's successes alarmed their opponents in Kyiv, supporters of "Rusness." This brief period of liberalization was followed by a new and even more brutal prohibition (1876) against the public use of the Ukrainian language.[77]

Owing to these circumstances, the Kyiv Hromada decided to transfer the base of its activities outside the borders of the Russian Empire—westward. This task was assigned to Mykhailo Drahomanov, who was the first Ukrainian figure to fall victim to the renewed repressions when he was dismissed from his position as associate professor of Kyiv University "because of his socialist tendencies and Ukrainian separatism." Without waiting to be exiled officially, Drahomanov went abroad at the beginning of 1876. Before his departure the members of the Kyiv Hromada appointed him as their emissary and promised to provide financial support for his activities in the West.[78]

Drahomanov's first stop on his way to the West was Lviv, where Ivan Franko first met him when he sat in on Ohonovsky's class and afterward made that devastating assessment of the Lviv University professor.[79]

Drahomanov the skeptic had long been aware of the low level of intellectual life among the Galician Ruthenians. He first visited the Galician capital in 1873, and he was shocked by what he saw in Lviv. A native of the town of Hadiach in the Poltava region, in his childhood years Drahomanov had developed a profound aversion to card games, the favorite occupation of the provincial intelligentsia. In Lviv he visited Ruska Besida (Ruthenian Conversation), one of the centers of the populist movement, where he witnessed the following scene:

> Here in Lviv, a university city in the freer part of our Rus, in a semipolitical society, I see card tables, and well-known patriots, professors, writers, politicians are sitting at them, for them [cards] they foreswear all conversation about the most burning issues—patriotic, popular, literary. When I was coming back to my hotel after the first evening at Besida, I thought: "But this is old Hadiach, the county town of the Nicholas era! [that is, the reign of Tsar Nicholas I of Russia, 1825–1855—Y. H.]—this is where I have returned after having traveled so extensively!"[80]

This episode aptly conveys the difference between "Ukrainians from the Dnipro region" and "Galician-Ukrainians." Despite the fact that Galician-Ruthenian politicians and intellectuals lived in one of the most modern cities in all of Eastern Europe, they remained among the least intellectually modernized groups in this part of the world: the new literary, artistic, and political currents simply bypassed them. In this respect, they were very different not just from the local Polish and progressive Jewish elites but from the Ukrainians of Kyiv as well. Young Galician Ruthenians experienced this at first hand. Ostap Terletsky, a member of the Vienna-based Ruthenian student organization *Sich*, wrote the following letter to a friend after his visit to Kyiv in 1874: "I will tell you the sincere and explicit truth, that before the Kyiv community in Kyiv and all Ukrainians I too stood in opposition to the current conduct of national affairs in Lviv. With my very own eyes I became convinced that the Lviv people have become lazy and reduced themselves to nothing, as well as the entire party that must of necessity rely on them. And what a huge contrast between Lviv and Kyiv! What tireless work goes on in Kyiv—I did not want to believe my eyes."[81]

Mykhailo Pavlyk shared Terletsky's opinion. Although he never managed to move to Kyiv (despite several attempts), he formed his image of Ukraine, and Kyiv, with the help of visiting Ukrainians. His encounters with them led him to make certain negative comparisons. "Your people are great (although not all) but ours are trash. We need people like yours in Galicia…I tell you, I don't know what I would have done if I had not gotten to know Ukrainians."[82]

Thus, it is no surprise that under these circumstances Drahomanov was able to make such a great impact on young Ruthenian intellectuals. Initially, he was counting on the Galician-Ruthenian students based in Vienna: the members of Sich. The main battle took place in May 1873, when the "progressivists" succeeded in transforming this populist society into a scholarly association. It was headed by Ostap Terletsky, who later became a librarian at the University of Vienna [ZT 33:322].

Drahomanov made the biggest splash in Lviv. In 1874 Rev. Ihnatii Onyshkevych, a Ruthenian language teacher at the Lviv Gymnasium, published an article in one of the first issues of *Druh*, titled "Novoe napravlenie ukrainskoi literatury" (A New Trend in Ukrainian Literature). Onyshkevych's article summarized two of Drahomanov's articles that had been published in Kyiv about the relationship between Russian, Great Rus, and Little Russian (Ukrainian) literatures. Correcting the widespread notion that Ukrainian literature emerged as a result of a "Polish intrigue," Drahomanov proposed studying this literature as part of the broader literary process in the Russian Empire. In his opinion, Ukrainian literature was *prostonarodna* (of the common people), adapted exclusively in order to instill awareness in and enlighten the common Little Russian people. Great Russian literature had the very same status—it was a literature aimed at instilling awareness among the Great Russian people. Both of these literatures were parts of the single Russian literary current, which was supposed to be superior because it was aimed at the educated classes, who had more developed aesthetic sensibilities. If Galician Ruthenians wanted to draw closer to Russian literature, then it would be natural for them to benefit from Ukrainian literature, as Little Russian activists and scholars in the Russian Empire were already doing. Onyshkevych's article concludes with an entreaty to all Galicians, in emulation of Drahomanov's appeal, to reflect on the linguistic uniformity of all Ruthenian publications in Galicia. But as a genuine "hard-line Ruthenian," he opposed Drahomanov's idea of replacing the "etymology" with "phonetics."[83]

Onyshkevych's article provided Drahomanov with an excellent opportunity to get involved in Galician-Ruthenian affairs. His reaction took the form of three letters to the editorial board of *Druh*. Dated 1875–1876, these letters were part of a clever plan that he had formulated as early as 1872:

"to spread a Ukrainian trend in Galicia through the new Rus (Great Rus) literature, which, with its secular character, will undermine Galician clericalism and bureaucratism, and help turn young people toward the demos; and since the people there are Ukrainian, Ukrainian national awareness will be achieved in and of itself." Drahomanov was convinced that young Galician Ruthenians, despite their leanings toward Russia and Russian culture, in fact had no knowledge of either the Russian language or Russian literature. But as soon as they acquainted themselves with Russian literature they would instantly grasp the degree to which Galician-Ruthenian literature differed from Russian. Moreover, their familiarity with the works of Russian populist writers, such as Herzen, Chernyshevsky, and Dobroliubov, would cause them to abandon their intention of creating a "salon literature" and to turn in the direction of the people; and this orientation toward the people would inevitably lead to the victory of the Ukrainian current.[84]

Despite its apparent complexity and strained intellectualism, Drahomanov's plan worked. A number of students treated his letters to the editors of *Druh* as a revelation. Whereas the journal's editors still sought to debate Drahomanov's second letter,[85] they published his third one without any rebuttal, because they were in complete accord with the main thrust of his argument—"the need to study the progression of leading European ideas with a passionate feeling for *narodnist'* [the national spirit; the people]."[86] Under Drahomanov's influence, a revolution took place in the Russophile Academic Circle. In October 1875, the advocates of an accord with the Ukrainophile current succeeded in gaining seats on the board of the society. At their urging, in early 1876 thirteen populist students joined the society. Thanks to this maneuver, the "conciliators" managed to outvote the "hard-liners." They completely took over first the editorial board of *Druh* and, later, the Academic Circle itself; Drahomanov was proclaimed an honorary member.[87]

These transformations are best documented on the pages of its publishing organ, *Druh*. Beginning in 1876, the bulk of this journal consisted of literary criticism and discussions, rather than literary works, including novels, short stories, and poetry. Even the very tenor of the journal changed—from an ingratiating salon tone, with which the "quiet and sincere *Druh*" pandered to public tastes (especially those of "young Russian beauties")[88] to one that was aggressively insolent, aimed at asserting a new program: "Work for the good of our people, the uplifting and enlightenment of the local Ruthenian element in its own language."[89]

The first harbinger of change was a brief article by Mykhailo Pavlyk, titled "From the Lips of the People," which was published in April 1876. It featured the texts of three folksongs, two of them recorded by Pavlyk and the third by his sister Anna. He concluded his article with an appeal to young people to record songs, urging anyone who could not do so in Cyrillic to use the Latin script.[90] Soon Pavlyk launched a personal crusade against the old symbols and old idols. In one of the journal's May issues he published a review of three new publications: Omelian Ohonovsky's *Zhytie Tarasa Shevchenka* (The Life of Taras Shevchenko); Oleksandr Stefanovych's brochure, *Pianstvo i pohybel' naroda* (The People's Drunkenness and Perdition); and Ivan Verkhratsky's *Baiky i povistky* (Fables and Novellas). Out of the three authors of these publications, Pavlyk spared only Ohonovsky, merely stating: "Everything that is written should be important for both 'ordinary' and 'educated' people; it should have equal value for both the people and the intelligentsia." Verkhratsky got the brunt of Pavlyk's criticism. This self-proclaimed poet had no poetic talent, wrote Pavlyk, who suggested that, instead of writing poetry, Verkhratsky would be better off compiling a terminological lexicon or a dictionary of the Little Russian language, or writing a natural history.[91] In Pavlyk's view, the criterion for poetic talent was the ability to recreate the spirit of folksongs: "A short folksong will put to shame the 'necessary' literature of Mr. V[erkhratsky], the 'language expert.' There is life here—but in Mr. V[erkhratsky]'s 'necessary literature' the corpus of words is a corpse."[92]

As Pavlyk began to launch galling and merciless blows at his opponents, without a care for the kinds of arguments he was wielding, his reviews began to resemble a kind of literary hooliganism. In a review titled "The Novellas of Volodymyr Pasichynsky" he writes that "in the circumstances of the terrible literary poverty of our land, just trash is being published."[93] In his rebuttal, Verkhratsky declared that Pavlyk's "disgusting and superficial" critique "does not explain anything, does not reveal anything beside the correspondent's shallowness and malice."[94] In a separate brochure decrying the harmful literary tendency evident on the pages of *Druh*, Verkhratsky concluded with an appeal to the clergy: "Do not subscribe to *Druh*! Away with *Druh*!"[95]

The editors of *Druh* received a harsh response from another leader of the populist current, the Rev. Stepan Kachala. He wrote that, despite being gladdened initially by the news that the Academic Circle and *Druh* had switched their allegiances to Ukrainophilism, he was saddened to read the letters written by Drahomanov, "that Muscovite nihilist...who garbs himself in the fine feathers of European civilization and scholarship, all the while ignoring the national spirit and everything that [is] sacred to man." Until recently, supporters of Ukrainophilism had been reproached for advocating first political separatism and then Polish patriotism. Now that a takeover had taken place at *Druh*, the Ukrainian orientation would in future be linked to socialism, communism, and nihilism, wrote Kachala. In conclusion, he declared: "Woe to us! One cannot go along with the direction set by the hard-liners [Russophiles—Y. H.], but it is worse to go along with the young, among whom such pernicious tendencies are being manifested."[96]

The Russophile camp, too, had harsh words for *Druh*. According to the editors of *Slovo*, the leading Galician Russophile newspaper, the nitpicking that was evident on the pages of *Druh* plays a base and harmful role because it implants in young people's hearts "hatred of generally revered Russian institutions" and demoralizes young female readers. The Russophiles fired a separate broadside at Pavlyk for the coarse and unseemly tone of his articles. In terms of policy, they reproached *Druh* for its cosmopolitanism (they claimed that more was written on its pages about "Paris, Warsaw, Wiesbaden, George Sand, et al.," yet "not a single word is mentioned in *Druh* about the Russian princes, about our glorious past") and for its orthographic inconsistency (the editors of *Druh* do not even know how to write "such a holy word as 'Russian'"). In their polemic with *Druh*, the editors of *Slovo* chose to adopt a pose of injured dignity: in answer "to the coarse, unseemly insults of juveniles, which are incompatible with the truth, the only possible response is: let the youngsters amuse themselves!"[97]

A crucial role was being performed by the statements issued by Pavlyk and his fellow thinkers: they were creating new fields of discourse that had not existed previously in Galician-Ruthenian political writings. Their provocatively offensive tone forced their opponents to defend themselves with words, thereby increasing the number of articles that were published on the nature and tasks of literature; and the scandal accompanying the publication of these articles inevitably attracted the local reading public's attention to the issues being raised.

Pavlyk did not merely engage in criticism; he also tried to create a positive action program. On 12 (24) July 1876, during an evening of music and poetry dedicated to the thirty-third anniversary of the death of Markiian Shashkevych, he delivered a speech titled "Pro potrebu etnohrafichnoi roboty v Halychyni" (On the Need for Ethnographic Work in Galicia). In many respects, his lecture reiterated the arguments that Drahomanov had already laid out in his three letters. Pavlyk's main thesis was the lack of folk literature in Galicia, which could serve the broad masses and offer them valuable knowledge. Only ethnographic work can create such a literature, he argued. Ethnography would, on the one hand, reveal the genuine needs of the people, and on the other, steer the attention of the Ruthenian intelligentsia to progressive European ideas. On the whole, it would ignite a mass movement in Galicia, comprising champions of the people's cause, as was already the case throughout Europe and in Russian-ruled Ukraine. According to a report that *Druh* published about Pavlyk's lecture, "the public received [it] with genuine rapture, which to us is a guarantee that similar ideas will now be quickly adopted among young people."[98]

The twenty-three-year-old Pavlyk became the leader of the new movement. His name was connected with the reincarnation of the Academic Circle, whose course had been shunted "onto the Drahomanov path."[99] Compared to Pavlyk, Franko was a hazy, bland public figure. He was the librarian of the society, and in late February 1876 he was appointed secretary of the editorial board of *Druh* (Antin Dolnytsky headed both the society and the journal). Although Franko could rightly boast of the largest number of literary works published in *Druh*, and his first collection came out in the summer of 1876,[100] not a single one of these publications brought him greater success, nor did it place him in the focal point of the public's attention.[101] His theatrical debut was the play *Try kniazi na odyn prestol* (Three Princes for One Throne). Premiering on 9 March 1876, it was a failure bordering on a total flop, mainly—according to *Druh*—because the administration of the Polish theater had refused to loan costumes to the actors, but also because of the playwright's mistakes and the weaknesses in the plot.[102]

The history surrounding the longest of Franko's works during this period, the novel *Petrii i Dovbushchuky* (The Petriis and the Dovbushchuks) is significant. Franko began writing and publishing it in *Druh* even before Drahomanov's letters appeared in the journal, and he completed it only in late 1876, after the takeover of the Academic Circle.[103] The main plot line concerned the enmity between two families, the Petriis and the Dovbushchuks, and the treasures buried by Oleksa Dovbush (1700–1745), the local Robin Hood, who was celebrated in the local folklore. Written in the spirit of E. T. A. Hoffmann and Eugène Sue, the novel was full of fantastic elements, the most emblematic of which is, arguably, one of the main characters, the 150-year-old Dovbush. Antin Dolnytsky, the editor of *Druh*, had to excise entire sections of the plot because they were so implausible. The narrative, generously studded with the amorous billing and cooing of the main characters, is weighed down by the author's moralizing tone and long-winded lyrical passages.[104]

Franko was clearly trying to satisfy the tastes of the Galician readership, which was the main target of Drahomanov's letters to the editors of *Druh*:

> The target of literary work in Galicia is the Ruthenian public, which was formed almost exclusively by its unfortunate history: priests trembling before consistories; functionaries clinging to their "positions," having long ago consigned to oblivion their seminary and university notebooks, and not thinking about following the course of European thought, barely maintaining their appetite for literature with Polish and German newspapers and journals in coffee houses; and "beauties," who are seen as cooks in Galicia, in the German fashion, or concubines and salon chatterboxes in the Polish magnate fashion; "beauties" who have never read anything but a prayer book and the Polish "Miscellanies." And the literary ideas and tastes of this public are becoming the legislators of your writers![105]

As usual, the editors of *Druh* added a preface to Drahomanov's letter: "Although the opinions expressed in [the letter] may be excessively harsh in places, nevertheless they so deserve closer examination and attention that we are offering it to our public *and particularly to our young writers* [my emphasis—Y. H.], among whom, in the current period of transition of our literature, many a one does not know which path to step onto and in which direction to go so that his work will not be futile, and so that at least with his sincere willingness he will help realize the great, vital idea: the genuine enlightenment and uplifting of our people."[106]

In the spring of 1876 Pavlyk discussed the novel *Petrii i Dovbushchuky* with Franko's stepfather during a visit to Nahuievychi. As Pavlyk described in a letter to Drahomanov, "He and I started talking, and he says to Franko: leave those Doboshchuks [*sic*] alone, it is not realistic, get to work on something more sensible.…And this is what a literate peasant says about the literature in *Druh*.…You see what kinds of writers the gymnasium produces, those who are incapable of writing something normal."[107] In his letters to Drahomanov, Pavlyk was unstinting in his criticism of his colleague. He rebuked Franko for conformism and called him an "opportunist," "two-faced," "restless," and "false." In one case, he even goes so far as to accuse him of being an informer and a plagiarist.[108]

The reasons behind Pavlyk's exasperation were of a programmatic character, so to speak. He believed in the special vocation of the new intelligentsia of peasant background. Raised to do the heavy work of peasants, it now had to repay them a debt of gratitude. It was futile to expect anything of the Lviv students, because they had a condescending attitude to the Galician peasantry. Even the very word *khlop* (peasant) made them laugh, and students in Lviv were occasionally heard using the expression *khlop-byk* (peasant-bull), likening a peasant to a beast of burden. Pavlyk even coined terms to define this particular environment: *shliakhetstvo* (nobility) and *popivs' ka shliakhta* (clerical nobility). According to Pavlyk, among the editors of *Druh* were "the best of the [young] peasant Lvivites," that is, Pavlyk, Belei, and Franko.[109] But Franko's stance both astonished and irritated him. For example, Franko once objected to the publication of the Russian anticlerical novel *Otravlennyi Diakon* (The Poisoned Deacon), which was reprinted in *Druh* on Drahomanov's insistence. Speaking with a fellow editor out of Pavlyk's earshot, Franko tried to halt its publication: "This is dangerous, there will be a revolution; don't let this happen."[110]

Nevertheless, Franko's views were changing. This is eminently clear from the evolution of the plot line of his novel, *Petrii i Dovbushchuky*. A new, and no less implausible, plot line appears in the second part of the novel, which was written after the change of orientation that had taken place within the Academic Circle: the main hero, the peasant Andrii Petrii, marries the daughter of a countess! Franko introduced this particular plot line in order to demonstrate the folly of the "lordly life" and its sway over an individual who traces his ancestry from the common people. In the novel, the hero's wife betrays him and nearly causes his death after she allies herself with the Polish rebels in 1863. The rebels are depicted in an extremely negative light and are described as a pack of haughty, pusillanimous nobles. By introducing this plot reversal, Franko was supposedly pointing to the chasm that had now opened up between him and the noble class, of which he himself was a descendant. The novel ends with reconciliation between the two families, as represented by Oleksa Dovbushchuk, the son of the brigand, and Andrii Petrii, who sold his estate and returned to the village in order to work on the people's behalf. Both agree on this issue: "We must propel the people not with the aid of Dovbush's money…but with our own forces, our own sacrifice, our own work, and only such a cause will be blessed by God" [*ZT* 14:242].

Franko's ultimate conversion in the direction of "radicalism" may be dated to the fall of 1876. We find evidence of this in a letter that Pavlyk wrote to Drahomanov on 2 November 1876:

> New ideas are being disseminated among the youth imperceptibly but vigorously, so much so that the young party (the populists) is already explicitly saying that the Lviv populists lag far behind in terms of learning, and they recognize that it is necessary to study. They would not recognize Dolnytsky—or Franko either. At one time he wanted to take his life;[111] this is what he thought and wrote and said earlier: that Dolnytsky was to blame for this.[112]

As proof of the fact that Franko had "turned himself around," Pavlyk cites his new poems, "Naimyt" (The Hired Hand) and "Postupovets'" (The Progressivist), both of which had a folk theme. The two poems were published in *Druh* in October–November 1876 and signed with a new pseudonym: "Myron ***."[113] There are serious grounds for assuming that Franko's choice of Myron as a pseudonym was part of his far-reaching program to "discover" his peasant identity. But this name did not simply signify a peasant background. If this were true, it would have been enough for Franko to adopt his first name, Ivan, as a pseudonym. In both folk and high culture, that name betokened a rural simpleton (sometimes contrasted with *Ivan-pan*, Ivan the lord).[114] The pseudonym "Myron" supposedly concealed a message: the name that was given only to bastards signified individuals who were of peasant background, yet stood out from other "normal" peasant children. Their abnormality lay in their exceptional giftedness, which caused them difficulties in their relations with their peers, and even their parents. But once they grew up, they bore the gospel of truth back to the peasants' thatched homes. Many were not able to carry out this noble mission: either they did not receive the necessary support and education in a timely manner, or they retreated in the face of social pressure. Only a handful of individuals, Franko among them, were able to stand their ground and become apostles of the new teachings. Franko sought to persuade his readers that Galician villages were filled to the rafters with children who resembled him when he was a child. As soon as social barriers are dismantled in Galicia, he writes, an entire nation of "Myrons" will emerge—peasants who will become enthralled by the "truths of knowledge" and desire to "turn them into reality" [*ZT* 15:71].

Franko's transformation into a Ruthenian-Ukrainian peasant was accompanied by more than a simple change of literary pseudonym. From that time onward he never again appended the patronymic "Yakovlevych" to his name. Many years later, when one of several Russians with whom he corresponded wanted to address him in this manner, Franko rebuffed the salutation, declaring: "In our country we do not use the patronymic" [*ZT* 50:222]. He also changed his surname: in Franko's village his surname was pronounced with the stress on the first syllable. Now, he began pronouncing his name Ukrainian-style, with the stress on the last syllable.[115]

Even before his ultimate conversion, which took place in February 1876, Franko stopped writing letters in German to his sweetheart. In connection with this decision, he wrote in a letter addressed to her:

> You may ask: why am I writing now in Ruthenian and not in German? It's simple. For me, German conversation is like a fashionable tuxedo that is donned by the kind of *Stutzer* [Ger.: dandy—Y. H.] in whose pockets the wind whistles. But for me, Ruthenian conversation is like one's favorite clothing worn at home, in which every person shows himself to another the way he really is, and in which I love you best! Ruthenian conversation is the conversation of my heart! [*ZT* 48:46]

An 1881 photograph of Franko reveals that his words were truthful in yet another sense: his bohemian outfit—"the fashionable tuxedo" had disappeared, replaced by an unpretentious embroidered shirt, a symbol of the Ukrainian peasant culture.[116]

Under Drahomanov's influence Franko abandoned his idea of writing exclusively for the intelligentsia. This was more than a straightforward change of literary benchmarks. It was the rediscovery of his peasant identity, from which he had increasingly distanced himself during his studies, but "discovered" as a result of his conversion. Henceforth, every single thing that he wrote fostered the consolidation of Ukrainian culture as a modern culture, the kind that answered the needs of the modern city of Lviv.

Chapter 8

At the Forefront of the Socialist Movement

According to an anecdote circulating in Galicia, a Polish socialist émigré from Warsaw who had been forbidden to reside in the Austro-Hungarian Empire appealed to the viceroy of Galicia, Prince Eustachy Sanguszko. "Please tell me how you picture socialism," the viceroy asked the socialist, who replied: "Socialism is the struggle between capital and labor." Sanguszko replied: "Ah, if that is the case, then you may obtain citizenship, because we have no capital and no one [here] wants to work!"[1]

It is impossible to determine how much truth there is to this story. But one can state with certainty that the statements attributed to the viceroy reflected the mindset of many educated people in Galicia.[2] One of the most knowledgeable experts on social relations in the territory, Stanisław Szczepanowski, was convinced that "socialism, just like Jesuitism, capitalism, and many other 'isms,' is merely a touch of foreignness, the grafting onto our soil of alien beliefs that emerged in completely different conditions and which are in conflict with our own civic traditions and ideas on social organization."[3]

Kornylo Sushkevych, one of the leaders of the "Ukrainian Piedmont," declared that "there is no social question in our country."[4] Volodymyr Barvinsky was convinced that the individualistic character of the Ruthenian-Ukrainian people was an opponent of communist and socialist ideas. In his view, the chief ideal of the people was not the destruction of classes but the free and completely unfettered movement from one class to another and the free development of the individual. In comparing Ukrainian Cossackdom to the French Revolution, he concluded that in its efforts to attain this ideal, Ukraine had overtaken France and the entire Western world by at least a hundred years, and therefore Ukrainians did not need to copy the great communist and socialist upheavals that had taken place in the West.[5]

There was general agreement on the circumstance that, because of Galicia's economic backwardness and the ingrained nature of traditional religious values, socialism would not have a chance to take root in the local soil.[6] Until the 1870s, the terms "socialism" and "communism" were used only as a tool to stigmatize individuals or groups, not to define concrete political currents.[7] At the same time, the level of public information about the ideology of socialism was very low, and the Galician public was ready to pitch rocks at anyone who even accidentally mentioned the phrase "social question."[8]

The Arrests and First Trials of Galician Socialists

Given the public mood, it is no surprise that socialism was imported into Galicia. This Western ideology was brought to Galicia by two émigrés from the Russian Empire: the Pole, Bolesław Limanowski, stood at the cradle of the local socialist movement, while the Ukrainian, Mykhailo Drahomanov, played an indirect role.

Drahomanov's role in the socialist conversion of Franko and other young Galicians may be acknowledged only according to the degree to which he precipitated the first trials for socialism of young Galician Ruthenians. From the mid-1870s, Galicia became the staging area for political émigrés from the Russian Empire continuing to head to various points in Europe. Among them were Polish socialists, Russian populists, and members of the Ukrainian Hromada of Kyiv—everyone who was fleeing westward to evade the escalating repressions in the Russian Empire. In the summer of 1876, Drahomanov rented an apartment in Lviv for Pavlyk, which was supposed to serve as a kind of hostel for people arriving from Russia. Moving in the reverse direction—from Vienna and Geneva through Lviv to Kyiv—were revolutionary works published in the Ukrainian and Russian languages. Thus, the apartment was also a storehouse of revolutionary literature. It is not surprising, therefore, that because of the intense movement of people and books, as well as the young Galicians' lack of conspiratorial experience, these activities quickly came to the attention of the Austrian police.

The first victim was Ostap Terletsky, who was arrested in Vienna in 1876 for circulating so-called "butterflies" (*metelyky*), small brochures intended to be used as socialist propaganda among Ukrainian and Russian peasants. Pavlyk's turn came in early 1877, when he was arrested in Lviv. In a café in Lviv a couple of Pavlyk's Russian lodgers, Aleksandr Cherepakhin and Sergei Yastrembsky (Jastrzębski), got into a fistfight with a police agent.

Following the altercation, a search of Pavlyk's apartment uncovered a stack of a thousand brochures penned by Drahomanov and another member of the Kyiv Hromada, the Marxist Serhii Podolynsky. The police arrested Pavlyk, and the verdict handed down at the end of the trial (17–20 March 1877) netted him eight days in prison.[9] After these two arrests it was easy for the police to establish who was standing behind the entire revolutionary transport scheme. After that, every letter written by Drahomanov to his Galician correspondents was perlustrated.

A letter written by Drahomanov to Pavlyk on 25 May 1877 played a very significant role in subsequent events and in Franko's personal destiny. The letter contained instructions to the Galicians concerning their further activities. One of their tasks was to spread the new ideas to the new territories of Bukovyna and Transcarpathia. Drahomanov was bound to the latter region by strong emotional ties. During his visit to Transcarpathia in 1875–1876 he was shocked by the poverty and ignorance of the local Ruthenian population, and dismayed by the disdain that the Hungarians and Jews had for the Ruthenians and by the egotism and faintheartedness of the local Ruthenian intellectuals. Under the sway of these impressions, Drahomanov made "Hannibal's oath to himself that he would do something for Hungarian Rus—at the very least to dispatch a few individuals to undertake real work for the people in the democratic-progressive direction."[10] Between the summer of 1876 and the beginning of 1877, Drahomanov managed to dispatch several emissaries to Transcarpathia. However, his efforts did not produce any significant results.[11] In his May letter to Pavlyk, Drahomanov had appointed Franko as his new emissary. Franko was supposed to travel to Transcarpathia to establish contact with the local youth and to collect ethnographic materials.[12]

Franko was not aware of the contents of this letter and the mission that had been placed on his shoulders. However, he knew he was under police surveillance because of Pavlyk's arrest. Fearing further arrests, for a time Franko and his friends stopped corresponding with people who lived abroad. To make matters worse, the rumor was that they would be instantly arrested as soon as they set foot in Russia.[13] All these scares and rumors strengthened Franko's idea that he absolutely had to attain a more stable situation and more respectable name; then it would be more difficult to harass him [*ZT* 48:53–54, 69].

Meanwhile, Franko's fame was growing. His Boryslav stories, published in 1877, garnered much attention. They were written primarily in order to illustrate the acuteness of the social question in Galicia.[14] The naturalistic depiction of the daily lives of Boryslav workers shocked readers and sparked, according to Franko, "a complete succès de scandale among the Galician public" [ZT 49:245]. Some priests mounted protests, claiming that such depictions demoralized women. Yosyf Sembratovych himself, the metropolitan of the Greek Catholic Church, issued instructions that he be brought copies of Druh along with the young author's Boryslav stories, "in order to see what kind of animal it was" [ZT 48:64].[15]

Inspired by his success, Franko decided to write a novel featuring the Boryslav theme, which would be titled Boa Constrictor. He shared his plans with Olha Roshkevych. Already in May 1876, Franko had asked her father for her hand in marriage [ZT 48:51]. The answer was hopeful, judging by the fact that, as before, Franko, together with Pavlyk and other friends, continued to be entertained at the Roshkevych home in Lolyn. The pair's youthful flirtation had developed into passionate love, and, as the correspondence between Olha Roshkevych and Ivan Franko indicates, it was around this time that their relations stopped being purely platonic.

One way or another, on 12 June 1877 Franko returned to Lviv from Lolyn where, according to his later statements, he had spent the happiest moments of his life. "En route," Franko recalled, "I wrote up the plan for Boa Constrictor and in the following days wrote the first part, but a week later I was arrested and propelled into the very depths of misfortune, into such an abyss that even today I cannot think about it without my heart shuddering and growing faint" [ZT 48:458].

At the very moment Franko was returning to Lviv, the Polish socialist, Erazm Kobylański, arrived in the city bearing an ill-fated letter from Drahomanov. His person, like his very arrival, was veiled in mystery. No one knew his real name, and in the socialist milieu he went by the name of Michał Koturnicki. He arrived in Lviv under the assumed name of Stanisław Barabasz.[16] After registering at a hotel, he began attracting attention by his suspicious behavior: he locked himself in his room, where he wrapped books in linen to send by post. The hotel staff denounced him to the police. A search of his room uncovered a revolver, a dagger concealed inside a walking-stick, and a small flask of poison. The arrest of "Barabasz-Koturnicki" sparked an investigation lasting nearly half a year. On the basis of Drahomanov's letters and various denunciations, some eighty to a hundred house searches were carried out in nearly every corner of Galicia, on top of the searches that took place in Lviv and Vienna. There were many dramatic, and often tragicomic, twists and turns in the investigation. Two members of the Sich Society, Ostap Terletsky and Shchasny Selsky, were taken in chains from Vienna to Lviv. Mykhailo Pavlyk was arrested right in the hospital where he was laid up. Owing to the similarity of their names, a Mykhailo Pavliuk was subjected to a search in Vienna, and in Lviv the home of a Yohan Franko was searched.[17]

In and of itself Kobylański's arrest was such a minor incident that, if not for the strange confluence of several factors, there might not have been any consequences.[18] The persecution of socialists in Austria had begun in 1870, when several Viennese socialists were accused of state treason. Other repressive measures followed their arrests, in particular, Ostap Terletsky's trial in 1876.[19] But the central government did not take the socialist threat too seriously. It is enough to say that until 1877 the foreign ministry archives did not even have a separate rubric for "socialist propaganda." All matters pertaining to Galician socialists were filed under "Polish Conspiracies in Vienna and Lviv." The documents in the case of "Barabasz and Associates" (as it was officially called) indicate how little Vienna understood the contemporary socialist movement. For example, the Austrian police regarded Koturnicki, who had been arrested in Lviv, as an emissary of the Russian and Polish sections of the International, which was allegedly headed by Drahomanov.[20]

Several factors served to bring wide public attention to this case. One of them was the expectation of war between Austria and Russia. At this time, the Russian army was in the Balkans fighting against the Ottoman Empire under the slogan of liberation of the Slavs from the Islamic yoke. Austria feared the prospect of Russian domination in the Balkans and the creation there of a large Slavic state. The question of a possible war with Russia was discussed with great gravity in Vienna. One of the causes for concern was the fear that war would be waged in Galicia, a border province where, owing to the Ruthenian population's sympathies for Russia, the Austrians' chances for victory would be slim.[21] The Russian army was passing very close to the Austrian border, and some of its technical equipment was being transported by a Galician railway into Romania. A rumor was circulating in Galicia that Muscovite agents were traveling throughout the region. There were fears that the arrival of the Russian army could spark an anti-Polish peasant uprising in Ruthenian counties. Ivan Horbachevsky (1854–1942), the future Austrian health minister, who was then a student at the University of Vienna and a member of the Vienna-based Sich Society, wrote a letter to Drahomanov dated 5 November 1877:

> Very strange and interesting things have emerged in Galicia—namely, to this
> day there is still great panic around socialism. Wherever there was a live
> Ruthenian, if he were not jailed, then at the very least he would be searched.
> They harass completely innocent people, officials, university students, high
> school students, teachers, etc.—the devil knows why. The most varied news is
> circulating everywhere in the villages. In one place it is said that people have
> consecrated knives; in another, that gunpowder has been found, etc. Who
> is inventing such tales? It seems that the Jews have contributed a lot to that,
> and also the Poles themselves, who are dispatching gendarmes throughout
> the villages—and they are questioning peasants in connection with certain
> matters about which the peasants have never heard in their entire lives.[22]

In the perception of the Galician public the Balkan war, socialism, Polish rebels, Russian agents, and rebellious peasants all melded together. The ensuing investigation could have developed any one of these lines. It began with the "Polish connection": the first people to be arrested by the police were the Polish socialist Bolesław Limanowski and August Skerla, the director of the local branch of Ognisko, the Polish workers' organization. Kobylański visited both of them immediately after arriving in Lviv. Three other Poles were arrested: their addresses were found during a search of Kobylański's lodgings and the Ognisko premises. Yet only one of them was considered suspect and sent to the prison in Lviv.[23]

However, the Polish line of investigation was quickly abandoned and the case was characterized as a Ruthenian plot. After a brief period of imprisonment Limanowski was released. Out of the seven defendants who were tried on 14 January 1878, only two—Kobylański and a worker named Anton Perebendowski—were Poles. The other five—Mykhailo Pavlyk, his sister Anna Pavlyk, Ostap Terletsky, Ivan Mandychevsky, Shchasny Selsky, and Ivan Franko—were Ruthenians, and four of them were members of Ukrainophile student organizations.[24]

It was convenient for the Polish territorial administration to present the case in such a way as to show that the sole reliable bulwark of state power in Galicia was the Polish nobility [ZT 33:348].[25] Thus, the local authorities, in their report to Vienna, usually portrayed the Ruthenian movement as a Muscophile threat. In 1877 this threat could be presented as a bona fide reality because the arrested Ruthenians were operating according to instructions sent by a citizen of Russia, Mykhailo Drahomanov. Rumors, possibly fabricated by the police, were circulating throughout Lviv that an organization serving Russian goals had been uncovered. The Vienna police had reportedly received a denunciation, according to which even the editor of *Slovo* was a socialist.[26] On their part, the Russophiles sought to shift the blame onto the Ukrainophiles, pointing out the natural link between Ukrainophilism and nihilism and socialism. Without a doubt, the scale of the arrests was influenced by the denunciations that were made by Russophile students, who were thus taking revenge for their defeat in the Academic Circle in 1875–1876. The Lviv-based Polish newspaper, *Dziennik Polski*, wrote that the Russophiles always knew one day in advance about every new search and arrest, which gave grounds to assume that their denunciations were sparking searches and arrests.[27] The Russophile students at the Lviv Theological Seminary even denounced their Ukrainian fellow seminarians, as a result of which eighteen of them were expelled from the seminary.[28]

During the arrests the police confiscated 199 books on socialist and Ukrainophile topics.[29] Since not one of these books was banned in the Habsburg monarchy, it was no crime to possess them. But the fact that there were several copies—and sometimes several dozen or hundred—of each book led the police to assume that this literature was meant for distribution, which required special permission. The detained individuals did not have any such permission, and thus on these grounds alone they could be tried for engaging in criminal activity. However, the illegal distribution of books was still not proof of the existence of a secret organization. The difficulty in proving such an allegation lay in the fact that in order to confirm the existence of a secret society Austrian legislation required the submission of minutes of a meeting held by a society and proof that the suspects had paid membership dues. The investigation lasted so long precisely because there was a lack of facts on which an indictment could be based. Bolesław Limanowski believed that the arrested Ruthenians would have been released if not for the perfidious testimonies of the Russophile students: thanks to them the Academic Circle, following the Ukrainophile coup, was presented as a secret society.[30]

That the case had been fabricated was clear even from the detail that Franko had met his "party comrade," Ostap Terletsky, only during the investigation. The arrested Ruthenians were tried on indirect grounds. Zborowski, the prosecutor, built his case on a syllogism: all the accused were socialists, and since socialist ideas were spread mostly by illegal means, then it stood to reason that they were members of a secret society.

As Pavlyk noted during his statement to the court, on these grounds one could indict all singers and musicians: all of them sing and play the same notes, ergo they are plotters. Both the judges and the Galician public had only a foggy notion of what socialism was and what exactly constituted its criminal nature.[31]

Franko scholars have depicted Ivan Franko as the main figure in this story. This portrayal was reflected in the title assigned to the literature connected with the legal proceeding: "The Trial of Franko and His Friends."[32] In reality, this was a gross exaggeration: the "starring" role in the trial was played by the twice-arrested Ostap Terletsky, whose sincere and persuasive statement to the court made such a vivid impression that the judges acquitted him.[33] Pavlyk, in turn, captured the attention of the judges and the press with his statements about free love, which shocked the public and gave rise to jokes about him.[34]

There are conflicting descriptions of Franko's conduct during the trial. Some observers claim that his speeches made a big impression,[35] while others do not mention him at all.[36] The press singled out Franko from among the other defendants because of his youthful, dreamy, and cheerful countenance. It seemed as though he were pleased to be at the center of attention, and he answered the judges' questions in Ruthenian with naïve frankness.[37] Originally, Franko had attracted the attention of the investigators wholly because of that agitation mission in Transcarpathia, which Drahomanov had assigned to him.[38] But during his imprisonment he saddled himself with another accusation. In his cell he had tried to strike up a conversation with the other prisoners, three peasants and a kitchen boy and thief named Karol Skamina, and to tell them a bit about socialism. Of his four cellmates only Skamina turned out to be a careful listener, but not in the way that Franko desired. The thief instantly reported on the contents of Franko's conversation to the court.[39] As a result, Franko was accused not only of belonging to a secret society, but also of attempting to recruit new members to that society.[40]

With the exception of Mandychevsky,[41] all the defendants confessed to harboring socialist views, but none admitted their guilt with regard to their membership in a secret society. The court sentenced Franko to six weeks' imprisonment and fined him five guldens. Compared to the others, his sentence was neither the severest nor the lightest: Koturnicki and Pavlyk were sentenced to three months in prison, while Mandychevsky, Selsky, and Pavlyk's sister received a one-month sentence.[42] Franko remained in prison until early March 1878, which means that, together with the time already served while awaiting his trial, he spent a total of nine months incarcerated.[43] Franko spent his time in prison reading, writing, and even collecting oral materials from the other prisoners for his literary and ethnographic works.[44] But, for the most part Franko's experience of prison was not an easy one. He wrote:

> The nine months spent in prison were torture for me. I was treated like a common thief, placed only among thieves and vagabonds, of whom there were about 14–18 in one cell with me, transferred from cell to cell, [subjected] to constant inspections and harassments (because of what I "had written," that is, songs and proverbs from the lips of my fellow prisoners, or even my own poems jotted down on pieces of paper acquired by chance, with a pencil acquired by chance). I spent several weeks in a cell that had only one window and housed twelve people, eight of whom slept on the trestle bed and four underneath the bed, for lack of space. For my protection, for fresh air, my fellow prisoners gave me the "best" spot for sleeping—beneath the window, opposite the door; and since the window had to be open day and night because of the stuffiness, every morning I woke up with snow on my head that had blown through the window. [ZT 49:245]

From the perspective of the twentieth century, with its Nazi and Soviet concentration camps, such complaints about the brutality of the Austrian penitentiary system may strike some as laughable. But one should not forget that prison is prison, and even a few weeks spent in poor sanitary conditions in a jail can cause lasting health problems and, in certain cases, a fatal illness, such as tuberculosis or pneumonia (which is what happened to Volodymyr Naumovych, the son of the well-known Russophile figure, Ivan Naumovych, who was imprisoned together with his father in 1882,[45] and to Franko's friend, the peasant Hryn Rymar, who was arrested and tried in 1886).[46]

The prisoners suffered most from the bad food. Right after Bolesław Limanowski's sister visited him in the Lviv prison, she wrote: "The poor fellow looks bad, the prison walls must have a bad effect on him, and actually that's what I'm afraid of, that if he has to be imprisoned longer….I am sending him food from home."[47] It should be kept in mind that Limanowski spent less time in prison than Franko, and—as he admitted—in rather comfortable conditions thanks to the constant care provided by his wife and sister, who regularly sent him food, money, and books.[48] During Pavlyk's first imprisonment, the same role was performed by Franko, who purchased food with money supplied by Drahomanov and took it to his friend. The concurrent imprisonment of Franko and the two Pavlyks, brother and sister, was even more difficult because there was no one to bring them care packages. Omelian Ohonovsky, Pavlyk and Franko's university professor, refused to forward the money that Drahomanov had sent for the two prisoners.[49]

But, as Franko said, "prison itself was not the heaviest affliction: the verdict of the criminal court and especially that which I encountered out in the world was a hundred times worse, and the most unjust condemnation of the entire society, which was flung at us, hurt me terribly" [ZT 49:245–46]. This condemnation was palpable even during the trial, as evidenced by newspaper commentaries and the jeering cries from the spectators during the courtroom proceedings.[50] People either avoided Franko or, if they had to consult with him on some matter, met him in secret. Olha Roshkevych's father forbade Franko to visit his home and refused to allow him to marry his daughter.[51] Franko was expelled from the Prosvita Society and banned from the Ruska Besida. Andrii Chaikovsky recalled that during one soiree Leonid Zaklynsky made the following request: "Friend, give me something for poor Franko. He has left prison in such a state that he doesn't even have a shirt on his back." Chaikovsky gave Zaklynsky a couple of small coins and suggested that he go into the crowd in the hall, where he might collect more donations. "What an idea!" Zaklynsky retorted. "If I did that, they would throw me out. Don't you know that everybody is giving Franko the evil eye?" This mood also infected the students. Chaikovsky recalled that when he was the head of Druzhnii lykhvar, he was pressured by the other members to expel Franko from the society, which earned him praise from the "elder citizens."[52]

It is only fair to say that the populist camp hoped that Franko would turn away from the path onto which he had been propelled by circumstances. Of all the socialists, the populists clearly rejected Pavlyk, whom they considered an out-and-out "red communist" and anticlerical figure. Yet they clung to the hope that Franko could be returned to the fold, as his writer's talent indicated intelligence and morality, traits that were considered incompatible with socialism.[53]

The social ostracism directed against Franko and Pavlyk was their punishment for violating the code of behavior upheld by Galician-Ruthenian educated society. Austrian Ruthenians cared about their reputation as the

"Tyroleans of the East"—that is, members of the most loyal ethnic group, and in return for this loyalty they expected support from Vienna for their national and cultural struggles against the ruling Polish stratum. In their daily lives they expected an untroubled and secure existence. According to Andrii Chaikovsky, the general ideology lay in the following formula: "The greatest joy for a Ruthenian is to finish university and with both hands grasp the emperor's doorknob and become a functionary...importance, advancement, status, pension, retirement..."[54]

Before his acquaintance with Drahomanov, Franko had shared this ideology. He dreamed of becoming a fashionable "salon" writer, marrying the daughter of a priest, and getting a job teaching in a gymnasium. Between 1876 and 1878 all these possibilities fell away, one by one. The socialist process proved to be very useful to Franko in leading him beyond the state career path and providing him with a relatively independent, albeit socially insecure, status in society. As late as 1891 he wrote:

> Galicia has relatively few people in positions, and very few in independent situations—that is, those in which a man might say fearlessly and clearly: I uphold such and such political views, I belong to that party, and who can do anything to me?...Our young people were going, and are still going, into the priesthood (a superficially independent position, but in fact a very dependent one), into teaching (an utterly slave-like position)[55] or officialdom (courts, administrations, etc., also a very dependent position)....We have only a few lawyers and two journalists in independent positions (as much as P[avly]k's situation may be called a position, rather than a mirage). [ZT 49:292–93][56]

To Franko and his friends this new, independent situation opened up the possibility to generate new ideas and new forms and ways of conduct. Deprived of the opportunity to earn a living in government service or in civic institutions, Galician socialists merely in order to survive had no other choice but to create their own means of existence, even though these were not very stable and quite limited[57]—and at the same time to build a new society, an alternative to the old Ruthenian one. From this point, Franko's career becomes less and less of a personal vocation and increasingly a social issue.

"The Well-known Demoralizer of Rus"

The trial of 1878 confirmed two new terms in Galicia's political lexicon: socialism and nihilism. Both of them were linked primarily to "the well-known demoralizers of Rus, Ivan Franko and Mykhailo Pavlyk."[58] After they were released from prison, the two men resumed the publication of *Druh*, which now had a different name: *Hromadskyi druh* (Community Friend). This name was supposed to indicate both the journal's affinity to the journal *Hromada* (Community), published by Drahomanov in Geneva, and its socialist character. *Hromadivstvo*—the desire to live in the form of communities—was supposed to become the Ukrainian version of the word "socialism." In addition, the word *hromada* was regarded as the counterpart to the French term *commune*; thus, the new name of the Lviv journal was linked to the Paris Commune.[59]

The first issue of the revamped journal had a print run of 400 copies. It is difficult to determine how many ended up in the hands of readers, because the entire run was confiscated two weeks after it was published.[60] The same fate befell the second issue.[61] In order to avoid further confiscations, the editors resorted to subterfuge: they decided to publish each issue under a different title, like a separate almanac. Thus, two collections titled *Dzvin* (The Bell) and *Molot* (The Hammer) appeared in 1878. In the second half of 1878 Franko also began publishing a series of popular booklets under the general title of *Dribna biblioteka* (Small Library), as a counterweight to the serial publications of the Prosvita Society. The new tactic did not produce results, however, and *Dzvin* and *Molot* shared the same fate as *Hromads'kyi druh*. The commissioner of the Lviv police declared, in the name of the authorities, that they would sort out "those Lviv Bebels and Liebknechts; we confiscated the first issue, and we will confiscate 2nd, 3rd, 4th, etc."[62]

Franko later said that the prosecutor's office confiscated these publications not because they were promoting in Galicia the works of well-known European socialists, such as Albert Eberhard Friedrich Schäffle and Friedrich A. Lange, but because they were publishing the belles-lettres and political essays of Franko and Pavlyk.[63] Thus, the authorities were letting it be known that they were prepared to tolerate socialism as a theory, but would crush any attempts to adapt it to Galician conditions. This line corresponded to the mood of a significant proportion of the Galician public. *Dziennik Polski* appealed to its readers "not to underestimate that movement, responsibility for which should fall on the well-known demoralizers of Rus....What can one expect from the future when seditious fragments from brochures like *Dzvin* will be read to ignorant peasants, who by their very nature have a propensity for every kind of pessimism? With regard to socialism in Germany and nihilism in Russia, we must not stand with folded hands; we are not, nor do we wish to be, angels that turn into a block of wood in the face of destruction by the enemy—but here in our land we cannot gaze indifferently upon the work of half-baked individuals who are threatening society."[64] In a letter to Meliton Bachynsky, Volodymyr Barvinsky wrote: "One must absolutely not permit our people, our youth, and our very selves to turn into beasts. But I already see a trace of such beastliness even in the Small Library."[65]

In the summer of 1878 Franko and Pavlyk were in a difficult situation, which occasionally drove Franko to despair and to contemplating suicide.

> Once in a while [one hears] outlandish tales around the city: that we have already been arrested or will be arrested, watch out, or be hanged, or a case will be cobbled together on grounds of *Hochverrat* [state treason—Y. H.], etc. But this is all foolishness, if it did not lead to bad consequences from the other side. Young people, who are flocking quite eagerly to *Hrom[ads'kyi] druh*, are being kept in check, anyone who joins us is threatened with expulsions and arrests, they are dragged around offices and questioned— well, it's hell, that's all there is to it! [*ZT* 48:84]

The Austrian government kept a vigilant eye on Pavlyk, who held all the threads of socialist agitation in his hands. Police reports characterized his activities as the Galician connection in an international socialist conspiracy that was masterminding a revolutionary coup all over the continent and manifesting itself, among other things, in the attempt of the German socialist Karl Nobiling to assassinate the German emperor, Kaiser Wilhelm I, in the summer of 1878.[66] Franko was overshadowed by his friend, Pavlyk. However, in the eyes of the police it was Franko who became the main promoter of socialism in Galicia in late 1878 and early 1879. On 1 October 1878, on orders of the Galician authorities, Limanowski was forced to leave Lviv and the Habsburg monarchy altogether. He went to Switzerland, where the socialist emigration from the Russian and Austrian empires sought refuge. In late January 1879, following in Limanowski's footsteps, Pavlyk left for Geneva in order to evade another prison term after the latest trial [*ZT* 48:153, 156].

Before his departure, Limanowski organized a farewell supper, to which he invited Franko and Pavlyk, as well as the Polish socialists Antoni Mankowski, Józef Danyluk, Bolesław Czerwieński, and Adolf Inlender. During the meal, the host and his guests agreed to found a society in order to spread socialist ideas throughout the land. Franko was assigned to write a brief socialist "catechism," along the lines of Louis Blanc's socialist doctrine. As Limanowski recalled, Franko gave his agreement, adding: "To tell the truth, I myself do not understand socialism well, but I will learn it as I write."[67]

It is difficult to ascertain the veracity of Limanowski's recollections.[68] If his version is accepted, then it is not clear why the task fell to Franko: were the assembled guests interested in him only because of his literary talent, or was their choice a kind of recognition that he was well versed in socialist works? Either way, Franko acquitted himself brilliantly in the task assigned to him. His Polish-language *Katechizm socjalistów* (The Socialists' Catechism; alternate title: *What Is Socialism?*), written and published in Lviv[69] in late 1878, enjoyed great popularity. "Everyone here [in Lviv—Y. H.] is saying that it is quite understandable, and workers are praising it a lot," Franko wrote to Olha Roshkevych in late 1878, describing his book's success [*ZT* 48:133]. Until the publication of Simon Młot-Dickstein's book *Kto z czego żyje?* (Who Lives Off What?, 1881), Franko's "catechism" was considered the best popular exposition of Marxian economic theory in the Polish language.[70]

Over a period of six months, roughly between the summer of 1878 and the early months of 1879, Franko was transformed from a little known, young Ruthenian writer into the leader of the Galician socialist movement. In the summer of 1878, printing workers in Lviv began publishing the newspaper *Praca*. Franko and Pavlyk's collaboration with this paper dates to the very first issues.[71] Toward the end of the year the workers appointed Franko as the newspaper's silent editor. He began his editorship in the new year [*ZT* 48:129–30]. On 1 January 1879 *Praca* came out with a new sub-masthead: "A bi-monthly devoted to issues of the laboring classes." From a professional newspaper produced by Lviv printers, *Praca* had turned into a general workers' organ.

There is no concurrence in scholarly literature on the question of who initiated this reform. The juxtaposition of two events—Franko's appointment to the post of editor of *Praca* and its transformation into a newspaper focused on general workers' issues—seems to denote that the idea to reorganize the newspaper came from the editor himself. This is the view of Ukrainian scholars, Soviet and post-Soviet alike.[72] However, the prominent Polish researcher of the socialist movement in Galicia, Walentyna Najdus, insists that Franko's role was minimal, claiming that the change in the newspaper's focus was due to the Polish revolutionary Ludwik Waryński, who in October 1878 visited Lviv, where he held lengthy discussions with Galician socialists.[73] As corroboration, Najdus cites a fragment from a letter that Franko wrote to Drahomanov on 16 January 1883, in which he claimed that he was never the editor of *Praca* and had no decisive voice on the editorial board [*ZT* 48:347]. But Franko's words should be treated with caution: he had to defend himself from Drahomanov's accusations, and therefore his arguments are exaggerated. The facts prove that during his editorship (from August 1878 to the end of that year) he published thirty-five articles, a considerable number of which were of a programmatic nature. The converse is also true: nearly all the programmatic articles published in *Praca* were written by Franko.[74]

The newspaper's transformation into a general workers' organ became a noticeable tendency as early as August 1878, when Mykhailo Pavlyk declared that *Praca* would champion the interests of all workers. In 1880, in an article that was not yet published at the time, he insisted that he was the one who had succeeded in persuading the publisher, a worker named Józef Danyluk, to change the direction of the newspaper.[75] But that same year Franko set about responding to Pavlyk's accusations concerning *Praca*, and he did so in the name of the paper's editorial board [*ZT* 48:231, 234]. Pavlyk's statements indicate that an important role was also played by Danyluk, who not only edited the newspaper but also did the typesetting in his free time, evenings, and nights. Danyluk's apartment housed both his large family and the editorial board; at the same time, it served as a refuge for the newspaper's employees who were penniless and homeless, including Franko and Pavlyk [*ZT* 48:267, 280].

This brief survey of various versions regarding the transformation of *Praca* into a general workers' newspaper offers some idea of the editorial board, which was neither a permanent nor a homogeneous one. The balance of relations among the board members had its own dynamics. Franko's most potent influence was felt from early 1879 to early 1880. The editorial board was designed to be the legal cover of a socialist committee, the ruling body of the socialist movement in Galicia, which in fact did not exist. Franko and Ludwik Inlender, Adolf's brother, were the main ideologists of this committee because they had the best theoretical background. In 1879–1880 both of them taught political economy in various workers' self-education circles [*ZT* 48:249]. By December 1880, Franko and Inlender, joined by the socialist poet Bolesław Czerwieński, finished writing the first programmatic document of the Galician socialist move-ment, titled "Program of the Polish and Ruthenian Socialists of Eastern Galicia."[76] Franko left the editorial board in the early 1880s, partly for per-sonal reasons and partly as a result of his disagreement with other members about the character of the socialist movement in Galicia. But he maintained direct links with the workers' milieu at least until 1886.[77]

Franko's activities were severely restricted by the local authorities. He was under constant surveillance by the police, which searched his vari-ous lodgings from time to time.[78] Intermittently, he faced the threat of confiscations, arrest, and new court proceedings. In March 1880 he was arrested near the city of Kolomyia, where he had gone to help prepare a local schoolteacher, Kyrylo Genyk, for his matriculation. A few days before he arrived, an incident occurred nearby, in the village of Moskalivtsi near Monastyryska: a peasant named Dmytro Fokshei shot the local reeve, severely wounding him. A search of Fokshei's home revealed socialist pub-lications from Geneva as well as issues of *Hromadskyi druh* and *Dzvin*. The police decided that it had uncovered a socialist conspiracy. Pavlyk's sister Anna was arrested in Kosiv, and Franko was arrested because he was found in the "field of action."

The investigation in Kolomyia lasted three months. The court proved that Fokshei had shot the reeve of his own free will, not at someone's behest. Franko was released, but since he was not a resident of Kolomyia County, he was treated as a "vagabond without a passport" and forced to make the journey on foot to his native village of Nahuievychi—accompanied all the way by a gendarme. Franko later described this journey:

> This transport under police escort in Kolomyia, Stanyslaviv, Stryi, and Drohobych was one of the most difficult moments of my life. By the time I arrived in Drohobych, I was already running a high fever. There I was stuffed into a pit, described in my short story "Na dni" [At the Bottom]; from there that very day (thanks to someone's intercession) I was sent on foot with a policeman to Nahuievychi. Along the way it started to rain and I got completely soaked. I got a high fever and spent a week at home in very unpleasant conditions, returned to Kolomyia in order to meet up with Genyk, spent a horrible week in a hotel there, wrote the short story "At the Bottom," and with the last of my money sent it to Lviv, and later survived for three days on three cents found on the sand near the Prut River, and once they were gone, I locked myself in

my small hotel room and lay feverish and hungry for a day and a half, awaiting death, helpless, and discouraged about life. [*ZT* 49:247]

Franko was rescued by a hotel servant, who sometimes brought a few spoonfuls of soup to his room. Three days later Genyk appeared at the hotel. He helped Franko return to Drohobych for his passport and then put him up in his house in Nyzhnii Bereziv. When the starosta of Kolomyia learned of Franko's presence in the area, he ordered Franko to be brought to Kolomyia at once. But since he did not have any money to pay for a cart, the gendarme forced Franko, who was still ailing, to make the journey on foot in the blazing heat of summer. As a result of this arduous trek, all of Franko's toenails fell off. Once the starosta saw his passport, he had no choice but to release him. Without waiting for further unpleasantness, Franko returned to Nahuievychi under his own steam.

"At the Bottom," the story describing these adventures, was published 1880 as the last, fourteenth, issue of the Small Library. In the story, Franko portrayed himself as a young intellectual and idealist, full of love for the people. Guided by his noble intentions, he ends up at the very "bottom" of Galician society—in jail, where he dies at the hands of a prisoner, who had become a feckless criminal by force of social circumstances. The story made a strong impression on readers. An anonymous reviewer in the populist journal *Zoria* prophesied that Franko's socialism would lead him irrevocably to the tragic finale described in his short story. It would be a crying shame, wrote this reviewer, if the educated Ruthenian-Ukrainian community of Galicia lost such a great literary force. The article ends on this note: "We highly value Mr. Franko's talent and his industriousness, and we think that precisely for the sake of this talent and this work the unanimous cry, 'Return as quickly as possible!' will spill from a thousand breasts."[79]

The reviewer cited the main character's idea: "The minute our path turns out to be incompatible with the natural laws of general evolution, with eternal human aspirations to goodness and universal happiness, we must turn back instantly" [*ZT* 15:158]. The review touched Franko to the quick. He wrote a sharply worded reply to the editor of *Zoria*, Omelian Partytsky, whom he believed to be the anonymous reviewer. Franko's ad hominem attack on Partytsky aside, his reply boils down to one point: no one can convince him that the path he has chosen is incompatible with the natural laws of evolution: "We have not seen this, and it looks like we shall never see it....Don't you know that everything that teaches people how to think, to reason, to look around at the world, that all this liberates them more and more from the oppression of authorities, draws them closer to progress, draws [them] closer to socialism? Don't you know that ordinary literacy spread among the people is a huge support for us because it enables us to disseminate our ideas through writings and books?" [*ZT* 48:249–50].

To what degree was Franko's optimism justified? The first, and most natural, answer is: to the degree that he himself believed in what he wrote. In his poem "The Stone-Crushers" (1878), Franko describes a strange dream: he sees himself chained to a rock, clasping a sledge hammer. He hears a voice telling him: "Shatter this rock!"

> Then, as one man, we raised our hands aloft;
> Thousands of hammers crashed against the stone;
> The battered fragments lashed at us as oft
> We smote the mountain; at despair we scoffed;
> And broke that stony brow's primeval bone.
>
> Like a loud cataract, like battle's din,
> Our sledges' blows incessantly resound:
> And foot by foot a further space we win,
> And splinters gashed at many a cheek and chin—
> But nothing stayed us in our ceaseless round.
>
> [...]
>
> Thus we go on, chained in a single mind
> By holy faith, with hammers in our hands.
> Let us be cursed, forgotten by mankind—
> A mountain-road to justice we will find
> That, though we die, will bless our sacred lands.[80]

The inspiration for this poem was the real image of workers who smashed rocks on the roadside, clearing the way for a railway tunnel through the Carpathian Mountains [*ZT* 1:423].[81] But this image can in no way be used for assessing the milieu in which Franko and his friends lived: he could have seen this only in a dream. The numbers of Galician socialists, together with all their supporters, were reckoned not in thousands and not even hundreds, but, at the very most, a few dozen: that was the number of workers who gathered at a demonstration to bid farewell to Limanowski as he was about to leave Galicia.[82] In 1879 the Lviv socialists attempted to create a workers' organization modeled on the British trade unions, and Franko even wrote a special article about them for *Praca*.[83] The results of these efforts were paltry: a grand total of thirty workers attended the general meeting of the newly created organization in January 1882, whereas the "official" tradesmen's association, *Gwiazda* (The Star) boasted nearly a thousand members. At about this time, the Galician socialist committee set about creating a party of workers and peasants belonging to all three nationalities. Initially, the workers' meetings that were convened to further this goal were very well attended: 300 people in January 1881 and 700 in June 1881. It is difficult to determine whether this was a new, stable trend, because all the subsequent Lviv meetings (October–December 1881 and April–June 1882) were either banned by the police or dispersed after the first few speeches were made.[84]

On 19 February 1880, Franko wrote to Pavlyk:

> Not much can be said about the relations between our people and Lviv workers. For who are our people? Students, academics, but what is their connection to workers? If they get together, then each one does so privately.... If there were a publishing house, then our people would start conducting a more detailed study of workers' lives (living quarters, food, earnings, etc.),[85] but now that everything is coming apart and undone, it is hardly possible to contemplate such systematic work. [*ZT* 48:233]

The environment with which the Galician socialists were dealing consisted of literate typesetters, who comprised a kind of "working-class aristocracy" (and an impoverished one at that, for it was a Galician aristocracy!).[86] There were practically no contacts with more distant areas in the province, besides the Drohobych and Kosiv areas, Franko's and Pavlyk's native places, where they distributed socialist literature.

Therefore, the activities of the Galician socialist committee were turned inward. Danyluk typeset his own newspaper and distributed it free of charge, and young intellectuals read brochures at secret meetings and occasionally shared a beer with the odd worker. Naturally, even this kind of humble activity was not entirely safe and demanded courage.[87] Nevertheless, all claims about the existence of a socialist movement in Galicia, the founding of a socialist party, and the distribution of socialist literature were nothing more than giving small things inflated names.

Galician socialists did not have the strength or numbers either to become an important party throughout Galicia—as a group, like the

Polish-Ruthenian-Jewish union—or in order to take control, individually, over their respective national camps—the Poles, Ruthenians, and the Jews. In their attempts to build independent institutions that would spread the new ideas, on the one hand, and ensure their existence, on the other, Franko and his associates failed. In April 1881, after several months of a half-starved existence, Franko decided to leave Lviv and return to Nahuievychi "without the hope of ever returning here again" [*ZT* 48:283].

However, what Franko succeeded in doing in Lviv in the three years after his release from imprisonment was to gather around himself several dozen young people who, in their turn, managed to make an impact on the lifestyle and mindset of educated Galicians—primarily, but not exclusively, the Ruthenians.

Chapter 9

"A Journal, All We Need Is a Journal!"

The emergence of the socialist movement in Galicia was part of the great transformation of political life that began in the 1860s as a result of reforms in the Habsburg monarchy. These changes may be conceptualized as the emergence of "public space."[1] Until that time, there was little if any public life in Galicia: most activities were concentrated in government bureaus.[2] The reforms put an end to the period of state guardianship of society, "when the government was everything and the people were nothing, when even the most trivial public issue was in the government's hands."[3]

The concept of public space is fairly applicable to the story of Franko's life during the first half of the 1880s. Central to it are his "journal plans."[4] In fact, journals, or the world of literature in the broader understanding, are at the center of public space. The degree of its development is usually assessed by the number of publications and the size of the reading public. This, in turn, is regarded as a decisive factor in the success of every movement, above all a national movement.[5] The society of the time understood this. "A journal, all we need is a journal!" wrote Ivan Belei in 1884 in a letter to Oleksandr Konysky, a member of the Kyiv Hromada.[6] A more fleshed-out version of this idea was expressed by Konysky when he was trying to persuade Franko to remain on the editorial board of the populist journal, *Zoria*: "The point here is not about *Zoria* but about the whole issue of awakening the somnolent, feeding the hungry, and raising our literature to the degree that it will resemble European [literature] at least somewhat. For me this issue is the most important one in Ruthenian national life at the present time."[7] For his part, Drahomanov demanded that Franko found a journal that would accelerate the formation of a "radical-progressive party" in Galicia, like the ones "that exist in all of Europe and which will take state power into their hands in Western Europe (England, France, Italy), if not today, then tomorrow.[8]

The discussion around the founding of a new journal, along with the names that were proposed for it (*Literary Review*, *Literary Notes*, *Notes*, or *Thought*), shows that what the Galician populists and radicals and the Kyiv Hromada members had in mind was a so-called "thick journal" (*tovstyi zhurnal*), a type of periodical that emerged in Russia in the 1830s and 1840s and then spread to neighboring countries.[9] Selecting the most important texts from the wealth of existing literature, these journals formed literary tastes, conducted polemics for the sake of formulating a generalized view, created a hierarchy of respected figures and values, and, finally, transformed diverse readers into a public. For the educated populations of Eastern and Central Europe, whose access to the sphere of active politics was closed or restricted, literary journals performed a role akin to a parliamentary party, and for the various peoples that were divided by state borders, like Poles or Ukrainians—a quasi–national parliament as well. A key role was played by editors, whose task it was to infuse their journals with a certain "party" line. In order to do this they had to immerse themselves in the submitted articles, often altering them beyond all recognition. In and of itself, the position of editor did not grant the holder the right to do this, it was only possible if both authors and the reading public recognized that person as a literary authority.[10]

It was precisely Franko's literary prestige that legitimized him as an editor, and by virtue of that esteem he became the central figure at the birth of various new journals. Franko the editor "dragged [new people into literature] by the ears." These were often people of average talent, and Franko had to revise their works considerably.[11] In addition, he filled the pages of the journal with his own works, shaking ready material out of his sleeve, as people said of him.[12] This is a particularly fascinating aspect of Franko's biography. His literary and organizational talents made him a desirable object of simultaneous competition within several political milieus: Ruthenian-Ukrainian populists and radicals; Ukrainian-Polish-Jewish socialists; and Polish liberals.

Between the Radicals and the Populists

For Franko, his enforced sojourn in Nahuievychi was neither long nor completely different compared to what he had been doing in Lviv. The only significant change was that he had to perform agricultural work in order to support himself, because his stepfather refused to support him.[13] He was free to do his literary work only in the evenings or on days when bad weather stopped all work on the homestead. "Well, here I am, quite busy, as God is my witness. I take the horses to pasture for entire days, or I [work] on the hay or in the forest; in the evening the lights are not lit in our house, so you have to go to bed; but even if the lights were on, a man is tired like a hundred devils; nevertheless, sometimes I snatch at least enough time to write a short article or to read something," Franko wrote to his friend, Ivan Belei, in a letter dated June 1882 [ZT 48:312].

The list of everything that Franko wrote and published during the nearly two years he spent in Nahuievychi is very long: it includes two novels, *Boryslav smiietsia* (Boryslav Is Laughing) and *Zakhar Berkut*; a cycle of poems titled *Vesnianky* (Spring Songs); a Ukrainian translation of Goethe's *Faust*; and dozens of articles on literary and political topics—altogether 106 entries, double the output of the two preceding years that he spent in Lviv. Franko's talent was growing and strengthening, and the change in his life circumstances had no effect on his industriousness. The same kind of continuity may be seen in the ideological aspect: the majority of what he wrote in Nahuievychi more or less overtly promoted socialism.[14]

Real changes began taking place in early 1883, after Franko returned to Lviv. He bargained for his return by agreeing to collaborate with his former opponents, the Galician populists. This collaboration offered him stable earnings and the possibility of supporting himself in the city. However, these changes were born not solely out of his penury: they were dictated by a turn of events in the Ruthenian-Ukrainian camp.

Until the early 1880s, there was a kind of division of labor in this camp: the Russophiles held the monopoly on political activity, while the populist leaders barely intruded into political work, focusing their efforts instead on cultural enlightenment. The Russophiles built their policies on an alliance with the German liberal centrists in Vienna as a counterweight to Polish dominance in the land. However, in 1879 the Viennese liberals lost their influence in the government, which deprived Ruthenian politicians of a strong ally in the center and left them at the mercy of the Polish parties in Galicia. During the elections to the Galician parliament in 1879 only three Ruthenian candidates were elected, compared to the sixteen who were elected in 1873.[15] Three years later, in June and July of 1882, a group of Russophile leaders were tried on charges of state treason, accused of trying to detach the Ruthenian lands under Austro-Hungary and annex them to the Russian Empire. This trial put an end to the political dominance of the Russophiles, who suffered further defeats in the local parliamentary elections in 1883 and 1885. In addition, their supporters were dismissed from their high positions in the church hierarchy, and the movement itself was discredited as politically unreliable.[16] One manifestation of this crisis was the drop in the number of Russophile publications. The biggest newspaper, *Slovo*, was constantly losing readers (from 1,200 subscribers in the early 1860s to some 300–400 in the early 1880s), and it finally stopped publishing in 1887.[17]

The crisis "at the top" in the Ruthenian-Ukrainian camp contrasted with the dynamic development of infrastructures "at the bottom," primarily the dynamic spread of a network of rural reading rooms. The first reading rooms appeared in the early 1870s, and between the years of 1879 and 1887, 600 more were opened.[18] The question was: which Galician grouping would transform the awakening peasantry into political capital? The socialists failed to become one of those groups. Franko had complained on several occasions to the editors of *Praca*, accusing them of ignoring the peasant question and underestimating its importance [*ZT* 48:347]. In addition to *Praca*, Franko planned to publish a bimonthly aimed at peasants, which would be modeled on that newspaper [*ZT* 48:298]. However, the funds for this undertaking were not found.

Also doomed to failure were Franko's efforts to mobilize the milieu of Ruthenian-Ukrainian radicals. In 1881–1882, in collaboration with Ivan Belei, he published a journal called *Svit*, which continued the *Hromadskyi druh* line but adopted a much softer tone. The periodical ceased publication not because of political persecution but from public apathy: aimed at young Ruthenian-Ukrainian intellectuals, it barely managed to circulate 150 copies.[19]

Of all the Galician groupings, only the populists had the best chance, as exemplified by the success of their newspaper, *Batkivshchyna*, which began appearing in the fall of 1879 especially for the peasants. Franko recalled later, probably on the basis of his own observations in Nahuievychi, that the newspaper "was awaited by whole groups of people way beyond the village, sending a courier, who was supposed to bring the issue from the post office; it was read by literate people in graveyards near the church on Sundays to the entire assembled community, which, listening to the unusual words, news, and advice, forgot about food and Sunday rest. Its word was sacred;

every community, wherever there were at least a few people with a live-lier personality, considered it a point of honor to describe their domestic order or woes [on the pages of] *Bat'kivshchyna*; in whatever county, from whichever corner there was no news in *Bat'kivshchyna* and news written almost exclusively by peasants,[20] there people walked as though shamed in the entire society, throughout the land" [*ZT* 41:487–88].

Starting in January 1880, the populists began publishing, in addi-tion to *Bat'kivshchyna*, a newspaper called *Dilo* (Deed), which was aimed at the educated public.[21] The paper was designed as an alternative to the Russophile *Slovo*, which was implied by its very name: deed vs word. The editor of *Dilo*, Volodymyr Barvinsky, the former editor of *Pravda*, believed that the task of the new paper was to "liberate the broad public from *Slovo*'s mischief-making and terrorism and slowly to bring the Ruthenian forces together."[22] In order to bring the Russophiles over to their side, he was pre-pared to accept far-reaching compromises. Barvinsky thus invited the "red" Ivan Belei to join the editorial board and was even banking on Franko's participation [*ZT* 49:249], even though he considered Franko's influence on young people to be harmful and therefore sought to overcome it.[23] Franko himself was quite skeptical of Barvinsky and the new paper, which he called "conciliatory" and "colorless" [*ZT* 48:226].

Franko became more amenable in the last months of 1882, when the imminent end of *Svit* became obvious. He was accepted to the editorial board of *Dilo* under Belei's protection [*ZT* 48:340]. Franko contributed articles on political and economic topics. In a letter written in November 1883 to his friend Yulia Schneider (Uliana Kravchenko), he commented: "Sometimes, when you read *Dilo*, you should know that all the most bor-ing articles, the ones that women never read and men rarely understand, all of them come from my hands" [*ZT* 48:375]. Franko was being coy: his articles were indeed being read, and his participation in *Dilo* even brought more subscribers to the paper [*ZT* 48:347; 49:249]. At this time Franko was invited to join the new literary journal, *Zoria*, which, like *Dilo*, began appearing in 1880.[24] Franko became the soul of yet another populist peri-odical, the satirical journal *Zerkalo* (1882–1883; called *Nove Zerkalo* [New Mirror] from 1884).[25] He also published the Small Library and edited the almanacs *Vatra* (Bonfire, 1886) and *Pershyi vinok* (First Wreath, 1887).[26]

Among educated Galician Ruthenians the conviction was growing that Franko's participation in any kind of publication was a guarantee of read-ership. "We do not have an abler and more lively and intelligent worker than Franko," wrote Ivan Belei to Oleksandr Konysky on 26 December 1884.[27] "Without Franko any other collection [of articles] would be nothing," Volodymyr (Lukych) Levytsky declared in 1885.[28] In a letter to Franko dated 3 August 1884, Natalia Kobrynska conveyed this idea in her typically uncompromising manner: "I consistently said of *Zoria* that if one were to excise from it everything that you write, the rest could easily be sold by weight."[29]

Franko's prolific writing had its shortcomings, such as extraordinarily scattershot production, lack of weighty topics, and many factual errors. In a letter to Franko from September 1884, Drahomanov wrote:

> My dear! You do not respect and look after yourself! First of all, you take on everything; you are wasting your energy even on programs of travel in verse,[30] which are reminiscent of those that concierges in Germany distribute to apartment residents at the New Year, when they convey their best wishes so as to receive a tip to buy some schnapps. Is this what you write, what with your talent as a novelist and ability as a researcher?! Next, you ask [me] to point out the errors in your articles. To do this one would need to write practically a whole volume because your articles...are teeming with errors.[31]

Above all, Franko was becoming exhausted and plagued with ill-health: sometimes blood seeped from his mouth and he suffered attacks of frustration or depression. At times he thought he was going mad or that his end was near. "God forbid that you should be as busy as I am," he wrote to Drahomanov's sister, Olena Pchilka, in a letter dated 29 November 1885. "Sometimes it simply reaches the point that you're sitting around and you begin writing letters to fantasy people and about completely far-fetched matters simply in order to escape from your own thoughts and from your own nerves" [*ZT* 48:580]. The constant reminders of doctors and friends that he should take care of his health, get some exercise, and take restorative baths were ignored.[32] It would appear that, despite his complaints, this condition appealed to him; at any rate, he had no intention of taking serious steps to change it.

The true nature of Franko's writings for the populist journals is one of the controversial questions in his biography. Soviet literary scholars preferred to view this cooperation as a tactical step that allowed Franko to reach the mass reader in order to criticize the "capitalist order."[33] However, a survey of Franko's articles in *Dilo* creates the impression that he was not some kind of socialist "Trojan horse" in the populist camp. A contemporary historian of *Dilo* describes the period of Franko's collaboration as an entire stage in the history of that newspaper.[34] Franko wrote editorials and prepared programmatic speeches—that is, to a great degree he determined the policies of the populist camp. For a mass popular assembly held in June 1883, Franko wrote the main speech on economic affairs, but, owing to his reputation as a socialist, he could not deliver it himself. The speech was delivered by his friend, Vasyl Nahirny.

Drahomanov and Pavlyk regarded Franko's work in *Dilo* as unprincipled opportunism. They were especially up in arms about Franko's elegy written upon the death of Volodymyr Barvinsky on 22 January 1883.[35] In this poem Franko calls Barvinsky *bat'ko*, father (even though the deceased was only six years older than Franko), a "friend" and "brother" [*ZT* 18:227–28]. According to Pavlyk, after Barvinsky's death the entire editorial board of *Dilo* consisted of "Belei + Franko under the supervision of the older populists." The irony lay in the fact that this populist publication was edited by two radicals. Belei and Franko's politics were putting at risk the existence of the radical camp because the two men had abandoned the idea of putting out a radical newspaper without pursuing their own line in *Dilo*. Pavlyk pointed to himself as an example of a viable other line: after returning penniless from Geneva to Lviv in early 1883, Pavlyk did not visit the populists "to make an obeisance," but set about editing the workers' newspaper, *Praca*. Pavlyk's goal was to make this paper a counterweight to *Dilo* by bringing Franko over to his side, "because otherwise he will fundamentally perish, but he is a literary force nonetheless."[36]

Franko was more amenable to compromise, as he viewed the differences between the populists and the radicals not as antagonism between two camps but as a difference within the *single* Ukrainian camp [*ZT* 48:335]. The price of this compromise was Franko's silent assent to pass through the populists' internal censorship [*ZT* 48:454, 456]. On their part, the populists turned a blind eye to Franko's minor violations of editorial discipline [*ZT* 48:479].

Between the Ukrainians and the Poles

The disturber of the peace turned out to be Mykhailo Pavlyk. His participation in the editing of *Praca* was short-lived, and by the summer of 1883 he was unemployed. Franko and Belei persuaded the board of *Dilo* to hire Pavlyk, but in such a way that the public would not find out. Pavlyk justified his collaboration with the populist camp by declaring that his goal was to help the populists transform themselves into a true people's party.[37] But Pavlyk's days at this paper were also numbered. Gentle and even timid in his private conduct, he had a special talent for provoking public scandals. In the fall of 1884, Pavlyk published an article titled "Moskvofil´stvo i ukrainofil´stvo sered sil´s´koho liudu v Halychyni i na Bukovyni" (Muscophilism and Ukrainophilism among the Rural Folk in Galicia and in Bukovyna), in which he rated the Russophile Ivan Naumovych higher than the late Volodymyr Barvinsky with respect to the issue of the people's enlightenment. His article also praised Franko for his decisive influence on the reorganization of the Galician Ukrainophiles.[38] Adding fuel to the fire was the fact that his article had been published in the Polish newspaper, *Kurjer Lwowski*—that is, it had brought out the Ruthenians' "domestic affairs" for public discussion, and now "the enemies not only of any party but the enemies of Galician Rus in general can only rub their hands in glee."[39] The offended populists reacted sharply to Pavlyk's article. Franko rose to Pavlyk's defense even though he acknowledged the fallacy of his arguments. Yet Franko's defense of Pavlyk failed to extinguish the furor, and only exacerbated the conflict. Franko ended up quarrelling with Belei, his only ally, who until recently had been successful in reducing the friction between Franko and the rest of the editors at *Dilo*.[40]

Another huge scandal erupted almost at the same time as the publication of Pavlyk's article. In November 1885, the populist Adolf Narolsky died in Lviv. Although he was a populist, over the years he had drawn closer to the radicals and contributed articles to *Hromadskyi druh*. Narolsky, who was an atheist, had left instructions in his will to be buried without the services of a priest. At his graveside a small group of some ten to fifteen students sang the national hymn, "Ukraine Has Not Yet Perished," and Mykhailo Pavlyk gave the eulogy. Gossip about the funeral began spreading to the effect that the young people at the graveside had been smoking cigarettes. The Russophile press capitalized on this story in order to brand the Ukrainophiles as "socialists," "nihilists," and "atheists."[41] Rebutting these accusations, *Dilo* called Narolsky's funeral a "demonstration of two doctrinaires," and issued the following warning: if young doctrinaires do not refrain from "fanatical demonstrations that are lethal to the general cause," then "society will be capable of eliminating such people from its company."[42]

These two cases decided Franko's fate. As it was, he had already been complaining that it was becoming increasingly difficult to work at *Dilo*. By early 1885, when the disagreements had become intolerable, he left the newspaper and never returned. The populists gave him a final admonishment "for the road": "Go, and do not admit that you are a Ruthenian."[43] Just as in 1878, the populists blocked Franko's access to their institutions.[44] For Franko, the most painful repercussion of both scandals was losing the opportunity to edit the journal *Zoria*. Omelian Partytsky, owner and editor of the journal, had been about to hand it over to Franko, but "the elders" feared that he would turn *Zoria* into a mouthpiece of socialist opinion: "Look at how 'they' are writing now!...And what are they going to write when they get *Zoria* into their hands!" it was said in the populist camp. "We lifted them out of the mud, warmed them up and fed them, but look how 'they' are repaying us" [*ZT* 48:498]. Under pressure from the majority Partytsky transferred *Zoria* to the ownership of the Shevchenko Society. Franko could have stayed on the editorial board, but under the strict control of the "elders." His function would have boiled down to the role of a "work ox" or an "editor's servant" [*ZT* 48:549, 583, 595]. When he refused to accept such a role, he was shown the door.

Nevertheless, the populists did not have complete freedom in handing down decisions. They were financially dependent on the Kyiv Hromada, and the populists' narrow party stand did not please the Kyivites: they saw *Zoria* as the main organ of Ukrainian forces not only in Galicia but all of Ukraine.[45] They insisted on Franko's participation, regarding it as a guarantee of success. After learning of Franko's departure from the journal, some Ukrainian authors were loath to continue writing a single line for *Zoria*. Oleksandr Konysky, the principal liaison between Kyiv and Lviv, who had devoted the most effort to ensuring the organizational and financial security of the populist publications, was devastated.[46] For his part, Volodymyr Antonovych, the leader of the Kyivites, was greatly alarmed by the prospect of the spread of "Muscovite centralism" to Galicia. A rumor was circulating in Kyiv that the Russian government had provided a large sum of money (1.5 million rubles) to the Russophiles to offset the harm that had been caused by the trial of 1882. In Antonovych's opinion, this could be stemmed only by a mouthpiece that was "clearly and boldly anti-Muscovite"—a periodical founded by the "progressivists," Franko and Pavlyk.[47]

The Kyivites set about reconciling Franko with the populists. They put pressure on Franko to agree to cooperate with the populists, at the same time insisting that the populists stop putting pressure on Franko. In February 1885, Franko set out for Kyiv to take part in negotiations with the Hromada concerning the founding of his own journal [*ZT* 48:525]. Nothing came of this, and in September of that year he returned to *Zoria* as the de facto (but unsigned) editor [*ZT* 48:548].

This compromise angered Drahomanov. He regarded Franko's alliance with *Zoria* as a deal between "fire and water" that had not only been struck without his (Drahomanov's) input, but was also directed against him personally. His journal, *Hromada*, had ceased publication in Geneva in 1882, and already by the spring of 1884 Drahomanov proposed to replace it with an "all-Ukrainian and progressive" journal headed by Franko. He had even chosen a name for it—"Postup" (Progress)—and written its program. He had authorized and recommended Franko to negotiate with the Kyivites on two conditions: first, the journal was to promote a radical program in the spirit of the Kyiv Hromada's declaration of 1873 (federalism, democratism, rationalism), and second, the journal was to have no connection with the Galician populists (whom he called *lux non lucendo*, "a light that does not shine"). Drahomanov complained that Franko's alliance with the populists, undertaken on the initiative of the Kyiv Hromada, "helped to wreck the matter of founding *Postup* and engineer a hybrid *Zoria*."[48]

Drahomanov despised what he called "Barvinshchyna," a conservative trend within the populist movement, which was identified with its leaders, the two Barvinsky brothers, Volodymyr (1850–1883) and Oleksandr (1847–1926).[49] In addition to his principled reasons, he had personal ones. He had expended much energy on creating populist organizations in Lviv in the early 1870s in the hope that they would start promoting "progressive" ideas throughout the region. These hopes were not unfounded: early populism appeared on the scene armed with quite radical ideas and plans. However, their organizational weakness, above all the lack of structures in the provincial backwaters, pushed them into an alliance with Ukrainian Greek Catholic clergymen, the main group from which Ruthenian national patriots were recruited. (As Ivan Belei wrote in a letter to Oleksandr Konysky, "Galician Rus may be the only place in the whole world where neither literature nor politics is possible without priestly support".)[50] This circumstance inevitably estranged them from the 1873 program, blunting social aspects at the expense of national ones. The only thing that the populists do, wrote Drahomanov, is discuss their own house, but they do not know how to furnish this house. Their journal cannot enjoy any success either in Galicia, where the dissatisfaction of the mass of burghers and peasants with the secular and ecclesiastical orders is increasingly felt, and even less so among the "progressive" youth of

Dnipro Ukraine, which, owing to the lack of a healthy Ukrainophile and radical alternative, is becoming "Russified."[51]

Drahomanov aimed similar accusations against the members of the Kyiv Hromada. In the period between his emigration and the mid-1880s, the Hromada's character had changed: many of its original members had died or left the Ukrainophile movement, opting for a state career. The remaining members preferred restricting their activities to cultural and scholarly work, and they were exasperated by Drahomanov's political declarations, which were apt to provoke the Russian government into introducing new anti-Ukrainian repressions. The other side of the coin was the intensification of nationalistic positions within the Hromada. This was manifested, in particular, in Konysky's persistent advice to make the national question the lynchpin of *Zoria* and to proclaim "Galician Rus for Galician Ruthenians." Drahomanov did not agree with this position, considering it harmful to the future journal:

> The nationalists are mistaken in thinking that the public can live off nationalism every day, always think about "their own house"....In public life a man is more often a gentleman, or a peasant, or a liberal, or an absolutist, a rationalist, or a cleric, etc., and very rarely a Ruthenian or a Pole [or] a Muscovite. And it is from literature that a man desires, above all, to learn about farming, or politics, or religion, etc., and only then to satisfy his national feeling even when it is awakened in him—and because of that he will gladly read foreign publications, when they teach him something that is interesting to him.[52]

A wall of misunderstanding and estrangement was rising between Drahomanov, who believed that even Antonovych had become "harmful to progress and a non-European," and the Kyiv Hromada. Finally, after a harsh exchange of letters full of mutual recriminations, the two men severed relations in 1886–1887.[53]

Drahomanov was banking on the younger generation in Galicia, attributing to them all the positive changes that had taken place in the Ruthenian-Ukrainian camp, which had emerged in the late 1870s under the direct influence of Franko, whom it considered its leader. The "juniors" did not acknowledge the populists' moral right to lead the Ruthenian camp and called them "Ukrainophile *katsapy*" (a derogatory Ukrainian term for Russians), considering them the same type of obscurantists as the Russophiles.[54] By the mid-1880s, when, according to their estimates, the number of "juniors" had outstripped their elders, they devised a plan to publish their own mouthpiece of the "young Rus," and invited Franko to be the editor. Organizational sponsorship and funds for the journal were supposed to be provided by the Women's Society of Stanyslaviv, headed by Natalia Kobrynska [*ZT* 48:525].

In the end, the Women's Society refused to provide assistance, the plan fizzled, and the "younger" Galicians changed their line, issuing a demand in the form of an ultimatum to the "elders" to recall Franko to *Zoria* [*ZT* 48:540–42].[55] Despite the fact that Franko shared Drahomanov's opinion, he tended toward agreement and sought to enlist his Geneva-based mentor's cooperation with *Zoria*. Franko saw the new *Zoria* as a compromise between the line pursued by *Pravda* and that of *Hromadskyi druh*. It was supposed to be neither nationalist nor strictly socialist. Furthermore, as Franko wrote, it was "not to curse or spit on any other 'isms'" in the name of a particular "ism" [*ZT* 48:483].

Drahomanov, along with his plan to publish *Postup*, was sidelined. Since he considered Franko to be head and shoulders above all the other young radicals, he held him chiefly responsible for the failure to get *Postup* off the ground. "I tell you: repent of your sins…; you have committed a great sin and taken great responsibility upon yourself in the future….You have sunk our newspaper."[56] In April 1886, Drahomanov announced that he was severing his relations with Franko: "We are now polar opposites" and "our former friendship is not possible."[57]

Yet it never came to a complete break between the two men: as in the earlier (1883) quarrel with Pavlyk, Drahomanov's gesture was more an expression of extreme exasperation than a serious declaration. However, nothing came of the idea to edit *Zoria*, because Franko was forced to leave the journal, and not of his own free will. The "populist super-editorial board" reprimanded him for publishing "immoral" materials in *Zoria*. Because he had shown them to the editor in chief before they were published, these accusations were formal and unjust [*ZT* 49:250]. But they were enough to compel Franko to leave the editorial board, and it appears that neither party regretted this.[58] Franko's departure from the populist periodicals marked the consolidation of the internal divisions within the Ruthenian-Ukrainian camp: "Retrograde elements have pushed the younger generation away, and the break becomes absolute by the end of the 1880s" [*ZT* 41:150].

Even though Franko had rid himself of his work with the populists, he was not left without the means to support himself: he was promptly engaged by Polish periodicals. As early as 1879, he had begun submitting articles to Polish journals and newspapers, first to those in the Russian Empire and later to those based in Galicia. Franko was a correspondent for the Warsaw-based newspaper *Prawda*[59] and the St. Petersburg weekly *Kraj*.[60] His main—and sole—place of employment during the next decade (1887–1897) was *Kurjer Lwowski*, the newspaper put out by Polish liberals. Of all the newspapers and journals where he had worked, Franko published the largest number of articles, approximately 900, in this newspaper.[61] In due course, he called his work for Polish periodicals "hired work for neighbors," implying its compulsory nature. However, Franko's feeling of duress did not emerge until several years later, when a wall of mutual estrangement and antagonism had built up between Franko and the Polish liberals and socialists.

But in the mid-1880s, he and his fellow radicals worked with the Polish periodicals in harmony with their own views. It is noteworthy that *Prawda* and *Kraj* published Franko's articles criticizing the state of relations in Galicia, which could hardly be expected of the populist periodicals. His articles provoked irritation among the populists and further deepened the internal divisions within the Ruthenian-Ukrainian camp. Putting distance between himself and the populists, Franko drew closer to Polish "progressive elements." Their collaboration was based on the idea of a possible compromise for the sake of "achieving a joint goal—the defeat of nobiliary and reactionary rule in the land."[62]

Franko's collaboration with the Lviv-based journal *Przegląd Społeczny* (Social Observer) was intellectually stimulating, albeit short-lived (1886–1887). Its editor was a Polish émigré named Bolesław Wysłouch. A year older than Franko, Wysłouch was a descendant of an impoverished noble family from Polissia, a Ukrainian–Belarusian ethnic borderland in the Russian Empire. He moved to Lviv with his wife, Maria, whom he met in Warsaw during his imprisonment for disseminating socialist propaganda. His apartment in Lviv was a drawing card for local leftist intellectuals of all nationalities.[63] For their newspaper, the Wysłouch couple managed to enlist the collaboration, along with Franko's, of such former members of the editorial board of *Praca* as Ludwik Inlender; Bolesław Czerwiński; Mykhailo Pavlyk and his sister Anna; Franko's friend and classmate from Lviv University Henryk Bigeleisen; the brothers Feliks and Ignacy Daszyński, young Polish socialists; the poet Jan Kasprowicz (who, like Franko, was dubbed "a peasant's son"); Alfred Nossig, one of the first Zionist leaders in

Galicia; and distinguished Polish, Russian, and Ukrainian émigrés, including Bolesław Limanowski, Georgii Plekhanov, Mykhailo Drahomanov, and others.

Franko was the most productive writer at the journal.[64] One Ukrainian scholar went so far as to call him the coeditor of *Przegląd Społeczny*.[65] Although this statement does not reflect the truth, to a certain degree it reflects the level of his engagement in the publication of the journal. Franko did not determine its ideological-programmatic face; that was Bolesław Wysłouch's role. But the journal published Franko's programmatic articles on the agrarian and Jewish questions. Despite the fact that the journal lasted only eighteen months, and eleven out of eighteen issues were confiscated, it came to occupy a notable place in the intellectual history of Galicia and neighboring lands.[66] After the first year of publication, Wysłouch wrote that *Przegląd* had helped introduce a complete sea change in social life and literature: "a shift in the center of gravity of national life to the lower social strata…which is becoming an inexhaustible source of solid and strong democracy."[67]

Of all the journalistic projects in which Franko was engaged in the years 1883–1886, *Przegląd Społeczny* lay closest to his ideal of a periodical publication in terms of both content and form. Its format was that of a "thick journal," and it was aimed at developing civic thought,[68] while its ideological principles were similar to those espoused on the pages of *Praca*. However, it was rather critical of Marxism and saw the main political force as residing in the peasantry. Like the Geneva and Galician radicals, the journal promoted rationalism and positivism.[69]

With respect to the national program, Wysłouch upheld the ethnic principle and recognized Eastern Galicia and Lviv as Ukrainian territory. Here he not only disagreed with Drahomanov, he went even further by criticizing his federation plans for their inadequate attention to the national question. (Drahomanov proposed to build a federation according to the territorial, not national, principle.)[70] The editors and writers of *Przegląd Społeczny* comprised a truly international community, and it was very likely the last of its kind in Galicia.

In summarizing Franko's plans for working in various journals and newspapers from 1881 to 1886, one cannot fail to be amazed by their extraordinary multidimensionality and scattershot approach. Franko was able to work simultaneously with Ukrainian radicals and Galician (non-Ruthenian) socialists, as well as with Ukrainian nationalists and Polish democrats both from Austro-Hungary and the Russian Empire. If one adheres to the thesis that mass publications were the chief instrument of the creation of modern "imagined communities," then the newspapers and journals that were edited by Franko, as well as their authors and reading public, represented two different projects: a federative Polish-Ukrainian-Jewish community created on the basis of the horizontal integration of the "laboring strata" of diverse ethnoreligious backgrounds, and a vertically integrated Ukrainian nation. In other words, Franko sought to unite socialism with nationalism, and this melding was the nucleus of his vision of modern Ukrainian identity.

PART 2
Franko and His Society

Chapter 10

Franko and His World Perception

No account of the young Franko's life is possible without a general description of his world perception. It must be noted, first and foremost, that his views did not form a complete system. Attempts to define Franko's views as "his own, evolutionarily complex philosophical system [called] *Frankizm*," are unconvincing.[1] Efforts to "systematize" Franko reflect a hagiographic tendency in current Franko studies rather than Franko's worldview.

In the history of Ukrainian political thought, two individuals who may be rightly called systematic thinkers are often singled out: the left-liberal Mykhailo Drahomanov and the right-liberal Viacheslav Lypynsky.[2] Franko's case is different. Just as he had never written a long-form literary work (a novel), neither Franko's political activity nor his views conformed to any kind of system. In order to assess his world perception, one may apply the image that Isaiah Berlin used in his famous essay on Leo Tolstoy, in which the British philosopher and historian of ideas divides all thinkers into "hedgehogs" and "foxes" according to the principle that the fox knows many things, while the hedgehog knows one big thing:

For there is a great chasm between those, on one side, who relate everything to a single central vision, one system less or more coherent or articulate, in terms of which they understand, think and feel—a single, universal, organizing principle in terms of which alone all that they are and say has significance—and, on the other side, those who pursue many ends, often unrelated and even contradictory, connected, if at all, only in some *de facto* way, for some psychological or physiological cause, related by no moral or aesthetic principle; these last lead lives, perform acts, and entertain ideas that are centrifugal rather than centripetal, their thought is scattered or diffused, moving on many levels, seizing upon the essence of a vast variety of experiences and objects for what they are in themselves, without, consciously or unconsciously, seeking to fit them into, or exclude them from, any one unchanging, all-embracing, sometimes self-contradictory and incomplete, at times fanatical, unitary inner vision.[3]

Franko was a classic "fox," and both his supporters and his opponents reproached him for the inconsistency and changeability of his views, accusing him of making huge "leaps" and calling him a "little flag" that flutters whichever way the wind is blowing.[4] No matter how just or unjust these accusations, they reflected the unpredictable ("artistic" or "poetic," as some of his contemporaries put it) nature. Therefore, a study of Franko's world perception, just like the foxhunt, requires a special technique, one that entails the repudiation of all attempts to reduce it to some kind of "-ism." It is important to distinguish the various sources of its formation, the different contexts of its functioning, and, consequently, the various ways of interpreting it.

Spokesman of Progress

Despite the variableness of Franko's worldview, it had a definite, stable, and central focus. This focus may be described with the aid of a caricature that Franko drew for the satirical Lviv journal *Nove Zerkalo* (The New Mirror). It shows a locomotive with the inscription "Postupus," a Latinized version of the Ukrainian word for progress: *postup*. Two bulls, one of them representing the Austrian foreign minister, Count Gyula Andrássy, and the other the German chancellor, Otto von Bismarck, are butting up against the locomotive, trying to stop it from moving forward. Their efforts are observed by a couple of peasants, one of whom remarks to the other: "Ni, Semene, ne spynyt′ tota para totu paru" (No, Simon, that pair will not stop that steam [steam locomotive]—a play on words based on the Ukrainian homonyms, *para* / pair and *para* / steam) [ZT 41:445].[5]

This cartoon reflects the main elements of Franko's world perception: belief in progress and its relentless power; condemnation and mockery of "reactionary forces" that seek in vain to stop it; the conviction the people (peasants) will have the last word on this matter and that, ultimately, it is ordinary people who will gain the most from large-scale, "progressive" changes. The only thing lacking is a "machinist"—leading intellectuals who are called upon to pave a new way and explain the people's mission to the people. Franko included himself among these intellectuals.

There is no way of knowing whether Franko did this deliberately, but his cartoon was a parody of the theme of a painting that had just been created in the studio of the famous Polish artist Jan Matejko. In the 1870s, when a new building was being constructed for the Lviv Polytechnic, the Austrian education ministry had commissioned Matejko to create a large mural to decorate the main hall. The Lviv Polytechnic was producing engineering graduates whose mission was to introduce modern technologies in the backward agrarian region. Matejko's task was to present this mission in allegorical form. One of his paintings shows a handcar moving along a railway track. Running in front of it is a little boy symbolizing the power of the steam locomotive. Seated on the pump trolley are a man and woman, who symbolize emancipation: thanks to technological progress, the man is releasing the woman from the burden of domestic chores and opening up new horizons for her. In the background are factory chimneys that contrast with the monotonous rhythm of rural life, which is symbolized by the figures of two peasants, who are plowing and sowing. Far away in the distance is a steamship, another symbol of progress.[6]

Matejko's paintings illustrated—without conscious premeditation, of course—a quotation from Marx's *Das Kapital*: "The country that is more developed industrially only shows, to the less developed, the image of its own future."[7] The resemblance among Matejko, Marx, and Franko may be explained by the belief in universal progress on the part of a significant proportion of educated, nineteenth-century Europeans. Developed Western countries, such as Great Britain and Prussia, or the central provinces of the Austro-Hungarian Empire, were showing the future to such backward regions as Galicia.

The train was the central symbol of progress; a better image of the stark changes brought about by the latest discoveries in technology could hardly be found. Twenty years after the opening in 1830 of the Liverpool and Manchester Railway, the world's first intercity passenger railway, the English newspaper *The Economist* wrote:

In *locomotion by land* [emphasis in the original, here and below—Y.H.]... our progress has been most stupendous—surpassing all previous steps since the creation of the human race....In the days of Adam the average speed of travel, if Adam ever did such things, was four miles an hour; in the year 1828, or *4,000 years afterward, it was still only ten miles,* and sensible and scientific men were ready to affirm and eager to prove that this rate could never be materially exceeded;—in 1850 it is habitually forty miles an hour, and *seventy* for those who like it.[8]

A train is depicted in a logotype that appeared in the Warsaw weekly *Przegląd Tygodniowy*, whose founding date of 1866 marks the birth of Polish Positivism. The weekly laid special emphasis on the use of steam power and railways as the prerequisite for the rebirth of the Polish nation.[9] After returning from his lengthy exile in 1857, Ukraine's national poet, Taras Shevchenko, prayed for the soul of the inventor of the steam engine.[10] Writing about the steamboat and the draught power of steam, he declared that this "young child, growing not by the day but by the hour, will soon devour the knouts, thrones, and crowns, and will merely snack on diplomats and landowners—amuse himself, like a schoolboy with a lollipop."[11]

Whereas Shevchenko commented only once on this question, Franko developed his views on technological progress into a consistent and well-thought-out program. One Franko biographer calls the poetization of technology one of the characteristic features of his work set against the background of all of nineteenth-century Ukrainian literature.[12] For Franko, the "invention of steam-powered machines, telegraphs, phonographs, microphones, electric machines, etc., is introducing into the world perhaps a greater revolution than the entire bloody French Revolution" [*ZT* 48:111]. Franko poetizes the train as an "iron horse" that finds the earth a crowded place because of its speed. Shattering limits and age-old obstacles, the railway was "uniting all the lands, all the peoples into one family" [*ZT* 1:201].

Of course, not everyone in Galicia shared Franko's optimism concerning the opening of railways and historical progress. In a letter to the Russian historian and journalist, Mikhail Pogodin, Denys Zubrytsky complained that the railway was one of the two greatest ills besetting Galicia (the second one was Jews), because it was advantageous only to entrepreneurs, factory owners, and carefree wanderers, but left millions of people without bread. He objected to the introduction of the railway in Russia because the only people who would gain from this would be "enlighteners," who were none other than "Jews, who periodically take over German literature."[13] In a similar vein, the Russophile leader Rev. Ivan Naumovych cursed Western science with its technical discoveries, contrasting it to the unspoiled nature of "holy Rus":

> There are holy matters in our country
> We have the wisdom of books;
> You are schooled in machines,
> But we, Rus, [are schooled] in these books.[14]

There were also those who simply feared the railway. In 1886, the Lviv newspaper Zoria published a short story by Natalia Kobrynska, titled "Iak stara Ianova ikhala zaliznytseiu z Kolomyi do Burshtyna" (How Old Ianova Traveled by Railway from Kolomyia to Burshtyn), in order to show "how bitterly ordinary people sometimes perceive progress and the inventions of civilization." Kobrynska tells the story of a simple woman named Granny Iustyna, who decides to visit her son by taking "some kind of train." She feared the railway as she would a "madman": to travel the ninety kilometers to Burshtyn was "such a great distance that when you think about it, your veins turn to ice." When, after many adventures, the old woman finally arrived at her destination, she "thanked the Lord for bringing her there safely." This short story illustrates the fear of the railway that older Galicians experienced in the 1880s. A Greek Catholic priest, the father of one of Franko's friends, never traveled by train and tried to discourage his son from train travel: "Hey, take care, take care, son, it's dangerous to travel this way; every day the newspaper reports some kind of railway accident."[15]

These examples help throw into sharp relief the radical nature of Franko's world perception: he was fascinated by progress, which many of his contemporaries viewed as undesirable, and even dangerous. "Progress" was the chief category around which Franko's world perception was formed both in his youth and, with certain caveats, in adulthood.[16] The emphasis on the primacy of progress separated him and his friends—at least in his imagination—from their closest allies in the Ruthenian camp, the Galician populists [ZT 48:188–89]. Franko was known as "one of the most dedicated spokesmen for progress in our land."[17]

It is difficult to glean Franko's own views on progress from the mass of articles that he wrote as a young man, in which he reviewed and recapitulated the views of other thinkers, inserting his own commentaries only here and there. He does this in his long, unfinished essay titled "Mysli o evoliutsii v istorii liuds´kosty" (Thoughts on Evolution in the History of Mankind), which was published in 1881–1882 in the journal Svit. The essay lacks originality, and for the scholar of Franko's ideas it is important only insofar as it helps to confirm the fact that Franko did not accept the idea of one-way linearity of development; he distinguished "forward progress" from "backward progress." Nevertheless, in his view the norm was only "forward progress," while "backward progress" was "a later and unhealthy manifestation" [ZT 45:81–82, 117–18].

Franko's vision of progress is more original when it is garbed in his poetic images. From this perspective the programmatic poem "Himn" (Hymn; also known by its alternate title, "Vichnyi revoliutsioner" [The Eternal Revolutionary]) merits special attention. Written in 1880 and first published in the Lviv workers' newspaper, *Praca*, two years later,[18] and set to music in 1905 by Mykola Lysenko, this work, according to Franko's contemporaries, burst on the scene like a "bombshell."[19] This poem, which opens his collection *Z vershyn i nyzyn* (From the Heights and the Depths, 1887), is a summary of his literary work, "dictated by the sincere desire for the common good and progress, by a sincere love for [his] people and [his] native land..." [*ZT* 1:21]. Thus, Franko's "eternal revolutionary" is "the spiritual force that stirs man up to stress / To liberty and happiness (Dukh, shcho tilo rve do boiu, / Rve za postup, shchastia i voliu). This spiritual force (*dukh*) is everlasting and nothing can destroy it: "For neither racks of priestly courts, / Nor tsarist dungeons' dark resorts, / Nor soldiers trained to crush revolt / With cannons' deadly thunderbolt, / Nor spy's device can overthrow (Ni popivs´kii tortury / Ni tiuremni tsars´ki mury / Ani viis´ka mushtrovani / Ni harmaty lashtovani / Ni shpions´ke remeslo). It is omnipresent: it can be heard "in the poor peasant's smoky cot, / In busy shop, in factory hot, / And in dark haunts of grief and tears" (Po kurnykh khatakh muzhyts´kykh, / Po verstatakh remisnyts´kykh, / Po mistsiakh nedoli i sliz). And it is relentless: it rolls like an avalanche, and there is no force in the world "to stop that fury in its course / And quench the sun's resistless ray / That brightens to a perfect day" (Shchob v bihu ii spynyla / Shchob zhasyla, mov ohen´, / Rozvydniaiushchyisia den´) [*ZT* 1:22, 24].[20]

There are parallels between Franko's "Hymn" and the poem "Odpowiedź na Psalmy przyszłości" (Answer to the "Psalms of the Future"), written by the Polish *wieszcz* (poet-prophet), Juliusz Słowacki: the two poems express a similar revolutionary mood, present a common hero—the Eternal Revolutionary—and even feature the same rhythm.[21] Yet, despite their formal resemblance, each of these two poems is written according to a different literary convention and world perception. Słowacki's Eternal Revolutionary is a metaphysical spirit that rises to the very heavens, from where "it delivers whirlwinds of comets and flames," and predicts a bloody battle—the Apocalypse—in which "no one will benefit from graves."[22] Franko's Eternal Revolutionary does not strive to unattainable heights. On the contrary, he is very "down to earth" and focused on concrete human actions. His victory is not the end of human history but the start of a new era of the "dawning day."

Słowacki was a romantic poet, and his poem is regarded as one of the clearest manifestations of romantic thought.[23] Even though Franko was strongly influenced by Romanticism, he belonged to the Positivist school, which emerged in reaction to the Romantic trend in literature. The Positivist vision also differed from the original idea of progress that arose during the Enlightenment: for the Positivists, the end goal of progress was not simply the emancipation of the human mind, which they required, but the rational organization of society. Accordingly, the carrier of wisdom is not the lone individual but an entire class that is called upon to carry out this great goal.[24]

In contrast to Polish intellectual history, there was no Ukrainian branch of Positivism. In the Ruthenian-Ukrainian case, what may be called a counterpart to Positivism acquired the form of so-called radicalism (understood as the name of a separate sociopolitical current rather than the expression of certain extremist views). It was a synthesis of several currents, including Polish Positivism. The influence of the Polish Positivists on Franko is unmistakable:[25] he was drawn to them by the desire to spread education and culture among the common people; the idea of working among the peasantry; the impetus to broach the workers' theme; and the need to democratize social relations, emancipate women, and grant equal rights to Jews.[26] The Polish Positivists had learned a bitter lesson from the defeat of the 1863 uprising and demanded a change from revolution to positive ("organic") work, the importance of which lay in the belief in work, science, and education as the main engines of civilization. Like them, Franko hoped to overthrow the social order "Not with weapons, not with the force / Of fire, iron and war, / But with truth, and work, / And science" (Ne zbroieiu, ne syloiu / Ohniu, zaliza i viiny, A pravdoiu, i pratseiu, / I naukoiu) [*ZT* 1:53]. However, just as the Ukrainian and Polish situations after 1863 were very different from each other, Franko's views differed substantially from those held by the Polish Positivists.[27]

It may be said, rather, that Franko and the Polish Positivists referred to the same sources: the works of Auguste Comte, Herbert Spencer, Charles Darwin, Thomas Huxley, Henry Thomas Buckle, Ernest Renan, and their many popularizers. According to the reminiscences of a contemporary, of all these distinguished writers it was Auguste Comte, the very creator of the term "Positivism" and its principal ideologist, to whom the young Franko accorded first place.[28] Comte is regarded as the embodiment of the nineteenth century, when the decline of faith in God was not accompanied by the emergence of a new, universal legitimization of the sociopolitical order. Comte, in fact, set about constructing a philosophical system that could, to use the words of a later scholar, reconcile "destruction with reconstruction, negation with affirmation, science with religion, the head with the heart, the past with the present, order with progress."[29] Of all the great ideological visionaries of the nineteenth century, he was the first to comprehend that the new world needed a new religion that would be consonant with the general scientific spirit of the age. Belief in progress was supposed to become this religion. The French Revolution appealed to principles that were to destroy the *ancien régime*. Yet even that revolution had given rise to new "metaphysical" dogmas that were obstacles to progress. To the "fruitless metaphysics" of the earlier philosophical idealism Comte opposed a system of "positive" knowledge—that is, knowledge hostile to speculative thinking and based exclusively on facts. He united knowledge of all the natural sciences into one system and expanded its method to encompass history, politics, and morality, thus creating—according to his own admission—the new science of "sociology" (a term that he himself devised). Positivism demanded that social phenomena be studied the same way as the phenomena of physics and chemistry. Engagement in sociology was aimed at introducing order to that part of nature which heretofore had been the most imperfect: human society.

Comte's philosophy is permeated with the Christian idea of universal love, but the general good of all society occupies the place of God as the central object of love. "To live for the sake of others" became the leading maxim. Positivism was supposed to extend to all spheres of human life, even art, which, liberated from the fetters of theology, could perform its function of the "idealization of real life" in a new manner. Within this philosophical system even poetry and poets were charged with their own, "real," mission: they became the priests, so to speak, of the new religion of Positivism, adjured to show the beauty and grandeur of human life.[30]

This selective and simplified account of Comte's system is crucial to recognizing the "Positivist" sources of Franko's views on society and literature, which will be discussed in greater detail later. It has not been established with any certainty that Franko read Comte, none of whose books were in Franko's personal library, which contained, however, several books written by two of Comte's popularizers: *The Sociology of Auguste Comte*, by Bolesław Limanowski (1875), and *August Comte and Positivism*, by John Stuart Mill (1874). The publication dates of both these books lead one to assume that

Franko acquired them early in his life. This is further implied by Franko's notes in the margins of Mill's book, which clearly indicate that Franko was making his first acquaintance with Comte: all the main terms and concepts as well as the principles of his philosophy are underlined in pencil.[31] The discussions of Positivism that were taking place in Lviv and Warsaw were typically marked by philosophical dilettantism, as indicated by the example of Bolesław Limanowski. A later expert on the Polish socialists expressed skepticism about the depth of his familiarity with Comte. With his weak knowledge of the French language, Limanowski had become acquainted with Comte's sociology "secondhand," through German writers.[32]

Was Franko's case any different? In connection with the formation of his philosophical views, it has been noted that he was a graduate of the universities of Lviv and Vienna, two centers that were associated with the development of Positivist systems.[33] However, this argument is outdated, inasmuch as the Lviv-Warsaw philosophical school of thought, which was close to the linguistic Positivism of Wittgenstein and the "Viennese group," was formed later, during the interwar period. The only thing that may be said of Franko with any certainty is that he was student of the star of Polish Positivism, Julian Ochorowicz, who had taught briefly at Lviv University. True, the first books by Spencer and Marx appeared in Franko's library in the spring of 1877, most likely thanks to Drahomanov's influence—that is, nearly a year before Franko registered for Ochorowicz's courses.[34] But Ochorowicz began to promote Positivism later, once Franko began attending his lectures after his first arrest and prison sentence. Thus, one cannot exclude Franko's university studies in his formation as a Positivist, which, in turn, means that he was not entirely a self-taught dilettante.

We see evidence of the fundamental principles of Positivism in one of the first articles that Franko wrote for *Praca* in 1878:

> Real science has nothing in common with any supernatural forces, with any innate ideas, with any inner worlds that control the external world. It only deals with the external world, with nature, understanding that nature as broadly as possible, that is, including in it everything that falls under our cognition; as well as people with their progress, history, religion, and all those countless worlds that fill space. The individual per se is only one of nature's incomplete creations. Only nature offers man the means of survival, the fulfillment of his needs, luxuries, and happiness. Nature is everything for man. Outside of nature there is no cognition, no truth. And only nature is

that book which the human being must constantly read because only with it can blessed truth appear to man. [*ZT* 45:32]

The fact that Franko was inspired by Comte and other Western Positivists is what distinguished him from the older generation of Ukrainophiles, the Galician populists. The populists of the 1860s and 1870s were the first people with a Galician-Ruthenian orientation to emphasize the need for "organic work," progress, and Western enlightenment, and they sought to introduce scholarly discourse into popular publications. They adopted these ideas and approaches from Polish Positivism, which had its debut in Galicia even earlier than in Warsaw, the Mecca of Polish Positivists.[35] However, it is almost impossible to find any references to Comte, Darwin, or Marx in the their works. It is likely that the older populists first became familiar with these names only in the late 1870s, when they initiated discussions with the younger radicals, including Franko. However, as Franko himself indicated, in these debates they expressed their opinions on questions that they did not understand and discussed books that they had not read [*ZT* 45:58–68]. Omelian Ohonovsky wrote that Franko the student liked sociology, familiarity with which could hardly be expected of him, a professor of philology.[36]

In any case, the number one philosopher for Franko was Comte, not Marx, as Soviet-era Franko specialists assiduously argued. Marxism, in Franko's view, was only a branch of Positivism; a transference and application of Positivist approaches with respect to understanding society. "The Program of the Galician Socialists" (1881), cowritten by Franko, states that it was Karl Marx who raised the theory of socialism to the status of a Positivist science [*ZT* 45:449].

True, there were many similarities between Positivism and Marxism. It was a rare Marxist who in his youth had not read or become fascinated by the writings of Comte, Spencer, Mill, Buckle, and others. In the mid-1870s, the young Karl Kautsky called Comte's students the "brothers" of the Marxists.[37] Positivism formed a view of the development of society being the result of objective actions independent of human will and historically determined factors, thereby laying the groundwork for the reception of socialism. What is particularly important in the context of this account of Franko's worldview is that Positivism and Marxism shared a common belief in the special social mission of the intelligentsia as a group that should reveal to society its historic mission.

Socialism as the Foundation of "Love of the People"

Socialism—in all its varieties, all the way to Marxism—was the second most powerful source of Franko's world perception. As Franko later claimed, socialism was the first ideology that provided him and Pavlyk with a strong foundation for their love of the people (*narodoliubstvo*). Franko gave the fullest exposition of his socialist ideals in a letter written to Olha Roshkevych on 20 September 1878. According to Franko, at the core of the construction of the new order lay social ("community") ownership of the means of production. Society was to consist of communities with equal rights, which would elect their own leaders. All the fruits of labor should belong to those who work. Class privileges and inequality would disappear, matters of general state importance (the development of schools, museums, institutes, and the like) were to be financed with public funds, and a civic militia would replace the army. The socialist order would guarantee the free development of all nations that together would create a "free federation." Unrestricted freedom of the individual would be instituted; unequal, arranged marriages would disappear; and children were to be raised on wise, progressive, and scientific notions, and never forbidden to acquaint themselves with other, opposing, ideas [*ZT* 48:113].

There was much in the young Franko's world perception that contradicted Marxism. For example, he agreed with certain principles of Lassallism, a socialist current to which Marx was hostile. In one of his later articles Franko, following in the footsteps of the Austrian socialist, Heinrich Oberwinder, even wrote about Ferdinand Lassalle's "superiority" to Marx. In borrowing his theories "partly from Marx, [Lassalle] had laid the foundations of practical socialism."[38] Franko uses hardly any of the terms that are central to Marxism: "class struggle," "proletarian (or "communist," as in the *Manifesto*) revolution," and so on.[39] "By the [term] 'world revolution' I do not understand the worldwide revolt of the poor against the wealthy, a global massacre; only universal [*sic*—Y. H.] Ruthenians, the feeble-minded, and policemen understand this as revolution," he wrote in his letter to Olha Roshkevych. "By revolution I understand precisely a whole great array of such cultural, scholarly, and political facts, be they bloody or not at all, which change all prior concepts and shunt both the foundation and the entire development of a nation onto an entirely different path....I am convinced that the final act of the great socialist revolution will be as gentle, yet carried out more wisely and more profoundly, as education and science will be able to elucidate the goal and ways of this issue to the laboring people" [*ZT* 48:111–12].

Franko's most significant departure from Marxism may be noted when he tries to adapt it to Galician conditions. Marx, Comte, Spencer, and Buckle—none of them offered any answers to the question of what to do with their theories here and now in a society that was merely "gazing at a picture of its future"—that is, where technological progress, industrialization, the bourgeoisie and the proletariat, modern science, and other strident phrases sounded like a dream list, not like realities of life. In the Galician socialists' program the following notation, believed to have been penned by Franko, was made next to the words "we aspire to create a strong workers' party": "Perhaps the name 'people's' party would be better suited to our relations. For at a time when in the West the cadres of the future fighting army of the proletariat are being created out of factory workers, in our country this role seems to be played by the peasant folk....Obviously, in our country the proletarian movement will be, first and foremost, an agrarian one" [*ZT* 45:455].

Franko's conflict with the editorial board of *Praca* lay precisely in his efforts to adapt socialist propaganda to the needs of the peasantry. Of all Franko's articles, the editors chose to reject the very one in which he "urged to write in a more peasant style, to discard all foreign terminology, and to try to modify the very theory of socialism so that it will better suit our agrarian and petty bourgeois circumstances than Marx's factory socialism" [*ZT* 48:347].

In Franko's statements from this period may be seen the influence of Drahomanov, who opposed the mechanical adaptation of Marxism to Eastern European conditions. Among Drahomanov's friends in the Kyiv Hromada were Mykola Ziber, one of the first popularizers of Marxist economic theory in the Russian Empire, and Serhii Podolynsky, "the 'purest' socialist of his era."[40] Both of them sought to create something along the lines of a Ukrainian version of Marxism. Podolynsky, in particular, explained the laws of Marxism as a consequence of the theory of energy conservation, which did not go unremarked by Marx.[41] Drahomanov, Podolynsky, and Ziber were Ukrainians by patriotic conviction and cosmopolitans by their lifestyle: they studied or worked as interns in Berlin, Heidelberg, and Paris, and their articles were published in French, German, Italian, and Russian émigré periodicals. Thus, they were notable figures in the pan-European intellectual milieu,[42] and their works even made their way into one of Ochorowicz's seminars in Lviv, during which, as Franko wrote later, Podolynsky's work on socialism and Darwinism elicited heated debates for a period of two weeks [*ZT* 48:213–14].

The commingling of nationalism and socialism was characteristic of several generations of Ukrainian intellectuals who, following in the footsteps of Drahomanov, Franko, and Pavlyk, embarked on political and cultural activism between the 1860s and the 1910s. Of course, this combination was not a uniquely Ukrainian phenomenon, but rather one that was typical of the members of assorted (for example, Polish and Jewish) socialist movements in Central and Eastern Europe. However, this was a "contradiction in terms," and not just in the sense in which Isaiah Berlin understood it— that not all the highest values to which humanity aspires are compatible with each other.[43] In the real conditions that existed in Central and Eastern Europe during the second half of the nineteenth century and the beginning of the twentieth, something different was at stake: socialist theories and the political movements that were formed on their basis had an indifferent, even hostile, attitude to the national aspirations of so-called "stateless nations" (*nederzhavni narody*). As early as 1848–1849, Friedrich Engels had argued in a number of articles ("The Magyar Struggle," "Democratic Pan-Slavism," and others) that the Slavs, with the exception of the Poles and Russians, could not play a progressive role in the general course of historical development and were therefore doomed to perish as independent nations.[44] This view was shared by Ferdinand Lassalle, Petr Lavrov, and other ideologists of the socialist movement. According to them, the only mission of "stateless" nations was their dilution (assimilation) within "state-embodied" nations (*derzhavni narody*). "These were no national great-state whims, merely the influence of a completely entrenched view of the course and interests of historical development," wrote Eduard Bernstein some forty years later, recalling the atmosphere in the international socialist movement during the late 1870s and early 1880s.[45]

The situation in which the Ukrainian socialists found themselves was complicated by a specific stance on the Ukrainian movement, one adopted by their closest allies, the Polish and Russian socialists: the latter regarded the Ukrainian socialist movement as a rupture with international solidarity in favor of petty, particular interests. In the view of the Russian and Polish socialists, there was a risk that the Ukrainian socialist movement could deprive them of one of their largest territorial bases in Central and Eastern Europe; from this perspective, the existence of a separate Lithuanian or

Estonian movement represented a less significant threat. As Kelles-Krauz reported from London in 1901, the Russian social democrats who gathered around Lenin rejected in principle the existence of a separate Ukrainian social democratic party. In the view of Lenin and his comrades, permitting the Ukrainians to have their own party would be tantamount to "political suicide."[46]

Thus, the leading figures of the Ukrainian socialist movement faced a dilemma: should they speed up the global victory of socialism by sacrificing their particular national aspirations, or should they work on behalf of their national revival, risking a conflict with the socialist movements in the neighboring nation-states? In practice, this dilemma dictated the crucial need to make a choice: to preserve their own organizational separateness or to work with socialist organizations based in nation-states? It goes without saying that choice of organizational structure defined, a priori, the character of the future state order in the Ukrainian lands in the event of the anticipated victory of the socialist revolution in this region: a unitary or federal structure of the socialist movement envisaged a unitary or federal character of the future Polish-Ukrainian (or Russian-Ukrainian) socialist state, while the existence of a separate Ukrainian socialist party could become the guarantor of Ukraine's political independence.

In all these arguments, the young Franko, like Pavlyk, was strongly influenced by Drahomanov, who not only devised a formula for fusing socialist interests with national ones, but also elaborated the organizational foundations of the functioning of the Ukrainian socialist movement. In his view, Ukrainian patriotic socialists should aspire to create a federal party that would unite Ukrainian peasants with Russian, Jewish, and Polish workers, the most populous non-Ukrainian ethnic groups on the Ukrainian ethnographic territory. As an antidote to Polish and Russian territorial claims, Drahomanov advanced the following principle: to uphold federal relations only with those Polish and Russian socialists who uphold the ethnographic, not historical, principle of building the future state. He considered the natural allies of the Ukrainian movement to be the "stateless" peoples of Russia: the Finns, Estonians, Moldovans, the "peoples of the Caucasus," and, among the Russians, those distinct groups that had strong regional traditions—for example, the peoples of the Don River and Ural regions, and the Siberians.[47]

It was no mean feat to implement this formula, which encountered strong resistance from the supporters of strict centralization of the socialist movement. As was to be expected, Drahomanov was severely criticized by Lenin. As Ivan Lysiak-Rudnytsky noted, "Drahomanov and Lenin, who held opposing positions on the question of centralization, agreed in one respect: the 'organizational structure of a revolutionary movement a priori determines the character of the system generated by the victorious revolution.'"[48]

Franko was destined to witness the negative attitude toward Ukrainian socialism very early on. Russian socialists stopping over in Lviv in the late 1870s en route to the Balkans, where they were planning to build a socialist republic, ridiculed the Galician socialists' efforts to conduct propaganda in the Ukrainian language; their position was that "small nations must join large [ones] and learn their language. This is the simplest road to universal equality."[49]

The Ukrainian socialists of Galicia were able to find support among their Polish colleagues. In the Polish movement, especially within its liberal and left wings, the idea of a federation garnered strong support. The authors of the "Program of the Polish and Ruthenian Socialists of Eastern Galicia" explicitly stated that they did not share the views that were prevalent among Marxists concerning the division into "nation-states" and "stateless nations," and into large and small nations: "For there are no higher and lower nations: all are equal and have equal right to free development." In Galicia, which was home to several nations, the socialists of each nationality were to create their own federal union, retaining the right to autonomy in internal affairs and enjoying "freedom to join related groups, no matter where they existed." Thus, the Ukrainian socialists who were members of the editorial board of *Praca*, together with Polish socialists, had the right to unite with Drahomanov's Hromada group in Geneva, and the Polish socialists with socialists in Warsaw and Cracow and other groups. Their relations in Galicia were regulated thus: "In those areas inhabited exclusively by Polish people, Poles engage in activity; where there are exclusively Ukrainian people—Ukrainians [engage in activity]; in mixed communities, propaganda is conducted by joint forces" [*ZT* 45:456, 461].

However, when the Program was about to be published, an incident took place demonstrating that upholding equal rights in the relations between Polish and Ukrainian nationalists was no simple matter. The text was sent to Geneva, where Bolesław Limanowski was responsible for seeing it into print. Limanowski made a major change to the title of the program by deleting the word "Ruthenian." The activists in Lviv, aghast at this modification, refused to accept the print run. Then, in order to conceal the altered title, Limanowski simply glued a strip of paper printed with the words "Program of the Galician Socialists" on each printed copy. Since the strip of paper with the crudely improvised title was easy to remove, everyone could read the title underneath and see that the program referred only to Polish socialists. Did Limanowski deliberately snub the Ruthenian socialists, or was this simply an unfortunate error, as he claimed? Franko was under the impression that Limanowski's mistake was no accident, and for many years afterward he was in the habit of recounting this incident as an example of the Polish socialists' unscrupulousness. For his part, Limanowski does not even mention it in his memoirs.[50]

This episode highlighted the difference between the Ukrainian and Polish points of view: what Limanowski regarded as trivial was a fundamental issue in the eyes of the Ruthenian-Ukrainian socialists in Lviv and Geneva. A few months later, at an international socialist conference held in the Swiss city of Chur (Coire), Limanowski repeated his earlier "mistake": appearing as a delegate of *Praca*'s editorial committee, he spoke about the existence in Galicia of only the Polish socialist movement. The Chur congress was the site of a clash between two conceptions within the Polish socialist movement. Limanowski was the spokesman of the current that regarded the national question as fundamentally important. Marshaling arguments to support his idea, he referred to the "Program of the Galician Socialists," among other things. His main opponent, Ludwik Waryński, believed that national liberation must not be one of the programmatic tasks of the Polish socialist movement. In his view, this was a secondary question that would be resolved automatically once the socialist question was settled. The conference participants supported Waryński, passing a resolution declaring that the "liberation struggle is a struggle of classes, not nationalities," thus throwing into sharp relief the vulnerable position of the Ukrainian socialists: not only could they not picture Waryński as their ally, it was also difficult for them to find a common language with his opponent, Limanowski.

Be that as it may, the Ukrainian socialists were fated to engage in the most important debates with Russian, not Polish, revolutionaries. Drahomanov had a particularly long history of conflict with left-wing Russians: his first clash with "Great Russian centralism and all-Russian Jacobins" took place as early as 1869 in Kyiv, during a discussion with a delegate from a students' group based in St. Petersburg. These disagreements continued after he moved to Switzerland, the Mecca of the Russian revolutionary movement. In order to organize the "Westernizing-federated undermining" of the policy of the "selfhood" and "Russification" of the Russian Socialist Revolutionaries, in 1879–1881 Drahomanov established closer ties with the Geneva-based anarchists and Proudhonites. He actively promoted the creation of an "Eastern European International Federation" that would be composed of socialists in the Russian, Austro-Hungarian, and German empires, as well as in Romania. The first step on this path was to be the founding of a literary union of socialist publications in all the Eastern European languages, both "plebeian" and "nation-state" ones. In a separate circular titled *Vnimaniiu sotsialistov-immigrantov iz Rossii* (To the Attention of Socialist Émigrés from Russia) Drahomanov substantiated the principle that socialist parties should be organized by natural (geographic, economic, national) regions, not on the basis of state borders.[51]

Among the Russian revolutionaries who promoted ideas of federalism were the members of the organization *Chernyi peredel* (Black Partition), which championed "Westernism" and was constantly evolving in the direction of Marxism. According to its leader, Georgii Plekhanov, "Only the federal principle in the political organization of a people that has liberated itself…can guarantee the normal course of development of national life."[52] Another *Chernyi peredel* member, Pavel Akselrod, even supported Drahomanov's plan and then departed to the Russian Empire, returning to Geneva with the program of the South Russian (Odessa) branch of *Chernyi peredel*, which recognized the principle of federalism.[53]

What happened next is difficult to ascertain, as both parties to this incident provided different versions. What is clear, however, is that in the summer of 1880 an acrimonious discussion took place in Geneva between Drahomanov and Pavlyk, who faced off against Plekhanov. The main issue was the need to conduct socialist propaganda in the Ukrainian language. Discussion of this question had been initiated by Pavlyk, who had given a lecture on the development of the Galician socialist movement during a joint meeting of Polish and Russian socialists, which took place in one of Geneva's many coffeehouses. During his lecture he used Galicia as an example of a movement in the ranks of which the principle of conducting propaganda in various languages was already being put into practice. Plekhanov, who argued in favor of the principle of building socialist organizations according to state, not ethnographic, borders, made the following notations in his notebook: "We could have understood the adaptation to the feelings of oppressed peoples, but since this is superfluous, it is necessary to pass directly to the economic question."[54]

The position of *Praca*'s editorial board on questions that were raised in discussions abroad was ambiguous. On the one hand, its members supported the idea of creating socialist organizations in line with the national-federal principle, and on the other, they, like Plekhanov, were convinced that, owing to the small membership and organizational weakness of the Galician socialist movement, the resolution of this task was a question of the distant future. Franko agreed with this point of view. When Pavlyk became offended because *Praca* had carelessly used the term "Poland" with regard to Eastern Galicia, Franko replied to him in the name of the editorial committee: *Praca* "does not wish to and cannot play around with national questions, which are mostly inaccessible and completely unnecessary for workers" [*ZT* 48:234].

Another incident involving Pavlyk indicates that Franko's response was not simply a justification but the expression of his position. After Pavlyk sent him Ivan Nechui-Levytsky's manuscript on Ukrainian hetmans for publication, Franko scolded him: "Why the devil did you send me an article about the hetmans? Do you really think there is nothing better to print here than that swinishness that no one cares about besides Barv[insky] and comp[any]?…The devil take all of history! We have to offer more important things now—as it is, our unfortunate and poorly understood history has led to that *absurd nationalism and independence movement*, upon which *Pravda* prides itself, like a piglet in a top hat [*ZT* 48:190–91; my emphasis—Y. H.].

Franko was prepared to sacrifice national ideals to socialist ones. But did he feel psychologically at ease in making this sacrifice? There are grounds to assume that he did not. In the early 1880s, Franko wrote a poem called "Ne pora" (Now Is Not the Time, in literal translation):[55]

> "Ne pora, ne pora, ne pora,
> Moskalevi i liakhovi sluzhyty!
> Dovershylas´ Ukrainy kryvda stara,—
> Nam pora dlia Ukrainy zhyty.
>
> Ne pora, ne pora, ne pora
> Za nevyhlaskiv lyt´ svoiu krov,
> I liubyty tsaria, shcho nash liud obdyra,—
> Dlia Ukrainy nasha liubov" […]

It is time, it is time, it is time
To refuse to serve Russian and Pole!
For an end is at hand to the past and its crime;
Our Ukraine claims your life and your soul.

It is time, it is time, it is time
All our alien bonds to disprove,
And to cast off the tsar, a despoiler in crime
Our Ukraine lives alone in our love.[56]

Whether this poem was Franko's response to Drahomanov and Pavlyk's quarrels in Geneva with the Russian and Polish socialists is anyone's guess. Set to music in the early 1900s, "Ne pora" became one of the most popular hymns of the Galician-Ukrainians, especially among nationalistic students, whose youthful gatherings rarely began or ended without a rendition of this unofficial hymn.[57]

The changeability of Franko's views is perhaps nowhere as evident as in the fact that he was the author of two popular Ukrainian hymns: the revolutionarily "cosmopolitan" "Eternal Revolutionary," which was sung on par with the "Internationale," and the national hymn, "Ne pora," sung together with the official Ukrainian national hymn, "Shche ne vmerla Ukraina" (Ukraine Has Not Yet Perished). It is noteworthy that both these poems, so different in their content, were written in the same period.

As mentioned earlier, this dualism was germane to the entire Ukrainian socialist movement. The internal classification of its leading figures may be determined according to the degree of their closeness or distance from the two poles of nationalism or socialism. Podolynsky and Ziber were more socialist than nationalist, and above all they regarded their Ukrainianness as a revolutionary matter.[58] Drahomanov's views were a balancing act between socialism and nationalism. The young Franko vacillated between nationalism and socialism, and there was no clear-cut system behind his vacillation. Drahomanov also reproached him for his ambiguous national position in his relations with the Polish socialists in Lviv and for his far-reaching compromises during his collaboration with the populists. However, under certain circumstances this "systemless" position gave Franko an important advantage over Drahomanov: not hamstrung by any system, he could evolve easily and quickly, thereby entering new spheres in the development of Ukrainian political thought.[59]

However, it must be emphasized that during his young adulthood Franko was building, first and foremost, not the Ukrainian nation but a Ruthenian-Polish-Jewish community, an alliance of workers, peasants, and progressive intellectuals from all three nationalities against the wealthy classes of these same nationalities. It is another question altogether whether his literary works and political essays of the 1870s and 1880s were helping young cosmopolitans discover their sense of being Ukrainian; but again, their Ukrainianness was part of the international progressive movement.

Post Scriptum

Drahomanov and Franko's discovery—not an original discovery, but one that is important in the Eastern European context—was their confirmation of the fact that the process of raising the masses to the level of general culture and civilization could only take place on national foundations. Or, to use the images depicted in Franko's cartoon, the universal train of progress must necessarily move along national rails, that is, it must be *postupus*, not *progressus*. As socialists, Drahomanov and Franko sought to disprove that part of Marx's theory which negated the workers' need for a national fatherland.

By the late nineteenth century, this ethos also emerged among the socialists in the Austro-Hungarian Empire. Meanwhile, in the Russian Empire the question of the relationship between the social and the national remained deeply contentious.[60] Suffice it to say that after the adoption in 1899 of the Brünn (Brno) Program, one of the defining features of Austrian Marxism was the peaceful division into various national social democratic parties, and that after the reestablishment of the Russian Social Democratic Party in 1903, the first big scandal erupted when the party leadership refused to recognize the Jewish Labor Bund as an autonomous national entity. Hans Mommsen, one of the most distinguished experts on Austrian Marxism, sees a similarity between the Brünn Program and the earlier Program of the Galician Socialists.[61] There is no telling whether this is merely a coincidence involving the influence of the Ukrainian and Galician socialist movements, in general, and Drahomanov and Franko, in particular, or, rather, that the similarities between these two texts are the result of their arising in one and the same mental atmosphere, yet independently of each other.

In the Russian and Polish cases, the influences of Drahomanov and Franko are more obvious, although not necessarily in the same sense as the Austrian case. Just as Lenin criticized Drahomanov for his views on federalism, Feliks Kon (1864–1941), another Bolshevik leader, accused Franko and Drahomanov of plotting to weaken the forces of the Polish socialist movement by breaking it up organizationally and subordinating it to national tasks. Kon's accusations were so extreme that he even called Franko a forerunner of Józef Piłsudski.[62]

Kon had firsthand knowledge of the early history of the socialist movement and the Galician situation. In his youth he had belonged to the Polish party Proletarjat (1882), led by Waryński, and after the defeat of the Russian revolution of 1905–1907 he hid out in Galicia for some time. In 1920, he was in charge of the efforts to create the Communist Party of Western Ukraine.[63] His accusations against the two Ukrainian socialists were voiced immediately after the Russian Bolsheviks' victory in the war against the Polish–Ukrainian alliance concluded between Piłsudski and Petliura (1920). In this context, the comparison of Franko with Piłsudski, one of the greatest foes of the Bolshevik regime, sounded rather ominous: if Franko had still been alive and within arm's reach of the Bolshevik government, Kon's article would have been described as a political denunciation.

Conspicuous in the young Franko's thinking is his inattention to the state as an obligatory factor of change. A certain tendency is noticeable in the modernization of nineteenth-century Europe: the farther east you went the stronger the role of the state as an *agens movens* of industrialization. In various countries and territories where, as in the Russian Empire, the emancipation of the peasants had arrived tardily, the state acted as the main modernizing factor until the end of the century.[64] Objectively, this was supposed to drive the progressivists to conclude an alliance with the state, which was indeed the case with the Russian Westernizers or the Polish liberals in the Austrian Empire.[65] Instead, in their modernizing projects, the Russian revolutionaries, Polish socialists, and Ukrainian patriots regarded the common people as a top priority, thereby transforming these projects into a beautiful but unrealistic utopia.

It is obvious that responsibility for this does not fall on them. They were provoked by the foreign and repressive character of the state of which they were subjects. Owing to this, in their mind's eye state modernization took the shape of "Genghis Khan with a telegraph."[66] However, when and how Franko's Seméns and Myrons could take advantage of the telegraph, steamship, and railway without the help of a Bismarck or an Andrássy remained open questions. The young Franko chose to answer this question in a way that seemed to postpone its solution *ad calendas graecas* (that is, never):

> In the future, freedom in our—Ukrainian—house is impossible without concomitant freedom in all our neighboring Slavic houses, and even then it is impossible without freedom in all of Europe, in all of humanity. This means that if freedom, liberty is to be genuine, complete freedom in our country, it must be founded on international, universal freedom. [*ZT* 26:162]

In his writings during his mature years Franko overcame these utopian features of his youthful world perception and derided them. However, even at age thirty there were still no traces of this later self-irony: the young Franko was deadly serious about his beliefs.

This brief survey of Franko's world perception does not permit me to dwell on many important topics, such as his attitude to religion, his views on the mechanism of social change, history, and the like. But the most notable point is that this survey says nothing about the people (*narod*) as the focal point of Franko's worldview. This topic is the subject of the next chapters in this volume, which will reveal his attitudes to four groups, on which the Positivists of Franko's day focused keen attention: peasants, workers, women, and Jews.

Chapter 11

Franko and His Peasants

One of the most widespread identities associated with Ivan Franko is that of a peasant's son. As it happens, it was Franko who was largely responsible for creating and disseminating this image. In various circumstances and on numerous occasions, he called himself a *muzhyk* (peasant) [*ZT* 2:186], wrote or talked about himself as having been nourished by "black peasant bread and the labor of strong peasant hands" [*ZT* 31:31], declaring that he was a "peasant's son, who was always close to the lives of his brothers and relatives [garbed] in peasant caftans," and that he was ready "to devote his energies to the service of peasant interests" [*ZT* 34:373]. Ukrainian Franko specialists, both Soviet and non-Soviet, emphasized Franko's "peasant background," which satisfied both the former and the latter, affording them a convenient starting-point for constructing an appropriate narrative. For Soviet scholars, Franko was a spokesman of an oppressed class, the peasantry, which was not quite a proletariat, but close. For non-Soviet Ukrainian scholars, he was the spokesman for a nation of oppressed peasants (stateless, unhistorical, plebeian) nation, and his personal triumphs were identified with the successes of an injured nation looked down upon by everyone.[1]

In many respects, Franko's peasant self-identification was farfetched, a result of the ideological evolution that he had experienced during his youth, when he began, under Drahomanov's influence, to identify himself with the peasantry and peasant concerns. Franko's transformation has already been discussed in chapter 7. Two other issues must be raised here. First, how did this transformation affect Franko and his creativity? Second, to what extent was this peasant image of Franko's successful or convincing to peasants and intellectuals, the two groups that were to be the main consumers of the myth of "Franko, a son of the peasantry"?

The Great Transformation

Throughout the "long" nineteenth century, the peasantry of Central and Eastern Europe experienced a huge transformation that markedly changed its way of life and turned it into a politically significant force.[2] The emancipation of the peasants from their landowners may be considered the starting point of these changes. The general transformational trend was as follows: the earlier the emancipation, the more profound were the inner transformations experienced by the peasants. Galicia differed from the norm in one major way: this process took place there gradually, over an extended period of time. It began with the advent of the Habsburgs, when the peasants were freed from personal dependence, and its main features disappeared during the Revolution of 1848 with the abolition of the corvée. However, the long shadow of serf dependence lingered until the First World War, and the peasants continued to pay for their emancipation; in fact, they would have had to pay for their freedom for an even longer stretch of time if not for the collapse of the monarchy.

Official statistics and other sources of information record significant changes that had already occurred a few decades after 1848. The consequences of the abolition of serfdom may be generally described as two mutually contradictory trends: on the one hand, the impoverishment of the peasantry and the lack of all prospects for the growing numbers of emancipated peasants to earn a living from their homesteads, and on the other, the slow but steady improvement in their living standards, the spread of new, "civilized," living conditions, and changes in mass consciousness. Emphasizing only one of these two trends inevitably distorts the general picture of peasant life in Galicia, while attempts to establish equilibrium between the two are hindered by the lack of relevant research.[3] The following discussion does not pretend to be an exhaustive description of the transformation of the Galician peasantry in the post-reform decades. Rather, the goal here is to identify those extreme poles in the broad spectrum of those changes, in between which fitted the lives of the majority of Galician peasants during Franko's lifetime.

One of the stable trends dating from the mid-nineteenth century is the pauperization of the peasantry, which was most evident in the shrinking size of peasant farmsteads. Scholarly works on this subject differ in terms of concrete data. According to one assessment, between 1857 and 1896 the size of the average peasant farm shrank by 14.5 times; according to another, the pace of the contraction was less precipitous, with peasant farms shrinking by 2.4 times between 1857 and 1889.[4] No matter which of these estimates is chosen, the same conclusion will be reached: already by the 1880s the average statistical farmstead could barely feed a single family.

There was another, more reliable, criterion of peasant prosperity: the pervasiveness of starvation during the period when food supplies from the old harvest were becoming depleted, while the new harvest was still ahead. According to contemporary accounts recorded a few years before the abolition of serfdom, local peasants regarded as wealthy those who did not starve before the new harvest and had no need to purchase or borrow grain or flour.[5] Such a description of the status of a "wealthy peasant" implies that the period of starvation was a regular occurrence in the lives of most peasants. As indicated in official reports, the situation had changed little by the late 1870s: periods of starvation occurred regularly every year and affected the majority of peasant households.[6]

The result of peasant pauperization was a large number of peasants who, in order to survive, were forced to seek additional earnings. In 1869 there were 0.8 million of them;[7] by the beginning of the twentieth century this number had grown to 1.2 million.[8] There are several causes behind the mass impoverishment of the peasants, such as the disadvantageous conditions that were stipulated by the 1848 reform, which left them without access to significant sections of land (forests and pasturelands) that they had once used together with landowners; lack of funds in peasant households to pay off taxes and loans; absence of industry, which could have provided the peasants with alternative ways to earn a living; and the prevalence of alcoholism, that eternal scourge of poor people, especially in Galicia, where drunkenness was a veritable plague because of *propinacja*, the licensing of the monopoly on the production and sale of alcoholic beverages. However, two things should be kept in mind: first, while many individual peasants were brought to ruin, the amount of land they had at their disposal as a social group was constantly growing; and second, the debt level of landowners' estates was much higher—as a matter of fact, it was three times higher than that of rural inhabitants, per one hectare of land in the early twentieth century.[9] In other words, the Galician peasantry had adapted itself to life in the new, post-reform, conditions—at least better than the landowners.[10]

The causes of agrarian overpopulation were not so much economic factors as extraeconomic, one of which was a demographic boom that resulted in a sharp increase in the numbers of peasants and peasant families. This, in turn, led to the shrinking of rural farmsteads. Already by the late 1870s the lands being farmed by peasants throughout Galicia little resembled the land allotments in the age of serfdom. The small size of farmsteads also restricted the peasants' ability to obtain cattle; this meant that they did not have manure with which to fertilize their fields, and this in turn reduced the harvest yield.[11]

Another problem was the extensive character of agricultural technology. Agricultural historians maintain that the level of agrotechnical culture in mid-nineteenth-century Galicia did not differ appreciably from the one that existed, say, in the twelfth or thirteenth centuries. The impact of large land ownership on the change in the method of farming was insignificant because it too was based on practically the same extensive methods. The first changes began to make themselves felt only in the 1860s–1880s, when the iron plow began to replace the wooden plow, and some farmers began to use mineral fertilizers.[12] These innovations became widespread in the last decades before the outbreak of the First World War. During Franko's youth, it was still premature to speak of any breakthrough in farming methods in Galicia. As was mentioned in chapter 3, in the Czech lands, where the soil was worse but where more up-to-date technology and farming methods were being used, 17.4 centners of wheat per hectare were being harvested in the 1890s, as opposed to 12.2 centners per hectare in Galicia, 12.5 in Bukovyna, and 8.5 in the mountainous section of the Carpathians.[13] Or, to give another example: German colonists in Galicia farmed much more efficiently than the local peasants. Nearly all German farmers adopted technological innovations and mineral fertilizers, and they almost never starved in the interharvest period.[14]

The state of rural agrotechnology was influenced by the peasants' mentality—namely, their mistrust of change and fear of taking risks, which are inevitable during a switch to new forms of farming.[15] The introduction of innovative agricultural technology also required investments, yet peasants mostly did not have enough cash to purchase agricultural equipment and mineral fertilizers. In other words, the circumstances demanded the creation of a system of advantageous, long-term loans, but for a long time neither the government nor civic institutions even considered pursuing such a goal. Therefore, peasants were most often forced to borrow money from rural moneylenders, and they did so not so much in order to purchase new technology as to be able to survive the period in between harvests or to pay off their taxes. They were usually given short-term loans at a high interest rate, so a debtor became quickly ensnared in debt, from which it was very difficult to extricate himself without losing part, or all, of his farm.[16]

The Galician peasants became victims of the liberal era after 1848, when land was recognized as the unrestricted property of individuals with full right to exploit and overexploit. On paper, this liberal policy formally abolished many restrictions that had bound peasant farmsteads. In reality, however, it placed the peasants at the mercy of a competitive struggle marked by unequal means and chances of success. The peasants could have taken advantage of the new conditions if the government had adopted some kind of affirmative action for their benefit. But, since this was not the case, the Galician peasants became mass victims of these changes, and some were even heard to say that "it was better under serfdom" [ZT 44/1:546–48].

There were, however, some improvements. The first one was related to the mass migrations to North America that started in the 1890s. Despite the immense suffering and distress experienced by migrants heading for that continent, many succeeded in saving their earnings, which they sent back to their families in Galicia. These funds were mostly used to purchase land. An additional and noteworthy factor in the improvement of the peasants' lot was the spread of the cooperative movement in the countryside. Cooperatives offered peasants advantageous loans and promoted new technology and innovative farming methods.[17] As a result, "even the poorest [peasant] can live even if he only has a pair of strong hands and a willingness to work" [ZT 19:346–47], a peasant radical told Franko in the 1890s.

The gradual improvements in the daily life of the peasantry took on the quality of civilizational changes. The rural population was increasing mainly thanks to a drop in the mortality rate. This meant that by and large peasants began to eat better and take greater care of their personal hygiene. They continued to consume a mostly vegetarian diet, and meat appeared on the dinner table as rarely as before. But they began to eat larger quantities of food than prior to 1848, and they baked bread from higher-quality flour. Their day-to-day conditions also changed for the better: fewer farmers now kept cattle inside their homes; their houses now consisted of two rooms instead of one, and they had glass windowpanes. According to official reports, increasingly more peasants sought to make their homes pleasant for living. One particular sign of this was that peasant homes now had furniture manufactured and purchased in a city, and paintings hung on walls next to the requisite icons. Glass and faience were increasingly seen, as well as metal utensils in place of the usual wooden spoons and dishes, oil lamps, and wall clocks. Whereas in the past peasants wore their own home-spun clothing, now they were becoming accustomed to buying ready-made clothes, especially women, who now took pleasure in buying stockings and even French-made dresses. The most hopeful change was the arrival in some farmsteads of a type of furniture that had never before graced the interior of peasant homes: bookshelves, which served as proof of the peasants' newly acquired habit of reading.[18]

The fragmentary nature of historical accounts makes it impossible for researchers to determine with any certainty the scale of these changes and their dynamics. Very likely, they pertained above all to those first peasant households whose members had the most frequent dealings with the city: seasonal workers and urban servants. However, it would not be an exaggeration to say that the Galician peasants were experiencing a situation that was typical of the majority of peasants in Eastern and Central Europe: at the beginning of the twentieth century, the peasant world became "young, filled to the brim with energy, a society that was decisive in overcoming obstacles that were arresting its development."[19] An important question remained unanswered, however: who would best convert the social energy of the post-reform peasantry into political capital?

The Galician peasants had an enduring and radical tradition of peasant protests. The largest and bloodiest of them was the armed uprising of 1846, the Greater Poland Uprising, known as *mazurs'ka riznia* (the "Mazurian [Polish] massacre"). It brought European notoriety to the Galician peasants, and the memory of the uprising served as a bogeyman to frighten Galician landowners and the local administration until the very end of Habsburg rule.[20]

The Galician peasants made their political—and quite raucous—debut in the Austrian parliament in 1848.[21] When the Galician parliament convened in 1861, the administration was still not interfering in elections, which is why eighteen Polish and seventeen Ukrainian peasants were elected out of a total of 150 delegates. The majority of the speeches made by the peasant delegates concerned those feudal holdovers that allowed landowners to retain privileges at the expense of the peasantry.

Although the peasants' activities in the parliament did not represent a threat to the political monopoly held by the great landowners, at the very least they were an irritant. In opposition to the peasant slogan of "Peasants, elect peasants!" the nobility put forward its own slogan: "The peasant is the enemy." In a variety of ways—through bribery, administrative pressure, or simply violence—elections were held in such a manner that during the next two convocations (1876–1889) there was not a single peasant deputy.[22]

The political debut of the Ruthenian-Ukrainian national movement in Galicia brought the first hopeful results of cooperation between the intelligentsia and the peasantry. But this cooperation was short-lived. A period of postrevolutionary reaction ensued in the 1850s, and their paths diverged. The main question that concerned the peasants at the time was the struggle for the so-called *servituty* ("servitudes," that is, forests and pasturelands)—lands that the peasants had used jointly with the landowners until 1848, but the reform had put an end to this arrangement. The struggle for forests and pasturelands was at its most intense from the early 1850s to the late 1860s, and abated in the 1870s.[23] At the peak of peasant activity, however, the Ruthenian intelligentsia was concerned with its own affairs, with the so-called "alphabet war," a struggle against the attempts of the Polish administration in Galicia to introduce the Latin alphabet into the Ruthenian language [*ZT* 47:549–650].

"The intelligentsia's alienation from the common people, its life and interests, was complete," wrote Franko about the days of his youth. "Both the Ukrainianness of the populists and the Russianness of the Muscophiles were in equal measure purely theoretical....No one tried to explain to the people either the foundations of constitutional life or the alphabet of economic and social sciences. Until the very year of 1880 the entire mass of our people lived according to the beliefs that the emperor has supreme and sole power, that he can do everything, and everything depends on his will" [*ZT* 41:473–74].

Although Franko's assessment was correct, it was too general and harsh. In fact, among both the populists and the Russophiles were prominent individuals who were seriously engaged in the peasant question. A significant proportion of the Ruthenian intelligentsia shared the ethos of enlightenment and worked among the peasants regardless of whether it had any political weight. For example, there was a group of "people's priests" in the bosom of the Greek Catholic Church.[24] One of its leading members was Rev. Ivan Naumovych, who in the 1870s was instrumental in writing, compiling, and publishing popular works written in the simple "peasant language." Spreading enlightenment among the common people was also the goal of the Ukrainophile Prosvita Society (1868) and the Russophile Mikhail Kachkovsky Society (1873). In the 1860s, the top ranks of the Greek Catholic clergy launched a struggle against alcoholism, which it regarded as the main cause of the material and spiritual decline among the Ruthenian peasants. The publications issued by the above-mentioned societies had a print run of between 1,000 and 5,000 copies, and 45,000 copies were printed of a little book titled *Hramota tverezosty* (Charter of Sobriety), which gives an approximate idea of the possibilities of mobilizing the peasants.[25]

However, the Ruthenian intelligentsia's attitude to the peasants in the 1860s and 1870s smacked of paternalism, and there was little understanding and sympathy. Rev. Osyp Levytsky, the priest in Nahuievychi who had baptized Franko, is a typical example. Levytsky was one of the first of the so-called national awakeners and the renowned author of a Galician-Ruthenian grammar. Even though he was regarded as a "defender of the people," as soon as he was assigned to the parish in Nahuievychi he began to arouse the enmity of a significant number of his parishioners. The image of Nahuievychi that emerged from Rev. Levytsky's self-vindicating statements to the Przemyśl Consistory was that of a dissolute village rife with drunkenness, where morality was declining by the day. The villagers flocked eagerly to the Jewish tavern, where they drank away their farmsteads. One time, the priest happened to pass by the school in Nahuievychi, where he found an unmarried village girl in the throes of labor pains: she was afraid to give birth at home, where her parents would witness her dishonor.[26]

The degree of veracity of Rev. Levytsky's description of Nahuievychi is not germane to this discussion. What is important is that this is how the priest viewed both the parish that had been assigned to him, and the local peasants. There are many such examples. In August 1875, the town of Halych was the site of a people's assembly convened by the Kachkovsky Society. When Mykhailo Pavlyk introduced a proposal to publish the Bible in the Ruthenian language, the priests who belonged to this society, which had been founded in order to spread enlightenment among the people, declared: "In principle, we should not permit any popularization or even a translation of the Bible in the common people's Galician language, because a church reformation and peasant wars will ensue from them, just as in Germany in the sixteenth century."[27] One of the leaders of the other educational organization, Prosvita, declared at a general meeting that "our peasant is like a farmyard animal: if we give him knowledge systematically, he will croak."[28] Another Prosvita leader explained that the poverty of the Ruthenian people was caused by their laziness, profligacy, and drunkenness.[29]

Such pronouncements came from the mouths of patriots, who believed (and, most likely, very passionately) that "our foundation is the people:

their customs, moods, conventions, etc."[30] The discrepancy between the real and invented image of the peasant was manifested particularly vividly in belles-lettres. In the nineteenth century the peasantry became a central theme in Ruthenian-Ukrainian literature. Until then, peasants were rarely encountered in literary works, and if they were, they were portrayed as decorative, sentimental *paysans* (as in Sebastian Fabian Klonowicz's Latin poem "Roxolania," written in 1584; Seweryn Goszczyński's "Kaniv Castle"; and Mickiewicz's *Pan Tadeusz*), or as a savage rabble, *haidamaky* (brigands), or half-witted drunkards, as in Jesuit dramas and Christmas carols (*koliady*) that were prevalent in the Ruthenian lands of the Rzeczpospolita. A turning point came with the age of Romanticism, with its fascination with folklore and peasant mores as the foundation of national life. Although not all main literary romantic heroes were now peasants, even "nonrural" characters in literature worked in the countryside, where they lived among the peasants and were involved in the problems of peasant life.[31]

Ruthenian-Ukrainian literature had a vibrant romantic tradition. In the early 1860s, Anatol Vakhnianyn, a member of the younger generation of Ukrainophile populists, wrote that the

> Little Russian man…conceals his immaculate paternal heritage…in his heart and on his lips underneath the peasant thatch. There he lives, grateful to his grandfathers; there he creates songs and *dumas* [folk ballads] about them in order to transmit the immortal memory to their grandchildren. In the little peasant house he produces geniuses; produces Taras [Shevchenko] and others, produces Markiian [Shashkevych]—various sons [of the same family—Y. H]. Through them he sings to the world about his fate and misfortune, through them he transmits the future destiny of heroes and their immortal memory.[32]

In keeping with the lively nature of Romanticism, for a long period of time the peasant theme in Ukrainian literature was limited to ethnographic descriptions and, frequently, to superficial depictions of the life of the common folk. It became almost mandatory "to look at the world and at people through the eyes of a singing peasant, to affect peasant naïveté" [*ZT* 33:238]. Writers and literary critics who championed realism as the principal creative method rose up in opposition to this type of writing. They referred to the authority of Taras Shevchenko, who was the first to ridicule such romantics:

> They read the *Eneida* [Ivan Kotliarevsky's travesty of *The Aeneid* by Virgil, which is considered the first work of modern Ukrainian literature—Y. H.]

syllable by syllable and hung around the tavern, so they think they have gotten to know their peasants. Oh, no, my brothers, read the *dumy*, the songs, listen how they sing, how they talk to each other without taking off their hats, or how they recall the old times at a friendly banquet and how they cry, as though they are truly in Turkish captivity or dragging the chains of a Polish magnate....That's how it is, my beloved brothers. In order to know people you have to live with them for a while. And in order to record them, you yourself need to become a man, and not a waster of ink and paper.[33]

The Making of the Ukrainian Peasantry

In the 1870s, the apt comments that emerged from time to time in Shevchenko's writings became an extensive program for the new generation of Ukrainian writers. Franko described this generation thus: "Mostly peasant sons by birth, socialists by conviction, the young writers have set about depicting the life that they knew best—rural life. The socialist critique of the social order offered them guidelines on where to seek contrasts and conflicts in that life, which are necessary for a work of art."[34]

This description was autobiographical. In the early 1880s, when Franko was attempting to create a brief definition of the radical movement, he named "love of the peasant" as one of the top three priorities (two others were "criticism of the work of the intellectual strata around [the question of] raising the people" and "education on the basis of European positivist knowledge").[35] According to these principles, the entire surrounding world acquired a new perspective in the mirror of Franko's literature: it was clearly polarized into peasants, as positive heroes, and their enemies, as negative heroes. Franko rewrote real-life stories in such a way as to accentuate this polarization. The hero of his short story "The Priest-Humorist" is the "peasant's son" Voliansky, who dies as a result of a beating administered by his teacher, a monk. Franko based his story on several true accounts from his school days (see chapter 4). But Novoselsky, the pupil from the school in Drohobych who had died from having been beaten by his teacher, was not a peasant's son; neither were either of the two real Volianskys, where one father was a priest and the other a salt miner. On the other hand, the death of Franko's classmate who was a peasant's son had nothing to do with teachers' brutality.[36]

In like fashion, Franko rewrote another story that he had heard in the home of his fiancée, Olha Roshkevych. When he was a little boy, her brother, Franko's pupil Yaroslav Roshkevych, liked to bury himself in the snow in the wintertime. One day a village boy came to the Roshkevych house, wearing only a shirt, the way mountain children were usually dressed. Yaroslav promised the boy a *halahan* (a coin worth four kreutzers) if he buried himself in the snow, which he did. Yaroslav's younger sister Mykhailyna told her mother about this prank, and Yaroslav got a scolding from his mother. In Franko's account the story takes a tragic turn: a six-year-old peasant boy is running barefoot over the snow, following a boy from a wealthy family, who is wearing shoes. The rich boy promises the peasant boy a halahan if he catches him. The peasant boy catches a chill and dies at home, clutching the coin, a present from the rich boy, who caused the tragedy [*ZT* 1:180]. Mykhailyna Roshkevych, who had recounted the real story to Franko, was very surprised by his ending. She pointed out the boy, who was alive and now grown up, and asked Franko: "Why was it necessary to portray it so tragically"?[37]

In his early short stories Franko does not depict peasants solely as victims of landowners' arbitrariness; he also introduces a new image of the peasant as a fighter for social justice. The representation of an entire gallery of "peasant protesters" is considered a national feature and achievement of modern Ukrainian literature.[38] Franko cannot be credited with introducing this image: the Ukrainian writer Panas Myrny did this in his 1875 novel *Khiba revut' voly, iak iasla povni?* (Do the Oxen Bellow When the Mangers Are Full?), as did Ivan Nechui-Levytsky in his novel *Mykola Dzheria* (1876). With Franko, however, this image acquired a new dimension. In contrast to Nechui-Levytsky and Myrny's anarchist rebels, Franko's hero in the short story "Moia stricha z Oleksoiu" (My Encounter with Oleksa) is ready for deliberate, organized action. The story is apparently autobiographical: the narrator is a man named Myron, who has just been released from prison, where he was incarcerated on charges of promoting socialism. "Outlawed" by the authorities and society, he returns to his native village to live with his stepfather, stepmother, and two of his younger biological brothers. "The stepfather, a man at the peak of his power, was reckoned as one of the most respectable and honest farmers…with unusual tact he evaded questions about my 'transgressions' and about my 'punishment'" [*ZT* 15:49–50]. But Myron's encounter with a distant relative named Oleksa Storozh, who was known for his rebellious character and thirst for justice, turns into an emotional discussion about socialism:

> During my conversation Oleksa's face brightened, became suffused with blood—he got up from the stool and, after I finished, he grabbed his forehead

and shouted: "Do you hear? Do you hear, Kateryna? [Oleksa's wife]. Listen to what he's saying! Do you understand everything? Oh, brother, dear brother! Perhaps, God willing, one day there may be some kind of benefit from our Storozhes, at least a poppy seed's worth! May God keep you on that path now that you have stepped onto it!" He rushed to embrace and kiss me. Wiping her tears, Kateryna also came up to me, and the little Storozhes surrounded me, chirping and gazing up at me. For the first time in two long, long years, pure tears of emotion spurted into my eyes. The entire world brightened for me, I felt a new strength rising in me, as though each of those poor people, downtrodden and disdained, was pouring part of their life, their hopes, and their strength into me!...But, what of it, good people! Such moments are experienced only by the "outlaws," just as the one who has stood beneath the executioner's knife feels the beauty of life ten times more vividly! True enough, the life of an "outlaw" is sometimes sad and difficult, but in our rotten circumstances it can only be called life. Inner peace, strength, and clarity of convictions, a clean conscience and struggle, an eternal ceaseless struggle against darkness, falsehoods, and parasitism! And on top of it, there are those moments in which one stands for all of life, life in a poisoned, suffocating air of ignorance! Hey, good people, for the struggle itself, for several such moments it is worth spitting on all "shackles," it is worth becoming an "outlaw"! [*ZT* 15:57–58]

"My Encounter with Oleksa" is regarded as the first depiction in Ukrainian literature of the ideal of a socialist society.[39] However, none of the materials connected with Franko's sojourn in his native village following his release from prison include a single statement attesting to such an enthusiastic reaction on the part of the Nahuievychi peasants.[40] Franko certainly provided the young villagers with socialist literature. For example, he sent books and journals to his childhood friend Ivan Yatsuliak. But when Franko began to be persecuted for his socialist views, Yatsuliak took all the literature and burned it in a field, which later earned him a rebuke from Franko. After his 1880 imprisonment, Franko went to visit him, recounting "all sorts of things about poor people, how they are suffering all kinds of injuries. He said that one day human misery must come to an end, as Taras Shevchenko predicted in his works." But there is nothing in Yatsuliak's reminiscences that even comes close to the plot of "My Encounter with Oleksa."[41]

Another important indication of the peasants' reaction to Franko during his brief stay in Nahuievychi (1881–1883) is found in the reminiscences of the lawyer Ivan Kobyletsky, who was born in the neighboring village of Yasenytsia Silna and was a preschool child when Franko returned to the village:

> One time in the autumn I was with my father doing the fall plowing in the field. A neighbor came up to us, a peasant, and a long conversation ensued, during which this neighbor asked my father: "Will you definitely be sending your boy to school?" pointing at me. "I'm not sure yet," my father replied. "Hey, you should give it a rest with those schools," the neighbor says, "look at what happened to Franko: he withdrew from God, the Lord sent repentance upon him—he lost his mind....He's gone off his head, off his head; he should have stayed home quietly. People from Sloboda [the hamlet where Franko's family lived] are saying such things about him that your hair stands up on your head. They say that day after day he roams around the woods, like someone out of his mind, so people are afraid to go into the forest. They say that at night he walks around the house, he talks to himself, smiles, sits down at the table and writes something, then he gets up again and walks, and he does this the whole night. One time he frightened me. I'm going to Boryslav, and he is on Popelivka Mountain, coming from Boryslav. He's as bushy-haired as an old man, he had rolled his trousers up to his knees, his boots were hanging off a staff, and he's talking to himself and laughing; well, I crossed over to the other side of the road and took to my heels. And why send children to school now?"[42]

These reminiscences may be a description of Franko's technique of writing poems: he would compose them while walking, talking, or humming lines and verses to himself before sitting down and committing them to paper.[43] But the peasants, who were not privy to the "secret of poetic creativity," regarded this behavior as a sign of madness, which frightened them. In any case, they did not understand him and clearly treated him as an outsider.

Dobrivliany and Volia Yakubova as a Touchstone of Ruthenian-Ukrainian Radicalism

Franko's failed attempts to spread socialism among the peasants of Nahuievychi and Yasenytsia Silna may be written off with the well-known observation, "Never a prophet in his own land." The irony lay in the fact that for the young Franko, this was the only arena in which socialist propaganda could be disseminated among the peasants. Ukrainian socialism in Galicia spread from islet to islet, and all these islets emerged, as Mykhailo Pavlyk wrote in the early 1880s, "near the birthplace of the socialists [who sprang] from the people";[44] in other words, in those places where Galician socialists lived or visited from time to time: Lviv, where most of them lived; the Kosiv and Kolomyia areas, where Pavlyk worked among the peasants; and the Drohobych area, where Franko was born.[45] In his small fatherland, Franko enjoyed the greatest success in two neighboring villages: Dobrivliany and Volia Yakubova.

Much has been written about the history of the local socialist movement, including the memoirs of eyewitnesses who came from these locales.[46] According to these reminiscences, Franko's propagandistic activities attain gigantic dimensions: in 1882–1886 secret congresses took place in Dobrivliany, with the participation of Franko and his city colleagues; the peasants printed and distributed agitational brochures and appeals written by Franko, and posted them along roads, brought them to outlying villages, or threw them into wagons on market days. The district was saturated with news of this activity. Peasants who had attended the secret congresses told others about the meetings, repeating verbatim the speeches of urban agitators, who had declared that things could not continue as they were, while peasants who had not attended the congresses added their own remarks. The peasants said that these young people were calling upon the common folk to awaken, to stop tending to their own affairs, but to unite with everyone into a single community for the purpose of joint work.[47]

The documents from the investigation of the "peasant socialists" from Dobrivliany and Volia Yakubova (1886)[48] and the memoirs of one of these peasant socialists, Hryhorii (Hryn) Rymar,[49] as well as other related materials, are helpful in comparing these reminiscences with the eyewitness testimonies of the members of this group. Their greatest value lies in their usefulness in analyzing the limits and nature of Franko's influence on the local peasantry.

Dobrivliany and Volia Yakubova had a reputation of being "revolutionary villages" long before Franko. Volia Yakubova was the site of peasant protests in 1819 and 1843,[50] while Dobrivliany was renowned for its local community, which, after the introduction of autonomy, arrived at its own interpretation of the idea of self-rule; for six years, from 1867 to 1873, the villagers lived and meted out justice according not to Austrian laws but to their own natural laws, "justly, according to God's commandments."[51] Both of the villages were large: Dobrivliany had a population of 1,600 and

Volia Yakubova, 1,000.[52] Most farmers (in the case of Dobrivliany, nearly two-thirds of the population) were not able to feed themselves and their families from their own plot of land and had to look for extra income from weaving and carting. The peasants transported their own produce and Drohobych salt to neighboring villages and also to the markets in Drohobych, Sambir, and Stryi. Some went as far as Lviv, Transcarpathia, Bukovyna, and Hungary [ZT 44/1:502–4]. In any event, the local peasants were now spending more time in the city, they saw more of the world, and they sent their children more readily to public school—even high school—and were thus prepared to accept new ideas. In the late nineteenth–early twentieth centuries both villages, especially Dobrivliany, were constantly at the forefront of the national, political, and educational movement—so much so that, in the view of Galician radicals, they were too left-leaning.[53]

In the late 1870s and early 1880s, the village of Dobrivliany became a Mecca for young Ruthenian-Ukrainian activists, both socialists and populists. This happened thanks to the efforts of the local parish priest, Rev. Anton Chapelsky. In his youth Chapelsky belonged to a group of so-called "early ritualists," Greek Catholic reformist priests whose goal, among other things, was to spread enlightenment among the common people. This group of priests formed a kind of center located between Sambir and Drohobych. In the early 1880s, when he was already in his late seventies, Rev. Chapelsky still had the reputation of a "progressive priest." Evidence of his "progressiveness" is the fact that he was not afraid to host Franko, Pavlyk, and the young Polish socialist Ignacy Daszyński in his home (he even hid the latter two from the gendarmes).[54] His son Ivan was Franko's friend when both attended the Drohobych Gymnasium.[55] Thanks to Chapelsky, Dobrivliany became a drawing card for young Ruthenian-Ukrainian intellectuals, who flocked to the village. According to the members of the Chapelsky family, at one time Franko was thinking of marrying the daughter of the elderly priest, a story that is difficult to verify. What is certain, however, is that in the 1880s Franko was considering buying some land and settling down in Dobrivliany or Volia Yakubova, and founding a commune with his friends.[56] During those years two other fiancées of Franko's, Olha Bilynska and Yulia Schneider (Uliana Kravchenko), taught school in Dobrivliany. They were visited by Bilynska's cousin, Volodymyr Kotsovsky, who was Franko's best friend and one of the leaders of the younger generation.[57] Another figure with active contacts with Dobrivliany and Volia Yakubova was Edmund Leon Solecki, the editor of the Drohobych biweekly newspaper, *Gazeta Naddniestrzańska*.[58]

Village reading rooms were the main venue for meetings and exchanges of ideas between the intelligentsia and rural activists. It has not been established whether their emergence may be connected with Franko, and if so, to what degree. Franko began to visit Dobrivliany on a regular basis in 1878.[59] The reading room in Volia Yakubova was founded a year earlier, in 1877. However, for the first four years after its founding it existed only on paper. Its reinauguration took place on 21 August 1881. The reading room in Dobrivliany opened on 22 May 1881; in other words, both reading rooms opened their doors a few months after Franko, unable to earn a living in Lviv, moved back to Nahuievychi [ZT 48:283]. It is not clear whether "after" means "as a result of." Documents on the founding of the two reading rooms do not mention Franko among the founders. Of course, the initiators could simply have agreed—with Franko's blessing—not to include him in the official lists: the very mention of the name of this prominent socialist, who was under police surveillance, could have damaged the entire project. Documents indicate that the idea to found a reading room in Volia Yakubova was proposed by the students Pavlo Harbinsky and Danylo Lepky and its statute was written by Franko's friend from the gymnasium Mykhailo Zubrytsky. But the greatest assistance in launching the reading room was rendered by the Lvivites Ivan Kuziv and Mykhailo Strusevych.[60] The reading room in Dobrivliany was founded by three local peasants: Hryn Rymar, Hryhorii (Hryn) Berehuliak, and Ivan Stupak.[61] Franko knew them all: he and Rymar were schoolmates at the Drohobych Gymnasium, and Franko knew the other two through workers based in Boryslav and Drohobych, and Edmund Solecki.[62]

Two important details are noteworthy. The first is the young age of the activists. Ten out of the twenty members of the Dobrivliany reading room were unmarried youths, of which there were fewer—five out of forty—among the members of the reading room in Volia Yakubova. The latter, however, had a "Youth Brotherhood" that functioned jointly with the reading room but operated without a statute. The rest of the members were married. Those who can be identified were more or less Franko's peers, only a few years older or younger. The second detail (which is connected with the first) is the split that quickly formed in the two village communities over the reading rooms. The main dividing line lay between the younger and older villagers. In a report on their work, the Volia Yakubova activists wrote that "from its founding…until the present day [the reading room] has been struggling with enemies." The main opponent was the village reeve,

Panas Zubrytsky, who was also the leader of the older householders, and whose authority was threatened by the activities of the much younger reading room members. His ally was the local priest, Rev. Mykhailo Harbinsky, who initially supported the reading room movement but eventually turned against it because the reading room members had asked him to reduce his service fees, in accordance with the requirements of the Austrian legislation. The priest's son Pavlo, one of the founders of the reading room, rose to the defense of its members, for which his father banished him from the family home. At first, Pavlo lived among the peasants, and later he was hired as a railway worker. The moving spirit of the opposition was a young (twenty-one years old in 1882) peasant named Atanasii Melnyk. In 1883, his associates organized a coup in the reading room by electing Melnyk as head and expelling seven of his opponents. Melnyk accused the old administration of misusing community funds. During the 1884 election his party obtained a majority in the village council (ten out of eighteen seats), and in 1885 he missed being elected village reeve by one vote.[63]

At first, the situation in Dobrivliany was comparatively calmer. "The reading room here does not have many supporters mostly because there is no one to lead it and to interest and excite people to become members. The movement is generally very sluggish," local leaders acknowledged in response to a questionnaire about the state of the reading room movement.[64] Social harmony was maintained thanks to Rev. Chapelsky, who was recognized and loved in the village for his good nature (in particular, he did not accept any fees from poorer peasants). Chapelsky treated Hryn Rymar, the head of the local reading room, like his own son: when Rymar was a little boy, the priest had noticed his innate talents and insisted that he be sent to the gymnasium. Even after Rymar completed his military service and became a gendarme and, later, the community scribe, he maintained friendly relations with Rev. Chapelsky. In 1884, the elderly and now ailing priest resigned from his parish in favor of his son-in-law, Rev. Yosyf Yavorsky, and the situation changed for the worse. The cause of tensions in the village was the same as in Volia Yakubova: the young priest turned out to have a grasping personality. His replacement by Rev. Hrabovensky did not improve the situation, because the conflict between Rev. Yavorsky and the villagers had gone on too long. Finally, the priests of both villages denounced the harmful "socialist agitation" in the reading rooms to the bishopric in Przemyśl, which forwarded the denunciation to the starosta of Drohobych for investigation. In March 1886, Melnyk,

Rymar, and three other peasants were arrested and then brought to trial in Sambir.[65]

The struggle of the "peasant socialists" (as they were called in official documents and newspapers) for power in the community and the conflict with the priest were only the tip of the iceberg. The illegal activities of Franko and other local intellectuals remained hidden, and their names never even came up during the investigation. Today it is possible to recreate the situation only on the basis of materials available in personal archives and later reminiscences. The number and repetitive nature of statements concerning Franko's role in this story leaves no doubt that his role was very important, if not central. He met with Melnyk and his friends in the Drohobych reading room, at Ignacy Daszyński's apartment in that city, and the Kossak family home in Drohobych.[66] As mentioned earlier, Franko supposedly wrote several small brochures for the peasants and attended secret peasant meetings in Dobrivliany. At one of them he reportedly talked about the land issue and the state of affairs in North America and Switzerland.[67]

It is more than likely that a letter titled "Sprava tserkovna u Skhidnii Halychyni" (The Church Issue in Eastern Galicia), which was published in the Ukrainian language by *Praca* on the insistence of "friends from the provinces," is connected with the activities of the reading rooms in Dobrivliany and Volia Yakubova. The letter advocates the need to separate the church from the state, and its author expresses the conviction that "one day art and science will reign instead of religion."[68] It may also be assumed that Franko's authorship of a brochure titled *Conversation about Money and Treasures with an Introduction about the Founding of the Dobrivliany Reading Room* (1883) was directly influenced by his Drohobych acquaintances. The brochure was a reworking of a textbook that he wrote in 1879 for the workers of Lviv, in which he laid out, in popular form, the principles of political economy from the works of Mill, Marx, and Chernyshevsky [*ZT* 49:248].[69]

Whereas it is highly likely that there is a connection between these two publications and Franko's activities in the rural reading rooms in the Drohobych area, in the case of the popularity of Shevchenko's poem *Maria* the connection is not entirely definite. In the late 1870s, Fedir Vovk, a member of the Kyiv Hromada, got the idea to use the works of Shevchenko, "the great peasant poet," to promote socialist ideas among the Ukrainian peasantry of the Austro-Hungarian and Russian empires. Mykhailo Drahomanov objected not so much to the idea as to the method of its implementation. In his view, "the most seditious, the least censurable things in Shevchenko are not the slightest bit suitable for dissemination in their entirety among the common people, without an index and footnotes." He therefore proposed to select from the *Kobzar* "the best pages, the most simply written and clearest as to their ideas, and to insert them into short stories that will teach, in a knowledgeable way, the history of Ukraine, state and civic orders, etc."[70]

Pursuing such a principle, in 1882 Drahomanov published Shevchenko's poema as a separate booklet in Geneva, under the title *Mary, the Mother of Jesus*. He chose this particular work because it recounted the well-known Gospel story in a new, "revolutionary," version. In Shevchenko's poem, Mary gives birth to Jesus, who is fathered by a young apostle who travels from village to village, preaching the arrival of the Messiah. The poem has a simple message: Jesus Christ was of earthly origin, close to the people, just like Mary, the defender "of robbed, blind slaves" and his "peasant"-apostle.[71] In Shevchenko's poem, the life of the Holy Family resembles that of the average Ukrainian peasant family. As Drahomanov wrote in the introduction to this publication, "Therefore, Shevchenko too recounted the story of Jesus and his mother Mary according to his own belief, according to his own thoughts and desires, and created a kind of Gospel, in which he placed his ideas and desires. And Shevchenko wanted all people, not just people of one faith or tribe (nation), to be free and equal both in terms of rights and property, so that neither priests, nor lords or tsars would govern the people."[72]

Shevchenko's poem was published as a brochure in the Ukrainian language rendered in Roman letters according to Polish transcription so that it would be understandable not only to Ruthenians but also to Poles and Jews.[73] It became one of the most popular publications used by Galician socialists in their propaganda activities.[74] Franko claimed that the poem enjoyed great popularity among the peasants. "I am rereading the *Kobzar*," he wrote in a letter to Ivan Belei in late 1881. "You cannot grasp the impression that the second volume [of the *Kobzar*] made on our people here, who were guests at our place [at Franko's brother's wedding].[75] I read them some small pieces: 'Maria,' 'The Dream,' 'The Caucasus,' and others. They were simply astounded that something like this could be written in our language!" [*ZT* 48:301]. In a letter to Drahomanov written one year later (4 December 1883), Franko informed him that "Shevchenko's poem" was being distributed en masse throughout the villages of Drohobych, Stryi, and Przemyśl counties, "among peasants, reading rooms, and priests," and in Drohobych it was being read by tradesmen, and even Jews. "I talked about 'Maria' with a peasant, a thinking man and one well informed on church matters, and also a bit on secular [matters] (when I was little, he taught me to read in two weeks). He was very surprised by the introduction and complained, [saying] how could it be that one evangelist said one thing, and another—something different. 'So with this kind of method, where is the truth?'" [*ZT* 48:387].[76]

Shevchenko's poem *Maria*, the anthologies *Molot* and *Dzvin*, as well as two other brochures that were published in Geneva (*Pro khliborobstvo. Rozmova tretia. Iak de zemlia podilena i iak treba ii derzhaty* [in Ukrainian: About Farming. Third Conversation. How the Land is Divided and How It Must Be Maintained]; and *Jan Brzoska* [in Polish]) were found hidden in a barrel of sauerkraut in the home of one of the three peasants who were arrested. These publications were used as the main pieces of evidence against them. Owing to its heretical content, Shevchenko's poem sparked most of the negative publicity around the case. Witnesses testified that Atanasii Melnyk had brought the Geneva edition of *Maria* and a copy of the Talmud to the reading room, where he read from them in order to point out the contradictions in Christian dogmas and to prove the earthly, rather than divine, origin of Jesus Christ. "At every favorable opportunity [the arrestees] claimed that everything that the priests are teaching is false, they denied God's existence, they taught that man does not have a soul and expires like an animal."[77]

The trial of the "peasant socialists" from Dobrivliany and Volia Yakubova, which was held in the Sambir county courthouse, lasted from 30 May to 3 June 1886. The accused were tried as serious criminals: the trial took place behind closed doors, and the press was forbidden to report on its proceedings. The defendants were accused of inciting the public against various social strata and against property ownership, ridiculing religious rites and religion per se, and insulting the honor of the Austrian emperor. Owing to the lack of proof, the jury acquitted the defendants of illegal socialist propaganda, but found them guilty of other charges in the bill of indictment. Hryhorii Rymar and Hryhorii Berehuliak were sentenced, respectively, to two years and to eighteen months, strict regime. The other defendants received different sentences, and one was acquitted.[78]

The Sambir trial sparked a public reaction. The discussions in Galician newspapers focused mainly on who should be held responsible for the destructive propaganda. The conservative Polish newspaper *Czas* accused the Ruthenian populists and the Russophiles of deliberately waging an anarchist propaganda campaign among the peasants, and demanded that all Ruthenian reading rooms in Galicia be closed.[79] The Russophile newspaper *Novyi prolom* (The New Breakthrough) placed the blame squarely on the populists, noting that not a single Russophile publication had been uncovered during the search of the two reading rooms.[80] In its turn, *Dilo* denied the culpability of the populists, considering the real culprit to be the "nihilistic influence" of Boryslav and Drohobych on the rural district.[81] According to Franko, the main significance of the trial lay in the fact that it served as a touchstone of the Galician intelligentsia's attitude to village reading rooms. He wrote: "One may boldly state that the intelligentsia has taken a position that absolutely does not do it honor and demonstrates an extraordinarily low level of understanding of freedom, reveals to us in all its nakedness the falseness of those noisy phrases about the people's need for enlightenment on broad foundations."[82]

Nevertheless, for the Ukrainian radicals Dobrivliany and Volia Yakubova were an acid test that was supposed to determine the degree to which they were influencing the Ruthenian peasantry and whether they could count on it for social support. In this affair Drahomanov saw only the germination of a new movement—"It will not end with this, but the cause will go further"—and he demanded more vigorous action from Franko and the other "young people." He had a hard time defining this movement, which to him appeared to be the beginning of a radical *Stunde*,[83] a sectarian movement that was widespread in southern Ukraine among German colonists and, through their influence, among local Ukrainian peasants.[84] This movement, Drahomanov anticipated, would lead to the reformation of the Greek Catholic Church in Galicia, similar to the one that had taken place within the Roman Catholic Church in Germany. He welcomed such a development, seeing a great future in it for Ukraine and the Ukrainian movement.[85]

Other individuals who were closely involved in the activities of the reading rooms were more skeptical. Edmund Solecki called the literature confiscated during the search, which led to the arrest and trial of the defendants, "stupid brochures that the common folk do not understand, but which, nevertheless, expose them needlessly to criminal culpability, while the frivolous sowers of these brochures are sitting safely behind the stove."[86] Solecki's words are echoed later in the statements of the leading figure of the trial, Hryn Rymar. A few years after completing his sentence, he wrote: "They made a lot of noise in standing water, [I] was turned into some kind of creature dangerous to society and the church; and that affair was conducted so successfully that the result of that turned out very unpleasantly for me....The trial is not at fault, or very little, but the one who is most at fault for it, that should no longer be recalled today."[87]

Rymar paid dearly for this affair: in prison he contracted tuberculosis, which led to his death at the age of forty-two.[88] After his death, Rev. Mykhailo Zubrytsky wrote: "This man, with all his talents, could have been instrumental in raising the peasants in his area if someone had been found who could have indicated the path to this and worked together with him."[89] Like Rymar and Franko, Zubrytsky had studied at the Drohobych Gymnasium, and the three of them knew each other. His sorrow over Rymar's fate may also be interpreted as sadness at the fact that, as Zubrytsky clearly expected, Franko had not become such a mentor for Rymar.

The affair of the "peasant socialists" from Dobrivliany and Volia Yakubova demonstrates that Franko's ideological influence even on "progressive" peasant youth was rather limited. Of all the ideas that he and his comrades disseminated in the village reading rooms, only anticlericalism took a firm hold, and for the most part the peasants turned a deaf ear to socialist slogans.

The Original Misapprehension: Analogies and Parallels

In order to get a clearer picture of what happened in Dobrivliany and Volia Yakubova in 1882–1886, broader comparisons should be introduced. I will leave the arena of hard facts and enter the fragile plane of analogies and interpretations. The reward for taking this risk may be a better understanding of the facts, which have less weight when they are not framed in the proper context. The first analogy may be illustrated by data on the reception of Shevchenko's works among the Ukrainian peasants, which, however, pertain not to Galicia but to Russian-ruled Ukraine, as well as to a later period. Immediately after the abolition, during the Revolution of 1905, of restrictions on the publication of Ukrainian-language literature in the Russian Empire, the Ukrainian writer and political activist Borys Hrinchenko organized a survey of rural schoolteachers, who were asked to report on the extent to which the peasants understood Shevchenko. The survey answers led Hrinchenko to draw some interesting conclusions. The main one of these contradicted the belief that Shevchenko was a "people's poet," who wrote for the "common folk," who therefore understood him. According to Hrinchenko, there was no such thing as a uniform perception of Shevchenko's poetry.

Shevchenko's most popular poem was "Kateryna," the tragic story of a young girl who is seduced and then abandoned by a Russian officer. Its first four lines—"Kokhaitesia, chornobryvi / Ta ne z moskaliamy / Bo moskali—chuzhi liude, / Robliat´ lykho z vamy" (My dark-browed beauties, fall in love, / But love no Muscovite / For Moscow troopers aliens are / And court in your despite)[90] may be read as a political manifesto of Ukrainian nationalism (another interpretation is that Shevchenko meant Russian soldiers, since in Russian-ruled Ukraine, Russian soldiers and ordinary Russians alike were called *moskali*). However, there is no evidence of such a "national" interpretation on the part of the peasants, whose perceptions of Kateryna differed. Girls and young women cried over her fate; some girls in a village in the Katerynoslav region even set the beginning of the poem to music and sang the newly created song. Young unmarried men also read the poem eagerly, but laughed at Kateryna's sin. In contrast, older, "respectable," peasants were irritated by the poem and denounced it for its "immoral content": "And why did he [Shevchenko] write it? It's not a nice book."

In general, peasants found it interesting to listen to readings of Shevchenko's poetry with lyrical themes and mores similar to "Kateryna,"—such as "Naimychka" (The Hired Girl), "Prychynna" (The Bewitched Woman), "Utoplena" (The Drowned Maiden), and "Topolia" (The Poplar)—which they called "fairy tales" (*kazky*). Shevchenko's poems with historical themes were more difficult for them to understand, as some knowledge of history was required: the educated classes (including Shevchenko) had it, but not the peasants. Hrinchenko recounted a conversation with an educated young peasant girl, who loved reading the *Kobzar* and historical books, and writing poetry. However, she had great difficulty understanding Shevchenko's historical poems. She was interested not so much in the descriptions of hetmans and concrete historical events from Cossack history as in the lyrical adventures of Shevchenko's main heroines. For the most part, this peasant girl did not know when these events had occurred and gave only approximate answers to Hrinchenko's questions: "When people were still not the lords' [that is, serfs]." In the historical poem "Hamaliia" she readily identified the Dnipro River, but did not know what a harem was ("like a Turkish building"), Byzantium ("a Turkish boat"), or the island of Khortytsia, where the Cossacks lived ("It's a kind of boat on which the Cossacks sailed"). She was completely in the dark with regard to the Dardanelles. Neither this young woman nor any other peasants understood anything from the "Introduction" to Shevchenko's most popular poem, "Haidamaky" (The Haidamaks). Their attitude to the haidamaks was not uniformly positive: they were not convinced that these rebels were engaged in a good cause, since "so many people perished" because of them. Peasants often interrupted public readings of the poem with accounts of their personal affairs if they were even slightly connected to the subject. Based on his analysis of the popularity of Shevchenko's *Kobzar* in the countryside, Hrinchenko drew the following conclusion: "We truly have a great poet, but he is still unknown or poorly understood in the peasant's house."[91]

The parallel between Hrinchenko's peasants who read Shevchenko and the "peasant socialists" from Dobrivliany and Volia Yakubova is obvious: in both cases, the intelligentsia and the peasantry, reading one and the same texts, understood them differently. It is not a question of "correct" or "incorrect" interpretations. In fact, a text may have any number of interpretations; hence, there is little sense in reflecting on the "correctness" or "incorrectness" of Shevchenko's reception. The crux of the problem lies in the fact that, in reading or listening to one and the same text written in the same language, the intelligentsia and the peasantry had different interpretations of the same words and concepts (with the peasants sometimes not understanding at all).

Another illustration of this phenomenon is a memorandum that was written by the political intelligence department of Great Britain's foreign affairs ministry about the military situation in the former Russian-ruled Ukraine in May 1918. At the time, the local provinces were engulfed in peasant uprisings against the occupying German armies. The anonymous author of the memorandum thus focused particular attention on the moods of the peasantry:

> Were one to ask the average peasant in the Ukraine his nationality, [the peasant] would answer that he is Greek Orthodox; if pressed to say whether he is a Great Russian, a Pole, or a Ukrainian, he would probably reply that he is a peasant; and if one insisted on knowing what language he spoke, he would say that he talked "the local tongue." One might perhaps get him to call himself by a proper national name and say that he is "russki," but this declaration would hardly yet prejudge the question of a Ukrainian relationship; he simply does not think of nationality in the terms familiar to the *intelligentsia*.[92]

The final phrase—that the peasant does not think in the same catego-ries as the intelligentsia—may serve as a key to understanding the relation-ship between urban intellectuals and their rural adepts. This phenomenon is well known to historians of the French Revolution of the late eighteenth century and the 1917 Russian Revolution. In an article exploring the lan-guage of the revolution Orlando Figes noted:

> Language was the key to cultural integration of the peasantry. The dissemination of the Revolution's rhetoric to the countryside—the development of a national discourse of civic rights and duties—would create the new political nation dreamed of by the leaders of democracy. Here again there were clear parallels with France. For just as in France there was an enormous gulf between the French written culture of the Revolution and the patois oral culture of the peasantry, so in Russia there was an equal divide between the political language of the towns and the terms in which the peasants couched their own moral and political concepts....In Ukraine, the Baltic lands, and the Caucasus, where the urban elites were ethnically different from the native peasantry, it was literally a foreign language.[93]

This observation may also be applied to peaceful, "nonrevolutionary" times, but in that case it will not have such a dramatic character for the polit-ical destiny of one country or another, and will therefore attract less atten-tion. In 1875, the newspaper *Kievlianin* wrote: "There are cases when officials and peasants, speaking about one and the same thing, simply do not under-stand one another..., and from simple words the peasants sometimes draw rather original conclusions."[94] The history of the Ruthenian provinces of the Habsburg monarchy offers many examples of this type of misapprehension. An anonymous contributor to a Ukrainian newspaper wrote about question-ing the residents of a Galician village who were leaving church one Sunday: "So, does the reverend father speak the truth?" "He speaks beautifully." "And what did he say?" "It's not for us, simple people, to understand this."[95]

Another newspaper contributor recounted a similar incident in Bukovyna: "One time in court I ask the witness Vasyl Hamaliak, a twenty-three-year-old Orthodox man from Rohizna: 'Are you of the Orthodox faith?' 'Ha! God forbid! I still haven't had any protocol [that is, never been tried], this is the first time I'm in court!' Another time in court I am questioning the witness Maryna Solohub, a forty-year-old Orthodox woman from Raranche: 'What faith are you?' 'I am Danko's daughter,' she replied. Then I ask the thirty-two-year-old Orthodox farmer, Tanasko Yaremko: 'What faith are you?' 'The blacksmith's,' he replies."[96]

The author of the article laid the blame for this situation on Orthodox priests, who were not taking care of the people's enlightenment and opposed the founding of reading rooms in the countryside lest the peasants convert to the Uniate faith (the implication here being that some Ukrainian activists in Bukovyna were of Galician descent, that is, Greek Catholics). Data on church visitations indicate, however, that Greek Catholic peasants often could not point to any difference between their faith and the Orthodox religion. Their understanding of the differences between the two faiths boiled down to external trappings (for example, Orthodox priests wore beards, while Greek Catholic clergymen, in emulation of Roman Catholic priests, were clean-shaven). Furthermore, villagers frequently did not understand the basic symbols of the faith. A pastoral visitor writing in the late eighteenth century commented thus: "It often happened that during catechism, in answer to the question, what is the Holy Trinity, people replied: the Mother of God; and who is Christ?—the Holy Trinity. Or in another city: are you a Christian? [Yes], a Christian. And do you believe in Christ? Yes, I believe. And who is Christ? That I don't know. Does the soul die? God knows. Will the body be resurrected at God's Judgment? It will not, etc."[97]

The folklore materials collected by Franko reveal that little had changed in a hundred years. He cited examples of how peasants distorted the simplest of prayers as a result of their incomprehension. Franko concluded that "people listen to the writings because this is the Holy Book, not because they understand what is being read" [*ZT* 35:241].[98]

On the basis of these numerous statements, spread over time and space, it is possible to trace a certain tendency of "original misapprehension" that was typical of the communication between educated and uneducated classes at the very moments when they were seeking to bridge the gap between them for the sake of common (or so they thought) goals. Was Franko a victim of such misapprehension? He was—and frequently, to boot. To the above-listed examples from his youth may be added the following, later, example, related by Ivan Kobyletsky:

> At the end of 1900 or in early 1901 I succeeded in opening a Prosvita reading room in Yasenytsia Silna. I invited Franko to the opening, and Mykhailo Kobyletsky, who was still alive and who at the time was a functionary in Horodok-Yahailonsky, and both of them came. In my opinion, this arrival is very important for explaining the psychology of our peasant at the time. Franko brought with him a whole pile of books as a present for the reading

room, so the reading room in Yasenytsia had the best library in the Drohobych area. All those present listened to Franko's speech with their mouths gaping open, extremely attentively. After finishing his speech, Franko explained the books that he had brought, how to read and understand them. Those present at the meeting did not react to all this with any applause. Mykhailo Kobyletsky, excited by Franko's present, pulled out 20 crowns and donated them to the reading room. Then all those present began to shout *"slavno"* (great) and to clap so hard that the windows tinkled. Franko realized that his books were worth nothing compared to Mykhailo Kobyletsky's 20 crowns, so he too pulled 20 crowns out of his pocket and donated them to the reading room, and only then did all those present honor him with loud applause.

This incident sparked great indignation against the peasants among the sandal-nobles, and this indignation settled on me. After the ceremony to launch the reading room ended, the noblemen who had hosted the event gathered at my father's house and together with him reproached me, [saying] why had I invited Franko to such a discrediting [event]. "What does the peasant need books for," they said, "just give him a *shistka* [small coins] and he will howl like a dog." Mykhailo Kobyletsky himself told me afterwards that if he had known how things would turn out, he would have handed over the money later. Let this incident stand as proof of what kind of icebergs must be broken in order to get through to the *khlop* [bumpkin].[99]

It must be assumed that after this incident Franko began reviewing his experience of communicating with the peasants. In 1902, he wrote an introduction to a collection of poems specifically aimed at "Ruthenian peasants and burghers." His introduction contained advice on what should be published for peasants, and in what form. He emphasized that the "common folk" prefer three types of writing that they consider

"intelligent," useful literature, the kind that is fit for an upright and dignified man to take into his hands. These are "writings" (religious publications on the word of God and the truth of religion), "rights" (laws and duties governing life in the state), and "*kazety*" [gazettes] (periodicals with news about what is happening in the world). Meanwhile, the peasants have a different view of those books that narrate invented adventures or are printed in verse, like songs. People call the former "fables" and the latter "songs." The peasants very much like to read fables, especially when it is a story about some real individuals, about strange, scary, or funny adventures, and when it is narrated in a lively, not boring, manner. Our people read such stories very eagerly, and sometimes they consider them the honest truth, but at other times they see in them a representation of genuine human relations, passions, desires, and strivings. But peasants do not like to read poems. "This is for girls, for children," respectable farmers often say whenever such a book falls into their hands. Even about poems like Shevchenko's they say: "What is there for us to read here! These are songs, and we, old people, have no more use for songs." [*ZT* 33:417–18]

Franko's observations are supplemented by those of his contemporary, Prof. Franciszek Bujak, the historian of the Galician countryside, who was himself a peasant by birth. He wrote: "In books, the common folk, like…the mass of educated people, seek first and foremost a nice, interesting plot that is provided to them by historical short stories and novels; scholarly publications whose goal is to disseminate beneficial knowledge, they value less."[100]

Three of Franko's works were especially popular in village reading rooms, since they fitted the categories of literature that he himself had defined as being of particular interest to peasants: the first two were his historical novel *Zakhar Berkut* and his recasting of the medieval poem *Reineke Fuchs* titled *Lys Mykyta—Baiky* (Mykyta the Fox—Fables). The third was a work featuring a "representation of genuine human relations": *Panshchyna ta ii skasuvannia 1848 r. u Halychyni* (Serfdom and Its Abolition in 1848 in Galicia). Each of these three works has a distinct tendency: socialist in *Zakhar Berkut*, anticlerical and antinobiliary in *Lys Mykyta* [*ZT* 49:201], and socialist and anticlerical in *Panshchyna*. But nowhere does Franko pursue any of these tendencies overtly, masking each one with an interesting story that absorbs the reader.[101]

Despite Franko's self-proclaimed peasant identity, one can say with certainty that from his younger years his relations with the peasants were problematic. However, this is not to say that Franko's "peasant project" was an utter failure. Here too one must resort to an analogy. The classic example of misapprehension between the intelligentsia and the peasantry is the campaign of "going to the people," which the Russian populists launched in 1874. Donning peasant clothing, the populists settled in villages, where they worked physically and led a simple life in the somewhat naïve expectation that they would thus earn the "people's" trust and enlist them in the antiautocratic movement. According to received wisdom, the peasants stubbornly rejected the revolutionaries, and even denounced them to the police. Recent studies show that the situation was much more complex. On the one hand, the populists were aware of the gulf between the educated public and the common folk, which is why they were exceptionally circumspect in establishing contact with the peasants. On the other, the peasants not only did not denounce the populists, but occasionally even tried to shield them from the authorities. If some people did denounce the populists, they were not peasants but merchants, priests, estate managers, or landowners. In the context of the present topic, it is important to note that during investigations the peasants demonstrated selective memory: they had a good recall of the populists' slogans and speeches, but they claimed to have "forgotten" their surnames and other circumstances connected with their sojourn in the village. It is easy to understand the motives behind such behavior: the peasants were simply trying to evade criminal culpability.[102]

Peasant resistance typically took the form of cunning tricks and a game in which they pretended to be nincompoops—"weapons of the weak."[103] It must be assumed that this type of behavior was exhibited by the "peasant socialists" during the trial of 1886. First of all, the investigation did not uncover the name of Franko. Everyone understood that the mere mention of his name would only make their position all the more difficult because their activities would be branded as illegal. Second, the young peasants who were embroiled in the affair were no ignoramuses. Hryhorii Rymar had completed two years at a gymnasium, and he supplemented his education during his military service in Vienna. Less than a year before his death, Rymar filled out a questionnaire about his education, in which he wrote: "I do not have any higher education…[but] by reading books and newspapers, [I] became a bit smarter, at least [smarter] than a stupid man."[104] Finally—and most importantly—there is evidence that the peasants had some grasp of the ideas that the socialists sought to transmit to them. For example, Anna Pavlyk's article had such an impact on Atanasii Melnyk that he wanted to marry her. In his memoirs, Petro Berehuliak was able to recapitulate rather accurately the content of Franko's speech in Dobrivliany even several decades after the described events.[105]

Like their memory, peasants' understanding was selective: they accepted that part of the socialist message which resonated with their expectations and world perception, and ignored or demonstrated a poor grasp of general abstract principles. Franko liked to quote the German reformer Michael Flirscheim, who said that *Deutschland* was really

Deutsch Land (German land), that is, not the land where Germans live but the land that Germans own [*ZT* 44/2:109]. In order to help resolve the land question in Galicia, Franko proposed a similar principle: "Polish land for the Poles and Ruthenian [land] for the Ruthenians" [*ZT* 44/1:573]. This formula combined the social and national questions in an image, one that was easily grasped by the peasants, of their new fatherland where they would own land. It was precisely this combination that ensured success for the Ukrainian socialists' propaganda campaign during the revolution in Russian-ruled Ukraine, and assured them a victory in the elections to the Constituent Assembly.[106] In Austrian Galicia, it became the foundation of the activities of the Ruthenian-Ukrainian Radical Party, which was created in 1890 for the political mobilization of the local peasantry. Franko was one of the party's founders, and the main points of its economic program were based on his works and experience dating to the mid-1880s.[107]

Post Scriptum

The Galician Ruthenian-Ukrainian radical movement arose only in the late 1870s. Therefore, it is premature to judge its success among the peasantry by the mid-1880s. Similarly, it is difficult to assess peasant consciousness several decades after the abolition of serfdom launched its transformation. Detailed analysis of texts that emerged in the milieu of the so-called rural "notables" shows that by the mid-1880s social identification of this most sentient segment of the Galician peasantry predominated over national identification,[108] even though unmistakable traces of the former and the latter can be seen. One may confidently assume that peasant consciousness was characterized by ambivalence and that it showed little of what could be clearly described as a "class" or "nation."

For that reason, Franko's successes and failures with regard to the creation of a modern ("conscious") peasantry should have corresponded to this ill-defined and ambivalent state. However, even this judgment would not be entirely correct, because it is constructed on the fallacious assumption that the peasantry necessarily had to go through an evolution, the end point of which was that it become conscious of itself in the image and likeness that were created for it by the intelligentsia. In fact, even in its "unconscious" state the peasantry managed to adapt quite well to the new conditions. There were no "objective reasons" why it had to enlist in the intelligentsia's project.

The creation of modern identities was not a unilateral process from "top to bottom." Rather, one may speak of mutual attempts on the part of peasants and intellectuals to adapt to each other and to shrink—through trial and error—the great distance between them. It is worth emphasizing that Franko's "peasant project" was not aimed exclusively at the peasantry. His own contemporaries unmasked Franko: he claimed, they said, that he was writing "for the peasants," but for whom was he writing those lengthy articles that the peasants certainly did not understand?[109] His works were designated above all for the Ruthenian-Ukrainian intelligentsia, especially the generation that was emerging on the civic and political stage in the latter third of the nineteenth century. For young people, Franko served as a certain role model, which they sought to emulate through their activities and creativity. He performed this role not as the real, physical Ivan but as the imaginary Myron, a definite archetype that, on the one hand, personified the finest traits of the peasantry and, on the other, legitimized the intelligentsia's work among the common folk.[110]

What did the peasants receive in exchange? The simplest answer is: certain habits and the educated classes' way of thinking.[111] The peasants' capacity and desire to identify themselves according to terms and categories that were alien to their normal experience are viewed as extraordinarily significant in the formation of modern nations.[112] At the same time, it was important for them to be able to feel equal to the educated classes and share an identical sense of self-worth. Franko's role as a "son of the peasantry" was exceptionally important as a living symbol of success achieved by a highly creative person who had sprung from the "common people."

To illustrate the latter thesis one may use the example of language as a key factor of the peasantry's cultural integration. Franko was the unquestioned leader in the formation of the Ukrainian literary language both in Galicia and in the entire sphere of the potential Ukrainian nation. He used the peasant vernacular as its basis, but he constantly enriched it with words and forms that were germane to the "high" German, Russian, and Polish languages. The result was not always pleasing to his contemporaries, but there existed something along the lines of a general consensus (and astonishment) that one could write works of such sophisticated form and content in this peasant language.[113] This was a feeling that the Ruthenian-Ukrainian peasants in the Austro-Hungarian and Russian empires shared with the intelligentsia. Listening to this language, filled with abstract notions, people born under peasant thatches felt as though they were dressed not in peasant shirts but in "German" clothing.[114]

In that sense, Franko's activities from the time of his conversion to Ukrainianness and radicalism may be characterized by a simple metaphor: he took off his German tailcoat and placed it on the peasants' shoulders in order to bestow a sense of personal dignity on them.

Chapter 12

Franko and His Boryslav

In the literary formation of Ivan Franko no other cycle of works played as important a role as his Boryslav stories and novels.[1] It was these works, not the sentimental poems of Franko's youth or the indigestible novel *The Petriis and the Dovbushchuks*, which introduced the reading public to his real literary talent. His work on Boryslav themes was not simply a literary endeavor for Franko, but part of his broader agenda to offer the people "a developed, rich literature along with the resolved social question" [*ZT* 35:371]. Two decades later Franko commented ironically on these plans, deeming them full of the same naïveté that had characterized the Russian populists of 1873–1874, who went to the people "in order to preach the socialist gospel" [*ZT* 35:371]. But during his socialist youth Franko took these plans very seriously. He not only wrote about Boryslav, but had the burning desire to accelerate, by means of his writings, the transformation of Boryslav into a center of an organized socialist movement in Galicia.

Establishing the differences between the real Boryslav and the Boryslav that was created by Franko's imagination is a very promising research topic. Unfortunately, this subject has been largely neglected until recently. Ukrainian prerevolutionary and émigré Franko specialists tended to ignore the Boryslav cycle because it did not correspond to the prevailing national paradigm: in honoring Franko as a "national poet" and a "Ukrainian Moses," they treated his early socialist works as the "sins of youth."[2] Soviet Franko studies, however, intensively mined the Boryslav cycle in order to prove that Franko was a forerunner of communism in Ukrainian intellectual history[3] and so-called Socialist Realism—and not just in Ukrainian literature but in world literature as well.[4] These trends in Soviet Franko studies were matched by Soviet historical research on the Boryslav oil field. Writing on that subject, Soviet historiography did its best to show the existence in Galicia of a strong workers' movement that was "heading toward the Great October."[5] It also created its own "Boryslav myth," but, in contrast to Franko, Soviet historians did this with the aid of blatant falsifications and much less talent.[6]

In the last two decades, the publication of new studies on Franko and Boryslav has effected a gradual change in the situation. However, critical works that aim to correlate Franko's texts with the context in which they emerged are still all too rare.[7] The following reflections are the result of such a correlation, which allows for the possibility of tracing how Franko's ideas evolved when new facts were forcing him to make a serious revision of his original notions.

The Boryslav That Really Was

Franko was a peer of the industrial city of Boryslav. In the 1850s, several technological discoveries led to the birth of the Subcarpathian oil extraction industry. In 1852–1853 two Lviv apothecaries, Jan Zeg and Ignacy Lukasiewicz, discovered a way to distill oil, which could then be used in specially constructed lamps.[8] As early as 1853, such lamps were providing illumination for a Lviv pharmacy and the operating room of one of Lviv's hospitals, and by 1854 they began to be used for lighting railway stations. Soon oil lamps spread throughout the Austrian Empire and were a common feature even in peasant homes.[9]

The increasing use of oil as a lighting source sparked the first wave of "oil fever" in the mid-1850s and Boryslav became its center. Zeg and Lukasiewicz conducted their experiments with Boryslav oil, which served as the raw material for the distillate that they used to light railway stations. In 1856, the year Franko was born, up to 500 kg of oil per week was being extracted in Boryslav. Two years earlier, during an 1854 oil exploration expedition, the Lviv manufacturer Robert Doms discovered large deposits of a naturally occurring mineral wax called ozocerite. This discovery had no practical application until a method was discovered for producing paraffin from ozocerite in 1862. The ozocerite industry comprised the lion's share of Boryslav's industrial development until the late 1880s.[10]

The industrial boom rapidly transformed Boryslav from a small village of 759 inhabitants (1850) into a large industrial center with a population of 12,439 (1900; see table 5). Oil and ozocerite were extracted in sixteen villages of Drohobych County. The main center, however, remained Boryslav, along with the neighboring villages of Mraznytsia, Tustanovychi, Skhidnytsia, and Volianka.[11] The Austrian government tried to nationalize the local oil and ozocerite deposits, but failed: legislation at the time specified that they belonged to the owners of the land on which they had been discovered. However, lacking the necessary capital to launch industrial drilling, most local peasants were not able to take advantage of these discoveries. Superstition also played a role: many people considered it a sin to exploit land in ways other than according to its natural designation. The only ones who became rich from the industrial exploitation of Boryslav were local reeves, who notarized contracts, and a handful of peasants who were lucky enough to lease their lands for advantageous fees.[12] Most peasants lost their land as a result of fraud or violence committed by industrialists [*ZT* 26:189].

The early decades of Boryslav's industrial development could serve as an illustration of Marx's pronouncement that "the methods of primitive accumulation are anything but idyllic."[13] Boryslav drew all kinds of people who were not particular about how they earned their money, as long as they obtained a lot of it.[14] Indeed, profits promised to be high: by 1865 they stood at an average of 62 percent. Both foreign and local observers described the relations in the city as exceptional, even unique. Boryslav was the embodiment of the cult of strength and the culture of violence, and it gained notoriety as the "Galician California" or "Austrian Sicily."[15] A local Polish industrialist, who had spent a few years in California during the Gold Rush when the pistol and the fist were the only sources of law and order, said that back in California he had not seen a tenth of what he witnessed in Boryslav.[16]

Boryslav was a classic example of "predatory industry" (*Raubbaubetrieb*): extraction took place with minimum investment, and with no regard for long-term—and ecological—consequences. The shallow depths of the local deposits opened up the opportunity for people to get rich quickly: the discovery of a rich vein of mineral wax (a "motherlode") or an oilfield was the ticket to becoming incredibly wealthy in a single day or overnight.

Thus, local industrialists were in no hurry to introduce technological innovations. In 1865, a local engineer described the local oil extraction method: "Two workers, who are accompanied by an overseer, carry all the mining equipment, which consists of a horizontal brace, a hand crank, and a rope, in which there is not even an atom of iron. The next minute they place it over the well and extract oil."[17]

In the late 1890s, heavy physical labor performed by workers was much cheaper than using machines.[18] Safety measures in the workplace were extremely primitive, which led to many accidents, including fatal ones.[19] The hiring of laborers was more reminiscent of slave markets in antiquity or medieval times than a modern-day practice. Joseph Muck, a German engineer who spent several years in Boryslav, described his impressions: "Anyone walking on the streets of Boryslav at five o'clock in the morning or the evening would encounter a slave market. Many hundreds of men and women dressed in wretched rags stood or sat along the road, waiting for someone to hire them for the new shift. Then, a whole crowd of overseers, who are gesticulating, bargaining, and shouting, 'having purchased' (as it is customarily said here) a group of people, are driving them like a herd of slaves to the mines."[20]

Another eyewitness added a few of his own details to this picture: "Whoever has not seen the workers' market in Boryslav has not observed how the overseer examines the hands [and] shoulders of the one being hired for work, and then places him aside, saying, 'You will go to the mine,' does not know the most unattractive side of our California."[21]

Boryslav turned into the largest labor force market in all of Galicia. In the second half of the nineteenth century, between 5,000 and 8,000 workers toiled there, depending on the season (see table 6). Boryslav was outstripped only by the capital city of Lviv, which was home to between 20,000 and 22,000 workers. But the proportion of hired laborers relative to the entire population (nearly 50–60 percent) in Boryslav was much higher than in Lviv (nearly 10 percent). Moreover, Boryslav workers labored in industry while a significant proportion, if not the majority, of the labor force in Lviv consisted of domestic servants.

However, it would be a gross exaggeration to call the Boryslav workers an industrial proletariat. Most of them were peasants: local Ruthenians from Drohobych and the neighboring counties of Sambir, Stryi, and Turka, as well as "Mazurians," that is, Poles from Western Galicia. They were hired for seasonal work during breaks from their agricultural labors, and once it ended they went back home. These seasonal peasant workers comprised three-quarters of the workers employed in the ozocerite industry. Their numbers shrank only in the late 1890s, when the majority of the ozocerite mines were shut down (more on this later). However, even at the beginning of the twentieth century they comprised the majority of oil industry workers.[22] Only one-sixth to one-fifth of all workers had permanent employment; the majority of them were local Jews mostly from neighboring Drohobych, one of the largest Jewish shtetls in all of Galicia. The rest were trained workers from the central provinces of Austro-Hungary (Bohemia and Moravia) or Prussia, who serviced the technical equipment.[23]

During the second half of the nineteenth century and the beginning of the twentieth, Ruthenians (Ukrainians) comprised nearly half (45–50 percent) of the entire labor force. The other half was divided almost evenly between Poles and Jews (20–30 percent of the labor force).[24] There was a certain correlation between the ethnic and professional structure. Ruthenian and Mazur peasants were hired for the most taxing and most dangerous work of digging mine shafts and extracting the mineral wax from underneath the ground. They also worked above ground, raising the extracted ore to the surface. Women carried out the primary processing of the extracted hunks of mineral wax, picking the soil out of it. Jewish workers were engaged mostly, but not exclusively, in the transportation or distillation of oil and ozocerite.[25] The ethnic diversity of the labor force hindered the formation of solidarity, which "would envelop all workers and force them to act unanimously."[26] If there were a few cases of group solidarity in Boryslav, they were more along ethnic and religious lines than class ones: for example, Jewish workers banded together and succeeded in their demand for higher wages on Sundays and Christian holidays, when most Ukrainian and Polish peasants refused to work.[27]

Boryslav became equated with "Jewish economy," in contrast to the extraction of oil in other areas of Galicia (Sloboda Rungurska in Stanyslaviv County and Bibrka in Krosno County), where Polish capital was predominant. The majority of local Jewish industrialists lacked sufficient capital to maintain even one mine for an entire year, but they could hang on by merging their modest capital with individuals who had similarly patchy finances. Thus, some mines had between twenty and thirty owners.[28] In 1873, there were 779 small Jewish industrialists in Boryslav. Jews were also the owners of the largest ozocerite factory and of Gartenberg, Goldhammer, Lauterbach & Company, which founded the first large oil company in Boryslav.[29]

The Jewish community was far from homogeneous. Industrialists represented one end of the spectrum, while thousands of workers were positioned on the opposite end. Situated between these two poles were overseers, cashiers, and owners of taverns and workers' lodgings. Owing to frequent and unexpected changes of fortune, people could rise up the social ladder, and fall down it, relatively easily.[30] There was also a sizeable Jewish lumpenproletariat, the scourge of Boryslav, the so-called *kochyniry* (Pol. *kuczynierze*), who were frequently hired by local industrialists to terrorize recalcitrant workers or competitors.[31]

Demoralization was one of the key words used to describe workers' relations in Boryslav. The old patriarchal way of life had forever disappeared, and along with it those moral restrictions that had bound the former inhabitants of Galician villages or shtetls. The difficult and dangerous work, the atmosphere of violence, and the easy accessibility of cheap entertainment were creating norms of behavior in which honesty and sobriety, and even life itself, counted for little. What remained of the old order, however, was the protective mechanism of self-abasement. "A single *kreutzer*, one cigarette, or even a kind word transforms them into obedient slaves. The result of such ingratiation is terrible self-abasement that appalls everyone who is not used to it. Despite your protestations, they kiss your hand, falling on their knees; and if you walk away, for a long time you will still hear, behind your back, the words of a grateful prayer for such unheard-of generosity," wrote an Austrian social democrat about the peasant workers of Boryslav in the 1890s.[32]

It is thus no surprise that to the very end of the nineteenth century there was no organized workers' movement in Boryslav. By the early 1880s only two or three minor workers' strikes had taken place in the city, all of which ended in failure.[33] Workers' protests mostly took the form of spontaneous disorder or individual acts of vengeance targeting industrialists or overseers.

The situation began to change gradually with the penetration of large capital, which squeezed out petty industrialists. In 1882, there were forty-eight large and 340 small companies in Boryslav; by 1890 the balance had changed, respectively, to fifty-nine and thirty.[34] Small industry was severely affected by the new mining legislation of 1897, which introduced the requirement that mines be separated from each other by a minimum of sixty meters and the need for modern equipment and mandatory safety measures. The majority of small enterprises could not fulfill these conditions and were forced to shut down.[35] These closures spelled the end of the "Jewish economy" in the history of Boryslav: having lost their livelihood, small Jewish industrialists and their sizeable clientele began to leave the local industry.[36]

By the beginning of the twentieth century the oil basin was in the hands of large overseas companies. The introduction of new and expensive extraction technology—the so-called "Canadian system" of drilling—made it possible to exploit the deep and particularly rich oil deposits. The Boryslav-Drohobych oil basin became the third largest oil extraction center in the world. As a result of these changes, trained workers gradually squeezed out untrained peasants. A stratum of permanently employed workers was also formed of workers' families.[37]

The growth of industry and the formation of a cadre workers' nucleus led to the birth of an organized mass workers' movement in the late nineteenth and early twentieth centuries. Starting in the late 1890s, Polish, Ukrainian, and Jewish social democrats began flocking to the industrial region, where workers' organizations were founded, and political meetings (for example, May Day celebrations) began to take place.[38] The peak of the workers' movement was the general strike of oil workers, which took place in Boryslav in the summer of 1904; it culminated with the oilfields being set on fire. However, the new strike movement did not put an end to spontaneous acts of worker violence. Despite the concerted efforts of Galician social democracy, the Boryslav-Drohobych oil basin never became the center of an organized workers' movement.[39]

The early twentieth century was both the peak of the development and the beginning of the end of Boryslav as a large industrial center. Control of Boryslav's oil was at the center of geopolitical disputes that were deciding the fate of Galicia during and after the First World War.[40] However, intensive exploitation was gradually exhausting the oil deposits. The local oil basin still attracted large investments that were arriving here owing to inertia and unjustified expectations. Even though industrial extraction of oil continued until Soviet times (the early 1960s), Boryslav never regained its former status. By the time of Franko's death in 1916 its glory days were numbered.

The Boryslav That Should Have Been

Franko worked on his Boryslav cycle throughout his active creative life, from 1876 until 1908 (in 1908, his capacity for work was markedly curtailed when his illness took a turn for the worse). He had heard stories about Boryslav since his childhood: it was a major topic of conversation among the peasants in Nahuievychi, who gathered in the smithy owned by his blacksmith father.

> Only some murky bubbles, so to speak, of that new phenomenon reached our smithy. This week five men perished in the pits, and sometimes three were suffocated in a single pit, and this one or that one had fallen from a kibble [egg-shaped iron bucket used to hoist rocks and tools up and down shafts—Trans.] and was torn to pieces on the fenced *kishnytsia* [wattled lining made with switches—Y. H.], which served as a plank well-cover in

those extremely primitively built pits. This was the one constant theme of the stories. And the second subject was: this Boryslav resident hit the road; that one started drinking; people say that the Jews got that one drunk and pushed him into a pit. And endless, fragmented stories continued about the Jews' swindles, about the drinking sprees of the oilfield workers, about their good wages and the frittering away of earned money, about explosions of naphtha in the excavations at the fifth, tenth, twelfth *sazhen* [1 *sazhen*=7 feet—Trans.].

I listened to those stories, which were like fantastic fairy tales about faraway, enchanted countries. Boryslav with its fights, coarse jokes, and wild twists of fortune, with its strange commerce, strange method of working, and bizarre people filled my imagination. [*ZT* 21:164]

Later, when Franko was a pupil at school in Drohobych, and later still at the gymnasium, he had many opportunities to visit Boryslav, where he observed the lives of the workers. His stepfather, Hryn Havrylyk, and the father of his friend Yasko Romansky once worked there. During the cholera epidemic of 1873, Franko spent a few weeks in Boryslav, according to a folk belief that naphtha emissions offered protection against this disease.[41] One of the most vivid memories of his youth was the huge three-day fire in Boryslav, which he observed from one of the foothills near Drohobych [*Mozaika* 346].

By the time Franko embarked on his literary career, he was already very familiar with the conditions in Boryslav. But he discovered Boryslav as a literary topic only in 1876, after his ideological conversion to socialism and his abiding interest in it. The most intensive period of work on the Boryslav cycle coincided with the very years during which Franko participated directly in the Galician socialist and workers' movement (1876–1883). This concurrence was not accidental: while Galician industrialists were prospecting for oil in Boryslav, Galician socialists were looking for a working class in that town. Their critics reproached them, declaring that because of the region's economic backwardness and lack of industry there was no social question in Galicia, at least not in the form in which it existed in Western Europe. Socialism, which had emerged in the West as a reflection of Western circumstances, could never be grafted onto Galician conditions. According to Franko and other Galician socialists, Boryslav was supposed to serve as empirical evidence of the correctness of socialist theories. Furthermore, in Franko's imagination Boryslav was emerging as a prototype of Galicia's future. In the introduction to the earliest publication of his works on the Boryslav cycle (January 1877), Franko wrote:

> Truly, not a single place in all of Galicia presents a greater field of studies, not so much poetic as social. Where our region is concerned, the working class is most strongly represented in Boryslav, and the destitution, loss of energy and health, people's descent into depravity from the moral standpoint are portending most harshly and loudly that which will befall our tillers of the soil during the next two decades, when the lack of fields, bread, and money, when the consequences of all manner of shortcomings of the current social order will force them to seek factory work, sell their health and their strength for a miserable subsistence. And the fact that it is precisely now that things are most heading to this not only in Western Europe but in our parts is shown by everyday experience, shown by the increasingly larger mass of workers who are flocking from our villages to all the factory plants. [ZT 14:275]

Franko was especially attracted by the existence of a factory proletariat in the Boryslav-Drohobych oil basin, which, by its very designation, was called upon to stand at the forefront of the movement for "progress and the liberation of the working class" [ZT 44/1:52]. In describing conditions there, Franko made use of Marxist terminology [ZT 44/1:56–57] in order to show once again the applicability of "Western" socialist theories to Galician realities. When Franko was already at work on the Boryslav cycle, he began translating Marx's Das Kapital into Ukrainian—the chapter about the primitive accumulation of capital [ZT 44/1:32–33, 581–609]. The plots of Franko's first short stories from the Boryslav cycle (1877) and his first novel, Boa Constrictor (1878)—about the simultaneous impoverishment of the local peasants and the fantastic rise to riches of industrialists—are also connected to this process. The concurrence between what Franko was writing and what he was translating could hardly have been accidental.[42] Marx's Das Kapital facilitated his understanding of these processes not simply as local phenomena but as events that were part of a worldwide process, in which Boryslav was merely one of the links in the consolidation of the "capitalist method of production" on the planet.

For the embodiment of capitalism Franko used the image of a boa constrictor that crushes all feelings in individual human beings and leads them to perdition. The main hero of Franko's novel is a Jew from Drohobych named Herman Goldkremer, who is orphaned at an early age. In order to survive, he tries his hand at various jobs, finally achieving success in Boryslav. In the race for wealth, he becomes alienated from his community and his own family, and nearly dies at the hands of his demoralized son Gottlieb. At the end of the novel, Goldkremer realizes the destructive force of capitalism and destroys the painting of a boa constrictor hanging in his office.

For the young Franko, the Boryslav theme was not simply a path to literary success; it also provided a marvelous opportunity to promote the new ideas. In the summer of 1879, he wrote the outline of *Boryslav Is Laughing*. Franko described the plot in a letter that he wrote to Olha Roshkevych in September 1879: "This will be a novel on a somewhat broader scale than my earlier novels, and besides the lives of the Boryslav workers it will also present 'new people' at work—this means that it will present not the fact but, so to speak, the development of that which now exists in its germinative state....The main thing is to present what is realistically extraordinary amidst the ordinary and in the adornment of the commonplace" [*ZT* 48:205–6].

This novel, Franko's only attempt to portray the organized workers' movement in the oil basin, is the exception among his Boryslav works. As with his earlier novel, *The Petriis and the Dovbushchuks*, Franko wrote *Boryslav Is Laughing* especially for a journal, which published it in installments from January to November 1881. However, in contrast to *The Petriis and the Dovbushchuks*, this novel was supposedly based on real events: the great workers' strike that culminated in the huge fire in Boryslav. On various occasions, Franko emphasized the reality of the events described in the novel [*Mozaika* 346; *ZT* 41:460; 48:197–98].

Research on the history of the workers' movement in Boryslav casts doubt on the veracity of Franko's statements. None of the documented workers' protests could have provided the historical basis of *Boryslav Is Laughing*. It is worth mentioning that Franko himself did not provide an exact date for the "great Boryslav fire." His literary works mention at least three different years: 1868, 1871–1872, and 1873. Historical documents indicate that there were three fires in Boryslav: in 1866, 1874, and 1876, all of which were the result of carelessness, not arson. Indirect accounts have allowed researchers to determine that Franko used the fire of 1874 for his novel. But this does not change the fundamental fact that he invented the link between the strike and the fire.[43]

Why did Franko feel the need to create a literary mystification? The answer is straightforward, and he did not take any pains to conceal it: he did it in order to present what was "realistically extraordinary amidst the ordinary and in the adornment of the commonplace." The strike was that element which was "realistically extraordinary." As the history of the workers' movement in Boryslav reveals, at least twenty years would elapse before one actually took place, and Franko simply wanted to speed things up. His 1880–1881 report on the working and living conditions among the workers employed at the biggest factory in Drohobych, Gartenberg, Goldkremer, Lauterbach & Company, concludes with these impatient words: "And you, brothers, Drohobych workers, do you not sense your misfortune, do you mean to bend your necks forever and bow patiently, has your misery not convinced you that the current 'obedient calf' does not only not suckle two mothers but not even one?" [*ZT* 44/1:65].

Franko's novel may be read as a manual on how to organize a strike. The main hero is a worker named Benedio Synytsia, who is injured at a construction site in Drohobych. Unable to find a job, he heads for Boryslav, where he experiences the full array of the horrors of working in the mines. In utter desperation he gets the idea to establish a self-help fund together with his brothers in misfortune, and to call a strike once enough money has been collected. His idea quickly becomes a reality: the workers declare a strike, and the fund allows them to survive without working and to ignore pressure from the owners. The strike succeeds, but the workers' joy is ruined when one of the overseers steals the cash-box. Benedio falls into depression because his idea of an organized struggle has failed. A fellow striker named Andrus Basarab appeals to the workers to set fire to Boryslav, at which point the novel ends. According to the plot outline, the next chapters were supposed to recount the great fire in Boryslav and Basarab's trial [*ZT* 15:499].

Franko's contemporaries pointed out that there was little resemblance between the heroes of his novel and Galician workers. Volodymyr Barvinsky called Franko's workers "too wise and filled with the associative spirit of Western European workers, who understand the fate of workers and reflect on ways to help [them], which probably do not even flicker in the minds of Galician workers."[44] Omelian Ohonovsky evinced doubt that "Benedio is a believable type of Boryslav oilfield worker. Only a Belgian, not a poor Ruthenian worker, who to this day has not had the opportunity to learn about the achievements of modern sociology, could have been such a clever worker."[45] Barvinsky and Ohonovsky's skepticism is only partly justified: although there could not have been many clever workers in Boryslav, there were some intelligent ones who stood out from the several thousand laborers in that city. Franko recalled at least one (unfortunately, he does not provide his surname), with whom he participated in the socialist movement in Boryslav from the early 1880s.[46] Franko's son Taras wrote that Benedio Synytsia was an autobiographical character based on Franko himself.[47] As for other "brothers in arms," Franko's correctness may be acknowledged only if one considers his artistic plan to present the "extraordinary amidst the ordinary and in the adornment of the commonplace."

The Boryslav That Should Not Have Been

Franko's socialist convictions allowed him to see things that did not exist, or that existed only in their germinative state. His perception of socialism in the days of his youth was sincere and almost fanatical. The young Franko and his comrades dreamed of the great socialist revolution prophesied by Marx and Engels. Some saw its commencement in the assassination of Tsar Alexander II and the wave of anti-Jewish pogroms that swept the Ukrainian lands in 1881. Drahomanov and Franko's close associates, Serhii Podolynsky and Mykhailo Pavlyk, who were in Geneva at the time, were making plans to move to Romania, which was closer to the Russian border. For Pavlyk, Romania's proximity to the Ukrainian ethnographic lands that were located in both empires had a strategic importance: he hoped that the revolutionary wave would soon flow across the Russian–Austrian border.[48]

And while his fellow socialists were filled with enthusiasm, Franko ended up in dire straits. In April 1881, at the very time that he was working on *Boryslav Is Laughing*, he found himself with no means of support, and was forced to abandon Lviv and return to his village of Nahuievychi. However, because he had moved not just anywhere but to the vicinity of Boryslav, he treated his move as a new opportunity. The proximity of Boryslav and Drohobych provided him with new material for articles that were published in *Praca* [ZT 26/186–93, 44/1:52–65]. He even suggested that Pavlyk should join him and move the center of their joint activities there. As arguments in favor of his plan he offered the "nearness of Boryslav, a mass of Jews, and a significant number of progressive people among them, and even socialist elements among the young people—all this would cement our activities in Drohobych on an intertribal–federal foundation" [ZT 48:325–26].

Police reports indicate that the local authorities were alarmed by this very prospect. The starosta administration of Drohobych was ordered to conduct daily surveillance of Franko, a "well-known socialist agitator," and to pay special attention to "whether he is wandering around the area, particularly to Boryslav, in order to make contact with workers in the oil mines." The starosta administration of Drohobych sent reports on a regular basis, but they were all rather repetitive: "Franko stays constantly at his stepfather's house.…He has not been spotted in Boryslav to this time, and at home he is always writing some kind of studies.…In Nahuievychi he is always occupied with some kind of writing, he has no friends and does not go anywhere."[49]

Official reports said little about Franko's real activities. In the winter of 1882, the young gymnasium student, Ignacy Daszyński, the future leader of the Polish social democrats, moved from Stanyslaviv and settled in Drohobych with his mother and brother Felix. He became acquainted with Franko and fell under his influence. In his memoirs he wrote: "That surveillance provided us with a pretext to engage in merry pranks. The considerate police reported to the authorities, for example, 'Franko is plowing' or 'Franko is digging a well'! But the police did not know about the wonderful poems or about the amazing novels, like *At the Bottom* or *Boryslav Is Laughing*."[50]

Franko's expectations of turning Drohobych into a new center of the socialist movement were entirely justified. Local relations prodded every unbiased observer toward radicalism. "The atmosphere in Drohobych incited me to rebellion," Daszyński recalled. "The brutality of the malevolent double-dealers who were then making a career in Drohobych was so blatant and public that one did not even have to be a socialist in order to hate that criminal 'production' which was based on the natural treasures of Mother Earth and on the unlimited exploitation of the Ruthenian peasants, who were extracting mineral wax in Boryslav."[51]

By the early 1880s, Drohobych was no longer the sleepy provincial town of Franko's school days; it had become the capital of an industrial region that was expanding at a rapid pace. Drohobych, in contrast to other Galician cities, was a center of a small but dynamic socialist movement. In 1880–1881, the editors of *Praca* launched the so-called assembly campaign, a series of workers' meetings in Lviv whose aim was to bring about the creation of a Polish-Ukrainian workers' party. The people of Drohobych also responded to this call.[52] At around this time, as may be deduced from police reports, Franko's *Catechism* and Polish socialist publications were being disseminated in the city.[53] In Drohobych Franko recorded a song that was popular among poor local Jews (*kaptsany*): it contained a glimmering of what could be called "class consciousness," and at the very least showed their alienation from the world of wealthy Jews.[54] The awakening of consciousness among the workers was also confirmed by a correspondent of *Praca*.[55] In his memoirs, Daszyński recalled that in the early 1880s he became acquainted with several educated local Jewish workers in Drohobych, one of whom even wrote the occasional article for socialist newspapers in Vienna.[56]

Another Drohobych resident with whom Franko and Daszyński were in close contact was a local architect named Edmund Leon Solecki. A convinced liberal, he was an implacable critic of local relations and the personal enemy of several wealthy industrialists.[57] In the mid-1870s, a group of local intellectuals formed around Solecki, whose goal was "to normalize relations in Boryslav." Powerful antagonism arose between the members of this group and the "Semitic-Jesuitical state of king Hersh"—that is, Goldhammer, cofounder of the first local large oil company, who accused Solecki and his associates of "socialist demagogy."[58]

In the first months after his move to Nahuievychi, Franko took part in the activities of the small socialist group in Drohobych. It remains unclear whether Franko created a new group or simply joined the existing socialist milieu. However, what is definitely known is that this group had an international flavor: its members included workers, peasants, high school students, and local intellectuals of all three nationalities.[59] Similar illegal groupings also emerged in other Galician cities, primarily in Lviv but also in Dubliany, Przemyśl, and Stanyslaviv, and they all maintained links with each other.[60] However, the Drohobych group was distinguished from the others by its active links with the local peasantry, above all with young activists from Volia Yakubova and Dobrivliany. Young reading room members also maintained links with Solecki, who, after Franko's return to Lviv, founded the biweekly newspaper *Gazeta Naddniestrzańska*, which was published in Drohobych from 1884 to 1889. One of the main thrusts of the newspaper was exposing scandals in Boryslav, and it regularly published statistics on accidents that local entrepreneurs had tried to conceal. The editors were closely linked to the group of which Franko was a member. No matter how naïve the attempts of Galician socialists in the early 1880s to create a socialist Ukrainian-Polish-Jewish workers' and peasants' community may have appeared, this program seemed to work in Drohobych.

Expectations that Boryslav would be transformed into a center of the workers' movement were also panning out. On 15 May 1881, an event took place in the city, which left a noticeable trace on the development of the workers' movement in Galicia: during the weekly disbursement of wages at the French mineral wax company a conflict arose between the workers and the administration. The directors summoned the police. When the gendarmes arrived, the workers, shouting "Hurray!" rushed to disarm them. The policemen opened fire and fatally wounded one of the attackers.[61] This "baptism by fire" inaugurated a new and heroic period in the history of the Galician socialist movement.[62] For Franko, the rebellion organized by the workers employed by the French company was proof that the peaceful relations that had existed heretofore between the workers and company owners were not durable [ZT 26:190], and that one could expect a new wave of worker protests, after which Boryslav would become the center of the socialist movement.

But subsequent events took a completely different turn. Reeling from the 1881 revolt, the French company decided to "civilize" its relations with the workers. In order to prevent any reoccurrence of such events, it launched the creation of a workers' mutual aid society and set about constructing dormitories for the workers. This initiative posed a threat to local industrialists, who had neither the desire nor the funds to build housing for their workers. But the workers were becoming less tractable, and from their new employers they expected benefits similar to the ones offered by the French company.

There was a factor in the relationship between workers and entrepreneurs that made their dealings particularly dangerous: the majority of small industrialists were Jews, while most workers were Christians: Ruthenian or Mazur peasants or trained Czech workers. Social antagonisms overlaid religious and ethnic stereotypes, and with every escalation in tensions the situation became explosive.

In the summer of 1884, Boryslav was shaken by a conflict the Galician press dubbed "the Boryslav war." It is difficult to reconstruct the exact course of events because various sources offer differing interpretations. On 18 July 1884, a conflict erupted between Christian workers and two Jewish overseers in the village of Volianka, near Boryslav. The next morning an anti-Jewish pogrom took place in Volianka. A mob broke into Jewish homes, smashing doors and windows and destroying furniture, and attacked a synagogue, where they ripped up prayer books, but left the Torah untouched. According to statements given by Jewish eyewitnesses, the attackers were workers employed by the French company. Solecki and his *Gazeta Naddniestrzańska* conducted their own investigation. The fact that the Torah was not destroyed led them to conclude that the attack was a provocation carried out on the orders of local Jewish industrialists.

The situation escalated, and that afternoon an act of vengeance took place, when 3,000 Jews and workers from Jewish mines (between 5,000 and 6,000 thousand according to other sources), armed with axes and staves, attacked the dormitories of the French company. The mob dealt harshly with those Christian workers who were not able to escape, and destroyed the dormitories and other property belonging to the French company. Thirty-four workers were seriously wounded, five of whom succumbed to their injuries. This "anti-Christian" pogrom was halted by local gendarmes, who arrived late at the scene and then opened fire on the crowd. Two attackers were wounded and the rest scattered. Thirty attackers were arrested and later sentenced to various terms of imprisonment.[63]

Gazeta Naddniestrzańska denied that antisemitism was the main cause of the "Boryslav war." The newspaper claimed that Jewish capital stood on both sides of the barricades. The owners of the French company were wealthy Jewish capitalists from Paris and Vienna, while the leaders of the opposing side were local Jewish industrialists. Moreover, the newspaper's editors claimed, the Boryslav war was no spontaneous outburst of violence: it had been planned long in advance. Back in March 1884, the owners of the French company, fearing a possible attack on their property, requested that a police station be set up in Volianka, but the Drohobych County administration did not respond to their request. The Boryslav workers who had taken part in the attack on the dormitories were offered beer and hard liquor and were accompanied by their minders to Volianka. Local hooligans had also been hired, including a gypsy named Hryn Latsko, who was renowned for his physical strength. Thus, *Gazeta Naddniestrzańska* concluded that the main cause of the explosion of violence was competition between big and small capital: the Boryslav war had been provoked by local Jewish industrialists, who had thus visited retribution on their competitors.

Most of the Galician press accepted the version of events suggested by *Gazeta Naddniestrzańska*. *Praca* initially characterized the Boryslav war as a workers' protest, which assessment it was forced to recant in its very next issue: "This was a struggle between the exploited and the exploited, a struggle inspired and carried out by the bourgeoisie, a struggle in which both sides were fighting for an alien and hostile cause."[64]

The article in *Praca* about the violence in Boryslav was headlined "The First Warning for the Bourgeoisie." These events were no less a warning for

Galician socialists, showing them that internal ethnic-religious divisions among Galician workers were more powerful than class solidarity.[65] The "working class," especially the "industrial workers in Boryslav," on whom the Lviv socialists were counting so much, turned out to be an abstraction greatly removed from Galician realities. This set back the question of a proletarian revolution for many years, placing the very creation of a mass socialist movement in Galicia at risk.

At Whom Was Boryslav Laughing?

It may be assumed that this crisis also affected Franko, who was well informed about local events. A few days after the Boryslav war ended, he and a group of young friends visited Boryslav and Volianka as part of a Ruthenian youth excursion that he organized. Franko accepted *Gazeta Naddniestrzańska*'s version of events[66] and praised it for its objective description of the upheavals in Boryslav [*ZT* 44/1:401]. By the end of the year he wrote his own description of these events:

> The Jews stick to us no less than the Bernardines.[67]
> In Boryslav—dear God!
> They so stuck onto working folk
> That they mortally wounded thirty![68]

The anti-Jewish pogroms that took place in the Russian Empire in 1881 and the Boryslav war of 1884 challenged the very idea of a common international action. Once things had reached the point of mass workers' actions, it was not so much socialism and strikes that were attractive to the workers as interethnic hostility and pogroms. To what extent did these events force Franko to change his opinion of Boryslav? Nowhere did he express his views overtly, and so this question cannot be answered in full. But his views may be extrapolated hypothetically by analyzing the chronology of the Boryslav cycle. His novel *Boryslav Is Laughing* remained unfinished because the journal *Svit*, where it had been published, went into decline. Franko said that the novel's conclusion was supposed to be based on real events. At approximately this time he began planning the sequel to *Boryslav Is Laughing*, the story of the ideological maturation of his "brothers in arms" following his imprisonment, which would be called *Andrus Basarab*. These three novels—*Boa Constrictor*, *Boryslav Is Laughing*, and *Andrus Basarab*—were to form a trilogy united by common heroes and plot lines.[69]

A second edition of *Boa Constrictor* was published in 1884, a few months before the outbreak of the Boryslav war.[70] It differed little from the first edition, and the changes were principally along linguistic lines. The only major plot change was a new ending for the novel. In the second edition, Herman Goldkremer's repentance turns out to be short-lived; he soon reverts to the person he once was—a cold, heartless speculator indifferent to the sufferings and tears of his victims. Franko's archives do not contain any manuscript of the second edition or other related materials, and thus it is difficult to ascertain the reasons behind his decision to change the novel's ending. He probably altered the image of his main character in order to introduce some inner logic to the Boryslav trilogy—to justify and establish the foundations of Goldkremer's conduct in *Boryslav Is Laughing*, in which he appears as the principal enemy of the Boryslav workers.[71]

Franko never completed *Boryslav Is Laughing* and did not even begin work on *Andrus Basarab*. The last time that he mentioned his plan to sit down and write a new novel was in the spring of 1884. Already then he felt that the novel would never be written, citing lack of time because of his duties as editor of the literary journal *Zoria* [ZT 48:426]. For three years he did not publish a new work in the Boryslav cycle, returning to this theme only in 1886, after he abandoned his work with the populists. At that point he began working for Polish periodicals, where he published two short stories, "Yats Zelepuha" (1887; Yats Zelepuha was the name of the protagonist) and "Zadlia prazdnyka" (For the Sake of the Feast Day, 1891). In 1899, Franko published the last two stories of the Boryslav cycle, "Poluika" and "Vivchar" (The Shepherd). But even in these stories he used no material dated later than 1882, and he never reverted to his plan of writing a larger literary work about the organized workers' movement, which was supposed to be the main theme of *Andrus Basarab*. One may speculate that this was Franko's delayed reaction to the Boryslav war: in its aftermath, writing anything about an organized workers' strike would have struck him as far-fetched.

In 1907, Franko published the last, third, edition of *Boa Constrictor*. However, it had undergone such a major revision that it may rightly be called a new novel. The main change concerns the image of Herman Goldkremer, who was now portrayed both as an entrepreneur and an organizer of large industry, and as someone who cares about the welfare of his workers, who respond to him with gratitude and sympathy, to the point of calling him "our father and protector." Goldkremer's main enemy—and the main negative character of the novel—is a small-time industrialist and fraudster named Izyk Zahnschmerz, who tries to steal ozocerite from Herman's mine, which he then proceeds to blow up. Both business rivals are killed in the explosion, and their deaths mark the end of the saga [*ZT* 22:109–207].

Franko was working on the third edition of *Boa Constrictor* at a time when Boryslav seemed to be justifying the expectations of his socialist youth: the Boryslav-Drohobych basin had become the arena of a mass workers' movement. In the new version, however, there is not even a hint of class conflict.[72] On the contrary, it depicts class harmony between Goldkremer and his workers. According to one theory, Franko embarked on such a radical revision of *Boa Constrictor* and, accordingly, the character of Herman Goldkremer, after reading the works of Bolesław Prus.[73] However, this hypothesis ignores the most natural reason: the ideological evolution that Franko had undergone in the 1890s placed the nation, not class, at the center of his new world perception.

Franko's evolution was also reflected in other stories that are linked, directly or obliquely, to the set of Boryslav-related subjects. The hero of his short story "The Shepherd" is a young Boryslav worker who works in a mine deep underground, where he recalls the happy days he spent as a shepherd in a mountain pasture. Abandoning that life, the shepherd headed for Boryslav in the naïve hope of earning some money to buy a plot of land. There he realizes that his old life will never be restored, but the sheer memory of it warms his heart, fills him with enchantment, and enlivens the "darkness and loneliness of his new life" [*ZT* 21:69]. The story contains a message that was untypical of the young Franko: the author sings the praises of the old patriarchal life and ranks its values higher than the new transformations. He seems to be discouraging the peasants from coming to Boryslav to start their lives as workers.

The Boryslav of Others

Franko's struggles with the Boryslav material are no less interesting than its result, his Boryslav cycle of short stories and novels. In order to assess his efforts to master this subject matter, it is worthwhile comparing Franko's works with the writings of other people who wrote about Boryslav. The first thing that catches one's eye is the relatively weak presence of the Boryslav theme in the national literatures of the three ethnic groups that are so massively represented in Boryslav: Ukrainians, Poles, and Jews. This theme is almost completely missing in Russophile literature, and its absence cannot be explained if one adheres to the "national" paradigm: the Russophiles were known for their virulent antisemitism,[74] so from this standpoint Boryslav was a vein of gold that could be successfully mined. The Russophiles' neglect of the Boryslav theme was most likely determined by the antimodernist orientation of this cultural and literary current. Support for this assumption is found in the facts relating to the life of Franko, who discovered the Boryslav theme only after he abandoned the Russophile camp—at Drahomanov's urging—and became a Ukrainian writer and socialist.

Nor is the Boryslav theme present in Jewish literature. Its absence provides a stark contrast to the strong presence of Jewish authors in Galician literature and literature about Galicia.[75] As in the case of the Russophiles, here too we are very likely dealing with the phenomenon of the marginalization of the theme, inasmuch as it was not part of the political and artistic agenda of assimilated Galician Jews.[76] In this connection it is interesting to compare the images of Drohobych in Franko's Boryslav cycle with those in the works of Bruno Schulz, another famous Drohobychite. Such a comparison reveals a cardinal difference in the aesthetic conception of two famous authors who were making use of the same material to a certain degree. In the literary topography of *Boryslav Is Laughing* and *Boa Constrictor* Drohobych appears as a closed and clearly structured space, within which the drama of modernization is unfolding. The narrator positions himself unmistakably in this space: he is on the side of the exploited victims. This is not the case with Bruno Schulz: his Drohobych is more like a bewildering labyrinth, where there are no clear-cut landmarks and dividing lines. His modern world is not the world of the construction of identity, as in Franko's works, but its continuous deconstruction.[77]

In Jewish belles-lettres the Boryslav theme emerged only after the Holocaust, and then only in connection with the destruction of Jews from this area during the Second World War;[78] until very recently, no mention has been made of Boryslav's early industrial history.[79] Whether this silence was accidental is anyone's guess. One probable explanation is that such works might have been written in Yiddish and Hebrew and thus were not accessible for a larger audience that did not have command of these languages.[80] It also can be explained by the fact that the majority of Galician-born Jewish authors lived outside their "small fatherland," and their life experiences had no direct connection with Boryslav.[81]

This factor was decisive for those Polish and Ukrainian authors who wrote on the Boryslav theme. Like Franko, one way or another they were linked to Boryslav, either by virtue of having been born there or having built their careers in this area. A comparison of their biographies reveals another common thread: their engagement with the Boryslav theme had explicitly ideological underpinnings.[82] One of the main plot lines in Polish literature became the struggle between Polish and Jewish capitalists. One example is the novel *W piekle Galicyjskim* (In the Galician Hell, 1896) by Józef Rogosz (1844–1896). To some extent Rogosz was Franko's alter ego. Like Franko, he was born into a noble family, worked in a variety of Polish left-wing and liberal newspapers, and was a very productive writer. At the beginning of his literary career, Rogosz was a supporter of Polish-Ukrainian unity, but in his mature years he adopted nationalistic positions. In addition to their shared Boryslav theme, the literary paths of Rogosz and Franko converged during the so-called Kukizow trial of the members of a Polish noble family, who were accused of trying to murder a wealthy local priest in order to save themselves from financial ruin. This is where the similarities end and the essential differences begin. It suffices to compare Rogosz's novel *Grabarze* (The Gravediggers), which was based on the Kukizow trial, with Franko's novel *Osnovy suspil'stva* (The Foundations of Society): whereas Franko tries to show the depths of the fall of the aristocratic defendants, Rogosz seeks to whitewash them, accusing the lower depths of society of causing their fall.

The differences in the treatment of the Boryslav theme are even more noticeable. In his novel *In the Galician Hell*, Rogosz recounts the story of a Boryslav peasant named Fedko Jacyszyn, who has lost his land, his father, his family, and his health through the deception and fraud of Jankiel Feigl, a local Jew. After finding a job at the French company, Fedko becomes friendly with some intelligent workers, who form the nucleus of the working class, according to Rogosz. They open Fedko's eyes to the fact that their common enemy is the Jew, and the peasant-turned-worker now has a new goal in life: to avenge the wrongs that were done to him. Fedko, accompanied by several of his fellow workers, goes to Jankiel's mine to settle accounts with him. En route they encounter a mob of several thousand Jews. Fedko is seriously injured and loses an arm. Although he survives, he is forced to become a beggar.

The entire novel is written as an illustration to antisemitic propaganda. Rogosz contends that even the poorest Jews are not accustomed to earning a living through honest work: "Jehovah created the goy in order to work; the Jew, in order to live off the goy's work." Peasants do not have the slightest chance of resisting the Jews. Rogosz stereotypes not only Jews but Ruthenian-Ukrainian peasants as well: Fedko, the hero of his novel, is stubborn yet passive and apathetic. The peasants' only salvation is to unite with educated Poles. In Vienna, Fedko is given a son's welcome by a Roman Catholic priest (even though Fedko is a Greek Catholic). He finds a sympathetic ear in a Polish judge, and the narrator himself has known Fedko for twenty years. There are no socialists in the entire novel—no Polish socialists, let alone Ukrainian or Jewish ones.

The Polish–Jewish conflict is depicted even more vividly by Rogosz's contemporary, the Polish writer Artur Gruszecki (1852–1929). Gruszecki was born in Sambir, and he spent his childhood there. After completing his studies in Lviv, he lived in Warsaw, central Ukraine, Cracow, and then returned to Warsaw late in his life. Gruszecki's creative method was a blend of naturalism and Positivism, from which he borrowed the treatment of literature as an element in the propagandization of ideas. He is also credited with introducing the theme of the industrial proletariat into Polish literature. Although Gruszecki was a promising writer, he did not leave a lasting mark on literature; he wrote too much, too quickly, and too easily, paying little attention either to narrative form or psychological characterization.[83]

The hero of Gruszecki's long novel *Dla miliona* (For a Million, 1900) is a Boryslav Jew named Krausberg, who earns his million-zloty capital any way he can.[84] His main opponents are the Polish industrialists Bratkowski and Florenski and a Belgian engineer named Van Hecht (the latter was a real person, who also appears in Franko's Boryslav cycle). Krausberg vows to make their life unbearable because the goyim have no place in "Jewish" Boryslav. Other Jews in the city gladly assist him in this goal. In contrast, the Christian industrialists have no one on whom they can rely. The peasants who work in Boryslav do not like the Jews, but neither do they want to help Bratkowski because they view him as a lord, who is not one of them, a "Christian." Unable to reach an understanding with one another, both the main heroes and the peasant-workers are killed as a result of Krausberg's duplicity. Like Franko, Gruszecki presents the "extraordinary amidst the ordinary": using real historical material, he ignores certain events and fleshes out others, embellishing them with his imagination in order to sustain the designated ideological line. The story of Van Hecht is noteworthy: the author places the Belgian in the Polish camp, having forced him to fall in love with Bratkowski's daughter. However, the author overlooks the fact that Poles, along with Jews, figure among the members of the "Drohobych clique," to which Van Hecht fell victim. Furthermore, in order to maximize the distinction between righteous Poles and Jewish criminals, the author has Krausberg murdering Van Hecht with his own hands.

In Ukrainian literature, Stefan Kovaliv may be positioned alongside Franko as an author who wrote a considerable number of works on the Boryslav subject. Kovaliv was born into a peasant family in the vicinity of Drohobych, studied in a Basilian school in Drohobych, and after graduating from the Lviv Teachers' Seminary was assigned to teach in Boryslav. "Here I saw wonders that before now I had no occasion to see, I met various foreigners from America, even from Australia, I saw destitution, the demoralization of our poor, defenseless people, and could not shout: 'Why are you beating [us]? Oh, why are you beating [us]…,' so I began to write and that calmed me down," he wrote in his autobiographical letter.[85]

Kovaliv's biographers call him "Franko's pupil."[86] Aside from the fact that Kovaliv knew Franko and had great respect for him, this is a questionable assertion. There is no trace of socialist ideology in Kovaliv's writings, even though he began to write in the early 1880s, when Franko had already published his first Boryslav works, which have a clearly socialist orientation. Kovaliv "photographed" reality, he did not create it.[87]

Kovaliv wrote stories and sketches exclusively, creating nearly a hundred during his decades-long literary career. These stories may be treated as cycles, with some characters migrating from story to story: in one story they play the role of secondary characters, in another they are the main heroes. The grouping of various short stories according to common characters and common plots creates the impression of one lengthy novel about Boryslav. The main themes of Kovaliv's short stories are very similar to Franko's: the vanishing traditional world of the Galician-Ruthenian (Ukrainian) peasantry as a result of the development of industry and the general demoralization of the population. However, unlike Franko's works, Kovaliv's lack "new heroes"—workers who are aware of their human rights and are prepared to launch an organized struggle. Kovaliv visits the theme of workers' protests only once, in "Khto vynen?" (Who Is Guilty?), in which he describes a pogrom organized by Mazur workers. He writes about the Boryslav war,[88] and his treatment corresponds almost completely to what was reported in *Gazeta Naddniestrzańska*.[89]

To Kovaliv's mind, the main guilty party was Jewish industrialists, and he does not refrain from depicting these "personified sons of hell" in the blackest hues. His stories are strongly antisemitic; this antisemitism, however, is not racially based but instead is selective: it is directed against those Jews who are the representatives of the "Galilean culture with its Asiatic character"[90]— wild, completely unbridled capitalism that destroys everything, primarily Galician peasants. In another story, Kovaliv creates a totally positive image of a young Jew named Shloim Brudergreber, the beloved pupil of a Boryslav teacher (very likely modeled on Kovaliv himself). After completing school, Brudergreber continues to study conscientiously in Vienna, Paris, Hamburg, and Berlin, and becomes a Jewish industrialist of the new European type. This image was supposed to illustrate Kovaliv's thesis that the only way out of the situation was to develop education. Another hero, similar to Brudergreber, is a Boryslav peasant named Lytiuk, who has become wealthy from leasing his lands. Despite his wealth, he behaves laudably, never lording it over his fellow countrymen, with whom he feels solidarity. Kovaliv makes it clear that the reason behind Lytiuk's commendable behavior is his education: he completed several years of gymnasium studies and "clearly understood the power of steam and electricity."[91]

Comparing Franko's Boryslav cycle with other writers' works allows us to establish certain common and dissimilar features in approaches to this theme. The literary works of each of these writers may be considered part of the broader modernizing project. None of these authors come out openly against civilizational progress, which entails the development of industry. They are not gratified solely by the concrete forms that industrialization acquired in Galicia in general and Boryslav in particular. But while Rogosz, Gruszecki, and, to some extent, Kovaliv consider the main guilty party to be "uncivilized," "semi-Asiatic" Jewish capital, the young Franko points the finger at the capitalist method of production in general. As he demonstrates in the first and second editions of *Boa Constrictor*, industrialists, and not just workers, can become victims of capitalism. It was the third edition of this novel that brought Franko closer to the camp of those critics of social relations in Boryslav who saw the source of misfortune in the dominance of small, uncivilized capital. However, in contrast to Gruszecki and Rogosz, he does not attribute a purely Jewish character to this uncivilized capitalism: Franko's main (positive) hero, who dies at the hands of Jewish capital, is also a Jew.

For Rogosz and Gruszecki the main conflict resides within the struggle between "uncivilized" Jewish and "civilized" Polish industrialists, while

Franko and to some extent Kovaliv view this conflict as springing from antagonism between the exploiters and the exploited. The "discovery" of Boryslav led, among other things, to the introduction of the workers' theme in literature. Franko and Rogosz constructed a certain ideal type of socially aware worker, from whom a modern working class was being forged. In Rogosz's works this is a worker whose understanding is that his main enemy is the Jew. Of all Franko's characters, perhaps only Andrus Basarab may be placed alongside Rogosz's "conscious workers." This type of workers' consciousness is unambiguously opposed by the character of Benedio Synytsia. His remedy for the workers' misfortunes is not revenge, which will not change anything in the established order of things, but organized legal labor. In Rogosz's works the rise of workers' consciousness was supposed to lie in the transformation of workers of the Fedko Jacyszyn type into one resembling Franko's Andrus Basarab. Clearly, Franko was not satisfied with such a transformation: Basarab was a "semi-fabrication" and in order to become a conscious worker, he would have to undergo the "purification" of prison and then turn into a Synytsia.

The development of the workers' movement in Boryslav seemed to follow the scenario that was written for it by Franko: workers become aware under the influence of socialists and organize a strike (the similarity between Franko's novel and the real strike of 1904 is all the more astonishing because this workers' protest ended with a huge fire). Franko should have experienced a sense of triumph: that which in the days of his youth was the "extraordinary amidst the ordinary" had become completely "ordinary." The irony of the situation lay in the circumstance that by the time the workers of Boryslav had traversed the long road of transformation from Jacyszyns to Synytsias, Franko had lost his interest in the workers' topic.

Out of all the images of Boryslav that sprang up in Ukrainian and Polish literatures, Franko's Boryslav turned out to be the most vital and most admired. The popularity of Franko's cycle was determined to a great extent by the fact that his Boryslav was well suited as a tool of propaganda for two ideologies—socialism and nationalism—that dominated Ukrainian political life in the twentieth century. However, the success of Franko's cycle cannot be explained by ideological reasons alone. The artistic worth of these works, which demonstrate his consummate literary skills, is beyond question. Thus, a certain paradox must be noted: where Franko experienced failure as a social activist, he attained the greatest success as a writer.

Chapter 13

Franko and His Women

Renowned for his sense of humor, the Polish writer Tadeusz Boy-Żeleński claimed that every poet, before becoming a real man, must first become a ladies' man. Therefore, every poet has a bit of Rasputin in him.[1] Franko was no exception. He was full of love for women and, naturally, this love frequently served as a source of inspiration. The following dialogue between him and the first Galician Ruthenian-Ukrainian feminist, Natalia Kobrynska, is characteristic in this regard:

> Kobrynska: "Are you in love with me?"
> Franko: "Not just with you but with many others. I have to be in order to write love poems."

This dialogue was recreated in the notes of Vasyl Shchurat, who was getting ready to write his reminiscences about Franko and his women. The only part of the plan ever to materialize was a list of Franko's "sweethearts." Shchurat totted up eight names.[2] In view of other existing materials, one must conclude that this list is far from complete.

Franko studies have traditionally focused on his relations with the three women for whom he acknowledged his love in his poem "Trychi meni iavlialasia liubov..." (Thrice Love Appeared to Me...) [ZT 2:160–62]: Olha Roshkevych, Józefa Dzwonkowska, and Celina Zygmuntowska. It is noteworthy that Franko did not mention his wife, Olha Khoruzhynska, in this list; however, this did not prevent Franko specialists from including her among Franko's loves.[3] Sometimes, two young Ukrainian poets whom Franko had inducted into the world of literature would appear— Yulia Schneider and Klymentyna Popovych—as well as Natalia Kobrynska, cooperation with whom led to the emergence of the feminist movement in Galicia. However, a number of other women would remain completely in the shadows and outside the canon of Franko studies, because Franko's relationships with them offer a different image of the poet—an image that is not quite suited to glorification and beatification, yet presents him as a full-bodied and likable individual.

In fact, Franko's relations with his "main women" were subjected to strict censorship. The poet and his women had much to conceal from the public, which placed under taboo many topics and situations that inevitably arise in relations between a man and a woman. Suffice it to recall the fate of his love letters. Until the end of her life Olha Roshkevych refused to make public her correspondence with Franko. In her last will and testament, she decreed that these letters be placed inside the coffin with her—which was done.[4] There are large gaps in the extant correspondence between Franko and Yulia Schneider, whose husband, a Polish teacher by the name of Niementowski, engaged in censorship with the aid of a pair of scissors.[5] The broken engagement between Franko and Olha Bilynska led to the mutual return of letters, which were eventually burned.[6] In 1926, Franko's letters to Celina Zygmuntowska ended up in the hands of Denys Lukiianovych. After familiarizing himself with their contents, he refused to forward them to the Shevchenko Scientific Society (NTSh) in Lviv, the owner of the Franko archive, for fear that, if the Society published the letters, they would damage Franko's reputation. The matter was handed over to an informal court made up of Franko's friends. After reading the letters, the court head, Kyrylo Studynsky, who was also a Franko specialist and the then head of the NTSh, expressed the opinion that they should not be revealed to the public. The originals of the letters were destroyed, as was the diary of Vasyl Shchurat, which mentions another of Franko's romances dating from the days when they were both living in Vienna in 1892–1893.[7]

Franko's biography resembles a cupboard filled with women's skeletons. It should be opened not in order to spark a scandal, although it is to be expected that, sooner or later, someone will try to do this simply for the sake of causing a sensation. Franko's relationships with women are crucial to understanding the key moments of his biography, particularly to the assessment of the success or failure of his efforts to reform the society in which he lived in keeping with the new ideas and images that captivated him in his youth.

Franko's Experiences in Childhood and Youth

At the time when Franko was born, marriage was the instrument and condition of daily survival. Therefore, it was constructed not so much on feelings as on internal family solidarity. Every member of a family was supposed to provide assistance to others, and to obtain it in return. The intensity of this help depended not on the affection of one family member for another but on the degree of blood ties. Love—no matter whether it was platonic or physical—was not considered a basis for creating a family. More often than not, the choice was made by the families of the man and his fiancée. It was they, in fact, who were "marrying," not their children. The income of the fiancé or fiancée's family was one of the main selection criteria. But such factors as physical health, character, and the local reputation of the family were also taken into consideration—these were a kind of capital that the new member was contributing to the general family property. Young people could rebel against the choice determined by their parents, but under the threat of forfeiting property rights and their family's care. The young girl was the main object of the transaction, and therefore her opinion was given the least consideration. In the new family she had to subordinate herself not only to her husband but also to his parents and elderly relatives. This subordination was particularly manifested in such blatantly unattractive features of everyday family life as the husband's legitimized violence. Work was divided into men's and women's categories, with the stipulation that the wife was doubly burdened: she had to carry the main responsibility for raising the children, but at the same time no one released her from work in and around the home.[8]

For the most part, these were not strictly Galician attributes; they were a manifestation of the universal patriarchal model. One can speak of Galician characteristics by superimposing religious, customary, and regional differences onto this general model. From the religious standpoint, what was important was that Eastern Galicia was part of the Eastern Christian tradition. This tradition shared the negative dictates of Christianity with regard to female corporeality, but, to a certain extent, it was pushing those dictates to the extreme. It was particularly distinguished by its phobia regarding sex, which primarily repressed women's sexuality. Church canons did not regard the emotional link between a man and a woman as an essential factor in a marriage's strength and quality. The concept of romantic love, which emerged in the Catholic West in the Middle Ages, was to a significant degree alien to the Eastern Christian world.[9] It was equally alien to Orthodox Jews, who considered it a "German concept" suitable only for the world of (Catholic) "lords."[10] Galicia, however, was a territory where both the Eastern Christian and Judaic traditions had undergone certain modifications thanks to the presence of the Greek Catholic Church and progressive Jews. It is believed, in particular, that this was reflected in a more tolerant attitude to women here than in the Russian-ruled territories.[11]

The norms governing local customs generally replicated the negative religious image of the woman as temptress, who is connected to the devil and is herself the embodiment of sin.[12] The folk tradition universally demanded severer punishment for a woman's premarital and extramarital relations than for a man's. But, at the same time, it took care to ensure that this punishment would not be excessive and would not drive the woman out of society.[13] Of course, customs differed from place to place. The Hutsuls, one of the ethnic groups of the Galician Ruthenians who lived in the northeastern part of the Carpathian Mountains, were renowned as the most sexual people in the Austro-Hungarian Empire. It was believed that Hutsul women had the greatest freedom and that "free love" reigned in Hutsul relationships.[14] The role and status of a woman within the family also changed according to life and age cycles, and family circumstances: before and after marriage, the birth of the first son, from the childbearing period to the time when the woman loses this ability, during the life and after the death of her husband, and the like. In summarizing all these traits, researchers of traditional culture in the Ukrainian lands have noted two mutually contradictory trends: a tendency toward egalitarian relations among married couples is observed along with the undeniable supremacy of men.[15]

Ivan Franko arrived at a similar conclusion on the basis of collected ethnographic materials and his own observations in the locales where he spent his childhood and youth. In the early 1880s, he wrote an article with the telling title "Zhinocha nevolia v rus´kykh pisniakh narodnykh" (Female Servitude in Ruthenian Folk Songs) in which he confirmed the predominance of the traditional model of arranged marriages:

> The mother carefully oversees her daughter's love. Her old, shrewd head… arranges in advance what the life of her child is to be like, she looks for a suitor according to her own taste or at least turns her away from love for a young fellow who is not her equal. The mother looks more at whether the suitor is wealthy, whether "he has oxen and cows," while the girl looks "at a fine waistline and at black brows"—this is the origin of the conflict, old as the hills, between emotion and intellect, between excessively passionate youth and excessively cold senescence. [ZT 26:213]

As an example of "free love," Franko cites a song "about a *shandar*" (gendarme), which was recorded in the village of Lolyn, about a villager named Nykolai, who kills his wife's lover, a gendarme. His wife asks that she be buried together with her lover.[16] Franko compares the heroine of this song with the well-known literary image of Katerina Kabanova from Ostrovsky's play *Groza* (The Storm): Katerina is married by design into a wealthy merchant family. After her marriage she falls in love with a young man, and when their relationship is discovered, Katerina cannot endure the terror wrought by the young man's family and she commits suicide. The Russian literary critic Dobroliubov canonized Katerina's image, calling her a "ray of light in the dark kingdom." Franko compares Katerina favorably to Nykolai's wife not because she is "lighter" but because, in his opinion, there is no such "dark kingdom" in Galicia as in Russia [*ZT* 26:250–51].

Franko made some interesting observations on the emergence of new trends in the marriage market. "Among the Ruthenian people we clearly have few cases of true coercion, where a girl is married against her will to a man she does not love," he wrote, "although, on the other hand, such incidents are increasing in the last while, particularly among poorer people" [*ZT* 26:213]. The reason lay not so much in folk traditions as in the pressure exerted by new economic circumstances that were leading to the pauperization of the local population. Under these conditions, a marriage of convenience "is often the parents' sole deliverance from economic disaster" [*ZT* 26:214].

Everyone has emotional and sexual attachments. But in traditional systems of family life, the small islands where these feelings could be revealed were limited in number. These were premarital relations; more rarely, relations between a man and a woman within marriage; and comparatively often, relations outside marriage. The history of the relationships in the family into which Franko was born and raised offers examples of both economic necessity and emotional attachment. Of the two men and three women who were his natural parents and stepparents, not a single one observed the one-year mourning period for his or her partner, as required by the church: Franko's father, Yakiv, remarried two weeks after the death of his first wife; his mother, Maria Kulchytska, remarried six months after the death of her first husband Yakiv; after Maria's death, her second husband, Hryn Havrylyk, remarried two and a half weeks later.

The marriage of Franko's biological parents bore all the hallmarks of a marriage of convenience. It is not precisely known whether the pragmatism behind this union was leavened with an emotional bond, which may have been hampered by the great difference in their ages. On the other hand, there is no evidence to indicate that Franko's father was ever violent or coarse toward his wife. In any case, if pragmatism lay at the foundations of their marriage, then this pragmatism turned out to be successful: Franko's mother married a man with a good and gentle nature, she lived in a well-to-do family, and, above all, she quickly bore sons and heirs for her elderly husband. Even if there was no love between the parents, there was still room for amicable relations, which in principle corresponded to the perceptions of the ideal family in those days.

Within the family, emotional connections most often formed along the line of "mother–children." Yet even here economic necessity exacted a tribute. A wife's domestic duties could stand in the way of her maternal obligations; the amount of time that a woman could devote to her child during the day was comparatively limited. The care of younger children was relegated to older children (the immediate family or close relatives) and grandmothers. "Folk pedagogy" prescribed both encouragement and physical punishment of children, and again this responsibility fell mainly on the mother. In those situations where mother-and-child contact was limited in terms of time and often carried a negative emotional coloration, the emotional link could become weakened and even acquire negative features.[17]

We see some of this at work in Franko's family. He wrote that his mother died prematurely from hard work [ZT 1:74]. He could not hope for special attention from his mother, all the more so as, until the time that he was sent to school, she had given birth to four more children. When his mother went into the fields, he was either left alone in the house or cared for by his older female cousin. He spent a lot of time with his grandmother's family in Yasenytsia Silna, and once he began his studies in Drohobych, with the exception of holidays, he rarely spent time at home. As mentioned, his story about "little Myron" contains allusions to the mother's exasperation with her son's "strange" behavior [ZT 15:69–70].

All this could have cast a pall on Franko's relationship with his mother. But in his memory his mother remained a thoroughly positive image. He wrote about this when he recalled the circumstances of her death:

> This was in 1872 [in fact, 1873—Y. H.], in the afternoon of the Saturday before Pentecost. The woman in question—my mother—lay dying. Early on

Saturday I was sitting in school, and I was overwhelmed by a fit of terrible, unnatural, and wild gaiety. I laughed nonstop from 8 am to 12 noon. Arriving at the station (in Drohobych) I heard—well, I don't know what I heard. I only know that it was raining, I was hungry, I had not eaten lunch, I wasn't looking at anything, but upon hearing that mama was dying, I ran instantly to Nahuievychi. I arrived in the afternoon, wet to the bone, and found mama dying. My stepfather was sitting near the window and carding wool. I came and stood next to the bed without saying a word—I was just shaking, not a tear fell from my eyes. I don't know what my face looked like then. Early the next morning my mother died. During the night she had talked with another woman (I was sleeping), and that woman conveyed the following words to me: "Oh, my God," the dead woman had said—"my little Ivan ran all the way from Drohobych and came and stood next to me, and, oh Lord, he was looking at me so angrily for some reason! What bad thing had I ever done to him?" [*ZT* 48:96]

Franko recalled this episode in order to illustrate the specific—or so he thought—quality of his love for women: "Whenever love or some other deep emotion takes the strongest hold of me, I cause pain to the person that is dearest to me" [*ZT* 48:95]. As confirmation of this statement, he described the death of another woman "whom [he] loved and who loved [him] very, very much"—his cousin and nanny Marysia Franko:

I still remember her short stature, her merry, staccato voice, her good-natured face—I loved her very much. She also died, and she died with a very unpleasant feeling toward me. She died of cholera. A few times during the cholera outbreak, when she was still healthy, she asked me: "Ivanchyk [dim. of Ivan], come when I fall sick (at the time everyone said 'fall sick' because no one knew 'either the day or the time') so that I can at least see you before my death!" I was going around to the houses of strangers who were dying, and a messenger came from the village, [saying] that Marysia had fallen sick, and he began to plead with me to go because she wanted to see me very much—I don't know why, but I refused to go. The messenger came three times and pleaded, he almost cried—no, I didn't go and never went. The fourth time he came and said that Marysia had died. He says, "The deceased was very regretful." You know how heavy those words are! I felt the whole weight of them the next day, when I saw Marysia's pitiful, painfully contorted face on which was seemingly frozen the pain that I had caused her until her final torments before death! [*ZT* 48:96–97]

Both of these fragments are from Franko's letter to his first love, Olha Roshkevych, the priest's daughter. Until that time, the circle of women whom he truly loved had been limited to the members of his own family. According to the reminiscences of his fellow villagers, as a young boy he had taken part in games that were organized by girls from the petty gentry at the house of his grandmother Liudvika Kulchytska. These games took place in the following manner:

> A fire was burning in the fireplace, and little Franko took a dishrag made from a bundle of mountain ash twigs onto a stick, held it over the fire, and said:
>
> > Why is the Gander not roasting?
> > Because the grease is not dripping from it.
> > The grease will start dripping
> > When the girls kiss me on the face.
>
> Then all the girls had to go and kiss him because, if they didn't, he would hit them in the face with the dishrag. During such games his old grandmother Liudvika would laugh and exult with her grandson.[18]

Such games are an important stage of young villagers' socialization and acquisition of sexual experience. There is no mention anywhere that, once Franko grew up, he took part in such amusements. It would appear that he lacked this experience, but it is hardly the reason why he left his village so soon. During his studies in Drohobych and Lviv he maintained contact with his childhood friends from the village. But there was not a single girl among them, neither then nor later, in 1881–1882, when, owing to the lack of means, he had to live for a year in Nahuievychi. Until his marriage in 1886, his chosen ones were mainly from the intellectual milieu—daughters of priests, young schoolteachers and, in one case, the daughter of a nobleman. As a suitor, Franko did not exist in the local rural marriage market, especially since, it would appear, that he himself did not aspire to this.

However, a sociological explanation does not suffice here; Franko avoided dealings with girls even when he was studying in Drohobych, although the conditions in which young *gymnasium* students lived easily afforded such opportunities. High school students started up "love affairs" with servant girls, students from the girls' school, and sometimes even the wives of their teachers. We find nothing of the kind either in Franko's memoirs or in his high school friends' reminiscences about him, even though he was generally a very friendly and cheerful child. His attention was entirely absorbed by literary and scholarly interests [*ZT* 21:317–18].

It is very likely that the paucity of Franko's connections with women in his teenage years may also be explained by reasons that are well known to psychoanalysts: in Franko's case, this was the psychological trauma that he experienced in his childhood and early adolescence. Within a short space of time everyone whom he had ever loved, and who loved him very much in return, had died: his father (1865), grandmother (1871), mother (1873), and female cousin (1874). The loss of the very people who were closest to him had to have established a link between love and death in his mind. In these circumstances, the defensive reaction was the desire to avoid excessive emotional attachment, and whenever it cropped up, there was a need to provoke the person to whom Franko was close into breaking off the relationship.[19] This may explain the trait to which Franko admitted to Olha Roshkevych: to cause the most beloved person pain at the very moment that he was most overcome by feelings of love.[20]

In any case, starting from an early age Franko did not have the requisite experience of "behaving around" women. "For a long time I have not had any luck with women, and I will never have any, and it's all because of my awkwardness!" he confessed in a letter to Yulia Schneider. "When I talk to them seriously, I bore them, and when I begin joking, then, like a bear, I offend them" [*ZT* 48:375]. There was another reason behind Franko's troubles: his looks or, rather, the lack of them. The beauty ideal in those days was associated with black hair and black eyes: both "low" (folk) and "high" cultures are unanimous in this. The only essential difference for men was that among the upper classes the fashion was to wear a black beard or black sideburns, whereas peasants were clean-shaven but sported a moustache. When he was young Franko tried to grow a beard, but to his distress it wouldn't grow. His most striking feature was his bright red hair. Red-haired, with a sparse little beard, freckles, and sickly, teary eyes, the young Franko's looks corresponded feebly to the existing ideals of male beauty. And if one added his lack of attention to his manners and clothing, one can easily understand how he must have shocked young girls during their initial encounters.[21] At least in one case, a young girl rebuffed Franko's wooing mainly because of his appearance,[22] and in another case, some older married women advised Franko's fiancée not to marry him because "he was not very handsome."[23]

However, the importance of this factor in his relationships with women should not be overemphasized. After all, strong charisma and talent can often override atypical physical features. Furthermore, in the period when Franko was maturing, educated Galician society was experiencing an acute change in attitudes and tastes. Hence, the concept of love was acquiring new and unprecedented dimensions, according to which the importance of a man's wealth or physical beauty could conceivably diminish.

The same system of relationships existed among educated Galicians as among the peasants. For example, for both these groups a girl's premarital conduct—first and foremost, the preservation of her virginity—played an important role. However, in educated families this rule was even more strictly upheld. Parents demanded that their daughters unswervingly uphold the standards that Stefan Zweig, in his memoirs about the last decades of the Habsburg monarchy, described: the "strict discipline, the pitiless surveillance, the social ostracism, applied only to the army of thousands and thousands, who defended, with their bodies and their humiliated souls, an old and long since undermined moral prejudice against free and natural love."[24] A girl could not appear on the street without her mother, aunt, or assigned servant girl, and the only male who could accompany her without her mother was her fiancé. Women could not visit men or accept their visits. No part of a woman's body, except for the face, could be uncovered. The wearing of gloves and long dresses covering the body from neck to feet was obligatory even in the worst heat. The contours of a woman's body had to be carefully hidden by a corset, so that even her suitor could not guess whether his chosen one was slender or plump, or had some kind of defect. The general rule was: the "grander" the woman the less natural she was supposed to look.[25] Andrii Chaikovsky recalled that it was extremely shameful for a girl even to utter the name of a crucial element of a man's wardrobe, without which one could not appear on the street or in the company of others.[26] Yulia Schneider described the scandal that erupted in Lviv around her behavior, when, as a young girl, she went unaccompanied to the library or met with the unmarried Franko in cafés or the editorial offices of the newspaper *Dilo*. Her conversation on the street with Franko's friend Kotsovsky led to the older Ruthenian-Ukrainian patriots' demand that he marry the young Ukrainian poet at once so as not to compromise her in the eyes of the hostile Polish public.[27]

In general, Galician standards reflected the universal requirements that were applied by the educated public to women throughout late nineteenth-century Europe. The closest parallel that comes to mind is British

Victorian society. However, in certain ways the standards in Galicia were stricter: whereas in Vienna a young woman could attend the theater alone, in Lviv this was regarded as a sign of loose conduct.[28] The singular rigorism of Galician customs was also discussed by Ukrainian patriots—émigrés from the Russian Empire, who were accustomed to "easier and freer friendly relations" between a man and a woman. They believed this to be the undeniable influence of Galician Polish society, because in these questions the Poles in the Russian Empire were considerably more emancipated.[29] Galician strictness and fastidiousness applied, however, strictly to women. Social morality was considerably more tolerant toward men, whose premarital and extramarital relationships were considered routine and straightforward, like one's "daily bread."[30]

New habits and a new morality were slowly but surely carving a path into Galician society. One of the first breakthroughs was the enactment of the liberal Austrian family code of 1868, which expanded the list of reasons permitting divorce. The code listed, although with certain reservations, the following reason: the couple's "invincible mutual antipathy." This meant, among other things, that the law recognized as standard a marriage founded on an emotional connection. The Roman and Greek Catholic churches protested against this liberal legislation and threatened violators of canon law with denial of the Holy Sacraments. However, the law established an important precedent that inexorably weakened the inviolability of the institution of marriage.[31]

Other changes were precipitated by the spread of consumerism. Railways brought in manufactured goods from the western industrial provinces of the Austro-Hungarian Empire, which sparked a vogue for new clothing, adornments, and cuisine. These changes are best documented in the families of Greek Catholic priests. The wives and daughters of priests exchanged their simple, homemade clothing for fashionable gowns from Vienna and Paris. They did this not just out of their own volition: the student sons of priests, who were living in the cities, looked askance, and even with derision, at their "rustic" sisters: disgruntled by their wardrobes, manners, and education, they pointed to young urban ladies as an example. The result was, among other things, the desire of educated young men to marry city girls. Under these conditions, a girl's wealth and her strict observance of morality alone were not enough to make her an attractive candidate for marriage. She also had to be fluent in foreign languages, know how to draw, to play a musical instrument, and she had to read widely and be conversant with fashionable literature. This necessitated the expansion of women's education, the possibilities for which were extremely limited in Galicia. On the other hand, it was not only a lack of education that could be a stumbling block, but also too much education: it was believed that an educated woman could not be a good mother and housewife. In the 1870s–1880s, the derogatory word "emancipatrix" spread throughout Galicia's high society: it was used to describe girls whose heads had been turned by various "new theories."[32]

Marital politics were marked by the penetration into Galicia of a new literature and modern ideologies. In young girls the reading of French and other Western novels inflamed the desire for romantic love. The passion for the works of Madame de Staël, George Sand, and Charlotte Brontë, and familiarity with the works of the Polish Positivists and Russian populists led to an understanding of the degraded status of women in society and to the desire to correct this injustice. The spread of nationalism also entered into the conflict with the standards of the day. This conflict may be shown in the example of interethnic marriages. Such marriages were rare in the countryside but widespread in cities, particularly in the capital city, Lviv, where the ratio hovered between one-third and two-thirds (see table 8). The development of the Ruthenian-Ukrainian movement was forcing people to ask themselves: can a Ruthenian patriot marry a Polish woman? It was firmly believed that a Polish wife would assimilate not only her children but her husband, who would thus be lost to the "national cause." Thus, for example, the members of the community of Ruthenian students in the Drohobych gymnasium in the 1860s swore an oath, "for the good of Rus," to marry only Ruthenian girls.[33] It is symptomatic that in a poem published by Volodymyr Barvinsky in the students' journal *Druh* in 1876, he asks people not to laugh at him for "having fallen in love with a *Liashka* [Polish girl]."[34]

Ruthenian-Polish antagonism was acquiring the dimension of a conflict between tradition and emancipation. The daughters of Ruthenian priestly and urban families, who were emulating the cultural examples of more emancipated Polish girls, were called "Wandas" (derived from the common Polish female name). They were the subject of numerous caricatures in Ruthenian newspapers and journals. It was believed that "Wandas"—in contrast to well-behaved Ruthenian "Olhas," who adhered to the old customs—did not want to marry Greek Catholic priests, and they spent most of their time playing the piano, reading "romance novels," and shirking domestic work.[35]

The Ruthenian family was supposed to become a bastion of the Ruthenian nation. Young girls, as future mothers and child-rearers, were called upon to carry out a particularly important role: to be the rock "on which the temple of future glory is being founded," with "the awakening of the spirit in women's hearts [as] the first safeguard of the future."[36] One of the chief tasks of the Ruthenian-Ukrainian movement was to tear Polish literature out of the hands of "Ruthenian beauties" and replace it with the national belles-lettres. The ideology and practice of nationalism did not so much eradicate "women's servitude" as change its form. To the traditional roles of "mother and wife" was added the role of "patriot," although the latter did not have independent significance: a woman was supposed to carry it out to the degree that she was the wife of a patriot and the mother of children raised in a patriotic spirit. Ultimately, those men who supported women's participation in the national movement did this on their own terms and advanced their own goals.[37] Under these conditions, many of the most active women could not remain in the national movement and went over to the more radical socialist movement, which offered greater freedom and equality. This was the fate of those Ukrainian girls who studied abroad: according to Drahomanov, there was not even a whiff of Ukrainianness among the members of the Russian female student community in Zurich, even though 75 percent of the students hailed from Ukrainian gubernias.[38] In the case of Galicia, a similar fate befell the first Ruthenian-Ukrainian feminist, Natalia Kobrynska: raised in a patriotic priest's family and introduced at an early age to civic activity, in time she became convinced that the national struggle was an "unwarranted, unnecessary waste of time." It was only the rumors about the 1878 trial of the young Franko and other Ruthenian-Ukrainian socialists and, later, her readings of Franko's works that helped her overcome "narrow nationalism" and form her convictions about the need to base her feminist activities on national soil.[39]

The Concept of Socialist Marriage:

Free Love and the Idea of Community (Obshchyna)

Franko and Pavlyk's debut on the political stage took place during the socialists' trial of 1878, when both of them were convicted of participating in an allegedly illegal society. The main scandal during the trial was Pavlyk's speech on the topic of "free love," in which he declared that sexual relations between people must be like those "of the birds."[40] Franko and Pavlyk led a frontal attack on the current idea and practice of marriage, particularly the secondary and humiliating role played by women in the "cemetery that is called the family"(a phrase coined by Pavlyk).[41] According to their view, marriage was supposed to be a union of equals, reinforced by feelings of love. Pavlyk cited the example of relations among young villagers who, in his opinion, were much nobler and sincerer compared to the hypocritical relations that existed between "young ladies" and their "lovers": "Rural love is often manifested more tenderly, although truth to tell, also more courageously than people of the higher estates can imagine for themselves.... Everything points to the fact that the peasant would not raise such a hue and cry against making women equal to men, as is done by the majority of men from the higher strata."[42]

The attack on relations between men and women was led by Pavlyk, who was handed down a prison sentence for his short story "Rebenshchukova Tetiana" (1878) about "women's servitude."[43] Franko was overshadowed by his more passionate friend. His short story "Lesyshyna cheliad'" (Les's Family), which was written earlier, in 1876, also features a discourse on free love [*ZT* 14:254–64]. However, its more restrained tone softened public reaction.[44] Franko advised Pavlyk not to put the women's question in first place; primarily, he believed this was a tactical error, since it was raising a storm of indignation among many citizens, including "our people." His second argument was that, in strategic terms, its importance gives way to other economic and cultural questions: "Believe me, you will turn women, particularly young ones, into socialists faster with the aid of physiology and economic theory than with the aid of no matter what kind of everyday vexatious images from the life of women. Vogt, Darwin, Lange, et al., will remake our women faster than George Sand and Ostrovsky" [*ZT* 48:215].

In the works of the young Franko the topic of "free love" emerges clearly and overtly only once—in his poem "Tovarysham z tiurmy" (To Comrades from Prison) in which he lists the slogans of the Galician radicals, which occupy last place in this poetic work:

Our goal is human happiness and freedom,
Powerful wisdom without the basics of faith
And great, universal brotherhood,
Free work and free love! [*ZT* 3:336]

Franko is much more eloquent in his private letters to his chosen beloveds. There he states explicitly that for him, sexual love alone (*geschlechtliche Liebe*) cannot serve as the basis for marriage. Out of all the forms of love, this is the lowest: from the standpoint of this type of love, a woman is nothing but a piece of "meat," and can one love meat? [*ZT* 48:377]. To sexual love Franko opposed "love for all people, especially for all those who are unfortunate, harmed, and humiliated," a feeling that is "much loftier and more sacred" [*ZT* 48:377]. He did not need "a female concubine" but a companion-in-arms and partner with whom he could work and study together [*ZT* 48:396]. It is no surprise, then, that after his conversion to the cause of radicalism Franko writes his fiancée a long letter containing his *profession de foi* in order to determine whether she agrees with his views if only in the most general ways—otherwise, their marriage simply makes no sense [*ZT* 48:108–19].

The question arises: for an individual possessing these kinds of views, how realistic for him was it to find a wife in the society of that time? Where Pavlyk is concerned, the answer is simple: he remained a lifelong bachelor. Franko's case, meanwhile, is much more complex and interesting—a constant conflict between theory and practice.

The source of Franko and Pavlyk's theoretical views on marriage was the literature Drahomanov recommended to them—above all, Chernyshevsky's novel *What Is To Be Done?*, which, according to their own admissions, exerted a great influence on them and their milieu. The story of a fictitious marriage contracted only in order to liberate the main heroine of the novel, Vera Pavlovna, from the tyranny of her family sparked the imagination. In the light of the new morality, divorce was not only permitted but also crucially necessary when there is no love between a husband and wife or when their feelings of love have become extinguished. This story was read as a revelation, practically with religious devotion, without a shadow of a smile on one's lips. The concept of "free love," widespread in the West, was not invented by Chernyshevsky.[45] What was a Russian invention, however, was the idea of the commune. Vera Pavlovna has three dreams that show her the socialist future and suggest to her the idea of the commune. As a result, she decides to establish a sewing cooperative for impoverished girls.[46]

Franko and Pavlyk obtained a copy of Chernyshevsky's novel in late 1876. Franko quickly translated part of it and published it in *Druh*. One of its first readers was Franko's fiancée, Olha Roshkevych, who was encouraged to read it, of course, by her lover.[47] During their sojourn in Lolyn, at Rev. Roshkevych's parish, Franko and Pavlyk drew up plans to found a commune together with their fellow thinkers: "A few of us will get together (P[avly]k, I, Bandrivsky, Poliansky, Oleskiv, Biletsky, the Ozarkevyches, Didytsky, Mokh, and a few others), we'll get married, with our collected money [we'll] buy a nice piece of land and a large manor, and begin farming. In the summer the men work with the peasants in the field, the women in the garden and the orchard, and in the winter [there will be] studies, literature, and in case of need, couples take their turns and move for a certain period of time to Lviv" [ZT 48:99–100].

In one of his later sonnets Franko celebrated these moments as a long-past idyll:

> Once upon a time, in a respectable Ruthenian home
> In the days of youth, days of happiness and love
> We read "What Is to Be Done?" and had conversations
> About future, unknown days. [ZT 1:155]

The realization of these plans was prevented by Franko's arrest, investigation, and imprisonment. As a result of these events, Rev. Roshkevych refused to give his daughter's hand in marriage to Franko and forbade him to visit his home. When Olha's parents learned that she was still seeing Franko, there was a huge family quarrel and she was confined to her home. At this point, she decided on a radical step, the one she had read about in Chernyshevsky's novel. In the summer of 1879, she concocted a plan to submit (ostensibly) to her parents' will, agreeing to marry a young priest named Volodymyr Ozarkevych in order to gain her freedom. She expected complete understanding from her future husband because he too had read Chernyshevsky.

In a letter to Franko, she writes: "Ivas [dim. of Ivan], I think that if you love me, then you should be happy about this. Then I will be free, independent, I will have a good life with him. Right? You desired freedom and for that you served eight months! But after all, Mr. Oz[arkevych] is not a prison, I will purchase my freedom in a better way. I love you, you showed me the path that I must traverse, and he [Ozarkevych] is opening the gates that are standing closed before me."[48]

Ozarkevych, too, was seeking personal freedom in his marriage to Olha. He was in love with the daughter of an impoverished priest's widow; his parents, however, were against this marriage, preferring the more convenient match with Olha Roshkevych.[49] In her letters to Franko, Roshkevych was constructing great plans for the future. She was planning to work on literary translations and to teach handicrafts to village girls. It was her intention to use her earnings to publish books, including Franko's. She also had plans to continue her studies, primarily mathematics and physics. But her main desire was to bring about in a couple of years "the [circumstance] that with their joint forces a few capable people will purchase a plot of land with a large farm and live in companionship there actively and well, as you said last year." Olha Roshkevych discussed these plans with Volodymyr Ozarkevych, who found them very appealing. He was ready to work on the land after abandoning the priesthood.[50]

On 14 September 1879, Roshkevych married Ozarkevych. The marriage was a fictitious one: the couple slept apart, initially in separate bedrooms. But when the days grew colder, they slept in the same room partitioned in two by a mountain of pillows placed on top of the piano, which reached all the way to the ceiling.[51] In early March 1880, Roshkevych, Ozarkevych, and Franko met in the city of Kolomyia "like good, old friends, who do not observe the rules of etiquette with each other. At that time I felt good and cheerful, and I felt happy when, gazing at both of you...I saw friendship between you. I thought how well they are suited to each other—it is good for me that I have such intelligent friends," she wrote later in a letter to Franko. "I don't remember if my heart ever felt so light as that evening; then passionate love also began to approach me. How wonderful it is for a woman to love!"[52]

However, great disappointment lay in store for Olha Roshkevych. Immediately after his meeting with her, Franko was arrested and sent to prison. This was one of the most tragic episodes of his entire life. In prison he became seriously ill and ended up at death's door. Because of these experiences, he ultimately decided to stop nurturing any illusions and forget about the idea of a fictitious marriage; at least this is what he writes to Olha. It still remains unclear whether Franko was being frank here or simply using his imprisonment as a pretext to break off his relations with a woman for whom his feelings had cooled.[53]

In any case, Roshkevych continued to struggle for her love for a long time, not believing that Franko had turned out to be unprepared to accept her great personal sacrifice. They exchanged letters, and in 1884 the three of them, including Volodymyr Ozarkevych, even met up at a ball in Kolomyia. However, Franko's stubborn refusal to adopt Chernyshevsky's formula led to the circumstance that, in time, Roshkevych's marriage to Ozarkevych became a typical one. The mountain of pillows between them disappeared. In 1886 she gave birth to a son, Ivan, probably named in honor of Franko.[54] Until the end of her life, however, Roshkevych held a "grudge against Franko for not loving her sincerely, since he had caused her such great vexations."[55]

While he was in the Kolomyia jail, Franko made a fresh decision: to marry Pavlyk's sister Anna, who had followed in her brother's footsteps and been arrested for engaging in socialist propaganda. Franko was rather skeptical about her personal qualities and did not love her. However, he was appreciative, despite certain reservations, of her lengthy article titled "Moi i liuds´ki hrikhy" (My and Other People's Sins) in which she recounts her conversion to socialism and the persecution by the government that she had suffered because of her convictions. Therefore, he decided to get married "not for love but for friendship" [*ZT* 48:101, 133, 242].

Deprived of a stable means of livelihood, Franko, Pavlyk and his sister, and another hero of the Lviv trial, Ostap Terletsky, rented an apartment together, which alone was a serious challenge to social morality. The young roommates dreamed of women who could become the center of their little group, along the lines of the "French female geniuses: Madame Rolland, Recamier, [de] Staël, and others." Anna Pavlyk could not fill this role because of her intellectual limitations, but she had an undeniable advantage: she was the only woman in this company of men. She was a ready, and sole, object of the new type of marriage—a marriage based "not on love but an idea." Ostap Terletsky and the peasant socialist Antin Melnyk, from Drohobych County, both vied for her hand.[56]

Anna refused both, preferring Franko. At the beginning of 1879, the group fell apart: Mykhailo Pavlyk left for Geneva in order to dodge another prison sentence, and Anna went back to her native village. But from the summer of 1880 Franko and Anna began discussing the idea of marriage.[57] Anna waited for Franko to propose, not daring to broach the idea herself: it was not appropriate for her to do this. Franko admitted to Mykhailo Pavlyk that he was struggling mightily with himself "so that our marriage will also be fortified by love as much as possible, but so far I have not succeeded" [*ZT* 48:283]. A solution appeared in the early spring of 1881, when Franko, owing to a lack of income, left for his native village of Nahuievychi, without the hope of ever returning to Lviv. At approximately the same time, Anna Pavlyk informed her brother that she no longer wanted to marry Franko.[58]

In the meantime, Franko became close to a group of socialists based in Stanyslaviv. This acquaintance led him to a new romance, with Józefa

Dzwonkowska, the sister of one of his Stanyslaviv socialist friends. Her late father was an impoverished Polish landowner from the Russian Empire who had taken part in the uprising of 1863, and after its failure he saved himself by escaping to Galicia. Józefa Dzwonkowska was noted for her extraordinary beauty, and Franko fell instantly in love with her. However, she never requited his love. It has not been possible to determine the reasons for her coldness: according to one theory, she was repelled by Franko's physical appearance, and according to another, she was put off by his low social status and the fact that he was not a Pole. Most probably, neither of these theories is accurate: the main reason was Dzwonkowska's incurable illness (tuberculosis), which forced her to contemplate her imminent death and to refuse all romantic overtures. Nevertheless, Franko did not think of giving up: with the help of his stepfather, he cobbled together plans to sell his share of his father's legacy and invest the money in the Dzwonkowski estate, which was mired in debts. This estate was to become the foundation of a new community, where Pavlyk and his sister would live with him and Dzwonkowska.[59]

Dzwonkowska's refusal exacerbated the dire straits that Ivan Franko was experiencing at this time. His thirtieth birthday was approaching, and he had neither permanent employment nor a family. Several themes are repeated in his letters from about the mid-1880s: his loneliness, intolerable living conditions, and a feeling of looming death. He was casting about feverishly for a wife so that he could experience domestic bliss before his death. However, rational considerations may be noted even in his heated search for a life partner: he restricted himself to the one sole category of intelligent women whose independence was tolerated by Galician society—schoolteachers. In late 1883, when the Dzwonkowska affair was still unresolved, he became acquainted with a schoolteacher named Yulia Schneider and, several months later, with two other schoolteachers, Klymentyna Popovych and Olha Bilynska.[60] By the summer of 1884, he had proposed to each of them, and rumors were circulating about his impending marriage.[61] All of his proposals ended in failure; they were based not on any deep emotion but rather on economic calculations that could hardly be expected to bring any results, inasmuch as the material situation of Franko and his fiancées—rural schoolteachers—left much to be desired. Capitalizing on his contacts, Franko tried to find Schneider and Popovych some employment in Lviv, but without any great or long-lasting success.

Out of the three women only Yulia Schneider truly loved Franko, yet not as a man but as a poet. She loved him platonically until the end of her life.[62] At this time Franko also fell in love with Natalia Chapelska, the daughter of a village priest, but she did not return his affections. Franko did not attract her as a man and frightened her as a poet: some kind of inexpressible strength wafted from his person and his speech, and she was frightened in his presence.[63]

One common trait emerges from the "collective portrait" of Franko's fiancées: all the women with whom he was involved seemed to become his alter egos, although, as one might expect, they were in no way his equals owing to their lesser talents, energy, and temperaments. As though with the wave of a magic wand, they discovered in themselves greater or lesser literary talents, becoming writers and contributors to the journals that he was publishing. This does not mean that a wife who was a writer was Franko's ideal. Rather, his choice was dictated by the social circumstances of the day: literary work, according to him, "for today's educated woman is the only livelihood that simultaneously ensures them a respectable name [and] public recognition, and does not make them into slaves." He also believed that literature was not an activity restricted to a few chosen individuals. The experience of European women's literature, where with a few exceptions, all female writers were (in Franko's opinion) minor talents, demonstrated that every educated woman in Galicia could also become a writer and thus forge a path to independence [ZT 48:134]. The young Franko was renowned as an organizer of women's talents. It is not surprising that in 1884, when discussions began about starting up a women's almanac with the goal of uniting female writers from the Austro-Hungarian and Russian empires, the initiator of the idea, Natalia Kobrynska, chose him to be the editor of this publication.[64]

Under Franko's influence, the majority of women did not merely write poems; they also engaged in social work in the "field of the people's welfare." Olha Roshkevych collected materials about the life of local peasants and workers, and she was a member of one of the first women's organizations in Galicia. Yulia Schneider was published in the Lviv socialist newspaper *Praca* and wrote verses for and about workers.[65] Klymentyna Popovych, together with Franko, provided assistance to the striking workers of Lviv.[66] Thus, it would be no exaggeration to say that all of Franko's relationships with women in 1876–1886 were more than mere romantic adventures. In their own way, they enlarged the sphere of the new social ethos that the first Ukrainian socialists developed.

One of the new elements of this ethos was transparency of relationships. Franko did not conceal his other romances from his lovers. He told

Olha Roshkevych that Anna Pavlyk was not indifferent to him. To Yulia Schneider he confessed that he was going off to marry Józefa Dzwonkowska. Olha Bilynska knew perfectly well that Franko was thinking of proposing to Yulia Schneider, to whom it was no secret that Bilynska, quite likely jealous of Franko's attentions to Schneider, was angered by the news about the possible marriage "with the poetess." This kind of relationship scheme was always painful and upsetting to the women for whose hand Franko was vying and who, in their turn, competed among themselves for his attentions. Franko reveals a tendency toward promiscuity. But the most symptomatic feature of adultery—the effort to keep one's relationships a secret—is missing from Franko's behavior. At any rate, at least one of his fiancées, Yulia Schneider, understood and excused his conduct:

> Such is the great love of great people. And the loyal Honoré de Balzac, despite his epistolary assurances sent to the distant Mme. Hańska, is interested in Caroline Marbouty, who traveled to Italy with him in 1836, dressed as a man. At this same time he is sympathetically attuned to the pretty Countess Visconti and to the romantic Madame de la Valette. In 1837 Balzac is absorbed in his correspondence with the mysterious Louise, and he wrote less often to Mme. Hańska. Dissonances arise. There is a moment of discouragement, but no: he, Myron [Schneider called Franko by his pseudonym—Y. H], is not a "Don Juan," not the kind of person to whom one can say: "Mischief-maker of this world, you disturbed my years..." He is sincere and so helpless: a genuine poor poet. He does not conceal anything. And he talks about Yuzia [Dzwonkowska—Y. H.] and about the letters that he writes to Olha [most probably, Schneider means Bilinska—Y. H.]. He has financial problems. His situation is hopeless owing to the lack of funds and material security. I understood him and excused him.[67]

A final point: the circle of Franko's women and friends was very closely interconnected. Olha Roshkevych married Volodymyr Ozarkevych, the brother of Natalia Kobrynska with whom Franko tried to launch a women's movement in Galicia. Mykhailo Pavlyk "cast a romantic eye" on Olha's younger sister during his stay in Lolyn. His sister Anna was wooed not only by Franko but also by Ostap Terletsky and Antin Melnyk, who was Franko's close friend. The entire socialist group in Stanyslaviv was in love with Józefa Dzwonkowska, including Franko's friend and translator Feliks Daszyński,. Together with his "great friend" Volodymyr Kotsovsky, Franko got into the habit of paying frequent visits to Maria Bilynska and Yulia

Karachevska. Both women were friends of Klymentyna Popovych and revealed her secrets to Franko [*ZT* 48:414, 421]. Maria Bilynska was the sister of Olha, another of Franko's loves. After she broke off her relations with Franko, Yulia Schneider "took her in hand"; it was she who found Bilynska a husband, Rev. Anton Chapelsky's long-standing assistant. This priest was another friend of Franko's—although much older than he was—and the father of Natalia Chapelska, another young lady whom Franko allegedly courted. Volodymyr Kotsovsky, together with Franko, helped relocate Yulia Schneider and Klymentyna Popovych to Lviv, and he married Yulia's younger sister.

Similar close links existed not just among the Galician socialists but among the leaders of the Russophiles and Ukrainophiles.[68] Franko's example shows that the young "alternative" elite instantly revealed a tendency toward strengthening internal solidarity through marriage, just like the older elite. This was indeed a case of *plus ça change, plus c'est la même chose.*

The Contracting of National Marriages:

The Concept of a Pan-Ukrainian Family

Despite his numerous Galician romances, Franko married outside of Galicia. Thanks to Drahomanov, Franko and Pavlyk had close ties with Kyiv and Geneva. They frequently encountered Russian and Ukrainian revolutionaries from the Russian Empire, who would stop over in Lviv en route to the West. Among them were many young women, primarily those who were on their way to attend university in Switzerland. These women shocked the Galicians with their unfettered behavior. Franko recalled that the new arrivals were

> proficient at loftily abstract, theoretical disputes, in theory they were appalling freethinkers, revolutionaries, and atheists, in their manners they were some kind of barbarians that did not acknowledge the friendly forms that were mandatory in Galicia, they carried axes around with them, yelled raucously in public lodging rooms, ladies arrived with cropped hair, free manners, ladies who entered the apartments of bachelors unaccompanied, traveled unescorted to distant Zurich for medical studies, did not care about their dress, about gloves, and often even about ordinary neatness; they boasted, "I simply adore going to taverns."[69]

The revolutionaries from Russia fascinated the young Galician radicals. Pavlyk even had a plan to get married in Ukraine, so that his wife would not lead him away from his chosen path.[70] When it comes to Franko, during his romance with Roshkevych, he became interested in one of the young girls who were traveling through Lviv on their way to their studies in the West. Recalling her later, he referred to her as a "saint," who was capable of encouraging any man to struggle [ZT 46:393].[71]

Under Drahomanov's influence, the Galician radicals became the left opposition to the populists in the Galician-Ukrainian camp. The rift in this camp was on the face of it a reflection and continuation of the internal division in the Hromada of Kyiv, where Drahomanov's radical current was in opposition to the moderate-liberal orientation headed by Volodymyr Antonovych. In this conflict, Franko occupied a particular position. Ideologically, he was on the side of the radicals, but institutionally, through his cooperation with populist publications, he was allied with Antonovych's group. Franko's name was primarily linked to the journal *Zoria*, which was dedicated to uniting talented Ukrainians on both sides of the Austrian-Russian border.

One of his most dynamic contacts was Yelysei Trehubov, a member of the Kyiv Hromada.[72] Franko stayed at Trehubov's house when he left for Kyiv in 1885. There, he met Olha Khoruzhynska, the younger sister of Trehubov's wife. Franko was attracted to Olha, and after his return from Kyiv, in early August 1885 he turned to Trehubov in connection with "a delicate matter": to let him know if Olha would agree to marry him.[73] One month later, on 4 September 1885, Franko wrote a letter to Olha Khoruzhynska in which he "theoretically and hypothetically" asked for her hand in marriage [ZT 48:542–45]. Olha did not answer right away, as she was waiting for the opinion of her guardian, her maternal grandfather, who was a general in the Russian army. After obtaining his permission in late October 1885, she sent Franko a positive answer. This news cheered him up immensely; at the start of his thirtieth year, he was hoping to launch a new, family, life [ZT 48:559].

Later, Franko confessed that he got married "without love, but for the sake of the doctrine according to which one must marry a Ukrainian woman and a more educated student to boot" [ZT 49:114]. Khoruzhynska was an orphan from a family of poor noblemen from Kharkiv gubernia, on the Ukrainian-Russian borderland. According to family lore, she and her three sisters were under the personal care of the Russian Tsar Alexander II: he had promised to repay his gratitude to their brother, who had died a hero's death during the Russo-Turkish War. Olha graduated from the Kharkiv Institute for Noble Maidens, which was subsidized by the tsar, and later completed Higher Women's Courses at the institute, which was the equivalent of a women's university and allowed her to become a teacher.[74]

Khoruzhynska was close to the Russian revolutionary movement. When Franko's non-Ukrainian friends from the Russian Empire visited him later in Lviv, they mentioned her as their long-standing acquaintance.[75] However, her sympathies—as she admitted in one of her letters to Franko, written characteristically in Russian—always tended more toward the "Little Russian [Ukrainian] people." When she was still studying in Kharkiv, she was particularly interested in lectures on Galicia, imagining this Austrian province as "something ideal."[76] Under the sway of her visit to the Trehubov family, Khoruzhynska experienced something akin to a national conversion and joined the Hromada of Kyiv.[77] It was here that she first heard about Franko and was attracted by his reputation as a poet and a socialist.[78]

From Franko the Trehubov family hid the fact that Olha suffered from a congenital nervous disorder. Even without this knowledge, Franko was eaten up with doubt about his choice. He consulted his Lviv and Kyiv friends about whether he should marry a Ukrainian from abroad.[79] In late 1885, after long "sleepless nights and days of reflection," Franko wrote a letter to Khoruzhynska, announcing he was breaking off the relationship so that their marriage "would not be the mutual purchase of a pig in a poke, so that our wedding would not be the prolog to a heavy, terrible drama" [ZT 48:591–93].

Khoruzhynska agreed to postpone the wedding: "I am not thrusting myself on you; I myself will succeed in living and earning a piece of bread for myself. In my opinion, there is one outstanding issue, if, in this state of affairs, you desire to renounce your idea, then I am not stopping you. And it will be better if we give each other peace and separate forever."[80]

Franko interpreted his fiancée's emotional reply as a sign that she was not indifferent to him: "After this kind of rather gross irritation on my part," he wrote to her, "your sincere and bright soul has shown itself to me in a good light. Having decided to set out on an unknown road with me, you do not even feel any doubts, although you know from the very start that this road is difficult" [ZT 49:16]. An important role in the further development of events was played by external factors. Franko's friend Volodymyr Kotsovsky had fallen in love with Khoruzhynska's girlfriend

Olena Dobrohraieva. Franko suggested to his fiancée that she move to Galicia not by herself but with Dobrohraieva, "and we could set up our life very nicely all together" [*ZT* 49:17].

He was also subjected to the indirect but rather considerable pressure from Ukrainian activists based in Kyiv. Marriages in the Hromada milieu were a continuation of the political line. The Drahomanovites, loyal to the idea of federalism, deliberately wed Russian women in order to underline the fact that "they are not Ukrainian chauvinists." "Timid Ukrainians" also married Russian women so as to deflect suspicions of Ukrainophilism. Meanwhile, in his anthropology lectures Volodymyr Antonovych argued that marriages between Ukrainians and Russians could not possibly be happy ones. In such marriages Ukrainians are purportedly culturally abased and they perish, becoming lost forever to the Ukrainian nation. Families issuing from such unions are always hostile to Ukrainians. Before becoming a historian, Antonovych was a medical student and then a doctor. Therefore, his lectures on anthropology were always perceived as being particularly trustworthy.[81]

Thus, in the marriage between Ivan Franko and Olha Khoruzhynska the Hromada members and the "culturalists" saw, first and foremost, the embodiment of all their theories. It was slated to be the first pan-Ukrainian (*sobornyi*) marriage uniting two Ukrainians from both sides of the Austro-Russian border. In that sense, this marriage was ostensibly a scaled-down model of the Ukrainian nation. The idea of uniting Austrian Galicia with Russian-ruled Ukraine in the image of Franko and Khoruzhynska was the leitmotif of the speeches and toasts during their wedding in Kyiv in 1886.[82] The entire history of Franko's marriage, from his declaration of intentions to the wedding, took place during two brief visits to Kyiv. The young members of the Hromada of Kyiv did not disguise their disappointment stemming from the circumstances of Franko's engagement to Khoruzhynska, which was done "indecorously" and "hastily." From that time onward, Franko's aura somewhat dimmed in their eyes.[83]

Franko's marriage was a symbol of the unification of the "two Ukraines," but it differed from the way its architects had planned. It symbolized those numerous cultural differences and obstacles that lay on the path to understanding between the "Westerners" and "Easterners."[84] These differences had already emerged during Franko's correspondence with Khoruzhynska before their marriage: he had reprimanded her for her lack of punctuality in corresponding with him, regarding this as a cultural difference—because in Europe and in Galicia this is not done [*ZT* 48:557, 591]. Galician society accepted Olha Khoruzhynska rather guardedly, as a "Russian," and rebuked Franko for not having married a "Galician girl."[85] To the Galicians, Franko's wife seemed to be too "progressive" in her views and conduct. That was why, it was claimed, she could not be a good housewife, did not know how to adapt to limited financial resources, and, in the final analysis, was unable to provide Franko with domestic happiness: "In Ukraine she would be completely at home, but in Galicia she did not know how to cope."[86]

Franko's home life was not without its joys. The couple had four children. His wife was very helpful in many civic matters, and he often heeded her advice, relying on her literary tastes. In the early years their relations were marked by love.[87] However, even during his engagement to Khoruzhynska Franko fell in love with another woman, Celina Zygmuntowska.[88] He kept falling in love later, searching for love outside the family. In the final analysis, both Franko and Khoruzhynska tended to view their marriage as a catastrophe—a kind of payback for their "marriage without love but for the sake of doctrine."

Postscript

Franko and Pavlyk's activity may be easily typologized: both of them were "men doing feminism." In discussions of this kind the question always arises: How sincerely can this be done by men, and, in engaging in such activities, are they not pursuing their own personal goals?[89] The ambivalence of this role is conspicuous where Franko and Pavlyk are concerned. On the one hand, both of them deserve credit for their undisputed achievements in fostering the rise of the Ukrainian women's movement in Galicia in the 1880s. On the other, they refuted the independent value of this movement, seeking to subordinate it to the goals of Galician radicalism. Naturally, from time to time, this sparked objections from Galician-Ukrainian feminists. Consequently, Franko and Pavlyk's relations with the women's movement were filled with mutual disappointments and resentments.[90]

Franko and, to a lesser degree, Pavlyk made their most enduring contribution to the development of so-called literary feminism, a trend that emerged in Galician-Ukrainian literature between the 1880s and the 1930s, which was represented by female writers who wrote frequently, albeit not exclusively, on women's themes.[91] For the most part, their works were not marked by extraordinary talent, but they played an important role as a link joining the Ukrainian national movement with the women's movement. The greatest achievements here belong to Yulia Schneider, the first Galician Ruthenian-Ukrainian female poet, who was known under the pseudonym Uliana Kravchenko. This protégée of Franko's became a role model for younger women, and she played an active role in spreading the cult of Franko during the interwar years.[92] However, neither in her writings nor in the works of other women do we encounter the ideas of fictitious or free marriage, which had so captured the imagination of Galician male radicals in the prewar years.

How vital were the new forms of relations between men and women, which the Galician-Ukrainian radicals were proposing? There are only fragmentary data on this question. However, there is sufficient information to form certain impressions and preliminary conclusions. These new forms were establishing the foundations of a new rituality: in 1885, one of Franko's friends organized a "bizarre wedding," without music, dancing, or girls, attended by a circle of "merry and intelligent people." The bride was wearing not a white dress but a national Ukrainian costume, while the bridegroom was dressed in an ordinary suit (Franko was the best man at this wedding).[93] At the same time, the radicals were firmly convinced that even a love marriage holds the risk of the betrayal of political ideals, when, with the onset of domestic bliss and material wellbeing, the husband "becomes a bourgeois" ("turns into a middle-class gentleman") and is a write-off where the political struggle is concerned.[94]

Therefore, the idea of free love remained popular among the Galician radicals: they constantly discussed this idea, contracted trial marriages for a certain period of time, lived with women without the benefit of marriage, and raised children without baptizing them.[95] Adultery was also not uncommon, although, of course, it was kept secret.[96] There are also examples of "united" (pan-Ukrainian) marriages. This type of marriage was embarked on by Teofil Okunevsky, one of the leaders of the radical movement, and by Roman Yarosevych, a member of the Viennese parliament, who was close to the radicals.[97] However, there is no information on the attempt to implement the formula of a family commune in Galicia.[98] It may be assumed that the fragmentariness of this data is itself proof of the marginality of these new forms of marriage: they performed the role of a marker of the left political milieu rather than a model suitable for wide-scale emulation. Indirect proof of this may be the cult of Franko that emerged in Galicia during his life and which blossomed after his death. Among the numerous publications on the subject of his life and activities we do not find a single one that mentions Franko's role in propagandizing the new forms of marriage and sexual relations. This topic was, and to a significant degree still is, taboo.

Even while Franko and Pavlyk were still alive, the second part of the idea of free marriage, namely, the right to divorce, was being practiced on a larger scale. As early as the final decades before the First World War, the weakening of family stability was on the rise. From that time, and during the entire interwar period, the number of marriages fell from year to year, while divorces caused by "invincible mutual antipathy" were increasing. During the brief existence of the Western Ukrainian National Republic in 1919, none other than the radical Kyrylo Trylovsky, Franko's pupil and follower, submitted a draft law that would permit full divorce and eliminate obstacles to remarriage caused by clergymen's or nuns' vows. However, the war prevented this draft law from making it onto the agenda of the Western Ukrainian parliament.[99]

The consolidation of the new trend was determined neither by the influence of ideology and the practice of Galician radicals, nor by the changes introduced to the Austrian civil code or that of the Catholic Church. Both codes were in effect even after the collapse of the Austro-Hungarian Empire in interwar Poland (1919–1939) and during the Nazi occupation of Galicia (1941–1944). The increase in the frequency of divorce was rather a manifestation of the *Zeitgeist*. A particular role was played by the increasing possibility for women of finding employment and thereby becoming economically independent.[100]

In those years, the Ukrainian national movement experienced an important inner transformation: in the general balance of political orientations, the influence of left-wing ideology increasingly diminished, to be replaced by right-wing, conservative, and integral nationalisms.[101] Under the conditions of this "turn to the right," the idea of national marriages underwent further transformation. A characteristic example is the writer Osyp Nazaruk, one of the main proponents of this idea in interwar Galicia. In his youth he had been a radical and helped spread the cult of Franko. After the First World War and the failure of Ukrainian national aspirations in 1917–1923, Nazaruk experienced a conversion to conservative Christian nationalism and, among other things, issued calls to "kill Franko," whom he characterized as a carrier of "the most terrible of all worldviews ever to emerge in humanity."[102] He claimed that interethnic marriages have more negative than positive sides, and he substantiated his thesis by using the examples of several Galician families.[103] On the other hand, he cautioned against marriages between Galician-Ukrainians, who were conservative by nature, and Ukrainians from Eastern Ukraine, who demonstrated a tendency toward "social chaos" (that is, Bolshevism), and therefore were a lower racial type (his formulation). He considered such marriages desirable if the Galician side was represented by a woman: "A Galician man who marries a woman from Dnipro Ukraine [Eastern Ukraine] will lose his Galician nature incomparably faster than a Galician woman who marries a man from Dnipro Ukraine. The logical consequence of this is that Galician men should not marry women from Dnipro Ukraine for loftier religious and national reasons, but should marry Galician women."[104]

It is not clear whether Nazaruk in his considerations meant Franko's family, the first example of a "united" marriage between a Galician man and a woman from Eastern Ukraine. At the time, Franko's wife, Olha Khoruzhynska, was living out the last years of her life. She had never assimilated into the Galician-Ukrainian milieu, forever retaining the traces of Russian culture.[105]

Franko's efforts to modernize relations between men and women brought certain but very limited success. His own failed quests for a bride, as well as his marriage, provide confirmation of this. Of course, this project failed not through his fault alone. Complicating the issue were various circumstances that were beyond his influence and control. The incongruity among the formulas that he proposed and the life that he was fated to live, and between the real and the imaginary, had a positive side: it served as the mainspring of his creativity. A lasting monument to this is, among other works, his *Ziv′iale lystia* (Withered Leaves), one of the finest collections of lyrical poetry in all of Ukrainian literature. One of the poems, titled "Iak pochuiesh vnochi krai svoioho vikna" (If One Night Near Your Window You Hear) [*ZT* 2:151], is full of sorrow over the fact that he and his beloved have forever parted ways. This poem was turned into a folksong that is still sung at weddings in Galicia as a sad reminder that love frequently does not last long, and domestic happiness is hard to achieve.

Chapter 14

Franko and His Jews

In Ukrainian intellectual history no other writer devoted more attention to Jewish subjects than Ivan Franko. The wealth of Jewish themes in his works contrasts sharply with the comparatively small number of studies that have been written on this topic.[1] An unspoken ban on researching Jewish topics was in effect in Soviet scholarship, which explains the prolonged silence on this issue. In Soviet Ukraine, in contrast with other Soviet republics, this tendency took an extreme form.[2] In the concrete case of Franko's legacy, the taboo led to the expunging from collections of his works of entire poems, short stories, and journalistic articles exploring Jewish subjects.[3]

Outside the borders of the USSR, Ukrainian scholarship in the humanities was unable to compensate for this shortcoming. Until 1939, gains in this field of studies were limited to the publication of several previously unknown articles by Franko and reminiscences about him,[4] and after 1945, to a small number of interesting, and somewhat apologetic, observations and articles on the Jewish question, which were published in the emigration.[5] Incidental references to Franko in relation to the Jews may be found in works written in the West by non-Ukrainians;[6] they are distinguished from works produced by Ukrainian diaspora scholars by the fact that Franko is mentioned only in passing (mostly in footnotes), and almost always presented as an antisemite.[7]

The notion of Franko's alleged antisemitism was reflected much more clearly in journalism. Two articles are worth mentioning. The first is an unsigned article titled "Franko and the Jewish Question," published in 1943 in *Krakivski visti* (Cracow News), on the eve of the final destruction of the Galician Jews. The article appeared to have been written to order, and its whole emotional thrust aimed at disproving the widespread image of Franko as a philosemite.[8] The second article, which appeared on the one hundredth anniversary of Franko's birth, was published in *Forverts*, the journal of progressive American Jews. Referring to Franko's novels of the

Boryslav cycle, which had been introduced into the Soviet school curriculum, the author argued that the Soviet government was wholeheartedly
spreading antisemitism among young people. He calls Franko a "*haidamaka* and a true heir of Khmelnytsky and Gonta, who in his works predicted
the pogroms and the destruction of the Jews," "a dirty pogromist," placing
the Ukrainian writer on par with the "*haidamaka* Nikita Khrushchev, in
whose blood roils the tainted blood of Bohdan Khmelnytsky."[9]

Both of these articles reflect the extreme end of the broad spectrum of
views on Franko's attitude toward the Jews, characterizing it in a range from
sincere Judaeophilism to radical Judaeophobia. This duality in the treatment
of his views became more distinct after the fall of the Communist regime
in Ukraine. With the disappearance of censorship, the majority of Franko's
texts, in which his favorable attitude to the Jews and Zionism is revealed, has
been commented and published (see *Mozaika*). The topic of "Franko as an
antisemite" also received a new lease on life: in a collection of articles published in Ukraine about the "harmfulness of Jews" one can find references to
Franko as a classic writer on this theme.[10] Both of these views are based on
a selective reading of Franko's legacy,[11] the difference being that in the latter
case, such articles are also poorly concealed political manipulations.[12]

The question of whether Franko was an antisemite is important, but
it is only one part of the broader topic, "Franko and the Jews."[13] It is no
less crucial to show how in his attitude to the Jews he was constructing the
limits of an imagined community that he called his "people." Franko's lifetime coincided with the period when the Jews were experiencing a decisive
transformation that was erasing their identification with Judaism. In the
new conditions, the term "Jew" was no longer only a self-identification: it
was also an identity that was foisted from outside on considerable groups of
people, mostly assimilated Jews. The attitude to the Jewish question defined
the limits of one's own identification. Therefore, discussions around the
question of "who was a Jew"—and, particularly, who was a "good Jew"—
revealed less about Jews and more about those who were engaged in discussing this question.

The Jewish Question in Autonomous Galicia

The changes that the Jews experienced during the nineteenth century may
be described with two words: emancipation and acculturation. However,
the changes in Western Europe had a different character from those that

took place in Eastern Europe. In Western Europe, emancipation was a one-time revolutionary act that resulted in the swift, mass assimilation of Jews into local societies, whereas in Eastern Europe emancipation was a lengthy process that lasted for nearly an entire century, and where successes were significantly more modest. As a result, the problem of the emancipation and acculturation of Eastern European Jews was a long-term process riven by conflicts.[14]

The difference between Western and Eastern European Jews carried no weight with antisemites: they rejected all forms of coexistence with any kind of Jews whatsoever. Antisemitism, like other modern ideologies, was imported to Eastern Europe from Western Europe. The "original" Eastern European contribution to the history of anti-Jewish persecutions was, first and foremost, the spontaneous pogroms that took place between the 1880s and the 1910s.[15] However, mass Jewish migration to the West, which was caused by these pogroms, contributed in its own way to the spread of anti-semitism. The arrival of a substantial number of unassimilated Eastern European Jews in such large cities as Vienna or Berlin created the image of a "Jewish threat." The role that the young Hitler's stay in Vienna in the early twentieth century played in the formation of his antisemitic and racist beliefs is well known. Although this is an extreme example, it is by no means the only illustration of how important Eastern Europe was in modern Jewish history.[16]

Galicia occupied a special place in this history. It was a land with one of the highest concentrations of Jews in the world. The Habsburg monarchy had the second largest Jewish population after the Russian Empire. The largest number of Jews lived in the Austrian part (Cisleithania) of the Austrian monarchy, while nearly two-thirds of Austrian Jews (66.2 percent in 1900) lived in Galicia; the largest concentrations of Jews in Galicia (75 percent in 1900) were found in the eastern (Ruthenian-Ukrainian) part. In the Austro-Hungarian Empire in the 1880s there was an average of one Jew for every twenty-six non-Jewish subjects. However, whereas in the Czech lands the ratio was 1:57, in Moravia 1:47, and in Lower Austria, 1:37, in Galicia the proportions were 1:9, and in Lviv, 1:3.[17]

As for the presence of Jews in everyday life, in the Galician case it was not just a question of their numerical strength. While Galicia had a bad reputation, *Galitzianers*—Galician Jews—suffered even more from this notoriety: in fact, they were the main personification of Eastern Europe's civilizational backwardness. With their clothing, manners, language, and adherence to Orthodox Judaism, they differed markedly from the rest of the population. In addition to cultural and religious differences, social differences played an important role in relations between Jews and non-Jews in Galicia. Since the majority of Jews (70 percent in 1900) lived in cities and town(let)s (shtetls) while the majority of Christians resided in the countryside, relations between the former and the latter acquired the features of the typical antagonism that existed between urban residents and peasants. Galician Jews followed the general trend of Jewish settlement throughout the world: within their milieu they developed a numerically large commercial and trading stratum whenever they ended up in a country with a predominantly agrarian population.[18] The social structure of the Jewish population seemed to be a reversed copy of the Christian society's structure: while nearly 80 percent of Ruthenians and Poles lived off the land, nearly 80 percent of the Jews earned a living from the proceeds of commerce and trade. This applied equally to both urban and rural Jews. The latter owned taverns and engaged in petty trade. In some Galician counties there was one Jewish trader for every eight to ten Christian families, and a village with eighty peasants might have between six and eight traders or tavern-keepers. Being engaged in trading did not necessarily signify wealth or high social status. Owing to the low purchasing power of the local population and aggressive domestic competition, most Jews who engaged in trading barely made ends meet: in the late nineteenth century, the total amount of property owned by the average Galician-Jewish trader did not exceed twenty US dollars, and in many cases, not even four.[19]

Nearly half the Galician Jewish population consisted of so-called *Luftmenschen*, people who lived "off air"—that is, they had no stable means of livelihood and their upkeep came from the Jewish community. Their poverty was horrifying. This is how the Ukrainian physician, Roman Yarosevych, a friend of Franko's, described his medical practice: "When I am summoned to a Jewish patient, I always give practically the same kind of prescription: food. The response to this prescription is a silent gesture. It says everything."[20]

The dramatic nature of the situation lay in the fact that the large Jewish population faced an even larger population of Ukrainian or Polish peasants, yet despite universal poverty, relations among these groups were rarely marked by feelings of solidarity. Here one can discuss the question of how large a role was played by religious differences. As it was, in the eyes of the Christians, the Jews were "Christ killers," while the Jews regarded Christians as pagans. Where the Ukrainian Greek Catholic Church was concerned, the religious factor carried little weight.[21] Instead, the negative image of Jewry dominated the so-called "folk religion": Jews were presented as the "absolute Other." But this image, like that of every "alien" in a traditional culture, was an ambivalent one: magical powers were ascribed to Jews, which could be either harmful or beneficial to Christians. Thus, peasants who were experiencing hard times could seek advice from *tzaddiks* (leaders of Hassidic communities) and rabbis, while peasant girls and women visiting the city were apt to light candles both in a church and a synagogue.[22]

The lack of solidarity between the Jewish and non-Jewish populations was chiefly determined by social causes. But, again, these were not social causes per se but their reflections in mass consciousness. The peasants remembered the role that the Jews had played during the days of serfdom—as stewards or managers of noblemen's estates. This memory of the Jews as "the lords' go-betweens" or "servants of the lords" was maintained and confirmed by the role of Jews as tavern owners: Jews had obtained permission to sell alcohol from Galician landowners, who held a monopoly over propination. At the same time, the Jews' historical awareness firmly preserved the image of their Christian neighbors as pogromists. Among other things, this was borne out by the popularity, in Ruthenian folk culture, of the "Cossacks" and "Ukraine," which, for the Jews, were indissolubly connected with the Cossack uprising led by Bohdan Khmelnytsky.

To the above-mentioned causes one should also add the fact that there were various gradations and manifestations of poverty in Galicia. The Jewish poor had one essential advantage: without any security for the future, they were forced to save more. These savings were in the form of cash, of which there was little in the hands of the Galician peasants, who continued to live in the conditions of natural economy. It was also easier for a poor Jew to endure his poverty than for a poor Christian because the former could rely on the support and assistance of his religious community.[23]

By virtue of its main features, the Jewish community in Eastern Europe was similar to a caste: affiliation to this closed (but not isolated) group was defined according to clear-cut criteria (most often religious ones) independently of place of residence. It was very difficult to cross the boundaries of this group, which were defined both internally and externally.[24] However, starting in the mid-nineteenth century they gradually began to corrode even in Galicia. The process of corrosion was launched by the spread of the idea of Jewish Enlightenment, the Haskalah, which called upon Jews to remain righteous at home but be "normal people" on the street. The Haskalah opened the doors to the assimilation of the Galitzianers initially into German and, later, into Polish society (after the introduction of Galician autonomy).[25]

The legal emancipation of the Jews played a considerable role in eroding internal boundaries. The turning point was the Constitution of 1867, which, however, recognized them as a separate religious community (*Religionsgemeinschaft*) rather than as a people (*Volksstamm*). Although the new constitution did not grant Jews equal rights as a group, they were now allowed to purchase land, join trade guilds, hold government posts, or be employed as university professors, and the like.[26]

Emancipation and assimilation sparked a certainty that the improvement of socioeconomic conditions would put an end to the Jews' isolation, just as the abolition of serfdom had instilled hopes for the integration of the peasants into a modern society. For the younger, emancipated, generation of Galician Jews in the 1880s this belief was as certain as the Marxists' confidence in the victory of the proletarian revolution.[27] To a certain extent these hopes were justified. In the final decades of the nineteenth century it was possible to speak of something resembling an exodus from the traditional Jewish society, mainly of young people filled with ambition to carve out a secular career for themselves.[28]

The irony of the situation lay in the fact that these liberal advances did not always ease tensions in relations between Jews and non-Jews. One example is the spread of usury. Two laws, passed on 14 June and 1 November 1868, permitted usurers to charge arbitrary rates of interest on loans and allowed peasants to dispose freely of their farms. Peasants were in constant need of money: in order to pay off taxes, feed their families in the periods between harvests, and pay for baptisms, weddings, funerals, and so on. Jews were most often the only ones to whom one could turn for help. Since no formal restrictions existed, a creditor charged a high rate of interest, often one that was higher than the profits that could be generated by a peasant farm. As a result, usury and auctions (*litsytatsii*), at which farms were sold to pay off debts, became one of the greatest social evils of the post-reform countryside.[29]

The transformation of the traditional roles of the Jewish and non-Jewish populations created new arenas of conflict. The purchase by Jews of lands owned by peasants and landowners, on the one hand, and the emergence of Christian trade cooperatives in the countryside, on the other, created the impression that each group was invading the living space of the other, and threatening the very foundations of its existence.[30]

By the end of the nineteenth century, images of the "typical Galician" feebly reflected the new social conditions, now that Galician Jewry was far from homogeneous. The families of wealthy secularized bankers, entrepreneurs, and landowners were divorcing themselves from that categorization socially and culturally, as was the growing stratum of representatives of the "free professions": physicians, lawyers, and secular intellectuals. Meanwhile, the social structure of Ruthenian society did not change in any fundamental way: the key figures were still the peasants and petty tradesmen, while bureaucrats comprised only 0.4 percent of the Ruthenian population (twelve times less than among Jews).[31] The differences in the pace and character of social transformation created the impression of "Jewish success" or "Jewish conspiracy," depending on the observer's attitude. This feeling was all the more acute because, politically, Jews remained a very insignificant force; therefore, "Jewish success" heightened suspicions of a "Jewish conspiracy."

In these circumstances it is easy to understand why the ideology of antisemitism became entrenched so quickly in Galicia. The first programmatic antisemitic works, including Teofil Merunowicz's book *About the Method and Goals of Research on the Jewish Question* (1879),[32] appeared in Galicia at the same time as German publications that mark the beginning of modern antisemitism (for example, Wilhelm Marr's *Path to the Victory of Germanicism over Judaism*).[33] By the early 1880s, antisemitism had penetrated every walk of Galician life.[34] Antisemitism was employed particularly vigorously as a tool in the political mobilization of both Polish and Ruthenian peasants.[35] From the late nineteenth century it became the heart of the ideology and practice of the Polish National Democratic Party, whose debut in the political arena marked the shift of Polish nationalism toward ethnic xenophobia.[36]

However, in characterizing the Jewish question in Galicia one must remember that, despite the high tensions that existed in the relations among Jews, Poles, and Ruthenians, until the First World War there were no mass large-scale pogroms in this part of the world, in contrast to the neighboring lands of the Russian Empire and the Hungarian part of the Habsburg monarchy.[37] The reasons behind this phenomenon require separate study. However, two are obvious. The first reason was the existence of a developed political and public life, which, like a lightning rod, transferred part of the conflict into the legal sphere, thereby easing tensions. The other was a trend common to all multiethnic regions, where the need to oppose a stronger opponent forced weaker parties to seek compromises with each other.[38] This was the nature of the Ruthenian–Jewish compromise. The first such alliance was established during the elections to the Galician parliament in 1873. As Polish antisemitism became stronger in Galicia in the late nineteenth century, in the Jewish and Ruthenian camps—the Zionist and Ukrainian movements, respectively—conditions were forming for the creation of a more durable Ukrainian–Jewish alliance based on antagonism toward a stronger foe: Polish nationalism. The Viennese parliament was the venue of an unprecedented event in 1907, when the Ukrainian deputy, Yulian Romanchuk, voiced a demand to recognize the Jews as a separate nation.[39]

In the broader context, the dynamics of relations at the center of the Galician ethnic triangle were acquiring increasingly greater importance for the future geopolitical configuration of all of Eastern and Central Europe. Ivan Franko was the unquestionable leader in the development of Ukrainian identity, and in his case the articulation of this identity was closely tied to the search for answers to the Jewish question, which is precisely what makes Franko's biography such an important research topic from the perspective of the history of Ukrainian–Jewish relations.

Young Franko's Encounters with Jews

Ruthenian-Ukrainian, Polish, and Jewish activists faced a crucial challenge: how to mobilize under their flags an uneducated and poor population that was mostly indifferent to the world of "high politics." The obvious answer was to capitalize on existing social, religious, and ethnic differences, ascribing ideological significance to them. The task of the intelligentsia was to minimize differences within its own national or social community (which had yet to be constructed!) and to capitalize on its real or imaginary differences from others.

Extant collections of folklore from that time reveal that the popular consciousness of Galician Ruthenians was replete with material for constructing this kind of distance from the Jewish community. This is attested in the collection of folk sayings and proverbs that Franko collected and published. Among the stereotypes were those of Jews being cowardly and feeble-minded, unable to perform the simplest kind of agricultural work; of Jews as controlling commerce, trading dishonestly, and thus a Jew becoming a synonym of a cheat; of being unclean, carriers of infectious diseases such as mange. References to uncleanliness abound in numerous sayings alluding to the most unclean functions of the human body. After perusing this list, it is not difficult to construe the insurmountable gulf between Galician Christians and Jews at that time: in the eyes of Christians, the Jews appeared to be almost a type of caste, and a caste of untouchables at that. However, they were imagined as a special type of caste that had risen above the Christians, extraordinarily quick-witted and prone to cheating, and that exploited the peasants mercilessly. Jews were seen as absolutely alien to the peasant also because of their religion, which allegedly commanded them to torment and even kill Christians. Jews would not attain salvation in the afterworld, and in this world they did not deserve Christian sympathy and help either. This explains why local sayings castigated those Christians who provided services to Jews or offered them assistance.[40]

Although the negative image of the Jew was predominant, it was not the only one. A separate group of proverbs portray Jews in neutral light. Some of them echo superstitions: it is a good omen to dream about a Jew or to see a Jew crossing a street. Other proverbs express the idea that a Christian is sometimes worse than a Jew, and that Jews are worthy of respect because they hold fast to their faith. Two proverbs that espouse tolerance are in a category all their own: "It is bad with the Jew but also bad without the Jew," and "Just as not every Jew is mangy, so too not every peasant is a pig" (the latter proverb was a response to the widespread Jewish anti-peasant stereotype).[41] Nevertheless, these proverbs do not refute the stereotype, but merely soften it.

Franko collected a substantial number of Jewish-themed proverbs in Nahuievychi and the neighboring village of Yasenytsia Silna. Familiarity with local moods based on these sayings suggests that at a young age Franko had a greater chance of becoming an antisemite than a philosemite. However, his childhood was relatively free of these stereotypes. One of his earliest memories of Jews is connected to the following incident: one day his mother brought a few Jewish breads from the village, which the female owner of the tavern in Nahuievychi had given to her:

> "Children," my mother shouted to me and my brothers and sister, "look what Sura [Sarah] gave me for you." She broke up the dried cakes and divided them up among us. "Eat, this is Jewish *paska*. Though people say it contains the blood of Christian children, that is nonsense." This was the first more lively impression of Jews that has remained from my childhood. At the same

time, it was the first inkling that I ever got about the blood tale. Mother
expressed her opinion of this so calmly and decisively that we only gaped in
wonder, without the usual horror into which, as it happens, older and much
educated people so often fall during conversations. At the same time mother
offered the best proof that she did not believe in the blood tale by eating with
us the pieces of bread that she had brought.[42] [*Mozaika* 338]

The Franko family lived on the outskirts of the village, where there
were no Jews or taverns. Franko gained his first experience of coexistence
with Jews when he began attending the school in Yasenytsia Silna. Among
the schoolchildren were two sons of the local tavern-keeper. One of them,
a precociously developed boy named Avramko, protected the shy Franko
from the taunts of the older schoolboys, and the two became friends.

Franko's real acquaintance with the world of the Galician Jews began
when he started his studies in Drohobych, where a pogrom had taken place
a year earlier, in 1863, provoked by patriotically inclined Polish gymnasium students. During his school years, Franko regularly witnessed fights
between the older pupils and local Jews. According to him, there was no violence between the Christian and Jewish pupils either in the Basilian school
or at the gymnasium. It is true, however, that the Basilian Fathers made the
Jewish children sit on separate bench and did not allow them to associate
with the Christian pupils. There was no segregation in the gymnasium. At
the time there was no trace of the national or confessional conflicts that
later flourished among young Galician gymnasium and university students.
In those days the only manifestation of this future conflict was the Polish-
Ukrainian discussions about history and literature. Although the Jewish
pupils did not take part in these debates, some of them enrolled in courses
of Ruthenian language or literature [*Mozaika* 340–42].

The reminiscences of Franko's peer Maurycy Gottlieb, who died prematurely (1856–1879), paint an entirely different picture: Gottlieb claimed that
he, like other Jewish children, suffered greatly at the hands of the Christian
pupils.[43] The incongruity between these two reminiscences does not necessarily mean that one of these two authors was not telling the truth. It may
simply be Franko and Gottlieb's different perception of what constituted
an insult or conflict. Incidentally, neither Franko nor Gottlieb makes any
detailed reference to the other; the two boys must not have associated with
each other. Franko's closest friend was Gottlieb's relative, Isaac Tigerman,
who showed a considerable aptitude for mathematics but opted for a career

as a lawyer; he too died prematurely, in Drohobych.[44] Some of the Jewish gymnasium students who studied later with Franko distinguished themselves in many walks of life. Among them were the Vienna-based journalist Henryk Monat[45] and the distinguished Polish classical philologist Leon Sternbach.[46]

That there was no great gulf between Jewish and Christian pupils is attested by the fact that most of Franko's clients, who hired him to tutor their children, were Jewish families in Drohobych. Based on his acquaintance with the family life of Galician Jews, Franko the pupil arrived at two important conclusions. First, Jewish children were more intellectually advanced than Christian children. He explained this circumstance to himself by the fact that Jewish boys devoted much time to their studies: besides their in-school work, they studied at home. Second, while visiting Jewish families in their homes, Franko was struck by the parents' capacity to rejoice at their children's successes, to offer them words of encouragement and praise, and sometimes even to exaggerate their real successes. Franko the pupil listened enviously to the praise that Sternbach's father, with tears of joy, lavished on his talented son, "because I, a poor boy, a prematurely orphaned peasant's son, had no one in the world to take an interest in my progress with such great love or at least half as much with such great understanding" [*Mozaika* 343].

Franko's observations of the differences between the Christian and non-Christian worlds sparked an interest in the culture of the East when he was still attending the gymnasium in Drohobych. Already in those years, he confessed, he was being "pulled toward the East." The Old Testament and the writers of antiquity made a huge impression on him: he devoured these works in Church Slavonic, German, and Polish translations, and eventually he did verse translations of much of the Book of Job and several chapters of the Book of Isaiah.[47] After reading Franko's translations of the Prophets, the father of his schoolmate Limbach asked him: "What are you looking for among the Jews? Are you capable of understanding their feelings and conveying them properly? And even if you were capable, then ask yourself: how would this come in handy? Who needs this? Does what those people were interested in thousands of years ago interest anyone nowadays?" [*ZT* 21:325]. Limbach often visited Franko, from whom he borrowed books of Western literature. Through Limbach, Franko became acquainted with the world of assimilated Jews, considerable numbers of whom lived in Drohobych.

After Franko enrolled at Lviv University, for some time he lost touch with the Jews. There were no Jews among the students who registered with him for courses on philology, just as there were none in the student societies of which Franko was a member [*Mozaika* 347]. At the time, the Ruthenian-Ukrainian student milieu was not free of antisemitic prejudices. Before the members of the editorial board of *Druh* were converted to championing all things Ukrainian, the journal advertised a translation of the Talmud aimed at ordinary people, so that they would know what "the Jews think about us, into what kind of diabolical nets they are seeking to enmesh every Christian."[48]

The renewal of Franko's contacts with the Jewish world is connected with the early years of his socialist activities. The goal of the Galician socialist committee that formed around the newspaper *Praca* was to create a Ruthenian-Polish-Jewish workers-peasant party. Therefore, socialist propaganda had to be conducted in the languages of all three groups. Two Jews were members of the editorial board: the Inlender brothers, Ludwik and Adolf. Franko, who was friends with them, later described Ludwik as a "sincere friend of our nationality, a thoroughly honest man with a broad education."[49] However, like other "progressive Jews," the Inlender brothers were not suited to playing the role of propagandists among unassimilated poor Jews. In a letter to Mykhailo Pavlyk, dated 5 June 1880, Adolf Inlender admitted:

> There are no progressive Jews who could implement the plan to create a separate Jewish current among working Jews: the ones that exist cannot be called Jews because they do not have a connection to the totality of Jews, specifically with the Jewish proletariat, and they could not even communicate with them because they do not know either the language or the customs.[50]

Paradoxically, it was Ivan Franko himself who, thanks to his fluency in Yiddish, made the biggest contribution to maintaining the "Jewish direction" in the activities of the Galician socialists, above all those who were based in Drohobych and Boryslav. During his involuntary stay in the Drohobych area in 1881–1883, Franko recorded a song that was circulating among poor local Jews (*kaptsany*), which he considered as a sign of the emergence of class feeling among the Jewish proletariat.[51]

Examples of Ukrainian-Polish-Jewish cooperation in the socialist arena were an anomaly of Galicia's sociopolitical life. Antisemitic moods especially affected all orientations within the Ruthenian-Ukrainian camp.

In his brochure titled *The Politics of the Ruthenians* (1873), the leader of the populists, Rev. Stepan Kachala, wrote that the question of the Ruthenians' relations with the Jews was not so much about the defense of their causes as about the very existence of the Ukrainian people, so quickly are they stripped of their property because of the Jews' "deceitful actions."[52] The Russophile cleric, Ivan Naumovych, made a direct link between the degree of demoralization of the Ruthenian-Ukrainian peasantry and Jewish influences. According to him, the least amount of demoralization could be seen among the Lemkos, the westernmost Ruthenian ethnic group, among whom only a few Jews lived. In the Lemko region little was heard about thieves and cheats, and there was much less of the drunkenness that was eroding the "healthy body of Galician Rus." The territory with the highest degree of demoralization, however, was the Hutsul region, which the Ruthenians at one time called their "Palestine flowing with milk and honey," but which was now truly a Jewish Palestine.[53] This observation was shared by the socialist Mykhailo Pavlyk, who was a native of the Hutsul region. In 1876, he wrote: "Soon there may be trouble in Galicia with the Jews: I see and know this according to what our people are saying."[54]

The spread of antisemitic moods was also noted by outside observers. Oleksandr Konysky, who visited Galicia in 1886, recorded in his travel notes that although religious intolerance between the local Christian and Jewish populations was not evident, neither the Poles nor the Ruthenians liked Jews:

> All well-known observers of Hutsul mores, especially parish priests, unanimously corroborate that the Jews have introduced terrible demoralization into the Hutsul milieu and are destroying their well-being. In point of fact, in the last ten years alone the Jews have multiplied so much in Hutsul settlements, especially, for example, in Zhabie [the largest village in the Hutsul region—Y. H.], that they comprise approximately 15 percent of the total urban population. Many entirely competent people told me that 'wherever a Jew shows up, drunkenness, debauchery, and extreme poverty crop up there among the Hutsuls and Lemkos![55]

In the second half of the nineteenth century there was a belief among Galician peasants that the day of retribution, when all Jews would be killed, was imminent. The peasants cherished hopes for the return of the army of the Russian tsar, who was supposed to give the peasants the lands belonging to the Polish lords and grant them permission to kill the Jews. After his visit to Galicia in 1875, Mykhailo Drahomanov recalled the words of a Hutsul about the future "war against the Jews," which "God may grant on the feast day of St. Nicholas."[56]

In any case, as an anonymous writer from Lviv wrote in 1884, anti-semitism was a universal feeling shared by everyone, from the poorest man to the heir to the throne, Crown Prince Rudolph. He cited Rudolph's comment about the Jews of northern Hungary (today, the Ukrainian region of Transcarpathia): "Living among the simple but honest Ruthenian folk, they issue orders according to their will and however it suits them, and in exploiting them at every step and acquiring power over them, they lead them to perdition, and before they [the Ruthenians] reach that point, they [the Jews] order them to serve them." The author of this newspaper report advised the Jews in Galicia "to sit quietly and be satisfied that everyone still opposes them in a legal manner, considering, furthermore, the example that in other lands efforts have been made in another manner to get rid of them, like, e.g., in Russia, Germany, or Hungary, all the more so as here, in Galicia, the jug is overflowing."[57]

Naturally, all these statements should be treated with caution: they reflect the contemporary thoughts of the Christian population rather than the real situation.[58] However, it is important to note that in popularizing Ruthenian-Jewish solidarity, Franko went dramatically against the prevailing mood. Thus, it is no wonder that he and his friends were called "sell-outs to the Jews, servants of the Jews, allies of the Jews, and God knows what other kinds of brothers to the Jews."[59] Franko himself was considered to be half-Jewish.[60]

Franko and the Jewish Question in 1881–1883

Even as Franko was taking an active part in forming a Ukrainian-Polish-Jewish party, the formula of solidarity among the working people of various nationalities, which he promoted, was severely tested. In the summer of 1881, a wave of anti-Jewish pogroms took place in the southern Ukrainian gubernias of the Russian Empire, which were caused or provoked by the assassination of Tsar Alexander II.[61] The Russian pogroms of 1881 were a watershed in the history of the Jews of Eastern Europe. On the one hand, they sparked the mass emigration of Russian Jews to Western Europe and North America and, on the other, they gave birth to Zionism as a response to the growth of antisemitic moods. The 1881 pogroms also had an impact on Galicia. Some Jews fleeing Russia to the West stopped over in Galicia, where they settled down. Their presence there led to renewed discussions of Jewish topics.[62] Both Jews and non-Jews awaited a repetition of the wave of violence that had passed through the southern Ukrainian gubernias.

Franko was well aware of the great apprehension felt by the Galician Jews, and commented later on this mood: "Strange rumors, frightening stories, ominous predictions were making the rounds" [*Mozaika* 27]. Franko reworked some Jewish songs from this period—imitations of the ancient psalms beseeching Jehovah's help—into a cycle of poems titled *Zhydivs'ki melodii* (Jewish Melodies). These poems are marked by Franko's sincere sympathy for the victims of the pogroms [*Mozaika* 27; *ZT* 31–32]. Nevertheless, his position on the Jewish question was ambivalent. For example, in 1883 he published in the Lviv newspaper *Dilo* an article titled "Pytannia zhydivs'ke" (The Jewish Question) whose tone was blatantly antisemitic. The article was published as a front-page editorial and, judging by its content, it claimed to have a programmatic character. The article, which was written in the wake of anti-Jewish pogroms in Hungary, also mentioned the recent pogroms in Russia. Franko was particularly concerned about Galicia, where anti-Jewish violence might be even larger in scale than in Russia.

The geography of the spread of the antisemitic movement led him to conclude that this movement was becoming universal, and therefore its causes could not be sought only in local conditions. Franko did not reduce these causes either to racial or religious hatred. In his opinion, they were much deeper and thus concealed the threat that such anti-Jewish violence would be repeated. According to Franko, the mass pogroms were primarily underpinned by economic motives, the "demoralizing dominance of Jewish capital and exploitation."[63]

There was nothing unexpected about this social diagnosis: emphasizing the economic foundations of any social phenomenon was part and parcel of socialist ideology, which Franko championed and promoted. However, Franko unexpectedly cites another main cause: "Jewish arrogance and provocation." Franko blamed the Jews for the pogroms—not in the sense that their exploitation had led to those social explosions, but that they themselves were provoking pogroms to their own advantage. He based his argument on a comparison of the losses suffered by the Jewish and non-Jewish populations as a result of the pogroms. Jewish losses, he argued, were limited to broken windows and damaged bed linen, clothing, or other belongings. Meanwhile, there was loss of life among Christians: when the army dispersed a group of pogromists in Katerynoslav, fourteen people died on the spot and twenty-eight were wounded, six of whom later died of their injuries. During the Jewish pogroms in Hungary, only Christian blood was spilled. Furthermore, the majority of the pogromists—mostly workers—lost their property and health as a result of arrest and imprisonment, while the real or false victims of the pogroms received financial assistance from the government, the municipal administration, and Jewish relief organizations (such as the World Union of Israelites), and some Jews even profited from this assistance.

Franko proposed a detailed action program aimed at averting the threat of anti-Jewish pogroms. Essentially, it boiled down to a legal struggle against Jewish capital: Christians were supposed to organize themselves in trade and economic unions and establish their own shops in cities and villages, which would compete with Jewish ones. Franko believed that more attention should be focused on workers by founding self-help societies for them and preventing their hard-earned money from being frittered away in Jewish taverns. Peasants had to be protected from the loss of their lands because of debts owed to Jews. Franko proposed that the Galician parliament adopt a law on the "homesteading right," similar to the one that existed in legislation of the United States. Such a law would not permit an owner to be alienated from the land he tilled, on which his well-being and that of his family depended.

These measures still fit within the socialist perceptual framework. However, Franko's other proposals were not so benign: he suggested restricting the right of Jews to be elected to public councils and to lease taverns and landowners' lands in villages. Capping off Franko's deviation from socialist principles was his advice to his "class enemies"—the Greek Catholic clergy—to ensure "that Christians did not serve Jews and become estranged because of this from their faith and their people."[64]

A detailed recapitulation of the main thrust of Franko's article is important because it has all the hallmarks of a program, and also because it markedly deviates from the author's image, which can be derived from a reading of his other works on the Jewish question.[65] This is not the only Franko work in which the specter of antisemitism is apparent. In 1884, Franko wrote a poem titled "Shvyndelesa Parkhenblyta vandrivka z sela Derykhlopy do Ameryky i nazad" (Schwindeles Parchenblut's Journey from the Village of Derykhlopy to America and Back), which was published in the humor magazine, *Nove Zerkalo*. The main character in the poem is a Jewish tavern-keeper who resorts to all kinds of chicanery in order to hang onto his livelihood in his village, the residents of which have sworn off alcohol under the influence of the local priest. The hero even resorts to seeking help from thieves. When all his efforts fail, he sets out for faraway America on the advice of the local tzaddiks.

The poem is artistically undistinguished, but it clearly appealed to the tastes of the reading public.[66] It should be noted that the name of the poem's hero is constructed on the basis of a couple of vulgar stereotypes of Jews as swindlers (Schwindeles) and "unclean" (Parkhenblyt). It is difficult to determine whether the Parkhenblyt character was Franko's own creation.[67] Shvyndeles Parkhenblyt appeared in various issues of *Zerkalo* and *Nove zerkalo* as one of "three friends of the peasants" (in reality, enemies), along with the Polish nobleman "Patriotnyk" (Patriot) and a Russophile named My (We).[68] Most probably, Franko used a ready image and then garbed him in literary robes. It is also difficult to figure out the target of Franko's satire. On the one hand, Parkhenblyt does not personify all Jews, only those who mercilessly dupe and exploit Ukrainian peasants; on the other, the title character does this by relying on the Talmud, which supposedly permits him to commit sins.[69] Since Parkhenblyt's behavior corresponded to the basic tenets of Judaism, the image created by Franko might therefore be easily extrapolated to all Jews.

The Discussion in *Przegląd Społeczny*

How could Franko advance such manifestly contradictory views on the Jewish question? A partial answer to this question may be found in the articles he wrote in 1886–1887 for the Lviv-based journal *Przegląd Społeczny*, where he made his first attempt to systematize his views. He was spurred to do this by the public discussion sparked by publication of the writings of the talented Jewish-Polish journalist Alfred Nossig, whose article "An Attempt at Solving the Jewish Question" appeared in the first volume of the journal. Because of the significant role this article played both in the reconfiguration of the Jewish question in Galicia and in Franko's intellectual life, the circumstances surrounding its publication warrant examination in greater detail. The publication of Nossig's article had a profoundly symbolic importance, as it connoted a move in the direction of Zionism of part of assimilated Jewish youth. Nossig was one of the main founders of the newspaper *Ojczyzna* and of the "progressive" society *Przymierze braci* (Covenant of Brothers), founded in 1882, both of which promoted Polish assimilation. However, in the mid-1880s, reacting to the escalation of anti-semitism, Nossig deplored assimilation as hopeless and then proceeded to write a lengthy article expounding the Zionist program.[70]

The central thesis of Nossig's article is the statement that the "Jewish question ... cannot be solved until the Jews are living entirely amidst foreign states and nations." His thesis was based largely on Malthusian theory and social Darwinism. He portrayed the life of Jews in Christian societies until now as an uncompromising struggle for survival by all possible means. Since Jews were always trapped in a worse situation, they had to develop traits that would help them to survive; for example, underhandedness, craftiness, and unscrupulousness toward Christians. However, in the conditions of this struggle they had forged a nation out of themselves.

Besides enumerating anthropological criteria (shared physiological and "biotic" traits based on tribal purity), Nossig emphasized the nation-building role of cultural and social factors: a shared language (Yiddish), internal self-organization, and the existence of their own education, literature, and art. If Jews are a nation, Nossig writes, then it is logical to recognize their rights to their own state. "As soon as its creation is recognized as a crucial necessity, a Jewish state will be established in Palestine. This land is the fatherland of the Jews that they abandoned a long time ago, which is hallowed by their national tradition and whose restoration they are anticipating on the basis of religious dogma." There is only one alternative left for those Jews who do not wish to move to Palestine: to set out on the path of consistent assimilation and dissolve without a trace as a result of the actions of "natural forces."[71]

The publication of Nossig's article was followed by a programmatic article by the journal's editors and a feuilleton authored by Franko, both of which fundamentally supported this new attempt to solve the Jewish question. All these articles sparked reactions both in Galicia and in the Polish part of the Russian Empire. The majority of Lviv- and Warsaw-based periodicals merely recapitulated the authors' arguments, and the only ones that unconditionally opposed them were the Jewish assimilationist periodicals, *Der Israelit* and *Ojczyzna*. Franko, along with Nossig, became a target of criticism. *Der Israelit* devoted an article to Franko,[72] and Karpel Lippe from Iaşi wrote a brochure that was published under the potent title *Symptome der antisemitischen Geisteskrankheit* (Symptoms of the Antisemitic Mental

Illness). The ensuing polemic, which occasionally took the form of ad hominem attacks against Franko and accusations of antisemitism, forced him to take up the pen and expound his views on the Jewish question in another article titled "Semityzm i antysemityzm u Halychyni" (Semitism and Antisemitism in Galicia; 1887).

The two most important points underpinning Franko's attitude to the Jewish question were by no means original: they reflected the position of Nossig and the editorial board of *Przegląd Społeczny*. The first point was his recognition of the Jews as a separate nation "based on their separate situation, tradition, lifestyle, and, independently of all that, a separate spiritual order, a separate view of the world, and a separate character." His second point flowed logically from the first with respect to the development in the direction that the Jews acknowledged as reasonable for themselves, along with the simultaneous recognition of the same rights for the Polish and Ruthenian-Ukrainian nations.

In the political and intellectual atmosphere that reigned in the Austro-Hungarian and Russian empires at the time, even recognizing the Jews as a separate nation with the right to their autonomous development was quite a novelty, and in this regard the contributions of *Przegląd Społeczny* and its writers were undeniable. However, the journal sought to translate these principles into everyday practice, and this is precisely what sparked the greatest discussions. In the view of Franko and other contributors to the journal, the main problem was the great incongruity between the statuses of the Jewish and non-Jewish populations: while the Jews were held in much less esteem in the social and confessional sphere than non-Jews, in the sphere of economics the situation was the exact reverse: 60 percent of industry and 90 percent of trade in Galicia were in the hands of the Jews. Therefore, in the noble cause of instituting equal rights, it was not only Jews but also non-Jews who needed intervention and protection.

Franko agreed with Nossig's main conclusion that the "Jewish type is on the average tougher in the struggle for existence, but stands morally lower than the non-Jewish [type], he has more swiftness and endurance, but also more arrogance, ambition, and unscrupulousness."[73] Their superiority lay not only and not so much in the national character of the Jews as in the confessional and religious principles underpinning the organization of the Jewish community, particularly in the existence of the *kahals* (assemblies), which safeguarded and strengthened the Jews' internal solidarity and gave them a competitive advantage over Poles and Ukrainians in the economic life of Galicia. Franko saw evidence of this superiority in how quickly the Jews were acquiring huge tracts of land in Eastern Galicia: according to his estimates, between 1872 and 1886 the number of larger properties located in eight mountain counties rose from 19 to 82; in areas along the Dnister River, from 66 to 105. In the majority of cases, Franko noted, these farms were being used unproductively, with no investments being made to raise the level of agricultural technology, all of which led to their rapid decline. Meanwhile, the majority of Polish and Ruthenian-Ukrainian peasants were suffering from severe land hunger.

Maintaining the economic superiority of Jews in Galicia would have been impossible without several external factors: the help of the Polish nobility, whose economic welfare often depended on leasing their rights to Jews to sell alcohol, and Jewish relief organizations such as the above-mentioned World Union of Israelites, which raised money from Jews all over the world "for Galician goals." But the main role in this superiority was played by the internal solidarity of the Jews as a religious community. Franko cited the Warsaw-based Jewish newspaper *Głos*, which declared that "Jews have created a particular collective organization whose sole mission was the exploitation of others. There are not only capitalists among the Jews but also proletarians; but this proletariat is a strange one, for even though it often starves to death, it usually finds the means for its existence only through the exploitation of foreign elements" [*Mozaika* 324]. Franko cited a considerable number of Galician examples to illustrate this thesis, including the Boryslav war of 1884.[74]

The key to understanding Franko's "antisemitism" lies precisely in these theses. Franko's socialist views led him to defend the weak and the downtrodden, and where the Jewish community was concerned, his sympathies lay with poor Jews who were exploited by wealthy Jews. But the need to defend the poor non-Jewish population forced him into a confrontation with the entire Jewish community which, in his view, demonstrated a high level of internal solidarity on the question of the exploitation of Ukrainian and Polish workers and peasants.

Franko proposed his own program for solving the Jewish question, which may be divided into a minimal program and a maximum program. The minimum requirements boiled down to two points: restricting Jews' rights to acquire land, and introducing laws that would forbid rabbis to support economic exploitation under the guise of confessional solidarity. In Franko's opinion, the implementation of these requirements would lead to the introduction of a real equalization of rights for the Christian and non-Christian populations, and proposals concerning these requirements were supposed to come from educated Jews who aspired to the implementation of equal rights.

The maximum program had a more far-reaching goal. Using different words, it reiterated Nossig's two main points: 1) the voluntary assimilation of a certain number of Jews into the local population; 2) emigration from Galicia of the majority of Jews "to such a land where they might live and develop comprehensively as an undivided and independent people." Franko's own contribution was a proposal to grant a certain number of Jews in Galicia who did not opt for either the first or the second option the status of "aliens"—that is, their civic rights would be somewhat restricted. However, even this point was not entirely original, but was an option discussed in the pages of Jewish newspapers in the Russian Empire on the eve of and during the 1881 pogrom; Franko referred to these discussions in his proposals.

Franko's originality lay primarily in his understanding of assimilation. By Jewish assimilation he did not mean "acceptance of baptism and the use of pork." On the contrary, he was in favor of safeguarding religious law and opposed all attempts to foist Christianity from above [*Mozaika* 326]. Franko also objected to the formula for assimilation proposed by the Haskalah.[75] The issue that sparked the most objections from Franko was the predictable—in those conditions—solidarity between assimilated Jews and the members of the ruling class of a given country, and their alienation both from the poor in general and the poor people of Christian "unhistoric nations." Franko proposed the following formula for Jewish assimilation: "Above all, this is a task of civic equalization on the basis of equal rights and equal duties....At the same time—and this must be emphasized!—it is not length of settlement, not land, not capital that makes one a citizen of a land, but only feelings of solidarity with the people's ideals and the work to translate them into reality" [*Mozaika* 328].

The presence in Franko's formula of the need for "solidarity with the people's ideals" diluted the very notion of assimilation to such a degree that, as the Ukrainian scholar Petro Kudriavtsev has written, Franko "interprets assimilation in such a way that there is nothing left of it."[76] However, this project cannot be regarded as all that utopian: in the late nineteenth and early twentieth centuries there was a small group of Jews in Galicia who called the Ruthenian language their language of conversation.[77] It is obvious, however, that compared to the Polish and German examples of assimilation, the scale of Ruthenian assimilation of Galician Jews was modest. In any event, whether intentionally or not, Franko greatly narrowed down the possibility of assimilation, even though he claimed that "no matter what, [it] must occupy the top place in our Jewish policies" [*Mozaika* 326].

In this context, Franko's programmatic demand that the majority of Jews should immigrate to a land "where they might live and develop comprehensively as an undivided and independent people" is intriguing. It was singled out by Ivan Lysiak-Rudnytsky, who described it as the seeds of the future Zionist program.[78] However, he failed to note that Franko was merely reiterating one of Nossig's theses. Zionism as a way of solving the Jewish question occupied a very marginal place in the young Franko's consciousness; he did not elaborate it anywhere at least until the mid-1890s. Even as late as 1893 he was still writing about Zionism as "the most dangerous of all trends" among Galician Jews, in keeping with his view that their plans to create a Jewish state was nothing more than "childish dreams."[79] He finally recognized the idea of an independent Jewish state only in 1896–1897, most probably under the influence of Theodor Herzl.[80] But before that time his world perception would undergo a fundamental alteration. The principal change would be the rejection of the populist paradigm within whose framework the "people's ideals" were the chief criteria for assessing any kind of political program and political activity.

Franko's Case in a Comparative Context

It is not difficult for historians of the Jewish question to define the views of the young Franko: they are a manifestation of what is known as "progressive antisemitism," whose goal is to exploit the Jewish question in order to spread revolutionary moods and activities. In contrast to "conservative antisemitism," the progressive variety is fundamentally opposed to chauvinism, racism, and "reactionary antisemitism"—that is, antisemitism that protects and legitimizes the old order, and supports the emancipation of the Jews.[81] However, in many respects Franko went beyond progressive antisemitism. In order to illustrate this point, it is worthwhile comparing Franko's views to those espoused by other famous intellectuals of the time, the various socialists and nonsocialists who were his peers and good friends. With each of them Franko operated to a certain degree on some shared plane: as a socialist, with the Austrian Social Democratic leader Victor Adler; as a writer, with the Polish poet Eliza Orzeszkowa; as a national ideologist, with the politician and later president of Czechoslovakia Tomáš Masaryk; and, finally, as an ideologist of Ukrainian nationalism, with his mentor, Mykhailo Drahomanov.

Victor Adler was of Jewish parentage; he even married his wife, Emma, according to the Jewish ritual. However, all three of his children were baptized. In this connection, Adler liked to repeat the words of Heinrich Heine: "Der Taufzettel ist das Eintrittsbillet zur europäischen Kultur" (baptism is the ticket to European culture). Like many young Jews of their generation, Victor and Emma Adler were fascinated by socialism, especially since it promised liberation not only to workers but also to Jews. Left-wing Jewish intellectuals regarded themselves as carriers of enlightenment, whose mission was to lead the Jews out of the premodern traditional society. However, in the company of his closest friends, Adler expressed his views in an antisemitic and even racist form—to the immense irritation of his wife.[82]

Eliza Orzeszkowa was the first Polish writer to treat Jewish topics systematically and with profound understanding. She noted a strange resemblance between Jewish history and culture and the fate of the Polish nation. Her works, like those of Franko, contain numerous examples of positive descriptions of Jews (Orzeszkowa's moralistic and didactic tone strengthens this resemblance). Like the young Franko, Orzeszkowa challenged the practical value of Zionism, believing that assimilation of the Jews was the best way to eradicate tensions in their relations with non-Jews. Unlike Adler, she was opposed to the conversion of Jews to Christianity. Nevertheless, she interpreted assimilation variously: in her view, this process should be nationally based: Jews should be integrated into the Polish nation. At the same time, she objected to the Jews' calling themselves a separate nation on the grounds that they did not have their own national language.[83]

Like Ivan Franko, Tomáš Masaryk was born in a village where from a young age he heard the stories of Jews using the blood of Christians to bake their Passover matzo. According to Masaryk's own admission, to the end of his life he never succeeded in overcoming certain anti-Jewish prejudices that were common among ordinary folk. Despite these prejudices, however, he remained a principled opponent of antisemitism. In 1900, he rose to the defense of a Jew who was accused of a ritual murder, and wrote a book exposing this blood libel. For his pains he was ostracized by his fellow professors, faculty, and students at Charles University in Prague.[84]

A comparison of the young Franko with Adler and Orzeszkowa clearly places him in the center of the "progressive antisemitism" current and reveals the distinctiveness or complete originality of his views with respect to at least two major points. The first lies in his rejection (in contrast to Adler) of the feasibility of the Jews' assimilation in the national or religious sense, and the second in his recognition (in contrast to Orzeszkowa) of the Jews as a separate nation. The Franko-Masaryk analogy is interesting from another perspective: both of them grew up in a milieu where it was far easier and simpler to become an antisemite than a philosemite. Thus, both of them were criticized by their fellow countrymen for their sympathies toward the Jews.

But in the Ukrainian context it is most productive to compare Franko with his intellectual mentor, Mykhailo Drahomanov, who was instrumental in formulating the Ukrainian movement's stance on the Jewish question. Recognition of the Jews as a separate nation was decisive. Here, the version of socialism as proposed by Drahomanov departed from many currents of European socialism, which regarded the assimilation of the Jews (as well as Ukrainians and others) into "historical nations" as the paramount task. Drahomanov placed social solidarity on a higher plane than national solidarity and therefore appealed to Ukrainian radicals to nurture "goodwill toward working Jews." At the same time, he struggled against the Russian populists' "Judaeophobia." Still, there was much utopianism, as well as quite a few contradictions, in his views on the Jewish question, especially with regard to his assessment of the Jewish nation in Ukraine as a "parasitic class" and his neglect of Judaism as the foundation of Jewish self-identity.[85]

Drahomanov's influence on Franko and the similarity of their views are obvious. There is a resemblance both in terms of the positive points in their attitudes toward Jews and certain antisemitic notes.[86] However, nowhere in Drahomanov's writings does any blatant antisemitism appear, as it does in Franko's article "The Jewish Question" and the poem "Shvyndeles Parkhenblyt." Some of Franko's antisemitic statements might be read as a manifestation of his solidarity with nationalism. Nevertheless, even the direct identification of antisemitism with nationalism does not work in Franko's case. One might expect that as Franko's attraction to nationalistic ideals grew in the late nineteenth and early twentieth centuries, so would his antisemitism. But this was not the case. On the contrary: in the writings of the later ("nationalistic") Franko it is difficult to find antisemitic declarations similar to the ones he made in his youth.[87]

Franko's example once again shows how attitudes to Jews among the progressive intelligentsia of that time could be complex and diverse, and therefore defy easy generalizations. His antisemitism corresponds to the conclusion reached by Peter Gay in his study of German antisemitism in the nineteenth century: "It was a culture in which clusters of ideas we would regard as grossly contradictory coexisted without strain in the same person."[88]

In view of the Galician situation and the circumstances of Franko's personal life, the occasional antisemitic notes in his work were simply inevitable. However, antisemitism constituted neither the nucleus of his views on the Jewish question nor his world perception: it was negated by his other declarations and political steps.

> Radicals are not antisemites. We say this clearly and openly. We are not the enemies of the Jews because they are Jews who come from Palestine, who wear peyos [side-curls] and caftans, and smell of onions. We are indifferent to this, and for such stupid reasons we shall certainly not be spreading among the people hatred of the Jews, the majority of whom in our land are even poorer and more miserable than our peasants....The radicals are appealing to and gathering the people not against the Jews but against Jewish parasitism and exploitation, against Jewish intrigue and mischief. But, no. Not just against Jewish parasitism but against all kinds of parasitism and exploitation, circumcised and uncircumcised, baptized and unbaptized, against all kinds of intrigue and mischief, whether they wear a caftan or a uniform or a cassock. And in coming out against the Jews the radicals know well how to distinguish, and they know that that Jewish *lapserdak* [black coat worn by Orthodox Jews—Y. H.] with peyos in a caftan and the smell of onions is much less of an enemy of the peasant than that civilized, tailcoat-wearing, and decorated Jewish financier, millionaire, speculator, and wholesaler, who turns over millions, who walks arm in arm with counts and ministers, whose hand is squeezed with a pleasant smile by bishops and metropolitans! The radicals come out strongest against those great bloodsuckers. They rail against those state and civic arrangements that allow those bloodsuckers to swan around like lords and guarantee them not only complete impunity but, in addition, all sorts of honors, respect, and medals.[89]

When Franko speaks in the name of the radicals, one must assume that he is speaking above all in his own name, for, as other documents from the radicals' milieu indicate, antisemitism was not at all alien to them.[90] Owing to the lack of studies on this subject, I cannot determine whether the radicals' position differed from the position held by the Polish peasant parties in Galicia, which exploited the image of the Jew in the traditional culture as a constitutional "other" in the formulation of their ideological principles and political mobilization of the peasantry.[91]

Franko, meanwhile, created a radical inversion of the traditional stereotype: in his view, the absolute "other" is the *pan* (lord), "exploiter," "parasite," and the like, while the Jews, under certain conditions, could be "ours." This conclusion becomes more apparent by moving from the domain of politics into the domain of literature. Aleksander Hertz, the author of studies on the image of the Jews in Polish culture, observed that, despite an abundance of Jewish themes, Polish literature presents Jews strictly from the Polish perspective, as part of the Polish landscape. Readers learn little or nothing about the life of the Jewish community, whether Orthodox or "progressive."[92] Hertz's observation makes it possible to assess Franko's originality in full: in having his main hero, whether it be Surka, a poor Jewish woman [*ZT* 1:215–23] or the Boryslav industrialist Herman Goldkremer, narrate the story, Franko allows the reader to view events through the eyes of the Jewish protagonist. This radical reconceptualization of Jews is regarded as one of the most interesting phenomena of modern Ukrainian thought.[93] The goal was to create the figure of a "Ukrainian Jew." That this process was full of contradictions and far from complete does not diminish Franko's role as the pioneer of such a reconceptualization in the nineteenth century, when this figure lacked the underpinnings of intellectual constructs.

Chapter 15

Franko and His Readers

On the last day of 1886, Franko, out walking, bumped into the gymnasium student Osyp Makovei and invited him home. Makovei stayed for many hours listening to his host talking about his life. Returning home, Makovei immediately recorded their conversation in his diary, which is how we know what the two men discussed.[1] As he was planning to give a lecture about Franko to his fellow gymnasium students in the next few months, he made detailed notes. But Makovei's conversation with Franko was important for another reason. Like most young and ambitious people, Makovei dreamed of a literary career. His contemporaries recalled that in the 1870s and 1880s the urge to write (*poezomaniia*) was so widespread among young people that it was a fad, or even a kind of epidemic, that affected if not every young person then every second one.[2] Thus, much could be learned about carving out a career as a successful writer from none other than Franko.

Makovei saw hope for success in the fact that his own life somewhat resembled Franko's. Like Franko, Makovei was born in the provinces, into an ethnically mixed family of a Ruthenian-Czech artisan. After he completed his studies at the school in Yavoriv, his parents heeded the advice of the boy's maternal uncle, a Czech landowner, and decided to send Osyp to the Lviv gymnasium. "If he passes the exams, that will be good, let him go [there], somehow we will push him forward; but if not, then at least he will have seen Lviv," they declared. Arriving in Lviv in 1879, Makovei, like Franko five years earlier, was bowled over by the city's grandeur. He began his studies at the Lviv Academic Gymnasium, the only Ruthenian classical high school in the city. In the upper grades, Makovei and a few other Ruthenian students formed a secret circle whose goal was "to gain preliminary practice in work in any kind of field, together to learn how to be useful to society." A total of fifty-eight students belonged to this group. They wrote works in the spirit of "realism and European liberalism," publishing them in illegal newspapers printed on hectographs.[3]

The circle was exposed after local Russophiles denounced it to the authorities, and an official investigation was launched in 1886. Among the accusations was the question of Makovei's relationship with Franko. They had met in late 1885 at the editorial offices of *Zoria*, where Makovei had brought his translations of German poetry. He became fascinated with Franko, and over time Makovei became one of his most ardent supporters. Their lengthy conversation in Franko's home resembled an encounter between one of the Apostles and a newly converted Christian; at the very least, there was mutual trust and openness between the two men.

On the day that Makovei was a guest in his home, Franko first reminisced about his years at the gymnasium and then turned to current events. "Now—he says—I am abandoning the editorship of *Zoria*. I do not wish to drink from this bitter cup, I will free myself." Franko wanted to move back to his native village, where he could work in peace. He was thinking of "earning a living from the Liakhs"—meaning from the honoraria that he was receiving from various Polish newspapers.

During his talk with Makovei Franko also talked about Ruthenian-Ukrainian literature in Galicia. He criticized the current crop of poets, among whom the populists bore the brunt of his critical comments. Makovei asked why the reading public had so little time and respect for great writers like Franko. "Who knows?!" Franko replied. "You live from year to year, and that's that…"

Then the two men began discussing Makovei's plans. Makovei admitted that he had been invited to work at *Zoria*, and Franko tried to dissuade him, urging him to complete his studies at the gymnasium and then study law at the university. He should first ensure that he had a profession that could provide him with a good living and, eventually, enough time to devote to his writing, Franko advised.

Finally, Franko began explaining religious and social issues to Makovei. But since the younger man was only interested in literary matters, he did not record this part of the conversation in his diary. His diary entry ends with the following reproach: "O Ruthenians! How gloriously you champion your own people—with hatred. You need colder blood. But in the meantime, because of Franko's sincerity I am becoming an increasingly greater friend of his."[4]

The close of 1886 marked the end of the first half of Franko's life. The years remaining before his death in May 1916 were approximately equal to the number of years that had elapsed since his birth. Of course, neither Franko nor Makovei could have known this. But, during his conversation with Makovei Franko spoke as though he were summarizing an entire period of his life. That much was true: the period of his unsettled and extremely eventful youth had just ended. He had just gotten married, attaining a certain level of stability in his life, and he enjoyed the reputation of a first-class writer.

In the following section I will endeavor to answer the following questions: What memories of himself would Franko have left behind if he had died in 1886 instead of 1916? Would a cult have still formed around his personality? What kind of influence would the works of the young Franko have exerted—if any at all—on the debates surrounding the identity of local Ruthenians?

Who Was Reading Franko?

Partial answers to these questions may be obtained by examining statistics on the production of printed matter. The Galician bibliographer, Ivan Levytsky, estimated that between 1801 and 1860—that is, before the birth of Franko—local Ruthenian-Ukrainian authors published a total of 1,352 works.[5] This is not a very impressive number, representing an average of twenty-two titles per year. There were years, even entire decades, when not a single work appeared.[6] Surveying the achievements of Ruthenian-Ukrainian literature during the first hundred years of Austrian rule, Franko declared that it would be an easy task to pile all those publications—especially truly valuable works that were not simply printed paper—onto a couple of wheelbarrows and transport them to Vienna as proof of the existence of Ruthenian-Ukrainian literature [ZT 41:21]. Meanwhile, the most complete bibliography of Franko's publications, covering the first thirteen years of his work (1874–1886), lists 572 titles, including 115 literary works.[7] Despite the fact that Levytsky's bibliography lacks thoroughness, not everything that the young Franko published may be regarded as valuable (he himself readily acknowledged this [ZT 1:19]). However, it may be stated with all certitude that in 1886 he alone could submit his book and journalistic writings as proof of the existence of Ruthenian-Ukrainian literature.

Of course, it makes more sense to compare Franko with his contemporaries rather than his predecessors. The specific moment when Franko appeared as a figure in the literary movement of the Galician-Ruthenian-Ukrainians in the mid-1870s was a turning point: from that point the number of printed works never fell below a hundred titles per year (see table 9). Between 1874 and 1886, 2,127 titles were published. Seventy-eight titles, or 6 percent of the total, belonged to Franko.[8] Considering that Levytsky's bibliography numbers several hundred authors, it is clear that Franko's contribution to the development of literature was greater than average—in fact, it was one of the largest.

The introduction of a general Ukrainian context does not change matters considerably: between 1871 and 1886 the young Franko became one of the thirty most productive Ruthenian-Ukrainian authors, editors, and publishers in the Austro-Hungarian and Russian empires (see table 10). Of course, it should be kept in mind that after the 1876 Ems Ukase the number of Ukrainian-language publications in the Russian Empire shrank significantly, which explains why the proportion of Galicians is inordinately high (numbering fifteen out of twenty of the most productive writers). However, it is worth remembering that, first of all, Galicia adopted the role of the "Ukrainian Piedmont," where not only Galicians but also Ukrainian authors—with increasing frequency—were published. Second, Franko's ratings continued to rise from that point (he occupied fourth place in 1887–1894, and a fixed first place during the next decade, 1895–1905).

In order to determine the specific importance of Franko's writings it is crucial to compare these data with readers' reception—that is, to answer the question, "Who was reading Franko?" The answer must begin with a general description of the reading market. Franko made his debut at a time that was quite favorable for writers like him: the local reading public was switching from reading foreign authors to reading the national literature. This is clear from research on tastes among users of the Ossoliński Library, the largest public library in Lviv. Whereas in the 1850s the most popular works were Defoe's *Robinson Crusoe* and the works of Goethe and James Fenimore Cooper, eventually the most popular works borrowed by readers were those by the Polish writers Józef Kraszewski, Józef Korzeniowski, Michał Czajkowski, and Henryk Sienkiewicz.[9]

Naturally, these data refer primarily to Polish readers, who were the main users of the Ossoliński Library. The Ruthenian case was simultaneously similar and different. Fylyp Svystun recalls that when he was studying at the Lviv gymnasium (1855–1864), his peers spent their free time in the Ossoliński Library, where they read almost exclusively Polish and German books; Ruthenian books did not appeal to their emotions. A sea change took place only in 1862, after Shevchenko's *Kobzar* appeared in Galicia. This book became the first national bestseller, and under its influence many young people switched to reading Ruthenian literature.[10] The switch to "national" reading is convincingly attested by the example of the self-organized students' library at the Drohobych gymnasium in the last years of Franko's studies there (1873–1874): its readers showed a greater keenness to borrow the works of Taras Shevchenko, Mykola Hohol (Nikolai Gogol), Panteleimon Kulish, and other Ukrainian authors than the works of Schiller and Goethe.[11]

Naturally, this trend should not be absolutized. For a considerable proportion of the educated public even *Robinson Crusoe* was heavy-going; at best, it was read as a sleep aid. Many educated members of the public read the same books as their servants: sensational novels with the characteristic titles *Simon and Maria, or the Cat's Eye, Princess Sirena, or the Cardinal's Secret*, and *Count Jan, or the Blind Slave Girl from Shiraz*.[12] As one Lviv newspaper complained in 1878, the Galician reading public had something like a strong and unassailable antipathy to reading, particularly works that were "serious, educational, their own."[13]

Franko and other Ruthenian-Ukrainian authors were read primarily by those members of the public for whom "reading is a moment of happiness and of dreams and plans for the future, not horror—fever—fainting."[14] These were members of the public who were engaged in civic work, and since they comprised a stratum that was "comparatively very impoverished, more patriotic than moneyed,"[15] every coin spent on a book or newspaper was practically an act of patriotism.

The weight of these facts should be particularly emphasized in view of the romanticized image of Austrian Galicia as a "national Piedmont" with a developed public space, mass publications, and large reading public. In reality, the reading public was limited, and print runs were modest. An accurate picture of their scope may be gained from the fact that in 1876 the government newspaper, *Gazeta Lwowska*, had a circulation of 7,000 copies, a figure that was considered very high.[16] For Ruthenian-Ukrainian publications the benchmark was the first mass-circulation newspaper, *Zoria Halytska*, which was published from 1848 to 1857. At the end of its first year of publication, the number of its subscribers (1,500) was the maximum by which the intellectual reading public was measured among Galician-Ruthenians for the next four decades (see table 11). Other publications enjoyed approximately the same circulation figures (1,000–1,500)—for example, the government's Ruthenian-language newspaper, *Visnyk*; the popular newspapers *Nauka* and Ivan Naumovych's *Russkaia rada*; and the first publications issued by the Kachkovsky and Prosvita societies. Of course, print runs were sometimes larger, reaching 5,000–6,000 copies, and even 10,000–15,000. But in those cases, considerable numbers of books remained unsold, or they were distributed over an extended period of time. In years marked by financial difficulties or simply a lessening of interest among readers, print runs could decrease to a minimum of 300–500 copies.[17]

Against this background, Franko's publishing activities enjoyed comparatively modest success: the print runs of his publications correspond to the minimum statistical indicator. The books from the Small Library, which were published under his editorship, were printed in runs averaging 300 copies each, regardless of whether a book had a larger print run of 1,000 or a smaller one [ZT 48:217, 275]. Sales statistics with regard to the publications of the Small Library are important in that until the late 1870s it was Franko's sole publishing venture that was not affected by censorship bans. Thus, it rather objectively reflects the size of the reading public with a radical orientation. The journal Svit, which Franko edited together with Ivan Belei, had a print run similar to the Small Library's [ZT 48:275], and the prosecutor's office never confiscated a single copy of the journal, which "was [eventually] extinguished as a result of public apathy."[18] Franko planned this kind of print run for his new journal, Postup (1886), which was designed to be the mouthpiece of the younger, radical generation. However, even this figure seemed inflated to him: "Three hundred subscribers is such a great feat that I don't even dare think about it" [ZT 49:92].

Franko's collection of poetry, Z vershyn i nyzyn (1887) had a larger print run of 600–1,000 copies, according to Bohdan Yakymovych's estimates.[19] This publication was the sum total of his "radical achievement" in the sphere of poetry. The larger print run of this poetry collection may be explained by the fact that, as one critic put it, whenever Franko forgot about his radicalism and naturalism, he created pearls of poetry,[20] and thus attracted not only the "radical" reader but also the wider reading public. Franko's almanacs, Veselka, Vatra, and Pershyi vinok, had roughly the same print runs.[21]

The nature of Franko's reading public may be illustrated by several concentric circles. The smallest circle, representing 300 people, comprised his closest radical milieu. Compensating for this small number was the high mobilizational level and young age of its members. Among this group of readers esteem for Franko bordered on piety, and his books and journals were preserved as reliquaries.[22] As regards Franko's literary works, the circle of his readers doubled in size. After joining the populist camp in the 1880s, Franko ended up in the "top league": their periodicals had print runs ranging between 1,000 and 1,500 copies.[23] This cooperation led to mutual benefits: Franko obtained access to a larger public, and his collaboration with populist periodicals boosted their popularity. For example, thanks to Franko's editorship, *Zoria*'s print run increased from 500 to 1,000 copies.[24]

Newspapers were the key to popularity among readers. Georg Brandes, the distinguished literary critic of the late nineteenth century, was convinced that 90 percent of people who knew how to read only read newspapers.[25] Brandes's assessment may be accepted, but with one serious reservation: even illiterate people participated in the reading of newspapers. The nineteenth century saw the rise of a new phenomenon whereby newspapers and magazines were read out loud in public. This is linked with the transition from the traditional peasant lifestyle to an urban one, even though the Galician experience shows that new forms of reading were also gaining popularity in the countryside.[26] In the hierarchy of print publications that were circulated among the peasantry, *kazety* (newspapers), featuring news about what was going on in the world, ranked high. They were read—from cover to cover—out loud outside churches after Sunday Mass or in rural reading rooms.

Estimates of the size of the peasant readership vary greatly. Mykhailo Pavlyk estimated the number of potential "readers" visiting Ruthenian-Ukrainian reading rooms during the mid-1880s at 9,050 people,[27] while the figure listed in official statistics is 29,500.[28] Pavlyk's estimate is probably more realistic, because he included those reading rooms that showed real signs of life, not those that existed merely on paper. Scant available sources provide grounds for concluding that the situation among the peasants was the same as among the intelligentsia, which consisted of several circles of readers. The nucleus was formed of "radical" peasants, most likely those who hailed from Franko and Pavlyk's areas. Pavlyk tried to convince Drahomanov that the "peasants…are flocking in great numbers to *Druh*,"[29] while Franko assured him that throughout the countryside there were one or two hundred people, at the very least, who read *Svit* [*ZT* 48:323].

There also existed a large number of readers who perused "nonrevolutionary" newspapers. Completed questionnaires about the state of rural reading rooms are included in the archive of Pavlyk, who tried to calculate the size of the reading room movement. These provide a good idea of which periodicals the peasants were reading and subscribing to (see table 12). The questionnaires do not contain any significant surprises; they merely confirm what is well known from other sources: the popularity of *Batkivshchyna* and *Nauka*, two newspapers that were published specifically for the peasants, and to which literate peasants regularly contributed materials. Franko did not collaborate with either of them. The populist periodicals *Dilo* and *Zerkalo* were a different matter: although they were not the most popular, they were in the top half of the list. Franko was a key contributor to both of these periodicals, although the need to conceal his identity with pseudonyms or to submit his materials completely unsigned did not foster his popularity. He was able to reveal his authorship in *Zoria*, and *Gazeta Naddniestrzańska* often wrote about him, but both these publications, as evidenced by the list, were rarely seen in rural reading rooms. The only extant list of books that were borrowed most frequently in reading rooms does not contain a single work by Franko, although this list reveals that literate peasants were definitely interested in the national literature and its authors (the list starts with a biography of Taras Shevchenko).[30]

On the basis of these few data it is possible to confirm the fact that peasants could have read Franko's writings in three mass populist periodicals: *Dilo*, *Zoria*, and *Zerkalo*. If so, then thanks to the peasantry, Franko's readership expanded to 11,500 people (based on Pavlyk's estimates) or even 31,000 (according to official data). But even this larger number was too small compared to, say, the 185,000 Ruthenian pupils and students of the mid-1880s.

The best indicator of the small reading market was the fact that not a single Galician author could earn a living through his or her writing. As Volodymyr Barvinsky, the editor of *Dilo*, was fond of saying, there was no benefit accruing to Galician literature—"not a crumb or a penny" (*ani krykhty, ani denezhky*).[31] In order to support himself and his family, every writer had to work in government service, devoting nine or ten hours a day to his job, and then work on his writing in his spare time. Thus, a writer in this position wrote sporadically, from time to time, and was unable to reflect or penetrate the essence of his subject with any profundity. As a result, a vicious circle was created in Galicia, from the time mass publications began appearing there in the mid-nineteenth century and lasting until the Second World War: the readers' market could not give rise to professional authors, and, owing to the impossibility of working professionally, writers were unable to create a mass readership.

Franko was the only successful exception: a professional writer who lived "by the pen."[32] His literary and scholarly work in the period from 1880 to 1920 was deemed the finest that Galicia was capable of producing.[33] But even the success that he enjoyed among the reading public—as regards its size—was comparatively modest, which is why he was utterly unable to support himself from the income generated from the Ruthenian-Ukrainian readers' market of Lviv and Galicia as a whole. His writings and editorial work for Lviv-based Ukrainian periodicals generated between half and three-quarters of his modest monthly earnings of sixty guldens [*ZT* 33:356; 48:554]. He could have survived on this amount if he had been a bachelor, but it was hardly sufficient for the needs of a growing family.[34] But even the small budgets of Galician periodicals could not have existed without the funds that they were sent by Ukrainian patriots in Kyiv or Geneva. It was expected that in exchange Galician publishers, editors, and writers would send their production eastward, across the Austrian-Russian border, beyond which lived up to 80–85 percent of the entire (potential) Ruthenian-Ukrainian nation. Franko hoped that literature would help bring down the border between Galicia and Ukraine [*ZT* 48:267].

However, the Ukrainian readers' market in the Russian Empire was even smaller than the Galician one. Its size was fatally restricted by two circumstances. First, the level of illiteracy in Ukrainian gubernias was higher than in Galicia. In the Kyiv educational district in 1885 there was one school serving a population of 2,500, while among Galician-Ruthenians the ratio was 1:1,100. The lack of schools could not be compensated for by rural reading rooms because, as an observer of education in Ukrainian gubernias has written, "you could sooner find a needle in a haystack than a people's reading room in Russia."[35] The second fatal circumstance was the unpublicized ban on the printed Ukrainian word. The ban was never a total one, and in 1881–1886 the newspapers *Dilo* and *Zoria* had permission to circulate their publications in the Russian Empire—from which newspapers, of course, the tsarist censors first excised offending articles by covering entire pages with black ink.[36] Franko's experience of censorship had more to do with Austrian censors than Russian ones.[37] However, the tsarist ban functioned in an indirect and more sophisticated manner: the Russian government viewed the very fact of subscribing to, or circulating, Ukrainian publications as a manifestation of political unreliability, suspicion of which could lead to a variety of problems, including dismissal from state service.[38]

A rough idea of the size of the reading market in the Ukrainian gubernias of the Russian Empire may be derived from data on the circulation of *Zoria*, which was under Franko's editorship: Konysky assured Franko that the journal could realistically count on 120–125 subscribers (See table 13). Franko claimed, however, that by the time Galician-Ukrainian publications were completely banned in the Russian Empire in 1894, *Zoria* had 600 subscribers scattered throughout its Ukrainian gubernias [*ZT* 48:479]. Of course, there were significantly more readers than subscribers: in 1884 Franko's local correspondents reported to him that issues of *Zoria* in Ukraine "went from hand to hand among the hungry populace."[39] The small chain of readers that was being formed during this process could have reached Moscow, Samara, and even Siberia.[40] But there could not have been all that many readers of *Zoria* there. The Ukrainian readers' market was an appendage of the Galician one, not the other way around. If one takes into account not only its patriotically inclined segment but also the general readership, it was oriented toward Russian publications. At the very best, the works of the Galician writer Franko, as well as local writers such as Ivan Nechui-Levytsky and Panas Myrny, and even Taras Shevchenko, were read as supplements to the spiritual nourishment that readers in the Russian Empire sought in Russian literature.[41]

What allowed Franko to earn a living as a professional writer was the fact that, starting in the late 1870s, he was constantly published in Polish periodicals. The Polish publishers' market in Galicia was larger than the Ruthenian-Ukrainian one: from the 1880s to the 1900s it surpassed the number of Ukrainian periodicals by some three to six times, while its print runs were seven or eight times larger. The Polish reading market also differed from the Ruthenian-Ukrainian one in that it served as a "balance" between "Austrian" and "Russian" publications. Despite the fact that a segment of the former markedly increased after the introduction of Galician autonomy, Warsaw remained the capital of Polish print production (Polish publications in the German Empire had a purely local significance; for that reason, they are not included in these figures).[42] In 1882, Oleksandr Barvinsky dreamed that all of Russian-ruled Ukraine would one day "produce even twice as little of the production that Warsaw alone offered to Poles."[43]

Franko took full advantage of the Poles' superior publishing market: his works were published by both Galician and "Russian" Polish periodicals. The largest and most mass-produced Polish periodicals were sociopolitical ones, which may be divided into four groups according to their political orientation: conservative, liberal-democratic, populist (*ludowa*), and socialist.[44] Franko collaborated with three out of four of the most important groups of periodicals: liberal-democratic (*Prawda* and *Kraj*), populist (*Kurjer Lwowski* and *Przegląd Społeczny*), and socialist (*Praca*).[45] In the latter three periodicals, he performed approximately the same role as in *Svit*, with its radical orientation, and the populist *Dilo* and *Zoria*: that of a leading writer whose various contributions (prose, poetry, and journalism) appeared in almost every issue; occasionally, he also wrote editorials. In the Warsaw-based *Prawda* and the St. Petersburg-based *Kraj*, his status was not as significant: there, he served as a Galician correspondent submitting reports on the state of affairs in the local Ruthenian camp.[46]

Franko's intensive collaboration with Polish periodicals led to the circumstance that from a certain point in time he began to be regarded as a part of both Ukrainian and Polish literature. Ludwik Inlender called Franko a "Ruthenian-Polish poet-sociologist" [*Mozaika* 325], and the Russophile Osyp Markov called him a pupil of the Polish school, who "wholeheartedly adopted its finest works."[47] The publication in *Przegląd Tygodniowy*, the leading mouthpiece of the Warsaw Positivists, of a very favorable article about Franko under the rubric "Dzieje Appollona" (Apollo's Deeds), which was devoted to Polish writers and artists, was an unprecedented event.[48] This was followed by an article published in late 1886 in *Kurjer Lwowski*, which noted that Franko enjoyed greater esteem among the Poles than among the Ruthenians.[49]

It should be kept in mind that the Polish-speaking readership was not just ethnically Polish. It also included many assimilated Jews from both empires, and whenever Franko broached the Jewish subject, they reacted sharply to those of his articles that were written in Polish.[50] Jewish authors, who usually did not read Cyrillic, completely ignored his Ukrainian-language publications on this topic, even the most controversial ones. A substantial proportion of the readership of Polish-language publications comprised educated Galician-Ruthenians, since the Polish language, as earlier, was still prevalent in the lives of many of them.[51] Therefore, in contributing articles to Polish newspapers and journals, Franko was also expanding his circle of Galician-Ruthenian readers.

The dynamic activity of the young Franko brought him to the attention of the editors of Czech- and German-language periodicals. However, their attempts to enlist his collaboration were mostly unsuccessful.[52] Franko's presence in the Russian-language market was equally insignificant. As he admitted in a letter to Drahomanov (10 May 1884), "at least a dozen times I have tried to write for Russian newspapers, but in the end I gave up without achieving either publication or a reply" [*ZT* 48:434]. Franko was not published at all in Russophile periodicals: his literary collaboration with them ended once and for all after the 1876 coup that took place in *Druh* (see chapter 7).

The important role of a reading market in an imagined national community is well known. The geography of Franko's publications and reviews of them (see table 14) confirms the conclusion that researchers on his readership have reached: he functioned mostly in two reading markets, the Ruthenian-Ukrainian and the Polish. In any case, the young Franko did not fit into the framework of one exclusive, national "imagined community," and in this sense he was truly a "Ruthenian-Polish poet."

Why Was Franko Read?

Statistics say a lot, but they do not tell the whole story; if print runs and the number of publications had decisive importance, then the reading market would be dominated by graphomaniacs. In order to determine Franko's influence, it is crucial to shift from the language of numbers to the language of citations from review articles and the reactions of readers who read the writings of the young Franko. One thing quickly catches the eye: among a significant proportion of readers, Franko had become the premier Ruthenian-Ukrainian writer as early as the mid-1880s. "Yours is a powerful talent, and it will continue to develop further," declared Ivan Nechui-Levytsky, a distinguished Ukrainian writer from the Russian Empire, in a letter he wrote to Franko on 28 July 1884, after reading his *Zakhar Berkut*. He continues: "The novel is read with great eagerness and pleasure....God speed! After you, the strongest talent is Sapohivsky, and it is a shame that he died prematurely."[53] In an undated letter written some time in the mid-1880s, Olena Pchilka gave the following endorsement of Franko's talent: "I place you as a writer higher than all those [authors] of ours who are writing both in Gal[icia] and in Ukraine: you are more talented than all of them."[54] In a letter dated 3 June 1886, Natalia Kobrynska wrote to Franko: "You are our ambition; hence we shall not stop working so that, sooner or later, we shall be granted unrestricted leadership in our literature."[55]

Similar things were said about Franko in private not only by his sympathizers and his opponents but also by his enemies. "We do not have a more capable, dynamic, and wiser worker than Franko," Ivan Belei wrote with conviction to Oleksandr Konysky, in a letter dated 26 December 1884.[56] In 1885, another populist editor, Volodymyr Levytsky, claimed that without Franko any kind of anthology would be nothing.[57] At a meeting of populists held in June 1886, Oleksandr Barvinsky declared that "in our land Franko alone is still able to construct—support—the building of a national program."[58] Although the organized community of Galician women acknowledged that Franko "is capable and may be the most capable of our young people," they shunned him only because he was "compromised": "If we embark on adventures [with Franko—Y. H.], then the entire world will point its finger at us."[59] Osyp Markov was convinced of Franko's "first-rate talents."[60] A Catholic priest named Walerian Kalinka, who criticized Franko frequently and acerbically, never acknowledged the correctness of his views. Yet even this clergyman acknowledged that "he possess[ed] indisputably both a higher intelligence and distinguished literary talent."[61]

In order to clarify the nature of Franko's impact, it is necessary to explain which of his many works made the strongest impression on readers, and why. As mentioned earlier, it was Franko's Boryslav cycle of short stories and novels that brought him literary fame.[62] Both "left-wingers" and "right-wingers" responded positively to these works. For some, Franko's works resonated with their own socialist credo. "After reading your *Boa* [*Constrictor*], I was gripped as though by a fever," wrote Felix Daszyński, brother of Ignacy, in a letter to Franko. "Show me a person that loves his people more, I will say that you are the only one."[63] At least in one case Franko's Boryslav cycle compelled a reader—Natalia Kobrynska—to reject internationalist rhetoric and adopt nationally oriented positions. "What is even more puzzling about this," Kobrynska wrote in a letter to Mykhailo Pavlyk on 28 November 1888, "is that in point of fact Franko, you, and others have introduced into Galicia generally European ideas which, in many respects, have become inimical to the reigning nationalism, but where I am concerned, the opposite happened."[64] For another reader, "the novels that have never before appeared in our land (Ivan Franko's *Boa Constrictor*)" furnished proof that Ukrainian literature had become fully fledged and competitive.[65] Various readers approached Franko's works from different positions: "cosmopolitan" or "national." However, they concurred in their view that Ruthenian-Ukrainian literature—along with the Ukrainian national project—could be both *Ukrainian* and *modern* at one and the same time.

Franko's poems and translations made an equally strong impression on his readers. Franko's translation of *Faust* was an important milestone. In Oleksandr Barvinsky's view, it was superior to the Polish translation published that same year in *Przegląd Polski*.[66] Franko's translation was read, among other reasons, in order "to learn Ruthenian speech."[67]

Franko's novel *Zakhar Berkut* was especially popular with readers. The novel netted positive assessments from a variety of readers, such as the members of *Zoria*'s competition committee ("This is a historical novel, extensive, wonderfully executed in every respect");[68] Ivan Nechui-Levytsky, Olha Roshkevych ("Your *Zakhar Berkut* is exceptionally written and everyone generally likes it"),[69] and a student named Anempodyt Dorodnytsky, a *Zoria* subscriber living in Sergiev Posad in the far-flung Moscow Gubernia.[70] According to Pavlyk, even the young Franko considered *Zakhar Berkut* to be his finest work.[71] This novel was also popular among peasants, who required that "a story be interesting, that it is narrated in a lively and gripping fashion" [*ZT* 49:406]. Franko's novel clearly satisfied these demands.

Finally, it seems that among the members of the Ruthenian-Ukrainian reading public there was a certain consensus with respect to his poem "Panski zharty." Critics wrote that, in creating this work, Franko had erected a *monumentum aere perennius* (a more lasting monument) to himself: "We do not hesitate to say that not since Shevchenko have we had a finer poem in Ruthenian literature."[72] After Franko's death the editors of *Zoria* placed this poem on the same plane as his Boryslav short stories and *Zakhar Berkut*, as works "unquestionably of first-rate beauty and the same kind of worth."[73]

The reception of Franko's other works was far from homogeneous. The works produced in those years, which may be divided into three groups, reflected the sharp polarization within the reading public (of course, this division is a provisional one, inasmuch as certain works could belong simultaneously to two or even all three groups). The first group consisted of works in which Franko, marching in the footsteps of Zola and other naturalists, offered detailed descriptions of violent scenes, murders, or sexual depravity. Foremost among them is the story "Na dni," as well as some of the Boryslav stories, which, as noted earlier, scandalized many readers. The second group includes Franko's "revolutionary" poems. Borrowing the title of Franko's poetry collection, *Z vershyn i nyzyn* (From the Heights and the Depths), Hryhorii Tsehlynsky called them the real "lower depths" of his oeuvre. According to Tsehlynsky, in these poems Franko revels in and plays with the word "revolution," like a "small child [playing with] a firearm."[74] As well, many readers were repelled by the "brutal" propaganda of atheism in those periodicals and anthologies that were edited by Franko.[75]

Besides the objectionable content of certain of Franko's works, the reading public was irritated by the very manner of his writing. Tsehlynsky, who was supposedly a "professional critic" of his works, wrote,

> The first thing that strikes every reader of his short stories is that remarkable falsehood: we hope to see a real world, but we see Franko's; we hope to see real people, but we see purely Franko's. The heroes in Franko's stories, whether they be workers, or lords, or priests, or peasants, are not people who result from an objective observation of life, but people who are real in name only, with their entire psychological makeup and world perception created by the writer's imagination, subjectively recreated.[76]

The situation sometimes became absurd. At one point, Oleksandr Borkovsky, the editor of *Zoria*, spent many hours observing bricklayers at work in order to gauge Franko's accuracy in his short story "Muliar." (The Mason). Not once did he see the brutality of apprentices and the defenselessness of workers as described by Franko. On the contrary, he saw lazy workers, who would have continued working slowly if an apprentice did not shout at them. Neither did Borkovsky notice any connection with "real circumstances" in another of Franko's stories, "Lel′ i Polel′," where he saw "much that is too fantastic, not in accord with the circumstances of Galician life, or is even completely incredible." The editor of *Zoria* thus rejected both stories.[77]

Critical remarks about Franko's tendentiousness were also heard in the writer's own milieu. Views similar to Borkovsky's comment were expressed by Pavlyk and Kobrynska.[78] Drahomanov advised other "progressive" writers to abandon "that Franko-style method of writing," in which the writer's pen produces "some kind of program, not a story."[79]

Franko's supporters were aware that in his writings he frequently departed from reality. Yet, in these shifts they perceived both shortcomings and certain values. Because his heroes often lacked "a sense of being rooted," they became universally human characters. As the Kyivan radical Ahatanhel Krymsky once commented on Franko's short stories, "With few exceptions, before us appear not just Ruthenians-Galicians but simply people—often a Ruthenian in Franko may be considered a Ukrainian, and a *Katsap* [a Russian], and a Pole, and a German, and an Italian—whoever you like!"[80] This assessment corresponds almost completely with the view of the Polish progressivist Stanisław Wasilewski, who focused on the fact that neither Andrii Temera, the main hero of "Na dni," nor the worker in "Muliar" were identified by nationality: they could have been either Poles or Ukrainians. "There are no Ruthenians, Poles, and Jews in his works— only ignorant and long-suffering people."[81]

Franko defended his writing style by pointing to readers' positive responses. Replying to Tsehlynsky, he wrote: "Thank God, the public for which I write is not turning away from me and does not object to the direction along which my conviction and personal temperament bid me to proceed."[82] The separation into sympathizers and antagonists was determined not by nationality but by other criteria. The first was the attitude toward progressive (Positivist and socialist) ideas. If the reading public may be likened to a "nation" which, in reading Franko, imagined its commonality of interests, then his was the "nation of progressivists." Nonradical Ukrainophiles clearly sought to diminish Franko's influence, as Volodymyr Barvinsky tried to do immediately after Franko's imprisonment.[83] Oleksandr Barvinsky, who had compiled a reader of Ruthenian-Ukrainian literature, claimed in this publication that the works of Franko and other young writers consist "mainly of reworkings and imitations"; and he expressed regret that these writers were cultivating "harmful radicalism" and waging a struggle "against the optimistic national enthusiasm of the Ruthenian populists," against "national sanctities," and even against the purity of the Ukrainian language.[84] Oleksandr Konysky's highly critical assessment of Franko's oeuvre was published in the Warsaw-based journal *Atheneum*.[85]

These negative reactions were in direct contrast to the positive reception of Franko in Polish left-wing and liberal circles. Examples of the latter include the enthusiastic reviews and articles about Franko that were published in the main organ of the Warsaw Positivists, *Przegląd Tygodniowy*,[86] in which such icons of Polish Positivism as Maria Konopnicka, Eliza Orzeszkowa, and Aleksander Świętochowski[87] offered high praise for Franko's talent; the initiatives with regard to the translation of *Boa Constrictor* and "Na dni," which were undertaken by Felix Daszyński and Ludwik Inlender, respectively; and, finally, the success of Franko's publications in *Prawda*, *Kraj*, and *Kurjer Lwowski*. Polish socialists and liberals supported Franko's activities because in him and other Ruthenian progressivists they saw no sign of the "nationalistic chauvinism" that was typical of other Ruthenian parties.[88] In addition to acquainting readers with Ukrainian literature, the publication of Franko's writings in Polish periodicals also carried out an important function in Polish literature by partly compensating for the lack of popular, propagandistic publications.[89] Franko's Polish-language writings had another, completely unexpected, impact—this time on young "progressive" Ruthenians: inasmuch as they considered the Polish press superior to the Ruthenian-Ukrainian press, the appearance of Franko's articles in leading Polish newspapers and journals ostensibly attested to the high quality of his production and focused attention on his oeuvre in general.[90]

Meanwhile, we can find nothing of the kind in Russophile publications. The Russophiles' initial reactions to the earliest works of the young Franko were moderately positive: Franko was called a promising but as yet little-known author.[91] The situation changed after the revolt in the ranks of the Academic Circle. One can only guess at the reasons behind the Russophiles' silence: as a "nihilist," Franko was subject to public anathema. It should be noted, however, that the Russophiles did not reject Ukrainophiles wholesale: on the grassroots level the differences between the two were negligible and often one and the same patriots worked in both Russophile and Ukrainophile organizations, while in the "upper levels," the Russophiles were prepared to include Taras Shevchenko in their national pantheon. But none of them considered it possible to place Franko alongside him.[92]

An analysis of Franko's reading public leads to several findings. The first is the extraordinarily successful nature of his literary career: thirteen years after his literary debut in 1874, he had already written several works that stood every chance of entering the literary canon of Ukrainian literature, regardless of the diverse aesthetic tastes and political views of his readers. The second conclusion is a reiteration of the one that was reached earlier on the basis of statistics on Franko's publications: Franko succeeded in embedding himself in two reading publics, the Ruthenian-Ukrainian space and the Polish-speaking one. At thirty years of age, Franko had still not achieved the fame of an "anti-Polish nationalist," which came to him in the 1890s, after the scandalous rift with the Polish milieu. Therefore, his cult could have existed not only in the Ukrainian cultural and political space but also in the Polish one. Finally, in the Ruthenian-Ukrainian space he was actively present in two out of the three rival camps: the radical and the populist. Although this duality did not afford him the comforts of life, it brought certain advantages. In this regard, it is worthwhile comparing the scope of Franko's influence on Galician society with that of the leading radicals, Mykhailo Drahomanov and Mykhailo Pavlyk, or the leading Russophile, Ivan Naumovych. To those three writers, access to populist periodicals was blocked. Meanwhile, Franko had never been subjected to complete anathema by the populists. Their periodical, *Pravda*, never stopped publishing Franko's works even after he ended up in prison, and during the highest point of tensions in Franko's relationship with the populists their doors remained open to him.

Typical in this regard is the secret group of students at the Lviv Academic Gymnasium, to which Osyp Makovei belonged. This high school was one of the main centers of the populist movement: the school's director, Rev. Vasyl Ilnytsky, and three of his professors—Yulian Romanchuk, Anatol Vakhnianyn, and Hryhorii Tsehlynsky—were well-known populist leaders. They were members of that "professorial clique" that held the reins of leadership in various populist institutions, including *Zoria*.[93] When the students' group was exposed following a denunciation by Rev. Ivan Naumovych, all the professors rose to the defense of the students. The populists clearly did not attach any significance to the circumstance that those high school students were associated with a "man who smells of socialism, like Franko." They pleaded the matter to the authorities in such a way that Franko was whitewashed, while Naumovych's reputation was blackened. It was a simple reckoning: the populists considered Naumovych to be a spent force in the national cause, while "some benefit could still be derived from Franko." They were convinced of this by his earlier important achievements: his translation of Goethe's *Faust*, his novel *Zakhar Berkut*, and the collection *Halyts′ki obrazky* (Galician Images), along with *Svit*, the periodical that Franko edited.[94]

An analysis of Franko's reading public also reveals certain limits of his success. This public was not very sizeable, and Franko was not the most popular author. What this analysis does not reveal is how, despite his rather limited circle of readers, Franko managed to exert such a powerful impact on the educated members of his society, and what the far-reaching consequences of his influence were. The following two chapters will examine these two questions.

Chapter 16

How Franko Became a Genius

In his memoirs about the late 1870s and early 1880s, the distinguished civic and political leader Yevhen Olesnytsky remarked that no one in Galicia had made a greater impact on young people than Ivan Franko. Several circumstances served to explain his influence, but foremost among them was Franko's individuality.

> [Our] acquaintance with Franko led us young people into a completely different world; his erudition, which was unusual for the times, his keen view of things and harsh but witty critique of contemporary relations impressed young people and united them around him....The Ukrainianness that reigned in the Lviv community and was confined to weak, purely formal, and even then infrequent and few manifestations could not satisfy the more capable and sincere youth. The school of Ivan Franko taught it to understand Ukrainophilism differently; it showed its true content, and Drahomanov's strong, merciless critique deepened it even more, and sparked a reaction against the formal Ukrainophilism that was still being manifested in Galicia. Under those influences took place the formation of those foundations on which we later based our work and activities in [our] subsequent life.[1]

Similar assessments may be found in the memoirs of other Galician figures of Ukrainian orientation whose high school and university years coincided with the period of the late 1870s–early 1880s.[2] Of course, it may be assumed that Olesnytsky's memoirs were written under the powerful sway of the subsequent Franko cult, which explains why they err anachronistically on the side of exaggeration. But this is not so. Convincing proof is found in Franko's correspondence with his younger colleagues, dating to the first half of the 1880s, in which they address him as their "Moses," call him their genius, compare him to Shevchenko, and the like.

Olesnytsky's memoirs enable scholars to form an accurate picture of how Franko managed to exert such a great influence over young people.

The nucleus around which the new community gathered was his library (one of the largest private libraries in Galicia).[3] Other methods included engaging young people as writers, correspondents, readers, and distributors of his writings; the organization of scholarly work that went beyond the framework of university and high school curricula; and, finally, regular youth trips, the first of which Franko organized in 1884.

However, these memoirs do not provide any explanation of the source of young people's inclinations to read, write, study, and travel under Franko's guidance. Student activism beyond the main obligations connected with university and high school studies was rather a rare phenomenon. It was customary for young men to seek out entertainment, patronize restaurants and coffeehouses, and engage in romances with girls. At least in the period preceding Franko's, there was not that much time for extra-curricular activities. Such situations became the rule later, during the years of mass politics; earlier, however, there were no cases of young people gathering around even an extremely talented individual. Therefore, in discussing the influence of the young Franko on his contemporary society, one must seek the motives and reasons that were connected not only with Franko but with the very age in which he lived.

How to Become a Genius

In order to understand the reasons behind Franko's success, the context must be enlarged. This goal is served well by the results of a comparative study, in which the author, German-born British psychologist H. J. Eysenck, studied the biographies of several hundred of the most renowned scholars and writers with the goal of arriving at a general formula for success. His formula may be summarized thus: "Works of genius depend on the confluence of certain personality variables (intelligence, creativity, persistence, etc.) and certain social conditions: Newton, Mozart or Shakespeare would not have been able to show their true genius in a primitive culture."[4]

Franko was blessed with many talents. But they could never have emerged, or at least would never have played such an important role, if the social circumstances were not right. It suffices to recall the heartrending fate of Franko's younger brother, Onufrii, who was also exceptionally gifted, but never got a chance in life. In order to explain Franko's opportunities, we must examine his biography in terms of the connections between micro- and macro-levels—between the facts of his personal life and broader social factors. The above-cited work points out several essential correlations between the former and the latter. The first is an individual's middle or upper-middle class origins. This factor was at work in Franko's case: he was born into a prosperous family of artisans and noblemen. His social origins played a decisive role in the trajectory of his early biography when his family decided to send him to school; the lower classes, especially peasants, were rarely in a position to do so.

This same factor may be used to explain the fate of Onufrii Franko. Like his older brother, he had been born into a middle-class family. But when it came time for him to start school, his tradesman father and noble-born grandmother died, and his mother's subsequent marriage to a peasant lowered her social status. They were thus transformed into a peasant family, and Onufrii was removed from school and brought back to the village to work on the family farm.

Another factor is gender: Franko was lucky enough to be born a man, not a woman. In those days, women rarely became geniuses. This factor is hardly biological: the difference between men's and women's life opportunities in a patriarchal society played an immense role—especially so in Galician society, where the possibilities for women to embark on an intellectual career were practically nonexistent.

If these two factors acted in Franko's favor, then the third one—the religious factor—worked against him: where achieving success is concerned, Catholics had fewer chances than Protestants, and Protestants had fewer chances than Jews. This is not the place to explain how this factor operated. Suffice it to say that Franko's chances as a Greek Catholic were even slimmer than if he had been a Roman Catholic. Nowhere in his biography is this imbalance more obvious than in the differences in scale between Polish and Ruthenian-Ukrainian cultural production and the two reading publics. If Franko had opted for Polish identity in his youth, his life opportunities would have been rosier. But he decided to become a Ruthenian poet, and his success, therefore, is all the more remarkable.

Franko's fateful decision is closely correlated with two other factors, motivation and invincible will, both of which are also crucial for a person with above-average talents to overcome the violent opposition that comes from average minds, as Einstein once justly noted. On his life's journey, Franko was forced to overcome such opposition to an excessive degree, to the point of being socially ostracized. He was constantly forced to pay for his social success with his turbulent personal life.

It may be assumed that Franko's will is connected to the circumstances of his childhood. Research has shown that very many distinguished, creative historical figures (according to one selected group, one in every four individuals) lost at least one parent in their childhood. The loss of a parent's care forces the child to rely on his own strengths. As in the preceding case, Franko had to pay for his social success with personal tragedies.

Finally, there is the age factor: talented people usually achieve success between the ages of twenty and forty, reaching their peak before their fortieth birthday, after which point their creative activity slowly declines. Although this "success curve" is universal, the peak of activity may vary depending on the nature of the activity. It is thought that success is achieved the earliest by individuals who engaged in poetic creativity and mathematics; at a later age, in other natural sciences, and latest in life, in the social sciences and the humanities. From this standpoint, the difference between the biographies of Franko and his contemporary Sigmund Freud is remarkable: whereas Franko was already enjoying popularity when he was twenty years old, and by the age of thirty he was ranked among the most famous individuals in the land, recognition came to Freud only at the age of forty.

This last factor indicates the close interdependence between the two key descriptions of Franko: "young" and "poet." The role of this interdependence further increases when we switch from examining "objective" factors to subjective factors—that is, to that which society at the time was prepared to recognize as the purview of geniuses. Historians of ideas have noted the powerful transformation of the concept of "genius" during a transition from a traditional to a modern society. The word "genius" derives from the name of a classical god from the Roman pantheon, who took care of either a single individual or an entire city. The other meanings of the word—above-average talent and, accordingly, a person who is endowed with such talents—emerged later, during the Renaissance and baroque ages. The Enlightenment ultimately changed the balance of meanings—from a guardian spirit to innate talent and a talented person. At the same time, the very object of the application of this term also changed: whereas earlier it was applied to anointed monarchs, now it was also applied to artists, including writers—above all to poets.[6]

The expansion of the framework encompassing the term "genius" to include poets signified a profound transformation of their perception by society. Until the late eighteenth and early nineteenth centuries, the word "poet" elicited in the public's imagination a rather unattractive image of a person with a not quite normal psyche and the actions of a liar (*poeta mendax*). The chief function of a poet was connected with religious cults

and court life: such an individual was required for church and court fes-
tivities, during which he was supposed to recite his made-to-order poems.
To be able to survive, a poet had to have a patron who commissioned these
poems and paid for them. The switch to a nonaristocratic society changed
the very concept of a poet and his functions. This pertained above all to the
very method of presenting poetry—not orally but in written form, through
the agency of text disseminated by printing. This change accompanied the
transformation of that which was "written": literature became a product
subject to the laws of the market, laying the groundwork for the profession-
alizing of the writer's occupation in the nineteenth century.[7]

At the same time, the social importance of these texts increased apace.
Thanks to the secularization of the educated strata, literature became a
replacement for religion; it was as though the sphere of literature had become
sacralized.[8] Henceforth, literature was supposed to be not simply a means of
entertainment and a way to fill one's free time but also a cultural phenomenon ordained to fulfill an important social role: defining new social ideals.
Poets began to be perceived as the natural leaders of society. Poetic genius
made them seemingly akin to God and bestowed on them the gift of prophecy. Even theologians were prepared to recognize this role. Poets, as one the-
ologian wrote, "have glimpses of truth in theology, as well as in philosophy
and physics. From their higher point of view, indeed, they sometimes descry
truths which are yet below the horizon of other thinkers."[9]

The onset of these changes is connected with the ideology of
Romanticism. The romantics not only created social conviction about the
fundamental difference between a poet and other people, they also cultivated this difference. They were convinced that poets not only reflect reality but create it. Shelley called poets the "unacknowledged legislators of
the world"; Hugo limned the portrait of a poet as a prophet who holds in
his hand a flaming torch, with which he illuminates the future. The image
of the poet as the central figure of literary and social life somewhat faded
during the Age of Positivism. However, in Central and Eastern Europe the
traditions of Romanticism were particularly dynamic: in that part of the
world it was something greater than simply a literary trend. Even the new
generation, which sought to draw literature closer to science, continued to
cherish the old concept of the poet as prophet.[10]

The fusion into one semantic field of the terms "poet–genius–prophet"
gave rise to new meanings. Literary scholars note the emergence in the nineteenth century of the archetype of a "poet-politician," a person whose literary

work was launched in early youth and who, once it brought fame, created the foundation on which he carried out an important social role. No matter how brilliant they were, the works themselves were not sufficient for this. The prophet had to be the carrier of lofty moral principles. And, inasmuch as the personal lives of poets were far from moral perfection, certain social strategies were put into operation, which could make the biography of a poet worthy of his prophetic gift. The main one was similar to the method of presenting the lives of saints and martyrs: moral purification through suffering.[11]

Arrest, exile, imprisonment, and early death all played a central role in the transformation of a poet into a national prophet. The "poet in prison" became the same kind of enduring archetype as the poet-genius, poet-prophet, and poet-politician. His prototype became the Italian poet and revolutionary nationalist Silvio Pellico. Imprisoned by the Habsburg government in 1820, twelve years later he published a book titled *Le Mie Prigioni* (My Prisons), a memoir about his time in a Venice prison, where both political prisoners and ordinary criminals were chained by the feet and forced to work for their bread and water. To nineteenth-century European intellectuals there was nothing nobler than to suffer in prison for liberty's sake. Until that time prisons were "open" to all, but a stint in prison did not transform a prisoner into a hero: he was regarded as an ordinary criminal. During the storming of the Bastille, and especially during the Romantic period, the prison became the central symbol of the struggle for personal and social liberty.[12]

In Eastern Europe, the concept of a "poet-genius" played a larger social role than in Western Europe. Although Shelley called poets "legislators of the world," few in England took his declaration seriously. Among the peoples of Central and Eastern Europe, literature to a large extent played the role of substitute politics, above all the politics of national identity.[13] Thus, for a local reading public a poet was a charismatic leader, the embodiment of the collective aspirations of the people, and therefore not only his works but his very biography became the stuff of legends. One example of this is the posthumous fame of Lord Byron, a poet and person of action: although his fame was insignificant in his homeland, his renown in Slavic countries practically bordered on divinity. As Czesław Miłosz put it, if raised on Polish literature, one can never rid oneself of the image of a poet as prophet. The Polish case may be regarded as unique because three poets were canonized as prophets in Poland: Adam Mickiewicz, Juliusz Słowacki, and Zygmunt Krasiński.[14] The image of a poet as a prophet inspired by divine powers was the central concept around which Russian literature was constructed.[15]

Ultimately, the need to have one's own national poet-prophet was connected with the key problem of identity for a society undergoing transformations: the creation of stable forms of social organization through the formation of a system of social myths.[16] In the case of Ukrainian nation building, the role of "poet-mythmaker" was performed by Taras Shevchenko.[17]

Evolving within a force field and in close interaction with Polish, German, Russian, and Ukrainian literatures, Galician-Ruthenian literature could not ignore the poet-prophet complex. In the writings of prominent figures of the nineteenth-century Ruthenian-Ukrainian movement one encounters a frequently repeated motif: expectation of the appearance of their own national poet, a "Galician nightingale." The poetry of such an individual was ordained "to inspire hearts" and to serve as a "push for daring deeds and ceaseless activity." Widespread among the intelligentsia of that time was the belief "that a people without poetry, without ideals is doomed to a pitiful existence and will never attain a prominent position in the world." From the very beginning of the "national revival" until the last third of the century, the Galician-Ruthenian public could not boast of a single prominent name whose works were capable of "stirring the mind" and "attracting the heart." Complaints were heard that the Ruthenians did not have their own Homer, their own Schiller, Pushkin, or Mickiewicz,[18] not even "at the very least a minor Kraszewski."[19] As Kornylo Ustyianovych wrote, the leaders of the time

> had neither a higher view of things nor breadth of thought—in a word, not a single one of them was a people's genius, all-loving, all-embracing, caring for everything, upon whom one could gaze as at an icon, whom one could recognize as an unquestionable authority and boldly follow him wherever he would lead.[20]

Expectations of a national poet were equated with expectations of the "Nazorei," the new Jesus Christ, without whom "it is impossible to raise Galician-Ruthenian literature to the level that is appropriate to the demands of the time."[21]

To a certain degree, these psychological requirements were fulfilled by the appearance in Galicia, in the early 1860s, of *Kobzar*, which led to the earliest attempts to create a cult of Shevchenko as a national Ruthenian-Ukrainian poet. However, in the late 1870s and early 1880s this cult did not extend beyond the milieu of its creators, young populists. The "peasant character" of Shevchenko's muse and the heretical content of his works were unacceptable to nonpopulists. Although the rest of the public did not object to this cult, neither did it wholeheartedly support it; they did not find Shevchenko's poetry a good fit for Galician conditions. At this very time the specifically Galician cults of Markiian Shashkevych,[22] Mykhailo Kachkovsky,[23] and Volodymyr Barvinsky[24] began forming, but with no great success.

The Struggle of the Poets

In any event, when Franko entered the Galician-Ruthenian literary arena, the position of national poet was vacant. Many were eager to fill it. Franko's gymnasium teacher, Ivan Verkhratsky, considered himself to be the greatest poet after Shevchenko. It was Verkhratsky, along with Fedkovych, who was chosen by Drahomanov at the time he was trying to create a "new breed" in Galicia—national poet—in keeping with examples from Russian literature. Verkhratsky refused to accept this role because, according to him, he "did not wish to light a fire under his own roof."[25] When Franko began publishing his works in *Druh*, the young Volodymyr Stebelsky dominated the pages of this periodical. Both Ukrainophiles and Russophiles placed their hopes on this "exceptionally talented poet." At the time, even Franko regarded Stebelsky as the "only star, apart from Fedkovych, in the wretched Galician-Ruthenian firmament." Yet, Stebelsky's talent never flowered, probably because he abused alcohol.[26]

When Franko achieved renown as a writer, his competitor in the field of poetry was Volodymyr Masliak. Masliak and his contemporary Ilarion Hrabovych belonged to the same generation and were the favorites of Omelian Partytsky, the owner of *Zoria*, who regarded them as great literary forces [*ZT* 41:432]. Franko collaborated with Masliak in the populist periodicals but had mostly a negative view of his work. As Franko declared sarcastically, Masliak was a salon poet who loved "meat"—women's physical beauty: "for being so rosy and white, and soft, and puffy, and for having such hair, and such eyes, and such hands....But he never mentions that that meat had neither heart, nor brain, nor character" [*ZT* 48:380]. For Franko, poetry had recently stopped being a "plaything for idlers, but had become a great matter, a civic duty," and for Galician-Ruthenians in particular—"a particle of that cultural progressive work to which we are all called, to which we are applying all hands" [*ZT* 48:406]. In contrast, from the poetry of Masliak and Hrabovych wafted the "reactionary, close, and stale spirit" of Ruthenianness, full of "hatred for socialism and all kinds of other isms"—a spirit that Franko considered to be the dominant one in the populist camp in the 1880s [*ZT* 41:478]. It is no accident that the board of the Prosvita

Society assigned a large quota for the printing of Masliak's collection of poetry (1886), at the same time expelling Franko after his trial in 1878 and refusing to renew his membership until the 1890s [*ZT* 49:325–26].

However, neither Verkhratsky nor Stebelsky nor Masliak could match Franko's popularity. None of them measured up to the notion of a national poet. This image was bound up with selfless service to social ideals, and such service was supposed to lead to suffering and persecution. From this perspective, Franko had only one real competitor, Rev. Ivan Naumovych. Naumovych wrote poems, and for some time, between 1849 and 1860 he tried to carve out a literary career for himself by writing poetry. But he was not, in truth, a poet; he was, at best, a minor one.[27] What boosted his esteem in the eyes of the public was his great personal charisma, which was enhanced many times over by his history of persecutions. Tall, long-haired and bearded, dressed in a cassock, he clearly stood out from both the secular intelligentsia as well as from run-of-the-mill Greek Catholic priests, who wore their hair short and were clean-shaven. Naumovych was a gifted autodidact. Despite having no medical training, he cured sick people with homeopathy. It was said that he exerted a magnetic force and healed people through the laying on of hands. He was also fascinated by astronomy and horticulture, and he was one of the first Galician-Ruthenians to take up photography.[28]

The Ruthenians regarded Naumovych as an authority primarily because of his energetic civic activities. For example, he is credited with founding the first enlightenment organization, the Mikhail Kachkovsky Society. When Franko was just launching his career, Naumovych was already known as the "Enlightener of Galician Rus." The following detail reveals the immense difference between the two men's importance in society: after electing Naumovych as its head, the third congress of the Mikhail Kachkovsky Society (1876) rejected the proposal of the Lviv students Vasyl Davydiak and Ivan Belei to elect Franko as his deputy on the grounds that "Mr. Franko is still unknown."[29] By the early 1880s, their positions were equal, and both writers were credited with making immense contributions to the cause of spreading enlightenment among the common people.[30] What placed them at the same height, unreachable by others, was the fact that both writers had suffered "for an idea." Naumovych was one of the main defendants in the trial of Olha Hrabar and her comrades, as a result of which he served a jail sentence of almost eighteen months, from December 1883 to August 1884.[31] Naumovych's popularity is illustrated by the fact that after his release from prison, he appeared at a banquet held by Galician-Ruthenians in Lviv. The guests grabbed him, hoisted him onto their shoulders and, to the tune of "Mnohaia lita" (Long Years), carried him around the banquet hall. Peasants who were at the banquet kissed his hands and were so moved that they wept.[32]

The relationship between Franko and Naumovych may be described as a competition between two charismatic individuals. The first to strike a blow was Franko. In 1878, he wrote a satirical poem titled "Duma pro Nauma Bezumovycha" (Ballad of Naum Bezumovych, a play on Naumovych's name based on the phrase "bez uma," meaning, brainless). The very distortion of his name was intended to be comical. Franko dethroned Naumovych as a Ruthenian patriot by pointing to his ultraloyal attitude to the Viennese government, implying that this loyalty was not selfless ("Bezumovych takes money, and the Ruthenians vote") [ZT 3:246]. This satire, together with another "sensational" one titled "Duma pro Maledykta Ploskoloba" (Ballad of Maledictus Sloping-Forehead, a reference to the editor of Slovo, Venedykt Ploshchansky), circulated among the students in Lviv and the provinces, and were very popular during the trial of Olha Hrabar and her comrades.

Naumovych could never forgive Franko for the "Ballad of Naum Bezumovych." He retaliated by denouncing the secret group in the Ruthenian gymnasium in Lviv, which led to an official investigation of Naumovych's accusation that Franko was spreading socialism and atheism among the students of that high school. The inquiry into the secret group was perceived as a manifestation of a struggle between two political trends "led by their two most determined representatives, who have already had a taste of prison"—Rev. Ivan Naumovych and Ivan Franko.[33]

The competition between Franko and Naumovych led to antagonism between these two trends which, until that time, had sought to avoid conflict. It is striking that, in his articles about the trial of Olha Hrabar and her comrades, Volodymyr Barvinsky tried to maintain a soft tone vis-à-vis the Russophiles, and when he died Ivan Naumovych and Venedykt Ploshchansky sent a telegram with condolences. Although Naumovych was the author of the well-known declaration (1866) stating that "we are not the Ruthenians of 1848, we are real Russians," nevertheless he refrained from proclaiming "Russian irredentism." The ability to speak obliquely was a typical feature of the Russophile movement, and Naumovych was skilled in this art. His indecisiveness was particularly revealed by the fact that for nearly two and a half years after the beginning of his excommunication from the Greek Catholic Church, he did not take the step of converting to Orthodoxy. After his conversion to that religion, in 1886 he abandoned Galicia and moved to Kyiv with his family. Numerous disappointments awaited him there. In his letters to Galician friends he complained about his poverty, about his new friends—whom he called "rogues"—about the absence of order, and about young people, who had "neither faith, nor honor, nor feeling." In a letter written to Kornylo Ustyianovych in 1889, he declares: "Poor Russia, with all its might it cannot be called great; it is not Russian, and God knows what it is." Nevertheless, he did not lose hope that one day it would be reborn. "But God does not abandon her. He has sent her a tsar who is doing everything in order to place her high, high—to resurrect her, make her Christian, not bureaucratic-Orthodox."[34] In the Russian Empire, Naumovych survived on a pension from the tsarist government. Owing to his restless personality, he became involved in the issue surrounding the resettlement of Ruthenian peasants in the Caucasus. He died in 1891, under mysterious circumstances (poisoning was suspected), and was buried on Askold's Mound in Kyiv.[35]

Naumovych's death gave new momentum for the creation of a cult. His apologists claimed that his influence on his generation could be compared with that of Shevchenko and Pushkin.[36] They maintained that in his publications for the peasantry he "was the creator of genius of that folk Russian literature, in which he had no equal in the entire Russian world."[37] This opinion was partly shared by the Ukrainophiles: although they were irritated by his radical Russophilism, they regarded him as a distinguished talent, a first-rate, popular writer, and a great spiritual authority.[38]

Naumovych's slogan, "Back to the people," was considered a singular achievement. This was the title of a series of his articles that were published in *Slovo* in 1881. Their main emotional thrust lay in the author's indictment of the secular intelligentsia whose members, for the sake of their careers, were forgetting about Rus and assimilating into the German and Polish cultures. According to Naumovych, only the peasants had preserved their Ruthenianness, which was manifested in their instinctive sympathy toward Russia and Ruthenian culture. He claimed that among the peasants in Galicia no one would say that "the Muscovite is alien to us, and his tongue is foreign to us." Naumovych did not believe that there would ever come a time when people in Galicia would say: "I am not Russian, I am Ukrainian." Furthermore, he had no doubt that a great future awaited Russia. His hopes were linked first and foremost to the Russian Empire's change of course after the ascent to the throne of Tsar Alexander III, who, as reported by Russophile newspapers in Galicia, proclaimed the slogan: "Back to the people's virtues—down with Western European corruption!"[39]

Naumovych's article and his above-cited letter from Kyiv clearly reveal the main collection of ideologemes underpinning Galician Russophilism: righteous anti-Westernism, conservatism, and emphasis on devotion to the Eastern Christian (Orthodox) faith and its teachings and rite. Their imaginary fatherland was not the Russian Empire, riddled with "Western European corruption," but "holy Rus," which did not exist but needed to be reborn. They were prepared to treat the Galician-Ruthenian peasant culture and peasant language as one of the manifestations of "Rusdom," but they were against Ukraine as a secularized Western model of national development.

That same year, 1881, Franko responded to Naumovych by writing an article titled "Should We Turn Back to the People?" His critique was aimed not so much at Naumovych's Russophile orientation as at his "rearview orientation"—that is, his conscious opposition of himself to social progress (the name that Franko devised for Naumovych is telling: "Rak Postupovych," Crab Progressive [*ZT* 3:242]). Franko agreed with Naumovych where the latter criticized the Ruthenian intelligentsia for having become estranged from the peasantry and where he called for the formulation of a new policy based on the people's interests. In this criticism he saw a reiteration of those theses that the young radicals had proclaimed in 1878. However, despite the superficial similarity between Naumovych and Franko, the two men were separated by an ideological chasm: whereas the former appealed to the intelligentsia to revive the "back to the people" movement, the latter proposed that it move "forward with the people." For Naumovych, "to turn back to the people meant that we, the sons and teachers of the Eastern, truly people's, church, which is filled through and through with love, should abandon once and for all time all the anti-Christian tendencies, which were imported to us from abroad, for the true Christian teachings." Franko criticized this position as intellectual insanity, with the help of which Naumovych, who was following in the footsteps of the Russian Pan-Slavists, "would like to turn Russia back to the pre-Petrine, purely Rus, era, so they thought." For Franko, the cure for national ills was supposed to be movement forward, for the sake of which the main achievements of Western civilization should be transplanted onto Ruthenian soil, "like an alien but strong plant": "all new thoughts, new ideas, everything that advances toward light, freedom, happiness"—in fact, everything against which Naumovych protested so vehemently—all the way to "freethinking in the economic field" [*ZT* 45:141–42, 146–49].

Franko's duel with Naumovych was not simply a struggle between two individuals filled with the ambition to become the "Galician genius." Each of them presented his model for the development of Galician-Ruthenian society, and these models differed from each other in fundamental ways. If, however, we abstract ourselves from their ideological orientation and focus on the scope of the popularity that the two writers enjoyed, then we surely have to conclude that both of them had equal chances for victory.

Franko and His Generation

The following question arises: if the social impact of Franko and Naumovych were equal in strength, then why did young people choose Franko? In seeking the answer to this question, it is worthwhile to try to recreate the collective biography of those people who acknowledged Franko as their "spiritual father." Most of these individuals were his peers, or younger or older by five to ten years (the oldest was Ostap Terletsky, born in 1850; the youngest was Kyrylo Trylovsky, born in 1864). Together with Franko they comprised a single generation. The younger generation's critical attitude to the ideals upheld by the older leaders of the Ruthenian-Ukrainian camp—not just the Russophiles but the Ukrainophiles as well—provides grounds for defining their relations according to the metaphor of "fathers and sons," borrowed from Russian literature (this metaphor is all the more apt because many young people from Franko's milieu deliberately modeled their lives on the heroes of Turgenev and other "progressive" Russian writers' novels). The debut of this generation on the public scene was connected with the revolution that had taken place in the Academic Circle and the first trials of the socialists. At least Franko thought so: "In the mid-[18]70s a new generation, the youngest, appeared on the scene in our land, in which I include myself," he wrote to Eliza Orzeszkowa in April 1886 [*ZT* 49:57]. The next generational change may be dated to the late 1880s, when there appeared a group of so-called "young radicals" who went much further than Franko and already had a skeptical attitude to his ideals.[40]

According to sociologists, the human personality forms between the ages of seventeen and twenty-five, when young people discover their identity.[41] A simple calculation helps to establish the fact that the formative years of "Franko's generation"—those people who were born between 1850 and 1865—were the 1870s and 1880s. Further discussion of Franko's role in restructuring the sociopolitical and cultural fields requires defining the key moments of their formative experience.

However, two caveats are in order. First, not all of Franko's peers in the Ruthenian-Ukrainian camp acquired their experience in the same way as Franko and the members of his milieu. Many were indifferent or even hostile to Franko's ideals and convictions.[42] Therefore, as far as Franko's fellow thinkers are concerned, it would be more correct to use the term "generation unit" or "cohort," rather than "generation." Second, a similar formative experience may also be noted among the younger generations of Poles and Jews in Galicia, and Ukrainians and Russians in the Russian Empire. Group experiences and common ideals led, among other things, to closer collaboration between Franko and his friends—his Polish, Jewish, and Russian peers—both in Galicia and beyond its borders. Thus, "Franko's generation" was both a narrower and broader concept compared to the biological generation of his Ruthenian-Ukrainian peers. Franko and his friends were united not simply by their shared experience but also by the way in which they had reacted to it.

The generation that was born in the 1850s was formed in an atmosphere of important political changes that were taking place on the European continent: the unifications of Italy and Germany, the Polish uprising of 1863 and the Balkan wars, the wide-scale reforms in the Russian and Austrian empires, the rise of the Paris Commune, the Internationale, and revolutionary terrorism. On the local level, this feeling was also connected with the cardinal changes that were transforming the way of life of the most populous groups in Galician society—peasants, landowners, tradesmen, and Jews—following the abolition of serfdom in 1848 and of the last remnants of anti-Jewish legislation, the technical revolution, and so on. In Galicia, the salient political features of the 1870s and 1880s were the introduction of autonomy and the creation of public space. The young people of Franko's generation experienced this process first-hand in the form of the Polonization of the educational system, which coincided with their high school and university years, as well as work in newly created civic institutions.

In its most general features this experience may be defined as a shared, albeit not entirely distinct, feeling that the old world was drawing to an end and a new one was being created right before their eyes. Oleksandr Kistiakivsky, a member of the Kyiv Hromada, recorded the following entry in his diary in the early 1880s: "You have to be dense not to see that the revolution began twenty years ago and is reaching a climax."[43] The generational group of Franko and his friends was defined precisely by their positive attitude to these changes. This feeling was the result of what they had experienced and read. Franko recalled the atmosphere of the late 1870s–early 1880s:

> Socialist ideals inflamed people to the point of fanaticism; at the same time, those ideas were far from that criticality which they took on later. Marx (and then only the first volume [of *Das Kapital*—Y. H.]) was the Gospel, and what was missing in it was supplemented by the imagination, by feeling. The great social upheaval was glimmering in everyone's reality; Engels and other Western European socialists had prophesied its emergence within ten years, and when those years had passed, they deferred the deadline for another ten years, etc.[44]

Belief in the inevitability of change was connected with personal life circumstances. According to sociologists, a particular penchant for extreme stances and radical ideology is demonstrated by elites that are formed as a result of upward or downward social mobility.[45] In the case of Franko's generation, this was the first generational group that differed from its parents in terms of activities and lifestyle. Some, like Mykhailo Pavlyk, came from the lowest social classes. In the majority of cases, young people were the sons of Greek Catholic priests, but were not priests themselves. This is evident from the changes in the administrations of the main national organizations of the Galician-Ruthenians: the "priestly" stage of the national movement in the late 1870s–early 1880s was succeeded by the so-called "professorial" stage, represented mainly by teachers ("professors") and, to a lesser degree, by lawyers, who took over the leadership by the turn of the twentieth century.[46] The young people who made their debut during this period clearly understood these changes. In their "Commemorative Letter of Lviv Populist Theologians to the Leaders of the People's Party" (1885), the authors—a group of individuals who supported Franko during his conflict with the populists—wrote that "those days have passed when priests, comprising the sole Ruthenian intelligentsia, were the main helmsmen, leaders of public life. It is true that now everyone's eyes are turned to the secular intelligentsia as the leading one…, and to the clerical [intelligentsia] as an auxiliary one."[47] The emergence of the new generation marked a break with an important tradition that may be conveyed through the words of a song sung in ancient Sparta: "We are those who you once were, you will be those who we are." Young people in the 1870s and 1880s had the feeling that they would be different, and therefore called themselves "new people".[48]

A similar tendency may be observed among Galician Jews. Starting in the early 1880s, the number of Jews working in secular professions began to increase. Often, those who opted for the new professions were the sons of rabbis.[49] The one fundamental trait that distinguished the new generation of "progressive Jews" from the preceding generation of Galician Jewish enlighteners was that they were not familiar with Jewish religious traditions and did not revere the ancient Jewish culture.[50] Their biographies reflected one of the main themes in the history of Eastern European Jewry: the search for a new ideology in a period of rapid changes.[51] Franko proclaimed the social ethos of his generation with this poetic formula: "To struggle means to live." This slogan corresponded almost literally to the words of the young assimilated Jew Wilhelm Feldman: "To be human means to struggle."[52]

Among the various circumstances in which the members of the new generation spent their youth, extreme poverty was most prevalent. The majority of these people were provincials. Studying at a gymnasium or university required moving to larger cities, including Lviv, where life, especially in the Galician capital, was expensive. Although cash infusions or food from home were a big help, such assistance was irregular; besides, it came from family savings, and such savings in the families of Greek Catholic priests, let alone peasants, could not have been that substantial. Thus, students led lives befitting the ancient Stoics. When Mykhailo Zubrytsky was studying at the Drohobych gymnasium, he was frequently so hungry that beggars offered him bread.[53] When he was a student at Lviv University, Volodymyr Navrotsky spent months subsisting on two cups of coffee whitened with milk a day, purchased on credit from a Viennese café. In the winter, he wore trousers with holes in them and a summer jacket, and lived in an apartment where the water turned to ice overnight.[54] Ludwik Krzywicki wrote the following description of the Daszyński brothers' studies in Lviv: "Both of them lived in abject poverty, and tea with bread and a bun on holidays comprised the main ingredients of their meals. The appearance of meat, cheese—those were holidays." In these same memoirs he recounts the bizarre behavior of Anna Pavlyk during an excursion that a group of Lviv socialists made to Vysokyi Zamok in Lviv. Apparently, she was in a state of such heightened emotion that she fainted. It turned out that she had not eaten anything for several days.[55]

For some people, like Volodymyr Navrotsky and Felix Daszyński, a life of poverty led to illness and premature death. For others, it left a permanent mark on their psyche. Andrii Chaikovsky recalled how he always killed his hunger by smoking cigarettes. After one such "breakfast" he went to see Kossak, the Ukrainian publisher, and found him and his wife eating a lunch of pork and cabbage. Chaikovsky was seized with spite at all those who were able to eat pork and cabbage. "It seems to me that before writing a single proletarian article, the apostles of socialism should first of all become very hungry and then watch how the bourgeois eat such a lunch."[56]

In their youth, the older Ruthenian activists had also experienced hunger and bad times, but the difference between them and Franko's generation was that their feelings were not sublimated to a new ideology—in this case, socialism. For the older generations Christianity was sufficient: it explained poverty and suffering, and in universal and morally attractive terms to boot. For people who in their youth had read Pushkin, Mickiewicz, or Shashkevych, "God still lived."[57] By the time Franko and his friends made their debut, things were different. The spirit of free-thinking that had been spreading in the West since the Age of Enlightenment and which had gained in intensity with the rise of Positivism led to a radical change in the intellectual climate. Readings of Henry Thomas Buckle and other Positivists markedly destabilized the religious world perception.[58] The new generation was affected en masse by religious skepsis, agnosticism, and even atheism. In his *Austro-Ruthenian Reminiscences*, Mykhailo Drahomanov recounted the following story: two residents of Kyiv, Mykola Ziber and Serhii Podolynsky, were on their way to Zurich via Vienna, where they attended a soiree held by Sich, the local Ruthenian-Ukrainian Student Society. Among the guests were several Greek Catholic priests who were deputies in the *Reichsrat*. The head of the Sich Society gave a speech, in which he spoke passionately about the friendly attitude of young Galicians to "their native church." "He's lying!" a member of Sich whispered to Ziber and Podolynsky. "He is the same kind of atheist as you and I! He's just saying that for the benefit of the guests!"[59] The same phenomenon was observed in Lviv in the early 1880s, when many of the older Ruthenian gymnasium students were "secret atheists."[60]

The shared experience of a generation may be defined through the literature that its members read with fascination. For the "generation of the 1860s," which was younger than the "generation of 1848" but older than Franko's, one such experience was the reading of Shevchenko's *Kobzar*.

Apart from their subsequent attitude to Shevchenko as a "Ukrainian prophet" or simply as one of the Slavic poets, they all remembered their first acquaintance with Shevchenko as a turning-point in their lives.[61] For their peers, Ukrainian patriots from the Russian Empire, Shevchenko was already passé. They were immersing themselves in the works of Russian "progressive writers" such as Herzen, Turgenev, and Chernyshevsky. This also distinguished them from the generation of their parents, "people of the [18]40s." The evolution of the "sons" led them in a harshly critical direction that was called "nihilism." In the Ukrainian version it boiled down to Positivism in philosophy and populism in politics. As Drahomanov recalled, this generation had

> neither its own poet, who would express in Ukrainian their special thoughts, nor a novelist, who would pluck from life and forever imprint types of new Ukrainian people parallel to the heroes of the novels of Turgenev, Chernyshevsky. Shevchenko could no longer respond to all the ideas that emerged in the period after his death: his finest thoughts are written according to the forms and ideas of the '40s, and his poems—of the '30s. The biblical-revolutionary mysticism or the idealization of the Cossack past by Shevchenko could no longer rule the minds of the university youth of the '60s.[62]

Galician radicals went through a comparable experience thanks to their similar social origins (like Galician radicals of the 1870s and 1880s, quite a few Russian and Ukrainian nihilists of the 1860s were *raznochintsy*—persons of non-noble origin[63]) and shared a fascination with Russian progressive writers. Thus, just as for Drahomanov's generation, Shevchenko could no longer serve as the undisputed authority for Franko's generation. Franko wrote about this when he recalled the discussions that were taking place in his milieu in the mid-1870s:

> I understand very well those blessed days when a few of us passionate patriots-idealists would get together and launch into a wide-ranging discussion of literature, about its lofty tasks and directions, the lofty ideals it was supposed to point out to a person, about the perfection of the artistic form and about the influence literature has on precisely the "leading" part of society. We talked loudly and passionately, we argued about extraneous questions and more removed ones, but we all agreed on the main thing, namely, that that influence is immense and beneficial, that those ideals are lofty, and the tasks are also lofty. True, in talking about such lofty matters, with the exception

of Shevchenko, we did not find anyone whom we could take as a model (and even Shevchenko—everyone according to his conscience—somehow did not suit here, did not "fit" somehow, like a square peg in a round hole), and for that, we usually placed foreign writers as models—Homer, Dante, Shakespeare, Goethe—i.e., such writers about whom we knew that they were "great," "geniuses," but did not know exactly in what their greatness lay, in what their genius had manifested itself. [*ZT* 26:5]

Drahomanov was the first to criticize Shevchenko for his "obsolescence."[64] Even harsher was his reaction to the clerics' version of the Shevchenko cult that the populists had created in Galicia.[65] His views were echoed by Pavlyk.[66] Franko's critique was neither so systematic nor radical [see *ZT* 26:161–62]. It was his function that was more important: he seemed to be supplementing what was missing in Shevchenko, adapting Ukrainophilism to the new circumstances. For his own generation he performed the same kind of function as Shevchenko did for his. When Franko was still a young man he was already being compared to Shevchenko. However, for the 1860s generation this comparison had more of a negative character. One of its leading representatives, Rev. Danylo Taniachkevych, wrote thus in a letter to the poet Yulia Schneider:

Child, in this man there is great strength, great work, and considerable talent! But despite that, he cannot be your entire model. There is no pure voice of our people's muse in him: he passed through a different school, he serves a different idea, to tell the truth, a very modified one now—which delights me indescribably, but you cannot follow that path. Your ideals must be different, a different song, other students. Your school is the folksong; your model: father Taras….But I feel sorry for poor Myron (Franko) that his poetic talent is so narrowed: his poems are so tormented, so tormented that one feels pity.[67]

For Rev. Taniachkevych the "highest poetry is God! The highest creation is prayer." But, according to him, "negation has nested itself" in Franko's heart.[68] Schneider did not bother listening to the rest of the good clergymen's advice. She compared Franko to Shevchenko in a thoroughly positive way: "You picked up the banner left by Taras; / like him, you grew under the burden of sorrow."[69]

For young people, Franko became a living symbol that could be used to explain their expectations. He embodied those radical changes that marked their generation, and formulated and disseminated an ideology that treated these changes positively. He thus occupied a very important niche in the psychological needs of this generation.

"The words of his songs lifted, awakened respect and the strange fear that he was one of the unattainable and inaccessible spiritual giants, that his ideas preceded the generation of his peers...," recalled Yulia Schneider.

> The aura of the revolutionary fighter for an idea attracted me. A young, freethinking girl, in her fascination with literature and revolutionary ideals, saw an ideal in him. Not officially acknowledged as a leader in literature at the time, he was for me the one who is introducing a new form and new content into poetry. And since an author lives in his works, a portrait of Franko rose up in my imagination. The hymn "Eternal Revolutionary" best characterized his figure and limned for me the spiritual face of the strong individualism of the Kameniar's [Stone-breaker's] strong individualism, who, having broken the circle of darkness, is showing people a new path.[70]

A similar view was expressed by the socialist, Ivan Maksymiak, who dedicated a poem to Franko, the son of peasants: "You magician of dear freedom and fraternity, / Whose hands, mouth, and eyes / Will not rest until / You free us of beggary."[71])

That Maksymiak and Schneider were not alone in these opinions is illustrated by the demand or even the ultimatum to support Franko's publishing plans that Ruthenian-Ukrainian young people put forward to the populists in late 1885. One of the authors of this ultimatum, Bohdar Kyrchiv, wrote to Franko about it, mentioning that it had been discussed during a meeting of populist leaders:

> There were some things [in the ultimatum] that were very sensitive for our old men; it was said that they had eliminated and shunted aside from the work on our people's behalf "our most brilliant people" [meaning Franko—Y. H.], the most capable people today are standing behind our doors—wandering, confusion without end, and the like....

> But facts are facts: our commemorative letter has become lodged in the throats of our Ukrainophile *katsaps* and is choking them to this day. The distinguished Tsehlynsky was supposed to have said not to provoke the youth because this youth may fall on those shoulders of Franko's and become enmeshed in his nets! The poor *katsap*! How I pity him! How afraid they are of your red hair! Well, let them talk, and young people, whether they are

[dressed] in short jackets or cassock-like black togas [that is, either students from the secular faculties or students of theology—Y. H.], will definitely not follow Mr. Ts[ehlynsky], even if his head were 20 times clearer—brighter—balder!

It is a fact that between the older and younger people a rift has emerged very clearly, and by and by our *katsaps* will become like a small blade of grass in the field! And when your Correspondences in the discussion in *Kraj* (nos. 19 and 20) provoked anathemizing hand-wringing over you, behind the doors of [the Academic] Brotherhood there were bravos and applause for you![72]

Kyrchiv expresses his fascination with Franko in the same kind of quasi-religious terms as Schneider. Addressing Franko, he says: "Perhaps you will lead us out of this oppressiveness, as Moses [led] Israel from the house of toil."[73] One other circumstance that is indicated in this letter is noteworthy: Kyrchiv calls the populists—above all, Franko's main critic, Tsehlynsky—"Ukrainophile *katsaps*," thereby creating the impression that a chasm lay between young people and Franko, on the one side, and the older Ukrainophiles, on the other: the latter were not even Ukrainians.

We now arrive at the final telling detail about Franko's influence over young people: even Naumovych's own son, Volodymyr, a student at the Lviv gymnasium, came over to Franko's side. Along with some of his fellow gymnasium students, he borrowed books from Franko's library and took part in the discussions in his apartment, which lasted deep into the night, until dawn. Under Franko's sway, the younger Naumovych wrote a paper for the Small Library and invited the writer to give a speech about Darwin to his group. Franko's speech sparked the most passionate discussion in the brief history of the group's existence.[74]

Franko was the victor in the polemic with Naumovych. In the second half of his life he would engage in a struggle with much more serious opponents: Shevchenko and Mickiewicz. The stakes in this struggle were different: it was not a struggle for influence among his contemporaries but for a place in the memory of future generations. But this is a different topic altogether.

Chapter 17

A Prophet in His Own Land

The Force of a Literary Genius

It would be fitting to conclude this account with reflections about the enduring significance of the young Franko's activities and writings. In order to avoid all speculation, we must examine sources from that period— above all letters, diaries, and memoirs, those contemporaneous documents featuring the greatest degree of outspokenness. We begin with the memoirs of Kornylo Ustyianovych, which were published in 1884. According to Ustyianovych, in the initial years following the introduction of autonomy and Polonization in Galicia, a generally pessimistic mood reigned in the Galician-Ruthenian camp. "Power is not ours, let's save ourselves," he writes. In the grip of this mood Ustyianovych left Lviv for the provinces. Nine years later, around the mid-1880s, again under the sway of those same despondent feelings, he came to Lviv, where he was ridiculed by his friends: "You don't know anything at all about what happened in those nine years when you were not here!"

> And it was in Lviv, as though it were the main headquarters, that I became convinced that our cause had progressed forward quickly along the entire line. It had progressed along a legal path; it had progressed without fruitless demonstrations, not through enmity toward the *Liakhs* or the government alone but through the enduring work of people of talent and sacrifice. Through our peoples' efforts we have already reached the point that we can acquire nearly all the world's knowledge in our native tongue. New literary talents are in the offing, novels that we have never had before have appeared (Iv[an] Franko's *Boa Constrictor*), dramatic writing has grown, our music has become enriched, Yevhen Zhelekhivsky's dictionary demonstrates the richness of our language....I became convinced that we have much to

boast of, there are people whom we can extol; there are people who can be honored.[1]

Similar positive changes were also described by Oleksandr Konysky in 1886:

In Lviv in the 1860s it was difficult, even impossible, for a newcomer who did not know Polish or German to manage solely with the Ruthenian language; in response to a question posed in Ruthenian to a Pole or a Jew, instead of an answer, people turned their backs on you, and if they deigned to hear you: "Nic nie rozumiem po rusku" [I don't understand Ruthenian], then this was already a great civility. In the homes of the Ruthenian clergy in Lviv none other than the Polish language was spoken. In fifteen years everything has changed; you will walk the entire breadth of eastern Galicia solely with the Little Russian language. In the capital of Galicia you will hear the Ruthenian language both in homes and in public places—restaurants, gardens, shops. Everyone will point out to you the location of the best Ruthenian editorial offices of newspapers, clubs (discussion), etc. In the Sejm itself, instead of the earlier shouts of "Niema Rusi" [There is no Rus] you will hear "Ruś żyje" [Rus lives] from the mouths of Poles, although not very many, it is true, and obtain advice, learn the literature of the Ruthenians, and reckon with the genuine needs of the Ruthenians.[2]

These travel notes, which were written by Konysky, a Ukrainian patriot from the Russian Empire, record that which is missing from the memoirs of the younger Ustyianovych,—namely, the changes that had taken place in the Galician countryside:

All of Galicia is an agricultural country, and especially its eastern part, which borders on our southwestern land. Within your first steps you cannot fail to note that the agricultural culture here is much superior to ours; villages are built more neatly, it is cleaner, gayer; somehow freer. Entering a house and speaking with the peasants, you will notice in their domestic everyday life certain signs of European culture and enlightenment, although they are still elementary; each peasant will tell you plainly and deliberately of what faith and nationality he is; he knows his Lviv champions of the people's rights; he even knows two or three of the best Ruthenian writers.

Nowadays, Galicia is covered with reading rooms, despite all kinds of opposition and constraint on the part of lower-ranking Polish functionaries and gendarmes.

You should see a local reading room, you should spend some time in it in order to grasp and assess its significance in the sense of resistance to the Polonization and Roman Catholicization of the Ruthenians! On holidays the reading room is full of people; even illiterates go [there]. Amidst the reverential quiet, one [peasant] reads and comments. After the reading, conversations take place about what was read and, finally, there is choral singing: "Ukraine Has Not Yet Perished," "Peace to You, Brothers," and the "Prayer." The "Prayer" appeared only in 1885; it is actually a short poem.

"God, the Sole Great One, / Protect Rus-Ukraine! / Spread freedom and the rays of the world over it." [3]

Even if these travel notes err on the side of exaggeration (for instance, it is unlikely that "every peasant" knew to which nationality he belonged), they are consonant with that part of Ustyianovych's memoirs in which he speaks of the great turning point that took place in the mid-1880s. Like Ustyianovych, Konysky links the positive changes with the fact that Ruthenian language and literature had attained the same kind of distinction as German and Polish. In particular, they observe that the language and literature of the Ruthenians had entered the public space of both cities and the countryside. Franko is present in these testimonies more or less implicitly: in Ustyianovych's memoirs he appears as one of those people of "talent and sacrifice" and "enduring work," thanks to whom the decisive turning point was achieved, and as the author of novels "that we have never had before." In Konysky's notes, Franko appears as one of the "Lviv champions of the people's rights" and "best Ruthenian writers," with whom Ruthenian peasants were acquainted.

By the mid-1880s, the Ukrainophile orientation in Galicia began to surpass the Russophile orientation. Although this was not yet an ultimate victory, it was the beginning of changes affecting the general balance of forces of the various national orientations within the Ruthenian camp. There are several interpretations of this transition in scholarly literature. In the view of John-Paul Himka, a decisive role was played by the external political factor: after the trial of 1882 the government began to persecute the Russophiles.[4] This explanation cannot be ignored. Indeed, the Russophiles never managed to recover from the heavy moral and physical blow they had suffered in the early 1880s, although in certain aspects (for example, the development of a network of reading rooms) they retained their supremacy until the early twentieth century. However, the story of

Franko may be cited as a counterargument. In the mid-1880s he had experienced more repression than Ivan Naumovych or any of the Russophile leaders: he was twice imprisoned, he was socially ostracized, his publications were confiscated regularly, and for many years he was under police surveillance. However, the current he personified did not lose its dynamic nature.

Another explanation is proposed by Paul Magocsi, who sees the reason behind the victory of the Ukrainophile orientation in the fact that the Ukrainophiles had the "force of a literary genius"—Ivan Franko—on their side. With his works Franko succeeded in demonstrating that the Ukrainian language was a vital tool for expressing all aspects of intellectual life.[5] This explanation underscores an important aspect of the national movement of "nonstate peoples," in which the linguistic question plays a particularly significant role as an integrating factor. However, this interpretation does not reckon with the definition of the concept of "genius," in those days, not only according to the scope and quality of literary production but also by subjective factors. In terms of those factors, the description of "literary genius" may be applied equally to the exceptionally prolific and extremely talented Ivan Franko, but also to Rev. Ivan Naumovych, who was Franko's inferior with regard to productivity and quality.

What Was in It for the Intelligentsia?

In the preceding chapter the comparisons drawn between Franko and Naumovych lead us to consider another factor: it was not just the particular language employed in writing one work or another that was important; the mission of each writer was no less significant. The difference between the young Franko and his predecessors is clearly evident in a parody that Franko wrote of Ivan Hushalevych's poem "Where Is the Ruthenian Fatherland?"

Ivan Hushalevych	*Ivan Franko*
Where Is the Ruthenian Fatherland?	Where is the Ruthenian Fatherland?
Where is the Ruthenian Fatherland?	"Where is the Ruthenian fatherland?
Where there is enough wheat,	Where are the wheat and barley?
Barley, and rye	And where is there enough rye,
Where hunger does not visit	Where hunger does not visit?"

Na-na-na-na-na-na

Oh, that is where the Ruthenian fatherland is!

Where milk and honey flow,

The forest, grove, and meadow bloom

Where there are mountains, valleys

And [where] stout cattle graze.

Na-na-na-na-na-na

Oh, that is where the Ruthenian fatherland is!

There is much from which

To forge sabers against the enemy,

Oh, there is also native salt

Foreign lands season with it

Na-na-na-na-na-na

Oh, that is where the Ruthenian fatherland is!

Where the San, Dnister, and Buh roar,

The Dnipro shakes its rapids,

Where the steppes are broad,

Where the Cossacks carouse

Na-na-na-na-na-na

Oh, that is where the Ruthenian
Fatherland is!

Oh, no, no! Oh, no, no!

It's in an entirely different place.

"There where freedom, our own courts,

Where all the sciences bloom,

Where every class enjoys prosperity,

Where each is master in his home?"

Oh, no, no! Oh, no, no!

It's in an entirely different place.

"Where is that Ruthenian fatherland?

Where all are drunk without wine,

Where the hungry peasant plows,

Where all bend their brow submissively."

Oh, no, no! Oh, no, no!

That is where the Ruthenian fatherland
is.

"Where falsehood spits on truth,

Where one can become a prophet

Without knowledge, without a
mind [*bez uma*—a reference to
Naumovych—Y. H.]

Oh, there, there! Oh, there, there!

Is where the Ruthenian fatherland is!

Where there has been discord since
ancient times,

They fight only for the "ь" and "ъ" [pro-
nounced "ir" and "ior," respectively—
Y. H.]

Where an incoherent one bamboozles
  the world,
And a blind man is the leader.
Oh, there, there you have it! Oh, there,
  there you have it!
That is where the Ruthenian fatherland
  is! [ZT 3:276–77]

In Franko's parody, "Rus" serves as a symbol of backwardness, poverty, and social injustice. He utterly desacralizes "Rus," ridiculing its ostensible wealth and grandeur and even writing the phrase "Ruthenian Fatherland" in small letters. In his writings, Franko opposed this image to "Ukraine" as an image of the future fatherland. This opposition should not necessarily be read in the context of the conflict between the Ukrainophile and Russophile orientations. Hushalevych wrote his poem when he was close to Ukrainophilism, and his "Rus" corresponds to "Ukraine" (Hushalevych, in fact, is credited with coining the term "Rus-Ukraine"). On the other hand, the image of Ukraine as a conservative utopia was not alien to the Ukrainophile movement either. It was further developed by one of the greatest Ukrainophile authorities, Panteleimon Kulish, who during the 1880s sought to influence events in the Galician-Ruthenian camp and even to rally Belei and other radicals under his leadership.[7] In criticizing Naumovych and Hushalevych, Franko did not refrain from directing his harsh criticism toward Kulish and his image of a "Ukraine filled with *khutory*" (farmsteads, as opposed to villages and cities) [ZT 26:161–79].

Franko's contribution to the Ukrainophile movement lay in the expansion of his ideological repertoire, particularly with respect to the creation of an image of Ukraine that was consonant with the new winds of change. Franko creates the impression that the triumph of this image is inevitable. With this goal in mind, he describes it practically in nature-related categories, comparing it to springtime, to a storm, and to a mighty oak. It is a symbol of the utmost loyalty. But this loyalty is in harmony with universal values and with the struggle of all oppressed people against all kinds of repressions:

In getting to know it, could I	Її пізнавши, чи ж я міг
Not come to love it sincerely,	Не полюбить її сердечно,
Not renounce my own joys,	Не відректися власних втіх,
In order to devote myself to it indispensably?	Щоб їй віддатись доконечно?
And having come to love it, could I	А полюбивши, чи ж би міг
Cast its godly likeness	Я божую її подобу
From my heart, regardless of all	Згубити з серця, мимо всіх
Sufferings and woes unto the grave?	Терпінь і горя аж до гробу?
And does this love contradict	І чи ж перечить ся любов
That other sacred love	Тій другій а святій любові
For all who pour their sweat and blood	До всіх, що ллють свій піт і кров,
For all who are enchained?	До всіх, котрих гнетуть окови?
No, he who does not love all brothers,	Ні, хто не любить всіх братів,
Like God's sun, everyone alike,	Як сонце боже, всіх зарівно,
Knew not how to love you,	Той щиро полюбить не вмів
Beloved Ukraine, sincerely.	Тебе, коханая Вкраїно! [*ZT* 1:83]

Before Franko's emergence on the literary scene, the image of Ukraine in Ruthenian-Ukrainian literature was represented most clearly in Shevchenko. Still, as already mentioned, although Ukraine exists in Shevchenko's work, there are as yet no Ukrainians in it. His ideological fatherland remains sparsely populated: the role of its population was performed, as in the folk literature, by mythologized Cossacks. Franko's conception of Ukraine is densely populated by "new people at work"— nationally aware peasants, intellectuals, women, and workers. His Ukraine is both a social and an ethnic category. His occasional statements on this theme indicate that, under certain conditions, even Galician Jews could be "citizen[s] of the land." According to Franko, the main criterion of belonging to a fatherland is not birth or ownership of land, "but only the feeling of solidarity with national ideals and work for their realization" [*Mozaika* 328]. The prerequisite of "solidarity with national ideals" is so diluted that it is impossible to apply it as a conceptual criterion. It implicitly envisages the existence of a social authority that will decide the applicability of this criterion in every concrete case. Obviously, these authorities are supposed to be the very people who propose this criterion—that is, the "progressive" intelligentsia.

Franko's image of Ukraine is very similar to the Christian Kingdom of God: in order to gain admittance to it, you must experience conversion—in fact, you must attest to the sincerity of your convictions—and experience the Final Judgment, a revolution that will ultimately separate the righteous from the sinners. Even Russophiles can go through this judgment, but only on the condition that they repent and begin to love "their people" in a genuine way [ZT 2:332]. However, Franko's proposal to the Russophiles went unheeded. But the point here is not national orientation. As mentioned earlier, the Russophiles did not fundamentally reject the Ukrainophiles, as the older, pragmatically oriented Ukrainophiles frequently dodged the harsh criticisms that the Russophiles aimed at them. After all, in Hushalevych's poem his fatherland is read as "Rus-Ukraine." Set to music, his poem became one of several unofficial Ruthenian hymns that were equally popular in both Russophile and Ukrainophile homes. If Konysky is to be believed, another of his poems, "Peace to You, Brothers" (Myr vam, brattia), as well as "Ukraine Has Not Yet Perished" (Shche ne vmerla Ukraina), was sung in rural reading rooms. What distinguished Franko's fatherland from the fatherland of the Russophiles and some Ukrainophiles was its radical social orientation. Illustrative in this respect is the case of Fylyp Svystun, one of the leading Russophile ideologists. Although Svystun was prepared to acknowledge Shevchenko as a national poet, he was categorically opposed to the nihilism that he associated with Drahomanov and his pupils: "We will have many more occasions to hear about the attempts to establish it [nihilism—Y. H.] in our land, but God willing, standing firmly with our church and nationality, we shall repulse all the encroachments of people who have forfeited all nobler feeling and who dream of…murders." [8]

Fylyp Svystun's writings explain why Franko-style Ukrainophilism was fundamentally unacceptable to the ideologists of Russophilism. They could tolerate it as a literary movement within the framework of the general pan-Slavic national awakening: the endeavor to write in the language of the common folk enriched the general Ruthenian culture. After all, a similar formula—Ukrainian literature as a part of general Rus literature, along with Belarusian and Russian—was proposed by none other than Drahomanov in his writings that were published in Galicia in the 1870s. To his mind, separating "Ruthenians" (*rus´kykh*: Ukrainians) from "Russians" (*russkikh*) was as nonsensical as separating "Franks" from "Frenchmen." However, the Russophiles of that time categorically disliked another of Drahomanov's formulas, his call to unite "passionate feelings for the people" with the propaganda of "leading European ideas," which was characteristic of "progressive" Russian literature.[9] From their perspective, the spread of realism and Positivism was tantamount to an assault on the very foundations of Russophilism, which saw itself as a conservative movement with a strong religious basis.[10]

This same idea, but in poetic form, was conveyed by Ivan Hushalevych in 1879. If he followed in the footsteps of the young "false prophets," then he "would probably be an unhappy man, / *An exile from [his] native land*, / Standing over the depths of an abyss [my emphasis—Y. H.]."[11] This verse appeared in the second volume of a collection of Hushalevych's poems, which was published in 1879, immediately after the trial of the Ruthenian-Ukrainian socialists ended. His philippics were directed at Franko, Pavlyk, Terletsky, and other radical Ukrainophiles, whom he labeled "traitors" who sow "hatred, spite, and nocturnal lies / And quarrels among the people's servants" (nenavist´, zlost´ i lzhi nochnyi / I spory mezh narodnykh slug). He called forth upon them "hungry serpents, the scourges of scorpions," "thunder," "the fires of Gehenna," and "all manner of torments."[12]

In order to illustrate that Svystun and Hushalevych's metaphors were not incidental occurrences but rather figures of speech that reflected a certain trend, I will cite here a fragment from a poem by the Russophile poet who titled himself Vladimir from the Carpathian Canyons (Yevhen Fentsyk), who objected to the "nihilists" even considering themselves "sons of Rus."

No, you are not sons of the Russian
People, they are alien to you.
A Ross [Russian] would not forget about God.
The heavenly voice is sacred to the Russians.
You want to tear to pieces
Or cripple your mother,
And turn the hundred-million-strong family
Into an eternal cripple.
You demand freedom,
And with a revolver in your hands.

Aimed at your own people, your mother—you monsters!

You bring forth death and fear.

Holy is Rus and all of Slavdom,

The entire birth family

Has proclaimed loudly, publicly

That you are enemies of hers.[13]

A comparison of Svystun, Hushalevych, and Fentsyk demonstrates another of the most radical differences between them and young left-leaning Ukrainophiles: revolutionary terror ("freedom with a revolver in your hand"), which does not shy away from assassinating tsars. The Russophiles' fatherland was poorly delineated in geographic terms. But it was clearly personified in the person of the "good monarch," the Austrian emperor or the Russian tsar. In organizing the assassination of an anointed monarch, revolutionaries were targeting the very heart of the Russophiles' fatherland. Meanwhile, for young socialists the assassination of the tsar was not only completely justified, it was also a desirable act, without which the dawning of freedom was impossible. In his "Prison Sonnets," Franko lionized the most famous of the tsar's assassins, Dmitrii Karakozov and Sophia Perovskaia, and appealed to his readers to avenge their torments: "Do not soften over time! Temper your strength! / Banish the beast, beat it, tear it with your teeth!" [ZT 1:172].

Ivan Maksymiak, one of Franko's epigones, appealed to his poetic muse in this tone:

You are that holy one, like the sole God,

You constantly shout for truth

With fiery word: Beat, stab

Murder the pious bloodsuckers

Tear down the thrones! And with your

Sincere word you praise those tsars' assassins

Who dedicated their lives to freedom![14]

What Was in It for the Peasantry?

What could Franko offer the peasantry? In truth, he did not have much to offer, apart from social demagogy. In his poems he resorts to one of the most beloved images in Ukrainian literature after Shevchenko, in which he compares Ukraine, the great fatherland, with a field on which a peasant is toiling. In Franko, this peasant is a hired laborer who "with a mournful song plows / That field, he does not plow for himself," "who pours rivers of sweat / Over someone else's field". But this field will become his when the storm—revolution—arrives.

He will conquer, tear the shells of idle talk—	Він побідить, порве шкарлущі пересуду,
And your own free field	І вольний, власний лан
You will plow once again—the owner of your labor,	Ти знов оратимеш—властивець свого труду,
And you will be the master in your own land!	І в власнім краї сам свій пан! [*ZT* 1:60–62]

In Franko, the image of Ukraine as a field has unmistakably socialist coloration: it is a field attained through joint effort and developed by collective labor.

I thought about the new human brotherhood,	Я думав про людське братерство нове,
And wondered: will it appear soon in the world?	І думав, чи в світ воно швидко прийде?
And in that thought I saw endless fields:	І бачив я в думці безмежні поля:
Worked by collective labor, that tillage Fed a happy, free nation.	Управлена спільним трудом, та рілля Народ годувала щасливий, свобідний.
Is this Ukraine, is this my native land. Robbed by foreigners and forgotten by the world?	Чи се ж Україна, чи се край мій рідний, Обдертий чужими і світом забутий?
Yes, this is Ukraine, free and new!	Так, се Україна, свобідна нова!
And the fierce pain in my heart began to ease.	І в мойому серці біль втишувавсь лютий. [*ZT* 1:186]

This poetic image could hardly fire up the peasants' imagination. Linking the new fatherland with revolutionary transformations could elicit healthy peasant skepticism. Franko later recalled how he had explained the theory of collective land ownership to an elderly farmer named Yatsko Zaparniuk, who was one of the most active peasant radicals. "The old man became firmly lost in thought, listening to my words, and then, smiling gently, he says: 'Yes, dear sir, this would be very good for lazy people!'" [15]

The Galician radicals encountered this peasant skepticism later, in the 1890s, once they got the chance to conduct their propaganda activities openly and legally. A brief period of popularity in some counties was followed by a backlash. "Ignorant peasants were enlisted to the national cause with the hope of material interest. This was demagogy of immense proportions," wrote Viacheslav Budzynovsky. "In profiting from the peasants [by enlisting them] under the national flag because it would provide material benefit, in the meantime the propagandists of the national idea themselves gave the peasant the right to abandon this flag at the very moment when it began to generate material losses, and when only *khrunivstvo* [switching to the opposing side for the sake of material interests—Y. H.] could provide benefits."[16] This shift in the events that were unfolding forced the radicals to seek a new method for arguing their views—by citing historical tradition. The Russophile, Osyp Markov, offered the following cue: "In agitating for your economic program, popularize history at the same time. Then the fire you have lit will not be of straw."[17]

In this respect, the young Franko's creative legacy includes a work that merits special attention: the historical novel *Zakhar Berkut* (1882). As mentioned earlier, it was popular among the peasants—and no wonder: it was a masterfully told story about the history of local districts and events, the "memory" of which lived on in the oral tradition. The plot interwove folk accounts of the drowning of the Mongol horde in the Carpathians with real events (the 1241 invasion of the Mongol armies led by Peta). But Franko would not be Franko if he had not used historical facts "for the embodiment of a certain idea in certain lively, typical personages" [*ZT* 16:7; see also *ZT* 16:481–82].

This embodied idea is "community" (*hromadstvo*), a neologism that, in the context of the novel, sounds like a synonym for the Western European word "socialism" (note that Drahomanov and Pavlyk linked the name of the journal *Hromadskyi druh* to the Paris Commune). During the Mongol horde's campaign throughout the Galician land only one mountain village, Tukhlia, offers resistance to the invaders. The villagers are victorious after they lure the Mongols into a ravine, where they drown. Their victory is not so much the result of their craftiness as their organized strength. In them lives the spirit of revolt and defiance of any power over them. They recognize only one power—that of their own community—which is personified by a local healer named Zakhar Berkut, a ninety-year-old man whom the peasants regard as their greatest authority and who is respected by all as the leader of their community. In his youth, he spent many years visiting one healer after another, traveling "over mountains and valleys" in order to learn the art of healing. He also visited Halych, the then capital of Red Rus, and even spent some time in Kyiv. Everywhere he saw the same thing: the princes and boyars of Rus were destroying public order throughout the countryside in order to turn the disunited peasants into their slaves and servants. During his travels, Zakhar Berkut heard much about the state of public affairs in northern Rus, in Novhorod and Pskov, where there was no princely rule, and about the local people's prosperity and burgeoning development. These accounts served to enflame his soul with one desire: "to devote his entire life to correcting and strengthening good civic order in his native Tukhlia region" [*ZT* 16:41].

Zakhar Berkut's main antagonist is a local boyar named Tuhar Vovk, not the Mongol military leaders. Under the pretext of protecting this area from foreign tribes, he gathers the surrounding lands under his control and ownership, thereby endangering the freedom and prosperity of the people of Tukhlia. When the time comes to resist the Mongols, Vovk goes over to the enemy's side, expecting that the superior forces will break the peasants' resistance. The romantic intrigue of the plot is the love between Maksym, the son of Zakhar Berkut, and Myroslava, the daughter of Tuhar Vovk. Myroslava sides with her lover and his father; she teaches the art of military subterfuge to the peasants, thereby greatly contributing to their victory.

The novel ends with the destruction of the Mongol army together with the traitor Tuhar Vovk and the marriage of Myroslava and Maksym, which is blessed by Zakhar Berkut. The joy of victory is dimmed by the imminent death of the ninety-year-old protagonist. On his deathbed, he addresses his fellow villagers; his farewell speech is worth citing here because it is clearly Franko's programmatic statement of what kind of fatherland the peasants should have:

> And now, children, come and lift me up a bit! Before my departure I would like to say something to the community that I sought to serve my entire life. Fathers and brothers! Today's victory of ours is a great deed for us. With what did we attain victory, with our weapons alone? No. With our cleverness? No. We triumphed through our community order, with our accord and friendship. Pay close attention to this! As long as you continue to live in community order, stay together in a friendly fashion, stand up unyieldingly for each other, one for all, no enemy force will ever defeat you. But I know, brothers, and my very soul feels this, that this was not the last blow struck at our community fortress, that it will be followed by others, and in the end

they will shatter our community. Bad times will come to our people. Brothers will become estranged from brothers, sons will cut themselves off from their fathers, and great quarrels and dissensions will commence throughout the Ruthenian land, and they will consume the people's strength, and then the entire people will end up in the captivity of foreign aggressors and their own ones, and they will turn it into an obedient servant of their whims and a laboring ox. But amidst those miseries the people will recalls its former community, and it will be a blessing if it recalls it swiftly and energetically: this will save it an entire ocean of tears and blood, entire centuries of slavery. But sooner or later, it will recall the life of its forefathers and will be seized with the desire to follow in their footsteps. Happy is he who is destined to live in those days! These will be beautiful days, days of spring, days of the people's rebirth! Pass down to your children and grandchildren tidings of the former life and former customs. May that memory live among them amidst the impending woes, just as a living spark is not extinguished amidst ashes. There will come a time when the spark will flare up into a new fire! Farewell! [*ZT* 16:154]

At first glance, Zakhar Berkut's deathbed vision seems to be another ideological utopia written by an intellectual for intellectuals. It is uttered by an individual who may be considered the prototype of a nineteenth-century intellectual: he was educated, having had to learn his trade, and he also traveled to various large cities; his power in the community is based not on his higher social origins but on his knowledge. In addition, his monologue echoes a quotation from modern revolutionary literature[18] and a general intellectual principle that was expressed by the Russian literary critic Vissarion Belinsky: "To love one's fatherland means to want passionately to see in it the realization of the ideal of humanity and to assist this to the degree of one's strength."[19]

But in Zakhar Berkut's monologue, as well as in the main idea of the novel, are aspects that were specifically aimed at the peasantry. It is normal for an intellectual or modernizer to shift his utopian vision into the future. Such a shift is based on a belief in historical progress and does not require additional legitimization. This is not the case in a traditional society, where every action has, or acquires, sense only when it existed and was repeated in the past. The main legitimization is the following: this is how our ancestors did it; this is why we do it that way. No other explanation is required. The past thus serves as a kind of matrix of human behavior.[20] In writing *Zakhar*

Berkut, Franko was projecting socialism into the future and presenting it as ostensibly deeply rooted in ancient Ruthenian mores, when "the community was both its own judge and arranger of all things" [*ZT* 16:41].

Also noteworthy is the fact that in Franko's novel the vision of the new order is expressed by a ninety-year-old man, not his son, a youth, or his beloved. The traditional world perception also mistrusts all kinds of innovations and the "new people" who want to introduce them. Innovations have a right to exist only when they emulate tradition. And tradition was the act that was allegedly first performed by a god, a hero, an ancestor.[21] All these three images are embodied in the figure of the community elder or a priest who is the main hero of Franko's novel. Through the character of Zakhar Berkut, Franko legitimizes a substantial number of new ideas: the utility of machines (Myroslava teaches the inhabitants of Tukhlia how to build machines), love as the foundation of marriage (the boyar's daughter marries the son of a peasant without her father's consent), and even pantheism, which is akin to atheism (Christianity is depicted as a "new religion from the East," a religion of submission, whose introduction aids the princes and boyars in enslaving the people; meanwhile, the inhabitants of Tukhlia serve the "ancient, free, purely communal religion" that "did not frighten people with punishments and torments after death, but regarded death as the greatest punishment, death of the body and the soul for unrighteous people" [*ZT* 16:122]). Zakhar Berkut approves of, and gives his blessing to, all these acts and deeds. Furthermore, he appears as the main and last priest of this "communal religion." The highest virtue is the good of the community, and everything must be subordinated to it, including even deep, sincere love. "You recognize only black eyes and a trim waistline," Zakhar Berkut tells Myroslava in response to her pleas for help for her lover, his son, "but I look at what is good for everyone. There is no choice here, daughter!" [*ZT* 16:150].

Franko places the good of the community higher than fealty to a monarch, because that is supposedly how it was in the "hoary past." This opposition of a republic to a monarchy (in Franko's words, "the struggle of the federal assembly element with the destructive princely-boyar [element]" [*ZT* 16:481–82]) appears twice in the novel: in the above-mentioned glorification of the city-republics of Novgorod and Pskov as an exemplary political model, and in his negative assessment of Prince Danylo of Halych. The prince is both indirectly and directly responsible for the dangers that the inhabitants of Tukhlia have encountered: indirectly because, like other princes of Rus, he was unable to protect them from the Mongol horde; and directly because he granted the community lands of Tukhlia to Tuhar Vovk. Although Danylo of Halych does not appear a single time in the novel (mentioned only in passing by the main characters), every mention of him is fraught with a negative meaning. The most significant condemnation is uttered by Zakhar Berkut, who says to Tuhar Vovk: "We do not recognize your prince as a father and a guardian, but as God's punishment sent upon us for our sins, from which we must absolve ourselves with annual tributes. The less we know about him, and he about us, the better for us. And if today our entire Rus could rid itself of him with all his gangs, then it would certainly still be happy and great!" [*ZT* 16:55].

This treatment of the most famous prince of Galicia was one of the reasons the editorial board of *Zoria*, in the person of Omelian Partytsky, delayed the novel's publication. To Partytsky and other Ruthenian patriots—no matter whether they were Ukrainophiles or Russophiles—Danylo of Halych "represent[ed] the light in [their] past....As attested by history, Danylo was a true 'king of the peasants.'"[22] Franko rejected this interpretation, but he agreed to meet privately with the editor in order to discuss possible changes. Finally, to Zakhar Berkut's words about Prince Danylo he added a note that somewhat softened the harshness of his assessment, but which generally justified it, once again citing historical tradition. As evidence of the "views of the people during that time" Franko cited a chronicle account of Mytusa's revolt against the Galician prince [*ZT* 16:55].

In *Zakhar Berkut*, Franko once again resorts to a method that he first used in his novel *Boryslav Is Laughing*: "to present what is realistically extraordinary amidst the ordinary and in the adornment of the commonplace" [*ZT* 48:206]. But, whereas in the Boryslav cycle he describes current events in order to prove the applicability of socialism to contemporary Galicia, in Zakhar Berkut he returns to the Galician past in order to show the rootedness of socialism in local historical tradition.

Zakhar Berkut was arguably the only work of Franko's that was popular among both the intelligentsia and the peasantry. Reading this novel, both intellectuals and peasants could be of one mind—although from diametrically opposing positions—about a single, common fatherland built on the principles of community.

Patria as Progress

Franko ends his novel with the following prophecy: "Much had changed since that time. The prophecies of the old citizen had come true, even too accurately. Like a hail cloud, great miseries passed over the Ruthenian land. The ancient community is long forgotten and buried, so it would seem. But, no! Was it not fated to be restored in our days? Is it not we who are living in that happy age of rebirth, of which Zakhar spoke when he was dying, or at least at the dawn of that happy era?" [*ZT* 16:154].

If this book had been written in the hagiographic genre, it would have ended with an exaltation of the young Franko as a righteous prophet. Indeed, he predicted what ended up happening a year or two after his death, but still within the life span of his generation: the fall of the Russian Empire in 1917 and the collapse of the Austro-Hungarian Empire in 1919, and from their remnants the rise of the Ukrainian states with a socialist orientation manifested to a greater (the Ukrainian National Republic and the Ukrainian Soviet Socialist Republic in the east) or lesser degree (the Western Ukrainian National Republic in the west). However, historians with a critically oriented perspective should have a more dispassionate attitude to Franko's prophetic talents: they should perceive them not as further proof of the fact that he was a genius but rather as a manifestation of a certain *Zeitgeist*. Specialists in late nineteenth-century history know that some historians or politicians of that period who were far from being geniuses made more or less accurate predictions. For example, Oleksandr Kistiakivsky was certain, judging from a journal entry in 1885, that

> a great future in Southern Russia awaits Ukrainophilism. It will come about willy-nilly through the energy of the public, which will be reckoned with very much. It has begun to play a role. But, partly as a result of its weakness, faintheartedness, and the vainglory of its leaders and those who side with them, partly as a result of the hatred for it of the surrounding world, it has suffered a serious collapse; but there is no doubt: it will rebound. [23]

On the other hand, we have the unrealized 1881 prophecy of the "genius," Ivan Naumovych, who declared that there would never come a time in Galicia when people would say, "I am not Russian, I am Ukrainian," or even that there would ever be a Ukraine in Transcarpathia.[24] From the perspective of the theory of probability, the chances of guessing which of the two opposing political currents would come to the fore are very high: 50 percent. As soon as the probable becomes real, there is always a temptation to call the supporters of one camp "visionaries." However, it is not worth limiting oneself to making trivial claims that all the actors enjoyed equal opportunities and that under certain circumstances history could have turned out differently. The historian's task is to show which circumstances are more relevant and which are less so. Naturally, the relevance of circumstances can change with the passage of time. Let's assume that Naumovych's prophecy in the 1860s looked far more probable and had better chances of coming true if not for the changes that took place in subsequent decades. Was there something about the circumstances during the latter third of the nineteenth century and the early decades of the twentieth that offered better chances for the prediction that is made at the end of *Zakhar Berkut* than for Naumovych's prediction?

Historians believe that it was precisely the period between 1867 and 1914 which saw the formation of movements and ideologies that were fully revealed only after the First World War. They claim that the connection between the past and the future was never as obvious as it was during this period. This was the classic era of progress, when Europe was changing more rapidly than ever before. The reverse side of this large-scale transformation was a profound identity crisis. Therefore, the solutions to this crisis that were then being proposed had an enduring impact throughout the twentieth century.[25]

Bismarck, who was one of the most pragmatic politicians of his time, was convinced that Europe would not rest easy until all its peoples became nations, or "tribes," as he called them disparagingly. This difference in the usage of terms, writes Bismarck's biographer, was not accidental. "The advocates of nationalism claimed to be preaching a high moral principle—Mazzini equating nationalism and Christianity merely carried this to its extreme. Bismarck did not regard nationalism as high or moral; he merely accepted it as inevitable and wished to be on the winning side."[26]

In the second half of the nineteenth century, nationalism entered into a struggle with a new and powerful competitor—Marxism. Marx and Engels's *Manifesto of the Communist Party* may be read as both an anticapitalist and an antinationalist manifesto. Each of these ideologies proposed a competing method of creating a modern society: vertical integration (nationalism) versus horizontal integration (Marxism). In the final analysis, it was a question of who would be the main actor of history—the nation or the class.[27]

The superiority of Franko's formula lay in the fact that it proposed placing both nation and class at the foundation of the new society. Ultimately, this formula united the conception of *patria* with the concept of progress, and it has been argued that this precise combination is a successful formula for nation building.[28] By the mid-1880s Ukrainophilism in Galicia was consonant with the new tendencies of social development, which fact was acknowledged by the Russophile Fylyp Svystun:

> Ukrainianism is the result of a new trend in the spiritual life of Europe, which, growing slowly since the second half of the eighteenth century, spread from the West to the East, and, having reached Russia, caused a revolution in the outlook of the educated classes of the Russian people. In the field of science it produced empiricism; in the field of literature, Romanticism; in the field of arts, realism; and in political and social relations it gave birth to the idea of personal freedom and the equality of all people.[29]

A similar view was expressed by Franko's peer, the Rev. Fylymon Tarnavsky:

> The first priority of the Muscophile idea was the Russification of the common masses, not the social question. For the Ukrainians, national issues went hand in hand with economic and social ones. The Ukrainian idea was more idealistic, it put deeper roots into the common masses and attracted workers who were devoted, while also appealing to those of a more idealistic character.[30]

The above-cited statements were made by people who were alien or even hostile to Franko and his radical movement. Kistiakivsky, who belonged to the moderate wing of the Kyiv Hromada, was irritated by Drahomanov as the "general of the revolution," while Franko annoyed Svystun with his talk of nihilism, and Tarnavsky with his discourse on atheism. If these statements are supplemented by a lengthy citation from Franko about the days of his youth, when socialist ideals enflamed his friends "to the point of fanaticism" and how they dreamt of a "great socialist revolution" (see chapter 16), then one gets the impression that the formula of an ideological fatherland, as proposed in *Zakhar Berkut*, corresponded to the ideas of a considerable part of the intelligentsia, regardless of which national orientation it espoused (Svystun was a Russophile) and to which lands (Kistiakivsky lived in the Russian Empire) or ideological group (Tarnavsky was a populist) it belonged.

Nevertheless, there was one significant problem with putting this formula into practice: the vitality of the traditional society. Although it is true that in the final decades of the nineteenth century and the first decades of the twentieth century Europe was becoming rapidly modernized, the degree of this modernization prior to 1914 should not be exaggerated. As Arno Mayer reminds us, out of the six superpowers that combined forces in the First World War—Austro-Hungary, Great Britain, Italy, Germany, Russia, and France—only France was not a monarchy (it had become a republic in comparatively recent times, in 1875); the industrial bourgeoisie and the middle class did not hold the reins of political power in any of these countries (including France and Great Britain); with the exception of Great Britain, each of the other countries' economies was dominated by the agrarian sector, and large industrial centers were ringed by an ocean of rural farms and traditional manufacturers; in their behavior, the new classes sought to imitate the aristocracy; classical models dominated cultural production, and the advocates of this culture enjoyed easier access to careers and official prizes. It took two world wars to eradicate the ancien régime in Europe.[31]

The young Franko's imagined community was a "nation of progressivists." If it is defined through its readers, then one cannot rid oneself of the impression that by the mid-1880s it was very small, economically weak, and politically marginalized. The situation could have changed fundamentally if it had been possible to speak to the hearts and minds of the numerically largest group, the peasantry. Franko placed the peasants at the center of his fatherland. But both Ruthenian and Polish peasants were powerfully bound up with the structures of their traditional societies. The language of "progress" was foreign to them, even hostile. Between the peasants and the intelligentsia lay a social chasm that could be overcome only by the spread of education and a gradual transformation of patterns of thinking.

Under these conditions, the Russophiles' conservative utopia continued to preserve its powerful influence. Their success in developing their institutional network in Galician cities and villages was a fact that could not be explained simply as the result of "Russian rubles"—that is, subsidies from the Russian imperial government. The effectiveness of their ideology and practice lay in the clever mix of tradition and modernity. The Russophiles were "modernizers," but in the conservative sense: they were advocates of a belated version of Josephinism, the goal of which was to introduce the traditions of the Enlightenment and rationalism into public discourses and public practices. In any case, they had the right to exist as long as the ancien régime existed.

The historical conjuncture changed fundamentally with the fall of the monarchies. In the Austrian part, things never reached the point at which the Russophiles' utopia came into being. The conservative wing of the Ruthenian-Ukrainian camp got its chance in Russian-ruled Ukraine, where it was represented as so-called "Little Russians," who, like the "Russophiles," were mostly from the petty nobility (if the Greek Catholic clergy in Galicia may be considered a quasi-nobility), combined their local patriotism (*Landpatriotismus*) with loyalty to the ruling dynasty, and were distinguished by their conservative stance.

In the spring of 1918, with the support of the German occupying regime, they brought down the government of the Ukrainian National Republic, established a new Ukrainian state under the leadership of Hetman Pavlo Skoropadsky, and ruled over the Ukrainian gubernias of the former Russian Empire until the entry of German troops. However, during the war and the Russian revolutions, the Ukrainian peasantry became much radicalized. Therefore, relations between the conservative Little Russian regime and the peasants were extremely problematic, to the point that the Ukrainian state turned into an arena of mass antigovernment peasant uprisings.[32]

The period of 1914–1923 became a touchstone for competing ideologies of the fatherland. War and revolution acted as powerful triggers activating the transformation of peasants into a nation. If the creation of modern nations was the result of modernizing processes, then it was precisely this war, thanks to the mass mobilization of peasants, which became the biggest mass incursion of the modern world into the traditional life of the countryside. The war also "nationalized" the peasantry, exposing it to the colossal national propaganda of the various warring sides, forcing it to cover huge distances as part of fighting armies or hordes of war refugees, and thereby expanding its geographic notions (the first mass contacts between the "Ruthenian" peasants of both empires took place during the Russian occupation of Galicia and the Austrian occupation of the Ukrainian gubernias, and so on).[33] Step by step, the peasants were arriving at the realization that they belonged to a larger fatherland. However, this did not help to lessen their alienation from the educated classes, so diverse were the images of ideological fatherlands that were nurtured by various strata.[34]

However, this does not mean that the degree of mutual alienation was equal in all cases. Some revolutionary regimes achieved success at least in terms of a short-lived mobilization of peasants. In this regard, an interesting example was the victory of the socialist parties in the Ukrainian gubernias during the elections to the All-Russian Constituent Assembly in late 1917. They won the support of the peasantry thanks to a blend—demagogical to a significant degree—of social and national slogans.[35] The peasantry's sensitivity to such a combination came to the fore during the anti-German and anti-Bolshevik uprisings of 1918–1920. The Ukrainian peasant movement during the revolution in the former Russian Empire was a singular phenomenon. Andrea Graziosi, a historian of this period, writes: "With the possible exception of the contemporary Mexican revolution, there developed the *first peasant-based national-socialist liberation movement* of a century which was to see so many of them. Of course, precisely because it was the first one, and because of Ukrainian peculiarities, its traits were sometimes ambiguous, though unmistakable."[36]

In the final analysis, the effectiveness of military and political control over Ukraine depended on the extent to which each of the warring sides was able to cope with the local peasantry, which had been jolted awake by war and revolution. The Bolsheviks, the main victors, were forced to embark on a far-reaching compromise with the Ukrainian peasants. The mass support that the peasantry in the Ukrainian gubernias provided to Ukrainian socialist parties in 1917 made a particularly strong impression on Lenin, who wrote: "In these circumstances, to ignore the importance of the national question in Ukraine…is a great and dangerous mistake. The division between the Russian and Ukrainian Socialist-Revolutionaries as early as 1917 could not have been accidental."[37]

The Bolsheviks supplemented the introduction of the New Economic Policy by creating the USSR, in which the autonomous Ukrainian SSR became the largest of the non-Russian republics. If one considers that the transformation of the Russian Empire into a federation was the main programmatic demand of the Ukrainian national movement before 1917, whereas the majority of the Russian parties, including the Bolsheviks, called for the preservation of a unitary state, then we are led to the paradoxical conclusion that the creation of the USSR was, at least partly, the realization of Ukrainian demands.

Our perception of the USSR and the Ukrainian SSR during the first postrevolutionary decade is poisoned by the later perspective of the 1930s–80s, when this compromise was abrogated by the forceful installation of the Soviet centralized regime. However, in the 1920s the historian and statesman Mykhailo Hrushevsky, the former head of the Central Rada, the parliament of the Ukrainian National Republic, had a different outlook on the phenomenon of the Ukrainian SSR. In 1925, he set about supplementing his national scheme of history with the events of the nineteenth century. He intended to show the "hundred-year process that had led Soviet citizenry, our working-peasant nation to today's positions." Hrushevsky generally regarded this process as the entwining of the national Ukrainian tradition with a new liberation movement that traced its beginnings to the French Revolution. He particularly acknowledged the achievements of those Ukrainian figures of the 1870s and 1880s who had merged these two points of origin. Of all these worthy individuals, it was Drahomanov whom Hrushevsky esteemed most highly.[38] Franko was not yet part of this schema. However, a year later, on the occasion of the 1926 celebrations marking the seventieth anniversary of Franko's birth and the tenth anniversary of his death, Hrushevsky wrote a lengthy eulogy titled "To the Apostle of Work," in which he straightforwardly and unambiguously proclaimed the link between the Ukrainian SSR and Franko's vision of a "united indivisible Ukraine from the San to the Kuban, an independent state of the Ukrainian working folk armed with the solid iron of European culture."[39]

It is too risky an endeavor to argue a connection between the views of the young Franko and that which took place in both neighboring empires two years after his death. If we consciously take this risky step, then we should do so not in order to prove the existence of a broad historical highway between one and the other, but to show that Franko's formula of a fatherland, no matter how naïve it may strike us today, had great mobilizational potential during the lifetime of his generation. It did not necessarily have to overcome competing conceptions, but the chances of its victory were higher than average.

Post Scriptum

To a considerable degree, these chances depended on the extent to which Franko's writings and activities enjoyed popularity and support among his readers. We are accustomed to literature reflecting reality. The thesis that literature alone can create this reality strikes us as strange, even absurd. But if we accept this thesis, then the focus on the successful nature of Franko's ability to see the future becomes more understandable: like a hypnotist, Franko himself called forth his own victory.

Instead of trying to guess what might have happened, let us examine what did happen by examining the collective biography of those individuals who were formed under the young Franko's influence. I will restrict myself to the high school circle, whose members included Osyp Makovei. In 1912 he published a book of memoirs based on his diary entries. Out of the thirty-four youths who matriculated in June 1887 along with Makovei, only twenty-eight were still alive at the time. Some of them had achieved renown. Yulian Bachynsky became a Marxist and the author of the book *Ukraina Irredenta* (1895), in which the postulate of Ukraine's political independence was first proclaimed. Bachynsky and his colleague Viacheslav Budzynovsky made a significant contribution to the founding of the first Ukrainian political parties: the Ruthenian-Ukrainian Radical Party (1890), the Ukrainian National-Democratic Party (1899), and the Ukrainian Social-Democratic Party (1899). Kyrylo Studynsky became an academic, and in the interwar years he would be appointed director of the Shevchenko Scientific Society. He and his younger colleague Vasyl Shchurat became the first professional researchers of Franko's oeuvre. Shchurat rose to fame as one of the finest literary scholars, and from time to time he committed the "sin" of penning his own works of literature. Osyp Nyzhankivsky, the conductor of a choir consisting of the members of the "underground" circle of gymnasium students, became a famous Ukrainian composer. He was summarily executed by Polish soldiers during the Ukrainian-Polish War of 1918–1919, and Kyrylo Studynsky was also shot—by the NKVD, during the first months of the Soviet-German War of 1941–1945.

Osyp Makovei, who also wrote a book of memoirs, tried his hand at working for several Ruthenian-Ukrainian periodical publications in Galicia and Bukovyna, and for some time coedited, with Franko, the most prestigious Ukrainian periodical, the *Literary Scientific Herald* (Literaturno-naukovyi vistnyk, or LNV). His literary works would be published and reissued during the rule of every regime throughout the twentieth century.

None of the former members of that Ukrainian gymnasium circle became a star of the first magnitude. Nevertheless, all of them held key positions in Ukrainian political, scholarly, and art institutions during the first two or three decades of the twentieth century. In point of fact, the strength of the Ukrainian movement in Galicia lay in the existence of a large number of secondary, albeit disciplined, figures. The members of this group nostalgically recalled their *Sturm und Drang* period, although not everyone remembered Franko with pleasure. His later illness had left a mark on his personality. There was hardly a single member of his former milieu with whom he had not quarreled at least once or completely severed ties. Makovei, Budzynovsky, and Shchurat were no exceptions. But one fact is unassailable: thanks to his activities, Franko created a social and cultural space in which they were able to carve out careers for themselves because they had Franko as a model they could emulate. Like Franko's hero Opanas Morymukha, real Lviv gymnasium students had found a "fatherland in his heart."

However, the question of who was to inhabit this fatherland, other than politically aware intellectuals, remained the subject of debate. At around the time Makovei published his memoirs, preparations were launched for marking the fortieth jubilee of Franko's literary activities, slated for 1913. A committee comprising representatives from all the Ukrainian parties was formed in Drohobych for this purpose. Its members could not agree on how to organize the jubilee procession. The social democrats insisted that Franko was a social writer, not a national one; they suggested, therefore, that the workers of Boryslav should march at the head of the procession. Their opponents declared that this would contradict the national character of the celebrations because the majority of Boryslav workers were Poles. Therefore, it made sense for Ukrainian intellectuals, Ukrainian peasants, and Ukrainian workers to march at the head of the procession. Volodymyr Byrchak, a professor at the Drohobych Gymnasium, set about resolving this conflict. He acknowledged the correctness of the social democrats' stance, taking their idea one step further by declaring that the workers of Boryslav should be followed by Jews, because Franko had also described them in his cycle of Boryslav stories. The Jews could be followed by the Basilian Fathers of Drohobych, and then by the women of easy virtue, whom Franko had also depicted, in his novel *For the Home Hearth* (Dlia domashnoho vohny-shcha), and others. Byrchak's intervention was a joke intended to extinguish the fires of conflict between the two sides. But there is a grain of truth in every joke. When the same question was addressed to Franko, he replied: "I am a poet not of a single stratum but of the entire nation."[40]

This response annulled the position he had adopted in his youth, when he placed the social factor if not higher than, then at least on a single plane with the national. However, much of Franko's literary oeuvre in his early years continued to function actively at the end of his life, and not just in the Austro-Hungarian Empire. In 1912, the Kyivan censor, Sergei Shchegolev, published a book about Ukrainian separatism in the Russian Empire. It appeared after the legal restrictions on Ukrainian-language publications were abolished as a result of the revolution of 1905–1907 in Russia. But, during the period of postrevolutionary reaction, as earlier, Ukrainianness continued to be treated as a threat to the unity of the empire. Shchegolev called Franko the leader of the Ukrainian irredentists and Russophobes, whose "tendentious" works, disseminated throughout a network of reading rooms, were destabilizing the very foundation of the Russian Empire. Among these works he named the hymn "Ne pora," which Franko wrote when he was a young man.[41] A list of the works that were being disseminated throughout the Russian Empire during this period may be compiled on the basis of indexes of popular works: these are the short stories "At the Bottom," "Les's Family," and "Little Myron"; the short stories anthologized in the collection *The Fatherland and Other Stories* (Bat´kivshchyna ta inshi opovidannia); reprints of individual poems from the collection *From the Heights and Depths*; and others—in other words, everything that Franko had written as a young man.[42]

In any event, even if Franko had died in his youth, he would still have given the Ukrainian national movement a selection of vivid literary images, from which peered the contours of a new fatherland. His biography would have offered excellent material for a cult of the national poet, which was to personify this fatherland, and the generation that had emerged from under his tutelage would have ensured the dissemination of his works and popularization of his cult. In other words, Franko did become a prophet: a prophet in his own land.

Conclusion

In the last third of the nineteenth century in Austrian Galicia, an event occurred that was destined to redefine the future geopolitical map of Eastern Europe: a new, dynamic Ukrainian national movement emerged, which was victorious over alternative models of identification among Galician Ruthenians. Its victory expanded beyond Galicia and influenced the Russian Empire, the government of which (correctly) viewed the Ukrainian movement as one of the chief threats to its very existence.

One cannot understand this event while remaining within the limits of only the national and imperial paradigms—that is, to interpret it as the result of the interaction of national movements and imperial governments. An adequate understanding requires us to widen the perspective and place national identity within a wider spectrum of other group identities. With this book, I have tried to prove the thesis that the transformation of identities (and correspondingly, the victory of the Ukrainian national movement) was the result of the emergence of a new, leftist culture. The very carriers of this culture called themselves Ruthenian-Ukrainian radicals and their own culture (correspondingly)—radical. It was built on models exported from Western Europe—a mix of agrarian socialism and nationalism. Some of these models came to Galicia from the east, from the Russian Empire, but this does not contradict the fact of their fundamentally Western origin.

This argument for the decisive role of radical culture rests on the example of the young Franko's biography. His life story reveals two parallel but mutually connected histories: on the one hand, how Franko went through his own evolution and became the main creator and central symbol of this culture; and on the other hand, how the appearance of a social actor such as Franko changed the real and imagined space around him.

The very terminology (actor, field) imposes the metaphor of the game, as I proposed at this book's beginning. Central to understanding the logic of this game is the question of stakes and prizes. In other words, why were Franko and his friends prepared to invest so much effort in the creation of a new culture? The example of his biography contradicts the oft-repeated viewpoint that leaders of national movements did this for their own immediate or later benefit. The conscious ideological choice that he made in his early years brought him numerous calamities in the form of arrests, imprisonment, confiscation of publications by the authorities, ostracism from society, material insecurity, and even existential threats to his very life. One can say confidently that with his rigor and work ethic, Franko would have made a decent career and attained a secure position had he stayed away from public activities.

Franko's case also does not work well with another thesis: that the intelligentsia of "peasant peoples" strove to create their own nation because they could not compete with the enlightened classes of the dominant nationality. In fact, Franko felt confident in three cultural spaces—Ukrainian, Polish, and German—becoming an example of a successful writer.

The stakes in this game were much higher. They amounted to the search for an answer to the challenge of modernization, which the local multiethnic traditional society faced in the last third of the nineteenth century. Because of a series of changes, in Austrian Galicia a severe imbalance developed between the population's size and its demands, on the one hand, and the possibility of satisfying them, on the other. This provoked a feeling of existential threat for the main traditional groups of Galician society: the local Polish nobles (*szlachta*), Galician Jews, and above all the Polish and Ruthenian peasants, on whose shoulders rested the entire agrarian society. In turn, this feeling of threat provoked a crisis of traditional values and identities—and the local intellectuals tried to solve this crisis.

For the scale of success of their activities, the transformation that the region's capital, Lviv, experienced was also important. Before the establishment of Galician autonomy (1867), it was a part of the German-speaking world, and within the framework of this world it remained a second-order periphery compared to the main centers of the ruling German-language culture of Berlin and Vienna. After the introduction of autonomy, Lviv became a center—a great Polish and Ruthenian-Ukrainian cultural metropolis—the influence of which radiated not only throughout Galicia, but to neighboring western border regions of the Russian Empire. In this way and others, in the last third of the nineteenth century, Galicia and Lviv came to comprise one of the central fields where the fate of the great game was decided.

The transformations outlined above relate to the stakes of the field. When we talk about the stakes of the player, we need to consider another circumstance. Central and Eastern Europe is usually considered a "historically backward region," lacking the necessary institutional preconditions for successful modernization. From this assumption flow two consequences that directly influenced the status of the Eastern and Central European intelligentsia. First: ideologies were used as one of the institutional substitutes. Even if they were borrowed from the West, in this part of Europe they played a different role: they became "the agents of modernization" and took on more radical forms in a more backward region.[1] Second: the struggle of ideologies took place, first of all, in the literary realm. Literature—not in the narrow sense of a corpus of artistic creations, but including newspaper and journal publications—was the chief means of formulating ideological tendencies; literary journals served as a substitute national parliament, and their readers as political parties.

Among all the genres, poetry had the greatest opportunity to articulate the "brave new world." Thanks to poetic license, it most anticipated the resistance to existing reality, while a radical transformation of the public image of poets elevated their writings to the status of prophecy. In any case, literary writers—and poets in the forefront—became the central players on the field.

One could say that, in the Ruthenian-Ukrainian case, the game was played between two teams: the "conservative utopia" of Rus and the "progressive utopia" of Ukraine. Of course, the very adjectives "conservative" and "progressive" are here quite conditional. Proponents of the conservative utopia relied on the ideology of the Enlightenment and the model of the enlightened monarchy, while the progressivists in their construction of Ukraine employed elements of the people's traditional culture. However, the dividing line between the first and second was the attitude toward the idea of progress as such—negative in the first case, positive in the second.

Franko experienced a quite dramatic ideological evolution from the conservative to the progressive model in his formative years, during studies at the gymnasium and in his first years at university. From the twentieth year of his life, he became a passionate proponent of the idea of progress—to the extent that contemporaries considered Franko the living embodiment of this idea. This evolution largely took place outside of his will, due to circumstances over which he had no influence. In any event, still during his youth—until his thirtieth year—Franko managed to accumulate great cultural capital as the most productive author of the most interesting creative works that appeared in the Galician literature of both Ruthenians and Poles at that time.

The facts reveal that his influence extended beyond the borders of one national literature: Ukraine was not his only or even his main fatherland. The international "fatherland of progressives" for him was no less important. In any case, nation was not a central category in the young Franko's consciousness. It was rather a necessary by-product—the main platform with the help of which a traditional society could enter the modern world. Accordingly, adding the concept of "progress" to the category "Ruthenians" almost automatically transformed them into "Ukrainians." But Franko also filled up his creative works with images of progressive women, workers, Jews, and others. They all posed as representatives of a fatherland that did not exist but had to be created—and the creator (prophet) was Ivan Franko.

Franko's personal success caused a rupture in the overall balance of forces between the Ukrainophile and Russophile movements in the mid-1880s, a shift that was later called the "Ukrainian conquest of Galicia." One should not exaggerate the scale of this success: Ukrainian nation-building remained a project whose influence did not extend beyond a few thousand (if not hundreds) of predominantly young intelligentsia. What is important, however, is that the majority of these young people, who from 1876 to 1886 read and worshipped Franko, became at the turn of the century the skeleton of a mass Ukrainian political movement. Even if Franko had died at a young age, his effect would have remained the same.

Moreover, Franko's very youthfulness was one of the preconditions of his success. He was not the only "national poet." One of his main opponents, Rev. Ivan Naumovych—the charismatic leader of the Russophiles, who articulated the model of a "conservative utopia"—also laid claims to this title. To a large extent, the victory of Franko's model meant that it better corresponded to the collective portrait of this generation. Besides youth, this generation shared other qualities with Franko. It was the first generation of secular leaders among a people of "priests and peasants." As a generation that knew social mobility, they were inclined to prefer an ideology that better reflected their lived experience—an ideology of progress. At the same time, though the majority of them were secular people, they continued to express themselves in quasi-religious terms: they called themselves "Christians," they read Shevchenko, Marx, and Chernyshevsky with religious awe, and related to Marxism and associated progressive ideologies (positivism, realism) as though they were modern religions. Franko's image attracted them because he was the secular equivalent of a religious martyr or almost a saint: he not only voiced his own ideas, but suffered for them, while remaining firmly his own person. By contrast, Ivan Naumovych, not possessing a similar firmness when it came to suffering repression, fled abroad.

Like other studies of nationalism, this book shows that the genesis of nationalism and national movements does not have a single general cause, nor their victory one general factor. Both the former and the latter are the consequences of a coincidence, sometimes accidental, of various political, economic, and cultural factors. However, the particular ambition of this investigation was to show that among all these factors, the cultural ones play a crucial role, and that they cannot be superseded (let alone replaced) by political and economic factors.

These conclusions concern the macro-scale of this book—that is, the history of nationalism. Concerning the micro-scale, the biography of Franko himself, it is necessary here to stress the following: he never considered himself among the greatest creators or geniuses. Franko counted himself to the group of writer-workers, "more or less hard-working, influential, popular, deserving, but not reaching the level of the masters." To his mind, the difference between the first and second group was that the life story of genius writers was "more interesting than their creative works," and their creative works were "only materials toward their characteristics, component parts of their life story."

> These are geniuses, chosen by fate, great and original in good and evil, in happiness and suffering. These were the coryphaei [luminaries] of literature, the creators of new directions. One can call them representatives of the time when they lived, and their life stories, in every case, enable one to enter more or less deeply into the secrets of the spirit of their days, because this spirit has been placed in them, and in them it seems to be recreated and finds its most vivid embodiment. It seems to me that only these writers deserve detailed and elaborate biographies with all the original sources, because their life itself is a kind of masterpiece, like their works, and even unsuccessfully described they enrich the treasury of the human spirit. [*ZT* 31:28]

Franko was wrong in his self-evaluation. He in fact belongs among those genius creators. His own biography is the empirical evidence of this, as it appears more fascinating than his creative works. As one of Franko's most serious critics, Mykhailo Rudnytsky, wrote, "the single work, above all others, more interesting than many of the most important artistic works of our literature, which Franko did not have the time or capability to equal, the unfinished work, over which one can think and argue in hypotheses and theses—is Franko himself."[2]

Tables

Table 1. Religious makeup of Galician population, 1857–?

Year	Roman Catholics	Greek Catholics	Jews	Protestants	Orthodox Christians	Other	Total
				absolute numbers			
1857	2,072,633	2,079,421	448,973	31,195	251	393	4,632,866
1869	2,509,015	2,317,884	575,918	39,746	1,495	651	5,444,689
1880	2,714,977	2,512,376	686,596	40,994	2,598	1,238	5,958,907
1890	2,999,062	2,792,316	770,468	43,804	1,907	230	6,607,816
1900	3,350,512	3,105,635	811,371	45,761	2,283	235	72,847,031
1910	3,731,569	3,381,105	871,895	37.698	2,818	609	80,256,751
				percentage			
1857	44.74	44.89	9.69	0.67	0.00	0.01	100
1869	46.08	42.58	10.57	0.73	0.03	0.01	100
1880	45.56	42.17	11.52	0.69	0.04	0.02	100
1890	45.39	42.26	11.65	0.67	0.03	0.00	100
1900	45.79	42.46	11.09	0.63	0.03	0.00	100
1910	46.49	42.13	10.86	0.48	0.03	0.01	100

Source: Krzysztof Zamorski, *Informator statystyczny do dziejów społeczno-gospodarczych Galicji* (Cracow–Warsaw, 1989), 70–71.

Table 2. Literacy among ethnic groups in the Austro-Hungarian Empire (1910)

	%	Rating
Czechs	97.6	1
Germans	96.9	2
Foreigners	92.8	3
Italians	89.7	4
Slovenes	85.4	5
Poles	72.6	6
Hungarians	63.6	7
Romanians	39.6	8
Ukrainians	39.0	9
Serbo-Croatians	36.3	10

Source: Adam Wandruszka and Peter Urbanitsch, eds., *Die Habsburgmonarchie 1848-1918*, vol. 3: *Die Völker des Reiches*, bk. 1 (Vienna, 1980), 77.
Official statistics did not recognize Jews as a separate ethnic group and counted them as Germans.

Table 3. Literacy among ethnic groups in the Russian Empire (1897)

	%	Rating
Estonians	94.1	1
Latvians	85.0	2
Germans	78.5	3
Lithuanians	48.4	4
Poles	41.8	5
Jews	50.1	6
Russians	29.3	7
Belarusians	20.3	8
Georgians	19.5	9

(continued)

	%	Rating
Ukrainians	18.9	10
Armenians	18.3	11
Tatars and Azeris	16.5	12

Source: Andreas Kappeler, *Rosiia iak polietnichna imperiia. Vynyknennia. Istoriia. Rozpad* (Lviv, 2005), 309.

Table 4. Magazines per capita, among various ethnic groups

Swedes in Russian Empire	1:11,000
Germans in Austro-Hungarian Empire (Moravia)	1:14,000
Germans in Russian Empire	1:15,600
Germans in Austro-Hungarian Empire (Bohemia)	1:16,000
Germans in Austro-Hungarian Empire (Hungary)	1:19,500
Hungarians in Austro-Hungarian Empire	1:28,400
Czechs in Austro-Hungarian Empire	1:30,840
Poles in Austro-Hungarian Empire	1:37,225
Finns in Russian Empire	1:55,000
Croatians in Austro-Hungarian Empire	1:60,000
Slovenians in Austro-Hungarian Empire	1:59,000
Poles in general	1:64,500
Poles in Russian Empire	1:85,800
Poles in German Empire	1:90,000
Slovaks in Austro-Hungarian Empire	1:13,200
Serbs in Austro-Hungarian Empire	1:133,000
Romanians in Austro-Hungarian Empire	1:136,000
Ukrainians in Austro-Hungarian Empire	1:164,000

Source: Korneli Heck, "Bibliografia Polska z r. 1881 w porównaniu z czeską, wegierską i rossyjską," *Przewodnik naukowy i literacki. Dodatek miesięczny do 'Gazety Lwowskiej'* X (1882): 1038–54.

Table 5. Population in the Boryslav-Drohobyvch oil basin

	1850	1869	1880	1890	1900
Boryslav	759	5,651	10,906	12,059	12,439
Drohobych	11,807	16,888	18,225	17,916	19,432
Nahuyevychi	2,238	1,656	1,652	1,828	2,081
Popeli	1,307	1,703	1,777	1,876	2,232
Skhidnytsia	520	750	988	1,275	5,912
Truskavets	136	1,131	1,170	1,587	1,630
Tustanovychi	1,102	2,313	3,220	4,085	4,334

Source: Ia. I. Hrytsak, *Rabochie Borislavsko-Drogobychskogo neftianogo basseina vo vtoroi polovine XIX–nachale XX veka: Formirovanie, polozhenie, klassovaia bor'ba* (Candidate of Historical Sciences diss., Lviv, 1986), table 4.

Table 6. Numbers of workers in the Boryslav-Drohobych oil basin

Year	Ozokerite Industry		Oil Industry		Together	
	Enterprises	Workers	Enterprises	Workers	Enterprises	Workers
1883	–	–	–	–	–	6,630
1884	–	–	–	–	–	8,211
1885	–	–	–	–	–	8,260
1886	89	6,872	48	504	137	7,736
1887	68	5,806	–	–	–	–
1888	70	5,632	53	538	128	6,170
1889	68	5,633	51	512	119	6,145
1890	71	6,069	–	–	–	–
1891	61	5,860	–	–	–	–
1892	64	4,655	–	–	–	–
1893	56	3,360	39	567	95	3,927
1894	44	4,778	47	881	91	5,661
1895	39	4,472	57	1701	96	6,173
1896	35	5,238	70	1841	105	7,079
1897	33	5,896	82	2454	115	8,350
1898	30	4,894	86	2725	116	7,619
1899	21	3,548	77	2609	98	6,187
1900	11	1,924	98	3128	109	5,059

Source: Ia. I. Hrytsak, *Rabochie Borislavsko-Drogobychskogo neftianogo basseina vo vtoroi polovine XIX–nachale XX veka: Formirovanie, polozhenie, klassovaia bor'ba* (Candidate of Historical Sciences diss., Lviv, 1986), table 6.

Table 7. Percentage of children born out of wedlock

Year	Parish of St. George Church in Lviv	Parish of St. Paraskevia Church in Lviv	Parish in Nahuievychi	Parish in Rechychany	Parish in Tukhlia
1846	34.5	30.7	7.2	9.50	*
1851	47.1	35.7	7.4	10.00	*
1856	45.0	41.6	6.5	11.70	*
1861	33.6	31.1	10.9	22.20	*
1866	33.0	25.0	9.2	13.04	9.9
1871	23.5	26.1	5.8	14.20	8.0
1876	18.4	18.8	2.9	10.70	12.7
1881	14.1	20.9	*	20.60	0
1886	13.0	20.3	*	6.25	1.8
1891	14.7	*	*	9.60	0
1896	13.3	22.8	*	10.80	0
1901	9.0	17.2	*	6.00	0

*No data available

Source: I. V. Kosyk, *Evolutsiia shliubu ta sim´i v Halychyni u druhii polovyni XIX stolittia (za materialamy metrychnykh knyh)* (Master's diss., Lviv, 2003), 69.

Table 8. Percentage of interdenominational marriages

Year	Parish of St. George Church in Lviv	Parish of St. Paraskevia Church in Lviv	Parish in Nahuievychi	Parish in Rechychany	Parish in Tukhlia
1846	31.25	*	0.00	0.00	0.00
1851	23.07	*	0.00	0.00	0.00
1856	34.88	*	0.00	0.00	0.00
1861	37.28	*	0.00	0.00	0.00
1866	48.48	*	0.00	0.00	0.00
1871	44.06	53.40	0.00	0.00	0.00
1876	48.78	53.60	0.00	0.00	0.00
1881	48.78	37.90	0.00	0.00	0.00
1886	49.05	68.75	0.00	0.00	0.00
1891	31.45	33.90	0.00	0.00	0.00
1896	31.89	21.10	0.00	0.00	0.00
1901	46.42	45.60	0.00	0.00	0.00

*No data available

Source: I. V. Kosyk, *Evolutsiia shliubu ta sim´i v Halychyni u druhii polovyni XIX stolittia (za materialamy metrychnykh knyh)* (Master's diss., Lviv, 2003), 71.

Table 9. Ruthenian and Ukrainian publications in the Habsburg Empire, 1800–1886

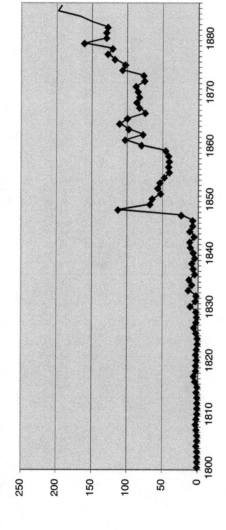

Source: Ostap Sereda, *Shaping of a National Identity: Early Ukrainophiles in Austrian Eastern Galicia, 1860-1873* (Ph.D. diss., Budapest, 2003), 60.

Table 10. List of the most active publishers and authors in the Ruthenian-Ukrainian language (by number of authored or published books)

1798–1869		1870–1886		1887–1894		1895–1900		1901–1905	
Iakhymovych H.	78	Bilous M.	156	Didytsky B.	91	Franko I.	94	Franko I.	77
Poremba M.	77	Poremba M.	65	Bednarsky S.	76	Shevchenko T.	68	Barsky P.	60
Holovatsky I.	67	Vaidovych A.	64	Bilous M.	64	Dzhulynsky M.	67	Shevchenko T.	55
Dziekovsky M.	55	Ploshchansky V.	45	Franko I.	62	Bilous M.	63	Korchak-Novytsky N.	53
Lytvynovych S.	54	Naumovych I.	43	Hrinchenko B.	54	Hrinchenko B.	59	Shyikovs'kyi V.	52
Bilous M.	47	Shevchenko T.	43	Parasavych Sh.	53	Didytsky B.	56	Bilous M.	50
Didytsky B.	44	Levytsky I.	40	Shevchenko T.	50	Hrushevsky M.	55	Nasalsky Yu.	49
Kvitka-Osnov'ianenko H.	38	Lysenko M.	38	Levytsky I.E.	44	Bednarsky S.	53	Hrushevsky M.	47
Shevchenko T.	38	Starytsky M.	38	Pelekh I.	39	Nasalsky IO.	52	Chokolov I.	40
Kulish P.	37	Sembratovych I.	37	Drahomanov M.	34	Lysenko M.	49	Manietsky	34
Huchkovsky S.	36	Nechui-Levytsky I.	35	Kotliarevsky I.	32	Sokalsky B.	49	Lysenko M.	32

(continued)

1798–1869		1870–1886		1887–1894		1895–1900		1901–1905	
Levytsky I.	33	Didytsky B.	34	Belei I.	31	Kotliarevsky I.	42	Khoinatsky A.	28
Levytsky M.	31	Labash S.	33	Levytsky I.	31	Levytsky V	38	Sheptytsky A.	28
Undolsky V.	27	Parasevych S.	32	Chopp H.	30	Shyikovsky V	31	Kotliarevsky I.	26
Venher N,	24	Vintskovsky D	30	Barvinsky Ol.	29	Konysky O.	30	Hrinchenko B.	25
Dukhnovych O.	24	Barvinsky V.	25	Popovych O.	29	Kulish P	28	Brauner V.	23
Ieher K.	24	Kotliarevsky I. Taniachkevych D.	24	Nechui-Levytsky I.	26	Pelekh I.	26	Hubanov T.	23
Poliansky T.	20	**Franko I.**	20	Chernetsky V.	26	Tomashivsky S.	25	Sytyn I.D.	23
Storozhenko O.	20	Lepkyi O.	19	Kvitka-Osnov'ianenko H.	25	Makovei O.	24	Mizevych A	23
Dobriansky A.	19	Petrushevych A.	19	Pavlyk M.	24	Andreichyn A.	23	Barvinsky O.	22
Shekhovych S.	19	Kulish P.	18	Dankevych I.	24	Bryk I.	22	Kvitka-Osnov'ianenko H	21
Grund L.	18	Okaz K.	18	Lysenko M.	22	Hnatiuk V	22	Budzynovsky O.	18
Estreicher K.	18			Manietsky V.	22	Manietsky V.	21	Veretelnyk A.	18

(continued)

1798–1869		1870–1886		1887–1894		1895–1900		1901–1905	
Karpenko S.	18	Partytsky O.	22	Horyshek K.	18	Pavlyk M.	18	Dzhulynsky M	20
Marko Vovchok	17	Barvinsky O.	21	Pankivsky K.	18	Hubanov T.	18	Kulish P.	18
Hrechulevych V.	17	Frits M.	21	Sembratovych S.	18	Krymsky A.	18	Lepkyi B	19
Malynoysky M.	17	Ilnytsky V.	19	Ohonovsky O.	17	Pankivsky K	17	Hnatiuk V	18
Bilous T.	15	Ohonovs'kyi O.	19	Vorobkevych I.	16	Shchurat V.	18	Shchurat V.	15

Source: L. I. Ilnyts'ka and O. I. Khmil', eds., *Repertuar ukrains'koi knyhy 1798–1916. Materialy do bibliohrafii*, vol. 1: *1798–1870* (Lviv, 1995); vol. 2: *1871–1886* (Lviv, 1997); vol. 3: *1887–1894* (Lviv, 1999); vol. 4: *1895–1900* (Lviv, 1999); vol. 5: *1901–1905* (Lviv, 2001).

Table 11. Ruthenian-Ukrainian periodicals in Galicia, 1880–1885

Title	Subscription price (1880)	Circulation (1880)	Circulation (1885)
Slovo	12 zr.	850	600
Pravda	4 zr.		
Lastivka (with Uchytel)	2,50 zr.		
Russkii Sion	4 zr.		
Nauka (with Slovo Bozhe)	4 zr.	100	600
Batkivshchyna	2,50 zr.	600	1500
Dilo*	8 zr.	550	1300
Zorya*	4 zr.	500	1000
Strakhopud	5 zr	500	
Ruska Rada	3 zr.	800	800
Vesna	3 zr		
Hospodar i promyshlennyk	2 zr		
Dennytsia	3 zr.		
Rodymyi lystok	5 zr.		
Karpat	7 zr.		
Novyi prolom		-	600
Nove zerkalo*		-	450

*Periodicals Franko contributed to

Source: John-Paul Himka, *Galician Villagers and the Ukrainian National Movement in the Nineteenth Century* (Edmonton, 1988), 68.

Table 12. Periodicals subscribed to by Ruthenian-Ukrainian village reading rooms in Galicia (1879–1884; number of reading rooms surveyed=50)

Titles	No. of reading rooms subscribing to the periodical
Batkivshchyna	40
Nauka	30
Dilo*	*27*
Hospodar i promyshlennyk	24
Ruska Rada	22
Zerkalo*	*10*
Prolom (Novyi Prolom)	6
Gazeta Naddniestrzańska	4
Zoria*	*3*
Viche	1
Illustriertes Blatt	1
Novosty	1
Sviashchenyk	1
Sztandar	1
Not identified	
incl. "Prosvita" Society publications	4
incl. Kachkovsky Society	1

*Periodicals Franko contributed to

Source: VR LNB, fond 160 (M. Pavlyk), file 64, folio 3.

Table 13. Subscribers to the journal *Zoria* in the Russian Empire, 1884

Place	Numbers of subscribers
Odessa	10–15
Kherson	4
Elysavethrad	**6**
Uman	6
Katerynoslav	15
Chernihiv	**10**
Poltava	4
Lubny	4
Pryluky	**3**
Eiery (?)	3
Samara	3
Kyiv	20
Others	20

Source: VR IL, fond 3 (Ivan Franko), file 1603, folio 367.

Table 14. Geography of Ivan Franko's Publications and their Reviews

I. Collection of Works

Year	Places, publications, numbers, and languages of publications									
	Lviv	Drohobych	Cracow	Kyiv	Warsaw	St. Petersburg	Vienna	Geneve	Berlin	Zurich
1876	1 U									
1879	1 U									
1883	1 U									
1884	1 U									
1885	1 U									

II. Belles-lettres

Year	Places, publications, numbers, and languages of publications										
	Lviv	Drohobych	Cracow	Kyiv	Warsaw	St. Petersburg	Vienna	Geneve	Berlin	Zurich	Przemyśl
1874	2 U										
1875	9 U										

(continued)

Places, publications, numbers, and languages of publications

Year	Lviv	Drohobych	Cracow	Kyiv	Warsaw	St. Petersburg	Vienna	Genève	Berlin	Zurich	Przemyśl
1876	15 U										
1877	3 U										
1878	9 U 3 P										
1879	1 U 1 P										
1880	1 U 2 P							1 U			
1881	51 U 2 P										
1883	36 U										
1884	32 U										
1885	4 U 1 P										
1886	5 U										1 P

III. Translations

Places, publications, numbers, and languages of publications										
Year	Lviv	Drohobych	Cracow	Kyiv	Warsaw	St. Petersburg	Vienna	Geneve	Berlin	Zurich
1875	1 U									
1876	7 U									
1877	10 U									
	19 U									
1879	2 P									
1880	1 U									
1881	2 U									
1882	2 U									
1883	4 U									
1884	1 U									
1885	10 U (1)									
1886	9 U (1)									

IV. Academic and journalistic works, reviews

Places, publications, numbers, and languages of publications

Year	Lviv	Drohobych	Cracow	Kyiv	Warsaw	St. Petersburg	Vienna	Geneve	Berlin	Praha	Leipzig
1875	1 U										
1876	9 U										
1877	4 U										
1878	16 U (2) 3 P (1)										
1879	13 U (2)12 P (5)										
1880	8 P (4)										
1881	14 U 3 P				1 P			1 P			
1882	10 U							1 R			3 н
1883	84 U 1 P							1 R			
1884	117 U				10 P						
1885	14 U 3 P				3 P	7 P (1)			1 U		
1886	63 U 8 P (2)		1 P		17 P	28 P					

V. Reviews on Ivan Franko

Year	Places, publications, numbers, and languages of publications									
	Lviv	Drohobych	Cracow	Kyiv	Warsaw	St. Petersburg	Vienna	Geneve	Berlin	Zurich
1875	3 U									
1876	7 U									
1877	1 U									
1878	2 U									1 G
1879	2 U									
1880	1 U									
1881			1 P		1 P		1 G	1 U	1 G	
1882	2 U			1 R		1 P		1 R		
1883	11 U				1 P					
1884	5 U	2 P	1 P	2 R	1 P	2 P				
1885	2				2 P	2 P		1 U		
1886	1 U			1 R	2 P					

Note:

G = in German language

P = in Polish language

R = in Russian language

U = in Ukrainian language

In brackets—publications attributed to Ivan Franko

Sources: M. O. Moroz, ed., *Ivan Franko. Bibliohrafiia tvoriv. 1874–1964* (Kyiv, 1966); O. Moroz and M. Moroz, "Materialy do bibliohrafii krytychnoi literatury pro Ivana Franka (1875–1938)," in *Ivan Franko: Statti i materialy* 9 (1962): 191–318; Mirosława Kosiecka and Zofia Żydanowycz, *Iwan Franko w Polsce* (Maszynopis. Biblioteka Narodowa. Zakład Informacji Naukowej), 107.

Notes

Introduction

1 See Natalie Zemon Davis, *The Return of Martin Guerre* (Cambridge, MA: Harvard University Press, 1983).

2 See John Davis, "An interview with Ernest Gellner," *Current Anthropology* 32, no. 1 (1991): 67.

3 "We Study Empires as We Do Dinosaurs: Nations, Nationalism, and Empire in a Critical Perspective, Interview with Benedict Anderson," *Ab Imperio* 3 (2003): 64.

4 Tom Nairn, "The Curse of Rurality: Limits of Modernization Theory," in *The State of the Nation: Ernest Gellner and the Theory of Nationalism*, ed. John A. Hall (Cambridge: Cambridge University Press, 1998), 107–34.

5 Iván T. Berend and György Ránki, *Economic Development in East-Central Europe in the 19th and 20th Centuries* (New York: Columbia University Press 1974), 17.

6 Roman Loth, *Młodość Jana Kasprowicza. Szkic biograficzny* (Poznań: Wydawnictwo Poznańskie, 1962), 5.

7 Ernest Gellner, *Nations and Nationalism* (Oxford: Basil Blackwell, 1983), 1.

8 Kazimierz Dobrowolski, "Peasant Traditional Culture," in *Peasants and Peasant Societies*, ed. Theodor Shanin (Middlesex: Penguin, 1971), 277–8.

9 See Ivan Franko, "Do istorii rus´koi tserkvy v poslidnykh chasakh Richypospospolytoi pol's'koi," *Zoria* 4 (1886): 67–68.

10 Barry Smart, "Modernity, Postmodernity, and the Present," in *Theories of Modernity and Postmodernity*, ed. Bryan S. Turner (London: Sage Publications, 1990), 16–17.

11 Hans-Ulrich Wehler, *Die Gegenwart als Geschichte. Essays* (Munich: C. H. Beck, 1995), 13–59.

12 Jacques Le Goff, *History and Memory* (New York: Columbia University Press, 1992), 21–50.

13 Zygmunt Bauman, "Modernity," in *The Oxford Companion to Politics of the World*, ed. Joel Krieger. 2nd ed. (Oxford: Oxford University Press, 2001), 551.

14 See Theodore H. Friedgut, *Iuzovka and Revolution*, vol. 1, *Life and Work in Russia's Donbass, 1869–1924* (Princeton, NJ: Princeton University Press, 1989).

15 Adrian Hastings, *The Construction of Nationhood: Ethnicity, Religion and Nationalism* (Cambridge: Cambridge University Press, 1997); see also Anthony Smith, "Adrian Hastings on Nations and Nationalism," *Nations and Nationalism* 9, no. 1 (2003): 25–28.

16 See Alexei Miller, *The Ukrainian Question: The Russian Empire and Nationalism in the Nineteenth Century*. Authorized translation by Olga Poato (Budapest: Central European University Press, 2003).

17 Shmuel N. Eisenstadt and Wolfgang Schluchter, "Introduction: Paths to Early Modernities—A Comparative View," *Daedalus* 127, no. 3: 14.

18 I borrowed this metaphor from Nancy F. Partner, "Historicity in an Age of Reality-Fictions," in *A New Philosophy of History*, ed. Frank Ankersmith and Hans Kellner (London: Reaktion Books, 1995), 22.

19 Pierre Bourdieu and Loïc J. D. Wacquant, *An Invitation to Reflexive Sociology* (Chicago: University of Chicago Press, 1992), 98–100.

20 Omelian Ohonovs´kyi, *Istoriia literatury ruskoi*, vol. 3 (Lviv: Tovarystvo im. Shevchenka, 1893).

21 Ivan Sverstiuk, "Ivan Kotliarevs´kyi smiiet´sia," *Suchasnist´* 5 (1972): 40.

22 Bohdan Krupnyts´kyi, *Istorioznavchi problemy istorii Ukrainy (zbirnyk statei)* (Munich: Ukrains´kyi Vil´nyi Universytet, 1959), 120–121.

23 Here I want to mention three books: Tamara Hundarova, *Franko—ne Kameniar*. 2nd ed. (Kyiv: Krytyka, 2006); Oksana Zabuzhko, *Filosofiia ukrainskoi idei ta ievropeis´kyi kontekst*. 2nd ed. (Kyiv: Fakt, 2006); Yaroslava Mel´nyk, *I ostatnia chast dorohy...Ivan Franko: 1908–1916* (Lviv: Kolo, 1999).

24 Yaroslav Hrytsak, *"...Dukh, shcho tilo rve do boiu..." Sproba politychnoho portreta Ivana Franka* (Lviv: Kameniar, 1990).

Chapter 1

1 For Karl Marx, see Tulo Nussenblatt, "Karol Marx potomkiem Żyda lwowskiego," *Chwila*, 11 February 1928 (no. 3194), 5; of Sigmund Freud, see Ernest Jones, *The Life and Works of Sigmund Freud*, ed. and abr. Lionel Trilling and Steven Marcus (New York: Basic Books, 1961), 4.

2 Galicia was the largest province in the Austrian (from 1867, the Austro-Hungarian) Empire: its total area—78,500 sq. km—was nearly equal to the total area of the second- and third-largest provinces of Bohemia (51,900 sq. km) and the Tirol (29,300 sq. km) combined; its population (6.3 million) surpassed that of Bohemia (5.9 million), and the total population of both these provinces equaled that of the other twelve territories of the Austrian part of the Habsburg monarchy. See map no. 5 in Anton Leo Hickmann, *Geographisch-statistischer Taschen-Atlas von Österreich-Ungarn* (Vienna: Freytag and Berndt, 1900). The reader will obtain a clearer picture from a comparison with today's countries: the total area of Austrian Galicia is equal to Austria or the Czech Republic and two times larger than Belgium, Armenia, or Georgia.

3 Cited in Józef Buszko, *Zum Wandel der Gesellschaftsstruktur in Galizien und in der Bukovina* (Vienna: Verlag der Österreichischen Akademie der Wissenschaften, 1978), 14.

4 Zbigniew Fras, *Galicja* (Wrocław: Wydawnictwo Dolnośląskie, 2000), 74.

5 Hickman, *Atlas*, maps nos. 13 and 15; V. Katz, "Die Bewegung der Bevölkerung in Galizien im Jahre mit Rücksicht auf die Confessionen," *Statistische Monatschrift* 9 (Vienna, 1888): 550; Wolfram Fischer, Jan A. Van Houtte, et al., eds., *Europäische Wirtschafts- und Sozialgeschichte von der Mitte des 19. Jahrhunderts bis zum ersten Weltkrieg* (Stuttgart, 1985), 88 [=*Kletta-Gotta Handbuch der Europäischen Wirtschafts- und Sozialgeschichte*, vol. 5].

6   Stanisław Szczepanowski, *Nędza Galicyi w cyfrach i program energicznego rozwoju gospodarstwa krajowego* (Lviv: Gubrynowicz i Schmidt, 1888), 22.

7   See Ivan Franko, *Zibrannia tvoriv u piatdesiaty tomakh*, vol. 44, bk. 1, 508–9. All subsequent references to this edition are marked by square brackets enclosing the abbreviation *ZT*, volume, and page(s), e.g., [*ZT* 44/1:508–9].

8   Istvan Deak, *Essays on Hitler's Europe* (Lincoln: University of Nebraska Press, 2001), 47–48.

9   Harald Binder, *Galizien in Wien. Parteien, Wahlen, Fraktionen und Abgeorgdneten im Übergan zur Massenpolitik* (Vienna: Verlag der Österreichischen Akademie der Wissenschaften, 2005), 13.

10 Mykhailo Vozniak, ed., *Materialy dlia kulturnoi i hromadskoi istorii Zakhidnoi Ukrainy*, vol. 1, *Lystuvannia I. Franka i M. Drahomanova* (Kyiv: Drukarnia Vseukrains'koi Akademii nauk, 1928) [=Vseukrainska Akademiia nauk. Komisiia Zakhidnoi Ukrainy. *Zbirnyk istorychno-filolohichnoho viddilu*, vol. 52; henceforward *Materialy*.]

11 Dmytro Doroshenko, *Moi spomyny pro davnie-mynule (1901-1914)* (Winnipeg: Tryzub, 1949), 52.

12 Cited in Jerzy Rudzki, *Świętochowski* (Warsaw: Wiedza Powszechna, 1963), 204.

13 Antoni Knot, introduction to *Pamiętniki. Galicja (1843–1880)*, vol. 1, by Kazimierz Chłędowski (Wrocław: Zakł. Narod. im. Ossol., 1951), xx; Keely Stauter-Halsted, *The Nation in the Village: The Genesis of Peasant National Identity in Austrian Poland, 1848-1914* (Ithaca, NY: Cornell University Press, 2001), 23.

14 Józef Burszta, *Wieś i karczma. Rola karczmy w życiu wsi pańszczyżnanej* (Warsaw: Spółdzielnia Wydawnicza, 1950), 200, 207–8; Józef Putek, *Mroki średniowiecza. Obyczaje. Przesądy. Fanatyzm. Okrucieństwa i ucisk społeczny w Polsce* (Warsaw: Państ. Instytut Wydawniczy, 1985), 395–402.

15 Wilhelm Feldman, *Stronnictwa i programy polityczne w Galicji 1846–1906*, 2 vols. (Cracow: Książka, 1907), vol. 1, 226, 231.

16 Zbigniew Pucek, "Galicyjskie doświadczenie wielekulturowości a problem więzi społecznej," in *Galicja i jej dziedzictwo*, vol. 2: *Społeczeństwo i Gospodarka*, ed. Jerzy Chłopiecki and Helena Madurowicz-Urbańska (Rzeszów: Wydawn. Wyższej Szkoły Pedagogicznej w Rzeszowie, 1995), 20–23.

17 It is noteworthy that even the term "traditional society" was formulated on the basis of ethnographic research that was carried out in Galicia. See Dobrowolski, "Peasant Traditional Culture," in *Peasants and Peasant Societies*, comp. Theodor Shanin, 277–98. When Ernest Gellner was formulating the image of Ruritania, he was probably thinking specifically of the Ruthenian population of Galicia and neighboring Slovakia. See Chris Hann, "Nationalism and Civil Society in Central Europe: From Ruritania to the Carpathian Euroregion," in *The State of the Nation: Ernest Gellner and the Theory of Nationalism*, ed. John A. Hall (New York: Cambridge University Press, 1998), 244.

18 Helena Madurowicz-Urbańska, "Perspektywy nowych badań nad społeczeństwem galicyjskim," *Pamiętnik XIII Powszechnego Zjazdu Historyków Polskich*, pt. 1 (Wrocław, 1986) 143.

19 A good introduction to this topic is Dietlind Hüchtker, "Der 'Mythos Galizien.' Versuch einer Historisierung," in *Die Nationalisierung von Grenzen. Zur Konstruktion nationaler Identität in sprachlichgemischten Grenzregionen*. Tagungen des Herder-Instituts zur Ostmitteleuropa-Forschung 16, ed. Michael G. Müller and Rolf Petri (Marburg: Herder-Inst., 2002). (I last accessed the online version of this publication found at: http://www.kakanien.ac.at/beitr/fallstudie/DHu_chtker2.pdf on 30 June 2006). Ewa Wiegandt, *Austria Felix, czyli o micie Galicji w polskiej prozie współczesnej* (Poznań: UAM, 1998).

20 Waltraud Heindl, *Gehörsame Rebellen. Bürokratie und Beamte in Österreich 1780–1848* (Wien: Böhlau Verlag, 1991); Valtraud Haindl [Waltraud Heindl], "Modernizatsiia ta teorii modernizatsii: pryklad Habsburz'koi biurokratii," *Ukraina moderna* 1 (1996): 89–100.

21 Krzysztof Pawłowski, "Narodziny nowoczesnego miasta," in *Sztuka 2 pol. XIX wieku,* comp. Jan Białostocki et al. (Warsaw: PWN, 1973), 57–58, 61–68.

22 For more specific details, see my chapter "Franko and His Boryslav." See also Alison Fleig Frank, *Oil Empire: Visions of Prosperity in Austrian Galicia* (Cambridge, MA: Harvard University Press, 2005).

23 Franciszek Bujak, *Z odległej i bliskiej przeszłości. Studia historyczno-gospodarcze* (Lwów: Zakład Narodowy im. Ossolińskich, 1924), 214–15.

24 Maria Kłańska, *Aus dem Schtetl in die Welt 1772 bis 1938: Ostjüdische Autobiographien in deutscher Sprache* (Vienna: Böhlau Verlag, 1994), 215.

25 Jolanta T. Pękacz, "Galician Society as a Cultural Public, 1771–1914," *Journal of Ukrainian Studies* 23, no. 2 (Winter 1998): 23–44; Walentyna Najdus, "Kształtowanie się nowoczesnych więzów społeczno-organizacyjnych ludności ukraińskiej Galicji Wschodniej w dobie konstytucyjnej," in *Lwów: miasto, społeczeństwo, kultura,* vol. 2, ed. Henryk W. Żaliński and Kazimierz Karolczak (Cracow: Naukowe Wydawnictwo WSP, 1998), 166–67.

26 See Binder, *Galizien in Wien*; Maciej Janowski, *Inteligencja wobec wyzwań nowoczesności: dylematy ideowe polskiej demokracji liberalnej w Galicji w latach 1889–1914* (Warsaw: Instytut Historii PAN, 1996); Kerstin Jobst, *Zwischen Nationalismus und Internationalismus. Der polnische und ukrainische Sozial-Demokratie in Galizien von 1890 bis 1914. Ein Beitrag zur Nationalitätenfrage im Habsburgerreich* (Hamburg: Dölling und Galitz, 1996); *Kai Struve, Bauern und Nation in Galizien. Über Zugerhörigkeit und soziale Emanzipation im 19. Jahrhundert* (Göttingen: Vandenhoeck and Ruprecht, 2005); Vasyl' Rasevych, "Ukrains'ka natsional'no-demokratychna partiia (1899–1918)" (Candidate of Historical Sciences diss., Lviv, 1996).

27 *Administrativ-Karte von den Königr. Galizien und Lodomerien mit dem Grossherzogthume Krakau u.d. Herzogthümern Auschwiz, Zator und Bukovina von Carl Kummers Ritter von Kummersberg* (Vienna, 1855), 6 sheets; Iakov Golovatskii [Iakiv Holovats'kyi], "Karpatskaia Rus'. Geografichesko-statisticheskie i istoriko-etnograficheskie ocherki Galichiny, Severo-Vostovchnoi Ugrii i Bukoviny," in *Slavianskii sbornik* 2 (1878): 58; Adam Wandruszka and Peter Urbanitsch, eds., *Die Habsburgmonarchie, 1848–1918,* vol. 3, *Die Völker des Reiches.* 1. Teilband (Vienna: Verlag der Österreichischen Akademie der Wissenschaften, 1980), table 1. It should be kept in mind that the population growth between the end of the eighteenth century and the middle of the nineteenth was also partly fostered by the expansions of the province's territory in 1809 and 1846.

28 Mykhailo Zubryts'kyi, "Tisni roky. Prychynky do istorii Halychyny 1846–1861," *Zapysky Naukovoho Tovarystva im. Shevchenka* (henceforward *ZNTSh*) 26 (1898): 1–16.

29 Bujak, *Z odległej i bliskiej przeszłości,* 214; Golovatskii, "Karpatskaia Rus'," 58.

30 Krzysztof Zamorski, "Zasadnicze linie przemian demograficznych Galicji w drugiej połowie XIX wieku i na początku XX wieku," in *Galicja i jej dziedzictwo,* vol. 2, 95–96, 105.

31 Jacek Kochanowicz, *Spór o teorię gospodarki chłopskiej. Gospodarstwo chłopskie w teorii ekonomii i w historii gospodarczej* (Warsaw: Wydawnictwo Uniwersytetu Warszawskiego, 1992), 195.

32 Madurowicz-Urbańska, "Perspektywy," 148.

33 See, e.g., Alfred Nossig, "Proba rozwiązania kwestji żydowskiej," *Przegląd Społeczny. Pismo naukowe i literackie* 2 (1887): 355–61; a speech given by Ostap Terletsky at a meeting of the Vienna-based student society "Sich," cited in Ivan Franko's article, "D-r Ostap Terlets'kyi. Spomyny i materialy" [*ZT* 33:325].

34 For a brief survey of the history of Galicia, see Paul Robert Magocsi, *Galicia: A Historical Survey and Bibliographic Guide* (Toronto: University of Toronto Press, 1990).

35 Józef Buszko, *Galicja 1859–1914. Polski Piemont?*, vol. 3, *Dzieje narodu i państwa polskiego* (Warsaw: KAW, 1989).

36 On the genesis of the idea of a "Ukrainian Piedmont," see Ihor Chornovol, "Politychni kontseptsii kyivs'koi 'Staroi Hromady,'" *Moloda natsiia*, Almanach 1 (2000): 27–28.

37 For more details, see Klaus Bachmann, *Ein Herd der Feindschaft gegen Russland. Galizien als Krisenherd in den Beziehungen der Donaumonarchie mit Russland (1907–1914)* (Vienna: Verlag für Geschichte und Politik; Munich: R. Oldenbourg Verlag, 2001); Alexander Victor Prusin, *Nationalizing a Borderland: War, Ethnicity, and Anti-Jewish Violence in East Galicia, 1914–1920* (Tuscaloosa: University of Alabama Press, 2005).

38 John-Paul Himka, "The Construction of Nationality in Galician Rus′: Icarian Flights in Almost All Directions," in *Intellectuals and Articulation of the Nation*, ed. Ronald G. Suny and Michael D. Kennedy (Ann Arbor: University of Michigan Press, 1999), 109–64.

39 Stanisław [Stanislaus] von Smolka, *Die Reussische Welt: Historisch-politische Studien* (Vienna: Zentral-verlagsbüro des Obersten polnischen Nationalkomittees, 1916), 103–20; Franciszek Bujak, *Galicya*, vol. 1 (Lviv: H. Altenberg, 1908–10), 94.

40 Norman Davis, *Orzel biały. Czerwona Gwiazda. Wojna polsko-bolszewicka 1919–1920* (White Eagle, Red Star), trans. Andrzej Pawelec (Cracow: ZNAK, 1997); Maciej Kozłowski, *Między Sanem a Zbruczem. Walki o Lwów i Galicję Wschodnią 1918–1919* (Cracow: ZNAK, 1990).

41 Mark R. Bessinger, "The Persisting Ambiguity of Empire," *Post-Soviet Affairs* 11, no. 2 (1995): 180; Alfred Rieber, "Struggle over the Borderlands," in *The Legacy of History in Russia and the New States of Eurasia*, ed. S. Frederick Starr (Armonk, NY: M. E. Sharpe, 1994), 61–90.

42 Iaroslav Isaievych, *Ukraina davnia i nova. Narod, relihiia, kul'tura* (Lviv: Instytut ukrainoznavstva im. I. Kryp′iakevycha NAN Ukrainy, 1996), 9–10.

43 Austrian official statistics used religious affiliation rather than nationality as a category. But since in the case of Galicia nationalities and religious groups largely coincided, it is plausible to characterize Roman Catholics as Poles and Greek Catholics as Ruthenians.

44 John-Paul Himka, "Dimensions of a Triangle: Polish-Ukrainian-Jewish Relations in Austrian Galicia," in *Focusing on Galicia: Jews, Poles, and Ukrainians, 1772–1918*, ed. Israel Bartal and Antony Polonsky, vol. 12 of *Polin: Studies in Polish Jewry* (London: Littman Library of Jewish Civilization, 1999), 25–48.

45 For more detailed discussion of the main ethnoreligious groups in Galicia, see the following survey works: Ivan L. Rudnytsky, "The Ukrainians in Galicia under Austrian Rule," in *Nationbuilding and the Politics of Nationalism: Essays on Austrian Galicia*, ed. Andrei S. Markovits and Frank E. Sysyn (Cambridge, MA: Harvard Ukrainian Research Institute, 1982), 23–67; Piotr Wandycz, "The Poles in the Habsburg Monarchy," in *Nationbuilding*, ed. Markovits and Sysyn, 68–93; Piotr Wróbel, "The Jews of Galicia under Austrian-Polish Rule, 1869–1918," *Austrian History Yearbook* 25 (1994): 97–138; Isabel Röskau-Rydel, "Galizien," in *Deutsche Geschichte im Osten Europas. Galizien. Bukowina. Moldau*, ed. Isabel Röskau-Rydel (Berlin: Siedler, 1999), 15–328.

46 Fernand Braudel, *The Mediterranean and the Mediterranean World in the Age of Philip II*, vol. 1 (New York: Harper and Row, 1972), 224; Bujak, *Galicja*, 53–66; J. G. [Johann Georg] Kohl, *Austria, Vienna, Prague, Hungary, Bohemia, and the Danube; Galicia, Styria, Moravia, Bukovina, and the Military Frontier* (London: Chapman and Hall, 1844), 433.

47 Józef Półćwiartek, "Miejsce religii w kształtowaniu oblicza etnicznego społeczności miast południowo-wschodnich obszarów Rzeczypospolitej w czasach nowożytnych," in *Miasto i kultura ludowa w dziejach Białorusi, Litwy, Polski i Ukrainy*, ed. Aleksandra Kowal-Kwiatkowska (Cracow: Międzynarodowe Centrum Kultury, 1996), 218.

48 Wróbel, "The Jews of Galicia," 106.

49 For more detail, see "Przesiędłanie się ludności w Galicyi zachodniej do wschodniej," *Wiadomości statystyczne o stosunkach krajowych* 15, no. 3 (1896): 35–76.

50 Tadeusz Pilat, "Najważniejsze wyniki spisu ludności Galicyi z 31. Grudnia 1880 według tymczasowych zestawień powiatowych," *Wiadomości statystyczne o stosunkach krajowych* 6, no. 2 (1881): 168–69, 174–75.

51 Władysław Zawadzki, *Pamiętniki życia literackiego w Galicji*, ed. Antoni Knot (Cracow: Wydawn. Literackie, 1961), 38.

52 Pękacz, "Galician Society," 32, 39.

53 Tadeusz Burdiewicz, "Sprawy narodościowy w utworach Jana Lama," in *Galicyjskie Dylematy. Zbiór rozpraw*, ed. Kazimierz Karolczak and Henryk W. Zaliński (Cracow: Wydawn. Naukowe WSP, 1994), 77–81. Jan Lam offers a snippet of conversation in this Galician version of Volapuk: "Wigejc Fraian Berta? Ach, że swi malaad, że la melankolik," in *Galicyjskie Dylematy*, ed. Karolczak and Zaliński, 83.

54 *Svoezhitevyi zapiski Bogdana Dieditskogo*, pt. 1, *Gde-shcho do istorii samorozvytiia iazyka i azbuky Galitskoi Rusi* (Lviv, 1906), 15–16, 52.

55 Kornylo Ustyianovych, *M. F. Raevskii i rossiiskii panslavizm. Spomynky z perezhytoho i peredumanoho* (Lviv: Nakladom K. Bednarskoho, 1884), 11.

56 "Pismo z-pod Lvova (Liubim i shanuimo svoiu rodnu besidu!)," *Batkovshchyna*, 1 October 1880, 150.

57 Antoni Podraza, "Uwarunkowania historyczne rozwoju kultury na ziemiach Dawnej Rzeczypospolitej," in *Miasto i kultura ludowa*, 20, 22. The civilizational map of this part of the world was actually even more diverse: one should not overlook the presence of the large Jewish community as well as smaller confessional communities, such as the Armenian Monophysites and the Karaims. I do not focus on the history of those communities because they are of tangential relevance to the topic of my book.

58 G. Fedotov, *Treasury of Russian Spirituality*, vol. 2 of *The Collected Works of George Fedotov* (Belmont, MA: Nordland, 1975), 32; Ihor Ševčenko, *Ukraine between East and West: Essays on Cultural History to the Early Eighteenth Century* (Edmonton: Canadian Institute of Ukrainian Studies, 1996), 24; Francis J. Thomson, *The Reception of Byzantine Culture in Medieval Russia* (Aldershot, UK: Ashgate, 1999), 2–3, 10, 108–9.

59 Cited in Markus Osterrieder, "Von der Sakralgemeinschaft zur Modernen Nation. Die Entstehung eines Nationalbewusstsein unter Russen, Ukrainern und Weissruthenen im Lichte der Thesen Benedict Anderson," in *Formen der nationalen Bewusstsein im Lichte zeitgenössischer Nationalismustheorien*, ed. Eva Schmidt-Hartmann (Munich: Oldenbourg, 1994), 207. In citing publishing statistics in the Muscovite tsardom, Osterrieder mistakenly listed the number of published books (20) as a print run. It should be noted that the maximum print run of books being published in Russia at that time was between 2,000 and 3,000; together this totals between 40,000 and 60,000 printed copies. I would like to thank Iaroslav Isaievych and Borys Gudziak for pointing out this error to me.

60 N. Miliukov, *Ocherki po istorii russkoi kul'tury*, vol. 2, pt. 26 (Moscow: Izd-vo MGTU, 1994), 352; Andreas Renner, *Russischer Nationalismus und Öffentlichkeit im Zahrenreich 1855–1875* (Cologne: Böhlau, 2000), 119–20.

61 Korneli Heck, "Bibliografia Polska z r. 1881 w porównaniu z czeską, węgierską i rossyjską," *Przewodnik naukowy i literacki. Dodatek miesięczny do "Gazety Lwowskiej"* 10 (1882): 1038–54, 1094–1128.

62 Arcadius Kahan et al., *Ost- und Südosteuropa 1850–1914* (Stuttgart: Klett-Gotta, 1980), 105–6; Fischer et al., eds., *Europäische Wirtschafts- und Sozialgeschichte*, 86, 88; Ivan T Berend and Gyorgy Ránki, *Europe Economic Development in East-Central Europe in the 19th and 20th Centuries* (New York: Columbia University Press,1974), 25–26.

63 Pilat, "Najważniejsze wyniki spisu ludności Galicyi," 172–73; Jerzy Potoczny, *Oświata dorosłych i popularyzacja wiedzy w plebejskich środowiskach Galicji doby konstytucyjnej (1867–1918)* (Rzeszów: Wydawn. Wyższej Szkoły Pedagogicznej), 1998), 87.

64 Josef Ehmer, "*Was There a 'European Pattern'?" Some Critical Reflections on John Hajnal's Model*, conference paper, Vienna, 2000; Zamorski, "Zasadnicze linie," 105.

65 For an interesting attempt at a conceptualization, see George Shoepflin, "The Political Traditions of Eastern Europe," *Daedalus: The Journal of the American Academy of Arts and Sciences* 19, no. 1 (Winter 1990): 55–90.

66 Cited in Ivan-Pavlo Khymka [John-Paul Himka], "Istoriia, khrystyians'kyi svit i tradytsiina ukrains'ka kul'tura: sproba mentalnoi arkheolohii," *Ukraina moderna* 6 (2001): 22.

67 Out of the rich corpus of literature on this topic I will cite only those works that helped me to formulate my own views (for which, of course, none of the authors cited below carry any responsibility). In addition to the above-cited works of Markus Osterrieder, Iurii (George) Fedotov, and Ihor Ševčenko, these are: John A. Armstrong, "Myth and History in the Evolution of Ukrainian Consciousness," in *Ukraine and Russia in Their Historical Encounter*, ed. Peter J. Potichnyj et al. (Edmonton: Canadian Institute of Ukrainian Studies Press, University of Alberta, 1992), 125–39; Michael Cherniavsky, *Tsar and People; Studies in Russian Myths* (New Haven: Yale University Press, 1961); and Leonid Heretz, "Russian Apocalypse, 1891–1917: Popular Perceptions of Events from the Year of Famine and Cholera to the Fall of the Tsar" (Ph.D. diss., Harvard University, 1993).

68 Armstrong, "Myth and History," 129–30. Absent among the versions listed by John Armstrong are national identities formed around smaller ethnic groups, such as the Polishchuks, who lived on the current Belarusian-Ukrainian border, or the Rusyns, who lived on the borders of Poland, Slovakia, Hungary, and Ukraine.

69 Roman Szporluk, "Ukraine: From an Imperial Periphery to a Sovereign State," *Daedalus: Journal of the American Academy of Arts and Sciences* 126, no. 3 (Summer 1997): 85–119.

70 Cited in Mykhailo Hrushevs'kyi, *Z pochyniv ukrains'koho sotsiialistychnoho rukhu. Mykh. Drahomanov i zhenevskyi sotsiialistychnyi kruzhok* (Vienna, 1922), 64.

71 Patrice M. Dabrowski, "'Discovering' the Galician Borderlands: The Case of the Eastern Carpathians," *Slavic Review* 64, no. 2 (Summer 2005): 380; Peter Sahlins, *Boundaries: the Making of France and Spain in the Pyrenees* (Berkeley: University of California Press, 1989), 271.

Chapter 2

1 The only exception to the rule is Oleksii I. Dei's work *Ivan Franko: Zhyttia i diial'nist'* (Kyiv: Vyd-vo khudozh. lit-ry "Dnipro," 1981), 8.

2   In his reminiscences of his childhood, dated 1902, Franko commented that "practically no trace is left of everything that was then the foundation of the quiet patriarchal life in our secluded corner" [*ZT* 21:169].

3   *Halyts´ko-rus´ki narodni prypovidky. Zibrav, uporiadkuvav i poiasnyv Ivan Franko*, vol. 2, bk. 1, *Dity–Kpyty* (Lviv, 1907), 25 [*Etnohrafichnyi zbirnyk* 23]. The Galician writer Stefan Kovaliv (1848–1920), who was also born in a village, used a similar plot in his autobiographical short story "Sil´s´ki zvizdari" (Rural Star Diviners): two neighbors—a peasant landowner and a German blacksmith—compete to see who can predict the time most accurately. The peasant does this according to the stars and the length of the shadow from the sun, while the blacksmith uses a mechanical watch. The blacksmith keeps losing and each time has to reset his timepiece. The story offers a detailed explanation of rural methods for estimating the time, and when the author, now an adult, recounts them to a specialist in astronomy, the latter acknowledges their correctness. See Stefan Kovaliv, *Tvory* (Kyiv: Derzh. vyd-vo khudozh. lit-ry, 1958), 270–328.

4   Franko himself used these names. See [*ZT* 4:401; 49:240].

5   The minute that a proportion of the urban population first tops 50 percent is believed to be the key criterion ("threshold") of modernization. See Karl Deutsch, "Social Mobilization and Political Development," *American Political Science Review* 55, no. 3 (September 1961): 495; for the application of this criterion to the Ukrainian case, see Bohdan Krawchenko, *Social Change and National Consciousness in Twentieth-Century Ukraine* ([Edmonton]: Canadian Institute of Ukrainian Studies, University of Alberta, in association with St. Antony's College, Oxford, 1987), 178.

6   Fischer et al., *Europäische Wirtschafts- und Sozialgeschichte*, 40–41; Paul M. Hohenberg and Lynn Hollen Lees, *The Making of Urban Europe, 1000–1950* (Cambridge, MA: Harvard University Press, 1985), 7–9, 106–7; Paul Bairoch, Jean Batou, and Pierre Chèvre, *La population des villes européennes, 800–1850: banque de données et analyse sommaire des resultats* (Geneva: Droz, 1988), 253–59, 267, 272.

7   More details are given in the chapter "Franko and His Boryslav."

8   Here is one example: in those Ukrainian lands that passed from the Rzeczpospolita to the Russian Empire, the percentage of the urban population at the beginning of the nineteenth century (5 percent) was two to three times lower than in the mid-seventeenth century (from 10 to 15 percent according to various estimates). See Krawchenko, *Social Change*, 6. Even Kyiv, the "mother of Rus cities," which in the early Middle Ages was one of the ten largest cities in the world, looked more like a large village in the nineteenth century. See Michael F. Hamm, *Kiev: A Portrait, 1800–1917* (Princeton, NJ: Princeton University Press, 1993), 21; Hohenberg and Lees, *The Making of Urban Europe*, 11.

9   David R. Brower, "Urban Revolution in the Late Russian Empire," in *The City in Late Imperial Russia*, ed. Michael F. Hamm (Bloomington: Indiana University Press, 1986), 319–53; Patricia Herlihy, "Ukrainian Cities in the Nineteenth Century," in *Rethinking Ukrainian History*, ed. Ivan Lysiak-Rudnytsky, with the assistance of John-Paul Himka (Edmonton: Canadian Institute of Ukrainian Studies, University of Alberta; Downsview, Ont.: Distributed by the University of Toronto Press, 1981), 152; Robert E. Johnson, "Peasant and Proletariat: Migration, Family Patterns, and Regional Loyalties," in *The World of the Russian Peasant: Post-Emancipation Culture and Society*, ed. Ben Eklof and Stephen Frank (Boston: Unwin Hyman, 1990), 81–99.

10   Rudolf A. Mark, *Galizien unter Österreichischer Herrschaft: Verwaltung, Kirche, Bevölkerung* (Marburg: Herder-Institut, 1994), 109–10.

11 Tomasz Gąsowski, "Struktura społeczno-zawodowa mieszkańców większych miast Galicyjskich w okresie autonomicznym," *Zeszyty Naukowe Uniwersytetu Jagiełłońskiego, Prace Historyczne* (Cracow) 123 (1997): 115–16; Tadeusz Pilat, "Obszar, zabudowa i ludność miast większych w Galicji," *Wiadomości statystyczne o stosunkach krajowych* 11, no. 3 (1890): 18f.

12 *Catalogus universi venerabilis cleri dioceseos Premisliensis graeci ritus catholicorum pro Anno Domini 1850* (Premisliae [Przemyśl], 1850), 73, 77–78, 88.

13 Ivan Franko, "Kontrakt oselennia Slobody bilia Nahuievychiv, Drohobyts´koho povitu, 1779 rik," *Studii z polia suspil´nykh nauk i statystyky*=Studien auf dem gebiete der Sozialwissenschaften und Statistik, published by the Statistical Commission of the Shevchenko Scientific Society, vol. 3 (Lviv: Tovarystvo im. Shevchenka, 1912), 1–4.

14 Hohenberg and Lees, *The Making of Urban Europe*, 5.

15 Boris N. Mironov, with Ben Eklof, *A Social History of Imperial Russia, 1700–1917*, vol. 1 (Boulder, CO: Westview Press, 2000), 286.

16 Vasyl´ Inkin, *Sil´s´ke suspil´stvo Halyts´koho Prykarpattia u XVI–XVIII stolittiakh: istorychni narysy* (Lviv: [Vyd-vo "Dobra sprava"], 2004), 62–63.

17 Hanna Hrom, *Nahuievychi* (Drohobych: Vydavnycha firma "Vidrodzhennia," 2002), 79–82.

18 See Frank's *Oil Empire*. See also my chapter "Franko and His Boryslav."

19 *Hacquet's neueste physikalisch-politische Reisen in den Jahren 1791, 1792, und 1793 durch die Dacischen und Sarmatischen oder nördlichen Karpathen*, vol. 3 (Nürnberg: Raspische Buchhandlung, 1794).

20 See Iwan Franko, "Mniemany bunt chłopski," *Kurier Lwowski*, 8 August 1890, 1–2; Larysa Chernyshenko, "Lysty Ol´hy Khoruzhynskoi do Ivana Franka," *Naukovyi visnyk muzeiu Ivana Franka u Lvovi* 2 (2001): 180–81.

21 Ewaryst Andrzej Kuropatnicki, *Geografia albo dokładne opisanie królestw Galicyi i Lodomeryi*, 2nd ed. (Lwów, 1858), 63–65.

22 Hohenberg and Lees, *The Making of Urban Europe*, 219; Fischer et al., *Europäische Wirtschafts- und Sozialgeschichte*, 41; Mark, *Galizien unter Österreichischer Herrschaft*, 117.

23 Jerzy Chłopiecki, "Galicja—skrzyżowanie dróg," in *Galicja i jej dziedzictwo*, vol. 2, 42.

24 Ludwik Dziedzicki, "Lwów," in *Słownik geograficzny*, ed. Filip Sulimierski, Bronisław Chlebowski, and Władysław Walewski (Warsaw: Druk. "Wieku"; nakł. Filipa Sulimierskiego i Władysława Walewskiego, 1880 ff.), vol. 5: *Kutowa Wola–Malczyce*, 508.

25 Dobrowolski, "Peasant Traditional Culture," 278.

26 I do not examine the definition of peasantry here, as it is a complex topic and not essential to this book. I accept the suggestion of those researchers who emphasize the predominance of common forms of the cultural behavior of peasants over economic differences. See Stauter-Halsted, *Nation in the Village*, 10. For a general discussion of this topic, see Michael Kearney, *Reconceptualizing the Peasantry: Anthropology in Global Perspective* (Boulder, CO: Westview Press, 1996).

27 For further details, see Krzysztof Ślusarek, "Włościańscy i niewłościańscy mieszkańcy wsi galicyjskiej w XIX wieku: wzajemne relacje," *Zeszyty Naukowe Uniwersytetu Jagiełłońskiego. Prace Historyczne* 126 (1999): 117. Ślusarek singles out only five groups, including peasants, but omits craftsmen, priests, etc.

28 O. I. Dei, comp., *Kolomyiky v zapysakh Ivana Franka* (Kyiv: Muzychna Ukraina, 1970), 27, 36, 46, 66, 69, 79, 81, 83, 97, 99–100, 102.

29 *Halyts´ko-rus´ki narodni prypovidky*, vol. 2, bk. 1, 275–76.

30 Franko's story about Yats (Yakiv) the blacksmith is recounted by one of his heroes: "Ho-ho / There is no richer man in the entire county than Yats the blacksmith / What does he

not have! Coins of beaten silver / cattle that would do a lord proud / and clothing and furs covered with broadcloth! / On holidays, when his wife dons her corals, her neck bends downward! / He is truly a wealthy man, one can gain benefit from him!" [*ZT* 4:409].

31 Franko described it in his memoir, "Moia vitsivs'ka khata" (My Father's House), published in *Materialy do ukrains'koi etnolohii* 18 (1918): 1–4. It was reprinted in Mykhailo Hnatiuk, comp., *Spohady pro Ivana Franka* (Lviv: Kameniar, 1997), 557–59.

32 Vasyl' Stefanyk, *Vybrane* (Uzhhorod: Vyd-vo "Karpaty," 1979), 237; Ivan Kossak, "Ivan Franko ta ioho braty," in Hnatiuk, *Spohady*, 47.

33 Franko described Sloboda in his unfinished novella "Hutak" (The Miner) [*ZT* 16:405, 420–21].

34 Roman Horak and Yaroslav Hnativ, *Ivan Franko*, bk. 1, *Rid Yakova* (Lviv: Vyd-vo ottsiv Vasyliian "Misioner," 2000), 76; Ivan Franko, "Moia vitsivs'ka khata," in Hnatiuk, *Spohady*, 557.

35 On the basis of the shape of Franko's head, even the anthropologist Fedir Vovk categorized him as a "German type." See Ivan Trush, "Z moikh spomyniv pro Franka," *Dzvin* 3 (2003): 124. Recollections of Franko's German background did not fade after his death. During the Second World War the Franko house in Lviv was purchased by a *Volksdeutscher*, the director of a perfume factory, who, under the impression that Franko was a fellow *Volksdeutscher*, completely renovated the building.

36 Viddil rukopysnykh fondiv i tekstolohii, Instytut literatury im. T. H. Shevchenka Natsional'noi akademii nauk Ukrainy (Department of Manuscript Collections and Textology, henceforward VR IL), fond 3 (Ivan Franko), file 1608, fol. 101; Ivan Puliui, *Zbirnyk prats'* (Kyiv: Vyd-vo "Rada," 1996), 547, 562; Mykhailo Vozniak, "Nimets'ka dopovid' Franka dlia shveda pro Ukrainu," *Lvivs'ki visti*, 18 June 1942.

37 Nowhere in Franko's writings is the blacksmith Ivan Herder identified with Yakiv Franko; this was inferred by later scholars.

38 Roman Horak, "'Ia ie muzhyk, proloh, ne epiloh': Povist'-dokument," *Kyiv* 9 (1989): 49–59.

39 a.b. z Sambora, "O prozvishchakh i imenakh," *Slovo*, 29 September (11 October) 1862.

40 Iulian Kostiovych Red'ko, *Slovnyk suchasnykh ukrains'kykh prizvyshch* (Lviv: TOV "Prostir-M", 2007), vol. 2, 1099; Oleksii S. Stryzhak, "Franky (materialy do Etymolohichnoho slovnyka etnonimiv Ukrainy)," in *Aktual'ni pytannia antroponimiky: Zbirnyk materialiv naukovykh chytan' pamiati Iuliana Kostiantynovycha Red'ka*, ed. I. V. Iefymenko (Kyiv: In-t ukrains'koi movy, 2005), 218–29; I. I. Triinyk, *Slovnyk ukrains'kykh imen* (Kyiv: Vyd-vo "Dovira," 2005), 395. I am grateful to Oleh Kupchynsky and Roman Ostash for directing my attention to these publications.

41 References to the fact that Franko's ancestors were recorded in birth registries as Frankiv or that a village named Frankivtsi existed near Rohatyn in the sixteenth century (see Horak, "Ia ie muzhyk," 59; Horak and Hnativ, *Ivan Franko*, bk. 1, 84, 96) cannot disprove the non-Slavic origins of this name. Slavicized forms of a non-Slavic root were quite widespread in the old Ukrainian language with its numerous borrowings from the German and Latin languages (G. Y. Shevelov, "Language, Ukrainian," in *Encyclopedia of Ukraine*, vol. 3, 44).

42 One of the earliest German composers, Magister Franco Teutonicus, came from Cologne. He lived for some time in Paris, the center of music in the twelfth and thirteenth centuries, where he earned the nickname "Franco," a Frenchman. See Franco de Colonia, *Magistri Franconis Ars cantus mensurabilis. Ausgabe von E. De Coussemaker nebst zwei handschriflichen Fassungen*, ed. Friedrich Gennrich (Darmstadt: 1957), 7. The two Frankos known in Polish history are the eleventh-century bishop of Poznan

and the thirteenth-century astronomer, both of whom came from the German regions of the Rhine and Silesia, respectively. See Zofia Kozłowska-Budkowa, "Franko, biskup polski," in *Polski Słownik Biograficzny*, vol. 7 (Cracow: Polska Akademia Umiejętności, 1948–1958), 82; Aleksander Birkenmajer, "Franko z Polski," op. cit., 93. The Croatian Franko or Frankopan family (known as Franov in Croatian) came from Italy. See Zvonimir Turina Křevan, *Liber roda Turinskog i Franko od nastanjivanja u primorskom kraju, te od 1673–1969* (Rijeka 1971), 85–88. Rumors circulated about General Franco's allegedly Jewish background both because of his physical appearance and because Franco was one of the most widespread Jewish surnames in Spain. See Paul Preston, *Franco: A Biography* (New York: Basic Books, 1994), 1.

43 I. Naumovych, "Nazad k narodu!" *Slovo*, 25 July (6 August) 1881, 2.

44 Walter Kuhn, *Die jungen deutschen Sprachinseln in Galizien. Ein Beitrag zur Methode der Sprachinselforschung*. Mit einem Vorworte von Univ.-Prof. Dr. Eduard Winter in Prag (Münster in Westfalen: Aschendorff, 1930), 135–38.

45 Magocsi, *Galicia*, 249.

46 Horak and Hnativ, *Ivan Franko*, bk. 1, 86, 95.

47 According to a legend, after the Siege of Vienna was lifted, Yurii Kulchytsky (Georg Franz Koltschitzky) was rewarded for his bravery with sacks of coffee that had been captured from the Turkish camp. He then opened the first coffeehouse in Vienna and, as was believed, in all of Europe, introducing a modern way to drink coffee: with cream and sugar (the Turks drank their coffee black). In fact, the first café was opened in Venice, most likely in 1647. This was followed by the opening of cafés in London (1652), Marseilles (1654), and Hamburg (1677). The Turks played a decisive role in the spread of coffee and coffeehouses in Europe. See Etienne François, "Das Kaffeehaus," in *Orte des Alltags: Miniaturen aus der europäischen Kulturgeschichte*, ed. Heinz-Gerhard Haupt (Munich: C. H. Beck, 1994), 111. For the longest time Polish and Ukrainian historians have fruitlessly discussed whether Yurii Kulchytsky was of Polish or Ukrainian background. For information on the Kulchytsky family, see Ivan Volchko-Kul´chyts´kyi, *Istoriia sela Kul´chyts´ i sela Draho-Sasiv (700-littia sela i 1000-littia rodu* (Drohobych: Vydavnycha firma "Vidrodzhennia," 1995); *Polska Encyklopedia Szlachecka*, vol. 7 (Warsaw: Instytut Kultury Historycznej, 1937), 217–18.

48 For elaboration of the maternal line of Franko's family, see Roman Horak, *Mariia, maty Frankova* [pt. 1] (Truskavets´, 1994), 8–13.

49 Fras, *Galicja*, 65; 23, n. 3; Edmund Lewandowski, *Charakter narodowy Polaków i innych* (London: Aneks, 1995), 138.

50 A. Fischer, *Zarys etnografii Polski południowo-wschodniej* (Lwów, 1939), 5.

51 Roman Kyrchiv, "Tsykl shliakhets´kykh povistei Andriia Chaikovs´koho," in Andrii Chaikovs´kyi, *Spohady. Lysty. Doslidzhennia*, vol. 3 (Lviv: Lviv. Nats. un-t im. I. Franka, NAN Ukrainy; Instytut ukrainoznavstva im. I. Kryp´iakevycha NAN Ukrainy; Nauk. Fundatsiia A. Chaikovs´koho, 2002), 351–53 [henceforward Chaikovs´kyi, *Spohady*].

52 In his sensational *Book of Plebeian Families* (*Liber chamorum*) the Polish nobleman Walerian Nekanda-Trepka listed 2,500 families of plebeian origins that had acquired noble rank with the aid of money, successful marriages, and intrigues. See Walerian Nekanda-Trepka, *Liber generationis Plebanorum*, 2nd ed. (Wroclaw: Ossolineum, 1995).

53 Ślusarek, "Włościańscy i niewłościańscy," 122; Petro Belz, "Storinky zhyttia ukrains´koi shliakhty ta ii vidobrazhennia u tvorakh A. Chaikovs´koho," in Chaikovs´kyi, *Spohady*, vol. 3, 374.

54 Ślusarek, "Włościańscy i niewłościańscy," 121; Belz, "Storinky zhyttia ukrains´koi shliakhty, 371, 374.

55 Tsentral'nyi Derzhavnyi Istorychnyi Arkhiv Ukrainy (Central State Historical Archive of Ukraine, henceforward TsDIAL, or TsDIAK if issued in Kyiv), Lviv, fond 201, list 41, file 6144.

56 Ivan Nehrebets'kyi, "Do rodovodu Ivana Franka," *Literaturno-naukovyi vistnyk* (henceforward: LNV) 90, bks. 7–8 (1926): 233.

57 Natalia Iakovenko, *Ukrains'ka shliakhta z kintsia XIV do seredyny XVII st. (Volyn' i Tsentral'na Ukraina)* (Kyiv: Naukova dumka, 1993), 271; Myroslav Trofymuk, "Natsional'na svidomist' cherez pryzmu zhyttia i tvorchosti Andriia Chaikovs'koho," in Chaikovs'kyi, *Spohady*, vol. 3, 332–38.

58 Antin Dol'nyts'kyi, "Spomyny pro molodoho Ivana Franka," in *Ivan Franko u spohadakh suchasnykiv*, comp. O. I. Dei and N. Korniienko (Lviv: Knyzhkovo-zhurnal'ne vyd-vo, 1956), 104; Ivan Kobylets'kyi, "Deshcho pro Franka," in Hnatiuk, *Spohady*, 37.

59 Kobylets'kyi, "Deshcho pro Franka," 37.

60 *Ivan Franko: Dokumenty i materialy, 1856–1965* (Kyiv: Naukova dumka, 1966), 26–27, 38.

61 Horak, *Mariia, maty Frankova* [pt. 1], 8; Mikołaj Kuplowski, *Iwan Franko jako krytyk literatury polskiej* (Rzeszów: Wydawn. WSP w Rzeszowie, 1974), 3.

62 Kobylets'kyi, "Deshcho pro Franka," 37.

63 Oleh Osypovych Pavlyshyn, "Formuvannia ta diial'nist' predstavnyts'kykh orhaniv vlady ZUNR-ZOUNR (zhovten' 1918–cherven' 1919 r.)" (Candidate of Historical Sciences diss., Lviv, 2000), 27.

64 Ivan Bylyna, "U kraini zahorodovoi shliakhty," *Dilo* (Lviv), 14 August 1937, 8.

65 Denys Lukiianovych, "Khto mav vyrishal'nyi vplyv na natsional'nyi kharakter Ivana Franka, *Krakivs'ki visti*, 7 April 1943, 4.

66 TsDIAL, fond 201, list 4a, file 4024, fol. 37v.

67 Viddil rukopysiv L'vivs'koi naukovoi biblioteky im. Vasylia Stefanyka NAN Ukrainy (Manuscript Division of the Vasyl Stefanyk Lviv Research Library, henceforward VR LNB), fond 29 (Mykhailo Vozniak), file 23 (P. 9), fol. 2 (rough draft of an unpublished work by Mykhailo Vozniak, titled "Vid dytynstva do povnolittia Ivana Franka").

68 See Horak, "Ia ie muzhyk," 49, 52, 58.

69 A second name could even have been non-Christian, pagan (i.e., not listed in the church calendar). There are many documented confirmations of this custom (e.g., the Cossack hetman Khmelnytsky is not known by his Christian name of Zynovii but by his Slavic name Bohdan). This practice has been preserved to our time among those ethnic groups that adopted Christianity late (e.g., the Yakuts). See M. O. Demchuk, *Slovians'ki avtokhtonni osobovi vlasni imena v pobuti ukraintsiv XVI–XVIII st.* (Kyiv: Naukova dumka, 1988), 13–33; Vasilii K. Chichagov, *Iz istorii russkikh imen, otchestv i familii: voprosy russkoi istoricheskoi onomastiki XV–XVII vv.* (Moscow: Gos. uchebno-pedagog. izd-vo., 1959), 11–28; Daniel H. Kaiser, "Naming Cultures in Early Modern Russia," in *Kamen Kraeogln: Rhetoric of the Medieval Slavic World: Essays Presented to Edward Keenan on His Sixtieth Birthday by His Colleagues and Students*, ed. Nancy Shields Kollman, Donald Ostrowski, Andrei Pliguzov, and Daniel Rowland (Cambridge, MA.: Harvard Ukrainian Research Institute, 1995), 271–91.

70 TsDIAL, fond 201, list 4a, file 6144.

71 For more detailed discussion, see Yaroslav Hrytsak, "History of Names: A Case of Constructing National Memory in Galicia, 1830-1930s," *Jahrbücher für Geschichte Osteuropas* 46 (2001): 163–77.

Chapter 3

1 Ivan Franko, *Mozaika: Iz tvoriv, shcho ne vviishly do Zibrannia tvoriv u 50 tomakh*, Z. T. Franko and M. H. Vasylenko, comps. (Lviv: Kameniar, 2001), 338. Henceforward, references to this publication are marked in the text by citations of the given volume and page of the *Zibrannia tvoriv* within square brackets.

2 This comment was made by Omelian Ohonovsky, one of the first researchers of Franko. See O. Ohonovs′kyi, *Istoriia literatury ruskoi*, vol. 3, 915–16.

3 M. S. Hrytsiuta, *Selianstvo v ukrains′kii dozhovtnevii literatury* (Kyiv: Naukova dumka, 1979); VR LNB, fond 206 (Vasyl′ Shchurat), file 340 (an unpublished article by Vasyl′ Shchurat titled "Narod v ukrains′kii literaturi XIX st.").

4 Hrytsiuta, *Selianstvo*, 41–44; M. M. Mundiak, "Opovidannia i povisti Ivana Franka z selians′koho zhyttia iak tvory krytychnoho realizmu," in *Doslidzhennia tvorchosty Ivana Franka*, ed. I. Krypiakevych (Kyiv: Vyd-vo Akademii nauk URSR, 1956), 108–18.

5 See, e.g., the story "Vivchar" (The Shepherd) with its idyllic depiction of the former life of a peasant now working in a mine in Boryslav [ZT 21:64–69].

6 For a list of natural cataclysms that afflicted Galician Subcarpathia between the thirteenth century and the first half of the nineteenth, see S. I. Kopchak, *Naselennia ukrains′koho Prykarpattia (istoryko-demohrafichnyi narys). Dokapitalistychnyi period* (Lviv: Vyshcha shkola, 1974), 87–89, 125.

7 Hanna Hrom, *Nahuievychi* (Drohobych: Vydavnycha firma "Vidrodzhennia," 2002), 106–7. These books were destroyed when the church burned down in 1996. The list is incomplete and fails to mention the failure of the potato crop in 1846 (see below).

8 B. N. Mironov, "Traditsionnoe demograficheskoe povedenie krest′ian v XIX–nachale XX vv.," in *Brachnost′, rozhdaemost′, smertnost′ v Rossii i SSSR: Sb. statei* (Moscow: Statistika, 1977), 94; William I. Thomas and Florian Znaniecki, "A Polish Peasant Family," in *Peasants and Peasant Societies; Selected Readings*, ed. Theodor Shanin (Harmondsworth [Baltimore]; Penguin, 1971), 23–29.

9 Roman Horak wrote a brief history of the Franko family on the basis of his genealogical research. See Horak and Hnativ, *Ivan Franko*, bk. 1.

10 S. Pavliuk, *Narodna ahrotekhnika ukraintsiv Karpat druhoi polovyny XIX–pochatku XX st. (Istoryko-etnohrafichne doslidzhennia* (Kyiv: Naukova dumka, 1986), 77, 83, 93; S. Pavliuk, *Tradytsiine khliborobstvo: ahrotekhnichnyi aspekt* (Kyiv: Naukova dumka, 1991), 131.

11 Zubryts′kyi, "Tisni roky," 2.

12 Stanisław Hoszowski, *Ekonomiczny rozwój Lwowa w latach 1772–1914* (Lwów: Nakładem Izby przemysłowo-handlowej we Lwowie, 1935), 47.

13 His father's adventures formed the nucleus of Franko's unfinished poem "The History of the Salt Cone" (Istoriia tovpky soli) [ZT 4:396–426].

14 Lev Kordasevych, "Spravy narodnii. Z Mokrianskoho dekanata Samborskoho okruha," *Vistnyk dlia rusynov avstriiskoi derzhavy*, 15–27 July 1850, 263. In a footnote to this article the editors of the newspaper noted the generosity of Yakiv Franko and other peasants as proof of the magnanimity that the peasant nation demonstrates "in its heart, when it sees a need for the benefit of a common cause." Ibid., 264.

15 Ivan Franko, *Halyts′ko-rus′ki narodni prypovidky*, vol. 1: *A–Dity* (Lviv, 1901), v.

16 Horak, *Mariia*, [pt. 2], 2.

17 Mykhailo Korinevych, "Spomyny pro Ivana Franka iak uchenyka himnazii," in Hnatiuk, *Spohady*, 57.

18 Mykhailo Vozniak, "Franko iak doslidnyk i istoryk ukrains´koi literatury," *Ukrains´ka literatura* 3 (1945): 99.

19 Franko, *Halyts´ko-rus´ki narodni prypovidky*, vol. 1, v.

20 According to the family's reminiscences, Havrylyk was cruel to his stepchildren, with the exception of Ivan. See Omelian Tvardovs´kyi, "Vasyl´ Franko rozpovidaie pro svoho stryika Ivana Franka," in *Drohobychchyna—zemlia Ivana Franka*, vol. 2, ed. Luka Lutsiv, *Ukrains´kyi arkhiv*, vol. 32 (New York: Naukove tovarystvo im. Shevchenka); Vasyl´ Chepurny, "Ivan Franko i fondy Chernihivs´koho literaturno-memorial´noho muzeiu-zapovidnyka M. M. Kotsiubyns´koho," *Naukovi zapysky Chernihivs´koho literaturno-memorial´noho muzeiu-zapovidnyka M. M. Kotsiubyns´koho* 1 (1996): 108.

21 Larysa Chernyshenko, "Lysty Ol´hy Khoruzhyns´koi do Ivana Franka (1892–1914)," *Naukovyi visnyk Muzeiu Ivana Franka u L´vovi.* 3 (2003): 202–3.

22 Antonina Trehubova, "Deshcho z zhyttia Ol´hy Frankovoi," in *Za sto lit: Materiialy z hromadskoho i literaturnoho zhyttia Ukrainy XIX i pochatkiv XX stolittia*, bk. 5 (Kyiv; Kharkiv: Derzhavne vydavnytstvo Ukrainy, 1930), 268.

23 Włodzimierz Mędrzecki, *Młodzież wiejska na ziemiach Polski centralnej, 1864–1939: procesy socjalizacji* (Warsaw: Wydawn. DiG, 2002), 40–41.

24 VR IL, fond 3 (Ivan Franko), file 207, fol. 10.

25 Volodymyr Kuz´movych, "Z iunykh lit Franka," *Novyi chas*, 2 May 1928, 9.

26 Trehubova, "Deshcho z zhyttia Ol´hy Frankovoi," 268.

27 Kuzmovych, "Z iunykh lit Franka," 8–9.

28 Karlo Bandrivs´kyi, "Spohady pro Franka-shkoliara," in Hnatiuk, *Spohady*, 49.

29 Trehubova, "Deshcho z zhyttia Ol´hy Frankovoi," 268.

30 Ivan Iatsuliak, "Spomyn z dytynnykh lit Franka," in Hnatiuk, *Spohady*, 43.

31 Kuzmovych, "Z iunykh lit Franka," 8.

32 VR LNB, fond 206 (Vasyl´ Shchurat), file 922, sub-file 27, fol. 11.

33 According to another version, Franko described an incident that took place not in his family but in the home of his maternal uncle, Pavlo Kulchytsky, from Yasenytsia Silna.

34 Iatsuliak, "Spomyn," 43.

35 Trehubova, "Deshcho z zhyttia Ol´hy Frankovoi," 268.

36 According to the strict rules governing the Lenten fast, no meat, fish, fats, eggs, or dairy products could be consumed during the seven-week period between Shrovetide and Easter Sunday.

37 Eugeniusz Chmielowski, *Czarownicy, strzygi, mamony czyli wierzenia i zabobony ludu galicyjskiego zebrane przez...w pierwszej połowie roku 1890* (Nowy Sącz: 1987), 8–9, 23; Volodymyr Hnatiuk, *Kupanie i palenie vid´m u Halychyni*, 2–3 (single copy; n.d.); Volodymyr Hnatiuk, *Narys ukrains´koi mifolohii* (Lviv: In-t Narodoznavstva Nats. Akademii nauk Ukrainy, 2000), 39, 224–31.

38 Lu. Dz., "Nahujowice," in Sulimierski et al., *Słownik geograficzny Królestwa Polskiego i innych krajów słowiańskich*, vol. 6, 882.

39 Roman Horak and Iaroslav Hnativ, *Ivan Franko*, bk. 2, *Tsilkom normal´na shkola* (Lviv: Vyd-vo ottsiv Vasyliian "Misioner," 2001), 84.

40 People resorted to black magic even in more prosaic situations. Neolithic axes found in Nahuievychi were used as healing aids for throat ailments. After the axes were blessed in church, water was poured over them and given to the sick person to drink. Little Franko was treated this way. See Ivan Franko, "Neolitychni znakhidky v okolytsiakh Nahuievych i ikh suchasne uzhyvannie," *ZNTSh* 103 (1911): 200–202.

41 Mędrzecki, *Młodzież wiejska*, 41.

42 Horak and Hnativ, *Ivan Franko*, bk. 1, 155; Hrom, *Nahuievychi*, 127.

43 Kossak, "Ivan Franko ta ioho braty," 45.

44 Iatsuliak, "Spomyn," 43.

45 Zenon Pelens'kyi, "Mizh dvoma konechnostiamy. Prychynok do sotsiolohii ukrains'koho natsional'no-vyzvol'noho revoliutsiinoho rukhu v Zakhidnii Ukraini mizh oboma svitovymy viinamy," in *Ievhen Konovalets' ta ioho doba* (Munich: Vydannia Fundatsii im. Ievhena Konoval'tsia, 1974), 513–16; Iu. Prysiazhniuk, "Mental'nist' ukrains'koho selianstva v umovakh kapitalistychnoi transformatsii suspil'stva (druha polovyna XIX–pochatok XX st.)," *Ukrains'kyi istorychnyi zhurnal* 3 (1999): 27.

46 VR LNB, fond 206 (Vasyl' Shchurat), list 922, file 27, fol. 4.

47 Ibid., fol. 6.

48 The following collective portrait of rural deacons-teachers emerges from the reminiscences of this era: "These were neither peasants nor educated people, neither lay people nor clerics. And their clothing was neither a peasant's nor an educated person's, or that of a lay person or a cleric's, but all mixed together....Among them were also some who were more competent and somewhat educated, but there were also ignorant people, who not only had never heard of these subjects, they could not even pronounce them. In response to the instruction to draw a circle, they would draw a wagon wheel, and about the ancient Romans, they said that they were still living in Napoleon's time." See Fylymon Tarnavs'kyi, *Spohady: Rodynna khronika Tarnavs'kykh iak prychynok do istorii tserkovnykh, sviashchenytskykh, pobutovykh, ekonomichnykh i politychnykh vidnosyn u Halychyni v druhii polovyni XIX storichchia i v pershii dekadi XX storichchia*, comp. and ed. Dr. Anatol' Mariia Bazylevych and Roman Ivan Danylevych (Toronto: Dobra knyzhka, 1981), 168–69.

49 Ł. H. Baik, "Z historii rozwoju ukraińskiej szkoły w Galicji," in *Galicja i jej dziedzictwo*, ed. Andrzej Meissner and Jerzy Wyrozumski, vol. 3: *Nauka i oświata* (Rzeszów: Wydawn. Wyższej Szkoły Pedagogicznej, 1995), 153.

50 R. Chmelyk, *Mala ukrains'ka selians'ka sim'ia druhoi polovyny XIX–pochatku XX st. (struktura i funktsii)* (Lviv: Instytut narodoznavstva NAN Ukrainy, 1999), 104–6.

51 Korinevych, "Spomyny pro Ivana Franka," 54.

52 Franko's acquaintances, the peasants Hryn Rymar and Hryn Berehuliak, were pupils of Rev. Chapelsky, who convinced their parents to send their gifted children to the gymnasium ("Pysmo z Drohobychchyny. Shcho hde-shcho pro sotsiializm i bohokhul'stvo v Dobrovlianakh i v Voli Iakubovii," *Bat'kivshchyna*, 24 [12] December 1886, 215). The patron of Osyp Markiv, who studied in the Drohobych gymnasium at approximately the same time as Franko, was Rev. Ivan Korostensky, the former secretary of the Sambir Ruthenian Council. See Andrii Zaiarniuk [Andriy Zayarnyuk], "Rus'ki patrioty v Halyts'komu seli 1860–1870-ykh rokiv: sviatoiurtsi, obriadovtsi, paternalisty i populisty (Na prykladi Sambirs'koi okolytsi)," *Ukraina moderna* 8 (2003): 113. At the urging of a local peasant-friendly landowner named Yosyp Teodorovych, who had taken part in Garibaldi's uprising and the Polish uprising of 1863, the father of the future distinguished Western Ukrainian writer Vasyl Stefanyk sent his son to school (see his autobiography in Vasyl' Stefanyk, *Vybrane* (Uzhhorod: Vyd-vo "Karpaty," 1979), 227). See also analogous Ukrainian and Polish examples from a later period: Viliam Nol [William Noll], *Transformatsiia hromadians'koho suspil'stva: Usna istoriia ukrains'koi selians'koi kul'tury 1920–30 rokiv* (Kyiv: Tsentr doslidzhen' usnoi istorii ta kul'tury Rodovid, 1999), 99, 106; Jan Jakóbiec, "Szkolna droga syna chłopskiego, 1882–1896," in *Galicyjskie wspomnienia szkolne*, ed. Antoni Knot (Cracow: Wydawn. Literackie,

1955), 404; Jan Madejczyk, "Dwa lata w szkółce wiejskiej, 1889–1891," in *Galicyjskie wspomnienia szkolne*, ed. Antoni Knot, 450–51.

53 Vasyl´ Nahirnyi, "Z moikh spomyniv," in *Nahirni, Levy—istoriia rodyny: Statti, spohady, naukovi rozvidky, arkhivni materialy* (Lviv: Skifiia, 2000), 61.

54 Prysiazhniuk, "Mental´nist´ ukrains´koho selianstva," 25.

55 B. Hrinchenko and M. Drahomanov, *Dialohy pro ukrains´ku natsional´nu spravu* (Kyiv: Natsional´na Akademiia nauk Ukrainy; Instytut ukrains´koi arkheohrafii, 1994), 38 [=*Dzherela z istorii suspilno-politychnoho rukhu v Ukraini 19–pochatku 20 st.*].

56 Ivan Makukh, who was the son of a peasant from the Sambir area and the first in his village to graduate from a gymnasium, claimed that one of the main reasons why peasants were loath to send their children to school was the fear that they would become atheists. "Parish priests pounded into the heads of the peasants the idea that an educated son would become an atheist, and that is why the peasants did not send their children to higher schools." Ivan Makukh, *Na narodnii sluzhbi: Spohady* (Kyiv: Osnovni tsinnosti, 2001), 10.

57 Heretz, *Russian Apocalypse*, 184–86.

58 See also the recollections of Franko's brother Zakhar, who claimed that when Ivan would come to Nahuievychi "for a vacation," he always went off fishing and mushroom-picking. "That's as much work as he did." See Kuz´movych, "Z iunykh lit Franka," 8.

59 Franko himself said that he was sent to school because he was a "feeble child unsuited to peasants' work" [*ZT* 31:29]. This statement, however, does not tally with the recollections of Franko's friends, who remember him as a physically healthy (but not strong) and agile boy.

60 It is significant that the adult Franko never mentioned his two sisters who died when he was six and ten years old, respectively, i.e., after he had already attained the age of reason. Similarly, his stories about little Myron, which he called "supplements" to his biography [*ZT* 48:559], contain no mention of his brothers, who stayed with their parents in Nahuievychi. This silence may be explained by the fact that Franko lived in the village for a very short time. Franko's other children's stories, "Hrytseva shkil´na nauka" (Hryts's School Education) and "Olivets´" (The Pencil), also reflect the Yasenytsia period of his life (see the draft copy of Mykhailo Vozniak's article, "Vid dytynstva do povnolittia Ivana Franka," which is stored at the VR LNB, fond 29 (Mykhailo Vozniak), list 23, file 9, fol. 16.

61 Roman Horak also doubts the veracity of this explanation. In his opinion, the cause was the acute conflict between the Nahuievychi community and its parish priest, Rev. Osyp Levytsky. Yakiv Franko, who was one of the most vociferous critics in the community, sent his son to school in a neighboring village, fearing possible retaliation from the priest, who had direct supervision over the local school. See Horak, "Ia ie muzhyk," 65–67. But this explanation is hardly persuasive: Rev. Levytsky died in 1860, and it is not clear why Yakiv Franko would still have been afraid of him in 1862.

62 The historian of the village of Nahuievychi claims that during Franko's childhood the local school was small and poor, and could not accommodate all the children. Therefore, some of the better-off children attended school in Yasenytsia Silna, and the poorer ones, after completing school in Nahuievychi, remained semiliterate (O. Tvardovs´kyi, "Nahuievychi—selo Ivana Franka," in *Drohobychchyna—zemlia Ivana Franka*, vol. 1, ed. Luka Lutsiv. *Ukrains´kyi arkhiv*, vol. 25. New York: Naukove tovarystvo im. Shevchenka, 1973.

63 Horak, "Ia ie muzhyk," 61, 64.

64 Nehrebets´kyi, "Do rodovodu," 233.

65 Franko's wife, who often spent the summer with her children in Nahuievychi with her brothers-in-law, recalled that they were uncultured and superstitious individuals; Trehubova, "Deshcho z zhyttia Ol'hy Frankovoi," 268.

66 Roman Horak, "Lysty rodyny do Ivana Franka," *Naukovyi visnyk Muzeiu Ivana Franka u L'vovi* 1 (2000): 121–208.

67 Ibid., 132, 134, 137–38, 172.

Chapter 4

1 See Jeffrey Brooks, *When Russia Learned to Read: Literacy and Popular Literature, 1867–1917* (Princeton: Princeton University Press, 1985), 55–56, 58; Natalie Zemon Davis, *Society and Culture in Early Modern France: Eight Essays* (Stanford: Stanford University Press, 1975), 196.

2 He left the school in Yasenytsia Silna at the end of first grade, after a conflict with one of his schoolmates. See Bandrivs'kyi, "Spohady," 49. Franko wrote that because he was "a small, unusually timid boy, [he] had to suffer a lot from the high-handedness of the other children" in the village school [*Mozaika* 340].

3 See *Ivan Franko: Dokumenty i materialy*, 20–23, 28.

4 In his reminiscences, Franko confirmed one of the incidents in this story: the punishment that Melko, the handwriting teacher, meted out to a Jewish pupil, who was writing from right to left [*Mozaika* 341].

5 Franko, *Halyts'ko-rus'ki narodni prypovidky*, vol. 2, bk. 1, 184.

6 Bandrivs'kyi, "Spohady," 49–51. Another example, based on her own observations of the educational practices in 1884, is cited by Yulia Schneider: a teacher struck a first-grade girl in the head with such force that she died. See Uliana Kravchenko, *Zamist' avtobiohrafii* (Kolomyia: Zahal'na knyhozbirnia, 1934), 306.

7 His roommate Mykhailo Korinevych, with whom Franko shared an apartment rented from a Drohobych shoemaker, recalled that Franko remarked several times how good it would be if property could be divided equally among everybody; if the common people could choose a ruler for themselves. See Korinevych, "Spomyny pro Ivana Franka," 57. However, there is no other trace of Franko's "elemental socialism" in his memoiristic literature or extant manuscripts from his school days in Drohobych.

8 Franko later admitted that "The Priest-Humorist" is almost completely memoiristic, while "Schönschreiben" contains an element of artistic fantasy [*ZT* 34:457]. Comparisons of Franko's reminiscences with official documents about the Basilian school reveal certain inaccuracies, and even tendentiousness. See Iosafat Skruten', "D-r Ivan Franko i vasyliiany," in Hnatiuk, *Spohady*, 604.

9 Bandrivs'kyi, "Spohady," 51.

10 See, e.g., I. I. Bass, *Ivan Franko: Biohrafiia* (Kyiv: Naukova dumka, 1966), 21–24.

11 The network of Basilian schools embraced the eastern borderlands of the former Rzeczpospolita—both the Austrian and the Russian parts. Their pedagogical activities were particularly successful in the Vilnius educational district, until both the Greek Catholic Church and the educational district were liquidated in the Russian Empire after the Polish Uprising of 1830. See Daniel Beauvois, *Szkoły podstawowe i średnie*, vol. 2 of *Szkolnictwo Polskie na ziemiach Litewsko-Ruskich, 1803–1832* (Lublin: Red. Wydawnictw KUL, 1991), 127, 148, 151, 177–87.

12 Baik, "Z historii rozwoju," 151; Jan Wierzbowski, "Klasyczne gimnazjum Galicyjskie 1872–1880," in *Galicyjskie wspomnienia szkolne*, ed. Antoni Knot (Cracow: Wydawn. Literackie, 1955), 386.

13 VR LNB, fond 41 (Hrushkevych), list 6, file 1, fols. 12–13.

14 Skruten´, "D-r Ivan Franko i vasyliiany," 604.

15 Bandrivs´kyi, "Spohady," 50.

16 *Ivan Franko: Dokumenty i materialy*, 20–21; Skruten´, "D-r Ivan Franko i vasyliiany," 605–6.

17 VR LNB, fond 266 (Ivan Shpytkovs´kyi), list 42, file 3, fol. 3.

18 W. F., "Klasyczne nauczanie w gimnazjach," *Gazeta Naddniestrzańska*, 15 December 1886, 1. This article recapitulates the main theses of a book that I was fortunate to locate: Prof. Dr. F. Schmeding, *Die klassiche Bildung in der Gegenwart* (Berlin: Gebrüder Borntraeger, 1885).

19 Wierzbowski, "Klasyczne gimnazjum," 388. Ivan Franko made a similar assessment of this system a few years after he graduated from the gymnasium: Mykyta [Ivan Franko], "Uchenytska biblioteka v Drohobychi," in *Molot: Halytsko-ukrainska zbirka*, ed. M. Pavlyk (Lviv, 1878), 127.

20 M. Drahomanov, "Dva uchyteli," in M. Drahomanov, *Vybrane...mii zadum zlozhyty ocherk istorii tsyvilizatsii na Ukraini* (Kyiv: Lybid, 1991), 578; Wierzbowski, "Klasyczne gimnazjum," 386–88.

21 See Jones, *Sigmund Freud*, ix; Drahomanov, "Dva uchyteli," 575–85; see also Drahomanov's "Avtobiograficheskaia zametka," in M. Drahomanov, *Literaturno-publitsystychni pratsi u dvokh tomakh*, vol. 1 (Kyiv: Naukova dumka, 1970), 39.

22 Bandrivs´kyi, "Spohady," 51.

23 This earliest attempt at writing has not been preserved. There is another identically titled poem by Franko, which was written in 1881 on an entirely different topic [*ZT* 1:176].

24 In a later autobiography Franko mistakenly said that he began writing in the lower gymnasium grades [*ZT* 49:242].

25 For detailed discussion, see Stepan Shchurat, "Pershi literaturni sproby Ivana Franka. Z dodatkom ioho lystiv do redaktsii zhurnalu *Druh* i Vasylia Davydiaka," in *Ivan Franko: Zbirnyk statei i materialiv*, vol. 2 (Lviv: Vyd-vo Lvivs´koho universytetu, 1949), 87–145.

26 Leszek Śliwa, "Gimnazja Galicyjskie w procesie kształtowania się inteligencji Polskiej," in *Galicja i jej dziedzictwo*, vol. 3, 163–64.

27 *Hickmann's...Atlas*, map no. 36.

28 Harald Binder, "Eine Provinzstadt in Galizien: Drohobycz in den letzten fünfzig Jahren österreichischer Herrschaft," [*separatum*], 4–5; Mark, *Galizien unter Österreichischer Herrschaft*, 92; Pilat, "Obszar, zabudowania i ludność miast," 18f–18i, 18l; Ignacy Weinfeld, "Ludność miejska Galicyi i jej skład wyznaniowy (1881–1910)," in *Wiadomości statystyczne o stosunkach krajowych* 24, no. 2 (1912): 34–35.

29 Tadeusz Pilat, "Materiały statystyczne do sprawy propinacyjnej," in *Wiadomości statystyczne o stosunkach krajowych* 11, no. 2 (1888): 6, 15.

30 Cited in Ezra Mendelsohn, *Painting a People: Maurycy Gottlieb and Jewish Art* (Hanover, NH: Brandeis University Press, Published by University Press of New England, c.2002), 20–21.

31 Pilat, "Obszar, zabudowania i ludność miast," 11.

32 Ibid., 12.

33 Ibid., 18e.

34 Ibid., 18b.

35 Makukh, *Na narodnii sluzhbi*, 12.

36 VR LNB, fond 41 (Hrushkevych), list 6, file 1, fols. 28–29; Ždisław Kultys, *Historya Gimnazyum Drohobyckiego* (Drohobycz: Komitet Jubileuszowy, 1908), 48–50, 56–61. Neither of these sources mentions anything about the Ruthenian students' participation in the pogroms.

37 Renata Dutkowa, *Polityka szkolna w Galicji między autonomią a centralizmem (1861–1875)* (Cracow: Księgarnia Akademicka, 1995), 151.

38 [Iwan Franko], "Emeryk Turczyński. Wspomnienia pośmiertne," *Kurjer Lwowski,* 16 April 1896, 2 (this article is unsigned; Franko's authorship was identified on the basis of Myroslav Moroz, *Ivan Franko: Bibliohrafiia tvoriv, 1874–1964* (Kyiv: Naukova dumka, 1966), 285).

39 Kultys, *Historya*, 23–24.

40 Ibid., 53.

41 Franko left a separate reminiscence about Hückel and Turczyński: see n. 38. The respect that both students and teachers had for Turczyński is attested by the following article that appeared in the local press: "Pan Emeryk Turczyński," *Gazeta Naddniestrzańska*, 1 November 1886, 7.

42 Franko turned Michonski into the hero of his short story "Borys Hrab" [*ZT* 18:177–90].

43 VR LNB, fond 206 (Vasyl Shchurat), list 922, file 27, fol. 7; Bandrivs´kyi, "Spohady," 51–53; Korinevych, "Spomyny pro Ivana Franka," 56–57.

44 Andrzej Śródka and Paweł Szczawiński, eds., *Biogramy uczonych polskich*, pt. 1, *Nauki społeczne*, bk. 3, *P–Z* (Wrocław: Ossolineum, 1985), 314–18.

45 Kultys, *Historya*, 83.

46 Antin Chernets´kyi, *Spomyny z moho zhyttia* (Kyiv: Osnovni tsinnosti, 2001), 19.

47 Kultys, *Historya*, 58.

48 Yaroslav Hrytsak, "*...Dukh, shcho tilo rve do boiu....*"

49 Andrii Chaikovs´kyi recalled that, during Franko's years at the gymnasium, the teachers in his own (Sambir) gymnasium told the more inept students: "Why are you tormenting yourselves here? It would be better if you went to Drohobych; there you will be top students." See Andrii Chaikovs´kyi, "Moi spohady pro Ivana Franka," in Hnatiuk, *Spohady*, 95. The low level of teaching in the Drohobych Gymnasium is also corroborated by the historian of this high school. See Kultys, *Historya*, 23–24, 44, 68–69, 71.

50 Among educated Galician Ruthenians trilingualism was quite common, but few were able to write well in German: this was a rarity among Slavs. (See, e. g., the comment about the "destructive nature" of the German language in Mykhailo Pavlyk, *Perepyska Mykhaila Drahomanova z Mykhailom Pavlykom (1876–1895)* [Chernivtsi: Tovarystvo "Rus´ka Rada," n.d.], vol. 3, 313.) A student's aptitude and industriousness played a decisive role here.

51 This statement should not be accepted as the gospel truth. In another article, written a few years after he graduated from the gymnasium, Franko states that the majority of the books in the library created by the Ruthenian students (138 out of 196) were Ruthenian-Ukrainian. See [Franko], "Uchenyts´ka biblioteka," 124. Complaining about the dearth of Ruthenian publications, Franko was probably referring above all to works of literature, which enjoyed the greatest popularity among the gymnasium students (ibid., 126).

52 Ipolyt Pohorets´kyi, "Franko v himnazii," in Hnatiuk, *Spohady*, 58.

53 At least that was the opinion of Mykhailo Korinevych, Franko's friend from the gymnasium days. See Korinevych, "Spomyny pro Ivana Franka," 56.

54 See "Kritika na 'Druha' i otzyvy o nem," *Druh*, 24 July (5 August) 1876, 239; Pavlyk, *Perepyska*, vol. 2, 34.

55 Ivan Verkhrats'kyi, *Zlobni vydumky d-ra Ivana Franka* (Lviv: Pechatnia V. A. Shyikovs'koho, 1907), 109.

56 Bandrivs'kyi, "Spohady," 52.

57 See, Mendelsohn, *Painting a People*, 28–44.

58 Until 1874, the proportion of Jewish students in gymnasiums never exceeded 20 percent. By 1881 there were twice as many Jewish students as Ruthenian ones, and nearly one and a half times as many Poles. See Kultys, *Historya*, 78.

59 Pilat, "Obszar, zabudowania i ludność miast," 18b.

60 W. C., "Niemieszczyzna w Drohobyczy," *Gazeta Naddniestrzańska*, 1 November 1886, 7–8.

61 Among the students at the Drohobych Gymnasium were Mykhailo Zubrytsky, the eminent Ukrainian ethnographer; Osyp Markov, the leader of the Russophiles; Hryhorii Rymar and Ivan Makukh, leading figures of the populist movement; Les Martovych and Vasyl Stefanyk, distinguished Ukrainian writers of peasant origin; and others. See VR LNB, fond 206 (Vasyl Shchurat), list 922, file 27, fol. 8; Kultys, *Historya*, 219, 222, 224; Makukh, *Na narodnii sluzhbi*, 16–17; Volodymyr Chapel's'kyi, *Ia liubyv ikh usikh: Z mynuloho Drohobychchyny* (Drohobych: Vydavnycha firma "Vidrodzhennia," 1997), 190–91.

62 The Ruthenian students' resistance to Polish assimilation is also indirectly attested by the fact that there were few Polish-language books in the public library which they founded: 19 vs. 67 German books, and 137 Ruthenian-Ukrainian works. Furthermore, Polish books were not among those most frequently borrowed. See [Franko], "Uchenyts'ka biblioteka," 124, 126.

63 A correspondent of the Russophile newspaper *Slovo* reported on the subsequent exacerbation of Ruthenian-Polish antagonism in the Drohobych Gymnasium. In 1876 a local teacher could tell a Ruthenian student: "I would hang those Ruthenians and Jews together on a dry branch." After Juliusz Turczyński left Drohobych and became the director of the teachers' seminary in Stanyslaviv, he opposed the introduction of the Ruthenian language into the curriculum. During classes he would deride the Ruthenian language in front of the students: "The Ruthenian language is the language of drunkards. Shevchenko himself was an ordinary peasant and a drunkard." See "Rovnoupravnenie ruskogo iazyka v shkolakh," *Druh*, 15 (27) September 1876, 285–86. In a letter to Ivan Franko, Kyrylo Tryliovsky, the future leader of the Radical Party, and at the time (1884) a student at the Kolomyia Gymnasium, described the attitude of Polish teachers to Ruthenians and the Ruthenian question: the history teacher "is distorting history; for entire hours he weaves the topic of 'Ruś, Polszcza i Litwa to odna mołytwa' ["Rus, Poland, and Lithuania are one prayer," a line from a poem by Platon Kostecki—Y. H.], makes fun of peasants, etc., without end. After a report was published about him in *Dilo* [a populist Ukrainian newspaper—Y. H.], Krucinski, the professor of drawing, called its editors 'palamarzami i kacapami' [sacristans and *katsaps*, the latter a derogatory Ukrainian and Polish term for Russians—Trans.]. Sokalski, the professor of mathematics, called one student from the V [class—Y. H.], whose surname ended in '-icz', as '-ski.' When he did not get up instantly, he made fun of him, [saying] 'You don't know mathematics, but you know how to speak Muscovite in the marketplace?' Vaitel, the professor of natural science, conducts himself the most treacherously.…He does not speak overtly, but in this manner, making fun of or distorting Ruthenian surnames and words, even using such words as 'Ivan crapped in his galoshes.'" See VR IL, fond 3 (Ivan Franko), list 1603, fol. 217.

64 Cited in Adam Mickiewicz, *Dzieła. Wydanie Rocznicowe. 1798-1998.* Ed. Czesław Zgorzelski (Warszawa: Czytelnik, 1993), 380.

65 "O. Teofan Hlyns´kyi," *Pravda* 17 (no. L, 1893): 232.

66 [Ios. Levyts´kyi], "Beseda hovorena dnia 22 maia 1848 roku v Drohobychy pry osnovanii komiteta russkoho" [n.d.], 11.

67 Viacheslav Budzynovs´kyi, "Latynka," *Novi shliakhy* 10 (1931): 317.

68 Bandrivs´kyi, "Spohady," 53.

69 Ibid.

70 Korinevych, "Spomyny pro Ivana Franka," 57.

71 VR IL, fond 3 (Ivan Franko), list 207, fols. 8, 13; Verkhrats´kyi, *Zlobni vydumky*, 44.

72 See Isidor Pasichyns´kyi, "Staryna," *Druh*, 1 (13) May 1874, 41 (n.).

73 For detailed discussion of the Drohobych Gymnasium community, see Ostap Sereda, "Shaping of a National Identity: Early Ukrainophiles in Austrian Eastern Galicia, 1860–1873" (Ph.D. diss., Central European University, 2003), 88–89, 95–96, 226.

74 VR LNB, fond 41 (Hrushkevych), list 6, file 1, fol. 41.

75 Chaikovs´kyi, "Moi spohady pro Ivana Franka," 95.

76 Franko recalled that during his years at the gymnasium there were three student societies of a scholarly-literary orientation and several societies of "gymnasium singing." None of them lasted long, and student activity began to decline with the advent of Polonization. The new teachers arriving at the gymnasium did not know how to spark the students' interest, and they spent their free time drinking. Their students followed in their footsteps, and the "former scholarly-literary societies turned into drinking groups," [Ivan Franko], "Dopys pro Drohobyts´ku himnaziiu," in *Dzvin: Halytsko-ukrains´ka zbirka* (Lviv, 1878), 267–68. (The article is untitled and unsigned; Franko's authorship was identified on the basis of Moroz, *Bibliohrafiia tvoriv*, 157.)

77 Anna Wendland, *Die Russophilen in Galizien:Ukrainische Konservative zwischen Österreich und Russland, 1848–1915* (Vienna: Verlag der Österreichischen Akademie der Wissenschaften, 2001).

78 John-Paul Himka, "The Greek Catholic Church and Nation-Building in Galicia, 1772–1918," *Harvard Ukrainian Studies* 8, nos. 3–4 (December 1984): 426–52.

79 *Ivan Franko: Dokumenty i materialy*, 38, 47–49; Pohorets´kyi, "Franko v himnazii," 57–58; Lev Shankovs´kyi, "Narys istorii Stryishchyny," in *Stryishchyna: istorychno-memuarnyi zbirnyk*, ed. Iryna Pelens´ka and Klymentii Babiak, vol. 1 (New York: Komitet Stryishchyny, 1990), 23.

80 Ivan Franko, "Shcho dumaie narod pro neustupchyvist´ mytropolyta Osypa Sembratovycha," in *Za sto lit*, bk. 4 (Kyiv: VUAN, 1929), 256.

81 Mykhailyna Roshkevych (Ivanets´), "Spohady pro Ivana Franka," in Hnatiuk, *Spohady*, 108.

82 See I. Slups´kyi, comp., *Ivan Franko: Dokumental´ni fotohrafii*, 2nd exp. ed. (Lviv: Kameniar, 1971), 23, 25.

83 Pohorets´kyi, "Franko v himnazii," 58.

84 Pavlyk, *Perepyska*, vol. 2, 10.

85 Ibid., vol. 3, 93.

86 Ibid., vol. 2, 57.

87 Ibid., 7, 8, 20, 36, 82.

88 Ibid., 57. According to another version, Franko said: "I was not thinking of writing in the peasant style, about the peasants and for the peasants," ibid., 96. Ivan Pankevych, a scholar of the young Franko's aesthetic views, believes that these words are a paraphrase of Goethe. In response to the question of whether his works can be popular, the German poet declared: "Sie sind nicht für die Masse geschrieben, sondern nur für einzelne Menschen, die etwas Ähnliches wollen und suchen, die in ähnlichen Richtungen

begriffen sind" (They are not written for the masses, but only for individual people who want and seek something similar that is grasped in similar ways). Pankevych notes that Franko's words generally reflected the views of young people at the time. See Ivan Pankevych, "Shche raz pro pytannia rishal'noho vplyvu na kharakter Franka v 1874–6 rokakh," *Krakivs'ki visti*, 24 May 1943, 4.

Chapter 5

1   Additional details may be found in the chapter "How Franko Became a Genius." See also Lilia Syrota, "Vid Frankovykh obraziv do obraziv Ivana Franka," *Ukraina: kul'turna spadshchyna, natsional'na svidomist', derzhavnist'* 9 (2001): 556–66.

2   On this topic, see the anthology of literary texts by Ukrainian, Polish, and Russian writers, *Vitchyzna; zbirnyk vyslovliuvan' diiachiv rosiis'koi ta ukrains'koi kultury pro Vitchyznu* (Kyiv: Derzh. vyd-vo khudozh. lit-ry, 1953), and Leon Radziejowski, ed., *Ojczyzna w poezyi polskiej: krótka antologia* (Kyiv, 1916).

3   Tadeusz Boy-Żeleński, *O Mickiewiczu* (Cracow: Czytelnik, 1949), 10; Aleksandr Gertsen, *Sobranie sochinenii v 30 t.*, 30 vols. (Moscow: Izd-vo Akademii nauk SSSR, 1954–65), vol. 2, 333; Knot, "Wstęp," in Chłędowski, *Pamiętniki*, vol. 1, xvii–xviii.

4   For more systematic discussion, see Roman Wapiński, *Polska i małe ojczyzny Polaków: Z dziejów kształtowania się świadomości narodowej w XIX i XX wieku po wybuchu II wojny światowej* (Wrocław: Zakład Narodowy im. Ossolińskich, 1994); Marian Mudryi, "Poniattia 'nasha zemlia' / 'nash krai' v ukrains'komu rusi Halychyny XIX–pochatku XX stolittia," *in Shliakhamy istorii: Naukovyi zbirnyk istorychnoho fakul'tetu LNU im. I. Franka; na poshanu profesora Kostiantyna Kondratiuka* (Lviv: Piramida, 2004), 160–77.

5   See Stanisław Ossowski, *O ojczyźnie i narodzie* (Warsaw: Państwowe Wydawn. Naukowe, 1984), 15–46.

6   See Antonina Kłoskowska, *National Cultures at the Grass-Root Level* (Budapest: Central European University Press, 2001), 42, 53; Benedykt Zientara, *Świat narodów europejskich: Powstawanie świadomości narodowej na obszarze Europy postkarolińskiej* (Warsaw: Państ. Instytut Wydawniczy, 1985), 26.

7   Maciej Abramowicz, "Patrie—"Ojczyzna"?, in Jerzy Bartmiński, ed., *Pojęcie ojczyzny we współczesnych językach europejskich* (Lublin: Instytut Europy Środkowo-Wschodniej, 1993), 241; Ernst H. Kantorowicz, "*Pro Patria Mori* in Medieval Political Thought," *American Historical Review* 56, no. 3 (April 1951): 472–92; Pasquale Policastro, "Patria, patriotyzm i lokalizm we Włoszech: Treści społeczne i polityczne," in Bartmiński, *Pojęcie ojczyzny*, 230–31.

8   Ewa Bem, "Termin 'ojczyzna' w literaturze XVI i XVII wieku: Refleksje o języku," *Odrodzenie i reformacja w Polsce* 34 (1989): 131–57.

9   Frank Sysyn, "'Otchyzna' v ukrains'kii politychnii kul'turi pochatku XVIII st.," *Ukraina moderna* 10 (2006): 7–19.

10 See the conclusion reached on the basis of a textual analysis of nineteenth-century Polish belles-lettres and political literature in David Althoen, "That Noble Quest: From True Nobility to Enlightened Society in the Polish-Lithuanian Commonwealth, 1550–1830," vol. 1 (Ph.D. diss., University of Michigan, 2001), 157–242. To date, no similar research in the domain of *Begriffgeschichte* has been done in Ukrainian historiography. Ukrainian researchers focus on another important aspect: the displacement in creative literature of the archaic term "oichyzna" by the modern term "bat'kivshchyna," and the increasing prevalence of the latter concept in the broader sense. See Michał Lesiów,

"Bat´kiwszczyna, witczyzna, ridnyj kraj: Ojczyzna w języku ukraińskim," in Bartmiński, *Pojęcie ojczyzny*, 93–104. A decisive role in the modernization of this concept is attributed to Taras Shevchenko (Bartmiński, *Pojęcie ojczyzny*, 95–96). However, in Shevchenko's poetry Ukraine as fatherland also has a territorial meaning, not a national one: he writes much about Ukraine, but not once does the term "Ukrainian" appear in his writings. See *Konkordantsiia poetychnykh tvoriv Tarasa Shevchenka = A Concordance to the Poetic Works of Taras Shevchenko*, comp. and ed. Oleh S. Ilnytzkyj and George Hawrysch, 4 vols. (Edmonton; Toronto: Canadian Institute of Ukrainian Studies Press, 2001), vol. 4, 2588–89, 2920, 3004, 3073.

11 See Andrzej Walicki, *Poland between East and West: The Controversies over Self-Definition and Modernization in Partitioned Poland* (Cambridge, MA: Harvard Ukrainian Research Institute, 1994).

12 Ernst Moritz Arndt, *Ausgewählte Gedichte und Schriften* (Berlin: Union Verlag, 1969), 67.

13 Ernst Moritz Arndt, "The German Fatherland," in *The Poets and Poetry of Europe*, with introductions and biographical notes by Henry Wadsworth Longfellow (Philadelphia: Carey and Hart, 1845), 322–33.

14 Johannes Paul, *Ernst Moritz Arndt: "Das ganze Teutschland soll es sein!"* (Göttingen: Musterschmidt, 1971), 11, 83, 86.

15 Tadeusz Namowicz, "Galizien nach 1772: Zur Enstehung einer literarischen Provinz," in *Galizien als Gemeinsame Literaturlandschaft. Beiträge des 2. Innsbrucker Symposiums Polnischer und Österreichischer Literaturwissenschaftler*, eds. Friedrun Rinner, Klaus Zerinschek (Innsbruck, 1988), 66, 70.

16 Hildegard Binder Johnson, "Geography in German Literature," *German Quarterly* 24, no. 4 (November 1951): 232; Hans Kohn, "Arndt and the German Character of German Nationalism," *American Historical Review* 54, no. 4 (July 1949): 798; Roy Pascal, "The Frankfurt Parliament, 1848, and the Drang nach Osten," *Journal of Modern History* 18, no. 2 (June 1946): 118–20.

17 Poems about Galicia as *Heimat*, which appeared only after the Second World War among Galician Germans who had been resettled in Germany, were an expression of their nostalgic yearning for their lost small fatherland. See *Heimat Galizien* (Stuttgart: [1959?]), 20; Josef Lanz and Rudolf Unterschütz, eds., *Heimat Galizien im Bild* (Stuttgart: Das Hilfskomitee, 1983), xxiv.

18 John W. Mason, *The Dissolution of the Austro-Hungarian Empire, 1867–1918* (London: Longman, 1985), 10–11.

19 Hubert Orłowski, *Z modernizacją w tle: Wokół rodowodu nowoczesnych niemieckich wyobrażeń o Polsce i o Polakach* (Poznań: Poznańskie Tow. Przyjaciół Nauk., 2002), 69.

20 Cited in Vadym Adadurov, "L´viv u napoleonivsku epokhu," in *L´viv: misto, suspil´stvo, kul´tura: Zbirnyk naukovykh prats´*, vol. 3, ed. Marian Mudryi (Lviv: Vyd-vo L´vivs´koho universytetu, 1999), 212.

21 Kohl, *Austria, Vienna, Prague*, 433, 451, 455–56.

22 For more details, see Larry Wolff, "Inventing Galicia: Messianic Josephinism and the Recasting of Partitioned Poland," *Slavic Review* 63, no. 4 (Winter 2004): 818–40.

23 Here I cite the introduction written by Archduke Rudolf, heir to the throne, to the multivolume publication, *The Austro-Hungarian Monarchy in Words and Pictures*, which was planned in the 1880s especially for the purpose of "increasing general love for the fatherland": *Die Österreichisch-ungarische Monarchie in Wort und Bild: Auf Anregung und unter Mitwirkung Seiner kaiserlichen und königlichen Hoheit des durchlauchtigtesten Kronprinzen Erzherzog Rudolf* (Vienna: K. K. Hof- und Staatsdruckerei, 1886), 5, 13, 16. For the history of this publication—in particular how, contrary to Rudolf's intentions, it

promoted the idea of national particularism—see Regina Bendix, "Ethnology, Cultural Reification, and the Dynamics of Difference in the *Kronprinzwerk*," in *Creating the Other: Ethnic Conflict and Nationalism in Habsburg Central Europe*, ed. Nancy M. Wingfield (New York: Berghahn Books, 2003), 149–66.

24 Galician identity—but as a regional identity, not national—emerged among all local Poles and Ukrainians only after the fall of the Austro-Hungarian Empire, to a significant degree in the orientalist discourse, which was directed against the Russians and their own "Russian fellow clansmen" (i.e., Poles and Ukrainians from the former Russian territories). See Yaroslav Hrytsak, *Strasti za natsionalizmom: istorychni esei* (Kyiv: Krytyka, 2004), 266–80; Jadwiga Kowalikova, "Słowo—Galicja—dawniej i dziś, czyli habent sua fata verba," in *Inteligencja południowo-wschodnich ziem polskich*, eds. Halina Kurek and Franciszek Tereszkiewicz (Cracow: Universitas, 1998), 211–19; Roman Szul, "Perspektywy regionalizmu Galicyjskiego w Polsce na tle tendencji międzynarodowych," in *Galicja i jej dziedzictwo*, vol. 2, 86–88.

25 Chłędowski, *Pamiętniki*, vol. 1, 41, 200; W. F., "Z okazji odbytego wiecu rabinów żydowskich i 'cudotwórców,'" *Przegląd Społeczny* 1 (1887): 76–80.

26 Chłopiecki, "Galicja—skrzyżowanie dróg," 37.

27 Ernest Gellner, *Nations and Nationalism*, 6.

28 These words, uttered by Maurycy Dzieduszycki, are cited in Fras, *Galicja*, 58.

29 Jerzy Holzer, "Von Orient die Fantasie, und in der Brust der Slawen Feuer... Jüdisches Leben und Akkulturation im Lemberg des 19. und 20. Jahrhunderts," in *Lemberg, Lwów, Lviv: eine Stadt im Schnittpunkt europäischer Kulturen*, eds. Peter Fässler, Thomas Held, and Dirk Sawitzki (Cologne: Böhlau Verlag, 1993), 75–91; Namowicz, "Galizien nach 1772," 72.

30 Typical in this respect is a historical anecdote that dates to the earliest appearance of the anti-Galician stereotype in Polish discourses: when a Polish Galician patriot visited Mickiewicz in Dresden in 1829, the poet asked him: "Well, what's new with you out in Galilee?" (Cited in Wiegandt, *Austria felix*, 10.) The implication is transparent: nothing good could come out of either Galicia or the biblical Galilee.

31 Daniel Beauvois, "Mit 'kresów wschodnich,' czyli jak mu położyć kres," in *Polskie mity polityczne XIX i XX wieku* (Wrocław: Wydawn. Uniwersytetu Wrocławskiego, 1994), 93–105; S. Makowski, "Musij Wernyhora i jego proroctwa w świetle badań polskich i ukraińskich," in *Druhyi mizhnarodnyi kongres ukrainistiv, L'viv, 22–28 serpnia 1993 r. Dopovidi i povidomlennia. Istoriia* 1, eds. Iaroslav Isaievych and Yaroslav Hrytsak (Lviv, 1994), 154–61; M. Masłowski, "Le Mythe de Wernyhora: Une Prophetie Polonaise sur la Coexistence de l'Ukraine et de la Pologne," in Isaievych and Hrytsak, *Druhyi mizhnarodnyi kongres*, 146–54.

32 Mirosław Ustrzycki, *Ziemianie Polscy na Kresach 1864–1914: Świat wartości i postaw* (Cracow: Wydawnictwo "Arcana," 2006), 176; Wapiński, *Polska i małe ojczyzny Polaków*, 207.

33 Ivan L. Rudnytsky, *Essays in Modern Ukrainian History* (Edmonton: Canadian Institute of Ukrainian Studies, 1987), 187–201.

34 Walerian Kalinka, *Dzieła*, vol. 4, pt. 2 (Cracow, 1894), 212.

35 Piotr Eberhardt, *Polska i jej granice: z historii polskiej geografii politycznej* (Lublin: Wydawn. Uniwersytetu Marii Curie-Skłodowskiej, 2004), 40–42.

36 Ladislas Mickiewicz, *La Pologne est ses provinces méridionales; manuscrit d'un Ukrainien* (Paris: E. Dentu, 1863), 5–6.

37 Rudnytsky, *Essays*, 22, 129–30, 437–38; Viktor Korotkyi and Vasyl' Ul'ianovs'kyi, comps., *Syn Ukrainy, Volodymyr Bonifatiiovych Antonovych*, vol. 2 (Kyiv: Zapovit, 1997).

38 Recent studies have shown that Orzechowski's position had nothing in common with the proclamation of the supremacy of nationality (*natione*) over birth (*gente*). On the contrary, Orzechowski was proud of his Ruthenian birth and valued it more than his membership in the ranks of the Polish nobility. The change of hierarchy—*natione* over *gente*—was a creation of nineteenth-century Polish patriots. See David Althoen, "Natione Polonus and the Naród Szlachecki: Two Myths on National Identity and Noble Solidarity," *Zeitschrift für Ostmittleeuropa-Forschung* 52 (2003): 475–508.

39 Cited in Ivan Franko, "Stara Rus'," *LNV* 10 (1906): 240–41. For information about Kostetsky, see Marian Tyrowicz, "Kostecki, Platon," in *Polski Słownik Biograficzny*, vol. 14 (Wroclaw: Wydawnictwo PAN, 1968–1969), 340–41.

40 Andrzej A. Zięba, "'Gente Rutheni, Natione Poloni': Z problematyki kształtowania się Ukraińskiej świadomości narodowej w Galicji," in *Prace Komisji Wschodnioeuropejskiej Polskiej Akademji Umiejętności*, vol. 2 (Cracow: Nakł. Polskiej Akademii Umiejętności, 1995), 61–77.

41 David Saunders, "Russia's Ukrainian Policy (1847–1905): A Demographic Approach," *European History Quarterly* 25, no. 2 (1995): 193.

42 A. Pietruszewicz [A. Petrushevych], *Słów kilka napisanych w obronie ruskiej narodowości* (Lwów, 1848), 47–48. Cited in O. Iu. Turii, "Hreko-katolyts'ka tserkva v suspil'no-politychnomu zhytti Halychyny, 1848–1867" (Candidate of Historical Sciences diss., Lviv, 1994), 131.

43 Hryhorii Il'kevych, comp., *Halyts'ki prypovidky i zahadky* (1841; reprint, Lviv: Vyd-vo L'vivs'koho universytetu, 1994), 11, 91.

44 For a general survey, see Ievhen Nakonechnyi, *Ukradene im'ia: Chomu rusyny staly ukraintsiamy* (Lviv: L'vivs'ka naukova biblioteka im. V. Stefanyka NAN Ukrainy, 2001), 33–70.

45 Nicholas Vakar, *Belorussia: The Making of a Nation: A Case Study* (Cambridge, MA: Harvard University Press, 1956), 2–3.

46 Borys Floria, "Evoliutsiia znachennia termina 'Rus'' i pokhidnykh vid nioho u skhidnoslovians'kykh dzherelakh XII–XIV stolittia," in Isaievych and Hrytsak, *Druhyi mizhnarodnyi konhres ukrainistiv*, 3; Omeljan Pritsak and John S. Reshetar, "Ukraine and the Dialectics of Nation-Building," in *From Kievan Rus' to Modern Ukraine: Formation of the Ukrainian Nation* (Cambridge, MA: Ukrainian Studies Fund, Harvard University, 1984), 24–25 (second pagination).

47 The possibility of such identification is implicit in one of the first grammars of the Ruthenian language, Ivan Mohyl'nyts'kyi's *Vidomosti o ruskom iazytsi* (1816–1824). See H. Iu. Herbils'kyi, *Rozvytok prohresyvnykh idei v Halychyni u pershii polovyni XIX st.: (do 1848 r.)* (Lviv: Vyd-vo L'vivs'koho universytetu, 1964), 58; Mikhael Mozer [Michael Moser], *Prychynky do istorii ukrains'koi movy* (Kharkiv: Kharkivs'ke istoryko-filolohichne tovarystvo, 2008), 337–38.

48 Bogdan A. Deditskii [Bohdan A. Didyts'kyi], comp., *Mikhail Kachkovskii i sovremennaia galitsko-russkaia literatura: Ocherk biograficheskii i istoriko-literaturnyi*, pt. 1 (Lviv: S pechati Instituta Stavropigiiskogo pod nariadom Stefana Rutkovskogo, 1876), 112. For detailed discussion of "Austro-Ruthenians," see Mariian Mudryi, "Avstrorusynstvo v Halychyni: sproba okreslennia problemy," *Visnyk L'vivs'koho universytetu, Seriia istorychna* 35–36 (2001): 571–604. For discussion of the potentially "subversive" character of the Ukrainophile movement with regard to the integrality of the Habsburg monarchy, see the conclusion submitted by the censor, Yerenei Kopitar, concerning the manuscript of the almanac *Zoria*, which was prepared by the Ruthenian Triad in 1834,

in F. I. Steblii, O. A. Kupchyns'kyi et al., comps., *"Rusalka Dnistrova": Dokumenty i materialy* (Kyiv: Naukova dumka, 1989), 52–53.

49 For detailed discussion, see Jan Kozik, *The Ukrainian National Movement in Galicia, 1815–1849* (Edmonton: Canadian Institute of Ukrainian Studies, University of Alberta; Downsview, Ont., Canada: Distributed by the University of Toronto Press, 1986), 83–125.

50 The origin of this term has been the subject of much discussion. Its introduction is most often attributed to Pavlyn Svientsitsky (see Nakonechnyi, *Ukradene im'ia*, 367), and, less often, to Oleksandr Barvinsky (see Ihor Chornovol, "Oleksandr Barvins'kyi u konteksti svoiei i nynishnioi epokhy," in *Oleksandr Barvins'kyi, 1847–1927. Materialy konferentsii, prysviachenoi 150 richnytsi vid dnia narodzhennia Oleksandra Barvins'koho, Lviv, 14 travnia 1997* (Lviv, 2001), 43; Mykoła Muszynka, "Towarzystwo Naukowe im. Szewczenki i jego rola w narodowym odrodzeniu Ukraińców na terenie Galicji," in *Galicja i jej dziedzictwo*, vol. 3, 70); Mykhailo Hrushevsky (see Barbara Łuczyńska, "Udział Towarzystwa Nauczycieli Szkół Wyższych w integrowaniu nauczycieli szkół średnich Galicji 1884–1909," in *Galicja i jej dziedzictwo*, vol. 3, 253); and even to Ivan Franko—see Katria Hrynevycheva, "Spomyny (I. Franko)," in Hnatiuk, *Spohady*, 144; and Mykhailo Mochul's'kyi, "Z ostannikh desiatylit' zhyttia Ivana Franka (1896–1916)," in Hnatiuk, *Spohady*, 369. However, Franko clearly stated that this term was first used by Ivan Hushalevych [*ZT* 35:7–73].

51 F. S. [Fylyp Svystun], *Chem est' dlia nas Shevchenko? Kritichnoe rozsuzhdenie* (Lviv, 1885), 5–6.

52 Taras Shevchenko, *Povne zibrannia tvoriv u shesty tomakh*, 6 vols. (Kyiv: Vydavnytstvo Akademii Nauk URSR, 1963–1964), vol. 4, 319; Mykola Dubyna, *Shevchenko i Zakhidna Ukraina* (Kyiv: Vyd-vo Kyivs'koho universytetu, 1969), 34.

53 Later generations of Ruthenian-Ukrainian patriots in Galicia—for the most part, Greek Catholic priests—had problems with the popularization of Shevchenko's works, not so much because of the anti-Uniate thrust of his poetry as because of the unorthodox nature of his Christianity, which bordered on heresy. See Y. Hrytsak, "Poshyrennia poemy 'Mariia' v Halychyni," *Radians'ke literaturoznavstvo* 3 (1986): 51–54.

54 Taras Shevchenko, *The Poetical Works of Taras Shevchenko: The Kobzar*, trans. C. H. Andrusyshen and Watson Kirkconnell (Toronto: Published for the Ukrainian Canadian Committee by the University of Toronto Press, 1964), 323.

55 See Volodymyr Navrots'kyi, "Ru'ska rodyna (Heohrafichnyi obzor zemli zaselenoi Rusynamy)," *Pravda*, 11 November 1867, 180–82; *Pravda*, 21 November 1867, 188–91; *Pravda*, 1 December 1867, 196–98; *Pravda*, 11 December 1867, 204–6; and *Pravda*, 21 December 1867, 211–13, reprinted in Volodymyr Navrots'ky, *Tvory: Vydanie posmertne z portretom i zhytiepysom. Zakhodom"Etnohrafichno-statystychnoho kruzhka*," vol. 1 (Lviv, 1885), 3–27.

56 Uliana Kravchenko, *Khryzantemy: povist'* (Chicago: M. Denysiuk, 1961), 130–31. Yulia Schneider (Uliana Kravchenko) describes how, as a little girl, she would crawl into the attic of her grandmother's house to read books, traveling throughout Ukraine and "moving her finger over the map."

57 Mykhailo Drahomanov, *Avstro-rus'ki spomyny (1867–1877)* (Kyiv: Naukova dumka, 2003), 62, 174; Ivan Franko, "Stara Rus'," *LNV* 34, bk. 6 (1906): 457, 460, 466.

58 S[vystun], *Chem est' dlia nas Shevchenko?*, 13–14.

59 O. A. Monchalovskii, *Zhytie i deiatelnost Ivana Naumovicha* (Lviv, 1889), 80.

60 Imenem mnohykh [Ivan Naumovich], "Pohliad v buduchnost'," *Slovo*, 8 August 1866, 1–2.

61 Cited in Rudnytsky, *Essays*, 331.
62 A. S. Pushkin, *Sochineniia, v trekh tomakh*, 3 vols. (Moscow: Gosudarstvennoe izdatel'stvo khudozhestvennoi literatury, 1955), vol. 1, 306.
63 Rudnytsky, *Essays*, 329–33; Wendland, *Die Russophilen in Galizien*, passim.
64 Osip Bodianskii [Osyp Bodians'kyi], "Predislovie" (Foreword) to Denys Zubritskii [Zubryts'kyi], *Kritiko-istoricheskaia povest' vremennykh let Chervonoi ili Galitskoi Rusi*, trans. from the Polish (Moscow: Obshchestvo istorii i drevnostei Rossiiskikh pri Moskovskom Universitete, 1845), vii.
65 I. Naumovich [Naumovych], "O Galitskoi Rusi," *Slavianskii sbornik* 1 (1875): 31.
66 N. V. Iastrebov, *Galitsiia nakanune Velikoi Voiny 1914 g.* (Petrograd: Tip. A. E. Kollins, 1915), vi–vii.
67 Maria Todorova, *Imagining the Balkans* (New York: Oxford University Press, 1997), 85. See the Ukrainian patriot Oleksandr Konysky's typical acknowledgment of the state of public awareness in Russian-ruled Ukraine: "In our country," he wrote to Ivan Franko in 1884, "people know far less about Galicia than about Paris." Cited in Mykhailo Vozniak, "Zhurnal'ni plany Franka v rr. 1884–1886," *Ukraina* 3 (1927): 30.
68 N. B., "Pisn' (na temu "Was ist des Teutschen Vaterland?")," *Słowianin, Dwotygodnik Polityczny* 1, no. 11 (1 June 1869): 175–76.
69 Cited in Drahomanov, *Avstro-rus'ki spomyny*, 85.
70 For detailed discussion of this, see the chapter "The Great Breakthrough."
71 For a comparison of all three poems, see Viktoriia Artemieva, "Ukrains'ki students'ki hurtky u Lvovi" (graduate thesis, Lviv 1996), 39–40. However, Artemieva indicates Stebelsky's authorship only with regard to the first two poems, failing to note that he was also the author of the third one, which was signed by the pseudonym "Ivan Iskra." For information on the decoding of this pseudonym, see O. I. Dei, *Slovnyk ukrains'kykh psevdonimiv ta kryptonimiv; XVI–XX st.* (Kyiv: Naukova dumka, 1969), 183.
72 For details on Volodymyr Stebelsky, see Gabriel Korbut, *Od roku 1864 do 1919*, vol. 4 of *Literatura Polska od początków do wojny światowej: książka podręczna informacyjna dla studjujących naukowo dzieje pismiennictwa polskiego*, 2nd ed. (Warsaw: Skład główny w Kasie im. Mianowskiego, 1931), 224–25; Iv. [Ivan] Franko, "Postscriptum pro Vol. Stebel's'koho," *LNV* 23, no. 12 (December 1905): 214–24.
73 Karl Marx and Friedrich Engels, "Manifesto of the Communist Party," in Karl Marx and Friedrich Engels, *Selected Works*, vol. 1 (Moscow: Progress Publishers, 1969), located at: http://www.marxists.org/archive/marx/works/1848/communist-manifesto/index.htm
74 Alina Molska, ed., *Pierwsze pokolenie marksistów polskich: wybór pism i materiałów źródłowych z lat 1878–1886* (Warsaw: Książka i Wiedza, 1962), vol. 1, 423.
75 Bolesław Limanowski, *Pamiętniki (1870–1907)* (Warsaw: Książka i Wiedza, 1958), vol. 2, 256–57; *Marks i Engels o Polsce: zbiór materiałów, ed. H. Michnik*, vol. 2 (Warsaw: Książka i Wiedza, 1960), 126–27; Molska, *Pierwsze pokolenie*, vol. 2, 761–65; Pavlyk, *Perepyska*, vol. 3, 291–93.
76 Pavlyk, *Perepyska*, vol. 2, 91–92.

Chapter 6

1 Ossowski, *O ojczyźnie i narodzie*, 15–46. See also a very interesting attempt to apply Ossowski's theory to Belarusian and Ukrainian peasants: Volodymyr Medzhets'kyi, "Seliany u natsiotvorchykh protsesakh Tsentral'noi i Skhidnoi Ievropy u druhii polovyni XIX–na pochatku XX stolittia," *Ukraina moderna* 6 (2001): 59–76.

2   Swietłana N. Tołstaja, "Ojczyzna w ludowej tradycji słowianskiej," in Bartmiński, *Pojęcie ojczyzny*, 17–22.

3   Dei, *Kolomyiky v zapysakh Ivana Franka*.

4   Franko, *Halyts'ko-rus'ki narodni prypovidky*, vol. 2, 484.

5   Ibid., 87–88.

6   Ibid., 246.

7   Ibid., 237.

8   Robert Thomas Anderson, *Traditional Europe: A Study in Anthropology and History* (Belmont, CA: Wadsworth, 1971), 141–51; Heretz, *Russian Apocalypse*, p. 130; Kłoskowska, *National Cultures*, p. 48; Alexander H. Krappe, *The Science of Folklore* (New York: Norton, 1964), 153.

9   *Litopys rus'kyi: za ipat'skym spyskom*, trans. Leonid Makhnovets' (Kyiv: Dnipro, 1989), 343, 375, 432, 434.

10 See Sysyn, "Otchyzna."

11 In individual cases its "high" origins are obvious. For example, listed among the proverbs in Matvii Nomys-Symonov's collection of Ukrainian proverbs and sayings, published in St. Petersburg in 1864, is a verbatim quotation from Samiilo Velychko's Cossack chronicle: "Bida v Ukraini: i ottol horiache, i otsel boliache" (There is calamity in Ukraine: on the one hand it [the situation] is impassioned, and on the other—painful.") See M. Nomys, comp., *Ukrains'ki prykazky, prysliv'ia y take ynshe: zbirnyky O. V. Markovycha y druhykh* (St. Petersburg: V drukarniakh Tyblena i komp. I. Kulisha, 1864), 15.

12 [Platon Lukashevych], *Malorossiiskiia i chervonorusskiia narodnyia dumy i piesni* (St. Petersburg: Tip. "Pratsia," 1836), 103.

13 Dei, *Kolomyiky v zapysakh Ivana Franka*, 34; Vasyl' Sokil, comp., *Narodni pisni z bat'kivshchyny Ivana Franka* (Lviv: Kameniar, 2003), 147, 187, 234, 302; see also O. I. Dei, *Spilkuvannia myttsiv z narodnoiu poeziieiu: Ivan Franko ta ioho otochennia* (Kyiv: Naukova dumka, 1981), 17.

14 Iurii Luts'kyi [George S. N. Luckyj], "Rozdumy nad slovom 'Ukraina' u narodnykh pisniakh," *Suchasnist'* 8 (1993): 117–22.

15 Franko, *Halyts'ko-rus'ki narodni prypovidky*, vol. 2, 58; Dei, *Kolomyiky v zapysakh Ivana Franka*, 13–14, 29, 45, 60, 76, 82, 86–87.

16 One Christmas *vertep* (Ukrainian puppet theater) comedy dating to 1600–1620 features a folksong whose words aptly convey the sense of this utopia: "Da ne bude luchche / Da ne bude krashche / Iak u nas na Ukraini,— / Shcho ne maie zhyda / Shcho ne maie liakha, / Ne maie Unii" [There will be nothing better / nothing finer / Than the day when in our Ukraine / There will be no Jew / There will be no Liakh / And no Union]. Cited in Drahomanov, *Vybrane*, 23.

17 Franko, *Halyts'ko-rus'ki narodni prypovidky*, vol. 2, 280–81; Dei, *Kolomyiky v zapysakh Ivana Franka*, 80, 121.

18 John-Paul Himka, "On the Left Hand of God: 'Peoples' in Ukrainian Icons of the Last Judgement," in *States, Societies, Cultures: East and West: Essays in Honor of Jaroslaw Pelenski*, eds. Janusz Duzinkiewicz et al. (New York: Ross, 2004), 324, 326. Of course, the image of the Cossacks is found only once in these icons and only in a specific context: as allies of the Tatars (which clearly reflects Cossack-Tatar alliances during the rule of hetmans Bohdan Khmelnytsky and Petro Doroshenko).

19 For examples of the use of this term prior to the nineteenth century, see Oleksandr Ohloblyn, *Liudy staroi Ukrainy* (Munich: Dniprova khvylia, 1959), 185, 217.

20 Tarnvas'kyi, *Spohady*, 171.

21 Dei, *Kolomyiky v zapysakh Ivana Franka*, 31, 116.

22　Franko, *Halyts'ko-rus'ki narodni prypovidky*, vol. 2, 526.

23　M. M. Kravets', *Selianstvo Skhidnoi Halychyny i Pivnichnoi Bukovyny u druhii polovyni XIX st.* (Lviv: Vyd-vo L'vivs'koho universytetu, 1964), 43.

24　Dei, *Kolomyiky v zapysakh Ivana Franka*, 48, 105, 107, 110, 112.

25　Franko, *Halyts'ko-rus'ki narodni prypovidky*, vol. 2, 284–85; Dei, *Kolomyiky v zapysakh Ivana Franka*, 81.

26　Dei, *Kolomyiky v zapysakh Ivana Franka*, 16, 19, 35–36, 38, 42–43, 58, 64, 81–82, 93, 100, 102, 105, 107, 120, 124.

27　For references to Boryslav in the local folklore, see Franko's survey published in the regular column "Znadoby do vyvchennia movy i etnohrafii ukrains'koho narodu" [Materials on the Study of the Language and Ethnography of the Ukrainian People] featured in the journal *Svit* (1882) [*ZT* 26:186–93].

28　Dei, *Kolomyiky v zapysakh Ivana Franka*, 56, 82, 100, 110, 114.

29　In the nineteenth century the border was not a significant obstacle for peasants. Denys Lukiianovych wrote a fact-based novella about the Podillian village of Vil'khivtsi, which was divided by the border into two parts: Austrian and Russian. The peasants on the Austrian side performed corvée labor for a Russian landowner until serfdom was abolished in the Russian Empire in 1861, despite the fact that the corvée had been abolished in Galicia back in 1848. For a long time after the abolition of serfdom the peasants were involved in a lawsuit against the landowner for the right to work the land on both sides of the border. See Denys Lukiianovych, "Za Kadyl'nu," in Denys Lukiianovych, *Vybrani tvory* (Kyiv: Dnipro, 1973), 17–113. In 1892, at the peak of the Galician-Ruthenian peasant immigration to the Russian Empire, the border was crossed by 6,000 peasants, of whom less than half (2,800) went back. See Tadeusz Pilat, "Wychodstwo z powiatów podolskich do Rosyi w roku 1892," *Wiadomości Statystyczne o stosunkach krajowych* 13 (1892): 229.

30　Franko, *Halyts'ko-rus'ki narodni prypovidky*, vol. 2, 560.

31　Dei, *Kolomyiky v zapysakh Ivana Franka*, 71.

32　Hohenberg and Lees, *The Making of Urban Europe*, 89–90, 94–95.

33　Fernand Braudel, *History and Environment*, vol. 1 of *The Identity of France*, 1st US ed. (New York: Harper and Row, 1988), 99.

34　Hernando de Soto, *The Mystery of Capital: Why Capitalism Triumphs in the West and Fails Everywhere Else* (London: Bantam, 2000), 81.

35　See Stauter-Halsted, *The Nation in the Village*, 26.

36　Susanne Luber, *Die Herkunft von Zaporoger Kosacken des 17. Jahrhunderts nach Personnennamen* (Berlin: Osteuropa-Institut; Wiesbaden: In Kommission bei Harrassowitz, 1983), 108–9.

37　Zamorski, "Zasadnicze linie," 104.

38　Willard Sunderland, "An Empire of Peasants: Empire-Building, Interethnic Interaction, and Ethnic Stereotyping in the Rural World of the Russian Empire, 1800–1850s," in *Imperial Russia: New Histories for the Empire*, ed. Jane Burbank and David L. Ransel (Bloomington: Indiana University Press, 1998), 176.

39　Benedict Anderson, *Imagined Communities: Reflections on the Origin and Spread of Nationalism*, rev. ed. (London: Verso, 1991), 53–56.

40　Antoni Mączak, *Odkrywanie Europy: Podróże w czasach renesansu i baroku* (Gdansk: Wydawnictwo Novus Orbis, 1998), 238–43.

41　John-Paul Himka, *Galician Villagers and the Ukrainian National Movement in the Nineteenth Century* (Edmonton: Canadian Institute of Ukrainian Studies, University of Alberta, in association with Macmillan Press, London, 1988), 10, n. 182; Ia. U. Holovatskii,

"Velykaia Khorvatyia abo Halychsko Karpatskaia Rus'," in *Vinok rusynam na obzhynky uplil...*, pt. 2, comp. Ivan B. U. Holovatskii (Vienna: 1847), 169–71.

42 Franko, *Halyts'ko-rus'ki narodni prypovidky*, vol. 1, 102; vol. 2, 67.

43 Dei, *Kolomyiky v zapysakh Ivana Franka*, 14, 16, 113.

44 Ibid., 100.

45 Holovatskii, "Velykaia Khorvatyia," 169.

46 Michael Cherniavsky, *Tsar and People: Studies in Russian Myths* (New Haven: Yale University Press, 1961), 104–20.

47 [Lukashevych], *Malorossiiskiia i chervonorusskiia narodnyia dumy*, 64; *Istoricheskiia pesni malorusskago naroda, s obiasneniiami Vl. Antonovicha i M. Dragomanova*, vol. 1 (Kyiv: Tip. M. Fritsa, 1874), 93.

48 Valiantsina Vasileuna Hryhorieva and Alena Mikalaeuna Filatava, "Kanfesiinae stanovishcha na Belarusi: XIX stahodze," in *Samoidentyfikacja mniejszości narodowych i religijnych w Europie Środkowo-Wschodniej; Problematyka atłasowa*, ed. Jan Skarbek (Lublin: IESW–Wydawnictwo Instytutu Europy Środkowo-Wschodniej, 1998), 88; Volodymyr Pashuk, *Zarobitchany Pravoberezhnoi Ukrainy: druha polovyna XIX st.* (Lviv: Instytut ukrainoznavstva im. I. Kryp'iakevycha NAN Ukrainy, 2001), 140; David Saunders, "What Makes a Nation a Nation? Ukrainians since 1600," *Ethnic Groups* 10, nos. 1–3 (1993): 111–12; Karel C. Berkhoff, *Harvest of Despair: Life and Death in Ukraine under Nazi Rule* (Cambridge, MA: Belknap Press of Harvard University Press, 2004), 206–7.

49 Heretz, *Russian Apocalypse*.

50 Natalia Kononenko, *Ukrainian Minstrels: And the Blind Shall Sing* (Armonk, NY: M. E. Sharpe, 1998), 70, 92–93. Another researcher of the folk bard culture excludes the western Ukrainian lands from the geographic range of its reach. However, he is not entirely certain about the Carpathian region. See William Noll, "The Social Role and Economic Status of Blind Peasant Minstrels in Ukraine," *Harvard Ukrainian Studies* 27, nos. 1–2 (June 1993): 51, 56.

51 Franko, *Halyts'ko-rus'ki narodni prypovidky*, vol. 2, 252.

52 Ibid., 302, 370.

53 Ibid., 252.

54 Ibid., 302, 370.

55 Myron [Ivan Franko], "Zamichatelnaia koliadka," *Kievskaia starina* 24, bk. 1 (1889): 232.

56 Volodymyr Hnatiuk, comp., *Halyts'ko-ruski narodni liegendy* (Lviv, 1902), 186 [*Etnohrafichnyi zbirnyk*, vol. 12].

57 Franko, *Halyts'ko-rus'ki narodni prypovidky*, vol. 2, 412.

58 Ibid., 419; vol. 3, 53.

59 Hnatiuk, *Halyts'ko-rus'ki narodni liegendy*, 187.

60 Franko, *Halyts'ko-rus'ki narodni prypovidky*, vol. 2, 247.

61 "Redaktor Osip Markov," *Russka Pravda* (Vienna) 1 (1889). (I am citing according to VR LNB, fond 167 (Ivan Levytsky), list 2, file 2102, sub-file 64 (Markiv [Markov] Osyp Andriiovych), fol. 8).

62 I. Naumovich, "Nazad k narodu!" *Slovo*, 19 (31) May 1881, 2.

63 John-Paul Himka, "Hope in the Tsar: Displaced Naïve Monarchism among the Ukrainian Peasants of the Habsburg Empire," *Russian History / Histoire Russe* 7, nos. 1–2 (1980): 125–38.

64 Hnatiuk, *Halyts'ko-rus'ki narodni liegendy*, 186.

65 Heretz, *Russian Apocalypse*, passim.

66 According to a folk song composed about the tragic death of Elisabeth (Sisi), the wife of Emperor Franz Josef, and recorded by Franko, "Our lady the empress is of Ruthenian origin" (in another version, she is of "human origin") and "she experienced tragic torment from her enemies" because "she was so good / like one's own mother," who "safeguarded the land" and "abolished all the shackles / of the streets and cudgels." In this song Emperor Franz Josef is portrayed as "first after God," who, together with his wife, sits in Vienna and only thinks, "Oh, what kind of presents should be given to those people." See Ivan Franko, "Zrazok novozlozhenoi nar. pisni," *LNV* 10, no. 4 (April 1900): 54. As a fascinating side-note, one may add the following fact: in the home of Mykhailo Pavlyk's father hung two portraits: one of the Russian tsar and the other of the Austrian emperor. See TsDIAL, fond 663, list 1, file 225, fol. 128. I am grateful to Ihor Chornovol, who pointed this out to me.

67 Semen Vityk, "Iz moikh spomyniv pro Franka," in *Ivan Franko u spohadakh suchasnykiv*, comps. O. I. Dei and N. P. Korniienko (Lviv: Kameniar, 1972), 48–49.

68 See the chapter titled "Franko and His Jews."

69 Franko, *Halyts'ko-rus'ki narodni prypovidky*, vol. 2, 370.

70 Bohdan Struminski, "Stereotyp Polaka w przysłowiach ukraińskich," in *Narody i stereotypy*, ed. Teresa Walas (Cracow: Międzynarodowe Centrum Kultury, 1995), 138.

71 Ibid., 140; Franko, *Halyts'ko-rus'ki narodni prypovidky*, vol. 2, 252, 302, 369–70. I must caution again that in researching stereotypes, it is not as important to determine the numerical quantity of each group of sayings as it is to reveal the diverse images and types that appear in them.

72 Franko, *Halyts'ko-rus'ki narodni prypovidky*, vol. 2, 569.

73 Ibid., 568.

74 Ibid., 569.

75 For detailed discussion, see Franz K. Stanzel, *Europäer: Ein imagologischer Essay*, 2nd updated ed. (Heidelberg: Universitäts verlag C. Winter, 1998). For information on the spread of this genre in the Rzeczpospolita, see Hubert Orłowski, *"Polnische Wirtschaft": Nowoczesny niemiecki dyskurs o Polsce* (Olsztyn: Borussia, 1998), 47.

76 Franko, *Halyts'ko-rus'ki narodni prypovidky*, vol. 2, 451, 568.

77 Ibid., 568.

78 Walter Connor, *Ethnonationalism: The Quest for Understanding* (Princeton, NJ: Princeton University Press, 1994), 103.

79 Franko, *Halyts'ko-rus'ki narodni prypovidky*, vol. 2, 568.

80 Sunderland, "Empire of Peasants," 180.

81 Cited in Andrii Franko, "Hryhorii Il'kevych iak etnohraf," *ZNTSh* 109 (1912): 109.

82 The censors removed this proverb from Ilkevych's collection. Ibid., 115.

83 Franciszek Bujak, *Żmiąca: wieś powiatu limanowskiego: Stosunki gospodarcze i społeczne* (Cracow: G. Gebethner, 1903), 132.

84 Oleh Turii, ed., *Holovna Ruska Rada (1848–1851): Protokoly zasidan' i knyhy korespondentsii* (Lviv: In-t istorii tserkvy Ukrains'koho Katolyts'koho Universytetu, 2002), 51–52, 56–57; Volodymyr Pylypovych, comp., *Za viru, narid i prava: Ruski Rady Nadsiannia 1848–1850 rr.* (Przemysl: Peremys'kyi viddil OUP, 2005), 87–93, 170–72, 190–91, 215–16, 232, 235–37, 240, 264–76.

85 Iurii Kmit, "Z sil's'kykh vidnosyn u Halychyni v seredyni XIX v.," *ZNTSh* 54, no. 4 (1903): 48.

86 Bujak, *Z odległej i bliskiej przeszłości*, 137.

87 Sahlins, *Boundaries*, 110–13.

Chapter 7

1   Rostyslav Chopyk, "Prychynky do flory i fauny Frankovoho L´vova," in *Henii mistsia: L´viv, Leopolis, Lemberg, Lwów*, ed. Taras Vozniak (Lviv, 2004), 205 [=*Yi, nezalezhnyi kul´turolohichnyi chasopys* 29 (2003)].

2   VR IL, fond 59, file 2753, fol. 193 (a fragment from the journal of Osyp Makovei, who arrived in Lviv to embark on his studies in September 1879); Mykhailo Vahylevych, "Denys: povist´," *Druh*, 15 [27] January 1876, 27; Stepan Shakh, *L´viv—misto moiei molodosty* (Munich: Khrystyians´kyi holos, 1955–56), 124.

3   Kohl, *Austria, Vienna, Prague*, 458; Walburga Litschauer, ed., *Dokumente zum Leben der Anna von Revertera*, vol. 2 of *Neue Dokumente zum Schubert-Kreis: aus Briefen und Tagebüchern seiner Freunde* (Vienna: Musikwissenschaftlicher Verlag, 1993), 16.

4   Iaroslav Dashkevych, "Davnii L´viv u virmens´kykh ta virmens´ko-kypchats´kykh dzherelakh," *Ukraina v mynulomu* 1 (1992): 7–13; Iaroslav Isaievych, "Iak vynyklo misto pid nazvoiu L´viv," in *L´viv: Istorychni narysy*, ed. Iaroslav Isaievych, Feodosii Steblii, and Mykola Lytvyn (Lviv: Instytut ukrainoznavstva im. I. Kryp´iakevycha NAN Ukrainy, 1996), 9–10, 20, 22; see also Isaievych's "Al´tana posered raiu: L´viv u 1582–1602 rr.," Iaroslav Isaievych, "Iak vynyklo misto," 35.

5   Hohenberg and Lees, *The Making of Urban Europe*, 1.

6   Braudel, *The Mediterranean*, vol. 1, 224.

7   See Yaroslav Hrytsak, "Lviv: A Multicultural History through the Centuries," in *Lviv: A City in the Crosscurrents of Culture* [=*Harvard Ukrainian Studies* 24 (2000), Special Issue], ed. John Czaplicka (Cambridge, MA: Harvard Ukrainian Research Institute, 2002), 47–73.

8   Stanisław Hoszowski, *Ekonomiczny rozwój Lwowa w latach 1772–1914* (Lviv: Nakładem Izby Przemysłowo-Handlowej we Lwowie, 1935), 107.

9   Ibid., 19, 56.

10 Mykola Bevz, "Ukrains´ki transformatsii tsentral´noi chastyny mista Lvova u XIX–XX st.," in *Arkhitektura Halychyny XIX –XX st.; Vybrani materialy mizhnarodnoho sympoziumu 24–27 travnia 1994 r., prysviachenoho 150-richchiu zasnuvannia Derzhavnoho universytetu "L´vivs´ka politekhnika,"* ed. Bohdan Cherkes, Martin Kubelik, and Elizabet Hofer (Lviv: L´vivs´ka politekhnika, 1996), 53–69; Olgierd Czerner, "Przekształcenia architektoniczne Lwowa w latach 1772–1848," ibid., 79.

11 Józef Szocki, *Księgozbiory domowe w Galicji wschodniej (1772–1918)* (Cracow: Wydawnictwo Naukowe Akademii Pedagogicznej, 2001), 81–82. See also Janina Kulczycka-Saloni, "Geografia literacka Polski pod zaborami," in *Polska XIX wieku: Państwo, społeczeństwo, kultura*, ed. Stefan Kieniewicz (Warsaw: Wiedza powszechna, 1977), 466–508.

12 During a brief period of liberalization in the first half of the 1870s, Kyiv became one of the centers of Ukrainian-language publishing. However, renewed repressions against the Ukrainian language (1876) nullified its importance. See Hamm, *Kiev: A Portrait*, 99–100. Unfortunately, I have not found any statistics on Jewish publication; the existing tally of Jewish book publications only goes up to 1863. See Yeshayahu Vinograd, *Otsar ha-sefer ha-Ivri: reshimat ha-sefarim she-nidpesu be-ot Ivrit me-reshit ha-defus ha-Ivri bi-shenat 229 (1469) ad shenat 623 (1863)*, 2 vols. (Jerusalem: ha-Makhon le-bibliyografyah memuḥshevet, 754, 1993), vol. 1, 24–37.

13 Heck, "Bibliografia Polska z r. 1881," 1096.

14 Maciszewski, "Kraków," in Sulimierski et al., *Słownik geograficzny*, vol. 4, 601; Kl. Przed., "Kijów," ibid., 90; Ludwik Dziedzicki, "Lwów," in Sulimierski et al., *Słownik geograficzny*,

vol. 5, 508; A. Załeski, W. Korotyński, J. Banzemer, and B. Chlebowski, "Warszawa," in *Słownik geograficzny*, vol. 13, 24; Józef Bielinski, "Wilno," ibid., 494; Herlihy, "Ukrainian Cities," 136; Paul R. Magocsi, *Historical Atlas of East Central Europe* (Toronto: University of Toronto Press, 1993), 96 (N.B.: Magocsi erroneously presents data for the year 1880 as data for 1870.); *Hickmann's...Atlas*, map no. 36; *Wiadomości statystyczne o stosunkach krajowych* 8, no. 1 (1883): 44–45.

15   With a population of 196,000 in 1910 and demographic growth at 125 percent in 1870–1910, in terms of one of these two indicators—demographic growth—Lviv still lagged behind Vienna (2 million and 143 percent, respectively); Budapest (880,000 and 175 percent); Prague (640,000 and 154 percent); Warsaw (512,000 and 114 percent); Odessa (520,000 and 181 percent); Wroclaw (512,000 and 114 percent); Lodz (352,000 and 803 percent [sic]); Kyiv (323,000 and 154 percent); Szczecin (236,000 and 191 percent); Vilnius (168,000 and 166 percent); Cracow (150,000 and 200 percent); and Minsk (100,000 and 178 percent). See Hrytsak, "Lviv," 67.

16   These statistics are cited in *Ludność podług zawodu i sposobu zarobkowania: Ludność przemysłowa. Wykaz przedsiębiorstw przemysłowych w całym kraju*, bk. 11 of *Rocznik statystyki przemysłu i handlu krajowego* (Lwów: Wyd. Krajowe Biuro Statystyczne [Oddział Statystyki Przemysłu i Handlu], 1888), 2–13, 16–17.

17   Roman Horak and Iaroslav Hnativ, *Ivan Franko*, bk. 4, *Universytet* (Lviv: Vyd-vo ottsiv Vasyliian "Misioner," 2004), 171.

18   Harald Binder, "Making and Defending a Polish Town: "Lwów" (Lemberg), 1848–1914," in *Austrian History Yearbook*, vol. 34, 2003, 57–81; Yaroslav Hrytsak and Victor Susak, "Constructing a National City: The Case of L´viv," in *Composing Urban History and the Constitution of Civic Identities*, ed. John J. Czaplicka and Blair A. Ruble; assisted by Lauren Crabtree (Washington, DC: Woodrow Wilson Center Press; Baltimore: Johns Hopkins University Press, 2003), 140–64.

19   Limanowski, *Pamiętniki*, vol. 1, 19–20.

20   Ievhen Olesnyts´kyi, *Storinky z moho zhyttia*, vol. 1: *1860–1890* (Lviv: Dilo, 1935), 127.

21   This phrase was used by Karl Stremayer, Imperial Minister for Education, in a letter that he wrote to Emperor Franz Josef on the occasion of the inauguration of the University of Chernivtsi. Cited in Fred Stambrook, "The Golden Age of the Jews of Bukovina, 1880–1914," Working Paper 03-2, Center for Austrian Studies at the University of Minnesota, October 2003, 9, 18.

22   Armand Freiherr von Dumreicher, *Die Verwaltung der Universitäten seit dem letzten politischen Systemwechsel in Oesterreich* (Vienna: A. Hölder, 1873), 106.

23   Xaver Liske, *Der angebliche Niedergang der Universität Lemberg: Offenes Sendschreiben an das Reichsrathsmitglied Herrn dr Eduard Suess prof. an der Universität Wien* (Lemberg, 1876), 5, 15.

24   Adam Wandruszka and Peter Urbanitsch, eds., *Die Habsburgermonarchie 1848–1918*, vol. 3: *Die Völker des Reiches*, pt. 1 (Vienna: Verl. d. Österr. Akad. d. Wiss., 1980), Table 10; Iwo Pollo, *Nauka i szkolnictwo wyższe w Polsce, a odzyskanie niepodległości* (Lublin: Wydawnictwa Uczelniane Politechniki Lubelskiej, 1990), 19.

25   Franko's view of Yevsebii Cherkavsky as a Polish chauvinist is not entirely just. It would be more correct to describe him as an individual who was extremely loyal to the government's policies, and whose views changed with every change in the official line. In 1859 he supported the introduction of the Latin orthography into the Ruthenian language, and two years later, in 1861, he opposed the introduction of the Polish language at the University of Cracow (which led to his beating at the hands of some Polish students). In 1868–1872 he advocated the introduction of the

Polish language at Lviv University. See Chlędowski, *Pamiętniki*, vol. 1, 35, 56; Antoni Knot, "Czerkawski, Euzebiusz," in *Polski słownik biograficzny*, vol. 4 (Cracow: Polska Akademia Umiejętności, 1938), 333–34.

26 Kazimierz Szmyd, *Twórcy nauk o wychowaniu w środowisku akademickim Lwowa, 1860–1939* (Rzeszow: Wydawn. Uniwersytetu Rzeszowskiego, 2003), 34, 59.

27 Omelian Ohonovskii [Ohonovs′kyi], *Istoriia literatury ruskoi*, 3 vols. (Lviv: Tovarystvo im. Shevchenka, 1887–93), vol. 3, 924–25.

28 Ibid., 925.

29 Iv. Franko, introduction to M. Drahomanov, *Lysty do Iv. Franka i ynshykh*, 2 vols. in 1, vol. 1: *1881–1886* (Lviv: Nakladom Ukrains′ko-rus′koi vydavnychnoi spilky, 1906–<1908>), 5–6.

30 Pavlyk, *Perepyska*, vol. 2, 77.

31 Mykhailo Rudnyts′kyi, *Pys′mennyky zblyz′ka: Spohady* (Lviv: Knyzhkovo-zhurnal′ne vyd-vo, 1958), 71.

32 Richard Stites, *The Women's Liberation Movement in Russia: Feminism, Nihilism, and Bolshevism, 1860–1930* (Princeton, NJ: Princeton University Press, 1978), 93.

33 Rudnyts′kyi, *Pys′mennyky zblyz′ka*, 72.

34 Zawadski, *Pamiętniki z życia literackiego*, 33–34.

35 V. Matula and I. Churkina, eds., *Zarubezhnye slaviane i Rossiia: Dokumenty arkhiva M. F. Raevskogo 40–80 godov XIX veka* (Moscow: Akademiia nauk SSSR, Institut slavianovedeniia i balkanistiki, Nauka, 1975), 139.

36 Hamm, *Kiev: A Portrait*, 63–64, 101; Brian Porter, *When Nationalism Began to Hate: Imagining Modern Politics in Nineteenth-Century Poland* (New York: Oxford University Press, 2000), 80–81.

37 See Janusz Krajewski's entry, "Ochorowicz, Julian," in *Polski słownik biograficzny*, vol. 23 (Wroclaw; Warsaw; Cracow; Gdansk: Wydawnictwo PAN, 1978), 499–505.

38 See Stauter-Halstead, *Nation in the Village*, 26.

39 See Stanisław Gąbiński's entry, "Biliński, Leon," in *Polski słownik biograficzny*, vol. 2 (Cracow: Polska Akademia Umiejętności, 1936), 97–98.

40 M. M. Parkhomenko, "Ivan Franko—student L′vivs′koho universytetu," in *Ivan Franko: Statti i materialy* 5 (1956): 191–92.

41 Vasyl′ Lukych, "Spomyny pro Ivana Franka," in Hnatiuk, *Spohady*, 61.

42 *Vulgo* (Latin): "put simply, put roughly, in the vulgate"; *Dzhedzhalyk*: Franko's pseudonym.

43 I suggest arguments for the concept of Lviv as a nationalizing city in my article, "Crossroads of East and West: Lemberg, Lwów, L′viv on the Threshold of Modernity," in *Austrian History Yearbook* 34 (2003): 103–9.

44 Mykhailo Hrushevs′kyi, *Z pochyniv ukrains′koho sotsiialistychnoho rukhu: Mykh. Drahomanov i zhenevs′kyi sotsiialistychnyi hurtok* [=Documents pour servir à l'histoire du mouvement social en Ukraine: Dragomanov et le groupe socialiste de Genève (Vienna: Institut sociologique ukrainien, Zakordonye [sic] biuro i sklad, 1922), 55.

45 Dol′nyts′kyi, "Spomyny pro molodoho Ivana Franka," 103.

46 Lukiianovych, "Khto mav vyrishalnyi vplyv," 6.

47 Artemieva, "Ukrains′ki students′ki hurtky u L′vovi," 42.

48 Lukych, "Spomyny pro Ivana Franka," 62. Vasyl Lukych (Levytsky), who corroborated the young Pavlyk's Russophilism, was not free of it himself. See Dolnytsky, "Spomyny pro molodoho Ivana Franka," 103. Yet Pavlyk claimed that Franko was already a populist, albeit a superficial one, when he was studying at the gymnasium. Proof of this, in Pavlyk's opinion, was that Franko wrote according to the phonetic orthography,

"which, for many at the time, was the sum of their populism." See Pavlyk, *Perepyska*, vol. 2, 7. See also the argument that took place later between Franko and Pavlyk about which orthography they had in fact used in their youth [*ZT* 35:44–46, 74].

49 The question of the influence and size of the subsidies that the Russian government awarded to Russophile organizations is still unresolved. There is no doubt, however, that these subventions did indeed exist (for documented testimonies from a later period, 1880–1910, see Oleksii Sukhyi, comp., *Moskvofil'stvo: Dokumenty i materialy* (Lviv: Vyd-vo L'vivs'koho universytetu, 2001), 89, 92–93, 100–107). However, it is difficult to establish their regularity and scale. On the other hand, it should be kept in mind that subsidies from the Russian Empire were also sent to populist institutions, but from Ukrainian activists. For example, the Shevchenko Society was founded in 1873 with funds supplied by the Poltava-based landowner Yelysaveta Myloradovych and several other donors. See Volodymyr Doroshenko, *Ohnyshche ukrains'koi nauky: Naukove Tovarystvo imeny T. Shevchenka z nahody 75-richchia ioho zasnuvannia* (New York: [Ameryka], 1951), 19.

50 Ievhen Olesnyts'kyi, "Z-ponad chetvertyny stolittia: Kartka z istorii ukrains'koi universytets'koi molodi," in Hnatiuk, *Spohady*, 66.

51 Artemieva, "Ukrains'ki students'ki hurtky," 48.

52 Lukych, "Spohady pro Ivana Franka," 62. It is worth noting that in their private conversations, Dolnytsky and Pavlyk called Franko a "chorągiewka"—i.e., an opportunist" or "shatashasia iazytsy" (wavering tongue). See Pavlyk, *Perepyska*, vol. 2, 58, 155, 160.

53 Dzhedzhalyk [Ivan Franko], "Napered!" *Druh*, 1 [13] October 1875, 40.

54 Dzhedzhalyk, "Pisnia Zadunaiskaia," *Druh*, 15 [27] January 1876, 33–34.

55 I. Sh., "Pis'ma o russkoi literature," *Druh*, 15 [27] April 1875, 190.

56 See M. O. (Myroslav Oleksandrovych) Moroz, comp., *Ivan Franko; bibliohrafiia tvoriv 1874–1964* (Kyiv: Naukova dumka, 1966), 18–19.

57 Iv[an] Franko, "Poeziia i iei stanovysko v nashykh vremenakh; Studiium estetychne," *Druh*, 15 [27] January 1876, 47.

58 Lukych, "Spomyny pro Ivana Franka," 63.

59 Franko was referring to Ustyianovych's poetic recasting of a story from the chronicles about Princess Olha's destruction of Iskorosten, the capital of the Derevlianian tribe. The last stanza of this poem features undisguised irony and the following condemnation: "And today the Drevi people / Exalt themselves as 'Ruthenians' / And call Olha / Beatific and holy…" See K. N. Ustyianovych, *Pys'ma*, vol. 1: *Poemy ystorychni* (Lviv: Tovarystvo im. Shevchenka, 1875), 368.

60 Osyp Nazaruk's words are cited in Artemieva, "Ukrains'ki students'ki hurtky," 25.

61 Ustyianovych, *M. F. Raevskii*, 48.

62 See, e.g., Himka, "Construction of Nationality," 109–64; A. I. Miller, *"Ukrainskii vopros" v politike vlastei i russkom obshchestvennom mnenii (vtoraia polovina XIX v.)* (St. Petersburg: Aleteiia, 2000).

63 Hans Kohn, *Nationalism: Its Meaning and History*, rev. ed. (Malabar, FL: Krieger, 1982), 38–49; Kozik, *Ukrainian National Movement*, 12; George S. N. Luckyj, *Between Gogol and Ševčenko; Polarity in the Literary Ukraine: 1798–1847*, Harvard Series in Ukrainian Studies, vol. 8 (Munich: W. Fink, 1971); Orest Pelech, "The State and the Ukrainian Triumvirate in the Russian Empire, 1831–47," in Bohdan Krawchenko, ed., *Ukrainian Past, Ukrainian Present* (New York: St. Martin's Press, 1993), 1–17. There are still many unresolved and conflicting aspects of the Brotherhood's history. For a brief survey of discussions on this topic, see Yaroslav Hrytsak, *Narys istorii Ukrainy: Formuvannia*

modernoi ukrains´koi natsii, XIX–XX stolittia (Kyiv: Vyd-vo "Heneza," 1996), 38–39; Orest Pelech, "The Cyril and Methodius Brotherhood Revisited," *Journal of Ukrainian Studies* 29, nos. 1–2 (Summer–Winter 2004): 335–44.

64 From a report sent by Illarion Vasilchikov, the governor-general of Kyiv, to the Ministry of Public Education (1862). Cited in Korotkyi and Ulianovs´kyi, *Syn Ukrainy*, vol. 2, 39.

65 From a denunciation written by the secret counselor, Mikhail Yuzefovich. Cited in *Serhii Podolyns´kyi, Lysty ta dokumenty*, comp. Roman Serbyn and Tetiana Sliudykova (Kyiv: TsDIAK, 2002), 435.

66 Drahomanov, "Avtobiograficheskaia zametka," 59; see also his *Avstro-rus´ki spomyny*, 219.

67 Drahomanov, "Literatura rosiis´ka, velykorus´ka, ukrains´ka i halyts´ka," in his *Literaturno-publitsystychni pratsi*, vol. 1, 117.

68 Volodymyr Mijakovskyj, "Kyivska Hromada (z istorii kyivs´koho hromads´koho rukhu 60–kh rokiv)" in his *Unpublished and Forgotten Writings: Political and Intellectual Trends of the Nineteenth Century; Modern Ukrainian Literature* [=*Nedrukovane i zabute: Hromadski rukhy deviatnadtsiatoho storichchia; Novitnia ukrainska literatura*], ed. Marko Antonovych (New York: Ukrainian Academy of Arts and Sciences in the US, 1984), 270.

69 According to stories circulating about Volodymyr Antonovych, he broke off relations with the members of the Kyiv Hromada (mostly likely with Professor Fedor Mishchenko of Kazan University) simply because the latter had dared place Dostoevsky on the same level as Dante. See Ihor Chornovol, "Mizh arkheolohiieiu ta politykoiu: Volodymyr Antonovych i pol´s´ke suspil´stvo (do 170-richchia vid dnia narodzhennia)," *Moloda natsiia* 32, no. 3 (2004): 134. For additional details of the Hromada members' discussions around the choice between the Western or Russian cultural model, see S. I. Svitlenko, *Narodnytstvo v Ukraini 60–80-kh rokiv XIX stolittia; Teoretychni problemy dzhereloznavstva ta istorii* (Dnipropetrovsk: Vyd-vo "Navchal´na knyha," 1999), 98–100.

70 A. M. Kruhlashov, *Drama intelektuala—politychni idei Mykhaila Drahomanova* (Chernivtsi: Vyd-vo "Prut," 2000), 123–25. Insight into Drahomanov's mode of thinking is provided by an episode from the early 1870s, which has come down to us in various versions thanks to two members of the Kyiv Hromada. At some meeting Drahomanov asked a sharply worded question about the inadmissibility of admitting the "bourgeoisie" to the Hromada; he was referring to the director of the Kyiv Industrial Bank, Vsevolod Rubinstein. Drahomanov also lambasted Viliam (William) Berenshtam, the owner of real estate in Kyiv; Mykhailo Starytsky, for his rusk-manufacturing business; and Luka Ilnytsky, about his bookstore. See A. F. Kistiakivs´kyi, *Shchodennyk (1874–1885): u dvokh tomakh*, comp. Valentyna S. Shandra et al., vol. 2: *1880–1885* (Kyiv: Naukova dumka, 1994–1995), 430–31; [V. Miiakovs´kyi], "Z opovidan´ Oresta Ivanovycha Levyts´koho," in *Naukovyi zbirnyk Ukrains´koi Vil´noi Akademii Nauk u Spoluchenykh Shtatakh Ameryky*, vol. 1 (New York: UVAN, 1952), 107.

71 Kisitakivs´kyi, *Shchodennyk*, vol. 2, 415–16, 455.

72 See *Arkhiv Mykhaila Drahomanova*, vol. 1: *Lystuvannia Kyivs´koi Staroi Hromady z M. Drahomanovym (1870–1895 rr.)* [=*Les archives de Michel Drahomanov*, vol. 1: *Correspondance avec les membres de l'association, Stara hromada de Kiev, Années 1870–1895*], ed. Roman Smal´-Stots´kyi (Warsaw: n. p., 1937).

73 Ihnat Zhytets´kyi, "Kyivska Hromada za 60-tykh rokiv," *Ukraina* 1 (1928): 95–96.

74 Kisitakivs´kyi, *Shchodennyk*, vol. 2, 455.

75 For detailed discussion, see Miller, "*Ukrainskii vopros*," 63–69. For detailed discussion of the support given by the Russian government and educated Russian society to Little

Russian culture in the earlier period, see Paul Bushkovits, "The Ukraine in Russian Culture 1790–1860: The Evidence of the Journals," *Jahrbücher für Geschichte Osteuropa* 39, no. 3 (1991): 339–63; Pelech, "The State and the Ukrainian Triumvirate," 3–6.

76 Geoffrey A. Hosking, *Russia: People and Empire, 1552–1917* (Cambridge, MA: Harvard University Press, 1997), 367–68.

77 For detailed discussion, see Miller, *"Ukrainskii vopros,"* 153–81.

78 Drahomanov, "Avtobiograficheskaia zametka," 62–63; *Mykhailo Drahomanov: Dokumenty i materialy, 1841–1994*, comp. Halyna Bolotova et al. (Lviv: [In-t ukrains'koi arkheohrafii ta dzhereloznavstva im. M. S. Hrushevs'koho], 2001), 94–107; R. P. Ivanova, *Mykhailo Drahomanov u suspil'no-politychnomu rusi Rosii ta Ukrainy (II polovyna XIX st.)* (Kyiv: Vyd-vo Kyivs'koho universytetu, 1971), 176–80.

79 Iv. [Ivan] Franko, introduction to M. Drahomanov, *Lysty do Iv. Franka*, vol. 1, 5–6.

80 Drahomanov, *Avstro-rus'ki spomyny*, 159.

81 TsDIAL, fond 152, list 2, file 14417, fol. 74.

82 Pavlyk, *Perepyska*, vol. 2, 33, 102.

83 Although this article was unsigned, the author's identity was later established on the basis of recollections. See Dol'nyts'kyi, "Spomyny pro Ivana Franka," 78.

84 Drahomanov, "Avtobiograficheskaia zametka," 55.

85 Ukrainets [M. Drahomanov], "Vtoroe pys'mo v redaktsiiu 'Druha,'" *Druh*, 1 [13] March 1876, 77–80; *Druh*, 15 [27] April 1876, 127–28; "Otpovid'" na 'vtoroe pys'mo' g. Ukraintsa," *Druh*, 1 [13] April 1876, 109–11.

86 "Tretie pys'mo Ukraintsa," *Druh*, 1 [13] July 1876, 201–3.

87 See Dol'nyts'kyi, "Spomyny pro Ivana Franka," 75–87; "Novynky," *Druh*, 15 [27] October 1876, 319; Franko, *Dokumenty i materialy*, 43–45, 49–51; Pavlyk, *Perepyska*, vol. 2, 24, 31, 38, 54, 99–100.

88 "Do rodymtsev, Pys'mo dlia beletrystyky i nauky," *Druh*, 1 [13] January 1876, 1.

89 "Krytyka na 'Druha' i otzyvy o nem," *Druh*, 24 July [5 August] 1876, 242.

90 Unsigned [M. Pavlyk], "Iz ust naroda," *Druh*, 1 [13] April 1876, 106–7.

91 "Literaturni pys'ma," *Druh*, 1 [13] May 1876, 140–44. The article was signed "Kh., Ch." because Pavlyk was afraid to sign it with his own name. The editors explained that these were two letters from their mailbag.

92 "Krytyka," *Druh*, 15 [27] June 1876, 191.

93 "Literaturni visti i krytyka," *Druh*, 1 [13] June 1876, 172.

94 "Nadoslane," *Druh*, 15 [27] May 1876, 159.

95 Ivan Verkhrats'kyi, *Odvit O. Partytskomu…i dekotry ynshy zamichania o lyteraturnoi stoinosty i tendentsiy 'Druha'* (Lviv: n. p., 1876).

96 "O. Stefan Kachala do redaktsii 'Druha,'" in Pavlyk, *Perepyska*, vol. 2, 78–81. Mykhailo Pavlyk found this unpublished letter among Drahomanov's papers after his death. Someone from the editorial board of *Druh*, most likely Volodymyr (Lukych) Levytsky, had forwarded this letter to Drahomanov. Ibid., 78.

97 "Nichto ob odnoi chasopisi: Iz Lvova," *Slovo*, 22 June [4 July] 1876, 1–2; *Slovo*, 25 June [7 July] 1876, 2–3; *Slovo*, 28 June [10 July] 1876, 2; *Slovo*, 1 [13] July 1876, 1–2; *Slovo*, 3 [15] July 1876, 2; *Slovo*, 6 [18] July 1876, 1–2; *Slovo*, 8 [20] July 1876, 1–2; "Ot Vostoka (Nichto o 'Druzi' i eho 'krytykakh,'" *Slovo*, 13 [25] July 1876, 3.

98 "Novynky," *Druh*, 15 [27] June 1876, 190. The audience gave Pavlyk a standing ovation. Bachynsky, the rector of the Lviv Theological Seminary, liked his speech so much that he invited Pavlyk to present it to the seminarians. See Pavlyk, *Perepyska*, vol. 2, 42–44, 50. For a reprint of the text of this speech, see Mykhailo Pavlyk, *Propashchyi cholovik: Opovidannia, povisti, publitsystyka* (Lviv: Kameniar, 1983), 295–322.

99 Pavlyk, *Perepyska*, vol. 2, 76.

100 Ivan Franko, *Pys'ma, [chast.] 1, Baliady i roskazy; Posviashcheno bl. divytse Nadezhde**** (Lviv: n. p., 1876). For the announcement about the appearance of this collection, see "Bibliohrafiia," *Druh*, 1 [13] July 1876, 207.

101 Dzhedzhalyk [Ivan Franko], "Pisnia Zadunaiskaia," *Druh*, 1 (13) February 1876, 33–34; see also his article, "Poeziia i ei stanovysko v nashykh vremenakh; Studiium estetychne," ibid., 44–47; and "Zhenshchyna-maty," ibid., 60–62.

102 "Novynky," *Druh*, 5 [27] March 1876, 96.

103 For detailed discussion, see S. V. Shchurat, "Povist' Ivana Franka 'Petrii i Dovbushchuky,'" in Franko, *Statti i materialy* 5 (1956): 191–215.

104 Franko eventually admitted this in the foreword to the second, revised, edition (1913) of his novel, calling this work "immature" [*ZT* 22:328–329].

105 "Vtoroe pys'mo v redaktsiiu 'Druha,'" *Druh*, 1 [13] March 1876), 79; M. Drahomanov, *Lysty do Iv. Franka*, vol. 2, 326.

106 Cited in Drahomanov, *Lysty do Iv. Franka*, vol. 2, 314–15.

107 Pavlyk, *Perepyska*, vol. 2, 26.

108 Ibid., 26, 30, 45, 47, 57–58, 63, 92, 123. In one of his autobiographies (1890) Franko wrote about his relationship with Pavlyk: "I became friendly with M. Pavlyk here [in Lviv after arriving from Drohobych—Y. H.]. Although we were both sons of peasants, our upbringing, evolution, and thought processes were very different, not to mention the great difference in temperament and habits. So it is no wonder that our friendship was actually an everlasting disagreement from the very beginning" [*ZT* 49:244]. These fractious relations persisted until Pavlyk's death in 1915. It is worth noting that, even though there was only a three-year age difference between the two men, they never addressed each other by the informal you (*ty*).

109 Pavlyk, *Perepyska*, vol. 2, 7–8, 61, 82.

110 Ibid., 57–58.

111 Pavlyk is probably not exaggerating: the desire to commit suicide is a frequent theme in Franko's correspondence, and it was particularly evident during the various dramatic reversals of his life [*ZT* 48:84, 95–96; 49:364, 461].

112 Pavlyk, *Perepyska*, vol. 2, 97.

113 *Druh*, 15 [27] October 1876, 312–13; *Druh*, 1 [13] November 1876, 321.

114 Il'kevych, *Halyts'ki prypovidky*, 39, 67, 73, 110, 116; Franko, *Halyts'ko-rus'ki narodni prypovidky*, vol. 2, 75, 106, 371. Mykhailo Pavlyk recounts a typical episode about one of the members of the Academic Circle, who was known for his "nobiliary venom": "My name is not Ivan, it is Ioann!" he shouted during a conversation with Pavlyk. See Pavlyk, *Perepyska*, vol. 2, 7.

115 VR LNB, fond 266 (Ivan Shpytkovsky), list 42, file 3, fol. 6; Kuz'movych, "Z iunykh lit Franka," 8.

116 Slups'kyi, *Ivan Franko: Dokumental'ni fotohrafii*, 27. From this day forward, Franko invariably appeared in public dressed in an embroidered shirt. But right before he died, he asked to be buried in an ordinary shirt, which request, however, was not carried out. See VR LNB, fond 192 (Ivan Franko Museum in Lviv), list 31, fol. 11.

Chapter 8

1 See Stanisław Grodziski, *W królewstwie Galicji i Lodomerii* (Cracow: Wydawn. Literackie, 1976), 265.

2   A similar story appears in the correspondence of Mykhailo Pavlyk, but that account concerns a real situation: in late 1876 a debate between socialist students and nonsocialists was to take place during a meeting of the Academic Circle. It did not lead to any clash, and after the meeting the government commissar who was present at the meeting, in accordance with Austrian law, said: "There's no way there are socialists in Galicia, especially among the Rusyns." Pavlyk commented: "It was a bitter thing to realize that he is telling the truth." See Pavlyk, *Perepyska*, vol. 2, 103.

3   Szczepanowski, *Nędza Galicyi*, 113.

4   Arkhiv Mykhaila Drahomanova, 37; Drahomanov, *Avstro-rus'ki spomyny*, 188–89.

5   Volodymyr Barvins'kyi, *Besida vyholoshena na muzykal'no-dekliamatorskim vecheri u L'vovi v XIV. rokovyny smerty Tarasa Shevchenka* (Lviv, 1875), 13, 16–17.

6   Michał Śliwa, "Ruch Socjalistyczny w Galicji w historiografii polskiej," in *Rocznik Naukowo-Dydaktyczny WSP w Krakowie*, vol. 26, bk. 13, Studia z dziejów Małopolski w XIX i XX wieku, ed. Ludwik Mroczek (Cracow: Wydawn. Naukowe Wyższej szkoły Pedagogicznej, 1992), 174.

7   *Svoiezhytievyi zapysky Bohdana Didyts'koho*, pt. 1, 52–53n; V. Z., "Respublika i komunizm!," *Vistnyk dlia rusynov avstriis'koi derzhavy*, 13 (25) June 1850, 205.

8   Leon Biliński, *O istocie, rozwoju i obecnym stanie socjalizmu* (Cracow, 1883), 11. Cited in Śliwa, "Ruch Socjalistychny w Galicji," 175.

9   For more detailed information on the trials of Terletsky and Pavlyk in 1876 and 1877, see Drahomanov, *Lysty do Iv. Franka i ynshykh*, vol. 1, 356–74; John-Paul Himka, *Socialism in Galicia: The Emergence of Polish Social Democracy and Ukrainian Radicalism (1860–1890)* (Cambridge, MA: Harvard Ukrainian Research Institute, 1983), 65; V. I. Kalynovych, *Politychni protsesy Ivana Franka ta ioho tovaryshiv* (Lviv: Vyd-vo L'vivs'koho universytetu, 1967), 13–32; and Franko's article, "D-r Ostap Terlets'kyi: Spomyny i materialy" [*ZT* 33:335–41].

10   Drahomanov, *Avstro-rus'ki spomyny*, 430.

11   For more detailed discussion, see Ia. R. Dashkevych, "Mykhailo Drahomanov i Zakarpattia," in *Shtrykhy do naukovoho portreta Mykhaila Drahomanova: Zbirnyk naukovykh prats'*, R. S. Mishchuk (Kyiv: Naukova dumka, 1991), 201–6; Oleh Mazurok, "Plata za vil'nodumstvo: Novovyiavleni dokumenty pro zv'iazky Mykhaila Drahomanova ta inshykh halyts'kykh diiachiv iz Zakarpattiam," *Novyny Zakarpattia* 8, nos. 20–21 (February 1997): 4.

12   The original copy of this letter has not survived. Its contents were recapitulated on the basis of a synopsis prepared during the trial. See Pavlyk, *Perepyska*, vol. 2, 199–202.

13   These rumors were not unfounded. The Department of Police of the Russian Empire, alarmed by the scale of the shipment of banned publications through Galicia, ordered the Russian ambassador in Vienna to discuss this question with high-ranking Austrian officials. Novikov, the Russian consul, met in Vienna with the Minister of Foreign Affairs, Baron von Hofmann, and the viceroy of Galicia, Baron Alfred Potocki. Novikov requested the Austrian government's assistance in the struggle against the distribution of this literature "not only through the maintenance of good neighborly relations but also from the standpoint of solidarity of the conservative origins and the mutual interests of both states." See Mazurok, "Plata za vil'nodumstvo," 4.

14   Detailed discussion of this question is found in the chapter titled "Franko and His Boryslav."

15   The compilers of vol. 48 of Franko's collected works, which contains the above-cited quotation, mistakenly attributed this story not to Yosyf Sembratovych, but to his nephew (and future metropolitan) Sylvester Sembratovych [*ZT* 48:625].

16 His real identity was established only in 1933. For detailed discussion of Kobylański and his links with Franko, see Mykhailo Pavlyk, "Khto sprychynyv areshtuvannia Franka i tovaryshiv v 1877 r.?" *Zhyttia i znannia* 5 (1936): 134–36; VR IL, fond 3 (Ivan Franko), file 1608, fol. 379; file 1618, fol. 125.

17 For detailed discussion of the investigation and subsequent trial, see Kalynovych, *Politychni protsesy*, 33–96; Kyrylo Studyns´kyi, "Ivan Franko i tovaryshi v sotsiialistychnim protsesi 1878," *Ukraina* 6 (1926): 56–114.

18 Hrushevs´kyi, *Z pochyniv ukrains´koho sotsiialistychnoho rukhu*, 64.

19 Herbert Steiner, "Die Wiener Hochverratsprozesse 1870," in *Sozialistenprozesse: Politische Justiz in Österreich, 1870–1936*, ed. Karl R. Stadler (Vienna: Europaverlag, 1986), 13–30; Karl Flanner, "Sozialistenprozesse in Wiener Neustadt 1870–1894," in Stadler, ed., *Sozialistenprozesse*, 31–52. Unfortunately, neither author examines the Viennese connection in the trials of the Galician socialists in 1876–1878.

20 Haus-, Hof- und Staatsarchiv, Informationsbüro des k.k. Ministeriums der *Äussern, 1960, 1982, 2174, 2262, 3306, 4559 / 70, 1877; henceforward: HHS*, Informationsbüro.

21 Gunther E. Rothenberg, *The Army of Francis Joseph* (West Lafayette, IN: Purdue University Press, 1976), 8–9.

22 Cited in Ivan Holovats´kyi, *Ivan Horbachevs´kyi, Zhyttiepysno-bibliohrafichnyi narys* (n.p. [Lviv], 1995), 91.

23 Studyns´kyi, "Ivan Franko i tovaryshi," 59–60; "Kronika Lwowska," *Dziennik Polski*, 10 June 1877, 3.

24 Studyns´kyi, "Ivan Franko i tovaryshi," 57–59.

25 See also Ivan Franko, "Mykhailo Pavlyk: Zamist´ iuvyleinoi syl´vetky," *LNV* 3 (1905): 163. Franko intended to write a separate study about the arrests and trial of 1877–1878; his archive contains a collection of documents on this topic.

26 *Slovo*, 24 January (5 February) 1878 (no. 9).

27 *Dziennik Polski*, 1878 (no. 175).

28 O. Obachnyi [D. Taniachkevych], *Sotsiialisty mezhy semynarystamy?! Studiia na nashom tserkovno-narodnom poli* (Lviv, 1877), 37.

29 VR IL, fond 3 (Ivan Franko), file 2323.

30 Limanowski, *Pamiętniki*, vol. 1, 174–81.

31 The editorial board of the popular Polish newspaper *Dziennik Polski* received letters with such questions as "What are socialists?" and "Why are they being imprisoned?" The editors responded jokingly, declaring that a socialist is the opposite of a deputy to the Austrian parliament. During the trial one of the judges, a good-hearted individual, asked his neighbor on the bench: "Tell me, colleague, what is socialism? I know that this is something worthy of punishment, but what are those socialists really after?" After the trial ended, the Russophile newspaper, *Slovo*, published a long article titled "Borot´ba z sotsiializmom" (The struggle against socialism), in which socialism was defined as the "thievish confiscation of ownership." It is worth noting that this article was reprinted in *Sankt-Peterburgskie vedomosti*. Yet none of the editors or contributors to *Slovo* managed to "elucidate" the essence of socialism. See Limanowski, *Pamiętniki*, vol. 1, 180; "Bor´ba s sotsializmom," *Slovo*, 5 (17) December 1878, 2; 8 (29) December 1878, 2–3.

32 See the works of V. I. Kalynovych and K. Studynsky cited here.

33 "Z izby sądowej: Proces socjalistów ruskich," *Dziennik Polski*, 19 January 1878, 2–3; Bolesław Limanowski, "Z chasiv pershoho areshtu," in Hnatiuk, *Spohady*, 93. Ostap Terletsky noted: "Every honest and sober thinking individual should therefore be a socialist if he does not wish to have on his conscience the responsibility for [the circumstance that], in witnessing injustice toward the people and knowing how to help,

they looked upon the people's decline with folded hands....I know full well that truth and justice are on my side, and because of that I will await your verdict utterly calmly." See Studyns′kyi, "Ivan Franko i tovaryshi," 105. At the end of his speech, Terletsky became so emotional that he nearly fainted. Another touching moment occurred when the Pole, Koturnicki, concluded his statement to the court by offering his hand to the Ruthenian defendants: he was convinced that national enmity would disappear among socialists because they were the enemies of all kinds of oppression and, therefore, the enemies of one nation's oppression by another. See Limanowski, "Z chasiv pershoho areshtu." Clearly, the trial was not lacking in drama.

34 "Z izby sądowej: Proces socjalistów ruskich," *Dziennik Polski*, 17 January 1878, 3; Limanowski, *Pamiętniki*, vol. 1, 181.

35 Ivan Kurovets recalled that Franko impressed young people with "his distinctiveness, his courageous statement to the court, and the passionate speech that he made in a ringing, metallic voice." See Ivan Kurovets′, "Ivan Franko v moikh zhadkakh," in Hnatiuk, *Spohady*, 71. The accuracy of these statements is negated by the following comment: "The other accused did not make a bigger impression on us" (ibid.). As we have seen, Ostap Terletsky made the most vivid impression. It is very likely that Kurovets was extrapolating his subsequent fascination with Franko onto an earlier period.

36 Limanowski, "Z chasiv pershoho areshtu," 93–94.

37 "Z izby sądowej: Proces socjalistów ruskich ," *Dziennik Polski*, 17 January 1878, 2.

38 In a letter to the Lviv prosecutor's office that was forwarded by Pavlyk, Drahomanov admitted that he had genuinely attributed "great importance to the person of Franko" because, based on his literary works, he saw in him "talent and the desire to look closer at the life of the people." See Pavlyk, *Perepyska*, vol. 2, 275.

39 *Ivan Franko: Dokumenty i materialy*, 51–53, 56–57. Scholars often cast doubt on the veracity of Skamina's testimony—e.g., Himka, *Socialism in Galicia*, 67. The compilers of the collection, *Ivan Franko: Dokumenty i materialy*, call him a provocateur outright (51, 56). Franko himself claimed that Skamina had misunderstood him and distorted his words. During his second interrogation Skamina admitted that he had a bad short-term memory and therefore could not repeat his testimony. He repeated his initial testimony only after the head of the court reminded him about the dangers of making false statements. Before repeating his statement, however, Skamina said that he did not want to do this because he was afraid that Franko would kill him after getting out of prison. See Studyns′kyi, "Ivan Franko i tovaryshi," 107. What strikes the eye—and the court did not fail to notice either—is that Skamina's account included accurate details that he could only have heard from Franko.

40 See the indictment of the state prosecutor's office, dated 10 October 1877, in *Ivan Franko: Dokumenty i materialy*, 57–58.

41 See his angry reply by letter to Drahomanov, dated 10 June 1877, in which Mandychevsky openly accused him of having caused all those problems for the young Galician Ruthenians. He told him: "Get away from us with your tendencies. Life is difficult enough as it is for us, and here you are sending the police after us." See Pavlyk, *Perepyska*, vol. 2, 218.

42 Studyns′kyi, "Ivan Franko i tovaryshi," 110.

43 The other defendants served their sentences later, in the second half of 1878. Each defendant's sentence was lengthened because of Ivan Mandychevsky's actions. Although Mandychevsky never spent any time in prison—his father, a deputy of the State Council in Vienna, managed to obtain his release—he submitted a protest against the verdict, which prolonged the trial for two more months.

44 Franko's prison notes were published in Mykhailo Vozniak, "Z pershoho zaareshtuvannia Ivana Franka," *Novi shliakhy* 10 (1931): 53–58, 170–82.

45 Wendland, *Die Russophilen in Galizien*, 234.

46 See the chapter "Franko and His Peasants."

47 Biblioteka Narodowa w Warszawie, Wydział Zbiorów Specjalnych (henceforward: BN WZS), II 2899, microfilm 41254, 248.

48 Limanowski, *Pamiętniki*, vol. 1, 173–75.

49 See M. Pavlyk, "Iz perepysky M. P. Drahomanova z D-rom Omelianom Ohonovs'kym," *Zhytie i slovo*, May–June 1897; for Omelian Ohonovsky's letter of refusal, see 369–70; see also Volodymyr Mykytiuk, *Ivan Franko ta Omelian Ohonovs'kyi: movchannia i dialoh* (Lviv: Vyd-vo L'vivs'koho universytetu, 2000), 41.

50 Negative commentaries were published in both the Ruthenian and the Polish press. On 22 January 1878 Pavlyk complained in a letter to Drahomanov: "In the newspapers we come out looking like a laughing-stock, so inaccurately and dishonestly do they write about us." Pavlyk, *Perepyska*, vol. 2, 284.

51 As Franko's correspondence with Olha Roshkevych reveals, the father's refusal was not final: he demanded that Franko continue his career and also "try to obtain a doctorate," but Franko rejected these conditions [ZT 48:76, 78, 86].

52 Chaikovs'kyi, "Moi spohady pro Ivana Franka," 96–97. Another contemporary, who was a student at the time, recalled: "The handful of 'proscribed individuals' was separated from us as though by the great wall of China." See Olesnyts'kyi, "Z-ponad chetvertyny stolittia," 69.

53 A. S., "Novynky. Sotsiializm. Protses vo L'vovi," *Ruskii Sion* 2 (1878): 62; Himka, *Socialism in Galicia*, 69, 199.

54 Chaikovs'kyi, "Moi spohady pro Ivana Franka," 97.

55 This thesis was sadly illustrated by the fate of the village schoolteacher, Lev Vasylevych, who had circulated Franko's brochures. Never able to find a permanent position and constantly transferred from one place to another, he died in abject poverty at the age of twenty-three. See Studyns'kyi, "Ivan Franko i tovaryshi," 84.

56 See also a similar opinion expressed by Yuliian Romanchuk, one of the leaders of the populists, in Pavlyk, *Perepyska*, vol. 3, 515.

57 The socialists themselves were aware of this task. After the trial these ideas were developed on the pages of *Dziennik Polski* by Bolesław Limanowski. See Limanowski, *Pamiętniki*, vol. 1, 182.

58 This appellation appeared in the 22 August 1878 issue of *Dziennik Polski*.

59 See Pavlyk, *Perepyska*, vol. 3, 516–17.

60 TsDIAL, fond 146, list 2, file 14628, fol. 2.

61 *Ivan Franko: Dokumenty i materialy*, 79–80.

62 Cited in O. I. Dei, *Ukrains'ka revoliutsiino-demokratychna zhurnalistyka: problemy vynyknennia i stanovlennia* (Kyiv: Vyd-vo Akademii nauk URSR, 1959), 200.

63 Franko, "Mykhailo Pavlyk," 167–68. Franko's view is corroborated by later research. See M. L. Butryn, "Tsenzurna istoriia zbirky 'Molot' (1878)," *Ukrains'ke literaturoznavstvo* 12 (1971): 46–50; Dei, *Ukrains'ka revoliutsiino-demokratychna zhurnalistyka*, 86–144; I. Denysiuk, "Do tsenzurnoi istorii 'Hromads'koho druha,' 'Dzvona' i 'Molota,'" in *Ivan Franko: Statti i materialy* 6 (1958): 49–73.

64 *Dziennik Polski*, 28 August 1878.

65 Cited in Dei, *Ukrains'ka revoliutsiino-demokratychna zhurnalistyka*, 331.

66 HHS, Informationsbüro, 1345, 1656, 1704, 1778, 3087, 3549, 3436 / 98, 1878.

67 Limanowski, *Pamiętniki*, vol. 1, 199.

68 Limanowski admitted that his description may not have been accurate. According to another version, the meeting took place in June 1878 (Himka, *Socialism in Galicia*, 71). Thus, it could not have been connected to his imminent departure (Limanowski received an order to leave Galicia in August 1878). He tried to refresh his memory of the soiree with the aid of a letter from someone who signed himself K...cki (Kulmatycki?) dated 7 November 1878. See Limanowski, *Pamiętniki*, vol. 1, 199; Marian Żychowski, *Bolesław Limanowski, 1835–1935* (Warsaw: Książka i Wiedza, 1971), 70. Unfortunately, I was not able to locate this letter, despite a thorough perusal of Limanowski's correspondence from this period, which is stored in the Manuscript Division of the National Library in Warsaw.

69 For conspiratorial purposes the title page did not indicate the author's name, and the place of publication is listed as Lipsk (Leipzig).

70 Józef Kozłowski, "Iwan Franko a polski ruch robotniczy w Galicji w latach siedemdziesiątych i osiemdziesiątych wieku XIX," *Kwartalnik Instytutu Polsko-Radzieckiego* 1, no. 6 (1954): 98. During the "great Cracow trial" of 1880, thirty-five socialists, headed by Ludwik Waryński, were considered living proof of their "activity [which is] dangerous to the state."

71 Józef Hudec, one of the founders of the Galician socialist movement, claimed that Franko and Pavlyk began working at the newspaper starting from the third issue. See *Praca*, 14 February 1892, 1.

72 H. D. Verves, "Ivan Franko u robitnychii hazeti 'Praca,'" in *Ivan Franko iak istoryk*, ed. I. O. Hurzhii, P. M. Kalenchenko et al. (Kyiv: Vyd-vo Akademii nauk URSR, 1956), 123; Himka, *Socialism in Galicia*, 72.

73 Walentyna Najdus, "Początki socjalistycznego ruchu robotniczego w Galicji (lata siedemdziesiąte–osiemdziesiąte XIX w.)," *Z pola walki* 3 (1960). Najdus cites one of the first histories of the Galician socialist movement: Emil Haecker, *Historja socjalizmu w Galicji i na Śląnsku Cieszyńskim* (Cracow: Nakł. Towarzystwa Uniwersytetu Robotniczego, 1933), 199; Feldman, *Stronnictwa*, vol. 1, 87. Hryhorii Verves writes ("Ivan Franko u robitnychii hazeti," 123) that *Praca* became a workers' newspaper thanks to the joint efforts of Franko and Waryński. Without undermining the scholarly value of Najdus's work, it must be noted, however, that the tendency to minimize Franko's impact on the socialist movement is also evident in another of her books, a biography of Ignacy Daszyński. In this one, she only makes a passing reference to Franko's relationship with Daszyński, neglecting to mention that Daszyński himself acknowledged Franko's decisive influence on the formation of his world perception in his youth. See Ignacy Daszyński, *Pamiętniki*, vol. 1 (Cracow: Z. R. S. S. "Proletarjat," 1925), 24–25.

74 Hryhorii Verves was the first scholar to draw attention to this fact. See his article, "Ivan Franko u robitnychii hazeti," 118.

75 Pavlyk, *Perepyska*, vol. 3, 186.

76 Franko claimed that this program "was written not by me but with my participation" [*ZT* 49:248]. However, the editors and compilers of the fifty-volume collection of Franko's works included the "Program" in one of the volumes, presenting it as a work written entirely by Franko [*ZT* 45:448–64].

77 Ia. I. Hrytsak and S. M. Trusevych, "Ivan Franko i robitnychyi rukh u Skhidnii Halychyni u 70–80-kh rokakh XIX st.," in *Ivan Franko i svitova kul'tura: materialy Mizhnarodnoho sympoziumu IuNESKO*, eds. I. I. Lukinov, M. V. Bryk et al. (Kyiv: Naukova dumka, 1990), 346.

78 Yaroslav Hrytsak, "Halyts'ka, 6. Iz l'vivs'kykh adres I. Franka," *Vil'na Ukraina*, 26 August 1987; Derzhavnyi arkhiv L'vivs'koi oblasti (State Archive of Lviv Oblast; henceforward DALO), fond 351, list 1, file 2375, fols. 1–3.

79 [Rets.], "Dribna biblioteka, knyzhka 14: 'Na dni'—suspilno-politychna studiia Yvana Franka," *Zoria*, 15 (27) October 1880, 272.

80 *The Ukrainian Poets, 1189–1962*, trans. C. H. Andrusyshen and Watson Kirkconnell (Toronto: Published for the Ukrainian Canadian Committee by University of Toronto Press, 1963), 206–8.

81 Ivan Kurovets claimed that Franko was inspired by the image of stone-crushers, who in the summer of 1878 were paving the road right beneath the Lviv apartment shared by Franko, Pavlyk, and Terletsky. See Kurovets´, "Ivan Franko u moikh zhadkakh"; in a subsequent reprint this fragment of his recollections was omitted. See Hnatiuk, *Spohady*, 69–74.

82 Limanowski, *Pamiętniki*, vol. 1, 202.

83 "Stowarzyszenia robotnicze angielskie (Trades-Union), ich cele i organizacja," *Praca* 8 (1879): 29–30; no. 9, 4–35.

84 Himka, *Socialism in Galicia*, 73–77.

85 Franko partially carried out this program in a series of articles on the material conditions of workers in Lviv, Drohobych, and Boryslav [*ZT* 26:186–93; 44/1:7–12, 52–65].

86 See Franko's article, "Zaribky i zhyttia l´vivs´koho zetsera," in *Molot*, 1878, 144–48, to which he affixed Józef Danyluk's name [*ZT* 44/1:7–12, 614].

87 In addition to the usual searches, arrests, and other kinds of persecutions, this type of activity sometimes led to tragic consequences. A student at the Lviv Polytechnic, who was a citizen of Russia, was slated to be handed over to the Russian authorities for engaging in socialist propaganda. Delivered to the Austro-Russian border, he threw himself under a train to avoid falling into the hands of the Russian police. The fate of Udalovych, a carpenter with socialist leanings, was equally tragic. Persecuted for his views, he was unable to find employment in Lviv and was forced to roam about in search of work. In the spring of 1891, he was found torn to pieces by wolves. See Feldman, *Stronnictwa*, vol. 2, 90–91.

Chapter 9

1 This concept proved to be very fruitful for conducting research on nineteenth-century political movements. See Geoff Eley, "Nations, Publics and Political Culture: Placing Habermas in the Nineteenth Century," in *Culture / Power / History: A Reader in Contemporary Social History*, ed. Nicholas B. Dirks, Geoff Eley, and Sherry B. Ortner (Princeton, NJ: Princeton University Press, 1994), 297–335. In recent years this concept has been applied successfully in research on the Ukrainian and Polish national movements in Galicia during the latter third of the nineteenth century and the early twentieth. See, e.g., Sereda, *Shaping of a National Identity*; Stauter-Halsted, *The Nation in the Village*.

2 Zawadski, *Pamiętniki życia literackiego w Galicji*, 38.

3 Ostap Terlets´kyi, *Halyts´ko-rus´ke pys´menstvo 1848–1865 rr. na tli tohochasnykh suspil´no-politychnykh zmahan´ halyts´ko-rus´koi inteligentsii* (Lviv: Vyd. red. Literaturno-naukovoho visnyka, 1903), 79.

4 For a detailed survey of these plans, see Vozniak, "Zhurnal´ni plany Franka," 17–88; see also Mykhailo Vozniak, *Iak diishlo do pershoho zhinochoho al´manakhu* (Lviv, 1937).

5 See, e.g., Althoen, *That Noble Quest*, 1–10; Rita Krueger, "Nationalizing the Public," in *Cultures and Nations of Central and Eastern Europe: Essays in Honor of Roman Szporluk*, ed. Zvi Gitelman et al. (Cambridge, MA: Harvard Ukrainian Research Institute, 2000), 360–61.

6   Mykhailo Vozniak, *Iv. Belei i Ol. Konys'kyi: Do zv'iazkiv Halychyny z Naddniprianshchynoiu v 80 rr. XIX v.* (Lviv, 1928), 19.

7   VR IL, fond 3 (Ivan Franko), file 1603, fols. 375–77.

8   *Materialy*, 110.

9   VR IL, fond 3 (Ivan Franko), file 1603, fols. 551–56. These names mimicked the titles of the Russian thick journals.

10   Cecylia Gajkowska, "Czasopiśmiennictwo literackie XIX wieku," in *Słownik Literatury Polskiej XIX wieku*, ed. Józef Bachórz and Alina Kowalczykowa (Wroclaw: Zakład Narodowy im. Ossolińskich-Wydawnictwo, 2002), 144–56; A. I. Reitblat, *Kak Pushkin vyshel v genii: Istoriko-sotsiologicheskie ocherki o knizhnoi kul'ture Pushkinskoi epokhi* (Moscow: Novoe literaturnoe obozrenie, 2001), 7–8, 80, 120–21, 124–25.

11   Uliana Kravchenko, "Shchyryi druh i vchytel'," in Hnatiuk, *Spohady*, 133–34.

12   Rudnyts'kyi, *Pysmennyky zblyzka*, 16.

13   This version appears in a report drawn up by the head (*starosta*) of Drohobych, dated 3 March 1882. (Cited in *Ivan Franko: Dokumenty i materialy*, 107.) In a letter to Belei (July-August 1881) Franko wrote that his stepfather wanted him to finish his studies and seek the emperor's favor in order to obtain a "government position" [*ZT* 48:286]. On the tense relations between Franko and his stepfather at that time, see Roman Horak, "Lysty rodyny do Ivana Franka," *Naukovyi visnyk Muzeiu Ivana Franka u L'vovi* 1 (2000): 150.

14   On Franko's stay in Lviv and Nahuievychi, see the two chapters in this book, "Franko and His Peasants" and "Franko and His Boryslav."

15   Kost' Levyts'kyi, *Istoriia politychnoi dumky halytskykh ukraintsiv, 1848–1914: Na pidstavi spomyniv* (Lviv: nakl. vlasnym, 1926–1927), 156, 168; Daniel Unowsky, "'Our Gratitude Has No Limit': Polish Nationalism, Dynastic Patriotism, and the 1880 Imperial Inspection tour of Galicia," *Austrian History Yearbook* 34 (2003): 148–49.

16   Wendland, *Die Russophilen in Galizien*, 193–234.

17   "Suchasna litopys'," *Pravda* 13, nos. 1–3 (1880): 64, 72.

18   Mykhailo Pavlyk, *Pro rus'ko-ukrains'ki narodni chytal'ni* (Lviv, 1887), 6.

19   Dei, *Ukrains'ka revoliutsiino-demokratychna zhurnalistyka*, 469–70; Himka, *Socialism in Galicia*, 109; Franko, *Moloda Ukraina*, 26.

20   These letters formed the nucleus of research on peasant participation in the national movement. See Himka, *Galician Villagers*.

21   Vasyl' Lukych, "Pershyi redaktor 'Dila' Volodymyr Barvins'kyi," *Dilo*, 14 January 1928, 4.

22   VR LNB, fond 1 (Barvins'kyi), file 3417, fol. 1.

23   Olesnyts'kyi, "Z-ponad chetvertyny stolittia," 67–68.

24   V. M. Iakovenko, "Do spivrobitnytstva Franka v 'Zori,'" in *Ukrains'ke literaturoznavstvo*, vol. 1 (Lviv: Vyd-vo L'vivs'koho universytetu, 1966), 64–69.

25   For a portrait of Franko as the "soul" of *Zerkalo*, see Ohonovs'kyi, *Istoriia literatury ruskoi*, vol. 3, 1069.

26   For detailed discussion, see Bohdan Iakymovych, *Knyha, prosvita, natsiia: Vydavnycha diial'nist' Ivana Franka u 70–80 rokakh XIX st.* (Lviv: Instytut ukrainoznavstva im. I. Kryp'iakevycha NAN Ukrainy, 1996).

27   Vozniak, *Iv. Belei i Ol. Konys'kyi*, 24.

28   VR IL, fond 3 (Ivan Franko), file 1602, fol. 149.

29   Ibid., fol. 241.

30   Drahomanov was referring to the versified program of a student trip that Franko wrote in 1884 and which was published as a separate brochure [*ZT* 3:250–62].

31   *Materialy*, 86.

32 VR IL, fond 3 (Ivan Franko), file 1603, fols. 355–57; file 1604, fol. 25; fond 132 (Uliana Kravchenko), file 171 (pages without any numeration).

33 See O. I. Dei, "Zhurnal 'Tovarysh' (Epizod iz zhurnalistychnoi diial´nosti I. Franka)," in *Doslidzhennia tvorchosti Ivana Franka*, 2nd ed. (Kyiv: Vyd-vo Akademii nauk URSR, 1959), 103.

34 Iu. H. Shapoval, *"Dilo," 1880–1939 rr.: postup ukrains´koi suspil´noi dumky* (Lviv: n.p., 1999), 28.

35 *Materialy*, 67; Pavlyk, *Perepyska*, vol. 4, 138.

36 Pavlyk, *Perepyska*, vol. 4, 134.

37 Ibid., 252, 264, 276–77, 280.

38 Ibid., 308.

39 "Perehliad chasopysei," *Dilo*, 5 (17) January 1885, 2.

40 VR IL, fond 3 (Ivan Franko), file 1603, fol. 363; M. F. Nechytaliuk, "Epistoliarna publitsystyka (Lysty Ivana Beleia do Oleksandra Barvins´koho)," in *Zbirnyk prats´ Naukovo-doslidnoho tsentru periodyky*, ed. M. M. Romaniuk et al. (Lviv: L´vivs´ka naukova biblioteka im. V. Stefanyka NAN Ukrainy, 1995), 397.

41 "Pokhorony bl. Adolfa Narols´koho…," *Dilo*, 22 November (4 December) 1884, 3; Pavlyk, *Perepyska*, vol. 4, 312; Ratai, "Zemletriastsi radykaly," *Nove zerkalo*, 1 (13) December 1884, 2; Franko, *Moloda Ukraina*, 34.

42 "V mutnii vodi…," *Dilo*, 8 (20) December 1884, 4. To the very end of this article it is not clear whether it was about Pavlyk and Franko or about the deceased's brother and his friend, both of whom had organized the community mourning-meeting. Franko did not attend Narolsky's funeral (Franko, "Mykhailo Pavlyk," 173).

43 M. Pavlyk, "Iz perepysky M. Drahomanova, III: Lysty M. Drahomanova do Oleksandra Borkovs´koho, redaktora "Zori" (1888–1889)," *Zhytie i slovo* 3, no. 6 (December 1896): 454.

44 M. O. Moroz, "Etnohrafichno-statystychnyi hurtok (do 100-richchia vid pochatku ioho diial´nosty)," *Narodna tvorchist´ ta etnohrafiia* 6 (1983): 45.

45 S. S. Kiral´, comp., *"…Viddaty zumiiem sebe Ukraini!": Lystuvannia Trokhyma Zinkivs´koho z Borysom Hrinchenkom* (Kyiv: Ukrains´ka Vil´na Akademiia nauk u SShA, 2004), 44.

46 VR IL, fond 3 (Ivan Franko), file 1603, fols. 375–77.

47 *Arkhiv Mykhaila Drahomanova*, 29–30.

48 Ibid., 34, 286, 312; VR IL, fond 3 (Ivan Franko), file 1608, fol. 383.

49 *Arkhiv Mykhaila Drahomanova*, 305.

50 Cited in Vozniak, "Zhurnal´ni plany," 48.

51 *Arkhiv Mykhaila Drahomanova*, 33–34; *Materialy*, 190.

52 Cited in Vozniak, "Zhurnal´ni plany," 29, 31.

53 *Arkhiv Mykhaila Drahomanova*, 270–82; *Materialy*, 190, 226–27, 264.

54 VR IL, fond 3 (Ivan Franko), file 1603, fols. 603–6

55 Ibid., fols. 607–8 ; fond 132 (Uliana Kravchenko), file 167, fol. 1

56 *Materialy*, 168–69.

57 Ibid., 179–80.

58 VR LNB, fond 29 (Mykhailo Vozniak), file 80, fols. 1–5. Franko's collaboration with the populists did not end here, as he returned to *Zoria* in the late 1880s (VR LNB, fond 29, file 169, fols. 1–15). But this collaboration was never again as systematic as it was in 1882–1886.

59 Ludwik Krzywicki, *Wspomnienia*, vol. 1: *1859–1885*, ed. Stanisław Stępowski ([Warsaw]: Czytelnik, 1947; Cracow: Druk. narodowa), 262.

60 Stefaniia Pushak, "Do pytannia pro spivpratsiu Ivana Franka z pol´s´kymy chasopysamy," in *Rocznik Europejskiego Kolegium Polskich i Ukraińskich Uniwersytetów* (Lublin: Wydawn. Uniwersytetu Marii Curie-Skłodowskiej, 2003–), 52–55. Despite the article's general title, it is mainly about Franko's collaboration with the editors of *Kraj*.

61 See M. Kosiv, "Ivan Franko proty reaktsiinykh krytykiv (z vystupiv na storinkakh 'Kurjera Lwowskiego,'" in *Ivan Franko: Statti i materialy* 9 (1962): 130–39; M. O. Moroz, "Do pytannia atrybutsii tvoriv I. Franka v hazeti 'Kurjer Lwowski,'" in *Pytannia tekstolohii: Ivan Franko*, ed. M. Ie. Syvachenko (Kyiv: Naukova dumka, 1983), 199.

62 Franko, *Moloda Ukraina*, 34–35.

63 Krzywicki, *Wspomnienia*, 259–61; Marja Wysłouchowa, *Wspomnienie pozgonne* (Lviv, 1905), 92.

64 During the eighteen-month existence of the journal, Franko published fifteen articles. The next most prolific authors were Bolesław Limanowski and Edward Przewóski, who published seven articles apiece. See *Przegląd społeczny, 1886–1887. Wstęp i antologię opracował Krzysztof Dunin-Wąsowicz. Bibliografię opracowała Jadwiga Czachowska* (Wroclaw: Zakład im. Ossolińskich, 1955), 187–201.

65 Ia. I. Shust, "Uchast´ Ivana Franka u prohresyvnomu zhurnali 'Przegląd społeczny' (1886–1887)," in *Pytannia slov'ianoznavstva: Materialy pershoi i druhoi slavistychnykh konferentsii, do V Mizhnarodnoho z'izdu slavistiv* ([Lviv]: Vyd-vo L´vivs´koho universytetu, 1962), 146.

66 Various Polish scholars have noted the journal's impact on the Polish public in Galicia and (the former) Polish Kingdom. See, among others, Andrzej Kudłaszyk, *Myśl społeczno-polityczna Bolesława Wysłoucha, 1855–1937* (Warsaw; Wroclaw: Państwowe Wydaw. Naukowe, 1978 (Wroc.: WDN)), 81–83; *Przegląd społeczny*, 39–42. However, it was not possible to locate any information on whether the journal was read in the Ukrainian gubernias of the Russian Empire. The journal's uniqueness, set against the background of the provincial intellectual life of the times, was recognized by both its supporters and its detractors. See BN, wźs, microfilm 67675 (a copy of materials held at the Ossolineum in Wroclaw: 14779 / II Stanisław Wasylewski: *Materiały i szkice dotyczące Iwana Franko*); Karpel Lippe, *Symptome der antisemitischen Geisteskrankheit* (Jassy: H. Goldner, 1887), 26.

67 [Bolesław Wysłouch], "Słowo wstępne," *Przegląd społeczny* 1 (1887): 3.

68 [Bolesław Wysłouch], "Szkice programowe, *Przegląd społeczny* 1 (1886): 329–30.

69 Kudłaszyk, *Myśl*, 64–69, 85; Stefan Józef Pastuszka, ed., *Szkice programowe Bolesława Wysłoucha* (Lublin: Wydawn. Lubelskie, 1981), 14.

70 Z. B. W. [Review], "M. Dragomanow, Nakanunie nowych smut (Genewa, 1886)," *Przegląd społeczny* 2 (1887): 155.

Chapter 10

1 Ivan Denysiuk, "Frankoznavstvo: zdobutky, vtraty, perspektyvy," in *Ivan Franko—pys´mennyk, myslytel´, hromadianyn. Materialy Mizhnarodnoi naukovoi konferentsii, L´viv, 1998*, 16. For a recent critique of this statement, see V. I. Mazepa, *Kulturotsentryzm svitohliadu Ivana Franka* (Kyiv: Vydavets´ PARAPAN, 2004), 227–28.

2 For detailed discussion, see Lysiak-Rudnyts´kyi, *Istorychni ese*, vol. 1, 299–347; vol. 2, 131–72.

3 Isaiah Berlin, *The Hedgehog and the Fox: An Essay on Tolstoy's View of History* (New York: Simon & Schuster, 1986), 1–2.

4 VR IL, fond 3 (Ivan Franko), file 1604, fol. 20; Pavlyk, *Perepyska*, vol. 2, 57–58; vol. 3, 109, 146.

5 Franko insisted that this caricature was published. A check of the entire set of *Nove Zerkalo* did not reveal it; very likely the caricature was confiscated.

6 This explanation appears in a brochure that was written to accompany Matejko's paintings. See Maryan Gorkowski, *Wskazówki do objaśnienia jedynastu obrazów Jana Matejki przeznaczonych do Politechniki lwowskiej* (Cracow, 1895), 8. There is another, simpler, interpretation: the man on the handcar is the symbol of fire, while the woman represents water. The fruit of their encounter is steam produced from boiling water (steam engine), symbolized by the child, who is paving the way for the train. I am grateful to Maciej Janowski for suggesting this interpretation. An exhibit of cartoons (sketches) of Matejko's paintings was held in Lviv in spring 1886. It is difficult to believe that Franko would not have known about it: the newspaper *Kurjer Lwowski*, where Franko was employed at the time, published a report about it, and the author of the article was Franko's friend Bolesław Spausta, who singled out, from all the sketches, the one picturing a railway. See Bolesław Spausta, "Kartony Matejki," *Kurjer Lwowski*, 18 April 1886, 2.

7 Karl Marx, 1867 preface to the first German edition of *Das Kapital*. Found at: http://www.marxists.org/archive/marx/works/1867-c1/p1.htm Accessed 14 February 2017.

8 Cited in Michael Crichton, *The Great Train Robbery* (New York: Knopf, 1975), xiv–xv.

9 Stanislaus A. Blejwas, *Realism in Polish Politics: Warsaw Positivism and National Survival in Nineteenth Century Poland* (New Haven, CT: Yale Concilium on International and Area Studies; Columbus, Ohio: Distributed by Slavica Publishers, 1984), 78.

10 Taras Shevchenko, *Povne zibrannia tvoriv u dvanadtsiaty tomakh*, 12 vols. (Kyiv: Naukova dumka, 2001–), vol. 5, 12, 320.

11 Ibid., 86–87.

12 Dei, *Ivan Franko*, 91.

13 Cited in *Pis'ma k M. P. Pogodinu iz slavianskikh zemel' (1835–1861)*, vol. 3 (Moscow, 1880), 601–2, 605.

14 Ivan Naumovych, "Chuzhyna," *Zoria Halytskaia iako al'bum na hod* (Lviv, n.d.), 68.

15 VR IL, fond 3 (Ivan Franko), file 1603, fols. 461–62. The extent to which the railway was a new and unreliable means of travel is clearly indicated by the fact that when the Chernivtsi-Iasi Railway was opened in 1870, rain turned out to be a serious impediment. See Chłędowski, *Pamiętniki*, vol. 1, 178.

16 The latest scholar to examine Franko's world perception reached the same conclusion. See Bohdan Tykholoz, "Ivan Franko-filosof (Do kharakterystyky styliu ta evoliutsii myslennia)," *Suchasnist* 12 (2002): 115.

17 *Kilka słów z powodu "Listu otwartego młodzieży akademickiej w sprawie artykułu Dra Iwana Franki"* (Lviv, 1897), 18. It is significant that one of Franko's pseudonyms was "Ignatsii Postupovsky." See Roman Dziuban, "Nevidomi lysty Ivana Franka do Tselestyny Zhuravskoi-Zygmuntovskoi," *Ukraina moderna* 10 (2006): 161–86.

18 *Praca*, 3 June 1882, 3.

19 "Ukrains'ki pisni-himny: Istoriia ta rodovid," *Ternopil'* 1 (1992): 24. After Franko's death this unofficial hymn was performed at the start of solemn gatherings devoted to his memory. In Soviet times it was canonized as a revolutionary song, along with the "Internationale."

20 I am citing a later version of the original poem because the changes that were made to it (reprinted in 1893 and 1903) do not fundamentally alter its gist. Ibid. The English translation is in: *The Ukrainian Poets, 1189–1962*, trans. C. H. Andrusyshen and Watson Kirkconnell (Toronto: Published for the Ukrainian Canadian Committee by University of Toronto Press, 1963), 208–9.

21 Kuplowski, *Iwan Franko jako krytyk*, 97; Ivan Hlyns´kyi, "Ivan Franko i Iuliush Slovats´kyi," *Vsesvit* 1 (1965): 85.

22 Juliusz Słowacki, *Liryki i inne wiersze*, ed. J. Krzyżanowski (Wroclaw: Wydawn. Zakł. Narodowego im. Ossolińskich, 1959), 262.

23 Ibid., 342.

24 Sidney Pollard, *The Idea of Progress: History and Society* (Harmondsworth, U.K.: Penguin, 1971), 116.

25 This was noted in particular by Vasyl Shchurat, one of the best Franko scholars during the latter's lifetime: "Franko was influenced by the Polish and German Positivists, I was under [the influence] of the French [Positivists]." Shchurat's assorted notes ("Okremi zapysy V. H. Shchurata"), which pertain to Ivan Franko's life and work, are stored in the private archive of the Shchurat-Seniv family.

26 Kuplowski, *Iwan Franko jako krytyk*, 132.

27 For detailed discussion of this question, see Vasyl´ Lev, *Ivan Franko ta pol´s´ki pozytyvisty* (Lviv, 1937).

28 Henryk Bigeleisen, "Moi spomyny pro Ivana Franka," in Hnatiuk, *Spohady*, 267; Severyn Danylovych, "Franko iak dukhovnyi bat´ko radykal´noi partii v Halychyni," in Hnatiuk, *Spohady*, 178–79.

29 Basil Willey, *Nineteenth Century Studies: Coleridge to Matthew Arnold* (New York: Columbia University Press, 1964), 188.

30 Mary Pickering, *Auguste Comte: An Intellectual Biography*, 3 vols. (Cambridge; New York: Cambridge University Press, 1993–2009), vol. 1, 691–710; Willey, *Nineteenth Century Studies*, 188–98.

31 John Stuart Mill, *August Comte und der Positivismus (1865)* (Leipzig: Fues's Verlag, 1874), 4, 6, 15, 67, 71. This book is stored in Ivan Franko's personal library housed at the Taras Shevchenko Institute of Literature at the National Academy of Sciences (NAN) of Ukraine (file 6012). It would be apropos to mention some of these underlinings as illustration of those aspects of Positivism that fascinated the young Franko: "The laws of phenomena are all we know respecting them"; it is necessary "to justify the science of sociology"; "The impulse to public life is germane to the individual"; "The collective organism is essentially composed of families which are its true elements" and "especially the institution of marriage"; "The obvious remedy is a large and liberal general education, preparatory to all special pursuits"; and "The main element in a person's development is intellectual education."

32 Zbigniew A. Żechowski, *Socjologia Bolesława Limanowskiego* (Poznan: UAM, 1964), 54, 57.

33 Ihor Zakhara, "Pozytyvizm u sotsiial´nii filosofii Ivana Franka," in *Ivan Franko—pys´mennyk*, 181.

34 They are mentioned in a list of books that were confiscated during a search of Franko's home. See TsDIAL, fond 152, list 2, file 14392, fols. 43–45; file 14496, fol. 69; file 14422, fol. 23; file 14423, fol. 55; Kalynovych, *Politychni protsesy*, 47.

35 Blejwas, *Realism in Polish Politics*, 25, 115; Halina Kozłowska-Sabatowska, *Ideologia pozytywizmu galicyjskiego: 1864–1881* (Wroclaw; Cracow: Zakład Narodowy im. Ossolińskich, 1978), 50–89.

36 Ohonovs´kyi, *Istoriia literatury ruskoi*, vol. 3, 924–25.

37 Kazimierz Kelles-Krauz, *Pisma wybrane* (Warsaw: Książka i Wiedza, 1962), vol. 1, 45.

38 For a discussion of the influence of Lassallism on Franko, see Verves, "Ivan Franko u robitnychii hazeti 'Praca,'" 132. The cult of Lassalle was widespread among Galician socialists. "The Workers' March," which sprang from the milieu of the Galician-Ukrainian social democrats, contained the following verse: "My ne damos´ voroham! / V borot´bi nam syl ne zhal´! / My idemo vsi po tym stezhkam / Shcho nam vkazav

Lassal´!" [We will not surrender to the enemies! / We do not spare our strength for the struggle! / We are treading the same paths / Indicated to us by Lassalle!]. See *Volia*, 1 December 1903, 7.

39 See Dei, *Ukrains´ka revoliutsiino-demokratychna zhurnalistyka*, 383–90.

40 Hrushevs´kyi, *Z pochyniv*, 15.

41 Roman Serbyn, "Zhyttia i diial´nist´ Serhiia Podolyns´koho: biohrafichnyi narys," in *Lysty ta dokumenty: Serhii Podolyns´kyi*, comp. Roman Serbyn and Tetiana Sliudykova (Kyiv: s.n., 2002), 54–55, 90–91.

42 Eduard Bernstein wrote to Petr Lavrov about Podolynsky: "I respect him very much for his magnificent sketch on the theme of Darwinism and socialism" (cited in Serbyn, "Zhyttia i diial´nist´," 82).

43 Isaiah Berlin, *Two Concepts of Liberty; An Inaugural Lecture Delivered before the University of Oxford on 31 October 1958* (Oxford: Clarendon Press, 1958).

44 For one of the best pieces of research on this topic, see Roman Rozdolski [Rozdol´s´kyi], *Engels and the "Nonhistoric" Peoples: The National Question in the Revolution of 1848*, trans., ed., and with an introduction by John-Paul Himka ([Glasgow]: Critique Books, 1986).

45 E. Bernshtein [E. Bernstein], "Spomyny pro Mykhaila Drahomanova i Serhiia Podolyns´koho," in Hrushevsky, *Z pochyniv*, 156.

46 Cited in Roman Szporluk, "The Ukraine and Russia," in *The Last Empire: Nationality and the Soviet Future*, ed. Robert Conquest (Stanford, CA: Hoover Institution Press, 1986), 156.

47 Lysiak-Rudnyts´kyi, *Istorychni ese*, vol. 1, 339.

48 Ivan Lysiak-Rudnyts´kyi, "Storichchia pershoi ukrains´koi politychnoi prohramy," *Suchasnist´* 3 (1979): 107.

49 Ivan Franko, "Perednie slovo," in Mykhailo Drahomaniv, *Shevchenko, ukrainofily i sotsiializm*, 2nd ed. (Lviv: Nakladom Ukrains´ko-rus´koi vydavnychnoi spilky, 1906), vi. Cf. the words that another Russian subject addressed to the young Franko: "And what are you writing and publishing? Everything that needed to be written has already been written by Marx and Chernyshevsky. Now, the only thing to do is to implement it!" (Franko, *Moloda Ukraina*, 2–3).

50 Some Polish historians tend to view this incident as the result of an ordinary printing error. They are convinced that Limanowski was always favorably disposed toward Ukrainians and the Ukrainian socialist movement, his friendly attitude persisting until the last days of his life. See Krzysztof Dunin-Wąsowicz, *Bolesław Limanowski a kwestia ukraińska* [Separatum, Biblioteka Uniwersytetu Warszawskiego, odbitka z "Międzymorze," 1995), 69–76; Michał Śliwa, *Bolesław Limanowski: Człowiek i historia* (Cracow: Wydaw. WSP, 1994), 64.

51 M. Dragomanov, *Istoricheskaia Pol´sha i velikorusskaia demokratiia* (Geneva: Tip "Rabotnika" i "Gromady," 1882), 434–37; Mykhailo Hrushevs´kyi, "Misiia Drahomanova," *Ukraina*, 2–3 (1926): 13; Drahomanov, *Lysty do Iv. Franka*, vol. 1, 133.

52 Georgii Plekhanov, *Sochineniia* (Moscow: Gosudarstvennoe izdatel´stvo, 1923), vol. 1, 108–9.

53 Drahomanov, *Lysty do Iv. Franka*, vol. 1, 133–34.

54 *Literaturnoe nasledie G. V. Plekhanova* (Moscow: Gos. sots.-ekon. izd., 1934–), 211.

55 Franko provided several different dates for this poem when it was reprinted in later editions of his collections, *Z vershyn i nyzyn* (1893) and *Mii izmarahd* (My Emerald, 1911). In the first case, he included "Ne pora" among the poems that he wrote between 1880 and 1882 (Ivan Franko, *Z vershyn i nyzyn*, 2nd exp. ed. [Lviv, 1893], 73). In the second case, he

erroneously dated the publication to 1890 (most likely a typographic error: the numeral "9" was printed instead of "8"). This was not the only error in the poem's attribution: Franko maintained that "Ne pora" was first published in the second edition of *Z vershyn i nyzyn*, although in fact it had already been published in his first collection in 1887; thus, it could not have been written as late as 1890. In addition, a comical proofreader's error inadvertently gave the lie to the erroneous date: the phrase, "written [napysano] in 1890," became "not written [nepysano] in 1890"; Ivan Franko, *Davnie i nove: poezii*, 2nd exp. ed of *Mii izmarahd* (Lviv, 1911), 255; Ivan Franko, *Z vershyn i nyzyn* (Lviv, 1887), 69–70. The final argument in favor of the poem's earlier dating is that in its patriotic tonality "Ne pora" is very similar to the poems "Moia liubov" (My Love), "Liakham" (To the Liakhs), and "Rozvyvaisia ty, vysokyi dube" (Grow, You Lofty Oak), which were written in 1880–1882 and joined together in one poetic text titled "Ukraina" (Franko, *Z vershyn i nyzyn*, 2nd exp. ed., 72–75). The editors of the later, posthumous, edition dated the writing of "Ne pora" to 1880 (Ivan Franko, *Z vershyn i nyzyn: zbirnyk poetychnykh tvoriv; v dodatku "Ziv´iale lystie" i "Velyki rokovyny"* [Kyiv; Leipzig, 1920], 175).

56 *The Ukrainian Poets, 1189–1962*, trans. C. H. Andrusyshen and Watson Kirkconnell ([Toronto]: Published for the Ukrainian Canadian Committee by University of Toronto Press, 1963), 210.

57 See "Ukrainski pis´ni-himny," 28–29.

58 Hrushevs´kyi, *Z pochyniv*, 81.

59 Franko's advantage over Drahomanov is clearly seen in his change of attitude to the idea of Ukraine's political independence in the 1890s. See my article, "Ivan Franko pro politychnu samostiinist Ukrainy," *Zeszyty naukowe Uniwersytetu Jagiellońskiego, Prace Historyczne=Universitas Jagellonica Cracoviensis Acta scientiarum litterarumque. Schedae historicae* 103 (1993): 45–53.

60 There is a large body of literature on this topic. Here I will cite a work that pertains directly to Galician and Ukrainian subjects: Timothy Snyder, *Nationalism, Marxism, and Modern Central Europe: A Biography of Kazimierz Kelles-Krauz, 1872–1905* (Cambridge, MA: Distributed by Harvard University Press for the Ukrainian Research Institute, Harvard University, 1997).

61 Hans Mommsen, *Das Ringen um die supernationale Integration der zisleithanischen Arbeiterbewegung*, vol. 1 of *Die Sozialdemokratie und die Nationalitätenfrage im habsburgischen Vielvölkerstaat* (Vienna: Europa-Verlag, 1963–), 241.

62 F. Kon, "Dragomanov i Franko v pol´skom rabochem dvizhenii," *Griadushchii mir* 1 (1922): 238–39.

63 *Velykyi Zhovten´ i hromadians´ka viina na Ukraini: entsyklopedychnyi dovidnyk*, ed. I. F. Kuras, et al. (Kyiv: Holov. red URE, 1987), 277; *Dovidnyk z istorii Ukrainy (A–IA): [posibnyk dlia serednikh zahal´noosvitnikh navchal´nykh zakladiv]*, ed. I. Pidkova and R. Shust, 2nd rev. ed. (Kyiv: Heneza, 2001), 338.

64 See Alexander Gerschenkron, *Economic Backwardness in Historical Perspective: A Book of Essays* (Cambridge, MA: Belknap Press of Harvard University Press, 1962), 16–21.

65 Janowski, *Inteligencja wobec wyzwań nowoczesności*; Svitlenko, *Narodnytstvo v Ukraini*, 117.

66 This image appears in Alexander Herzen's famous letter to Tsar Nicholas II. See A. I. Gertsen, *Sobranie sochinenii*, 30 vols. (Moscow: Akademiia nauk SSSR, 1954–66), vol. 13, 35–46.

Chapter 11

1   I too shared this view in the late 1980s, when I was writing a biography of Franko. See my *"...Dukh, shcho tilo rve do boiu...,"* 33.

2   There is an immense body of literature on this subject. Here I will mention only the most recent works on the Russian peasantry: David Moon, *The Russian Peasantry, 1600–1930: The World the Peasants Made* (London; New York: Longman, 1999); the Polish peasantry: Włodzimierz Mędrzecki, *Młodzież wiejska na ziemiach Polski centralnej, 1864–1939: procesy socjalizacji* (Warsaw: Wydawn. DiG, 2002); Jan Molenda, *Chłopi, naród, niepodległość* (Warsaw: Wydawn. NERITON, Instytut Historii PAN, 1999); Keely Stauter-Halsted, *The Nation in the Village: The Genesis of Peasant National Identity in Austrian Poland, 1848–1914* (Ithaca, NY: Cornell University Press, 2001); and the Ukrainian peasantry: Iu. P. Prysiazhniuk, *Ukrains'ke selianstvo XIX–XX st.: evoliutsiia, mental'nist', tradytsionalizm; navchal'nyi posibnyk dlia istorychnykh fakul'tetiv* (Cherkasy: Vidlunnia-Plius, 2002). See also Andriy Zayarnyuk, "Framing the Ukrainian peasantry in Habsburg Galicia: 1846–1914 (with a focus on the Sambir area)" (Ph.D. diss., University of Alberta, 2003). Each of these books contains a detailed bibliography.

3   The practice of emphasizing the constant worsening of peasant conditions, leading to the rise of class consciousness and class struggle among the peasants, was typical of Soviet historiography. See, e.g., Kravets', *Selianstvo Skhidnoi Halychyny*. John-Paul Himka's more sophisticated study (*Galician Villagers*) notes both tendencies, but its chronological framework does not extend past 1880. Positive changes in one particular region during a later period are most clearly presented in Stella Hryniuk, *Peasants with Promise: Ukrainians in Southeastern Galicia* (Edmonton: Canadian Institute of Ukrainian Studies, 1991).

4   Wilhelm Feldman, *Stan ekonomiczny Galicyi: cyfry i fakty* (Lviv, 1900), 13.

5   Cited in Kozik, *Ukrainian National Movement*, 122.

6   Józef Kieczynski, "Stosunki włościan w Galicji," in *Wiadomości statystyczne o stosunkach krajowych* 7, no. 1 (1881): 67.

7   Mieczysław Marassé, *Gospodarcze stosunki w Galicji* (Warsaw, 1874), 9.

8   Bujak, *Galicja*, vol. 1, 391.

9   H. I. Koval'chak, *Ekonomichnyi rozvytok zakhidnoukrains'kykh zemel'* (Kyiv: Naukova dumka, 1988), 147.

10 Franko reached the same conclusion in a lengthy article titled "Zemel'na vlasnist' u Halychyni," in which he analyzed the agrarian question in Galicia in the 1880s [*ZT* 44/1:562].

11 Kieczynski, "Stosunki włościan w Galicji," 5–6.

12 Bujak, *Z odległej i bliskiej przeszłości*, 108–10; Pavliuk, *Narodna ahrotekhnika ukraintsiv Karpat*, 67, 134–35.

13 Pavliuk, *Narodna ahrotekhnika ukraintsiv Karpat*, 93.

14 Kieczynski, "Stosunki włościan w Galicji," 20.

15 Franciszek Bujak, *Żmiąca: wieś powiatu Limanowskiego: stosunki gospodarcze i społeczne* (Cracow: G. Gebethner, 1903), 140; Kudłaszyk, *Myśl społeczno-polityczna*, 31. These traits were not exclusively "Galician" but were typical of all peasants who balanced on the knife-edge of survival.

16 Leopold Caro, "Lichwa na wsi w Galicji w latach 1879–1891," *Wiadomości statystyczne o stosunkach krajowych* 14, no. 2 (1893): 6–7.

17 Hryniuk, *Peasants with Promise*.

18 Kieczynski, "Stosunki włościan w Galicji," 66–69.

19 Andreas Gratsiozi [Andrea Graziosi], *Bol'sheviki i krest'iane na Ukraine, 1918–1919 gody: ocherk o bol'shevizmakh, natsional-sotsializmakh i krest'ianskikh dvizheniiakh* (Moscow: Airo-XX, 1997), 28.

20 According to accepted wisdom, the 1846 uprising did not spread to the eastern (Ruthenian) districts of Galicia. But recent studies show that this was not the case, at least not entirely. See Oleg Polianskii, "Kresti'anskoe vosstanie 1846 g. v Galitsii" (Candidate of Historical Sciences diss., Lviv, 1985); Zayarnyuk, *Framing the Ukrainian Peasantry*, 78–118.

21 European leftists were captivated by a speech made by a Ukrainian peasant named Ivan Kapushchak during a debate on the abolition of feudal service. The speech was later published in the *Neue Rheinische Zeitung*, the newspaper edited by Karl Marx. See Rozdolski, *Engels and the "Nonhistoric Peoples,"* 65–66; see also Roman Rozdolski, *Die Bauernabgeordneten im konstituierenden österreichischen Reichstag, 1848–1849* (Vienna: Europaverlag, 1976).

22 Krzysztof Dunin-Wąsowicz, *Dzieje Stronnictwa Ludowego w Galicji* (Warsaw: Ludowa Spółdzielnia Widawnicza, 1956), 24–29.

23 Franciszek Bujak, *Rozwój gospodarczy Galicji, 1772–1914* (Lviv: Księg. Polska B. Połonieckiego, 1917), 31; Kravets', *Selianstvo Skhidnoi Halychyny*, 151; see also his *Klasova borot'ba u skhidnohalyts'komu seli navkolo servitutnoho pytannia—realistychna osnova opovidannia I. Ia. Franka "Lisy i pasovys'ka" (Metodychna rozrobka dlia studentiv)* (Vinnytsia, 1981), 24.

24 Zayarnyuk, "Ruski patrioty v Halytskomu seli," 107–26.

25 Mykhailo Pavlyk, *Tvory* (Kyiv: Dnipro, 1985), 232–35, 261.

26 Horak, "Ia ie muzhyk…," 68.

27 TsDIAL, fond 663, list 1, file 154, fol. 249.

28 Cited in Pavlyk, *Perepyska*, vol. 2, 43.

29 Ibid., 80.

30 Ibid., 79.

31 Hrytsiuta, *Selianstvo*, 9–19; VR LNB, fond 206 (Vasyl' Shchurat), file 340, fols. 7–14 (manuscript of a Polish-language article written by Szczurat [Shchurat], titled "Lud w literaturze ukraińskiej XIX w.")

32 Cited in Steblii, Kupchyns'kyi et al., *"Rusalka Dnistrova,"* 281.

33 Taras Shevchenko, *Povne zibrannia tvoriv u dvanadsiaty tomakh* (Kyiv: Naukova dumka, 2001–), vol. 5, 208.

34 Franko, *Moloda Ukraina*, 37–38.

35 VR IL, fond 3 (Ivan Franko), file 2252, fol. 1.

36 Bandrivs'kyi, "Spohady pro Franka-shkoliara," 49–50; Horak and Hnativ, *Ivan Franko*, 107–14.

37 Roshkevych (Ivanets'), "Spohady pro Ivana Franka," 118.

38 Hrytsiuta, *Selianstvo*, 56.

39 M. N. Mundiak, "Rasskazy i povesti Iv. Franko iz krest'ianskoi zhizni kak proizvedeniia kriticheskogo realizma" (Candidate of Philological Sciences diss., In-t lit-ry im. T. H. Shevchenka Natsional'noi akademii nauk Ukrainy Kyiv, 1954), 12.

40 It is very likely that Franko based his story on an incident that happened to Mykhailo Pavlyk, not to him. See Pavlyk, *Perepyska*, vol. 2, 15.

41 Iatsuliak, "Spomyny," 42–44.

42 Kobylets'kyi, "Deshcho pro Franka," 39–40.

43 Vasyl' Shchurat, "Frankiv sposib tvorennia," in Hnatiuk, *Spohady*, 280–81.

44 VR IL, fond 3 (Ivan Franko), file 1605, fol. 3.

45 Semen Vityk, "V chasy Ivana Franka," *Kultura i pobut*, 16 May 1926, 3.

46 Himka, *Socialism in Galicia*, 129–38; Hrytsak, "Poshyrennia poemy 'Maria' v Halychyni"; Andriy Zayarnyuk, "The Dobrivliany Affair of 1886: A Nodal Approach to Consciousness Formation," http://www.univie.ac.at/spacesofidentity/_Vol_4_3/_ HTML/Zayarnyuk.html).

47 "Spomyny Petra Berehuliaka pro Ivana Franka," in Dei, *Ivan Franko u spohadakh suchasnykiv*, vol. 2, 43–46; Vityk, "Iz moikh spomyniv pro Franka," 50.

48 These materials are stored in the Franko archive (VR IL, fond 3, file 2322, fols. 208–13). This is a copy of the court case, made by an unknown hand, perhaps at the request of Franko, who was intending to write an article about the "peasant socialists" for the Vienna newspaper, *Neue freie Presse*, which was to be based on the bill of indictment [*ZT* 49:69].

49 VR LNB, fond 1 (NTSh), file 493 / 53, fols. 1–3.

50 *Klasova borot'ba selianstva Skhidnoi Halychyny: 1772–1849: dokumenty i materialy*, comp. O. A. Kupchyns'kyi, A. H. Silets'kyi, and F. I. Steblii (Kyiv: Naukova dumka, 1974), 99–100, 236, 531; Himka, *Socialism in Galicia*, 130.

51 See Franko's article, "Hromady Dobrovliany (Materialy do monohrafii)" [*ZT* 44/1:494–504]. A similar case of peasant self-rule was described by Mykhailo Pavlyk: the Ukrainian community in the village of Dobrostany, near Lviv, resisted the introduction of Polish autonomy, refusing to elect a community council because it believed that these changes spelled the "return of Poland," and for the peasants Poland meant serfdom. See Pavlyk, *Perepyska*, vol. 4, 153.

52 Konrad Oksza Orzechowski, *Przewodnik statystyczno topograficzny i Skorowidz obejmujący wszystkie miejscowości przysiołkami w Królewstwie Galicyi W. X. Krakowskiem i X. Bukowinie, według najświetszych skazówek urzędowych* (Lviv, 1872), 17, 91.

53 Franko, "Hromady Dobrovliany," 502–4; Makukh, *Na narodnii sluzhbi*, 11.

54 Zayarnyuk, "Rus'ki patrioty v halyts'komu seli," 113, 123; Chapel's'kyi, "Ia liubyv ikh usikh," 128–48; Volodymyr Chapel's'kyi, "Z rodynnoi khroniky," *Ameryka*, 18 July 1966; Himka, *Socialism in Galicia*, 134–35.

55 Pavlyk, *Perepyska*, vol. 4, 278; Makukh, *Na narodnii sluzhbi*, 11.

56 VR IL, fond 3 (Ivan Franko), file 1615, fols. 595–96.

57 See chap. 13, "Franko and His Women."

58 See chap. 12, "Franko and His Boryslav."

59 Chapelsky, "Z rodynnoi khroniky."

60 VR LNB, fond 160 (Mykhailo Pavlyk), file 64 / 3, fol. 59.

61 Ibid., fol. 88.

62 Vityk, "Iz moikh spomyniv pro Franka," 50.

63 VR LNB, fond 160 (Mykhailo Pavlyk), file 64 / 3, fol. 59; Himka, *Socialism in Galicia*, 132–34; Vityk, "Iz moikh spomyniv pro Franka," 51, 53.

64 VR LNB, fond 160 (Mykhailo Pavlyk), file 64 / 3, fols. 59, 88.

65 Himka, *Socialism in Galicia*, 134–37.

66 Kossak, "Ivan Franko ta ioho braty," 48; Daszyński, *Pamiętniki*, vol. 1, 25. The general atmosphere, which was marked by close, warm relations, is attested by the correspondence between Franko, who returned to Lviv in early 1883, and Daszyński and Melnyk, who remained in Drohobych and Volia Yakubova, respectively. See VR IL, fond 3 (Ivan Franko), file 1602, fols. 141–43.

67 "Spomyny Petra Berehuliaka," 44, 46. It may be assumed that Franko expounded on the principal theses of the resolution of the agrarian question in Galicia, because the

example of North America is ubiquitous in his journalistic works dating to the period 1886–86, all of which are devoted to this topic [ZT 44/1:475, 572–73; 44/2:107–88].

68 "Ze wsi i dla wsi," *Praca*, 26 February 1883, 16. For a discussion of the links between the editors of the newspaper and Franko, as well as the members of the Drohobych group, see 48:347, 357, 368; and TsDIAL, fond 146, list 4, file 3694, fol. 33. The claim by some Soviet Ukrainian historians that this article was written by Mykhailo Pavlyk is discussed in Ivan Denysiuk, *Mykhailo Pavlyk* (Kyiv: Derzh. vyd-vo khudozh. lit-ry, 1960), 27; Petro Manzenko, *Suspil'no-polityčni i filosofs'ki pohliady M. Pavlyka* (Kyiv: Akad. nauk URSR, 1962), 104–5; P. Iashchuk, *Mykhailo Pavlyk* (Lviv, 1959), 79. However, all three authors fail to provide convincing arguments. At the time, Pavlyk was the editor of *Praca* and living in Lviv. Therefore, from a purely formal standpoint he could not have been one of those "friends from the provinces" who had written that letter.

69 The introduction to this brochure contains autobiographical elements: it recounts the story of Ivan, a "blacksmith's son," who founded a rural reading room. Franko dated this text thus: "written in Dobra Volia in early 1883." See Ivan Franko, *Rozmova pro hroshi i skarby z peredmovoiu o zalozhenniu Dobrovlianskoi chytal'ni* (Lviv, 1883), 11, 24.

70 Drahomanov, *Literaturno-publitsystychni pratsi*, vol. 2, 14.

71 Shevchenko, *Povne zibrannia tvoriv*, vol. 2, 311, 377.

72 *Marija maty Isusowa: Wirszy Tarasa Szewczenka z uwahamy M. Drahomanowa* (Geneva, 1882), 59.

73 Mykhailo Drahomanov advised the editors of *Praca* to publish articles on Ruthenian topics in the Ruthenian language, but in the Polish alphabet. See Drahomanov, *Lysty do Iv. Franka*, vol. 1, 4–11. The editors took his advice and, using this system, later published Franko's "Hymn" and "Halahan," as well as a variety of articles.

74 For additional details, see Hrytsak, "Poshyrennia poemy 'Mariia' v Halychyni." Franko considered this poem to be "one of Shevchenko's finest and most deeply considered and harmoniously crafted poems," in which the image of the woman / mother "reaches the highest peak that the poet's fantasy could attain, and the finest apotheosis of that type" [ZT 39:300].

75 The reference is to the second volume of the Czech edition of Shevchenko's *Kobzar* (1876), which included some unpublished works.

76 This is clearly a reference to Pavlo Kulchytsky, Franko's maternal uncle, who taught him how to read.

77 VR IL, fond 3 (Ivan Franko), file 2322, fols. 210–11. Hryn Berehuliak expressed his view of Christ's origin even more harshly; owing to its extreme vulgarity, I will not cite it here (ibid.).

78 Edmund L. Solecki, "Wojna o 'Jura stolae,'" *Gazeta Naddniestrzańska*, 15 June 1886, 2.

79 *Czas*, 7 June 1886.

80 "Psevdo-deiateli," *Novyi prolom*, 18 (31) June 1886, 1.

81 "Protses selian z Drohobychchyny," *Dilo*, 7 (19) June 1886, 1.

82 Iwan Franko, "Włościańe socjaliści," *Prawda*, 17 July 1886, 339.

83 *Materialy*, 191, 194.

84 For a detailed discussion of this movement, see Sergei I. Zhuk, *Russia's Lost Reformation: Peasants, Millennialism, and Radical Sects in Southern Russia and Ukraine, 1830–1917* (Washington, DC: Woodrow Wilson Center Press; Baltimore: Johns Hopkins University Press, 2004).

85 For additional details, see Kruhlashov, *Drama intelektuala*, 190–96, 204.

86 Solecki, "Wojna o 'Jura stolae,'" 3.

87 VR LNB, fond 1 (NTSh), file 493 / 53, fol. 3.

88 Like Semen Vityk ("Iz moikh spomyniv pro Franka," 53), John-Paul Himka (*Socialism in Galicia*, 138) states incorrectly that Atanasii Melnyk also died as soon as he was released from prison. In the late 1890s, he was one of the leaders of the Ruthenian-Ukrainian Radical Party and a trusted confidant of Franko's, when the writer was standing as a parliamentary candidate during the 1897 election. Melnyk died in 1905. See TsDIAL, fond 663, list 1, file 179, fol. 1. In 1940 Melnyk's son Andrii (b. 1890) became the leader of the Organization of Ukrainian Nationalists. See O. Zhdanovych, "Velykyi i blyz'kyi," in *Nezhasnyi ohon viry: zbirnyk na poshanu polkovnyka Andriia Mel'nyka, holovy Provodu Ukrains'kykh Nationalistiv* (Paris, 1974), 518.

89 VR LNB, fond 206 (Vasyl' Shchurat), file 922, folder 27, fol. 8.

90 *Poetical Works of Taras Shevchenko*, 14.

91 Borys Hrinchenko, *Shevchenkiv "Kobzar" na seli* (Kyiv, 1914), 29–30. Hrinchenko arrived at a similar conclusion after analyzing the popularity, in the countryside, of the works of another apostle of modern Ukrainians, Shevchenko's companion in arms Panteleimon Kulish. See Borys Hrinchenko, *Kulishovi tvory i sil's'ki chytachi* (n.p, n.d, [written in Kyiv in 1906]).

92 Cited in Saunders, "What Makes a Nation a Nation?," 111–12.

93 Orlando Figes, "The Russian Revolution of 1917 and Its Language in the Village," *Russian Review* 56 (July 1997): 324.

94 Cited in Prysiazhniuk, *Ukrains'ke selianstvo XIX–XX st.*, 80.

95 "Z nad Dnestra," *Osnova*, 23 March (4 April) 1871, 2.

96 Zhuravel', "Pravoslavna kul'tura na Bukovyni (Nadoslane)," *Zerkalo*, 15 March 1883, 15.

97 M. O. [Mikhail Osipovich] Koialovich, *Istoriia vossoedineniia zapadnorusskikh uniatov starykh vremen (do 1800 g.)* (Minsk: Luchi Sofii, 1999).

98 These cases should be distinguished from examples of the deliberate distortion of prayers to achieve a comic effect. See Franko, *Halyts'ko-rus'ki narodni prypovidky*, vol. 2, 222–23.

99 Kobylets'kyi, "Deshcho pro Franka," 41–42.

100 Bujak, *Z odległej i bliskiej przeszłości*, 134.

101 Here and there are other comments attesting to the popularity of individual newspaper articles that were written by Franko. But there are too few of them to trace a specific tendency. See chapter 15, "Franko and His Readers."

102 Daniel Field, "Peasants and Propagandists in the Russian Movement to the People of 1874," *Journal of Modern History* 59, no. 3 (September 1987): 415–38.

103 James C. Scott, *Weapons of the Weak: Everyday Forms of Peasant Resistance* (New Haven, Conn.: Yale University Press, 1994).

104 VR LNB, fond 1 (NTSh), file 493 / 53, fols. 2–3.

105 "Spomyny Petra Berehuliaka pro Ivana Franka," 46.

106 Steven L. Guthier, "The Popular Base of Ukrainian Nationalism in 1917," *Slavic Review* 38, no. 1 (March 1979): 30–47.

107 Himka, *Socialism in Galicia*, 121.

108 Himka, *Galician Villagers and the Ukrainian National Movement*, 215.

109 Puliui, *Zbirnyk prats*, 549–50.

110 See, e.g., the lengthy excerpt from the memoirs of Yulia Schneider (Uliana Kravchenko) about her experience teaching in the Drohobych area: under Franko's influence, the rural schoolteacher discovered the world of the peasantry. The peasants, both young and old, were dear to her because they reminded her of Franko in the physical and psychological senses. See Uliana Kravchenko, *Pam'iaty druha: virshi v prozi, statti,*

spohady, lysty, comp. and ed. H. I. Ohryza (Lviv: Kameniar, 1996), 87–88. See also the letters of another rural schoolteacher, Olha Bilynska, who addressed Franko only as Myron: VR IL, fond 3 (Ivan Franko), file 1603, fols. 111–13.

111 I tried to illustrate this process with the example of how peasants began giving their children names, during the baptismal rite, that earlier were only common among the educated classes. See my article, "Iakykh-to kniaziv buly stolytsi v Kyievi?...": Do konstruiuvannia istorychnoi pam'iati halyts'kykh selian u 1830–1930-ti roky, *Ukraina moderna* 6 (2001): 87–88.

112 This is emphasized by Marc Raeff in his Afterword to *Culture, Nation, and Identity: The Ukrainian-Russian Encounter, 1600–1945,* ed. Andreas Kappeler, Zenon E. Kohut, Frank Sysyn et al. (Edmonton: Canadian Institute of Ukrainian Studies Press, 2003).

113 VR IL, fond 3 (Ivan Franko), file 1583, fols. 25 –26; Puliui, *Zbirnyk prats',* 532; Rudnyts'kyi, *Pys'mennyky zblyzka,* 43, 80–81. See also chapter 15, "Franko and His Readers."

114 Iurii Shevelov, *Ukrains'ka mova v pershii polovyni dvadtsiatoho stolittia (1900–1941): stan i status,* trans. Oksana Solovei ([Munich]: Suchasnist, 1987), 35.

Chapter 12

1   The Boryslav cycle consists of seven short stories, two novels (*Boa Constrictor* and *Boryslav smiiet'sia* [Boryslav Is Laughing]), and the poem "Maksym Tsiunyk." For the most complete survey of the Boryslav cycle, see S. V. Shchurat, "Boryslavs'kyi tsykl khudozhn'oi prozy Ivana Franka (Dzherela, problematyka, maisternist' i metod)," (Doctor of Philological Studies diss., Instytut suspil'nykh nauk, AN URSR, Lviv, 1970).

2   The lengthiest, but not the most complete, bibliography of works about Franko in the West does not cite any work devoted to the Boryslav cycle. See Myroslav Moroz, comp., *Zarubizhne frankoznavstvo: bibliohrafichnyi pokazhchyk* (Lviv: L'vivs'ke viddilennia In-tu lit-ry im. T. H. Shevchenka Natsional'noi akademii nauk Ukrainy, 1997).

3   V. (Volodymyr) Koriak, *Burzhuazne pys'menstvo,* vol. 2 of *Narys istorii ukrains'koi literatury: U 2 t.* (Kharkiv: Derzhavne vydavnytstvo Ukrainy, 1929), 436.

4   D. S. Nalyvaiko, "'Boryslav smiiet'sia' Ivana Franka v porivnial'no-typolohichnomu aspekti," in *Ivan Franko—maister slova i doslidnyk literatury (do 125-richchia narodzhennia),* ed. M. T. Iatsenko (Kyiv: Naukova dumka, 1981), 332–62. For a survey of Soviet literary studies, see Shchurat, *Boryslavs'kyi tsykl,* 4–75.

5   K. H. Kakovs'kyi, *Na shliakhu do Velykoho Zhovtnia: straikovyi rukh v Halychyni kintsia XIX–pochatku XX st.* (Lviv: Vyd-vo L'vivs'koho universytetu, 1970).

6   The Soviet scholar who most distinguished himself in this respect was the Lviv-based historian Yakiv Khonigsman. None of the "facts" pertaining to workers' strikes in Boryslav, cited in his book, have ever been corroborated (see Ia. S. Khonigsman, *Pronyknennia inozemnoho kapitalu v naftovu promyslovist' Zakhidnoi Ukrainy v epokhu imperializmu (do 1918 r.)* (Lviv: Vyd-vo L'vivs'koho universytetu, 1971). Later, these "facts" migrated to the works of other Soviet historians. See, e.g., V. Makaiev, *Robitnychyi klas Halychyny v ostanniii tretyni XIX st.* (Lviv: Vyd-vo L'vivs'koho universytetu, 1968), among others.

7   I made such an attempt when I examined Franko's novel *Boryslav Is Laughing.* See my article, "Istorychna osnova povisti I. Franka 'Boryslav smiiet'sia,'" *Ivan Franko: Statti ta materialy* 44 (1985): 3–9.

8   Z. Bielski, "W sprawie starzeństwa przemysłu naftowego," *Przemysł naftowy* 4 (1932): 90; A. Schreiner, *Boryslaw und seine Producte: Entdeckung und Entwicklung derselben* (Drohobych, 1886), 7–9; J. Malinowski, "150-lecie przemysłu naftowego—nowe spojrzenie na dawne dokumente," located at: http/www.orpatowski.pl.lib/kopalnictwo.html.

9   Stefan Piatka [Stefan Kovaliv], "Produktsiia nafty (skel'noho oliiu) v Boryslavi," *LNV* 22 (1903): 101–2; *Bericht der Lemberger Handels- und Gewerbekammer über den Handel un die Industrie, so wie deren Beförderungsmittel in ihres Kammerbezirks für den J. 1861– 1865* (Lviv, 1867), 207; H. Gintl, *Galizische Petroleum und Ozokerit* (Vienna, 1873), 4–5.

10   For detailed discussion of the development of the local ozocerite industry, see Joseph Muck, *Der Erdwachsbergbau in Borysław* (Berlin: Julius Springer, 1903).

11   TsDIAL, Microfilm Collection, fond 4, list 1, file 78, fols. 40–58; "O produkcyi nafty w Galicyi," *Dodatek tygodniowy do Gazety Lwowskiej*, 17 October 1868.

12   DALO, fond 1188, list 2, file 3476, fols. 1–2; TsDIAL, fond 146, list 30, file 2896, fol. 2; fond 242, list 1, file 33, fol. 48; fond 255, list 1, file 1631, fols. 1–2; Piatka, "Produktsiia nafty," 103. Franko claimed that some local Greek Catholic priests were involved in the oil extraction business. See I. Franko, "Shcho se za inteligentsiia halyts'ki popy," *Za sto lit*, bk. 4, 243.

13   K. Marks and F. Engels, *Tvory*, vol. 23 (Kyiv, 1963), 675. The English translation is located at: http://www.marxists.org/archive/marx/works/1867-c1/ch26.htm. Last visited 14 February 2018.

14   TsDIAL, fond 146, list 55, file 35, fol. 2.

15   Ignaz Leichner, *Erdöl und Erdwachs: Ein Bild galizischer Industrie* (Vienna, 1898), 22; Muck, *Der Erdwachsbergbau in Borysław*, 1; Arnulf Nawratil, *Bericht der k.k. Gewerbe- Inspektoren über ihre Amtsthätigheit im Jahre 1885* (Vienna, 1886), 385.

16   S. Wisnowski, "Listy Amerykanina z Galicyi," *Gazeta Polska*, 28 December 1877.

17   Cited in Muck, *Der Erdwachsbergbau in Borysław*, 5.

18   Leichner, *Erdöl und Erdwachs*, 27.

19   In one of his articles Franko cites statistics collected by the Drohobych City Hall (*magistrat*), which revealed that during the first twenty or twenty-five years of Boryslav's industrial development the number of accidents reached 10,000 [*ZT* 44/1:63–64]. Although these data may be inflated, there is no doubt that accidents were a common enough occurrence. An approximate idea of their number may be derived from the following statistic: between January 1884 and March 1886, there were 109 accidents at local enterprises; a little less than half of them (44 percent) led to loss of life. See Ia. Grytsak [Ia. Hrytsak], "Rabochie Borislavsko-Drogobychskogo neftianogo basseina vo vtoroi polovine XIX–nachale XX vv.: Formirovanie, polozhenie, klassovaia bor'ba" (Candidate of Historical Sciences diss., Lviv, 1986), 61.

20   Muck, *Der Erdwachsbergbau in Borysław*, 121.

21   Polifem [pseud.], "Obrazki z Borysławia," *Nafta* 16 (1895): 146.

22   *Berichte der k.k. Bergbehörden über ihre Tätigkeit im Jahre 1896 bei Handhabung der Bergpolizei und Beaufsichtung der Bergarbeiterverhältnisse* [henceforward *Berichte... im Jahre* with the indicated year] (Vienna, 1899), 462; *Berichte...im Jahre 1904* (Vienna, 1907), 417.

23   *Berichte...im Jahre 1885* (Vienna, 1886), 384–85; *Berichte...im Jahre 1896*, 462; TsDIAL, fond 146, list 4, file 3420, fol. 87; *Wiadomości statystyczne* 15, no. 3 (1896): 44; "Borysław: Opis nędzy 10000 robotników," *Praca*, 14 June 1891.

24   Bujak, *Galicya*, vol. 2, 174; Muck, *Der Erdwachsbergbau in Borysław*, 123.

25 Berichte...im Jahre 1896, 462; Berichte...im Jahre 1897 (Vienna, 1900), 193; Leichner, Erdöl und Erdwachs, 25; Muck, Der Erdwachsbergbau in Borysław, 123. This correlation had an approximate character: in 1898–1899 Jews comprised 17–18 percent of all workers laboring underground. See Berichte...im Jahre 1898 (Vienna, 1901), 709; Berichte...im Jahre 1899 (Vienna, 1902), 507.

26 "Korespondencje 'Prace': Borysław, d. 25 maja," Praca, 20 June 1883, 35.

27 Ż. D. [Ignacy Daszyński], "Borysław: Burżua i robotnicy," Gazeta Naddniestrzańska, 1 June 1884, 3.

28 TsDIAL, fond 146, list 4, file 3411, fols. 96–97; Władysław Szajnocha, Płody kopalne Galicyi, ich występowanie i zużytkowanie, vol. 2 (Lviv, 1894), 121–22.

29 E. Windakiewicz, Das Erdöl und Erdwachs in Galizien (Vienna, 1875), 7–8, 26.

30 E.g., the millionaire mayor of Boryslav, Moishe Itsyk Kornhaber, started out as a worker. See Piatka, "Produktsiia nafty," 102.

31 V. Iu. Pastushchin, "Byt rabochikh Borislavskogo neftianogo raiona (1915–1953)," (Candidate of Historical Sciences diss., Kyiv, 1954), 33; El., "Kasjer Borysławski," Gazeta Naddniestrzańska, 15 January 1886, 1–2; -H.-, "Borysławski 'kuczyner,'" Gazeta Naddniestrzańska, 1 January 1885, 2–3.

32 Leichner, Erdöl und Erdwachs, 13, 32.

33 Ż. D., "Borysław: Burżua i robotnicy," 3.

34 R. Zuber, "Borysław i tegoż przyszłośc," Nafta 5 (1894): 69.

35 Berichte...im Jahre 1898, 657; Berichte...im Jahre 1902 (Vienna, 1905), 446, 450; Berichte...im Jahre 1904, 427.

36 One fascinating episode in the history of Zionism is connected with this migration: the fate of the Boryslav Jews attracted the attention of Theodor Herzl, the founder and chief ideologist of the Zionist movement.

37 According to official statistics, 3,442 workers had permanent employment in 1900. See Österreichische Statistik, vol. 61, bk. 11 (Vienna, 1904), 6, 12.

38 TsDIAL, fond 146, list 25, file 483, fol. 3; file 3621, fols. 252–55; file 3623, fol. 75; Berichte...im Jahre 1901 (Vienna, 1904), 429; "Jak u nas swiecono 1 Maja," Robotnik, 7 May 1897, 4–5; Walentyna Najdus, Polska Partia Socjalno-Demokratyczna Galicji i Śląska, 1890–1919 (Warsaw: Państwowe Wydawn. Naukowe, 1983), 116, 169.

39 Alison Fleig Frank, "Austrian El Dorado: A History of the Oil Industry in Galicia, 1853–1923" (Ph.D. diss., Harvard University, 2001), 243–44, 254–69.

40 Ibid., 284–340; Zofia Zaks, "Walka dyplomatyczna o naftę wschodniogalicyjską, 1918–1923," Z dziejów stosunków polsko-radzieckich: Studia i materialy 4 (1969): 37–60.

41 Bandrivs'kyi, "Spohady pro Franka-shkoliara," 53–54.

42 According to Soviet literary scholars, Boa Constrictor was conceived under the direct influence of Marx's introduction to the first edition of Das Kapital. See Dei, Ukrains'ka revoliutsiino-demokratychna zhurnalistyka, 228–33; P. I. Kolesnyk, Ivan Franko: Literaturnyi portret (Kyiv: Dnipro, 1964), 117–19.

43 Hrytsak, "Istorychna osnova," 3–9.

44 Oleh [Volodymyr Barvins'kyi], "Ohliad slovesnoi pratsi avstriiskykh Rusyniv v rotsi 1882," Dilo, 8 (20) January 1883, 1–2.

45 Ohonovs'kyi, Istoriia literatury ruskoi, vol. 3, 999.

46 Ivan Franko, "Pershyi z'izd halyts'kykh sotsiial-demokrativ," Narod, nos. 5–6 (1892): 73.

47 Taras Franko, Pro bat'ka: statti, opovidannia, spohady, 2nd exp. and rev. ed. (Kyiv: Derzh. vyd-vo khudozh. lit-ry, 1954), 39, 49–50.

48 Hrushevs'kyi, Z pochyniv ukrains'koho sotsiialistychnoho rukhu, 86–87.

49 Ivan Franko, Dokumenty i materialy, 100, 107.

50 VR IL, fond 3 (Ivan Franko), file 2556, fol. 2. Franko described his experiences with the gendarmes in a letter to Ivan Belei, dated early October 1881: "The gendarmes come to our house often, they chat about this and that, they recount their adventures; some of their stories will come in handy for my sketches. Sometimes when they find me writing, they would be glad to know what I am writing, but it's unfortunate that they are Mazurs, they don't know how to read Ruthenian, so they leave without having satisfied their curiosity" [*ZT* 48:288].

51 Daszyński, *Pamiętniki*, vol. 1, 3.

52 This is attested by two congratulatory telegrams that the workers of Drohobych sent to the Lviv assembly in January 1881. See "Lwowskie zgromadzenie robotników," 10 February 1881, 7.

53 TsDIAL, fond 146, list 6, file 47–87 / d, fol. 258.

54 VR IL, fond 3 (Ivan Franko), file 294, fol. 128; Ivan Franko, "Zhydy bohachi i 'kaptsany' v Halychyni," in *Za sto lit*, bk. 4, 258–59; see also his "Iz zhydivs´koi poezii zhargonovoi," *Tovarysh, Vistnyk literaturno-naukovyi*, 10 July 1888, 89.

55 "Korespondencje 'Pracy': Borysław, d. 25 maja," *Praca*, 20 June 1883, 35.

56 Daszyński, *Pamiętniki*, vol. 1, 25.

57 *Gazeta Naddniestrzańska*, 14 July 1887. For more information on Edmund Leon Solecki, see my article, "Zabutyi pol´s´kyi perekladach T. H. Shevchenka," *Materialy zasidan´ Istorychnoi ta Arkheohrafichnoi komisii NTSh v Ukraini*, vol. 2 (1995–97) (Lviv, 1999), 111–16.

58 TsDIAL, fond 146, list 7, file 4166, fols. 66–81, 84–90; file 4312, fols. 1–15; [E. L. Solecki], "Kronika Tygodniowa. Drohobycz, 10 września," *Strażnica. Tygodnik dla obrony spraw ekonomiczno-społecznych*, 15 September 1878, 317–18; "Korespondencje. Drohobycz, Państwo semicko-jezuickie naszego króla Hersza I," *Strażnica*, 25 September 1878, 336; "Korespondencje. Drohobycz, dnia 8 maja. Klika semicko-jezuicka..." *Strażnica*, 10 May 1879, 77. All the articles are unsigned. See TsDIAL, fond 146, list 7, file 4166, fols. 66–81, 84–90; file 4312, fols. 1–15.

59 Daszyński, *Pamiętniki*, vol. 1, 24–25; TsDIAL, fond 146, list 4, file 3694, fol. 33; Franko, "Pershyi zizd," 73; Kossak, "Ivan Franko ta ioho braty"; "Spomyny Petra Berehuliaka pro Ivana Franka," 43–46; Mariia Bilets´ka, "Kartyna z zhyttia Ivana Franka," in Dei and Korniienko, *Ivan Franko u spohadakh suchasnykiv*, vol. 1, 153–59.

60 This is attested by Franko's correspondence with the members of the Stanyslaviv group. See VR IL, fond 3 (Ivan Franko), file 1618, fols. 125, 157–60.

61 "Różności. Z Borysławia," *Praca*, 30 May 1881, 26.

62 Haecker, *Historja socjalizmu w Galicji*, 273.

63 K., "Morderstwa w Borysławiu," *Gazeta Naddniestrzańska*, 1 August 1884, 4–5; 15 August 1884, 2–3.

64 "Zaburzenia w Borysławiu," *Praca*, 23 July 1884; "Pierwsza przestroga dla burżuazji," *Praca*, 25 September 1884.

65 A similar situation existed among workers in the Donbas region. See Theodore H. Friedgut, *Life and Work in Russia's Donbass, 1869–1924*, vol. 1 of *Iuzovka and Revolution* (Princeton, NJ: Princeton University Press, 1989–94); Charters Wynn, *Workers, Strikes, and Pogroms: The Donbass-Dnepr Bend in Late Imperial Russia, 1870–1905* (Princeton, NJ: Princeton University Press, 1992).

66 Myron [Iwan Franko], "Z Czerwonej Rusi," *Prawda*, 30 (18) August 1884, 415.

67 An allusion to the reform of the Greek Catholic monastic order of St. Basil (Basilians), which the Vatican instituted in cooperation with the Austrian government in the early 1880s. For detailed discussion, see John-Paul Himka, *Religion and Nationality in*

Western Ukraine: The Greek Catholic Church and the Ruthenian National Movement in Galicia, 1867–1900 (Montreal: McGill-Queen's University Press, 1999), 79–84.

68 Ivan Franko, "Suchasnyi litopys," in his *Davnie i nove* (1884; 2nd exp. ed. of *Mii Izmarahd: Poezii*, Lviv, 1911).

69 S. Shchurat, "Boryslavs´kyi tsykl," 399–400.

70 The last fragment of the novel was published in the February issue of the journal *Zoria* 4 (1884): 32.

71 See S. Shchurat, "Boryslavs´kyi tsykl," 268–85.

72 In 1930, Franko's son Petro revised *Boryslav Is Laughing* and wrote the ending for the novel, seemingly based on real events that his father had recounted to him. In Petro Franko's version, after the workers conclude their meeting (see chapter 20 [*ZT* 15:471–79] in the original novel), they grab homemade torches and march through Boryslav, along the way setting fire to all the mines, storehouses, and cisterns filled with oil. However, they are beaten to the punch by Gottlieb, who sets fire to Leon Hammershlag's property in revenge for his refusal to let him marry his daughter Fanny. In the general confusion of the fire the workers throw Mortko, the overseer who had stolen the workers' fund, into the flames. They nearly do the same thing to Gottlieb, who accidentally falls into their hands but is saved by Benedio. In the final scene Goldkremer and Hammershlag make peace both with each other and the workers, and they promise to create a fund for the workers. Benedio predicts that conditions in Boryslav will change only when new workers appear, "who are better suited to life." See Petro Franko, *Boryslav smiietsia: drama v 4 diiakh: pislia povisty "Boryslav smiietsia" Ivana Franka* (Ternopil: Nakladom Vyd-va "Podil´s´ka teatral´na biblioteka" v Ternopoli, 1930), 53–56. Critics noted the implausibility of such an ending. Franko's handwritten notes outlining the novel describe a completely different plot: it is not Mortko who dies but Leon and Matii. Benedio dies as a result of a mishap, and Andrus Basarab ends up on trial [*ZT* 15:499].

73 M. Stepniak, "Ivan Franko ta B. Prus (Shche do istorii 'Boa konstriktor')," *Chervonyi shliakh* 1 (1929): 174–86.

74 For detailed discussion, see Wendland, *Die Russophilen in Galizien*, 321–37.

75 For a general survey, see Stefan H. Kaszyński, "Der jüdische Anteil and der Literatur in und über Galizien, " in *Von Franzos zu Canetti: jüdische Autoren aus Österreich: neue Studien*, ed. Mark. H. Gelber, Hans Otto Horch, and Sigurd Paul Scheichl (Tübingen: Niemeyer, 1996), 129–40.

76 A perusal of the Lviv-based newspaper *Der Israelit* for the years 1873, 1875–1877, 1879–1881, and 1895–1899 reveals that the Boryslav theme occupied a marginal place in this periodical. Even the local assimilationist newspaper, *Drohobyczer Zeitung*, published far fewer articles than, say, the Drohobych newspaper, *Gazeta Naddniestrzańska*. I would like to take this opportunity to thank Dr. Claudia Erdheim of the University of Vienna for sharing this observation with me.

77 This interpretation was suggested by the German literary scholar Martin Sander, "Mehrdeutigkeit des Raum: die Einbruch der Modern als Problem der literarischen Topographie am Beispiel von Ivan Franko und Bruno Schulz," in *Literaturoznavstvo*, vol. 2 of *Druhyi mizhnarodnyi konhres ukrainistiv. L´viv, 22–28 serpnia 1993 r.: dopovidi i povidomlennia* (Lviv: Mizhnarodna asotsiatsiia ukrainistiv, Akademiia nauk Ukrainy 1993–), 266–67.

78 Henryk Grynberg, *Drohobycz, Drohobycz: Galizische Erinnerungen, Zwölf Lebensbilder* (Vienna: Szolnay Verlag, 2000).

79 To my knowledge, the first novel recounting the story of a Jewish family that enriched itself in Boryslav was Claudia Erdheim, *Längst nicht mehr koscher* (Vienna: Czernin, 2006).

80 The novel *Di Yiddishe naftamafgnatn*, by Julien Hirszhaut, was written in Yiddish and has been translated into English only recently: Julien Hirszhaut. *The Jewish Oil Magnates*, trans. Miriam Dashkin Beckerman, ed. Valerie Schatzker (Montreal: McGill-Queen's University Press, 2015).

81 A similar paradox may be noted in the literary representation of the pogrom theme: it is barely present in the works of Jewish authors in the last two decades of the nineteenth century and the beginning of the twentieth, even though that was precisely the period when two of the three largest explosions of anti-Jewish violence occurred (1881–1882, 1903–1906, 1917–1921). See Joachim Beug, "Pogroms in Literary Representation," in *Ghetto Writing: Traditional and Eastern Jewry in German-Jewish Literature from Heine to Hilsenrath*, ed. Anne Fuchs and Florian Krobb (Rochester, NY: Camden House, 1999), 83–96.

82 A. Marczak, "Motywy i watki 'naftowe' w tworczosci literackiej," *Technika Naftowa i Gazownicza*, nos. 2–3 (1989): 13; Aleksander Zyga, "Pisarstwo polskie o początkach przemysłu naftowego," in *Krosno: studia z dziejów i regionu*, vol. 3, ed. Stanisław Cynarski (Rzeszów: Krajowa Agencja Wydawnicza, 1995) 175.

83 Jan Kucharski, afterword to *Tam, gdzie się Wisła kończy* by Artur Gruszecki (Gdansk: Wydaw. Morskie, 1979), 267–313; Kazimierz Wyka, "Gruszecki, Artur," in *Polski Słownik Biograficzny*, vol. 9 (Cracow: Polska Akademia Umiejętności, 1960–61), 59–61.

84 Artur Gruszecki, *Dla Miliona, powieść* (Warsaw: Nakład Gebethnera i Wolffa; Cracow: G. Gebethner i Spółka, 1900).

85 VR IL, fond 59, file 1242; Stefan Kovaliv, *Opovidannia, kazky, lysty: z nedrukovanoi spadshchyny* (Lviv: Kobzar, 2003), 164, 166–68.

86 V. M. Lesyn, S. I. Dihtiar, "Litopysets′ revolutsiinoho Boryslava," in Stefan Kovaliv, *Tvory* (Kyiv: Derzh. vyd-vo khudozh. lit-ry, 1958), 19.

87 Osyp Makovei, "Stefan Kovaliv," *LNV* 11, bk. 2 (1900): 81–91.

88 Kovaliv, *Tvory*, 628–49.

89 Kovaliv was closely connected with this newspaper, which published some of his Boryslav stories in 1884–85. Kovaliv, *Tvory*, 394–95, 513.

90 Ibid., 668.

91 Ibid., 387.

Chapter 13

1 Tadeusz Boy-Żeleński, *O Mickiewiczu* (Cracow: Czytelnik, 1949), 19–20, 30.

2 Shchurat's notes on Franko, undated. The Vasyl′ Shchurat Archive.

3 See Roman Horak, *Trychi meni iavlialasia liubov* (Kyiv: Radians′kyi pys′mennyk, 1983).

4 The letters that are extant were taken from Roshkevych in 1926 by her nephew Stepan Ivanets′, at the urging of his teacher, the Franko specialist Mykhailo Vozniak. See Denys Lukiianovych, "Lysty Ol′hy Roshkevych do Ivana Franka," in *Ivan Franko: Statti i materialy* 6 (1958): 5–48.

5 D. Lukiianovych, "Lysty Franka do Uliany Kravchenko," in *Ivan Franko: Statti i materialy* 5 (1956): 141–44.

6 Mykhailo Vozniak, "Iz strakhu pered zhyttievoiu nezabezpechenistiu. Koly rozkhodylys′ Ivan Franko i Ol′ha Bilyns′ka," *Nazustrich* 11 (83), 1 June 1937, 2.

7   Iaroslava Mel'nyk, *Z ostannoho desiatylittia Ivana Franka* (Lviv: Vyd-vo L'vivs'koho universytetu, 1999), 73–74. The copies of the burned letters were found and finally published in Dziuban, "Nevidomi lysty Ivana Franka," 161–86.

8   O. R. Kis', "Zhinka v ukrains'kii selians'kii sim'i druhoi polovyny XIX—pochatku XX stolittia: genderni aspekty" (Candidate of Historical Sciences diss., Instytut ukrainoznavstva im. I. Kryp'iakevycha NAN Ukrainy, 2001), 35, 57, 97–100, 130, 133; William I. Thomas and Florian Znaniecki, "A Polish Peasant Family," in *Peasants and Peasant Societies: Selected Readings*, comp. Theodor Shanin (Baltimore: Penguin, 1971), 23–29.

9   Eve Levin, *Sex and Society in the World of the Orthodox Slavs, 900–1700* (Ithaca, NY: Cornell University Press, 1989), 162, 301–2; N. L. Pushkareva, "Sem'ia, zhenshchina i seksual'naia etika v pravoslavii i katolitsizme: perspektivy sravnitel'nogo podkhoda," *Etnograficheskoe obozrenie* 3 (1995): 55–70.

10 Ezra Mendelsohn, "Jewish Assimilation in L'viv: The Case of Wilhelm Feldman," in Andrei Markovits and Frank Sysyn, eds., *Nationbuilding and the Politics of Nationalism: Essays on Austrian Galicia* (Cambridge, MA: Harvard Ukrainian Research Institute, c1982), 102

11 Kis', "Zhinka v ukrains'kii selians'kii sim'i," 63–64.

12 Christine D. Worobec, "Temptress or Virgin? The Precarious Sexual Position of Women in Postemancipation Ukrainian Peasant Society," *Slavic Review* 49, no. 2 (Summer 1990): 227–28.

13 Kis', "Zhinka v ukrains'kii selians'kii sim'i," 106, 111–12.

14 Alexander Sixtus von Reden and Josef Schweikhardt, *Eros unter Doppeladler. Eine Sittengeschichte Altösterreichs* (Vienna: Ueberreuter, 1993), 92–96.

15 Kis', "Zhinka v ukrains'kii selians'kii sim'i," 138, 171–72.

16 Franko subsequently used the plot of this song as the nucleus of his play *Ukradene shchastia* (Stolen Happiness) [*ZT* 24:7–64].

17 Kis', "Zhinka v ukrains'kii selians'kii sim'i," 145–49.

18 Kobylets'kyi, "Deshcho pro Franka," 39.

19 I am grateful to Prof. Petro Rudnytsky for suggesting this interpretation.

20 He revealed this trait not only in relation to women but also to his closest male friends. His best friend, Volodymyr Kotsovsky, complained about this. See VR IL, fond 132 (Uliana Kravchenko), file 173.

21 See Hnatiuk, *Spohady*, 108–9, 125.

22 Chapel's'kyi, "Ia liubyv ikh usikh," 149–60.

23 Hnatiuk, *Spohady*, 155.

24 Stefan Zweig, *The World of Yesterday: An Autobiography* (New York: Viking, 1943), 85.

25 Ibid., 72–73.

26 Andrii Chaikovs'kyi, "Natalia Kobryns'ka," *Kalendar "Zhinocha Dolia"* (1931): 26. Cited in Irena Knysh, *Smoloskyp u temriavi: Natalia Kobryns'ka i ukrains'kyi zhinochyi rukh* (Winnipeg: Novyi shliakh, 1957), 61. Chaikovsky does not name this mandatory item of men's clothing.

27 Archiwum Ojców Bazylianów. WAW. Coll. XX, B 3 / 13, unnumbered pages ("U Uliany Kravchenko (Spomyny)." Recorded by I. Radlovska, undated typescript).

28 Viacheslav Budzynovs'kyi, *Iak cholovik ziishov na pana: Avtobiohrafiia avtora* (Lviv, 1937), 32–33.

29 Doroshenko, *Moi spomyny pro davnie-mynule*, 51–52, 56.

30 Chłędowski, *Pamiętniki*, vol. 1, 145–46, 151–52, 163, 188, 221.

31 TsDIAL, fond 201 (Greek Catholic Consistory), list 4-b, file 2754, fols. 19–22.

32 VR IL, fond 132 (Uliana Kravchenko), file 1, fol. 41; Natalia Kobryns´ka, *Vybrani tvory* (Kyiv: Derzh. vyd-vo khudozh. lit-ry, 1958), 377; Ohonovs´kyi, *Istoriia literatury ruskoi*, vol. 3, 1273.

33 Lukiianovych, "Khto mav vyrishal´nyi vplyv," 5.

34 "Z 'Al´boma' Volodymyra B.," *Druh. Pys´mo literaturne* (no. 22, 1876): 337.

35 Kobryns´ka, *Vybrani tvory*, 334–35.

36 "Ot redaktsii 'Druha,'" "Holos do rodymtsev," *Druh*, July 1875, 297–99.

37 Martha Bohachevsky-Chomiak, "How Real Were Nationalism and Feminism in 19th-Century Galicia?" in Sophia Kemlein, ed., *Geschlecht und Nationalismus in Mittel- und Osteuropa, 1848–1918* (Osnabrück: Fibre, 2000), 151; Oksana Malanchuk-Rybak, *Ukrains´ki zhinochi studii: istoriohrafiia ta istoriosofiia*" (Lviv: Tovarystvo im. Shevchenka, 1999), 17–22; B. M. Ianyshyn, "Narodovs´kyi rukh u Halychyni iak suspil´no-politychna techiia (70–80-ti roky XIX st.)" (Candidate of Historical Sciences diss., Kyiv, 2003), 53.

38 Drahomanov, *Avstro-rus´ki spomyny*, 106–07.

39 Kobryns´ka, *Vybrani tvory*, 376-77.

40 This speech became the target of numerous jokes. One of them went like this: Pavlyk is explaining the harmfulness of the institution of marriage. The judge asks him if he is married. Pavlyk says no. Then the judge says: "Aha, so you're not married. So how can you know what it is?" Cited in "Z izby sądowej. Proces socjalistów ruskich," *Dziennik Polski* (no. 14), 17 January 1878, 3. Ludwik Waryński, a Polish socialist from the Russian Empire, was visiting Lviv at this time. He attended the trial with his lover, a woman named Jankowska, who had abandoned her husband and two children for Waryński. Bolesław Limanowski recalled that after a session of the trial, when Waryński was recapitulating the gist of Pavlyk's speech, both he (Waryński) and his companion were killing themselves laughing. "Although I was quite tolerant of that which concerned sexual relations, nevertheless I thought to myself that it was not very correct on Jankowska's part to make fun of Pavlyk's 'silliness,'" Limanowski writes in *Pamiętniki*, vol. 1, 181.

41 Pavlyk, *Perepyska*, vol. 2, 477.

42 Cited in Knysh, *Smoloskyp u temriavi*, 91.

43 For more details, see Denysiuk, *Mykhailo Pavlyk*, 106–18. This short work is based on a true story about one of Pavlyk's female relatives, who was given in marriage to a man she did not love. Franko dedicated his poem "Tetiana Rebenshchukova" to her [1:97].

44 Ivan Franko, *Dobryi zarobok i ynshi opovidania* (Lviv: Nakladom Antona Khoinats´koho, 1902), pp.vi–vii.

45 It is believed that Chernyshevsky based his novel on real facts: the marriage between Maria Obrucheva, who was the sister of the Russian radical, and the medical student Petr Bokov, who married her on Chernyshevsky's advice in order to free her to engage in an affair with the famous psychologist Ivan Sechenov. See Stites, *The Women's Liberation Movement in Russia*, 89–99.

46 Communal living was widespread among the Russian intelligentsia in the 1860s. Among the residents of communes were such famous artists as Ilya Repin and Modest Mussorgsky. However, from the late 1860s the founding of communes became a hallmark of the Russian revolutionary milieu (Stites, *The Women's Liberation Movement in Russia*, 108–11). By the time the idea of communes became popular in Galicia it had become an anachronism in Russia.

47 Ivan Franko, "Shchyrist´ tonu i shchyrist´ perekonan," *LNV* 30, bk. 5 (1905): 109; Stepan Shchurat, "Ivan Franko i rosiis´ki revoliutsiini narodnyky," *Doslidzhennia tvorchosti Ivana Franka*, vol. 2 (Kyiv: Vyd-vo Akademii nauk URSR, 1959), 93–95.

48 Lukiianovych, "Lysty Ol´hy Roshkevych," 12–14.

49 Horak, *Trychi meni*, 38.

50 Lukiianovych, "Lysty Ol´hy Roshkevych," 19.

51 Ibid., 30.

52 Ibid., 42–43. Franko described his meeting in Kolomyia with Roshkevych in the short story "Na dni" (At the Bottom).

53 Even earlier, in the spring of 1879, a letter that Olha Roshkevych had written to a third party fell into Franko's hands. Suspecting that she was flirting with another man, Franko forwarded the letter to Pavlyk for arbitration. Pavlyk, who already felt a strong antipathy for Roshkevych, whom he called the "priest's daughter," turned out to be very harsh in his judgment: he advised Franko not to believe Olha when she said that she had to get married in order to remain with the man she loved. "Rest assured that this matter will end in a real 'marriage': a fictitious one requires a stronger character than Olha" (VR IL, fond 3 (Ivan Franko), file 1604, fol. 520.

54 Horak, *Trychi meni*, 54.

55 Ibid., 47.

56 VR IL, fond 3 (Ivan Franko), file 1602, fols. 141–43.

57 Pavlyk, *Perepyska*, vol. 3, 156, 200, 266, 333–35.

58 Ibid., 374–75, 428.

59 VR IL, fond 132 (Uliana Kravchenko), file 218; Horak, *Trychi meni*, 71–87.

60 M. Vozniak, "Lysty Ivana Franka do Klymentyny Popovych," in Ivan Franko, *Statti i materialy* 3 (1952): 54–66; Klymentyna Popovych, "Spomyny pro Ivana Franka," in Hnatiuk, *Spohady*, 123–31; Mariia Bilets´ka, "Kartyna z zhyttia Ivana Franka," in Hnatiuk, *Spohady*, 121; Vozniak, "Iz strakhu," 2.

61 VR IL, fond 3 (Ivan Franko), file 1603, fols. 267–69.

62 Uliana Kravchenko, *Pam'iati druha*; Uliana Kravchenko, "Z lit davnomynulykh," Archiwum ojców Bazylianów, Warsaw.

63 Chapel´s´kyi, *Ia liubyv ikh usikh*, 149–60.

64 This almanac, titled *Pershyi vinok* (First Wreath), came out in 1887. See Mykhailo Vozniak, *Iak diishlo do pershoho zhinochoho almanakha* (Lviv, 1937).

65 V. A. Goshovskaia, "Stanovlenie i razvitie rabochei pressy v Vostochnoi Galitsii v poslednei treti XIX veka," (author's abstract of her dissertation for a Candidate of Philological Sciences degree, Kyiv, 1983), 14.

66 Osyp Makovei, "Iz shchodennyka," in Dei and Korniienko, *Ivan Franko*, 217; Klymentyna Popovych, "Spomyny pro Ivana Franka," 129.

67 VR IL, fond 3 (Ivan Franko), file 1583, fols. 17–18.

68 Oleksa Volians´kyi, "Moi spomyny pro Ivana Franka," in Hnatiuk, *Spohady*, 491; Ianyshyn, *Narodovs´kyi rukh u Halychyni*, 54–55; Wendland, *Russophilen in Galizien*, 373. Franko complained about the nepotism among the older populists who, thanks to their family connections, restricted the radicals' access to publications [*ZT* 48:322].

69 Franko, *Moloda Ukraina*, 8.

70 Pavlyk, *Perepyska*, vol. 2, 33, 102, 111.

71 This is most likely Olha Hortynska (1855–?), the sister of P. Hortynsky, a member of the People's Will. Olha, who was a close friend of Pavlyk and Drahomanov, acted as liaison between the Hromada of Kyiv and the Geneva émigré community. She studied medicine in St. Petersburg and later completed her medical studies in Switzerland [*ZT* 48:646]; see also the Mykhailo Drahomanov Archive, 25–26, 267, 355, 408. Pavlyk believed that with her "lively temperament" she was a better match for Franko than Olha Roshkevych, with her "very slow movements and thoughts" (VR IL, fond 3 [Ivan

Franko], file 1604, fol. 519). Franko spotted Hortynska, or someone resembling her, in Vienna in 1892 and described the circumstances of this encounter in the poem "Pryvyd" (The Apparition). See Vasyl´ Shchurat, "Nimets´kyi p'ianytsia v ukrains´komu odiazi," in Dei and Korniienko, *Ivan Franko*, bk. 2, 95. The gist of the poem indicates that his acquaintance had become a prostitute, which tinged their encounter with a particular bitterness [*ZT* 2:134–36].

72 VR IL, fond 3 (Ivan Franko), file 1603, fols. 401–3, 517–18, 545.

73 Ibid., fol. 624. Olha's sister, Trehubov's wife Antonina, claims that her husband refused to help Franko because in their family it was not considered proper to interfere in the intimate affairs of adults. Trehubova, "Deshcho z zhyttia Ol´hy Frankovoi," in Hnatiuk, *Spohady*, 156. Trehubov's answer, sent by letter, does not confirm this version.

74 Anna Kliuchko-Franko, "Ivan Franko ta ioho rodyna," in Hnatiuk, *Spohady*, 484.

75 Krzywicki, *Wspomnienia*, 265.

76 VR IL, fond 3 (Ivan Franko), file 1603, fol. 864.

77 Irena Knysh, *Ivan Franko ta rivnopravnist zhinky* (Winnipeg: Novyi shliakh, 1956), 53.

78 Trehubova, "Deshcho z zhyttia Ol´hy Frankovoi," 156; VR IL, fond 3 (Ivan Franko), file 1603, fol. 624.

79 Lonhyn Ozarkevych, "Moi spomyny pro Franka," in Hnatiuk, *Spohady*, 92.

80 VR IL, fond 3 (Ivan Franko), file 1603, fol. 865.

81 Serhii Shelukhyn, "Ukrainstvo 80-kh rokiv XIX v. i moi znosyny z Iv. Frankom," in Hnatiuk, *Spohady*, 191–93. Shelukhyn, who was Antonovych's student and a "kul´turnyk" (culturalist) in his views, claimed that he could name around twenty mixed Ukrainian-Russian marriages and that all of them were unhappy. This same conclusion was purportedly confirmed by anthropological field studies in the Kherson region, located in the Ukrainian-Russian border area: according to birth records, in one village, which had a population of 20,000, there was only one mixed marriage. Shelukhyn published an article in the Lviv newspaper *Pravda*, which was based on a conspectus of a lecture by Antonovych. The "Drahomanovite" Fedir Vovk was angered by it, and he said as much to the author (ibid.). As Pavlyk's correspondence indicates, the "Drahomanovites" themselves were not free of these prejudices. In 1880, Pavlyk was living in the emigration with Serhii Podolynsky and his wife Natalia Yakymivna, who was an ethnic Russian. In his letters to Drahomanov he showed how Podolynsky's attitude to the Ukrainian movement depended on his wife's influence: before her arrival on the scene, and also during quarrels with her, he condemned the national intolerance of the Russian revolutionaries, but when their marital relations were beginning to improve, he justified their tactic and became hostile to the Ukrainian movement. See Pavlyk, *Perepyska*, vol. 3, 494.

82 Trehubova, "Deshcho z zhyttia Ol´hy Frankovoi," 157.

83 Shelukhyn, "Ukrainstvo," 191.

84 Hnat Zhytets´kyi, "Odruzhennia I. Ia. Franka," in Hnatiuk, *Spohady*, 161; Trehubova, "Deshcho z zhyttia Ol´hy Frankovoi," 156.

85 Trehubova, "Deshcho z zhyttia Olhy Frankovoi," 158.

86 Hryhorii Velychko, "Spomyny pro Ivana Franka," in Hnatiuk, *Spohady*, 290. See also Roshkevych (Ivanets´), "Spohady pro Ivana Franka," 115; Sofiia Oleskiv-Fredorchakova, "Iz spohadiv pro Ivana Franka," 434.

87 This is evident from their correspondence and from Franko's poem that was written half a year after his marriage [*ZT* 2:401].

88 For the history of this romance, see Horak, *Trychi meni*, 88–118; Dziuban, "Nevidomi lysty Ivana Franka," 161–86.

89 See Tom Digby, ed., *Men Doing Feminism* (New York: Routledge, 1998).

90 See Mykhailo Vozniak's unpublished article "Kobryns'ka, 'vil'na liubov' i radykaly (uchast' Franka v sprostuvanni Pavlyka)," which is stored in VR LNB, fond 29 (Mykhailo Vozniak), file 94.

91 Ievhen Hrytsak, *Vybrani ukrainoznavchi pratsi* (*Przemyśl*: n.p., 2002), 364–67, 370–75, 380–82

92 Martha Bohachevsky-Chomiak, *Feminists Despite Themselves: Women in Ukrainian Community Life, 1884–1939* (Edmonton: Canadian Institute of Ukrainian Studies, 1988), 105.

93 VR IL, fond 3 (Ivan Franko), file 1603, fols. 445–46, 455–57.

94 See Budzynovs'kyi, *Iak cholovik ziishov na pana.*

95 Denys Lukiianovych, "Trahediia Kobryns'koi (z nahody zhinochoho Kongresu)," *Dilo*, 24 June 1934, 3–4; Kliuchko-Franko, "Ivan Franko ta ioho rodyna," 469.

96 Kyrylo Trylovs'kyi, *Z moho zhyttia* (Toronto: Takson, 1999), 105–6.

97 Yarosevych's marriage ended in a fiasco: a few years into the marriage, Yarosevych's wife abandoned him for a lover with whom she returned to her motherland. This family catastrophe affected Yarosevych so much that he completely abandoned his political activity. Okunevsky's circumstances turned out to be happier, although people remained prejudiced toward his wife, who never learned to speak Ukrainian. Ibid., 79, 84–85.

98 The only known attempt to set up a family commune, which occurred much later, in the 1970s–1980s, was made by some Ukrainian Canadians from Alberta. A group of young leftist intellectuals and feminists set up a residential cooperative in the city of Edmonton, which sprang from the Hromada cultural society. All the members of the cooperative lived separately but in close proximity, which allowed them to raise their children in a leftist, Ukrainian-speaking milieu. One can speak of the influence of Franko and the Galician radicals only in relation to John-Paul Himka, the researcher of the Ukrainian socialist movement. Kobrynska was the role model for the women, while the other members of the cooperative were influenced by the traditions of the eastern Ukrainian left-wing movement of the twentieth century. (John-Paul Himka to the author, 16 September 2003).

99 Trylovs'kyi, *Z moho zhyttia*, 196.

100 TsDIAL, fond 201 (Greek Catholic Consistory), list 4-b, file 2754, fols. 51–52.

101 Alexander J. Motyl, *The Turn to the Right: The Ideological Origins and Development of Ukrainian Nationalism, 1919-1929* (New York: Distributed by Columbia University Press, 1980).

102 Cited in "Chy Franko zasluzhyv na nahrobnyk?" *Dilo* (no. 136), 23 June 1932, 1.

103 TsDIAL, fond 359, list 1, file 351, fols. 32–35. Nazaruk offered, however, two exceptions to this rule: the first concerned marriages among the "simple folk," while the second concerned daughters from interethnic marriages in the intellectual milieu. He cited the example of Milena Rudnytska, the leader of the Ukrainian women's movement, who was the product of a Ukrainian-Jewish marriage.

104 Osyp Nazaruk, *Halychyna i Velyka Ukraina: Traktat prysviachenyi ukrains'kym zhinkam i viis'kovym* (Lviv, 1936), 45–48.

105 The justness of the accusations that she never "learned the Ukrainian language well" is corroborated by her letters to Yulia Schneider, written in 1930 and 1932 (see IL VR, fond 132 [Uliana Kravchenko], file 2190), which are written in *surzhyk*, a mixed Ukrainian-Russian language; these letters also contain obvious traces of the psychiatric illness from which she suffered from the time she married Franko. Among other things, she cites from memory eighteen poems by Mikhail Lermontov, adding: "What could be better

than that?" At the same time, there is no doubt that Khoruzhynska was a Ukrainian patriot: "Proceeding consistently, we all champion an independent Ukraine," she wrote in one of these letters.

Chapter 14

1   To this day only one systematic analysis of the topic of Franko and the Jews has ever been published. This is a lengthy article by Petro Kudriavtsev, which was prepared for the Jewish Historical-Archaeographic Commission of the Ukrainian Academy of Sciences and published in 1929. See P. Kudriavtsev, "Ievreistvo, ievrei ta ievreiska sprava v tvorakh Ivana Franka," in *Zbirnyk prats' ievreis'koi istorychno-arkheohrafichnoi komisii*, vol. 2, ed. A. I. Kryms'kyi (Kyiv, 1929), 1.

2   See, e.g., Zvi Gitelman, "Soviet Reactions to the Holocaust, 1945–1991," in *The Holocaust in the Soviet Union: Studies and Sources on the Destruction of the Jews in the Nazi-Occupied Territories of the USSR, 1945–1991*, ed. Lucjan Dobroszycki and Jeffrey Gurock (Armonk, NY: M. E. Sharpe, 1993), 3, 9–11.

3   One example is the secret memorandum issued by Glavlit (the central censorship committee) of the Ukrainian SSR on 12 March 1953, "Pro shkidlyvu praktyku Instytutu ukrains'koi literatury Akademii nauk URSR" (On a Harmful Practice of the Institute of Ukrainian Literature of the Academy of Sciences of the Ukrainian SSR). The memorandum proposed, among other things, to halt the publication of a volume of Franko's works, which was supposed to include his long poem, *Moses*, because it was about the "'promised land' of the Jewish people of Palestine and the Jews' longing for Palestine, which to them is their native home, etc." See the Central State Archive of Civic Associations of Ukraine (Tsentral'nyi derzhavnyi arkhiv hromads'kykh ob'iednan' Ukrainy; henceforward TsDAHO Ukrainy), fond 1, list 24, file 2712, fol. 162). A list of Franko's works with Jewish themes was never published in the Soviet Union. See Zinoviia Franko, "50-tomne zibrannia tvoriv I. Franka v otsintsi sohodennia," *Suchasnist'* 10 (1989): 113–14; see also her "Peredmova" [*Mozaika* 10–12].

4   Ivan Franko, "Moi znaiomi zhydy," *Dilo*, 28 May 1936, 5–6; 29 May 1936, 5–6; 30 May 1936, 5–6 (trans. Mykhailo Vozniak; reprint, *Mozaika*, 335–47); Wasyl Szczurat, "Wtedy było to jeszcze mrzonką," *Chwila poranna*, 5 August 1937, 5.

5   For a bibliography of these articles, see Moroz, *Zarubizhne frankoznavstvo*, 41, 56, 63–64.

6   See Leila P. Everett, "The Rise of Jewish National Politics in Galicia," in Markovits and Sysyn, *Nationbuilding and the Politics of Nationalism*, 166–67; Jobst, *Zwischen Nationalismus und Internationalismus*, 82–83; Ezra Mendelsohn, "From Assimilation to Zionism in Lvov: The Case of Alfred Nossig," *Slavonic and East European Revue* 49, no. 117 (October 1971): 521–34.

7   The only exception is Asher Wilcher, "Ivan Franko and Theodor Herzl: To the Genesis of Franko's 'Mojsej," *Harvard Ukrainian Studies* 6 (1982): 233–43.

8   "Ivan Franko i zhydivs'ke pytannia," *Krakivs'ki visti*, 28 May 1943, 3–4. For the circumstances surrounding the publication of this article, see John-Paul Himka, "*Krakivs'ki visti* and the Jews, 1943: A Contribution to the History of Ukrainian-Jewish Relations during the Second World War," *Journal of Ukrainian Studies*, nos. 1–2 (Summer–Winter 1996): 81–95. Dr. Himka, who had access to the archive of *Krakivs'ki visti*, was able to identify the author of this article, but did not reveal his name until after his death in 2001. The author was Anatol Kurdydyk. See John-Paul Himka, "War

Criminality: A Blank Spot in the Collective Memory of the Ukrainian Diaspora," paper presented at the conference, Gespaltene Geschichtskulturen? Die Bedeutung des Zweiten Weltkrieges für die Etablierung Nationalstaatlicher Symboliken und Kollektiver Errinerungskulturen in Ostmitteleuropa, Lviv, 30 May–1 June 2003.

9   Cited in "Ivan Franko…antysemit," (unsigned), *Svoboda* 178 (1958).

10 Ivan Franko, *Zur Judenfrage=Do iudeiskoho pytannia: statti* (Kyiv: Mizhrehional´na akademiia upravlinnia personalom, 2002); Panteleimon Kulish, *Zhydotriepaniie* (Kyiv: MAUP, 2005); and Vasyl´ Iaremenko, *Ievrei v Ukraini sohodni: real´nist´ bez mifiv* (Kyiv: Mizhrehional´na akademiia upravlinnia personalom, 2003). All three books were published by the Interregional Academy of Personnel Management (MAUP), which is known for its efforts to spread antisemitism in Ukraine.

11 This is precisely why the compilers of an additional volume of Franko's "censored" works did not include his poems about Shvyndeles Parkhenblit or the articles "Pytannia zhydivske" (The Jewish Question) and "Mozes Mendelson—reformator zhydivs´kyi" (Moses Mendelson, the Jewish Reformer), and others. See Zinoviia Franko, "Peredmova," [*Mozaika* 11].

12 See my article about the recent dissemination in Lviv of antisemitic leaflets containing statements attributed to Franko: Iaroslav Hrytsak, "Namy znovu manipuliuiut´," *Postup*, 19 September 2003, 10.

13 In an article that was an early version of this chapter I tried to explain this question: Jaroslaw Hrycak, "Między filo-Semityzmem i antysemityzmem—Iwan Franko i kwestia żydowska," in *Świat niepożegnany: żydzi na dawnych ziemiach wschodnich Rzeczypospolitej w XVIII–XX wieku=A World We Bade No Farewell: Jews in the Eastern Territories of the Polish Republic from 18th to 20th Century*, ed. Krzysztof Jasiewicz (Warsaw: Instytut Studiów Politycznych PAN: Oficyna Wydawn. RYTM; London: Polonia Aid Foundation Trust, 2004), 451–80.

14 Artur Eisenbach, *Emancypacja żydów na ziemiach polskich 1785–1870 na tle europejskim* (Warsaw: Państ. Instytut Wydawniczy, 1988), 14–15, 21; Alfred Nossig, *Materialien zur Statistik des Jüdischen Stammes* (Vienna: C. Konegen, 1887); Prusin, *Nationalizing a Borderland*, 6.

15 For detailed discussion of this topic, see *Pogroms: Anti-Jewish Violence in Modern Russian History*, ed. John D. Klier and Shlomo Lambroza (Cambridge: Cambridge University Press, 1992).

16 For detailed discussion of this topic, see Shlomo Avineri, "The Presence of Eastern and Central Europe in the Culture and Politics of Contemporary Israel," *Eastern European Politics and Societies* 10, no. 2 (Spring 1996): 163–72.

17 Nossig, *Materialien zur Statistik*, 38–39, 59.

18 Peter Pulzer, *The Rise of Political Antisemitism in Germany and Austria*, rev. ed. (London: P. Halban, 1988), 3.

19 Raphael Mahler, "The Economic Background of Jewish Emigration from Galicia to the United States," in *East European Jews in Two Worlds: Studies from the YIVO Annual*, ed. Deborah Dash Moore (Evanston, IL: Northwestern University Press; [New York]: Yivo Institute for Jewish Research, 1990), 127, 134.

20 Cited in ibid., 134.

21 See John-Paul Himka, "Ukrainian-Jewish Antagonism in the Galician Countryside during the Late Nineteenth Century," in *Ukrainian-Jewish Relations in Historical Perspective*, ed. Howard Aster and Peter J. Potichnyj (Edmonton: CIUS Press, 1988). Franko claimed, however, that clergymen were active in spreading the tale of Jews committing ritual killings of Christians [*Mozaika* 338].

22 Kai Struve, "Gentry, Jews, and Peasants: Jews as Others in the Formation of the Modern Polish Nation in Rural Galicia during the Second Half of the Nineteenth Century," in *Creating the Other: Ethnic Conflict and Nationalism in Habsburg Central Europe*, Austrian Studies, vol. 5, ed. Nancy M. Wingfield (New York: Berghahn, 2003), 106–7.

23 Szczepanowski, *Nędza Galicyi*, 117–18.

24 Aleksander Hertz, *The Jews in Polish Culture* (Evanston, IL: Northwestern University Press, 1988), 84–85.

25 For detailed discussion, see Jerzy Holzer, "Zur Frage der Akkulturation der Juden in Galizien im 19. und 20. Jahrhundert," *Jahrbücher für Geschichte Osteuropas* 37 (1989): 217–27; Vladimir Melamed, *Evrei vo L´vove (XIII–pervaia polovina XX veka): Sobytiia, obshchestvo, liudi* (Lviv: Sovmestnoe ukrainsko-amerikanskoe predpriiatie Tekop, 1994), 107–36.

26 For detailed discussion, see Wróbel, "The Jews of Galicia," 101–2.

27 Mendelsohn, "Jewish Assimilation in L´viv," 106.

28 For a book exploring this process, based on an analysis of the autobiographies of those who left the shtetl, see Kłańska, *Aus des Schtetl*.

29 Caro, "Lichwa na wsi w Galicji," 4–11; Tadeusz Pilat, "Licytacye sądowe posiadłości włosciańskich i małomiejskich w latach 1880–1883 włącznie," *Wiadomości statystyczne o stosunkach krajowych* 8, no. 3 (1884): 139–41. The following fact should be noted: the increase in the permanent number of auctioned farms was accompanied by an increase in the number of Jewish merchants who were forced to sell off their stocks of merchandise. This suggests that the worsening situation of Christian peasants and tradesmen had a negative impact on the material circumstances of Jewish merchants, and even usurers, which fact demonstrates once again the degree to which the Jewish and non-Jewish economies existed in symbiosis and mutual dependence. See Pilat, "Licytacye sądowe, 157–60.

30 Himka, "Ukrainian-Jewish Antagonism," 114–15.

31 Józef Buzek, "Stosunki zawodowe i socyalne ludności Galicyi według wyznania i narodowości. Na podstawie spisu ludności z 31 grudnia 1900 r.," *Wiadomości statystyczne o stosunkach krajowych* 20, no. 2 (1905): 26.

32 Teofil Merunowicz, *O metodzie i celach rozpraw nad kwestią żydowską* (Lviv, 1879).

33 Wilhelm Marr, *Der Weg zum Siege des Germanenthums über das Judenthum* (Berlin, 1879).

34 Cited in Mendelsohn, "Jewish Assimilation in L´viv," 107.

35 Struve, "Gentry, Jews, and Peasants," 107–16.

36 See Porter, *When Nationalism Began to Hate*.

37 This fact was noted simultaneously by a number of researchers specializing in Galician-Jewish history: Ia. R. Dashkevych, "Vzaiemovidnosyny mizh ukrains´kym ta ievreis´kym naselenniam u Skhidnii Halychyni (kinets´ XIX–pochatok XX st.)," *Ukrains´kyi istorychnyi zhurnal* 10 (1990): 63–73; Kłańska, *Aus des Schtetl*, 224; and Claudia Erdheim, with whom I had private discussions.

38 Pulzer, *Rise of Political Antisemitism*, 135–36.

39 Everett, "Rise of Jewish National Politics in Galicia," 156–66; Porter, *When Nationalism Began to Hate*, 176–82; Lysiak-Rudnyts´kyi, *Istorychni ese*, vol. 1, 126–27, 440.

40 Franko, *Halyts´ko-rus´ki narodni prypovidky*, vol. 1, 106–16.

41 Ibid., 114. The lack of relevant studies makes it difficult to analyze anti-Christian stereotypes among Eastern European Jews. Nevertheless, there are occasional references to such stereotypes. See Mark Zborowski and Elizabeth Herzog, *Life Is with People: The Culture of the Shtetl* (New York: Schocken, 1962), 67, 144, 148, 152.

42 Franko was convinced that the "blood libel" was known throughout Ruthenian-Ukrainian villages. However, it elicited "neither deeper emotion nor fantastic hatred" in the peasants [*Mozaika* 338]. We found a completely different account in the memoirs of Franko's peer, Rev. Mykhailo Zubrytsky. The priest recalled the fear he experienced as a young boy the first time that he saw a lot of Jews in Przemysl. His father took him to a local tavern during a break from their journey to visit a distant relative. The little boy was told that "Jews catch small Christian children, put them inside a barrel pierced with nails, roll the barrel, and that's how they get blood from a child in order to mix it with their *paska*." The frightened boy fled from the tavern, and his father had to run to catch up with him (VR LNB, fond 206 [Vasyl´ Shchurat], list 922, file 27, fol. 4).

43 Mendelsohn, *Painting a People*, 26.

44 Franko was connected to the Tigerman family by long-standing ties of friendship: Isaac's father corresponded with Franko for many years. See VR IL, fond 3 (Ivan Franko), list 1603, fols. 209, 267–69. Isaac's mother had great respect for Franko and told local gymnasium students that "there is no other great mind in all of Austria, if not for socialism, long ago he could already have been a minister." See Stefanyk, *Vybrane*, 231.

45 In 1896, Monat published an article in Vienna about the most recent works of Ruthenian-Ukrainian literature, giving high praise to Franko. In 1897, Monat engaged in a discussion with Franko on the pages of the influential journal *Die Zeit* in connection with Franko's famous article about Mickiewicz, titled "Der Dichter Verrathers." For more information on Monat, see Aleksander Zyga, "Monat, Henryk," in *Polski Słownik Biograficzny*, vol. 21 (Cracow: Polska Akademia Umiejętności), 641–42.

46 For more information on Sternbach, see *Biogramy uczonych polskich: materiały o życiu członków AU w Krakowie, TNW, PAU, PAN*, ed. Andrzej Środka and Paweł Szczawiński, pt. 3 (Wroclaw: Zakład Narodowy im. Ossolińskich, 1983–), 314–18; Łuczyńska, "Udział towarzystwa nauczycieli szkół średnich Galicji 1884–1909," in *Galicja i jej dziedzictwo*, vol. 3, 265.

47 Kudriavtsev, "Ievreistvo, ievrei ta ievreis´ka sprava," 2.

48 *Druh*, 1 (13) October 1875, 295.

49 I[van] F[ranko], "Nekrology," *LNV* 10 (1900): 62. Ludwik Inlender partly financed the publication of "Na Dni," one of Franko's most famous short stories.

50 Pavlyk, *Perepyska*, vol. 3, 173–74.

51 Franko, "Zhydy bohachi i 'kaptsany,'" 258–59.

52 [Stepan Kachala], *Polityka rusyniv* (Lviv, 1873), 23.

53 I. Naumovych, "O Halytskoi Rusi," 38–40.

54 Pavlyk, *Perepyska*, vol. 2, 28.

55 Kn. [Oleksandr Konys´kyi], "Galichina i Rusiny. Iz dorozhnykh zametok i nabliudenii," *Vestnik Evropy* (September 1886): 126.

56 *Materialy*, 354.

57 "Korespondencje, Lvov, dnia 5 (17) lypnia 1884," *Gazeta Naddniestrzańska*, 1884, 4.

58 Cf. the observations of the Austrian ethnographer, Raimund Friedrich Kaindl, who lived for a considerable period of time among the Hutsuls. Kaindl mentions the widespread practice of childless peasants adopting nonfamily members, to whom they were prepared to bequeath their property on condition that the adoptee would support them until their death. Very often these adoptees were Jews, who were considered trustworthy. At the same time, the Hutsuls believed it was a sin to engage in sexual relations with a Jew. The Hutsuls had a much greater intolerance toward greedy priests and evangelicals (they disliked the latter because they did not observe the fasts). But most conflicts took place between neighbors; neighbors were usually not chosen to be

godparents, because quarrels between parents and godparents were regarded as a sin. See R. F. Kaindl, *Hutsuly: ikh zhyttia, zvychai ta narodni perekazy* (Chernivtsi: Molodyi bukovynets´, 2000), 40, 59, 98.

59 Cited in Ivan Franko, *Radykal´na partiia*, pt. 2, *Radykaly i zhydy* (Lviv, 1899), 9.

60 See chapter 2, "The Mysteries of Franko's Birth."

61 Irwin Michael Aronson, *Troubled Waters: The Origins of the 1881 Anti-Jewish Pogroms in Russia* (Pittsburgh, PA: University of Pittsburgh Press, 1990); Wynn, *Workers, Strikes, and Pogroms.*

62 The scale of Jewish immigration to Galicia has not been studied. This topic is mentioned in the Galician press of the time. The populist-oriented Ukrainian journal of humor, *Zerkalo* (more on this below), published the following joke: "What is the difference between Moses's Jews and Russian Jews? Those ones crossed the Red Sea, but the other ones crossed Red Rus [i.e., Russia]. And what is the difference between the Red Sea and Red Rus? The Pharaoh got stuck in the Red Sea, but in Red Rus Jews are the ones getting stuck." See *Zerkalo*, 1883 (no. 77).

63 [Ivan Franko], "Pytanie zhydivs´ke," *Dilo*, 20 August (1 September) 1884, 1.

64 Ibid., 2.

65 Petro Kudriavtsev doubts that Franko wrote this article because "it is difficult to square it with [his] basic democratic world perception." See Kudriavtsev, "Ievreistvo, ievrei ta ievreis´ka sprava," 72n.

66 Franko's contemporaries considered this poem to be lowbrow. See Volodymyr Doroshenko, "Ivan Franko (Zi spomyniv avtora)," *Svoboda*, 6 June 1957. However, the fact that the editors of the magazine's final issue of 1884 announced a "treat" to encourage readers to renew their subscriptions for another year (see "Ot redaktsii," *Nove zerkalo*, 15 (27) December 1884, 4) is a clear indicator of its popularity.

67 The magazine published the writings of Franko's friend Vasyl Nahirny, with whom he shared an apartment. Franko admitted later that some images and caricatures had appeared in *Zerkalo* and *Nove zerkalo* at his instigation. Omelian Ohonovsky claimed that in 1884 Franko was the soul of *Nove zerkalo* (see chapter 9, "A Journal, All We Need Is a Journal!"

68 "Ispyt," *Zerkalo*, 15 December 1882, 187; "Shvyndeles Parkhenblyt," *Zerkalo*, 15 February 1882, 29; 15 May 1882, 77; 15 June 1882, 92; 15 January 1883, 11; 15 March 1883, 53; and 1 May 1883, 68.

69 See *Zerkalo*, 15 December 1882, 187.

70 In addition to n. 6 in Mendelsohn's article, "From Assimilation to Zionism in Lvov," see also Shmuel Almog, "Alfred Nossig—A Reappraisal," *Studies in Zionism* 7 (1983): 1–29; Mitchell B. Hart, "Moses the Microbiologist: Judaism and Social Hygiene in the Work of Alfred Nossig," *Jewish Social Studies* 2, no. 1 (1995): 72–97; Janina Kulczycka-Saloni, *Na Polskich i europejskich szlakach literackich: z pism rozproszonych 1985–1998* (Warsaw: Antyk, 2000), 199–213.

71 Nossig, "Proba rozwiązania kwestji żydowskiej," 261, 286–93, 353–57, 370, 412–13.

72 *Der Israelit*, 26 November 1886, 1–2 (the article was published as an unsigned editorial).

73 *Przegląd Społeczny* 2 (1886): 232.

74 See chapter 12, "Franko and His Boryslav."

75 This topic was the subject of Franko's later poem "Asymiliatoram" (To the Assimilators; 1889). The poem begins with the following lines: "Pryhnuty zhydiv, pokoryty / Vy radi b pid vashi prava, / Ikh movu i zakon rozoryty?… / Pusti tse, bezumni slova." (You are keen to bend the Jews, / Submit them to your rights, / Destroy their language and law?… / These are empty, insane words) [*Mozaika* 33]. Franko devoted a separate article to Moses

Mendelssohn, the ideologist of the Haskalah. See Ivan Franko, "Zhydy v zhyttiu i literaturi: 1. Mozes Mendel´son, reformator zhydivs´kyi," *Zoria*, 1 (13) April 1886, 114–15.

76 Kudriavtsev, "Ievreistvo, ievrei ta ievreis´ka sprava," 79.

77 For detailed discussion, see Dashkevych, "Vzaiemovidnosyny mizh ukrains´kym ta ievreis´kym naselenniam," 66–67.

78 Lysiak-Rudnyts´kyi, *Istorychni ese*, vol. 1, 388.

79 Iwan Franko, "Żydzi o kwestji Żydowskiej," *Tydzień*, 20 March 1893, 93.

80 See n. 7 above.

81 Theodore R. Weeks, "Polish 'Progressive Antisemitism,' 1905–1914," *East European Jewish Affairs* 25, no. 2 (1995): 49–67.

82 Emma Adler, Vienna: Verein für Geschichte der Arbeiterbewegung, 1989, 2–3, 10, 14. This brochure contains extracts from some of her letters that are stored in the VGA; the Adler family has banned access to the complete archive.

83 Ursula Phillips, "The 'Jewish Question' in the Novels and Short Stories of Eliza Orzeszkowa," *East European Jewish Affairs* 25, no. 2 (Winter 1995): 69–90.

84 T. G. Masaryk, *President Masaryk Tells His Story*, recounted by Karel Čapek, trans. from the Czech (London: G. Allen and Unwin, 1934), 29; Robert S. Wistrich, "The Jews and Nationality Conflicts in the Habsburg Lands," *Nationalities Papers* 22, no. 1 (Spring 1994): 129, 136.

85 For the most extensive discussion of Drahomanov's attitude to the Jewish question, see Lysiak-Rudnyts´kyi, *Istorychni ese*, vol. 1, 117–20, 375–89, 391–97.

86 Antisemitic notes also emerge in their correspondence, particularly in descriptions of their close Jewish friends. See *Materialy*, 39, 129, and 251.

87 Cf., in particular, his later programmatic work: Franko, *Radykal´na partiia*. See n. 59.

88 Peter Gay, *Freud, Jews, and Other Germans: Masters and Victims in Modernist Culture* (New York: Oxford University Press, 1978), 15.

89 Franko, *Radykal´na partiia*, 12–13.

90 See, e.g., the poem (below) written by a peasant radical named Monastyrsky from the village of Soltsi, Drohobych County:

Пам'ятай наші що ся звали стане навіки

Бо ми хлопи радикали всіх урядах будемо стояти навіки.

Ой ви пани панички уже досить панських зисків навіки

Всі подяки усі треба позичь [sic!] і ше треба навіки.

І рекрута ми всі дали абись увсі вім нім мали навіки

А ті житки [євреї—Я.Г.] все ховаються і грішми

Підплачутся навіки

Ой житки багаті ви служете на етапі навіки

Усі хлопи гортаються у сотні записуються навіки

Чи, в Карпати чи під [С]трипу щоб зібрати більшу силу все треба…

А нам за се усе добре що Україна наша мати

Вона нам наша мати Навіки.

Remember our people, who always called themselves rebels / For we peasant radicals will occupy all posts for all time. / Oh, you gentlemen lords, enough of your eternal lordly exploitation. / For all benefits one needs loans and will still need them forever /

And we gave all the recruits so that you would have them for all time / But those Jews always hide and always pay money / O rich Jews, you are always serving at the back / All the peasants are assembling in the hundreds, are signing up for all time / Or, in the Carpathians or at the [S]trypa River in order to assemble an even larger force... / And for this it is good for us that Ukraine is our mother / She is our mother For All Time. (VR IL, fond 132 [Uliana Kravchenko], file 233).

91 Struve, "Gentry, Jews, and Peasants," 104–26.
92 Hertz, *Jews in Polish Culture*, 203, 216.
93 Yohanan Petrovsky-Shtern, "Reconceptualizing the Alien: Jews in Modern Ukrainian Thought," *Ab Imperio* 4 (2003): 519–80.

Chapter 15

1 VR IL, fond 59, file 2753, fols. 204, 286, 289–302. A large fragment was reprinted in Makovei, "Iz shchodennyka," 213–15.
2 "Lystuvannia Ivana Pan´kevycha z Antonom Dol´nyts´kym u 1940–1944 rokakh," *ZNTSh* 234 (2000): 558; Popovych, "Spomyny pro Ivana Franka," 124.
3 Makovei later published a history of this circle. See Osyp Makovei, *Istoriia odnoi studentskoi hromady* (Lviv, 1912).
4 VR IL, fond 59, file 2753, fols. 290–302.
5 Ivan Em. Levytskii (Ivan Omelianovych Levyts´kyi), *Halytsko-russkaia bybliohrafiia XIX stolitiia s uvzhliadnenniem russkykh izdanii poiavyvshykhsia v Uhorshchyni i Bukovyni* (1801–1886), vol. 1., *Khronolohycheskii spysok publikatsii* [1801–1860] (Lviv, 1888), ix, xx–xxi.
6 Ibid., xxi.
7 These estimates are based on Moroz, *Ivan Franko: Bibliohrafiia tvoriv*, 7–8, 18–39, 103–9, 155–93.
8 Levytskii, *Halytsko-ruskaia bybliohrafiia*. The discrepancy between Levytsky's bibliographic data (78 entries) and Franko's bibliographic data (572 entries) is explained by the use of different types of descriptive entries: in Levytsky's bibliography, an individual entry was the title of any kind of book or annual of a newspaper or journal.
9 Iryna Vushko, "Evoliutsiia chytats´kykh interesiv l´viv´ian u druhii polovyni XIX st. (Za danymy pro diial´nist´ Biblioteky Ossolins´kykh," *Ukraina moderna* 8 (2003): 127–41. (Vushko's article is based on her M.A. thesis.)
10 S[vystun], *Chem est´ dlia nas Shevchenko?*, 4–6.
11 Franko, "Uchenyts´ka biblioteka u Drohobychi," 126.
12 Uliana Kravchenko, *Spohady uchytel´ky* (Kolomyia: Nakl. Zahalnoi knyhozbirni, 1936), 222, 234.
13 "Wstręt do czytania," *Strażnica*, 16 February 1878, 52–53.
14 Kravchenko, *Spohady uchytel´ky*, 232.
15 [Oleksandr Barvins´kyi], "Ohliad slovesnoi pratsi avstriiskykh Rusyniv za rik 1881," *Dilo*, 2 (12) January 1882, 2. For discussion of authorial attribution, see [*ZT* 41:428].
16 Chłędowski, *Pamiętniki*, vol. 1, 201.
17 Pavlyk, *Tvory*, 193, 199, 225, 232, 235–36.
18 Franko, *Moloda Ukraina*, 26–27. For a detailed description of these publications, see Iakymovych, *Knyha, prosvita, natsiia*.
19 Iakymovych, *Knyha, prosvita, natsiia*, 183.
20 Hryhorii Tsehlyns´kyi, "Krytychni zamitky i bibliohrafiia," *Zoria*, 8 (20) July 1887, 241–42.

21 Iakymovych, *Knyha, prosvita, natsiia*, 195, 200, 206.

22 Kobylets´kyi, "Spomyny z dytynnykh lit Franka," 40.

23 For data on the print runs of populist periodical publications in 1880–1885, see Himka, *Galician Villagers and the Ukrainian National Movement*, 63.

24 *Materialy*, 75, 166.

25 Jerzy Brandes [Georg Brandes], *O czytaniu: odczyt wygłoszony d. 26 listopada r. 1898. w sali ratuszowej we Lwowie* (Lviv, 1899), 8, 13.

26 See Reitblat, *Kak Pushkin vyshel v genii*, 30–31.

27 Pavlyk, *Tvory*, 250.

28 "Prosvitnyi postup Halytskoi Rusy za poslidnee desiatyletie," *Zoria*, 8 (20) July 1887, 233.

29 Pavlyk, *Perepyska*, vol. 2, 97.

30 Nothing is known about the fate of a book written by the young Franko, which was part of a series of mass publications issued by the Prosvita Society: *Rozmova pro hroshi i skarby z peredmovoiu o zalozhenniu Dobrovlianskoi chytal´ni* (1883) [A Conversation about money and treasures with an introduction about the founding of the Dobrovliany reading room]. However, it may be assumed that this book, which was written in the form of a popular textbook on political economy for a narrow readership—"gymnasium students as well as for peasants who read a bit" [*ZT* 48:197]—could not have found a mass readership. For information on Franko in other publications issued by the Prosvita Society and their public reception, see [*ZT* 49:249].

31 VR IL, fond 3 (Ivan Franko), file 1603, fol. 739.

32 One example of a failed professional writer was Franko's younger colleague, Viacheslav Budzynovsky. The author of popular historical works, Budzynovsky barely eked out a living from his writing, and several times nearly starved to death. As his biographer later wrote, Budzynovsky "tried to live by the pen, but in our country this means 'extreme poverty.'" See Mykhailo Rudnyts´kyi, "Trahediia humorysta," in Budzynovs´kyi, *Iak cholovik ziishov na pana*, 11.

33 I. Svientsits´kyi, "Deshcho pro nauku, literaturu i mystetstvo Halyts´koi Ukrainy za ostannikh 40 lit," *Dilo*, 14 January 1928, 15.

34 Ievhen Olesnyts´kyi, *Storinky z moho zhyttia*, pt. 2, 1890–1897 (Lviv, 1935), 3.

35 Kost´ Odovets´, "Osvita na zakhidno-pivdennii Ukraini," *Zoria*, 8 (20) August 1887, 259–62.

36 In 1886 this was reported to Franko by Eliza Orzeszkowa, who was living in Grodno at the time. After reading a few issues of *Dilo*, which had been "processed" this way, she stopped reading this newspaper. (BN, wżs, mf 67675, 2–3).

37 The first piece of writing by Franko that did not make it past the Russian censors was an article titled "Luk'ian Kobylytsia," after the peasant rebel chieftain. It was supposed to be published in 1884 in *Przegląd Tygodniowy*, the mouthpiece of the Polish Positivists. See Stanisław Makowski and Tadeusz Styszko, "Z nie opublikowanej korespondencji Iwana Franki z Adamem Wiślickim," *Slavia Orientalis* 7, no. 1 (1958): 127–28). In 1887, Russian censors banned the publication of a Polish translation of Franko's short story "Muliar," which was slated to appear in the Warsaw-based newspaper *Prawda* (VR IL, fond 3 (Ivan Franko), file 1608, fol. 595). In 1888, the publication of his poetry collection *Z vershyn i nyzyn* was banned (see Franko, *Dokumenty*, 120–21). These works were banned because of their revolutionary content, not because they were written in Ukrainian. For the history of Franko works banned in the Russian Empire, see "Tsarskaia tsenzura o proizvedeniiakh pisatelia I. Franka: Vvodnaia statia Polianskoi," *Krasnyi arkhiv* 98, no. 1 (1940): 263–77; I. Kurylenko, "Zaborona tvoriv I. Franka tsars´koiu tsenzuroiu,"

Radians'ke literaturoznavstvo 1 (1959): 137–41; Hryhorii Pavlenko, "Ivan Franko i tsars'ka tsenzura (90-i rr. XIX st.)," *Ukrains'ke literaturoznavstvo: respublikans'kyi mizhvidomchyi zbirnyk: Ivan Franko: Statti i materialy* 26 (1976): 23–30; "Ivan Franko i tsars'ka tsenzura (1909–1914 rr.)," *Carpatica-Karpatyka* (Uzhhorod) 6 (1999): 204–9.

38 VR IL, fond 3 (Ivan Franko), file 1608, fols. 143–45.

39 VR IL, fond 3 (Ivan Franko), file 1608, fol. 387.

40 VR IL, fond 3 (Ivan Franko), file 1603, fol. 355; file 1608, fol. 323.

41 P. Lukashevych [Pavlo Tuchaps'kyi], "Ukrainskie natsional'nye partii," *Vistnyk" zhizni*, 30 March 1906, 40, cited in Olga Andriewsky, "The Politics of National Identity: The Ukrainian Question in Russia, 1904–1912" (Ph.D. diss., Harvard University, 1991), 193; Ievhen Malaniuk, *Knyha sposterezhen': Proza* (Toronto, 1962), 12. The theory that the young Franko was little known in the Ukrainian gubernias of the Russian Empire appears in the diary of Oleksandr Kistiakivsky. In his entries for the years 1880–1885, this intellectual, who was very supportive of the Ukrainian movement, was a member of the Kyiv Hromada, and had many contacts in Galicia, does not mention Franko and his works even once, as though they did not exist. See Kistiakivs'kyi, *Shchodennyk*, vol. 2.

42 For statistics dating to the early 1880s, see Heck, "Bibliografia Polska z r.," 1103–9.

43 [Oleksandr Barvins'kyi], "Ohliad slovesnoi pratsi avstriis'kykh Rusyniv za rik 1881," 4.

44 Aleksandra Garlicka, *Spis tytułów prasy polskiej 1865–1918* (Warsaw: PAN, IBL, 1978 [Warsaw: WDN]), 411.

45 Jerzy Jarowiecki, "Prasa ugrupowań politycznych we Lwowie w okresie autonomiji galicyjskiej (1867–1918)," in *Kraków–Lwów: Książki, czasopisma, biblioteki XIX i XX wieku*, vol. 5, ed. Jerzy Jarowiecki (Cracow: Wydawnictwo naukowe Akademii Pedagogicznej, 2001), 396, 411.

46 It is very likely that Franko himself proposed and carried out this role, above all for financial considerations. This is indirectly attested by the fact that he paid scant attention to the content of his contributions, often resorting to duplicating them, for which he received a (mild) reprimand from Erazm Pilc, the editor of *Kraj*, who demanded that he curb this practice. See VR IL, fond 3 (Ivan Franko), file 1608, fols. 161–63. The author of the biography of Aleksander Świętochowski, the editor of *Prawda*, regards this episode as evidence of rivalry between these two newspapers. See Maria Brykalska, *Aleksander Świętochowski: Biografia*, 2 vols. (Warsaw: Państ. Instytut Wydawniczy, 1987), vol. 1, 370.

47 VR LNB, fond 168 (Osyp Markov), file 188 / 7, fol. 1

48 Nie-Eol [Edward Przewóski], "Iwan Franko," *Przegląd Tygodniowy*, 27 November (7 December) 1894, 567–68. Przewóski's authorship was established by later researchers, who noted that the reason the article was so short was that it had been shortened by the censors. An even more abbreviated version of Franko's biography was republished in the St. Petersburg *Kraj*. See Makowski and Styszko, "Z nie opublikowanej korespondencji," 121–22.

49 "Postup," *Kurjer Lwowski*, 24 November 1886, 1.

50 See chapter 14, "Franko and His Jews."

51 Viacheslav Budzynovs'kyi, "Latynka: Spohad," *Novi shliakhy* 10 (1931): 66; Trylovs'kyi, *Z moho zhyttia*, 27, 30–31, 34–35, 37, 43, 122, 124, and 172.

52 The period in which Franko made substantial inroads into the Czech- and German-language market began somewhat later, in the late 1880s, and peaked in the 1890s. See *Zviazky Ivana Franka z chekhamy ta slovakamy*, comp. M. Molnar and M. Mundiak (Bratislava: Slovats'ke vyd-vo khudozh. lit-ry, 1957), 399–481; *Beiträge zur Geschichte und Kultur der Ukraine: Ausgewählte deutsche Schriften des Revolutionären Demokraten,*

1882-1915, ed. E. Winter and P. Kirchner (Berlin: Akademie Verlag, 1963). See also Moroz, *Ivan Franko: Bibliohrafiia tvoriv*, 164–65.

53 VR IL, fond 3 (Ivan Franko), file 1603, fol. 233.

54 VR IL, fond 3 (Ivan Franko), file 1603, fol. 838.

55 Vozniak, *Iak diishlo do pershoho zhinochoho al'manakha*, 45.

56 Vozniak, *Iv. Belei i Ol. Konys'kyi*, 24.

57 VR IL, fond 3 (Ivan Franko), file 1602, fols. 149–52.

58 VR IL, fond 3 (Ivan Franko), file 1603, fol. 605.

59 Vozniak, *Iak diishlo do pershoho zhinochoho al'manakha*, 51.

60 VR LNB, fond 168 (Osyp Markov), file 188, folder 7, fol. 1.

61 VR IL, fond 3 (Ivan Franko), file 1603, fol. 616.

62 See chapter 12, "Franko and His Boryslav."

63 VR IL, fond 3 (Ivan Franko), file 1603, fol. 55.

64 Natalia Kobryns'ka, *Vybrani tvory*, 402–3.

65 Ustyanovich, *Raevskii i rossiiskii panslavizm*, 75.

66 [Oleksandr Barvins'kyi], "Ohliad slovesnoi pratsi avstriis'kykh Rusyniv za rik 1881," 4.

67 VR IL, fond 3 (Ivan Franko), file 1603, fols. 543–44.

68 "Zamitky i visty," *Zoria*, 15 (27) February 1883, 64.

69 VR LNB, fond 29 (Mykhailo Vozniak), file 641, folder 147, fol. 10.

70 VR IL, fond 3 (Ivan Franko), file 1603, fol. 523.

71 VR LNB, fond 29 (Mykhailo Vozniak), file 169, fols. 1–15.

72 H[ryhorii] Ts[ehlyns'kyi], [Review of] "Z vershyn i nyzyn. Zbirnyk poezii Ivana Franka. L'viv, 1887," *Zoria*, 8 (20) July 1887, 242.

73 *Zoria*, 8 (20) August 1887, 271–72.

74 Ts[ehlyns'kyi], [Review of] "Z vershyn i nyzyn," 241.

75 Tarnavs'kyi, *Spohady*, 85; Chaikovs'kyi, "Moi spohady pro Ivana Franka," 97.

76 *Zoria*, 1 (13) June 1887, 194.

77 VR LNB, fond 29 (Mykhailo Vozniak), file 641, folder 169, fols. 2–4.

78 Ibid., fol. 4.

79 Cited in Vozniak, *Iak diishlo do pershoho zhinochoho al'manakha*, 45.

80 A. Khvan'ko [Ahatanhel Kryms'kyi], [Review of] "V poti chola: Obrazky z zhytia robuchoho liudu. Napysav Ivan Franko, L'viv, 1890," *Zoria* 12 (1891): 77. Krymsky's review was written in 1891, but it mostly concerns the short stories that Franko had written in his youth.

81 BN, wźs, mf 67675, 83–84, 90.

82 *Zoria*, 8 (20) July 1887, 271.

83 See chapter 9, "A Journal, All We Need Is a Journal!"

84 Cited in S. V. Shchurat, "Ivan Franko i Vasyl' Shchurat u literaturnykh zv'iazkakh ta lystuvanni," in *Doslidzhennia tvorchosti Ivana Franka*, ed. I. P. Kryp'iakevych (Kyiv: Vyd-vo Akademii nauk URSR, 1956–), 205–55.

85 [A. Koniski], "Zarys ruchu literackiego Rusinów," *Atheneum* 3 (1885): 350–51. The entry under "Franko Iwan" in the card catalog of the Institute of Literary Research at the Polish Academy of Sciences (Kartoteka im. Bara Instytutu Badań Literackich PAN) lists a different author: Czesław Neyman. See Franko's reply in *Zoria*, 1 (13) October 1885, 226–27.

86 "Czego chcą galicyjscy rusini," *Przegląd Tygodniowy*, 22 February (8 March) 1881, 2; E. Przeworski, "Działa Apołona XXV. Ivan Franko," *Przegląd Tygodniowy* 49 (1884): 567–68. For a bibliography of Polish responses to Franko and his works, as well

translations, see Mirosława Kosiecka and Zofia Żydanowicz, "Iwan Franko w Polsce do 1953" (MS., Biblioteka Narodowa, Zakład Informacji Naukowej).

87 BN, wźs, mf 67675, 74.

88 "Postup," *Kurjer Lwowski*, 24 November 1886, 1.

89 This was Felix Daszyński's chief motive concerning the translation of Franko's short story "Na dni." See Makowski and Styszko, "Z nie opublikowanej korespondencji," 126.

90 Viacheslav Budzynovs´kyi, *Ishly didy na muku: vvedennia v istoriiu Ukrainy* (Lviv: V-vo "Ukrains´ke slovo," 1925), 29.

91 "Iz L´vova ("Akademicheskii Kruzhok." Obshchee sobranie. Myzykal´no-deklamatorskii vecher)," *Slovo*, 13 (25) November 1875, 1; "Iz L´vova (Publichnoe chtenie v "Akademicheskom Kruzhke")," *Slovo*, 18 (30) November 1875, 1; "Treťe general´noe sobranie obshchestva imeni Mikhaila Kachkovskogo," *Slovo*, 12 (24) August 1876, 1–2.

92 See the next chapter, "How Franko Became a Genius."

93 VR IL, fond 3 (Ivan Franko), file 1603, fols. 430–31.

94 Vasyl´ Shchurat, "Ivan Franko i taini kruzhky v akadem. gimnazii," *Ukrains´ka shkola* 13–14 (1926): 6, 10–12.

Chapter 16

1 Olesnyts´kyi, "Z-ponad chetvertyny stolittia," 68.

2 Vasyl´ Bilets´kiy, "Spomyny pro moi vzaiemyny z d-rom Ivanom Frankom," in *Spohady*, 59 –60; Kurovets´, "Ivan Franko v moikh zhadkakh," ibid., 69–71; Kyrylo Studyns´kyi, "Iak ia stav uchenykom Franka," ibid., 100–4; Kobryns´ka, *Vybrani tvory* (1980 ed.), 317–18.

3 Józef Szocki, *Księgozbiory domowe w Galicji wschodniej (1772–1918)* (Cracow: Wydaw. Naukowe AP, 2001), 122.

4 H. J. Eysenck, *Genius: The Natural History of Creativity* (Cambridge: Cambridge University Press, 1995), 124.

5 Ibid., 126–47.

6 Robert Currie, *Genius: An Ideology in Literature* (London: Chatto and Windus, 1974), 11, 23, 48–51; Barbara Otwinowska, "Geniusz," in *Słownik literatury polskiego oświecenia*, ed. Teresa Kostkiewiczowa (Wroclaw; Warsaw; Cracow, 2002), 139; Stefan Treugutt, "Geniusz," in *Słownik literatury polskiej XIX wieku*, ed. Józef Bachórz and Alina Kowalczykowa (Wroclaw: Zakład Narod. im. Ossolińskich, 2002), 318–21.

7 Janina Kulczycka-Saloni, "Poeta mendax—i prawda polskich dziejów," in *Wiek XIX: Prace, ofiarowane Stefanowi Kieniewiczowi w 60 rocznicę urodzin*, ed. Barbara Grochulska, Bogusław Leśnodorski, and Andrzej Zahorski (Warsaw: Państwowe Wydawn. Naukowe, 1967), 439–49; Frank Muir, *An Irrelevant and Thoroughly Incomplete Social History of Almost Everything* (New York: Stein and Day, 1976), 104.

8 Reitblat, *Kak Pushkin vyshel v genii*, 57.

9 Augustus Hopkins Strong, *The Great Poets and Their Theology* (Philadelphia: American Baptist Publication Society, 1897), vii.

10 Kulczycka-Saloni, "Poeta mendax," 439–49; Muir, *An Irrelevant and Thoroughly Incomplete Social History*, 104; Reitblat, *Kak Pushkin vyshel v genii*, 57; Wiktor Weintraub, "Poeta," in *Słownik literatury polskiej XIX wieku*, 711–15; K. Wyka, "Warunki i przebieg rozwoju kultury polskiej w drugiej połowie XIX w.," in *Historia Polski*, ed. Żanna Kormanowa and Irena Pietrzak-Pawłowska, vol. 3, pt. 1 (1850 / 1864–1900) (Warsaw: Polska Akademia Nauk, Instytut Historii, 1967), 736.

11 Pamela Davidson, "The Moral Dimension of the Prophetic Ideal: Pushkin and His Readers," *Slavic Review* 61, no. 3 (Fall 2002): 506–14.

12 Jacques-Guy Petit, "Das Gefängnis," in *Orte des Alltags: Miniaturen aus der europäischen Kulturgeschichte*, ed. Heinz-Gerhard Haupt (Munich: C. H. Beck, 1994), 250–59.

13 Peter Brock, *The Slovak National Awakening: An Essay in the Intellectual History of East Central Europe* (Toronto; Buffalo: University of Toronto Press, 1976); George G. Grabowicz, "Province to Nation: Nineteenth-Century Ukrainian Literature as a Paradigm of the National Revival," *Canadian Review of Studies in Nationalism* 16, nos. 1–2 (1989): 117–32.

14 Czesław Miłosz, *The History of Polish Literature* (London: Macmillan, 1969).

15 Davidson, "Moral Dimension of the Prophetic Ideal," 490.

16 Paul Debreczeny, *Social Functions of Literature: Alexander Pushkin and Russian Culture* (Stanford, CA: Stanford University Press, 1997), 163–93; Reitblat, *Kak Pushkin vyshel v genii*, 209.

17 George G. Grabowicz, *The Poet as Mythmaker: A Study of Symbolic Meaning in Taras Ševčenko* (Cambridge, MA: Harvard Ukrainian Research Institute, 1982).

18 For the preceding quotations in the paragraph: S[vystun], *Chem est' dlia nas Shevchenko?*, 4, 11–12.

19 V. Stefanyk, "Poety i inteligentsiia," *LNV* 2, book 6 (June 1899): 23.

20 Ustyianovych, *Raevskii i rossiiskii panslavizm*, 42.

21 *Materialy*, 205.

22 M. Hvozdevych, "Kul´t Markiiana Shashkevycha u seredyni XIX–na pochatku XX st." (Diss., Lviv, 2004); Ihor Chornovol, "Markiian Shashkevych: mekhanizmy kul´tu," *Krytyka* 87–88, nos. 1–2 (2005): 30–31; *Rusalka Dnistrova*, 285–89.

23 See the biography of Kachkovsky that was specially written with this goal in mind: Bohdan A. Didyts´kyi, *Mikhail Kachkovskii i sovremennaia galitsko-russkaia literatura: Ocherk biograficheskii i istoriko-literaturnyi*, pt. 1 (Lviv, 1876).

24 Pavlyk claimed that there was a time when rural reading rooms esteemed the trinity of the Austrian emperor, Taras Shevchenko, and Volodymyr Barvinsky. But the latter's cult lasted only about a dozen or so months. See Mykhailo Pavlyk, *Propashchyi cholovik: Opovidannia, povisti, publitsystyka* (Lviv: Kameniar, 1983), 348.

25 Verkhrats´kyi, *Zlobni vydumky d-ra Ivana Franka*, 10–12; Drahomanov, *Avstro-rus´ki spomyny*, 18.

26 Iv[an] Franko, "Postscriptum pro Vol. Stebel´s´koho," *LNV* 12 (December 1905): 215; Iuliian Chaikovs´kyi, "Volodymyr Stebel´s´kyi," ibid., 81.

27 On Naumovych as a poet, see Ivan Franko, "Is istorii 'moskvofil´skoho' pys´menstva v Halychyni. III. Naumovych-poet," *LNV* 8, bk. 11 (1899): 53–65.

28 O. A. Monchalovskii, *Zhyte i diiatel´nost´ Ivana Naumovycha* (Lviv, 1889), 73–74.

29 "Tret´e general´noe sobranie obshchestva imeni Mikhaila Kachkovskoho," *Slovo*, 12 (24) August 1876, 1–2.

30 V. R. Vavrik, *Narodnaia slovesnost´ i seliane-poety* (Lviv, 1929), 16; Makowski and Styszko, "Z nie opublikowanej korespondencji," 125; Pavlyk, *Perepyska*, vol. 4, 308.

31 For further details, see Himka, *Religion and Nationality in Western Ukraine*, 94–96.

32 Monchalovskii, *Zhyte i diiatel´nost´ Ivana Naumovycha*, 84–86, 88.

33 Kurovets´, "Do pochatkiv 'Dila,'" 8; Makovei, *Istoria odnoi students´koi hromady*, 12; Shchurat, "Ivan Franko i taini kruzhky," 10–11.

34 VR IL, fond 3 (Ivan Franko), file 1619, fol. 2.

35 Himka, *Religion and Nationality in Western Ukraine*, 26–28, 94–98.

36 Monchalovskii, *Zhyte i diiatel´nost´ Ivana Naumovycha*, 71, 102, 112.

37 *Torzhestvennyi Literaturno-muzykal'nyi vecher, posviashchennyi pamiati I. G. Naumovicha v 100 letniuiu godovshchinu so dnia rozhdeniia 26.1.1826–26.1.1926. Programma* (Lviv, 1926) (no page numeration).

38 Kurovets', "Do pochatkiv 'Dila,'" 8. See also Pavlyk's assessment in chapter 9 of this book, "A Journal, All We Need Is a Journal!"

39 I. Naumovych, "Nazad k narodu!" *Slovo*, 5 (17) May 1881, 1; 19 (31) May 1881, 2; 28 May (9 June) 1881, 2–3; 5 (17) December 1881, 1.

40 Iaroslav Hrytsak, "'Molodi radykaly' u suspil'no-politychnomu zhytti Halychyny," *ZNTSh* 221 (2001): 71–110.

41 Marvin Rintala, "Generations in Politics," in *The Youth Revolution: The Conflict of Generations in Modern History*, ed. Anthony Esler (Lexington, MA: D. C. Heath, 1974), 17–20.

42 Illustrative from this standpoint are the memoirs of Rev. Fylymon Tarnavsky (*Spohady: Rodynna khronika*), a Ukrainian patriot whose life paths intersected with Franko's, but who was hostile to his ideas. Franko's reflections on his peers in the alien camp are best reflected in his series of short stories collectively titled *Rutentsi* (Ruthenians) [*ZT* 15:7–41].

43 Kistiakivs'kyi, *Shchodennyk*, vol. 2, 352.

44 Ivan Franko, "Perednie slovo," in Drahomanov, *Shevchenko, ukrainofily i sotsializm*, 6.

45 Daniel R. Brower, "A Sociological Analysis: Fathers and Sons in Tsarist Russia," in *Youth Revolution*, 62–81.

46 Iaroslav Hrytsak, "Ukrains'ke natsional'ne vidrodzhennia v Halychyni XIX–poch. XX st.: porivnial'nyi analiz sotsial'noho skladu patriotychnykh hrup," *Krakivs'ki Ukrainoznavchi Zoshyty* 5–6 (1996–1997): 283–85; Oleh Pavlyshyn, "Sotsial'no-politychnyi portret provodu Halychyny ta Bukovyny v revoliutsii 1918–1919 rr.," *Ukraina moderna* 4–5 (2000–2001): 195; Ianyshyn, "Narodovs'kyi rukh u Halychyni," 37–38, 46.

47 VR IL, fond 100 (Ivan Belei), file 2482.

48 *Materialy*, 2, 6–7, 28. See also chapter 12 in this book, "Franko and His Boryslav."

49 Kłańska, *Aus dem Schtetl in die Welt*, 113, 115, 118.

50 Mendelsohn, "From Assimilation to Zionism in Lvov," 521.

51 Ibid., 533.

52 Ibid., 524.

53 VR LNB, fond 206 (Vasyl Shchurat), file 922, folder 27, fol. 6.

54 Ostap Terlets'kyi, "Zhadka pro zhytie Volodymyra Navrotskoho," in *Tvory Volodymyra Navrotskoho vydane posmertne z portretom i zhytiepysom. Zakhodom Etnohrafychno-statystychnoho kruzhka*, vol. 1 (Lviv, 1884), xiv.

55 Krzywicki, *Wspomnienia*, vol. 1, 318–19.

56 Chaikovs'kyi, *Spohady*, vol. 1, 174.

57 Cited in Włodzimierz Mokry, *"Ruska Trójca": Karta z dziejów życia literackiego Ukraińców w Galicji w pierwszej połowie XIX wieku* (Wrocław: Wydawn. Uniwersytetu Jagiellońskiego: Fundacja Świętego Włodzimierza, 1997), 92.

58 Chłędowski, *Pamiętniki*, vol. 1, 90–91, 179.

59 Drahomanov, *Avstro-rus'ki spomyny*, 93–94, 183; *Materialy*, 164.

60 Tarnavs'kyi, *Spohady: Rodynna khronika*, 85–86.

61 See chapter 5 in this book, "Between Small and Large Fatherlands."

62 Drahomanov, *Literaturno-publitsystychni pratsi*, vol. 2, 113–14, 116–17.

63 Bianka Pietrow-Ennker, *Russlands "neue Menschen": die Entwicklung der Frauenbewegung von der Anfängen bis zur Oktoberrevolution* (Frankfurt: Campus, 1999), 61.

64 Drahomanov, "Shevchenko, ukrainofily i sotsializm," passim.

65 Mykhailo Drahomanov, "25-ti rokowyny smerty Szewczenka a halycki narodowci," *Praca* 3-4 (1886).

66 Pavlyk, *Propashchyi cholovik*, 337–47.

67 VR IL, fond 132 (Uliana Kravchenko), file 213, fol. 3.

68 Ibid., file 209, fol. 3.

69 Kravchenko, *Pam'iati druha*, 25, 28.

70 Ibid., 74, 76.

71 VR IL, fond 3 (Ivan Franko), file 1617, fol. 269.

72 Ibid., file 1603, fols. 605–6.

73 Ibid., file 1603, fol. 605.

74 Ivan Franko, "Spomyny pro Volodymyra Naumovycha," in Volodymyr Naumovych, *Velychyna i budova zvizdianoho svita. V dodatku spomyny pro Volodymyra Naumovycha napysav Ivan Franko* (Lviv, 1901), 24–27. Volodymyr Naumovych's role was very controversial: during the trial of the Russophiles in 1882, it was learned that after he left Lviv, he received remuneration (50 Russian rubles a month) from Myroslav Dobriansky for writing denunciations (*spravozdannia*) against the Galician socialists. Figuring in these denunciations was Franko as the individual around whom were gathered the Lviv "nihilists." Franko never showed any anger toward Naumovych. On the contrary, he pitied him, regarding him as an innocent victim of Russophile intrigues. Furthermore, Franko suspected that these denunciations were a fabrication engineered by the "heroes" of the 1882 trial, who sought to mask the real motives behind their activities by appearing to be loyal subjects of the Austro-Hungarian Empire and claiming to be keeping an eye on nihilist conspiracies. In any event, although Volodymyr Naumovych was cleared of all accusations, he left the courtroom to find himself the target of young people's general disrespect for his denunciatory activities. He died shortly after the trial ended and, as Franko later recounted, he suffered terrible agonies of remorse during the last months of his life: squeezing his head between his hands, he walked around the garden or paced up and down a room, repeating: "What have I done! What have I done!" See Franko, "Spomyny pro Volodymyra Naumovycha," 30–34.

Chapter 17

1 Ustyianovych, *M.F. Raevskii i rossiiskii panslavizm*, 74–75.

2 [Konys'kyi], "Galichina i Rusiny. Iz dorozhnykh zamitok i nabliudenii," 138.

3 Ibid., 135.

4 Himka, "Construction of Nationality in Galician Rus'," 148–49.

5 Paul Robert Magocsi, *The Roots of Ukrainian Nationalism: Galicia as Ukraine's Piedmont* (Toronto: University of Toronto Press, 2002), 96.

6 [Hushalevych], *Pisni na den 3 / 15 maia 1849*; no page numeration.

7 See VR IL, fond 3 (Ivan Franko), file 1604, fol. 17.

8 [Fylyp Svystun], "Nigilizm," *Slovo*, 2 (15) June 1879, 1. The attribution of this unsigned article was made on the basis of Levitskii, *Galitsko-russkaia bibliografiia*, vol. 2, 702.

9 See chapter 7, "The Great Turning Point."

10 [Fylyp Svystun], "Nigilisty," *Slovo*, 8 (20) March 1880, 1. The attribution of this unsigned article was made on the basis of Levyts'kyi, *Galitsko-russkaia bibliografiia*, vol. 2, 702. My interpretation here is based, with some minor reservations, on the main conclusions reached by Anna Veronika Wendland in her book on the Galician Russophiles. In my opinion, she somewhat simplifies Franko's relationship with the Russophiles. The

young Franko admitted that "there are honest and sincere people among them [the Russophiles—Y. H.]" (*Materialy*, 266). But his critique had primarily an ideological rather than a national character. In particular, calling the Russophiles *botokudy*, the name of a primitive tribe—which is emphasized by Wendland—was aimed at underscoring their "backward" nature. For further discussion, see [Iwan Franko], "Ferment w obozie ruskim," *Kurjer Lwowski*, 22 December 1890, 1 (unsigned); Vasyl´ Shchurat, "Ivan Franko i videns´ki moskvofily v 1893 r.," *Literaturno-naukovyi dodatok "Novoho chasu*," no. 21, 1939, iv–v. Wendland makes no mention of Franko's collaboration either with young Russophiles or with this current within the Russophile camp. See, e.g., Ivan Franko, "Stara Rus´," *LNV* 34, bk. 6 (1906): 456–73; 35, bks. 32–51; bk. 9: 382–92; 36, bk. 10: 66–79; bk. 11: 359–74; Ivan Franko, "Shchyrist´ tonu i shchyrist´ perekonan," *LNV* 30, bk. 5: 101–12.

11 I. N. Hushalevych, *Poezii*, pt. 2 (Lviv, 1879), 20.

12 Ibid., 12–13.

13 [Ievhenii Fentsyk], "Nigilistam," *Slovo*, 17 (29) May 1879, 2–3, signed by: "Vladimir iz ushchelii Karpat." The attribution of this poem is based on Levyts´kyi, *Galitsko-russkaia bibliografiia*, vol. 2, 611, 717.

14 VR IL, fond 3 (Ivan Franko), file 1617, fol. 272.

15 TsDIAL, fond 387, list 1, file 17, fol. 1.

16 Budzynovs´kyi, *Ishly didy na muky*, 36, 38.

17 Ibid., 80.

18 It is worth recalling here the glorification of community property, which European socialists in this period regarded as the starting point for the development of all societies ("from India to Ireland"), the "original communist society." (See Friedrich Engels's footnote in the English edition [1888] of the *Manifesto of the Communist Party*, cited on 31–32.) Also compare Berkut's phrase "the spark will flare up into a new fire" with a line from the famous poem, "From a Spark a Flame Will Blaze Up" (Из искры разгорится пламя), attributed to Pushkin [no it is from the Decembrists' response to Pushkin, penned by A.I. Odoevskii]. The comparison is all the more feasible because for the epigraph of his novel Franko chose the following lines from Pushkin: "The deeds of bygone days, / The legends of deep antiquity" (Дела давно минувших дней, / Преданья старины глубокой) [*ZT* 16:9].

19 *Vitchyzna: zbirnyk vyslovliuvan´*, 74.

20 Mircea Eliade, *The Myth of the Eternal Return: or, Cosmos and History*, trans. Willard R. Trask (Princeton, NJ: Princeton University Press, 1965), 22–27.

21 Ibid., 22; Le Goff, *History and Memory*, 22–29.

22 VR IL, fond 3 (Ivan Franko), file 1618, fols. 27–30. See also [*ZT* 16:482–83].

23 Kistiakivs´kyi, *Shchodennyk*, vol. 2, 165, 352.

24 See chapter 16, "How Franko Became a Genius."

25 Eric J. Hobsbawm, *The Age of Empire, 1875–1914*, 1st US ed. (New York: Pantheon Books, 1987), 6, 10; Norman Stone, *Europe Transformed, 1878–1919* (Cambridge, MA: Harvard University Press, 1984), 13; Pulzer, *Rise of Political Anti-Semitism*, ix.

26 A. J. Taylor, *Bismarck: The Man and the Statesman* (New York: Vintage, 1967), 63.

27 For detailed discussion, see Roman Szporluk, *Communism and Nationalism: Karl Marx versus Friedrich List* (New York: Oxford University Press, 1988); see also his article, "In Search of the Drama of History: or, National Roads to Modernity," *East European Politics and Societies* 4, no. 1 (Winter 1990): 134–50.

28 Yuri Slezkine, *The Jewish Century* (Princeton, NJ: Princeton University Press, 2004), 61.

29 S[vystun], *Chem est´ dlia nas Shevchenko?*, 24.

30 Tarnavs´kyi, *Spohady: Rodynna khronika*, 96–97.

31 Arno J. Mayer, *The Persistence of the Old Regime: Europe to the Great War* (London: Pantheon Books, 1981), 3–15, 329.

32 For detailed discussion, see Włodzimierz Mędrzecki, *Niemiecka interwencja militarna na Ukrainie w 1918 roku* (Warsaw: Wydawn. DiG, 2000).

33 Mark von Hagen, "The Dilemmas of Ukrainian Independence and Statehood, 1917–1921," *Harriman Institute Forum* 7, no. 5 (January 1994): 7–11.

34 See the wide-ranging discussion that took place in a 2002 issue of a leading journal of Slavic Studies: Josh Sanborn, "The Mobilization of 1914 and the Question of the Russian Nation: A Re-Examination," *Slavic Review* 59, no. 2 (Summer 2000): 267–89; Scott J. Seregny, "Zemstvos, Peasants and Citizenship: The Russian Adult Education Movement and World War I," ibid., 290–315; and S. A. Smith, "Citizenship and the Russian Nation during World War I: A Comment," ibid., 316–29. It would appear that alienation did not bypass even Galician peasants, who had a much longer experience of associating with urban intellectuals and were very active in the development of local institutions in the Western Ukrainian National Republic. See Pavlyshyn, "Formuvannia ta diialnist predstavnytskykh orhaniv vlady ZUNR-ZOUNR, 165–81.

35 Guthier, "Popular Base of Ukrainian Nationalism in 1917," 30–47.

36 Andrea Graziosi, *The Great Soviet Peasant War: Bolsheviks and Peasants, 1917–1933* (Cambridge, MA: Distributed by Harvard University Press for the Ukrainian Research Institute, Harvard University, 1996), 19.

37 V. I. Lenin, "Vybory do Ustanovchykh Zboriv i dyktatura proletariatu," in *Povne zibrannia tvoriv*, 50 vols. (Kyiv, 1974), vol. 40, 18.

38 Mykhailo Hrushevs´kyi, "1825–1925," *Ukraina* 6 (1925): 3–4.

39 Mykhailo Hrushevs´kyi, "Apostolovi pratsi," 217.

40 Volodymyr Byrchak, "Spohady pro I. Franka," in *Spohady*, 311.

41 S. N. Shchegolev, *Ukrainskoe dvizhenie, kak sovremennyi etap iuzhnorusskago separatizma* (Kyiv, 1912), 115–18, 126–27, 293, 296.

42 Moroz, *Ivan Franko: Bibliohrafiia tvoriv; Chto chitat´ narodu? Kriticheskii ukazatel´ knig dlia narodnago i detskogo chteniia*, vol. 3 (Moscow, 1906).

Conclusions

1 Gerschenkron, *Economic Backwardness*, 22–26; Richard Sylla and Gianni Tonniolo, "Introduction: Patterns of European Industrialization during the Nineteenth Century," in *Problems of European Industrialization* (New York: Routledge, 1991), 1–26.

2 Mykhailo Rudnyts´kyi, *Vid Myrnoho do Khvylovoho* (Lviv: Vydavnycha Spilka "Dilo," 1936), 181–82.

Bibliography

Abramowicz, Maciej. "Patrie—"Ojczyzna"? In Bartmiński, *Pojęcie ojczyzny*.

Adadurov, Vadym. "L′viv u napoleonivsku epokhu." In *L′viv: misto, suspilstvo, kul′tura: Zbirnyk naukovykh prats′*, edited by Marian Mudryi, vol. 3, 209–31. Lviv: Vyd-vo L′vivs′koho universytetu, 1999.

Administrativ-Karte von den Königr. Galizien und Lodomerien mit dem Grossherzogthume Krakau u.d. Herzogthümern Auschwiz, Zator und Bukovina von Carl Kummers Ritter von Kummersberg. Vienna, 1855.

Almog, Shmuel. "Alfred Nossig—A Reappraisal." *Studies in Zionism* 7 (1983): 1–29.

Althoen, David. "Natione Polonus and the Naród Szlachecki: Two Myths on National Identity and Noble Solidarity." *Zeitschrift für Ostmittleeuropa-Forschung* 52 (2003): 475–508.

Althoen, David. "That Noble Quest: From True Nobility to Enlightened Society in the Polish-Lithuanian Commonwealth, 1550–1830," vol. 1. Ph.D. dissertation, University of Michigan, 2001.

Anderson, Benedict. *Imagined Communities: Reflections on the Origin and Spread of Nationalism*. Rev. ed. London: Verso, 1991.

Anderson, Robert Thomas. *Traditional Europe: A Study in Anthropology and History*. Belmont, CA: Wadsworth, 1971.

Andriewsky, Olga. "The Politics of National Identity: The Ukrainian Question in Russia, 1904–1912." Ph.D. dissertation, Harvard University, 1991.

Arkhiv Mykhaila Drahomanova, vol. 1: *Lystuvannia Kyivskoi Staroi Hromady z M. Drahomanovym (1870–1895 rr.)* [=*Les archives de Michel Drahomanov*, vol. 1: *Correspondance avec les membres de l'association, Stara hromada de Kiev, Années 1870–1895*]. Vol. 37 of *Pratsi Ukrains′koho naukovoho instytutu*, edited by Roman Smal′-Stots′kyi. Warsaw: n. p., 1937.

Armstrong, John A. "Myth and History in the Evolution of Ukrainian Consciousness." In *Ukraine and Russia in Their Historical Encounter*, edited by Peter J. Potichnyj et al, 125–39. Edmonton: Canadian Institute of Ukrainian Studies Press, University of Alberta, 1992.

Arndt, Ernst Moritz. *Ausgewählte Gedichte und Schriften*. Berlin: Union Verlag, 1969.

Arndt, Ernst Moritz. "The German Fatherland." In *The Poets and Poetry of Europe*, with introductions and biographical notes by Henry Wadsworth Longfellow. Philadelphia: Carey and Hart, 1845, 322–33.

Aronson, Irwin Michael. *Troubled Waters: The Origins of the 1881 Anti-Jewish Pogroms in Russia.* Pittsburgh, PA: University of Pittsburgh Press, 1990.

Artemieva, Viktoriia. "Ukrains´ki students´ki hurtky u L´vovi v 1870–1882 rokakh." Graduate thesis, Lviv, 1996.

Avineri, Shlomo. "The Presence of Eastern and Central Europe in the Culture and Politics of Contemporary Israel." *Eastern European Politics and Societies* 10, no. 2 (Spring 1996): 163–72.

Bachmann, Klaus. *Ein Herd der Feindschaft gegen Russland. Galizien als Krisenherd in den Beziehungen der Donaumonarchie mit Russland (1907–1914).* Vienna: Verlag für Geschichte und Politik; Munich: R. Oldenbourg Verlag, 2001.

Baik, Ł. H. "Z historii rozwoju ukraińskiej szkoły w Galicji." In *Galicja i jej dziedzictwo*, vol. 3.

Bairoch, Paul, Jean Batou, and Pierre Chèvre. *La population des villes européennes, 800–1850: banque de données et analyse sommaire des resultats.* Geneva: Droz, 1988.

Bartmiński, Jerzy, ed. *Pojęcie ojczyzny we współczesnych językach europejskich.* Lublin: Instytut Europy Środkowo-Wschodniej, 1993.

Barvins´kyi, Volodymyr. *Besida vyholoshena na muzykal´no-dekliamators´kym vecheri u L´vovi v XIV. rokovyny smerty Tarasa Shevchenka.* Lviv, 1875.

Bass, I. I. *Ivan Franko: Biohrafiia.* Kyiv: Naukova dumka, 1966.

Bauman, Zygmunt. "Modernity." In *The Oxford Companion to Politics of the World*, edited by Joel Krieger. 2nd ed. Oxford: Oxford University Press, 2001.

Beauvois, Daniel. *Szkoły podstawowe i średnie.* Vol. 2 of *Szkolnictwo Polskie na ziemiach Litewsko-Ruskich, 1803–1832.* Lublin: Red. Wydawnictwo KUL, 1991.

———. "Mit 'kresów wschodnich,' czyli jak mu położyć kres." In *Polskie mity polityczne XIX i XX wieku*, 93–105. Wroclaw: Wydawn. Uniwersytetu Wrocławskiego, 1994.

Beiträge zur Geschichte und Kultur der Ukraine: Ausgewählte deutsche Schriften des Revolutionären Demokraten, 1882–1915. Edited by E. Winter and P. Kirchner. Berlin: Akademie Verlag, 1963.

Bem, Ewa. "Termin 'ojczyzna' w literaturze XVI i XVII wieku: Refleksje o języku." *Odrodzenie i reformacja w Polsce* 34 (1989): 131–57.

Bendix, Regina. "Ethnology, Cultural Reification, and the Dynamics of Difference in the *Kronprinzwerk*." In *Creating the Other: Ethnic Conflict and Nationalism in Habsburg Central Europe*, edited by Nancy M. Wingfield, 149–166. New York: Berghahn Books, 2003.

Berend, Iván T., and Gyárgy Ránki. *Economic Development in East-Central Europe in the 19th and 20th Centuries.* New York: Columbia University Press, 1974.

Bericht der Lemberger Handels- und Gewerbekammer über den Handel un die Industrie, so wie deren Beförderungsmittel in ihres Kammerbezirks für den J. 1861–1865. Lviv, 1867.

Berkhoff, Karel C. *Harvest of Despair: Life and Death in Ukraine under Nazi Rule*. Cambridge, MA: Belknap Press of Harvard University Press, 2004.

Berlin, Isaiah. *Two Concepts of Liberty: An Inaugural Lecture Delivered before the University of Oxford on 31 October 1958*. Oxford: Clarendon Press, 1958.

———. *The Hedgehog and the Fox: An Essay on Tolstoy's View of History*. New York: Simon and Schuster, 1986.

Bernshtein, E. [E. Bernstein]. "Spomyny pro Mykhaila Drahomanova i Serhiia Podolyns'koho." In Hrushevs'kyi, *Z pochyniv*, 153–161.

Bessinger, Mark R. "The Persisting Ambiguity of Empire." *Post-Soviet Affairs* 11, no. 2 (1995): 180.

Beug, Joachim. "Pogroms in Literary Representation." In *Ghetto Writing: Traditional and Eastern Jewry in German-Jewish Literature from Heine to Hilsenrath*, edited by Anne Fuchs, and Florian Krobb, 83–96. Rochester, NY: Camden House, 1999.

Bevz, Mykola. "Ukrains'ki transformatsii tsentral'noi chastyny mista L'vova u XIX–XX st." In *Arkhitektura Halychyny XIX–XX st.: Vybrani materialy mizhnarodnoho sympoziumu 24–27 travnia 1994 r., prysviachenoho 150-richchiu zasnuvannia Derzhavnoho universytetu "L'vivs'ka politekhnika,"* edited by Bohdan Cherkes, Martin Kubelik, and Elizabet Hofer, 51–69. Lviv: L'vivs'ka politekhnika, 1996.

Bielski, Z. "W sprawie starzeństwa przemysłu naftowego." *Przemysł naftowy* 4 (1932): 89–91.

Biliński, Leon. *O istocie, rozwoju i obecnym stanie socjalizmu*. Cracow, 1883.

Binder, Harald. *Galizien in Wien. Parteien, Wahlen, Fraktionen und Abgeorgdneten im Übergan zur Massenpolitik*. Vienna: Verlag der Österreichischen Akademie der Wissenschaften, 2005.

———. "Making and Defending a Polish Town: 'Lwów.' (Lemberg), 1848–1914." In *Austrian History Yearbook* 34 (2003): 57–81.

Biogramy uczonych polskich: materiały o życiu członków AU w Krakowie, TNW, PAU, PAN. Edited by Andrzej Środka and Paweł Szczawiński, pt. 3: P–Z. Wroclaw: Zakład Narodowy im. Ossolińskich, 1983–.

Blejwas, Stanislaus A. *Realism in Polish Politics: Warsaw Positivism and National Survival in Nineteenth Century Poland*. New Haven, CT: Yale Concilium on International and Area Studies; Columbus, OH: Distributed by Slavica Publishers, 1984.

BN WZS, microfilm 67675. A copy of materials held at the Ossolineum in Wroclaw: 14779 / II, Stanisław Wasylewski: *Materiały i szkice dotyczące Iwana Franko*.

Bodianskii, Osip [Bodians'kyi, Osyp]. "Predislovie" (Foreword) to Denis Zubritskii [Denys Zubryts'kyi], *Kritiko-istoricheskaia povest' vremennykh let Chervonoi ili Galitskoi Rusi*, v–xxii. Translated from Polish. Moscow: Obshchestvo istorii i drevnostei Rossiiskikh pri Moskovskom Universitete, 1845.

Bohachevsky-Chomiak, Martha. *Feminists Despite Themselves: Women in Ukrainian Community Life, 1884–1939*. Edmonton: Canadian Institute of Ukrainian Studies, 1988.

———. "How Real Were Nationalism and Feminism in 19th-Century Galicia?" In *Geschlecht und Nationalismus in Mittel- und Osteuropa, 1848–1918*, edited by Sophia Kemlein, 143–152. Osnabrück: Fibre, 2000.

Bourdieu, Pierre, and Loïc J.D. Wacquant. *An Invitation to Reflexive Sociology*. Chicago: University of Chicago Press, 1992.

Boy-Żeleński, Tadeusz. *O Mickiewiczu*. Cracow: Czytelnik, 1949.

Brandes, Jerzy [Georg Brandes]. *O czytaniu: odczyt wygłoszony d. 26 listopada r. 1898. w sali ratuszowej we Lwowie*. Lviv, 1899.

Braudel, Fernand. *History and Environment*. Vol. 1 of *The Identity of France*. 1st US ed. New York: Harper and Row, 1988.

———. *The Mediterranean and the Mediterranean World in the Age of Philip II*, vol. 1. New York: Harper and Row, 1972.

Brock, Peter. *The Slovak National Awakening: An Essay in the Intellectual History of East Central Europe*. Toronto: University of Toronto Press, 1976.

Brooks, Jeffrey. *When Russia Learned to Read: Literacy and Popular Literature, 1867–1917*. Princeton: Princeton University Press, 1985.

Brower, David R. "Urban Revolution in the Late Russian Empire." In *The City in Late Imperial Russia*, edited by Michael F. Hamm, 62–81. Bloomington: Indiana University Press, 1986.

Brykalska, Maria. *Aleksander Świętochowski: Biografia*. 2 vols. Warsaw: Państ. Instytut Wydawniczy, 1987.

Budzynovs'kyi, Viacheslav. *Ishly didy na muku: vvedennia v istoriiu Ukrainy*. Lviv: V-vo Ukrains'ke slovo, 1925.

———. "Latynka: Spohad." *Novi shliakhy* 10 (1931): 314–323.

———. *Iak cholovik ziishov na pana: Avtobiohrafiia avtora*. Lviv, 1937.

Bujak, Franciszek. *Żmiąca: wieś powiatu Limanowskiego: stosunki gospodarcze i społeczne*. Cracow: G. Gebethner, 1903.

———. *Galicya*, vol. 1. Lviv: H. Altenberg, 1908–10.

———. *Rozwój gospodarczy Galicji, 1772–1914*. Lviv: Księg. Polska B. Połonieckiego, 1917.

———. *Z odległej i bliskiej przeszłości. Studia historyczno-gospodarcze*. Lviv: Zakład Narodowy im. Ossolińskich, 1924.

Burszta, Józef. *Wieś i karczma. Rola karczmy w życiu wsi pańszczyźnanej*. Warsaw: Spółdzielnia Wydawnicza, 1950.

Bushkovits, Paul. "The Ukraine in Russian Culture 1790–1860: The Evidence of the Journals." *Jahrbücher für Geschichte Osteuropa* 39, no. 3 (1991): 339–63.

Buszko, Józef. *Zum Wandel der Gesellschaftsstruktur in Galizien und in der Bukovina*. Vienna: Verlag der Österreichischen Akademie der Wissenschaften, 1978.

———. *Galicja 1859–1914. Polski Piemont?*, vol. 3: *Dzieje narodu i państwa polskiego*. Warsaw: KAW, 1989.

Butryn, M. L. "Tsenzurna istoriia zbirky 'Molot' (1878)." *Ukrains'ke literaturoznavstvo* 12 (1971): 46–50.

Buzek, Józef. "Stosunki zawodowe i socyalne ludności Galicyi według wyznania i narodowości. Na podstawie spisu ludności z 31 grudnia 1900 r." *Wiadomości statystyczne o stosunkach krajowych* 20, no. 2 (1905): 1–51.

Bylyna, Ivan. "U kraini zahorodovoi shliakhty." *Dilo* (Lviv), 14 August 1937.

Caro, Leopold. "Lichwa na wsi w Galicji w latach 1879–1891." *Wiadomości statystyczne o stosunkach krajowych* 14, no. 2 (1893): 1–50.

Catalogus universi venerabilis cleri dioceseos Premisliensis graeci ritus catholicorum pro Anno Domini 1850. Premisliae [Przemyśl / Peremyshl], 1850.

Chaikovs´kyi, Andrii. "Natalia Kobryns´ka." *Kalendar "Zhinocha Dolia."* (1931): 29–36.

———. *Spohady. Lysty. Doslidzhennia.* 3 vols. Lviv: Vyd-vo L´vivs´koho universytetu; NAN Ukrainy; Instytut ukrainoznavstva im. I. Kryp´iakevycha NAN Ukrainy, Nauk. Fundatsiia A. Chaikovs´koho, 2002.

Chaikovs´kyi, Iuliian. "Volodymyr Stebel´s´kyi." *LNV* 12 (December 1905): 81–109.

Chapel´s´kyi, Volodymyr. "Z rodynnoi khroniky." *Ameryka*, 18 July 1966.

———. *Ia liubyv ikh usikh: Z mynuloho Drohobychchyny.* Drohobych: Vydavnycha firma Vidrodzhennia, 1997.

Chepurnyi, Vasyl´. "Ivan Franko i fondy Chernihivs´koho literaturno-memorial´noho muzeiu-zapovidnyka M. M. Kotsiubyns´koho." *Naukovi zapysky Chernihivs´koho literaturno-memorial´noho muzeiu-zapovidnyka M. M. Kotsiubyns´koho* 1 (1996): 107–110.

Chernets´kyi, Antin. *Spomyny z moho zhyttia.* Kyiv: Osnovni tsinnosti, 2001.

Cherniavsky, Michael. *Tsar and People: Studies in Russian Myths.* New Haven: Yale University Press, 1961.

Chernyshenko, Larysa. "Lysty Ol´hy Khoruzhyns´koi do Ivana Franka." *Naukovyi visnyk Muzeiu Ivana Franka u L´vovi* 3 (2003): 173–236.

Chichagov, Vasilii K. *Iz istorii russkikh imen, otchestv i familii: voprosy russkoi istoricheskoi onomastiki XV–XVII vv.* Moscow: Gos. uchebno-pedagog. izd-vo, 1959.

Chłopiecki, Jerzy. "Galicja—skrzyżowanie dróg." In *Galicja i jej dziedzictwo*, vol. 2, 27–48.

Chmelyk, R. *Mala ukrains´ka selians´ka sim´ia druhoi polovyny XIX–pochatku XX st. (struktura i funktsii).* Lviv: Instytut narodoznavstva NAN Ukrainy, 1999.

Chmielowski, Eugeniusz. *Czarownicy, strzygi, mamony czyli wierzenia i zabobony ludu galicyjskiego zebrane przez...w pierwszej połowie roku 1890.* Nowy Sącz: 1987.

Chopyk, Rostyslav. "Prychynky do flory i fauny Frankovoho Lvova." In *Henii mistsia: L´viv, Leopolis, Lemberg, Lwów,* edited by Taras Vozniak, 204–11. Lviv, 2004 [*Ї, nezalezhnyi kulturolohichnyi chasopys* 29 (2003)].

Chornovol, Ihor. "Politychni kontseptsii kyivs´koi 'Staroi Hromady.'" *Moloda natsiia* 1 (2000): 24–39.

———. "Oleksandr Barvins´kyi u konteksti svoiei i nynishnoi epokhy." In *Oleksandr Barvins´kyi, 1847–1927. Materialy konferentsii, prysviachenoi 150 richnytsi vid dnia narodzhennia Oleksandra Barvins´koho, L´viv, 14 travnia 1997*, 32–44. Lviv, 2001.

———. "Mizh arkheolohiieiu ta politykoiu: Volodymyr Antonovych i pol´s´ke suspil´stvo (do 170-richchia vid dnia narodzhennia)." *Moloda natsiia* 32, no. 3 (2004): 91–174.

———. "Markiian Shashkevych: mekhanizmy kul´tu." *Krytyka* 87–88, nos. 1–2 (2005): 30–31.

Connor, Walter. *Ethnonationalism: The Quest for Understanding.* Princeton, NJ: Princeton University Press, 1994.

Crichton, Michael. *The Great Train Robbery.* New York: Knopf, 1975.

Currie, Robert. *Genius: An Ideology in Literature.* London: Chatto and Windus, 1974.

Czerner, Olgierd. "Przekształcenia architektoniczne Lwowa w latach 1772–1848." In Cherkes, Kubelik, and Hofer, *Arkhitektura Halychyny XIX –XX st,* 71–86. Lviv: L´vivs´ka politekhnika, 1996.

Dabrowski, Patrice M. "'Discovering' the Galician Borderlands: The Case of the Eastern Carpathians." *Slavic Review* 64, no. 2 (Summer 2005): 380–402.

Dashkevych, Ia. R. "Vzaiemovidnosyny mizh ukrains´kym ta ievreis´kym naselenniam u Skhidnii Halychyni (kinets´ XIX–pochatok XX st.)." *Ukrains´kyi istorychnyi zhurnal* 10 (1990): 63–73.

———. "Mykhailo Drahomanov i Zakarpattia." In *Shtrykhy do naukovoho portreta Mykhaila Drahomanova: Zbirnyk naukovykh prats´* edited by R. S. Mishchuk, 201–6. Kyiv: Naukova dumka, 1991.

———. "Davnii L´viv u virmens´kykh ta virmens´ko-kypchats´kykh dzherelakh." *Ukraina v mynulomu* 1 (1992): 7–13.

Daszyński, Ignacy [Ż. D.]. "Borysław: Burżua i robotnicy." *Gazeta Naddniestrzańska,* 1 June 1884.

———. *Pamiętniki,* vol. 1. Cracow: Z. R. S. S. Proletarjat, 1925.

Davidson, Pamela. "The Moral Dimension of the Prophetic Ideal: Pushkin and His Readers." *Slavic Review* 61, no. 3 (Fall 2002): 506–14.

Davis, John. "An interview with Ernest Gellner." *Current Anthropology* 32, no. 1 (1991): 63–72.

Davis, Natalie Zemon. *Society and Culture in Early Modern France: Eight Essays.* Stanford: Stanford University Press, 1975.

———. *The Return of Martin Guerre.* Cambridge, MA: Harvard University Press, 1983.

Davis, Norman. *Orzel biały. Czerwona Gwiazda. Wojna polsko-bolszewicka 1919–1920.* Translated by Andrzej Pawelec. Cracow: ZNAK, 1997.

de Colonia, Franco. *Magistri Franconis Ars cantus mensurabilis. Ausgabe von E. De Coussemaker nebst zwei handschriflichen Fassungen,* edited by Friedrich Gennrich. Darmstadt: 1957.

de Soto, Hernando. *The Mystery of Capital: Why Capitalism Triumphs in the West and Fails Everywhere Else.* London: Bantam, 2000.

Deak, Istvan. *Essays on Hitler's Europe.* Lincoln: University of Nebraska Press, 2001.

Debreczeny, Paul. *Social Functions of Literature: Alexander Pushkin and Russian Culture.* Stanford, CA: Stanford University Press, 1997.

Deditskii, Bogdan A. [Bohdan A. Didyts′kyi], comp. *Mikhail Kachkovskii i sovremennaia galitsko-russkaia literatura: Ocherk biograficheskii i istoriko-literaturnyi*, pt. 1. Lviv: S pechati Instituta Stavropigiiskogo pod nariadom Stefana Rutkovskogo, 1876.

Dei, Oleksii I. *Ukrains′ka revoliutsiino-demokratychna zhurnalistyka: problemy vynyknennia i stanovlennia.* Kyiv: Vyd-vo Akademii nauk URSR, 1959.

———. "Zhurnal 'Tovarysh' (Epizod iz zhurnalistychnoi diial′nosti I. Franka)." In *Doslidzhennia tvorchosti Ivana Franka*, 103–132. 2nd ed. Kyiv: Vyd-vo Akademii nauk URSR, 1959.

———. *Slovnyk ukrains′kykh psevdonimiv ta kryptonimiv; XVI–XX st.* Kyiv: Naukova dumka, 1969.

———. *Ivan Franko: Zhyttia i diial′nist′.* Kyiv: Dnipro, 1981.

———. *Spilkuvannia myttsiv z narodnoiu poeziieiu: Ivan Franko ta ioho otochennia.* Kyiv: Naukova dumka, 1981.

Dei, O. I., comp. *Kolomyiky v zapysakh Ivana Franka.* Kyiv: Muzychna Ukraina, 1970.

Dei, O. I., and N. Korniienko. *Ivan Franko u spohadakh suchasnykiv*, vol. 1. Lviv: Knyzhkovo-zhurnal′ne vyd-vo, 1956.

———. *Ivan Franko u spohadakh suchasnykiv*, vol. 2. Lviv: Kameniar, 1972.

Demchuk, M. O. *Slovians′ki avtokhtonni osobovi vlasni imena v pobuti ukraintsiv XVI–XVIII st.* Kyiv: Naukova dumka, 1988.

Denysiuk, I. "Do tsenzurnoi istorii 'Hromads′koho druha,' 'Dzvona' i 'Molota.'" *Ivan Franko: Statti i materialy* 6 (1956): 49–73.

———. *Mykhailo Pavlyk.* Kyiv: Derzh. vyd-vo khudozh. lit-ry, 1960.

———. "Frankoznavstvo: zdobutky, vtraty, perspektyvy." In *Ivan Franko—pys′mennyk, myslytel′, hromadianyn. Materialy Mizhnarodnoi naukovoi konferentsii*, 12–18. Lviv, 1998.

Deutsch, Karl. "Social Mobilization and Political Development." *American Political Science Review* 55, no. 3 (September 1961): 495.

Die Österreichisch-ungarische Monarchie in Wort und Bild: Auf Anregung und unter Mitwirkung Seiner kaiserlichen und königlichen Hoheit des durchlauchtigetsten Kronprinzen Erzherzog Rudolf. Vienna: K. K. Hof- und Staatsdruckerei, 1886.

Digby, Tom, ed. *Men Doing Feminism.* New York: Routledge, 1998.

Dobrowolski, Kazimierz. "Peasant Traditional Culture." In *Peasants and Peasant Societies: Selected Readings, edited by Theodor Shanin*, 277–298. Baltimore: Penguin, 1971.

Doroshenko, Dmytro. *Moi spomyny pro davnie-mynule (1901–1914).* Winnipeg: Tryzub, 1949.

Doroshenko, Volodymyr. *Ohnyshche ukrains′koi nauky: Naukove Tovarystvo imeny T. Shevchenka z nahody 75-richchia ioho zasnuvannia.* New York: [Ameryka], 1951.

———. "Ivan Franko (Zi spomyniv avtora)." *Svoboda*, 6 June 1957.

Dovidnyk z istorii Ukrainy (A –IA): [posibnyk dlia serednikh zahal′noosvitnikh navchal′nykh zakladiv], edited by I. Pidkova and R. Shust. 2nd rev. ed. Kyiv: Heneza, 2001.

Drahomanov, Mykhailo. *Istoricheskaia Pol′sha i velikorusskaia demokratiia.* Geneva: Tip. Rabotnika i Gromady, 1882.

———. "25-ti rokowyny smerty Szewczenka a halycki narodowci." *Praca* 3–4 (1886).

———. *Lysty do Iv. Franka i ynshykh.* 2 vols. in 1. Vol. 1: *1881–1886.* Lviv: Nakladom Ukrains´ko-rus´koi vydavnychnoi spilky, 1906–<1908>.

———. "Avtobiograficheskaia zametka." In M. Drahomanov, *Literaturno-publitsystychni pratsi u dvokh tomakh,* vol. 1, 39–68. Kyiv: Naukova dumka, 1970.

———. "Dva uchyteli." In M. Drahomanov, *Vybrane...mii zadum zlozhyty ocherk istorii tsyvilizatsii na Ukraini,* 575–604. Kyiv: Lybid´, 1991.

———. *Avstro-rus´ki spomyny (1867–1877).* Kyiv: Naukova dumka, 2003.

Dubyna, Mykola. *Shevchenko i Zakhidna Ukraina.* Kyiv: Vyd-vo Kyivs´koho universytetu, 1969.

Dunin-Wąsowicz, Krzysztof. *Dzieje Stronnictwa Ludowego w Galicji.* Warsaw: Ludowa Spółdzielnia Widawnicza, 1956.

———. *Bolesław Limanowski a kwestia ukraińska.* [Warsaw: Separatum, Biblioteka Uniwersytetu Warszawskiego, odbitka z "Międzymorze"], 1995.

Dutkowa, Renata. *Polityka szkolna w Galicji między autonomią a centralizmem (1861–1875).* Cracow: Księgarnia Akademicka, 1995.

Dzhedzhalyk [Ivan Franko]. "Napered!" *Druh,* 1 / 13 October 1875, 40.

———. "Pisnia Zadunaiskaia." *Druh,* 15 / 27 January 1876, 33–34.

Dziuban, Roman. "Nevidomi lysty Ivana Franka do Tselestyny Zhuravs´koi-Zygmuntovs´koi." *Ukraina moderna* 10 (2006): 161–86.

Eberhardt, Piotr. *Polska i jej granice: z historii polskiej geografii politycznej.* Lublin: Wydawn. Uniwersytetu Marii Curie-Skłodowskiej, 2004.

Ehmer, Josef. *"Was There a 'European Pattern'? Some Critical Reflections on John Hajnal's Model."* Conference paper, Vienna, 2000.

Eisenstadt, Shmuel N., and Wolfgang Schluchter. "Introduction: Paths to Early Modernities—A Comparative View." *Daedalus* 127, no. 3: 1–18.

Eley, Geoff. "Nations, Publics and Political Culture: Placing Habermas in the Nineteenth Century." In *Culture / Power / History: A Reader in Contemporary Social History,* edited by Nicholas B. Dirks, Geoff Eley, and Sherry B. Ortner, 297–335. Princeton, NJ: Princeton University Press, 1994.

Eliade, Mircea. *The Myth of the Eternal Return: or, Cosmos and History.* Translated by Willard R. Trask. Princeton, NJ: Princeton University Press, 1965.

Emma Adler [brochure]. Vienna: Verein für Geschichte der Arbeiterbewegung, 1989.

Erdheim, Claudia. *Längst nicht mehr koscher.* Vienna, Czernin, 2006.

Everett, Leila. "The Rise of Jewish National Politics in Galicia." In Markovits and Sysyn, *Nationbuilding and the Politics of Nationalism,* 166–67.

Eysenck, H. J. *Genius: The Natural History of Creativity.* Cambridge: Cambridge University Press, 1995.

Fedotov, George. *Treasury of Russian Spirituality.* Vol. 2 of *The Collected Works of George Fedotov.* Belmont, MA: Nordland, 1975.

Feldman, Wilhelm. *Stan ekonomiczny Galicyi: cyfry i fakty.* Lviv, 1900.

———. *Stronnictwa i programy polityczne w Galicji 1846–1906.* 2 vols. Cracow: Książka, 1907.

Field, Daniel. "Peasants and Propagandists in the Russian Movement to the People of 1874." *Journal of Modern History* 59, no. 3 (September 1987): 415–38.

Figes, Orlando. "The Russian Revolution of 1917 and Its Language in the Village." *Russian Review* 56 (July 1997): 323–345.

Fischer, Wolfram, and Jan A. Van Houtte, Hermann Kellenbenz, Ilja Mieck, and Friedrich Vittinghoff, eds. *Europäische Wirtschafts- und Sozialgeschichte von der Mitte des 19. Jahrhunderts bis zum ersten Weltkrieg.* Stuttgart, 1985. [=*Kletta-Gotta Handbuch der Europäischen Wirtschafts- und Sozialgeschichte,* vol. 5.]

Fischer, A. *Zarys etnografii Polski południowo-wschodniej.* Lwów, 1939.

Flanner, Karl. "Sozialistenprozesse in Wiener Neustadt 1870–1894." In Stadler, *Sozialistenprozesse,* 31–52.

Floria, Borys. "Evoliutsiia znachennia termina 'Rus'' i pokhidnykh vid nioho u skhidnoslovians'kykh dzherelakh XII–XIV stolittia." In Isaievych and Hrytsak, *Druhyi mizhnarodnyi konhres ukrainistiv.*

François, Etienne. "Das Kaffeehaus." In *Orte des Alltags: Miniaturen aus der europäischen Kulturgeschichte,* edited by Heinz-Gerhard Haupt, 111–118. Munich: C. H. Beck, 1994.

Frank, Alison Fleig. "Austrian El Dorado: A History of the Oil Industry in Galicia, 1853–1923." Ph.D. dissertation, Harvard University, 2001.

———. *Oil Empire: Visions of Prosperity in Austrian Galicia.* Cambridge, MA: Harvard University Press, 2005.

Franko, Ivan. "Poeziia i iei stanovysko v nashykh vremenakh; Studiium estetychne." *Druh,* 15 / 27 January 1876, 44–47.

———. [Under the name Mykyta]. "Uchenyts'ka biblioteka v Drohobychi." In *Molot: Halyts'ko-ukrains'ka zbirka,* edited by M. Pavlyk, 123–128. Lviv, 1878.

———. [Under the name Józef Danyluk]. "Zaribky i zhyttia lvivs'koho zetsera." In Pavlyk, *Molot,* 144–48. Reprint [*ZT* 44/1:7–12].

———. [Unattributed]. "Dopys pro Drohobyts'ku himnaziiu." In *Dzvin: Halyts'ko-ukrains'ka zbirka, 266–269.* Lviv, 1878.

———. "Shvyndeles Parkhenblyt." *Zerkalo,* 15 February 1882, 29; 15 May 1882, 77; 15 June 1882, 92; 15 January 1883, 11; 15 March 1883, 53; and 1 May 1883, 68.

———. "Himn" [alternate title "Vichnyi revoliutsioner"]. *Praca,* 3 June 1882.

———. "Znadoby do vyvchennia movy i etnohrafii ukrainskoho narodu." *Svit,* 25 March 1882, 265–267. Reprint [*ZT* 26:186–93].

———. *Rozmova pro hroshi i skarby z peredmovoiu o zalozhenniu Dobrovlians'koi chytal'ni.* Lviv, 1883.

———. [Unattributed]. "Pytanie zhydivske." *Dilo,* 20 August / 1 September 1884.

———. [Under the name Myron]. "Z Czerwonej Rusi." *Prawda,* 18 / 30 August 1884, 415.

———. "Do istorii rus'koi tserkvy v poslidnykh chasakh Richypospospolytoi pol's'koi." *Zoria* 4 (1886): 67–68.

———. "Zhydy v zhyttiu i literaturi: 1. Mozes Mendel′son, reformator zhydivs′kyi." *Zoria*, 1 / 13 April 1886, 114–15.

———. [Iwan]. "Włościane socjaliści." *Prawda*, 17 July 1886, 339.

———. "Iz zhydivs′koi poezii zhargonovoi." *Tovarysh, Vistnyk literaturno-naukovyi*, 10 July 1888, 89–90.

———. [Under the name Myron]. "Zamechatel′naia koliadka." *Kievskaia starina* 24, bk. 1 (1889): 231–233.

———. [Iwan]. "Mniemany bunt chłopski." *Kurjer Lwowski*, 8 August 1890, 1–2.

———. [Unattributed]. "Ferment w obozie ruskim." *Kurjer Lwowski*, 22 December 1890, 1.

———. "Pershyi z'izd halyts′kykh sotsiial-demokrativ." *Narod*, nos. 5–6 (1892): 73.

———. *Z vershyn i nyzyn*. Lviv, 1887. 2nd exp. ed. Lviv, 1893.

———. [Iwan]. "Żydzi o kwestji Żydowskiej." *Tydzień*, 20 March 1893, 93.

———. [Iwan]. "Emeryk Turczyński. Wspomnienia pośmiertne." *Kurjer Lwowski*, 16 April 1896, 2 [unsigned article].

———. "Is istorii 'moskvofil′s′koho' pys′menstva v Halychyni. III. Naumovych-poet." *LNV* 8, bk. 11 (1899): 53–65.

———. "Zrazok novozlozhenoi nar. pisni." *LNV* 10, bk. 4 (April 1900): 54–55.

———. "Spomyny pro Volodymyra Naumovycha." In Volodymyr Naumovych, *Velychyna i budova zvizdianoho svita. V dodatku spomyny pro Volodymyra Naumovycha napysav Ivan Franko*, 24–27. Lviv, 1901.

———. *Dobryi zarobok i ynshi opovidania*. Lviv: Nakladom Antona Khoinats′koho, 1902.

——— [Iv.]. "Postscriptum pro Vol. Stebel′s′koho." *LNV* 23, no. 12 (December 1905): 214–24.

———. "Mykhailo Pavlyk: Zamist′ iuvyleinoi syl′vetky." *LNV*, no. 3 (1905): 160–186.

———. "Peredne slovo." In Mykhailo Drahomaniv, *Shevchenko, ukrainofily i sotsiializm*, III–XI. 2nd ed. Lviv: Nakladom Ukrains′ko-rus′koi vydavnchnoi spilky, 1906.

———. "Stara Rus′." *LNV* 34, bk. 6 (1906): 456–73; 35, bk. 7: 32–51; bk. 9: 382–92; 36, bk. 10: 66–79; bk. 11, 236–243; bk. 12, 359–374.

——— [Iv.]. Introduction to M. Drahomanov, *Lysty do Iv. Franka i ynshykh*. 2 vols. in 1. Vol. 1: *1881–1886*, 3–11. Lviv: Nakladom Ukrains′ko-rus′koi vydavnychnoi spilky, 1906–<1908>.

———. "Suchasnyi litopys." In Ivan Franko, *Davnie i nove*, 359–374. 2nd exp. ed. of *Mii Izmarahd*. Lviv, 1911.

———. *Davnie i nove*. 2nd exp. ed. of *Mii izmarahd*. Lviv, 1911.

———. "Neolitychni znakhidky v okolytsiakh Nahuievych i ikh suchasne uzhyvannie." *ZNTSh* 103 (1911): 200–202.

———. "Kontrakt oselennia Slobody bilia Nahuievychiv, Drohobyts′koho povitu, 1779 rik." *Studii z polia suspil′nykh nauk i statystyky = Studien auf dem Gebiete der Sozialwissenschaften und Statistik*, vol. 3, 1–4. Lviv: Tovarystvo im. Shevchenka, 1912.

———. *Z vershyn i nyzyn: zbirnyk poetychnykh tvoriv; v dodatku "Ziv′iale lystie" i "Velyki rokovyny."* Kyiv and Leipzig, 1920.

———. "Shcho dumaie narod pro neustupchyvist´ mytropolyta Osypa Sembratovycha." In *Za sto lit*, bk. 4, 256–58. Kyiv: VUAN, 1929.

———. "Moi znaiomi zhydy." *Dilo*, 28 May 1936, 5–6; 29 May 1936, 5–6; 30 May 1936, 5–6. Translated by Mykhailo Vozniak. Reprint [*Mozaika* 335–47].

———. *Mozaika: Iz tvoriv, shcho ne vviishly do Zibrannia tvoriv u 50 tomakh*, compiled by Z. T. Franko and M. H. Vasylenko. Lviv: Kameniar, 2001.

———. *Zur Judenfrage = Do iudeis´koho pytannia: statti*. Kyiv: Mizhrehional´na akademiia upravlinnia personalom, 2002.

———. *Zibrannia tvoriv u piatdesiaty tomakh*, edited by Ie. P. Kyryliuk et al. Kyiv: Naukova dumka, 1976–86.

———. "Hutak" [*ZT* 16:405, 420–21].

———. "Shcho se za inteligentsiia halyts´ki popy." *Za sto lit*, bk. 4, 228–251.

———. "Shchyrist´ tonu i shchyrist´ perekonan´." *LNV* 30, bk. 5, 101–12.

Franko, Petro. *Boryslav smiietsia: drama v 4 diiakh: pislia povisty "Boryslav smiietsia" Ivana Franka*. Ternopil: Nakladom vyd-va Podil´s´ka teatral´na biblioteka v Ternopoli, 1930.

Franko, Taras. *Pro bat´ka: statti, opovidannia, spohady*. 2nd exp. and rev. ed. Kyiv: Derzh. vyd-vo khudozh. lit-ry, 1954.

Franko, Zinoviia. "Peredmova." In [*Mozaika* 4–20].

———. "50-tomne zibrannia tvoriv I. Franka v otsintsi sohodennia." *Suchasnist´*, no. 10 (1989): 113–14.

Fras, Zbigniew. *Galicja*. Wrocław: Wydawnictwo Dolnośląskie, 2000.

Friedgut, Theodore H. *Iuzovka and Revolution*, vol. 1: *Life and Work in Russia's Donbass, 1869–1924*. Princeton, NJ: Princeton University Press, 1989.

Gąbiński, Stanisław. "Biliński, Leon." In *Polski słownik biograficzny*, vol. 2, 37–38. Cracow: Polska Akademia Umiejętności, 1936.

Gajkowska, Cecylia. "Czasopiśmiennictwo literackie XIX wieku," in *Słownik Literatury Polskiej XIX wieku*, 144–56.

Galicja i jej dziedzictwo, vol. 2: *Społeczeństwo i Gospodarka*, edited by Jerzy Chłopiecki and Helena Madurowicz-Urbańska. Rzeszów: Wydawn. Wyższej Szkoły Pedagogicznej, 1995.

Galicja i jej dziedzictwo, vol. 3: *Nauka i oświata*, edited by Andrzej Meissner and Jerzy Wyrozumski. Rzeszów: Wydawn. Wyższej Szkoły Pedagogicznej, 1995.

Garlicka, Aleksandra. *Spis tytułów prasy polskiej 1865–1918*. Warsaw: PAN, IBL, 1978.

Gąsowski, Tomasz. "Struktura społeczno-zawodowa mieszkańców większych miast Galicyjskich w okresie autonomicznym." *Zeszyty Naukowe Uniwersytetu Jagiellońskiego, Prace Historyczne* (Cracow) 123 (1997): 113–135.

Gay, Peter. *Freud, Jews, and Other Germans: Masters and Victims in Modernist Culture*. New York: Oxford University Press, 1978.

Gellner, Ernest. *Nation and Nationalism*. Oxford: Basil Blackwell, 1983.

Gerschenkron, Alexander. *Economic Backwardness in Historical Perspective: A Book of Essays*. Cambridge, MA: Belknap Press of Harvard University Press, 1962.

Gertsen, A. I. [Alexander I. Herzen]. *Sobranie sochinenii*. 30 vols. Moscow: Akademiia nauk SSSR, 1954–66.

Gintl, H. *Galizische Petroleum und Ozokerit*. Vienna, 1873.

Gitelman, Zvi. "Soviet Reactions to the Holocaust, 1945–1991." In *The Holocaust in the Soviet Union: Studies and Sources on the Destruction of the Jews in the Nazi-Occupied Territories of the USSR, 1945–1991*, edited by Lucjan Dobroszycki and Jeffrey Gurock, 3–28. Armonk, NY: M. E. Sharpe, 1993.

Golovatskii, Iakov [Iakiv Holovats'kyi]. "Karpatskaia Rus'. Geografichesko-statisticheskie i istoriko-etnograficheskie ocherki Galichiny, Severo-Vostovchnoi Ugrii i Bukoviny." *Slavianskii sbornik* 2 (1878).

Gorkowski, Maryan. *Wskazówki do objaśnienia jedynastu obrazów Jana Matejki przeznaczonych do Politechniki lwowskiej*. Cracow, 1895.

Goshovskaia, V. A. "Stanovlenie i razvitie rabochei pressy v Vostochnoi Galitsii v poslednei treti XIX veka." Author's abstract of her dissertation for a Candidate of Philological Sciences degree, Kyiv, 1983.

Grabowicz, George G. *The Poet as Mythmaker: A Study of Symbolic Meaning in Taras Ševčenko*. Cambridge, MA: Harvard Ukrainian Research Institute, 1982.

———. "Province to Nation: Nineteenth-Century Ukrainian Literature as a Paradigm of the National Revival." *Canadian Review of Studies in Nationalism* 16, nos. 1–2 (1989): 117–32.

Gratsiozi, Andreas [Andrea Graziosi]. *Bol'sheviki i krest'iane na Ukraine, 1918–1919 gody: ocherk o bolshevizmakh, natsional-sotsializmakh i krest'ianskikh dvizheniiakh*. Moscow: Airo-XX, 1997.

Graziosi, Andrea. *The Great Soviet Peasant War: Bolsheviks and Peasants, 1917–1933*. Cambridge, MA: Ukrainian Research Institute, Harvard University, 1996.

Grodziski, Stanisław. *W królewstwie Galicji i Lodomerii*. Cracow: Wydawn. Literackie, 1976.

Gruszecki, Artur. *Dla Miliona, powieść*. Warsaw: Nakład Gebethnera i Wolffa; Cracow: G. Gebethner, 1900.

Grynberg, Henryk. *Drohobycz, Drohobycz: Galizische Erinnerungen, Zwölf Lebensbilder*. Vienna: Szolnay Verlag, 2000.

Guthier, Steven L. "The Popular Base of Ukrainian Nationalism in 1917." *Slavic Review* 38, no. 1 (March 1979): 30–47.

Hacquets neueste physikalisch-politische Reisen in den Jahren 1791, 1792, und 1793 durch die Dacischen und Sarmatischen oder nördlichen Karpathen, vol. 3. Nürnberg: Raspische Buchhandlung, 1794.

Haecker, Emil. *Historja socjalizmu w Galicji i na Śląsku Cieszyńskim*. Cracow: Nakł. Towarzystwa Uniwersytetu Robotniczego, 1933.

Haindl, Valtraud, [Waltraud Heindl]. "Modernizatsiia ta teorii modernizatsii: pryklad Habsburz'koi biurokratii." *Ukraina moderna* 1 (1996).

Halyts'ko-rus'ki narodni prypovidky. Zibrav, uporiadkuvav i poiasnyv Ivan Franko, vol. 1: *A-Dity*. Lviv, 1901.

Halyts´ko-rus´ki narodni prypovidky. Zibrav, uporiadkuvav i poiasnyv Ivan Franko, vol. 2, bk. 1: *Dity-Kpyty.* Lviv, 1907. [*Etnohrafichnyi zbirnyk* 23.]

Hamm, Michael F. *Kiev: A Portrait, 1800–1917.* Princeton, NJ: Princeton University Press, 1993.

Hann, Chris. "Nationalism and Civil Society in Central Europe: From Ruritania to the Carpathian Euroregion." In *The State of the Nation: Ernest Gellner and the Theory of Nationalism*, edited by John A. Hall, 243–57. New York: Cambridge University Press, 1998.

Hart, Mitchell B. "Moses the Microbiologist: Judaism and Social Hygiene in the Work of Alfred Nossig." *Jewish Social Studies* 2, no. 1 (1995): 72–97.

Hastings, Adrian. *The Construction of Nationhood: Ethnicity, Religion and Nationalism.* Cambridge: Cambridge University Press, 1997.

Haus-, Hof- und Staatsarchiv, Informationsbüro des k.k. Ministeriums der Äussern, 1960, 1982, 2174, 2262, 3306, 4559 / 70, 1877. [Appears in text citations as *HHS*, Informationsbüro.]

Heck, Korneli. "Bibliografia Polska z r. 1881 w porównaniu z czeską, węgierską i rossyjską." *Przewodnik naukowy i literacki. Dodatek miesięczny do "Gazety Lwowskiej,"* 10 (1882): 1038–54, 1094–128.

Heindl, Waltraud. *Gehörsame Rebellen. Bürokratie und Beamte in Österreich 1780–1848.* Wien: Böhlau Verlag, 1991.

Herbil´s´kyi, H. Iu. *Rozvytok prohresyvnykh idei v Halychyni u pershii polovyni XIX st.: (do 1848 r.).* Lviv: Vyd-vo L´vivs´koho universytetu, 1964.

Heretz, Leonid. "Russian Apocalypse, 1891–1917: Popular Perceptions of Events from the Year of Famine and Cholera to the Fall of the Tsar." Ph.D. dissertation, Harvard University, 1993.

Herlihy, Patricia. "Ukrainian Cities in the Nineteenth Century." In *Rethinking Ukrainian History*, edited by Ivan Lysiak-Rudnytsky, with the assistance of John-Paul Himka, 135–155. Edmonton: Canadian Institute of Ukrainian Studies, University of Alberta; Downsview, Ont.: Distributed by the University of Toronto Press, 1981.

Hertz, Aleksander. *The Jews in Polish Culture.* Evanston, IL: Northwestern University Press, 1988.

Hickmann, Leo. *Geographisch-statistischer Taschen-Atlas von Österreich-Ungarn.* Vienna: Freytag and Berndt, 1900.

Himka, John-Paul. "Hope in the Tsar: Displaced Naïve Monarchism among the Ukrainian Peasants of the Habsburg Empire." *Russian History / Histoire Russe* 7, nos. 1–2 (1980): 125–38.

———. *Socialism in Galicia: The Emergence of Polish Social Democracy and Ukrainian Radicalism (1860–1890).* Cambridge, MA: Harvard Ukrainian Research Institute, 1983.

———. "The Greek Catholic Church and Nation-Building in Galicia, 1772–1918." *Harvard Ukrainian Studies* 8, nos. 3–4 (December 1984): 426–52.

———. *Galician Villagers and the Ukrainian National Movement in the Nineteenth Century.* Edmonton: Canadian Institute of Ukrainian Studies, University of Alberta, in association with Macmillan Press, London, 1988.

————. "Ukrainian-Jewish Antagonism in the Galician Countryside during the Late Nineteenth Century." In *Ukrainian-Jewish Relations in Historical Perspective*, edited by Howard Aster and Peter J. Potichnyj, 111–58. Edmonton: Canadian Institute of Ukrainian Studies, 1988.

————. "*Krakivs'ki visti* and the Jews, 1943: A Contribution to the History of Ukrainian-Jewish Relations during the Second World War." *Journal of Ukrainian Studies* 1–2 (Summer–Winter 1996): 81–95.

————. "The Construction of Nationality in Galician Rus': Icarian Flights in Almost All Directions." In *Intellectuals and Articulation of the Nation*, edited by Ronald G. Suny and Michael D. Kennedy, 109–64. Ann Arbor: University of Michigan Press, 1999.

————. "Dimensions of a Triangle: Polish-Ukrainian-Jewish Relations in Austrian Galicia." In *Focusing on Galicia: Jews, Poles, and Ukrainians, 1772–1918*, edited by Israel Bartal and Antony Polonsky, 25–48. Vol. 12 of *Polin: Studies in Polish Jewry*. London: Littman Library of Jewish Civilization, 1999.

————. *Religion and Nationality in Western Ukraine: The Greek Catholic Church and the Ruthenian National Movement in Galicia, 1867–1900*. Montreal: McGill-Queen's University Press, 1999.

————. [Ivan-Pavlo Khymka]. "Istoriia, khrystyans'kyi svit i tradytsiina ukrains'ka kul'tura: sproba mental'noi arkheolohii." *Ukraina moderna* 6 (2001): 7–24.

————. "War Criminality: A Blank Spot in the Collective Memory of the Ukrainian Diaspora." Paper presented at the conference "Gespaltene Geschichtskulturen? Die Bedeutung des Zweiten Weltkrieges für die Etablierung Nationalstaatlicher Symboliken und Kollektiver Errinerungskulturen in Ostmitteleuropa," Lviv, 30 May–1 June 2003.

————. "On the Left Hand of God: 'Peoples' in Ukrainian Icons of the Last Judgement." In *States, Societies, Cultures: East and West: Essays in Honor of Jaroslaw Pelenski*, edited by Janusz Duzinkiewicz et al. New York: Ross, 2004.

Hirszhaut, Julien. *The Jewish Oil Magnates*. Translated by Miriam Dashkin Beckerman. Edited by Valerie Schatzker. Montreal: McGill-Queen's University Press, 2015.

Hlyns'kyi, Ivan. "Ivan Franko i Iuliush Slovats'kyi." *Vsesvit* 1 (1965): 85–86.

Hnatiuk, Mykhailo, comp. *Spohady pro Ivana Franka*. Lviv: Kameniar, 1997.

Hnatiuk, Volodymyr. *Kupanie i palenie vid'm u Halychyni*. Single copy; n.d.

————. *Narys ukrains'koi mifolohii*. Lviv: In-t Narodoznavstva Nats. Akademii nauk Ukrainy, 2000.

————, comp. *Halyts'ko-rus'ki narodni liegendy*. Vol. 12 of *Etnohrafichnyi zbirnyk*. Lviv, 1902.

Hobsbawm, Eric J. *The Age of Empire, 1875–1914*. 1st US ed. New York: Pantheon Books, 1987.

Hohenberg, Paul M., and Lynn Hollen Lees. *The Making of Urban Europe, 1000–1950*. Cambridge, MA: Harvard University Press, 1985.

Holovatskii, Ia. U. "Velykaia Khorvatyia abo Halychsko Karpatskaia Rus'." In *Vinok rusynam na obzhynky uplil*, compiled by Ivan B. U. Holovatskii, pt. 2, 169–71. Vienna, 1847.

Holovats'kyi, Ivan. *Ivan Horbachevs'kyi. Zhyttiepysno-bibliohrafichnyi narys*. Lviv, 1995.

Holzer, Jerzy. "Zur Frage der Akkulturation der Juden in Galizien im 19. und 20. Jahrhundert." *Jahrbücher für Geschichte Osteuropas* 37 (1989): 217–27.

———. "Von Orient die Fantasie, und in der Brust der Slawen Feuer… Jüdisches Leben und Akkulturation im Lemberg des 19. und 20. Jahrhunderts." In *Lemberg, Lwów, Lviv: eine Stadt im Schnittpunkt europäischer Kulturen*, edited by Peter Fässler, Thomas Held, and Dirk Sawitzki, 75–91. Cologne: Böhlau Verlag, 1993.

Horak, Roman. *Trychi meni iavlialasia liubov*. Kyiv: Radians´kyi pys´mennyk, 1983.

———. "'Ia ie muzhyk, proloh, ne epiloh': Povist-dokument." *Kyiv* 9 (1989): 49–59.

———. *Mariia, maty Frankova*, pt. 1. Truskavets, 1994.

———. "Lysty rodyny do Ivana Franka." *Naukovyi visnyk Muzeiu Ivana Franka u L´vovi* 1 (2000): 120–208.

Horak, Roman, and Iaroslav Hnativ. *Ivan Franko*, bk. 1: *Rid Iakova*. Lviv: Vyd-vo ottsiv Vasyliian "Misioner," 2000.

———. *Ivan Franko*, bk. 2: *Tsilkom normal´na shkola*. Lviv: Vyd-vo ottsiv Vasyliian "Misioner," 2001.

———. *Ivan Franko*, bk. 4: *Universytet*. Lviv: Vyd-vo ottsiv Vasyliian "Misioner," 2004.

Hosking, Geoffrey A. *Russia: People and Empire, 1552–1917*. Cambridge, MA: Harvard University Press, 1997.

Hoszowski, Stanisław. *Ekonomiczny rozwój Lwowa w latach 1772–1914*. Lwów: Nakładem Izby Przemysłowo-Handlowej we Lwowie, 1935.

Hrinchenko, Borys. *Kulishovi tvory i sil´s´ki chytachi*. Kyiv: n.p., 1906.

———. *Shevchenkiv "Kobzar" na seli*. Kyiv, 1914.

Hrinchenko, Borys, and M. Drahomanov. *Dialohy pro ukrains´ku natsional´nu spravu*. Kyiv: Natsional´na Akademiia nauk Ukrainy; Instytut ukrains´koi arkheohrafii, 1994. [=*Dzherela z istorii suspil´no-politychnoho rukhu v Ukraini 19–pochatku 20 st.*]

Hrushevs´kyi, Mykhailo. *Z pochyniv ukrains´koho sotsiialistychnoho rukhu: Mykh. Drahomanov i zhenevs´kyi sotsiialistychnyi hurtok* [=*Documents pour servir à l'histoire du mouvement social en Ukraine: Dragomanov et le groupe socialiste de Genève*]. Vienna: Institut sociologique ukrainien, Zakordonye [*sic*] biuro i sklad, 1922.

———. "1825–1925." *Ukraina* 6 (1925): 3–4.

———. "Misiia Drahomanova." *Ukraina* 2–3 (1926): 3–28.

Hryhorieva, Valiantsina Vasileuna, and Alena Mikalaeuna Filatava. "Kanfesiinae stanovishcha na Belarusi: XIX stahodze." In *Samoidentyfikacja mniejszości narodowych i religijnych w Europie Środkowo-Wschodniej; Problematyka atłasowa* edited by Jan Skarbek, 82–88. Lublin: IESW–Wydawnictwo Instytutu Europy Środkowo-Wschodniej, 1998.

Hryniuk, Stella. *Peasants with Promise: Ukrainians in Southeastern Galicia*. Edmonton: Canadian Institute of Ukrainian Studies, 1991.

Hrytsak, Yaroslav. "Istorychna osnova povisti I. Franka 'Boryslav smiiet´sia.'" *Ivan Franko: Statti ta materialy* 44 (1985): 39.

———. "Poshyrennia poemy 'Maria' v Halychyni." *Radianske literaturoznavstvo* 3 (1986): 51–54.

——— [Ia. Grytsak]. "Rabochie Borislavsko-Drogobychskogo neftianogo basseina vo vtoroi polovine XIX–nachale XX vv.: Formirovanie, polozhenie, klassovaia bor´ba." Candidate of Historical Sciences dissertation, Lviv, 1986.

———. "Halyts´ka, 6. Iz l´vivs´kykh adres I. Franka." *Vil´na Ukraina*, 26 August 1987.

———. "*...Dukh, shcho tilo rve do boiu...*" *Sproba politychnoho portreta Ivana Franka.* Lviv: Kameniar, 1990.

———. "Ivan Franko pro politychnu samostiinist´ Ukrainy." *Zeszyty naukowe Uniwersytetu Jagiellońskiego, Prace Historyczne = Universitas Jagellonica Cracoviensis Acta scientiarum litterarumque. Schedae historicae* 103 (1993), 45–53.

———. *Narys istorii Ukrainy: Formuvannia modernoi ukrains´koi natsii, XIX–XX stolittia.* Kyiv: Heneza, 1996.

———. "Ukrains´ke natsional´ne vidrodzhennia v Halychyni XIX–poch. XX st.: porivnial´nyi analiz sotsial´noho skladu patriotychnykh hrup." *Krakivs´ki Ukrainoznavchi Zoshyty* 5–6 (1996–97): 283–285.

———. "Zabutyi pol´s´kyi perekladach T. H. Shevchenka." *Materialy zasidan´ Istorychnoi ta Arkheohrafichnoi komisii NTSh v Ukraini*, vol. 2: *1995–97*, 111–16. Lviv, 1999.

———. "History of Names: A Case of Constructing National Memory in Galicia, 1830–1930s." *Jahrbücher für Geschichte Osteuropas* 46 (2001): 163–77.

———. "'Iakykh-to kniaziv buly stolytsi v Kyievi?...': Do konstruiuvannia istorychnoi pam´iati halyts´kykh selian u 1830–1930-ti roky." *Ukraina moderna* 6 (2001): 87–88.

———. "'Molodi radykaly' u suspil´no-politychnomu zhytti Halychyny." *ZNTSh* 221 (2001): 71–110.

———. "Lviv: A Multicultural History through the Centuries." In *Lviv: A City in the Crosscurrents of Culture* [=*Harvard Ukrainian Studies* 24 (2000), Special Issue], edited by John Czaplicka, 47–73. Cambridge, MA: Harvard Ukrainian Research Institute, 2002.

———. "Crossroads of East and West: Lemberg, Lwów, L´viv on the Threshold of Modernity." *Austrian History Yearbook* 34 (2003): 103–9.

———. "Namy znovu manipuliuiut´." *Postup*, 19 September 2003, 10.

——— [Jaroslaw Hrycak]. "Między filosemityzmem i antysemityzmem—Iwan Franko i kwestia żydowska." In *Świat niepożegnany: żydzi na dawnych ziemiach wschodnich Rzeczypospolitej w XVIII–XX wieku = A World We Bade No Farewell: Jews in the Eastern Territories of the Polish Republic from 18th to 20th Century*, edited by Krzysztof Jasiewicz, 451–80. Warsaw: Instytut Studiów Politycznych PAN: Oficyna Wydawn. RYTM; London: Polonia Aid Foundation Trust, 2004.

———. *Strasti za natsionalizmom: istorychni esei.* Kyiv: Krytyka, 2004.

Hrytsak, Ya. I., and S. M. Trusevych. "Ivan Franko i robitnychyi rukh u Skhidnii Halychyni u 70–80-kh rokakh XIX st." In *Ivan Franko i svitova kultura: materialy Mizhnarodnoho sympoziumu IuNESKO*, edited by I. I. Lukinov, M. V. Bryk et al., 346. Kyiv: Naukova dumka, 1990.

Hrytsak, Yaroslav, and Victor Susak. "Constructing a National City: The Case of L´viv." In *Composing Urban History and the Constitution of Civic Identities*, edited by John J.

Czaplicka and Blair A. Ruble; assisted by Lauren Crabtree. Washington, D.C.: Woodrow Wilson Center Press; Baltimore: Johns Hopkins University Press, 2003.

Hrytsak, Ievhen. *Vybrani ukrainoznavchi pratsi*. Przemyśl, 2002.

Hrytsiuta, M. S. *Selianstvo v ukrains'kii dozhovtnevii literaturi*. Kyiv: Naukova dumka, 1979.

Hüchtker, Dietlind. "Der 'Mythos Galizien.' Versuch einer Historisierung." In *Die Nationalisierung von Grenzen. Zur Konstruktion nationaler Identität in sprachlich gemischten Grenzregionen*, edited by Michael G. Müller and Rolf Petri. Vol. 16 of *Tagungen des Herder-Instituts zur Ostmitteleuropa-Forschung*. Marburg: Herder-Inst., 2002. Accessed 30 June 2006 at http://www.kakanien.ac.at/beitr/fallstudie/DHu_chtker2.pdf.

Hundorova, Tamara. *Franko—ne Kameniar*. 2nd ed. Kyiv: Krytyka, 2006.

Hushalevych, N. I. *Poezii*, pt. 2. Lviv, 1879.

Hvozdevych, M. "Kult Markiiana Shashkevycha u seredyni XIX–na pochatku XX st." Dissertation, Lviv, 2004.

Iakovenko, Natalia. *Ukrains'ka shliakhta z kintsia XIV do seredyny XVII st. (Volyn' i Tsentral'na Ukraina)*. Kyiv: Naukova dumka, 1993.

Iakovenko, V. M. "Do spivrobitnytstva Franka v 'Zori.'" In *Ukrains'ke literaturoznavstvo*, vol. 1, 64–69. Lviv: Vyd-vo L'vivs'koho universytetu.

Iakymovych, Bohdan. *Knyha, prosvita, natsiia: Vydavnycha diial'nist' Ivana Franka u 70–80 rokakh XIX st.* Lviv: Instytut ukrainoznavstva im. I. Kryp'iakevycha NAN Ukrainy, 1996.

Ianyshyn, B. M. "Narodovs'kyi rukh u Halychyni iak suspil'no-politychna techiia (70–80-ti roky XIX st.)." Candidate of Historical Sciences dissertation, Kyiv, 2003.

Iaremenko, Vasyl'. *Ievrei v Ukraini sohodni: real'nist' bez mifiv*. Kyiv: Mizhrehional'na akademiia upravlinnia personalom, 2003.

Iastrebov, N. V. *Galitsiia nakanune Velikoi Voiny 1914 g.* Petrograd: Tip. A. E. Kollins, 1915.

Il'kevych, Hryhorii, comp. *Halyts'ki prypovidky i zahadky*. 1841; reprint, Lviv: Vyd-vo L'vivs'koho universytetu, 1994.

Inkin, Vasyl'. *Sil's'ke suspil'stvo Halyts'koho Prykarpattia u XVI–XVIII stolittiakh: istorychni narysy*. Lviv: [Vyd-vo Dobra sprava], 2004.

Isaievych, Iaroslav. "Iak vynyklo misto pid nazvoiu Lviv." In *L'viv: Istorychni narysy*, edited by Iaroslav Isaievych, Feodosii Steblii, and Mykola Lytvyn. Lviv: Instytut ukrainoznavstva im. I. Kryp'iakevycha NAN Ukrainy, 1996.

———. *Ukraina davnia i nova. Narod, relihiia, kul'tura*. Lviv: Instytut ukrainoznavstva im. I. Kryp'iakevycha NAN Ukrainy, 1996.

Isaievych, Iaroslav, and Yaroslav Hrytsak, eds. *Druhyi mizhnarodnyi konhres ukrainistiv, L'viv, 22–28 serpnia 1993 r. Dopovidi i povidomlennia. Istoriia*, vol. 1. Lviv, 1994.

Istoricheskiia pesni malorusskago naroda, s obiasneniiami Vl. Antonovicha i M. Dragomanova, vol. 1. Kyiv: Tip. M. Fritsa, 1874.

Ivan Franko: Dokumenty i materialy, 1856–1965. Kyiv: Naukova dumka, 1966.

Ivanova, R. *Mykhailo Drahomanov u suspil'no-politychnomu rusi Rosii ta Ukrainy (II polovyna XIX st.)*. Kyiv: Vyd-vo Kyivs'koho universytetu, 1971.

Janowski, Maciej. *Inteligencja wobec wyzwań nowoczesności: dylematy ideowe polskiej demokracji liberalnej w Galicji w latach 1889–1914*. Warsaw: Instytut Historii PAN, 1996.

Jarowiecki, Jerzy. "Prasa ugrupowań politycznych we Lwowie w okresie autonomiji galicyjskiej (1867–1918)." In *Kraków–Lwów: Książki, czasopisma, biblioteki XIX i XX wieku*, edited by Jerzy Jarowiecki, vol. 5. Cracow: Wydawnictwo naukowe Akademii Pedagogicznej, 2001.

Jobst, Kerstin. *Zwischen Nationalismus und Internationalismus. Der polnische und ukrainische Sozial-Demokratie in Galizien von 1890 bis 1914. Ein Beitrag zur Nationalitätenfrage im Habsburgerreich*. Hamburg: Dölling und Galitz, 1996.

Johnson, Hildegard Binder. "Geography in German Literature." *German Quarterly* 24, no. 4 (November 1951): 232.

Johnson, Robert E. "Peasant and Proletariat: Migration, Family Patterns, and Regional Loyalties." In *The World of the Russian Peasant: Post-Emancipation Culture and Society*, edited by Ben Eklof and Stephen Frank. Boston: Unwin Hyman, 1990.

Jones, Ernest. *The Life and Works of Sigmund Freud*, edited by and abr. Lionel Trilling and Steven Marcus. New York: Basic Books, 1961.

Kahan, Arcadius, Dietrich Beyrau, Ivan T. Bérend, György Ránki, Dimitrus J. Delivanis, and Holm Sunhaussen. *Ost- und Südosteuropa 1850–1914*. Stuttgart: Klett-Gotta, 1980.

Kaindl, R. F. *Hutsuly: ikh zhyttia, zvychai ta narodni perekazy*. Chernivtsi: Molodyi bukovynets´, 2000.

Kaiser, Daniel H. "Naming Cultures in Early Modern Russia." In *Kamen Kraeogln: Rhetoric of the Medieval Slavic World: Essays Presented to Edward Keenan on His Sixtieth Birthday by His Colleagues and Students*. Cambridge, MA.: Harvard Ukrainian Research Institute, 1995.

Kakovs´kyi, K. H. *Na shliakhu do Velykoho Zhovtnia: straikovyi rukh v Halychyni kintsia XIX–pochatku XX st.* Lviv: Vyd-vo L´vivs´koho universytetu, 1970.

Kalynovych, V. I. *Politychni protsesy Ivana Franka ta ioho tovaryshiv*. Lviv: Vyd-vo L´vivs´koho universytu, 1967.

Kantorowicz, Ernst H. "*Pro Patria Mori* in Medieval Political Thought." *American Historical Review* 56, no. 3 (April 1951): 472–92.

Karolczak, Kazimierz, and Henryk W. Zaliński, eds. *Galicyjskie Dylematy. Zbiór rozpraw*. Cracow: Wydawn. Naukowe WSP, 1994.

Kaszyński, Stefan H. "Der jüdische Anteil and der Literatur in und über Galizien." In *Von Franzos zu Canetti: jüdische Autoren aus Österreich: neue Studien*, edited by Mark. H. Gelber, Hans Otto Horch, and Sigurd Paul Scheichl, 129–40. Tübingen: Niemeyer, 1996.

Kearney, Michael. *Reconceptualizing the Peasantry: Anthropology in Global Perspective*. Boulder, CO: Westview Press, 1996.

Kelles-Kraus, Kazimierz. *Pisma wybrane*. Warsaw: Książka i Wiedza, 1962.

Khonigsman, Ia. S. *Pronyknennia inozemnoho kapitalu v naftovu promyslovist Zakhidnoi Ukrainy v epokhu imperializmu (do 1918 r.)*. Lviv: Vyd-vo L´vivs´koho universytetu, 1971.

Khvan´ko, A. [Ahatanhel Kryms´kyi]. [Review of] "V poti chola: Obrazky z zhytia robuchoho liudu. Napysav Ivan Franko, L´viv, 1890." *Zoria* 12 (1891): 77.

Kieczynski, Józef. "Stosunki włościan w Galicji." In *Wiadomości statystyczne o stosunkach krajowych* 7, no. 1 (1881): 67.

Kiral´, S. S., comp. *"...Viddaty zumiiem sebe Ukraini!": Lystuvannia Trokhyma Zin´kivs´koho z Borysom Hrinchenkom*, 44. Kyiv and New York: Ukrains´ka Vil´na Akademiia nauk u SShA, 2004.

Kis´, O. R. "Zhinka v ukrains´kii selians´kii sim´i druhoi polovyny XIX—pochatku XX stolittia: genderni aspekty." Candidate of Historical Sciences dissertation, Instytut ukrainoznavstva im. I. Kryp´iakevycha NAN Ukrainy, 2001.

Kistiakovs´kyi, A. F. *Shchodennyk (1874–1885): u dvokh tomakh*, compiled by Valentyna S. Shandra et al., vol. 2: *1880–1885*. Kyiv: Naukova dumka, 1994–1995.

Kłańska, Maria. *Aus dem Schtetl in die Welt 1772 bis 1938: Ostjüdische Autobiographien in deutscher Sprache*. Vienna: Böhlau Verlag, 1994.

Klasova borot´ba selianstva Skhidnoi Halychyny: 1772–1849: dokumenty i materialy, compiled by O. A. Kupchyns´kyi, A. H. Silets´kyi, and F. I. Steblii. Kyiv: Naukova dumka, 1974.

Klier, John D., and Shlomo Lambroza, eds. *Pogroms: Anti-Jewish Violence in Modern Russian History*. Cambridge: Cambridge University Press, 1992.

Kłoskowska, Antonina. *National Cultures at the Grass-Root Level*. Budapest: Central European University Press, 2001.

Knot, Antoni. "Czerkawski, Euzebiusz." *Polski słownik biograficzny*, vol. 4, 333–34. Cracow: Polska Akademia Umiejętności, 1938.

———. Introduction to *Pamiętniki. Galicja (1843–1880)*, vol. 1, by Kazimierz Chłędowski. Wrocław: Zakł. Narod. im. Ossol., 1951.

———, ed. *Galicyjskie wspomnienia szkolne*. Cracow: Wydawn. Literackie, 1955.

Knysh, Irena. *Ivan Franko ta rivnopravnist´ zhinky*. Winnipeg: Novyi shliakh, 1956.

———. *Smoloskyp u temriavi: Natalia Kobrynska i ukrainskyi zhinochyi rukh*. Winnipeg: Novyi shliakh, 1957.

Kobryns´ka, Natalia. *Vybrani tvory*. Kyiv: Derzh. vyd-vo khudozh. lit-ry, 1958.

Kochanowicz, Jacek. *Spór o teorię gospodarki chłopskiej. Gospodarstwo chłopskie w teorii ekonomii i w historii gospodarczej*. Warsaw: Wydawnictwo Uniwersytetu Warszawskiego, 1992.

Kohl, J. G. [Johann Georg]. *Austria, Vienna, Prague, Hungary, Bohemia, and the Danube; Galicia, Styria, Moravia, Bukovina, and the Military Frontier*. London: Chapman and Hall, 1844.

Kohn, Hans. "Arndt and the German Character of German Nationalism." *American Historical Review* 54, no. 4 (July 1949): 798.

———. *Nationalism: Its Meaning and History*. Rev. ed. Malabar, FL: Krieger, 1982.

Koialovich, M. O. [Mikhail Osipovich]. *Istoriia vossoedineniia zapadnorusskikh uniatov starykh vremen (do 1800 g.)*. Minsk: Luchi Sofii, 1999.

Kolesnyk, I. *Ivan Franko: Literaturnyi portret*. Kyiv: Dnipro, 1964.

Kon, F. "Dragomanov i Franko v pol´skom rabochem dvizhenii." *Griadushchii mir* 1 (1922): 238–39.

Konkordantsiia poetychnykh tvoriv Tarasa Shevchenka = A Concordance to the Poetic Works of Taras Shevchenko. 4 vols. Compiled and edited by Oleh S. Ilnytzkyj and George Hawrysch. Edmonton: Canadian Institute of Ukrainian Studies, 2001.

Kononenko, Natalia. *Ukrainian Minstrels: And the Blind Shall Sing.* Armonk, NY: M. E. Sharpe, 1998.

Korbut, Gabriel. *Od roku 1864 do 1919.* Vol. 4 of *Literatura Polska od początków do wojny światowej: książka podręczna informacyjna dla studjujących naukowo dzieje pismiennictwa polskiego.* 2nd ed. Warsaw: Skład główny w Kasie im. Mianowskiego, 1931.

Kordasevych, Lev. "Spravy narodnii. Z Mokrianskoho dekanata Samborskoho okruha." *Vistnyk dlia rusynov avstriiskoi derzhavy*, 15 / 27 July 1850.

Koriak, V. [Volodymyr]. *Burzhuazne pysmenstvo.* Vol. 2 of *Narys istorii ukrainskoi literatury: U 2 t.* Kharkiv: Derzhavne vydavnytstvo Ukrainy, 1929.

Korotkyi, Viktor, and Vasyl´ Ul´ianovs´kyi, comps. *Syn Ukrainy, Volodymyr Bonifatiiovych Antonovych*, vol. 2. Kyiv: Zapovit, 1997.

Kosiecka, Mirosława, and Zofia Żydanowicz. "Iwan Franko w Polsce do 1953." Ms., Biblioteka Narodowa, Zakład Informacji Naukowej.

Koval´chak, H. I. *Ekonomichnyi rozvytok zakhidnoukrains´kykh zemel´.* Kyiv: Naukova dumka, 1988.

Kovaliv, Stefan. *Tvory.* Kyiv: Derzh. vyd-vo khudozh. lit-ry, 1958.

———. *Opovidannia, kazky, lysty: z nedrukovanoi spadshchyny.* Lviv: Kobzar, 2003.

Kowal-Kwiatkowska, Aleksandra, ed. *Miasto i kultura ludowa w dziejach Białorusi, Litwy, Polski i Ukrainy.* Cracow: Międzynarodowe Centrum Kultury, 1996.

Kowalikova, Jadwiga. "Słowo—Galicja—dawniej i dziś, czyli habent sua fata verba." In *Inteligencja południowo-wschodnich ziem polskich*, edited by Halina Kurek and Franciszek Tereszkiewicz, 211–19. Cracow: Universitas, 1998.

Kozik, Jan. *The Ukrainian National Movement in Galicia, 1815–1849.* Edmonton: Canadian Institute of Ukrainian Studies, University of Alberta; Downsview, Ont., Canada: Distributed by the University of Toronto Press, 1986.

Kozłowska-Budkowa, Zofia. "Franko, biskup polski." In *Polski Słownik Biograficzny*, vol. 7. Cracow: Polska Akademia Umiejętności, 1948–58.

Kozłowska-Sabatowska, Halina. *Ideologia pozytywizmu galicyjskiego: 1864–1881.* Wroclaw: Zakład Narodowy im. Ossolińskich, 1978.

Kozłowski, Józef. "Iwan Franko a polski ruch robotniczy w Galicji w latach siedemdziesiątych i osiemdziesiątych wieku XIX." *Kwartalnik Instytutu Polsko-Radzieckiego* 1, no. 6 (1954): 98.

Kozłowski, Maciej. *Między Sanem a Zbruczem. Walki o Lwów i Galicję Wschodnią 1918–1919.* Cracow: ZNAK, 1990.

Krajewski, Janusz. "Ochorowicz, Julian." In *Polski słownik biograficzny*, vol. 23. Wroclaw: Wydawnictwo PAN, 1978.

Krappe, Alexander H. *The Science of Folklore*. New York: Norton, 1964.

Kravchenko, Uliana. *Zamist' avtobiohrafii*. Kolomyia: Zahal´na knyhozbirnia, 1934.

———. *Spohady uchytel´ky*. Kolomyia: Zahal´na knyhozbirnia, 1936.

———. *Khryzantemy; povist'*. Chicago: M. Denysiuk, 1961.

———. "Z lit davnomynulykh." Warsaw: Archiwum ojców Bazylianów, n.d.

———. *Pam'iaty druha: virshi v prozi, statti, spohady, lysty*, compiled and edited by H. I. Ohryza. Lviv: Kameniar, 1996.

Kravets´, M. M. *Selianstvo Skhidnoi Halychyny i Pivnichnoi Bukovyny u druhii polovyni XIX st*. Lviv: Vyd-vo L´vivs´koho universytetu, 1964.

———. *Klasova borot´ba u skhidnohalyts´komu seli navkolo servitutnoho pytannia— realistychna osnova opovidannia I. Ia. Franka "Lisy i pasovys´ka." Metodychna rozrobka dlia studentiv*. Vinnytsia, 1981.

Krawchenko, Bohdan. *Social Change and National Consciousness in Twentieth-Century Ukraine*. Edmonton: Canadian Institute of Ukrainian Studies, University of Alberta, in association with St. Antony's College, Oxford, 1987.

Křevan, Zvonimir Turin. *Liber roda Turinskog i Franko od nastanjivanja u primorskom kraju, te of 1673–1969*. Rijeka, 1971.

Krueger, Rita. "Nationalizing the Public." In *Cultures and Nations of Central and Eastern Europe: Essays in Honor of Roman Szporluk*, edited by Zvi Gitelman et al. Cambridge, MA: Harvard Ukrainian Research Institute, 2000.

Kruhlashov, A. M. *Drama intelektuala—politychni idei Mykhaila Drahomanova*. Chernivtsi: Vyd-vo Prut, 2000.

Krupnyts´kyi, Bohdan. *Istorioznavchi problemy istorii Ukrainy (zbirnyk statei)*. Munich: Ukrains´kyi Vil´nyi Universytet, 1959.

Krzywicki, Ludwik. *Wspomnienia*, vol. 1: *1859–1885*, edited by Stanisław Stempowski. [Warsaw]: Czytelnik, 1947.

Kucharski, Jan. Afterword to *Tam, gdzie się Wisła kończy* by Artur Gruszecki. Gdansk: Wydaw. Morskie, 1979.

Kudłaszyk, Andrzej. *Myśl społeczno-polityczna Bolesława Wysłoucha, 1855–1937*. Warsaw: Państwowe Wydawn. Naukowe, 1978.

Kudriavtsev, P. "Ievreistvo, ievrei ta ievreis´ka sprava v tvorakh Ivana Franka." In *Zbirnyk prats ievreis´koi istorychno-arkheohrafichnoi komisii*, vol. 2, edited by A. I. Kryms´kyi. Kyiv, 1929.

Kuhn, Walter. *Die jungen deutschen Sprachinseln in Galizien. Ein Beitrag zur Methode der Sprachinselforschung*, with Introduction by Univ.-Prof. Dr. Eduard Winter in Prag. Münster in Westfalen: Aschendorff, 1930.

Kulczycka-Saloni, Janina. "Poeta mendax—i prawda polskich dziejów." In *Wiek XIX: Prace, ofiarowane Stefanowi Kieniewiczowi w 60 rocznicę urodzin*, edited by Barbara Grochulska, Bogusław Leśnodorski, and Andrzej Zahorski, 439–449. Warsaw: Państwowe Wydawn. Naukowe, 1967.

———. "Geografia literacka Polski pod zaborami." In *Polska XIX wieku: Państwo, społeczeństwo, kultura*, edited by Stefan Kieniewicz. Warsaw: Wiedza powszechna, 1977.

———. *Na Polskich i europejskich szlakach literackich: z pism rozproszonych 1985–1998*. Warsaw: Antyk, 2000.

Kulish, Panteleimon. *Zhydotriepaniie*. Kyiv: Mizhrehional'na akademiia upravlinnia personalom, 2005.

Kultys, Ždisław. Historya Gimnazyum Drohobyckiego. Drohobycz: Komitet Jubileuszowy, 1908.

Kuplowski, Mikołaj. *Iwan Franko jako krytyk literatury polskiej*. Rzeszów: Wydawn. WSP w Rzeszowie, 1974.

Kuropatnicki, Ewaryst Andrzej. *Geografia albo dokładne opisanie królestw Galicyi i Lodomeryi*. 2nd ed. Lwów, 1858.

Kurylenko, I. "Zaborona tvoriv I. Franka tsars'koiu tsenzuroiu." *Radians'ke literaturoznavstvo* 1 (1959): 137–41.

Lanz, Josef, and Rudolf Unterschütz, eds. *Heimat Galizien im Bild*. Stuttgart: Das Hilfskomitee, 1983.

Le Goff, Jacques. *History and Memory*. New York: Columbia University Press, 1992.

Leichner, Ignaz. *Erdöl und Erdwachs: Ein Bild galizischer Industrie*. Vienna, 1898.

Lenin, V. I. "Vybory do Ustanovchykh Zboriv i dyktatura proletariatu." In *Povne zibrannia tvoriv*, vol. 40, 18. Kyiv, 1974.

Łesiów, Michał. "Bat'kiwszczyna, witczyzna, ridnyj kraj: Ojczyzna w języku ukraińskim." In Bartmiński, *Pojęcie ojczyzny*, 93–104.

Lesyn, V. M., and S. I. Dihtiar. "Litopysets revolutsiynoho Boryslava." In Stefan Kovaliv, *Tvory*.

Lev, Vasyl'. *Ivan Franko ta pol's'ki pozytyvisty*. Lviv, 1937.

Levin, Eve. *Sex and Society in the World of the Orthodox Slavs, 900–1700*. Ithaca, NY: Cornell University Press, 1989.

Levytskii, Ivan E. [Ivan Omelianovych Levyts'kyi]. *Halytsko-ruskaia bybliohrafiia XIX stolitiia s uvzhliadnenniem russkykh izdanii poiavivshykhsia v Uhorshchyni i Bukovyni (1801–1886)*, vol. 1: *Khronolohycheskii spysok publikatsii* [1801–1860]. Lviv, 1888.

Levyts'kyi, Kost'. *Istoriia politychnoi dumky halyts'kykh ukraintsiv, 1848–1914: Na pidstavi spomyniv [i dokumentiv]*. Lviv: nakl. vlasnym, 1926–1927.

Lewandowski, Edmund. *Charakter narodowy Polaków i innych*. London: Aneks, 1995.

Lippe, Karpel. *Symptome der antisemitischen Geisteskrankheit*. Jassy: H. Goldner, 1887.

Liske, Xaver. *Der angebliche Niedergang der Universität Lemberg: Offenes Sendschreiben an das Reichsrathsmitglied Herrn dr Eduard Suess prof. an der Universität Wien*. Lviv, 1876.

Literaturnoe nasledie G. V. Plekhanova. Moscow: Gos. sots.-ekon. izd., 1934–.

Litopys ruskyi: za ipats'kym spyskom. Translated by Leonid Makhnovets'. Kyiv: Dnipro, 1989.

Litschauer, Walburga, ed. *Dokumente zum Leben der Anna von Revertera*. Vol. 2 of *Neue Dokumente zum Schubert-Kreis: aus Briefen und Tagebüchern seiner Freunde*. Vienna: Musikwissenschaftlicher Verlag, 1993.

Loth, Roman. *Młodość Jana Kasprowicza. Szkic biograficzny*. Poznań: Wydawnictwo Poznańskie, 1962.

Luber, Susanne. *Die Herkunft von Zaporoger Kosacken des 17. Jahrhunderts nach Personnennamen*. Berlin: Osteuropa-Institut; Wiesbaden: Harrassowitz, 1983.

Luckyj, George S. N. *Between Gogol and Ševčenko: Polarity in the Literary Ukraine: 1798– 1847*. Munich: W. Fink, 1971.

Łuczyńska, Barbara. "Udział Towarzystwa Nauczycieli Szkół Wyższych w integrowaniu nauczycieli szkół średnich Galicji 1884–1909." In *Galicja i jej dziedzictwo*, vol. 3, 253.

Ludność podług zawodu i sposobu zarobkowania: Ludność przemysłowa. Wykaz przedsiębiorstw przemysłowych w całym kraju. Bk. 11 of *Rocznik statystyki przemysłu i handlu krajowego*. Lwów: Wyd. Krajowe Biuro Statystyczne [Oddział Statystyki Przemysłu i Handlu], 1888.

Lukiianovych, Denys. "Trahediia Kobryns´koi (z nahody zhinochoho Kongresu)." *Dilo*, 24 June 1934.

———. "Khto mav vyrishal´nyi vplyv na natsional´nyi kharakter Ivana Franka." *Krakivski visti*, 7 April 1943.

———. "Lysty Franka do Uliany Kravchenko." *Ivan Franko: Statti i materialy* 5 (1956): 141–44.

———. "Lysty Ol´hy Roshkevych do Ivana Franka." *Ivan Franko: Statti i materialy* 6 (1958): 5–48.

Lukych, Vasyl´. "Pershyi redaktor 'Dila' Volodymyr Barvins´kyi." *Dilo*, 14 January 1928.

Luts´kyi, Iurii. [George S. N. Luckyj]. "Rozdumy nad slovom 'Ukraina' u narodnykh pisniakh." *Suchasnist'* 8 (1993): 117–22.

Lysiak-Rudnyts´kyi, Ivan. "Storichchia pershoi ukrains´koi politychnoi prohramy." *Suchasnist'* 3 (1979): 107.

Mączak, Antoni. *Odkrywanie Europy: Podróże w czasach renesansu i baroku*. Gdansk: Wydawnictwo Novus Orbis, 1998.

Madurowicz-Urbańska, Helena. "Perspektywy nowych badań nad społeczeństwem galicyjskim." In *Pamiętnik XIII Powszechnego Zjazdu Historyków Polskich*, pt. 1. Wroclaw, 1986.

Magocsi, Paul Robert. *Galicia: A Historical Survey and Bibliographic Guide*. Toronto: University of Toronto Press, 1990.

———. *Historical Atlas of East Central Europe*. Toronto: University of Toronto Press, 1993.

———. *The Roots of Ukrainian Nationalism: Galicia as Ukraine's Piedmont*. Toronto: University of Toronto Press, 2002.

Mahler, Raphael. "The Economic Background of Jewish Emigration from Galicia to the United States." In *East European Jews in Two Worlds: Studies from the YIVO Annual*, edited by Deborah Dash Moore. Evanston, IL: Northwestern University Press; [New York]: Yivo Institute for Jewish Research, 1990.

Makaiev, V. *Robitnychyi klas Halychyny v ostannii tretyni XIX st.* Lviv: Vyd-vo L´vivs´koho universytetu, 1968.

Makovei, Osyp. *Istoriia odnoi students´koi hromady.* Lviv, 1912.

Makowski, S. "Musij Wernyhora i jego proroctwa w świetle badań polskich i ukraińskich." In Isaievych and Hrytsak, *Druhyi mizhnarodnyi konhres ukrainistiv,* 154–61.

Makowski, Stanisław, and Tadeusz Styszko. "Z nie opublikowanej korespondencji Iwana Franki z Adamem Wiślickim." *Slavia Orientalis* 7, no. 1 (1958): 127–28.

Makukh, Ivan. *Na narodnii sluzhbi: Spohady.* Kyiv: Osnovni tsinnosti, 2001.

Malanchuk-Rybak, Oksana. *Ukrains´ki zhinochi studii: istoriohrafiia ta istoriosofiia.* Lviv: Tovarystvo im. Shevchenka, 1999.

Malaniuk, Evhen. *Knyha sposterezhen´: Proza.* Toronto, 1962.

Malinowski, J. "150-lecie przemysłu naftowego—nowe spojrzenie na dawne dokumente." Accessed at http://www.orpatowski.pl.lib/kopalnictwo.html.

Manzenko, Petro. *Suspil´no-politychni i filosofs´ki pohliady M. Pavlyka.* Kyiv: Vyd-vo Akademii nauk URSR, 1962.

Marassé, Mieczysław. *Gospodarcze stosunki w Galicji.* Warsaw, 1874.

Marczak, A. "Motywy i watki 'naftowe' w tworczosci literackiej." *Technika Naftowa i Gazownicza* 2–3 (1989): 13.

Mark, Rudolf A. *Galizien unter Österreichischer Herrschaft: Verwaltung, Kirche, Bevölkerung.* Marburg: Herder-Institut, 1994.

Markovits, Andrei S., and Frank E. Sysyn, eds. *Nationbuilding and the Politics of Nationalism: Essays on Austrian Galicia.* Cambridge, MA: Harvard Ukrainian Research Institute, 1982.

Marks i Engels o Polsce: zbiór materiałów, edited by H. Michnik, vol. 2. Warsaw: Książka i Wiedza, 1960.

Marr, Wilhelm. *Der Weg zum Siege des Germanenthums über das Judenthum.* Berlin, 1879.

Marx, Karl. Preface, first German edition of *Das Kapital.* 1867. Accessed 14 February 2017 at http://www.marxists.org/archive/marx/works/1867-c1/p1.htm.

Marx [Marks], K., and F. Engels. *Tvory,* vol. 23. Kyiv, 1963.

Marx, Karl, and Friedrich Engels. "Manifesto of the Communist Party." In Karl Marx and Friedrich Engels, *Selected Works,* vol. 1. Moscow: Progress Publishers, 1969. Accessed at http://www.marxists.org/archive/marx/works/1848/communist-manifesto/index.htm.

Masaryk, T. G. *President Masaryk Tells His Story.* Recounted by Karel Čapek. Translated from the Czech. London: G. Allen and Unwin, 1934.

Masłowski, M. "Le Mythe de Wernyhora: Une Prophetie Polonaise sur la Coexistence de l'Ukraine et de la Pologne." In Isaievych and Hrytsak, *Druhyi mizhnarodnyi kongres ukrainistiv,* 146–54.

Mason, John W. *The Dissolution of the Austro-Hungarian Empire, 1867–1918.* London: Longman, 1985.

Matula, V., and I. Churkina, eds. *Zarubezhnye slaviane i Rossiia: Dokumenty arkhiva M. F. Raevskogo 40–80 godov XIX veka.* Moscow: Akademiia nauk SSSR, Institut slavianovedeniia i balkanistiki, Nauka, 1975.

Mayer, Arno J. *The Persistence of the Old Regime: Europe to the Great War*. London: Pantheon Books, 1981.

Mazepa, V. I. *Kulturotsentryzm svitohliadu Ivana Franka*. Kyiv: Vydavets´ PARAPAN, 2004.

Mazurok, Oleh. "Plata za vil´nodumstvo: Novovyiavleni dokumenty pro zv´iazky Mykhaila Drahomanova ta inshykh halyts´kykh diiachiv iz Zakarpattiam." *Novyny Zakarpattia* 20–21 (8 February 1997).

Mędrzecki, Włodzimierz. *Niemiecka interwencja militarna na Ukrainie w 1918 roku*. Warsaw: Wydawn. DiG, 2000.

———. *Młodzież wiejska na ziemiach Polski centralnej, 1864–1939: procesy socjalizacji*. Warsaw: Wydawn. DiG, 2002.

——— [Medzhets´kyi, Volodymyr]. "Seliany u natsiotvorchykh protsesakh Tsentral´noi i Skhidnoi Ievropy u druhii polovyni XIX–na pochatku XX stolittia." *Ukraina moderna* 6 (2001): 59–76.

Melamed, Vladimir. *Evrei vo L´vove (XIII–pervaia polovina XX veka): Sobytiia, obshchestvo, liudi*. Lviv: Sovmestnoe ukrainsko-amerikanskoe predpriiatie Tekop, 1994.

Mel´nyk, Iaroslava. *I ostatnia chast´ dorohy...Ivan Franko: 1908–1916*. Lviv: Kolo, 1999.

———. *Z ostannoho desiatylittia Ivana Franka*. Lviv: Vyd-vo L´vivs´koho universytetu, 1999.

Mendelsohn, Ezra. "From Assimilation to Zionism in Lvov: The Case of Alfred Nossig." *Slavonic and East European Review* 49, no. 117 (October 1971): 521–34.

———. "Jewish Assimilation in L´viv: The Case of Wilhelm Feldman." In Markovits and Sysyn, *Nationbuilding and the Politics of Nationalism*.

———. *Painting a People: Maurycy Gottlieb and Jewish Art*. Hanover, NH: Brandeis University Press, 2002.

Merunowicz, Teofil. *O metodzie i celach rozpraw nad kwestią żydowską*. Lviv, 1879.

Mickiewicz, Ladislas. *La Pologne est ses provinces méridionales; manuscrit d'un Ukrainien*. Paris: E. Dentu, 1863.

Mijakovskyj, Volodymyr. "Kyivs´ka Hromada (z istorii kyivs´koho hromads´koho rukhu 60-kh rokiv)." In *Unpublished and Forgotten Writings: Political and Intellectual Trends of the Nineteenth Century; Modern Ukrainian Literature* [=*Nedrukovane i zabute: Hromads´ki rukhy dev'iatnadtsiatoho storichchia; Novitnia ukrains´ka literatura*], edited by Marko Antonovych. New York: Ukrainian Academy of Arts and Sciences in the US, 1984.

Miliukov, N. *Ocherki po istorii russkoi kul´tury*, vol. 2, pt. 26. Moscow: Izd-vo MGTU, 1994.

Mill, John Stuart. *August Comte und der Positivismus (1865)*. Leipzig: Fues's Verlag, 1874.

Miller, A. I. *"Ukrainskii vopros" v politike vlastei i russkom obshchestvennom mnenii (vtoraia polovina XIX v.)*. St. Petersburg: Aleteiia, 2000.

———. *The Ukrainian Question: The Russian Empire and Nationalism in the Nineteenth Century*. Authorized translation by Olga Poato. Budapest: Central European University Press, 2003.

Miłosz, Czesław. *The History of Polish Literature*. London: Macmillan, 1969.

Mironov, B. N. "Traditsionnoe demograficheskoe povedenie krest'ian v XIX–nachale XX vv." In *Brachnost', rozhdaemost', smertnost' v Rossii i v SSSR: Sb. statei*. Moscow: Statistika, 1977.

Mironov, Boris N., with Ben Eklof, *A Social History of Imperial Russia, 1700–1917*, vol. 1. Boulder, CO: Westview Press, 2000.

Mokry, Włodzimierz. *"Ruska Trójca": Karta z dziejów życia literackiego Ukraińców w Galicji w pierwszej połowie XIX wieku*. Wroclaw: Wydawn. Uniwersytetu Jagiellońskiego, Fundacja Świętego Włodzimierza, 1997.

Molenda, Jan. *Chłopi, naród, niepodległość*. Warsaw: Wydawn. NERITON, Instytut Historii PAN, 1999.

Molska, Alina, ed. *Pierwsze pokolenie marksistów polskich: wybór pism i materiałów źródłlowych z lat 1878–1886*, vol. 1. Warsaw: Książka i Wiedza, 1962.

Mommsen, Hans. *Das Ringen um die supernationale Integration der zisleithanischen Arbeiterbewegung*. Vol. 1 of *Die Sozialdemokratie und die Nationalitätenfrage im habsburgischen Vielvölkerstaat*. Vienna: Europa-Verlag, 1963–.

Monchalovskyi, O. A. *Zhyt'ie i deiatel'nost' Ivana Naumovicha*. Lviv, 1889.

Moon, David. *The Russian Peasantry, 1600–1930: The World the Peasants Made*. London: Longman, 1999.

Moroz, M. O. [Myroslav Oleksandrovych], comp. *Ivan Franko; bibliohrafiia tvoriv 1874–1964*. Kyiv: Naukova dumka, 1966.

———. "Do pytannia atrybutsii tvoriv I. Franka v hazeti 'Kurjer Lwowski.'" In *Pytannia tekstolohii: Ivan Franko*, edited by M. Ie. Syvachenko. Kyiv: Naukova dumka, 1983.

———. "Etnohrafichno-statystychnyi hurtok (do 100-richchia vid pochatku ioho diial'nosty)." *Narodna tvorchist' ta etnohrafiia* 6 (1983): 45.

———, comp. *Zarubizhne frankoznavstvo: bibliohrafichnyi pokazhchyk*. Lviv: L'vivs'ke viddilennia In-tu lit-ry im. T. H. Shevchenka Natsional'noi akademii nauk Ukrainy, 1997.

Motyl, Alexander J. *The Turn to the Right: The Ideological Origins and Development of Ukrainian Nationalism, 1919–1929*. New York: Distributed by Columbia University Press, 1980.

Mozer, Mikhael' [Michael Moser]. *Prychynky do istorii ukrains'koi movy*. Kharkiv: Kharkivs'ke istoryko-filolohichne tovarystvo, 2008.

Muck, Joseph. *Der Erdwachsbergbau in Borysław*. Berlin: Julius Springer, 1903.

Mudryi, Mar'ian. "Poniattia 'nasha zemlia' / 'nash krai' v ukrains'komu rusi Halychyny XIX–pochatku XX stolittia." In *Shliakhamy istorii: Naukovyi zbirnyk istorychnoho fakul'tetu LNU im. I. Franka; na poshanu profesora Kostiantyna Kondratiuka*, 160–77. Lviv: Piramida, 2004.

———. "Avstrorusynstvo v Halychyni: sproba okreslennia problemy." *Visnyk Lvivskoho universytetu, Seriia istorychna* 35–36 (2001): 571–604.

Muir, Frank. *An Irrelevant and Thoroughly Incomplete Social History of Almost Everything*. New York: Stein and Day, 1976.

Mundiak, M. M. "Opovidannia i povisti Ivana Franka z selians koho zhyttia iak tvory krytychnoho realizmu." In *Doslidzhennia tvorchosty Ivana Franka*, edited by I. Kryp iakevych, 108–18. Kyiv: Vyd-vo Akademii nauk URSR, 1956.

Mundiak, M. N. "Rasskazy i povesti Iv. Franko iz krest ianskoi zhizni kak proizvedeniia kriticheskogo realizma." Candidate of Philological Sciences dissertation, Kyiv, 1954.

Muszynka, Mykoła. "Towarzystwo Naukowe im. Szewczenki i jego rola w narodowym odrodzeniu Ukraińców na terenie Galicji." In *Galicja i jej dziedzictwo*, vol. 3, 70.

Mykhailo Drahomanov: Dokumenty i materialy, 1841–1994, compiled by Halyna Bolotova et al. Lviv: [In-t ukrains koi arkheohrafii ta dzhereloznavstva im. M. S. Hrushevs koho], 2001.

Mykytiuk, Volodymyr. *Ivan Franko ta Omelian Ohonovs kyi: movchannia i dialoh*. Lviv: Vyd-vo L vivs koho universytetu, 2000.

N. B. "Pisn' (na temu 'Was ist des Teutschen Vaterland?')." *Słowianin, Dwotygodnik Polityczny* 1, no. 11 (1 June 1869): 175–76.

Nahirnyi, Vasyl'. "Z moikh spomyniv." In *Levy—istoriia rodyny: Statti, spohady, naukovi rozvidky, arkhivni materialy*. Lviv: Skifiia, 2000.

Nairn, Tom. "The Curse of Rurality: Limits of Modernization Theory." In *The State of the Nation: Ernest Gellner and the Theory of Nationalism*, edited by John A. Hall, 107–34. Cambridge: Cambridge University Press, 1998.

Najdus, Walentyna. "Początki socjalistycznego ruchu robotniczego w Galicji (lata siedemdziesiąte–osiemdziesiąte XIX w.)." *Z pola walki* 3 (1960).

———. *Polska Partia Socjalno-Demokratyczna Galicji i Sląska, 1890–1919*. Warsaw: Państwowe Wydawn. Naukowe, 1983.

Nakonechnyi, Ievhen. *Ukradene im ia: Chomu rusyny staly ukraintsiamy*. Lviv: L vivs ka naukova biblioteka im. V. Stefanyka NAN Ukrainy, 2001.

Nalyvaiko, D. S. "'Boryslav smiietsia' Ivana Franka v porivnial no-typolohichnomu aspekti." In *Ivan Franko—maister slova i doslidnyk literatury (do 125-richchia narodzhennia)*, edited by M. T. Iatsenko, 332–62. Kyiv: Naukova dumka, 1981.

Namowicz, Tadeusz. "Galizien nach 1772: Zur Enstehung einer literarischen Provinz." In *Galizien als Gemeinsame Literaturlandschaft. Beiträge des 2. Innsbrucker Symposiums Polnischer und Österreichischer Literaturwissenschaftler*, edited by Friedrun Rinner, Klaus Zerinschek. Innsbruck, 1988.

Navrotskyi, Volodymyr. *Tvory: Vydanie posmertne z portretom i zhytiepysom*. Zakhodom *"Etnohrafichno-statystychnoho kruzhka,"* vol. 1, 3–27. Lviv, 1885.

Nawratil, Arnulf. *Bericht der k.k. Gewerbe-Inspektoren über ihre Amtsthätigheit im Jahre 1885*. Vienna, 1886.

Nazaruk, Osyp. *Halychyna i Velyka Ukraina: Traktat prysviachenyi ukrains kym zhinkam i viis kovym*. Lviv, 1936.

Nechytaliuk, M. F. "Epistoliarna publitsystyka (Lysty Ivana Beleia do Oleksandra Barvins koho)." In *Zbirnyk prats' Naukovo-doslidnoho tsentru periodyky*, edited by M. M. Romaniuk et al. 2nd ed. Lviv: Lvivska naukova biblioteka im. V. Stefanyka NAN Ukrainy, 1995.

Nehrebets'kyi, Ivan. "Do rodovodu Ivana Franka." *LNV* 90, bks. 7–8 (1926): 233.

Nekanda-Trepka, Walerian. *Liber generationis Plebanorum.* 2nd ed. Wroclaw: Ossolineum, 1995.

Nie-Eol [Edward Przewóski]. "Iwan Franko." *Przegląd Tygodniowy,* 27 November / 7 December 1894, 567–68.

Noll, William [Vil'iam Noll]. *Transformatsiia hromadians'koho suspil'stva: Usna istoriia ukrains'koi selians'koi kultury 1920–30 rokiv.* Kyiv: Tsentr doslidzhen usnoi istorii ta kul'tury Rodovid, 1999.

———. "The Social Role and Economic Status of Blind Peasant Minstrels in Ukraine." *Harvard Ukrainian Studies* 27, nos. 1–2 (June 1993).

Nomys, Matvii, comp. *Ukrains'ki prykazky, prysliv'ia y take ynshe: zbirnyky O. V. Markovycha y druhykh.* St. Petersburg: V drukarniakh Tyblena i komp. I. Kulisha, 1864.

Nossig, Alfred. "Proba rozwiązania kwestji żydowskiej." *Przegląd Społeczny. Pismo naukowe i literackie* 2 (1887).

Odovets', Kost'. "Osvita na zakhidno-pivdennii Ukraini." *Zoria,* 8 / 20 August 1887, 259–62.

Ohloblyn, Oleksandr. *Liudy staroi Ukrainy.* Munich: Dniprova khvylia, 1959.

Ohonovskii [Ohonovs'kyi], Omelian. *Istoriia literatury ruskoi,* 3 vols. Lviv: Tovarystvo im. Shevchenka, 1887–1893.

Oleh [Volodymyr Barvins'kyi]. "Ohliad slovesnoi pratsi avstriis'kykh Rusyniv v rotsi 1882." *Dilo,* 8 / 20 January 1883, 1–2.

Olesnyts'kyi, Ievhen. *Storinky z moho zhyttia,* vol. 1: *1860–1890.* Lviv: Dilo, 1935.

———. *Storinky z moho zhyttia,* vol. 2: *1890–1897.* Lviv: Dilo, 1935.

Orłowski, Hubert. *"Polnische Wirtschaft": Nowoczesny niemiecki dyskurs o Polsce.* Olsztyn: Borussia, 1998.

———. *Z modernizacją w tle: Wokół rodowodu nowoczesnych niemieckich wyobrażeń o Polsce i o Polakach.* Poznań: Poznańskie Tow. Przyjaciół Nauk., 2002.

Orzechowski, Konrad Oksza. *Przewodnik statystyczno topograficzny i Skorowidz obejmujący wszystkie miejscowości przysiołkami w Królewstwie Galicyi W. X. Krakowskiem i X. Bukowinie, według najświetższych skazówek urzędowych.* Lviv, 1872.

Ossowski, Stanisław. *O ojczyźnie i narodzie.* Warsaw: Państwowe Wydawn. Naukowe, 1984.

Österreichische Statistik, vol. 61, bk. 11. Vienna, 1904.

Osterrieder, Markus. "Von der Sakralgemeinschaft zur Modernen Nation. Die Entstehung eines Nationalbewusstsein unter Russen, Ukrainern und Weissruthenen im Lichte der Thesen Benedict Anderson." In *Formen der nationalen Bewusstsein im Lichte zeitgenössischer Nationalismustheorien,* edited by Eva Schmidt-Hartmann. Munich: Oldenbourg, 1994.

Otwinowska, Barbara. "Geniusz." In *Słownik literatury polskiego oświecenia,* edited by Teresa Kostkiewiczowa, 139. Wroclaw, 2002.

Pankevych, Ivan. "Shche raz pro pytannia rishalnoho vplyvu na kharakter Franka v 1874–6 rokakh." *Krakivski visti,* 24 May 1943.

Parkhomenko, M. M. "Ivan Franko—student Lvivs´koho universytetu." *Ivan Franko: Statti i materialy* 5 (1956): 181–90.

Partner, Nancy F. "Historicity in an Age of Reality-Fictions." In *A New Philosophy of History*, edited by Frank Ankersmith and Hans Kellner. London: Reaktion Books, 1995.

Pascal, Roy. "The Frankfurt Parliament, 1848, and the Drang nach Osten." *Journal of Modern History* 18, no. 2 (June 1946): 118–20.

Pashuk, Volodymyr. *Zarobitchany Pravoberezhnoi Ukrainy: druha polovyna XIX st.* Lviv: Instytut ukrainoznavstva im. I. Kryp´iakevycha NAN Ukrainy, 2001.

Pastushchin, V. Iu. "Byt rabochikh Borislavskogo neftianogo raiona (1915–1953)," Candidate of Historical Sciences dissertation, Kyiv, 1954.

Pastuszka, Stefan Józefa, ed. *Szkice programowe Bolesława Wysłoucha.* Lublin: Wydawn. Lubelskie, 1981.

Paul, Johannes. *Ernst Moritz Arndt: "Das ganze Teutschland soll es sein!"* Göttingen: Musterschmidt, 1971.

Pavlenko, Hryhorii. "Ivan Franko i tsars´ka tsenzura (90-i rr. XIX st.)." *Ivan Franko: Statti i materialy* 26 (1976): 23–30.

Pavliuk, S. *Narodna ahrotekhnika ukraintsiv Karpat druhoi polovyny XIX–pochatku XX st. (Istoryko-etnohrafichne doslidzhennia).* Kyiv: Naukova dumka, 1986.

———. *Tradytsiine khliborobstvo: ahrotekhnichnyi aspekt.* Kyiv: Naukova dumka, 1991.

Pavlyk, Mykhailo. *Perepyska Mykhaila Drahomanova z Mykhailom Pavlykom (1876–1895).* Chernivtsi: Tovarystvo Rus´ka Rada, n.d.

———. *Pro rusko-ukrains´ki narodni chytalni.* Lviv, 1887.

———. "Iz perepysky M. Drahomanova, III: Lysty M. Drahomanova do Oleksandra Borkovs´koho, redaktora 'Zori.' (1888–1889)." *Zhytie i slovo* 3, no. 6 (December 1896): 454.

———. "Iz perepysky M. Drahomanova z D-rom Omelianom Ohonovs´kym." *Zhytie i slovo* (May–June 1897).

———. "Khto sprychynyv areshtuvannia Franka i tovaryshiv v 1877 r.?" *Zhyttia i znannia* (1936): 134–36.

———. *Propashchyi cholovik: Opovidannia, povisti, publitsystyka.* Lviv: Kameniar, 1983.

———. *Tvory.* Kyiv: Dnipro, 1985.

Pavlyshyn, Oleh Osypovych. "Formuvannia ta diial´nist´ predstavnytskykh orhaniv vlady ZUNR-ZOUNR (zhovten 1918–cherven 1919 r.)." Candidate of Historical Sciences dissertation, Lviv, 2000.

———. "Sotsial´no-politychnyi portret provodu Halychyny ta Bukovyny v revoliutsii 1918–1919 rr." *Ukraina moderna* 4–5 (2000–2001): 195.

Pawłowski, Krzysztof. "Narodziny nowoczesnego miasta." In *Sztuka 2 pol. XIX wieku*, compiled by Jan Białostocki et al. Warsaw: PWN, 1973.

Pękacz, Jolanta T. "Galician Society as a Cultural Public, 1771–1914." *Journal of Ukrainian Studies* 23, no. 2 (Winter 1998).

Pelech, Orest. "The State and the Ukrainian Triumvirate in the Russian Empire, 1831–47." In *Ukrainian Past, Ukrainian Present*, edited by Bohdan Krawchenko. New York: St. Martin's Press, 1993.

———. "The Cyril and Methodius Brotherhood Revisited." *Journal of Ukrainian Studies* 29, nos. 1–2 (Summer–Winter 2004): 335–44.

Pelens'kyi, Zenon. "Mizh dvoma konechnostiamy. Prychynok do sotsiolohii ukrains'koho natsional'no-vyzvol'noho revoliutsiinoho rukhu v Zakhidnii Ukraini mizh oboma svitovymy viinamy." In *Ievhen Konovalets' ta ioho doba*. Munich: Vydannia Fundatsii im. Ievhena Konoval'tsia, 1974.

Petit, Jacques-Guy. "Das Gefängnis." In *Orte des Alltags: Miniaturen aus der europäischen Kulturgeschichte*, edited by Heinz-Gerhard Haupt, 250–59. Munich: C. H. Beck, 1994.

Petrovsky-Shtern, Yohanan. "Reconceptualizing the Alien: Jews in Modern Ukrainian Thought." *Ab Imperio* 4 (2003): 519–80.

Phillips, Ursula. "The 'Jewish Question' in the Novels and Short Stories of Eliza Orzeszkowa." *East European Jewish Affairs* 25, no. 2 (Winter 1995): 69–90.

Piatka, Stefan. [Stefan Kovaliv]. "Produktsiia nafty (skel'noho oliiu) v Boryslavi." *LNV* 22 (1903).

Pickering, Mary. *Auguste Comte: An Intellectual Biography*, vol. 1, 691–710. 3 vols. Cambridge: Cambridge University Press, 1993–2009.

Pietrow-Ennker, Bianka. *Russlands "neue Menschen": die Entwicklung der Frauenbewegung von der Anfängen bis zur Oktoberrevolution*. Frankfurt: Campus, 1999.

Pietruszewicz, A. [A. Petrushevych]. *Słów kilka napisanych w obronie ruskiej narodowości*. Lviv, 1848.

Pilat, Tadeusz. "Najważniejsze wyniki spisu ludności Galicyi z 31. Grudnia 1880 według tymczasowych zestawień powiatowych." *Wiadomości statystyczne o stosunkach krajowych* 6, no. 2 (1881).

———. "Licytacye sądowe posiadłości włościańskich i małomiejskich w latach 1880–1883 włącznie." *Wiadomości statystyczne o stosunkach krajowych* 8, no. 3 (1884).

———. "Materiały statystyczne do sprawy propinacyjnej." In *Wiadomości statystyczne o stosunkach krajowych* 11, no. 2 (1888).

———. "Obszar, zabudowa i ludność miast większych w Galicji." *Wiadomości statystyczne o stosunkach krajowych* 11, no. 3 (1890).

———. "Wychodstwo z powiatów podolskich do Rosyi w roku 1892." *Wiadomości statystyczne o stosunkach krajowych* 13.

Pis'ma k M. Pogodinu iz slavianskikh zemel (1835–1861), vol. 3. Moscow, 1880.

Plekhanov, Georgii. *Sochineniia*. Moscow: Gosudarstvennoe izdatel'stvo, 1923.

Podraza, Antoni. "Uwarunkowania historyczne rozwoju kultury na ziemiach Dawnej Rzeczypospolitej." In Kowal-Kwiatkowska, *Miasto i kultura ludowa*.

Półćwiartek, Józef. "Miejsce religji w kształtowaniu oblicza etnicznego społeczności miast południowo-wschodnich obszarów Rzeczypospolitej w czasach nowożytnych." In Kowal-Kwiatkowska, *Miasto i kultura ludowa*.

Polianskii, Oleg. "Krest′ianskoe vosstanie 1846 g. v Galitsii." Candidate of Historical Sciences dissertation, Lviv, 1985.

Policastro, Pasquale. "Patria, patriotyzm i lokalizm we Włoszech: Treści społeczne i polityczne." In Bartmiński, *Pojęcie ojczyzny*, 230–31.

Polifem. "Obrazki z Borysławia." *Nafta* 16 (1895): 146.

Pollard, Sidney. *The Idea of Progress: History and Society*. Harmondsworth, UK: Penguin, 1971.

Pollo, Iwo. *Nauka i szkolnictwo wyższe w Polsce, a odzyskanie niepodległości*. Lublin: Wydawnictwa Uczelniane Politechniki Lubelskiej, 1990.

Polska Encyklopedia Szlachecka, vol. 7. Warsaw: Instytut Kultury Historycznej, 1937.

Porter, Brian. *When Nationalism Began to Hate: Imagining Modern Politics in Nineteenth-Century Poland*. New York: Oxford University Press, 2000.

Potoczny, Jerzy. *Oświata dorosłych i popularyzacja wiedzy w plebejskich środowiskach Galicji doby konstytucyjnej (1867–1918)*. Rzeszów: Wydawn. Wyższej Szkoły Pedagogicznej, 1998.

Preston, Paul. *Franco: A Biography*. New York: BasicBooks, 1994.

Pritsak, Omeljan, and John S. Reshetar. "Ukraine and the Dialectics of Nation-Building." In *From Kievan Rus′ to Modern Ukraine: Formation of the Ukrainian Nation*. Cambridge, MA: Ukrainian Studies Fund, Harvard University, 1984.

Prusin, Alexander Victor. *Nationalizing a Borderland: War, Ethnicity, and Anti-Jewish Violence in East Galicia, 1914–1920*. Tuscaloosa: University of Alabama Press, 2005.

Prysiazhniuk, Iu. *Ukrains′ke selianstvo XIX–XX st.: evoliutsiia, mental′nist′, tradytsionalizm; navchal′nyi posibnyk dlia istorychnykh fakul′tetiv*. Cherkasy: Vidlunnia-Plius, 2002.

———. "Mental′nist′ ukrains′koho selianstva v umovakh kapitalistychnoi transformatsii suspil′stva (druha polovyna XIX–pochatok XX st.)." *Ukrains′kyi istorychnyi zhurnal* 3 (1999).

Przegląd społeczny, 1886–1887, edited by Krzysztof Dunin-Wąsowicz and Jadwiga Czachowska. Wroclaw: Zakład im. Ossolińskich, 1955.

Przeworski, E. "Działa Apołona XXV. Ivan Franko." *Przegląd Tygodniowy* 49 (1884).

Pucek, Zbigniew. "Galicyjskie doświadczenie wielekulturowości a problem więzi społecznej." In *Galicja i jej dziedzictwo*, vol. 2.

Puliui, Ivan. *Zbirnyk prats′*. Kyiv: Vyd-vo Rada, 1996.

Pulzer, Peter. *The Rise of Political Anti-Semitism in Germany and Austria*. Rev. ed. London: Halban, 1988.

Pushak, Stefaniia. "Do pytannia pro spivpratsiu Ivana Franka z pol′s′kymy chasopysamy." In *Rocznik Europejskiego Kolegium Polskich i Ukraińskich Uniwersytetów*, 52–55. Lublin: Wydawn. Uniwersytetu Marii Curie-Skłodowskiej, 2003–.

Pushkareva, N. L. "Sem′ia, zhenshchina i seksual′naia etika v pravoslavii i katolitsizme: perspektivy sravnitel′nogo podkhoda." *Etnograficheskoe obozrenie* 3 (1995): 55–70.

Pushkin, A. S. *Sochineniia v trekh tomakh*. 3 vols. Moscow: Gosudarstvennoe izdatel'stvo khudozhestvennoi literatury, 1955.

Putek, Józef. *Mroki średniowiecza. Obyczaje. Przesady. Fanatyzm. Okrucieństwa i ucisk społeczny w Polsce*. Warsaw: Państ. Instytut Wydawniczy, 1985.

Pylypovych, Volodymyr, comp. *Za viru, narid i prava: Rus'ki Rady Nadsiannia 1848–1850 rr.* Przemysl: Peremys'kyi viddil OUP, 2005.

Radziejowski, Leon, ed. *Ojczyzna w poezyi polskiej: krótka antologia*. Kyiv, 1916.

Raeff, Marc. Afterword to *Culture, Nation, and Identity: The Ukrainian-Russian Encounter, 1600–1945*, edited by Andreas Kappeler, Zenon E. Kohut, Frank Sysyn et al. Edmonton: Canadian Institute of Ukrainian Studies, 2003.

Rasevych, Vasyl'. "Ukrains'ka natsional'no-demokratychna partiia (1899–1918)." Candidate of Historical Sciences dissertation, Lviv, 1996.

Redko, Iulian Kostiovych. *Slovnyk suchasnykh ukrains'kykh prizvyshch*, vol. 2. Lviv: TOV "Prostir-M." 2007.

Reitblat, A. I. *Kak Pushkin vyshel v genii: Istoriko-sotsiologicheskie ocherki o knizhnoi kul'ture Pushkinskoi epokhi*. Moscow: Novoe literaturnoe obozrenie, 2001.

Rieber, Alfred. "Struggle over the Borderlands." In *The Legacy of History in Russia and the New States of Eurasia*, edited by S. Frederick Starr. Armonk, NY: M. E. Sharpe, 1994.

Rintala, Marvin. "Generations in Politics." In *The Conflict of Generations in Modern History*, edited by Anthony Esler. Lexington, MA: D. C. Heath, 1974.

Röskau-Rydel, Isabel. "Galizien." In *Deutsche Geschichte im Osten Europas. Galizien. Bukowina. Moldau*, edited by Isabel Röskau-Rydel, 15–328. Berlin: Siedler, 1999.

Rothenberg, Gunther E. *The Army of Francis Joseph*. West Lafayette, IN: Purdue University Press, 1976.

Rozdolski [Rozdol's'kyi], Roman. *Die Bauernabgeordneten im konstituierenden österreichischen Reichstag, 1848–1849*. Vienna: Europaverlag, 1976.

———. *Engels and the "Nonhistoric" Peoples: The National Question in the Revolution of 1848*. Translated, edited, and with an introduction by John-Paul Himka. [Glasgow]: Critique Books, 1986.

Rudnytsky, Ivan L. "The Ukrainians in Galicia under Austrian Rule." In Markovits and Sysyn, *Nationbuilding and the Politics of Nationalism*.

———. *Essays in Modern Ukrainian History*. Edmonton: Canadian Institute of Ukrainian Studies, 1987.

Rudnyts'kyi, Mykhailo. *Pysmennyky zblyz'ka: spohady*. Lviv: Knyzhkovo-zhurnal'ne vyd-vo, 1958.

Rudzki, Jerzy. *Świętochowski*. Warsaw: Wiedza Powszechna, 1963.

Sahlins, Peter. *Boundaries: the Making of France and Spain in the Pyrenees*. Berkeley: University of California Press, 1989.

Sanborn, Joshua. "The Mobilization of 1914 and the Question of the Russian Nation: A Re-Examination." *Slavic Review* 59, no. 2 (Summer 2000): 267–89.

Sander, Martin. "Mehrdeutigkeit des Raum: die Einbruch der Modern als Problem der literarischen Topographie am Beispiel von Ivan Franko und Bruno Schulz." In Isaievych and Hrytsak, *Druhyi mizhnarodnyi konhres ukrainistiv*.

Saunders, David. "What Makes a Nation a Nation? Ukrainians since 1600." *Ethnic Groups* 10, nos. 1 –3 (1993).

———. "Russia's Ukrainian Policy (1847–1905): A Demographic Approach." *European History Quarterly* 25, no. 2 (1995).

Schmeding, Prof. Dr. F. *Die klassiche Bildung in der Gegenwart*. Berlin: Gebrüder Borntraeger, 1885.

Schreiner, A. *Boryslaw und seine Producte: Entdeckung und Entwicklung derselben*. Drohobych, 1886.

Scott, James C. *Weapons of the Weak: Everyday Forms of Peasant Resistance*. New Haven, CT: Yale University Press, 1994.

Serbyn, Roman. "Zhyttia i diial'nist' Serhiia Podolyns'koho: biohrafichnyi narys." In *Lysty ta dokumenty: Serhii Podolyns'kyi*, compiled by Roman Serbyn and Tetiana Sliudykova. Kyiv: TsDIAK, 2002.

Sereda, Ostap. "Shaping of a National Identity: Early Ukrainophiles in Austrian Eastern Galicia, 1860–1873." Ph.D. dissertation, Central European University, Budapest, 2003.

Seregny, Scott J. "Zemstvos, Peasants and Citizenship: The Russian Adult Education Movement and World War I." *Slavic Review* 59, no. 2 (Summer 2000): 290–315.

Serhii Podolyns'kyi: Lysty ta dokumenty. Compiled by Roman Serbyn and Tetiana Sliudykova. Kyiv: TsDIAK, 2002.

Ševčenko, Ihor. *Ukraine between East and West: Essays on Cultural History to the Early Eighteenth Century*. Edmonton: Canadian Institute of Ukrainian Studies, 1996.

Shakh, Stepan. *L'viv—misto moiei molodosty*. Munich: Khrystyians'kyi holos, 1955–56.

Shankovs'kyi, Lev. "Narys istorii Stryishchyny." In *Stryishchyna: istorychno-memuarnyi zbirnyk*, edited by Iryna Pelens'ka and Klymentii Babiak, vol. 1. New York: Komitet Stryishchyny, 1990.

Shapoval, Iu. H. *"Dilo." 1880–1939 rr.: postup ukrains'koi suspil'noi dumky*. Lviv: n.p., 1999.

Shchegolev, S. N. *Ukrainskoe dvizhenie, kak sovremennyi etap iuzhnorusskago separatizma*. Kyiv, 1912.

Shchurat, Stepan. "Pershi literaturni sproby Ivana Franka. Z dodatkom ioho lystiv do redaktsii zhurnalu *Druh* i Vasylia Davydiaka." In *Ivan Franko: Zbirnyk statei i materialiv*, vol. 2, 87–145. Lviv: Vyd-vo L'vivs'koho universytetu, 1949.

———. "Ivan Franko i Vasyl' Shchurat u literaturnykh zv'iazkakh ta lystuvanni." In *Doslidzhennia tvorchosti Ivana Franka*, edited by I. Kryp'iakevych. Kyiv: Vyd-vo Akademii nauk URSR, 1956–.

———. "Ivan Franko i rosiiski revoliutsiini narodnyky." *Doslidzhennia tvorchosti Ivana Franka*, vol. 2. Kyiv: Vyd-vo Akademii nauk URSR, 1959.

———. "Boryslavs'kyi tsykl khudozhnoi prozy Ivana Franka (Dzherela, problematyka, maisternist' i metod)." Doctor of Philological Studies dissertation, Lviv, 1970.

Shchurat, Vasyl'. "Ivan Franko i taini kruzhky v akadem. gimnazii." *Ukrains'ka shkola* 13–14 (1926).

——— [Wasyl Szczurat]. "Wtedy było to jeszcze mrzonką." *Chwila poranna,* 5 August 1937, 5.

Shevchenko, Taras. *Povne zibrannia tvoriv u shesty tomakh.* 6 vols. Kyiv: Vyd-vo Akademii nauk URSR, 1963–64.

———. *The Poetical Works of Taras Shevchenko: The Kobzar.* Translated by C. H. Andrusyshen and Watson Kirkconnell. Toronto: Published for the Ukrainian Canadian Committee by the University of Toronto Press, 1964.

———. *Povne zibrannia tvoriv u dvanadtsiaty tomakh.* 12 vols. Kyiv: Naukova dumka, 2001–.

Shevelov, George. S.v. "language." *Encyclopedia of Ukraine,* vol. 3, 44.

———. [Shevelov, Iurii]. *Ukrains'ka mova v pershii polovyni dvadtsiatoho stolittia (1900–1941): stan i status.* Translated by Oksana Solovei. [Munich]: Suchasnist, 1987.

Shoepflin, George. "The Political Traditions of Eastern Europe." *Daedalus: The Journal of the American Academy of Arts and Sciences* 19, no. 1 (Winter 1990): 55–90.

Shust, Ia. I. "Uchast' Ivana Franka u prohresyvnomu zhurnali 'Przegląd społeczny' (1886–1887)." In *Pytannia slov'ianoznavstva: Materialy pershoi i druhoi slavistychnykh konferentsii, do V Mizhnarodnoho z'izdu slavistiv.* [Lviv]: Vyd-vo L'vivs'koho universytetu, 1962.

Slezkine, Yuri. *The Jewish Century.* Princeton, NJ: Princeton University Press, 2004.

Śliwa, Leszek. "Gimnazja Galicyjskie w procesie kształtowania się inteligencji Polskiej." In *Galicja i jej dziedzictwo,* vol. 3, 163–64.

Śliwa, Michał. "Ruch Socjalistyczny w Galicji w historiografii polskiej." In *Rocznik Naukowo-Dydaktyczny WSP w Krakowie,* edited by Ludwik Mroczek, vol. 26, bk. 13: *Studia z dziejów Małopolski w XIX i XX wieku.* Cracow: Wydawn. Naukowe Wyższej Szkoły Pedagogicznej, 1992.

———. *Bolesław Limanowski: Człowiek i historia.* Cracow: Wydaw. WSP, 1994.

Słowacki, Juliusz. *Liryki i inne wiersze,* edited by J. Krzyżanowski. Wroclaw: Wydawn. Zakł. Narodowego im. Ossolińskich, 1959.

Słownik literatury polskiej XIX wieku, edited by Józef Bachórz and Alina Kowalczykowa. Wroclaw: Zakład Narod. im. Ossolińskich, 2002.

Slups'kyi, I., comp. *Ivan Franko: Dokumental'ni fotohrafii.* 2d exp. ed. Lviv: Kameniar, 1971.

Ślusarek, Krzysztof. "Włościańscy i niewłościańscy mieszkańcy wsi galicyjskiej w XIX wieku: wzajemne relacje." *Zeszyty Naukowe Uniwersytetu Jagiellońskiego. Prace Historyczne* 126 (1999): 117.

Smart, Barry. "Modernity, Postmodernity, and the Present." In *Theories of Modernity and Postmodernity,* edited by Bryan S. Turner. London: Sage Publications 1990.

Smith, Anthony. "Adrian Hastings on Nations and Nationalism." *Nations and Nationalism* 9, no. 1 (2003): 25–28.

Smith, S. A. "Citizenship and the Russian Nation during World War I: A Comment." *Slavic Review* 59, no. 2 (Summer 2000): 316–29.

Snyder, Timothy. *Nationalism, Marxism, and Modern Central Europe: A Biography of Kazimierz Kelles-Krauz, 1872–1905.* Cambridge, MA: Ukrainian Research Institute, Harvard University, 1997.

Sokil, Vasyl´, comp. *Narodni pisni z bat´kivshchyny Ivana Franka.* Lviv: Kameniar, 2003.

Śródka, Andrzej, and Paweł Szczawiński, eds. *Biogramy uczonych polskich,* pt. 1, *Nauki społeczne,* bk. 3: *P–Z.* Wrocław: Ossolineum, 1985.

Stadler, Karl R., ed. *Sozialistenprozesse: Politische Justiz in Österreich, 1870–1936.* Vienna: Europaverlag, 1986.

Stambrook, Fred. "The Golden Age of the Jews of Bukovina, 1880–1914." Working Paper 03-2, Center for Austrian Studies at the University of Minnesota, October 2003.

Stanzel, Franz K. *Europäer: Ein imagologischer Essay.* 2nd updated ed. Heidelberg: Universitätsverlag C. Winter, 1998.

Stauter-Halsted, Keely. *The Nation in the Village: The Genesis of Peasant National Identity in Austrian Poland, 1848–1914.* Ithaca, NY: Cornell University Press, 2001.

Steblii, F. I., O. A. Kupchyns´kyi, et al., comps. *"Rusalka Dnistrova": Dokumenty i materialy.* Kyiv: Naukova dumka, 1989.

Stefanyk, Vasyl´. *Vybrane.* Uzhhorod: Vyd-vo Karpaty, 1979.

Steiner, Herbert. "Die Wiener Hochverratsprozesse 1870." In Stadler, *Sozialistenprozesse,* 13–30.

Stepniak, M. "Ivan Franko ta B. Prus (Shche do istorii 'Boa konstriktor')." *Chervonyi shliakh* (1929): 174–86.

Stites, Richard. *The Women's Liberation Movement in Russia: Feminism, Nihilism, and Bolshevism, 1860–1930.* Princeton, NJ: Princeton University Press, 1978.

Stone, Norman. *Europe Transformed, 1878–1919.* Cambridge, MA: Harvard University Press, 1984.

Strong, Augustus Hopkins. *The Great Poets and Their Theology.* Philadelphia: American Baptist Publication Society, 1897.

Strumiński, Bohdan. "Stereotyp Polaka w przysłowiach ukraińskich." In *Narody i stereotypy,* edited by Teresa Walas. Cracow: Międzynarodowe Centrum Kultury, 1995.

Struve, Kai. "Gentry, Jews, and Peasants: Jews as Others in the Formation of the Modern Polish Nation in Rural Galicia during the Second Half of the Nineteenth Century." In *Creating the Other: Ethnic Conflict and Nationalism in Habsburg Central Europe,* edited by Nancy M. Wingfield. New York: Berghahn, 2003.

———. *Bauern und Nation in Galizien. Über Zugerhörigkeit und soziale Emanzipation im 19. Jahrhundert.* Göttingen: Vandenhoeck and Ruprecht, 2005.

Stryzhak, Oleksii S. "Franky (materialy do *Etymolohichnoho slovnyka etnonimiv Ukrainy*)." In *Aktual´ni pytannia antroponimiky: Zbirnyk materialiv naukovykh chytan´ pam'iati Iuliana Kostiantynovycha Red´ka,* edited by I. V. Yefymenko, 218–229. Kyiv: In-t ukrainskoi movy, 2005

Studyns'kyi, Kyrylo. "Ivan Franko i tovaryshi v sotsiialistychnim protsesi 1878." *Ukraina* 6 (1926): 56–114.

Sukhyi, Oleksii, comp. *Moskvofil'stvo: Dokumenty i materialy*. Lviv: Vyd-vo L'vivs'koho universytetu, 2001.

Sulimierski, Filip, Bronisław Chlebowski, and Władysław Walewski, eds. *Słownik geograficzny*. Warsaw: Druk. "Wieku"; nakł. Filipa Sulimierskiego i Władysława Walewskiego, 1880 ff.

Sunderland, Willard. "An Empire of Peasants: Empire-Building, Interethnic Interaction, and Ethnic Stereotyping in the Rural World of the Russian Empire, 1800–1850s." In *Imperial Russia: New Histories for the Empire*, edited by Jane Burbank and David L. Ransel. Bloomington: Indiana University Press, 1998.

Sverstiuk, Ivan. "Ivan Kotliarevs'kyi." *Suchasnist'* 5 (1972): 40.

Svientsits'kyi, I. "Deshcho pro nauku, literaturu i mystetstvo Halyts'koi Ukrainy za ostannikh 40 lit." *Dilo*, 14 January 1928, 15.

Svitlenko, S. I. *Narodnytstvo v Ukraini 60–80-kh rokiv XIX stolittia; Teoretychni problemy dzhereloznavstva ta istorii*. Dnipropetrovsk: Vyd-vo Navchal'na knyha, 1999.

Svoezhitevyi zapiski Bogdana Dieditskogo, pt. 1: *Gde-shcho do istorii samorozvytiia iazyka i azbuky Galitskoi Rusi*. Lviv, 1906.

Sylla, Richard, and Gianni Tonniolo. "Introduction: Patterns of European Industrialization during the Nineteenth Century." In *Patterns of European Industrialization: The Nineteenth Century*, edited by Richard Sylla and Gianni Tonniolo. New York: Routledge, 1991.

Syrota, Lilia. "Vid Frankovykh obraziv do obraziv Ivana Franka." *Ukraina: kul'turna spadshchyna, natsional'na svidomist', derzhavnist'* 9 (2001): 556–66.

Sysyn, Frank. "'Otchyzna' v ukrains'kii politychnii kul'turi pochatku XVIII st." *Ukraina moderna* 10 (2006): 7–19.

Szajnocha, Władysław. *Płody kopalne Galicyi, ich występowanie i zużytkowanie*, vol. 2. Lviv, 1894.

Szczepanowski, Stanisław. *Nędza Galicyi w cyfrach i program energicznego rozwoju gospodarstwa krajowego*. Lviv: Gubrynowicz i Schmidt, 1888.

Szmyd, Kazimierz. *Twórcy nauk o wychowaniu w środowisku akademickim Lwowa, 1860–1939*. Rzeszow: Wydawnictwo Uniwersytetu Rzeszowskiego, 2003.

Szocki, Józef. *Księgozbiory domowe w Galicji wschodniej (1772–1918)*. Cracow: Wydawnictwo Naukowe Akademii Pedagogicznej, 2001.

Szporluk, Roman. "The Ukraine and Russia." In *The Last Empire: Nationality and the Soviet Future*, edited by Robert Conquest. Stanford, CA: Hoover Institution Press, 1986.

———. *Communism and Nationalism: Karl Marx versus Friedrich List*. New York: Oxford University Press, 1988.

———. "In Search of the Drama of History: or, National Roads to Modernity." *East European Politics and Societies* 4, no. 1 (Winter 1990): 134–50.

———. "Ukraine: From an Imperial Periphery to a Sovereign State." *Daedalus: Journal of the American Academy of Arts and Sciences* 126, no. 3 (Summer 1997): 85–119.

Szul, Roman. "Perspektywy regionalizmu Galicyjskiego w Polsce na tle tendencji międzynarodowych." In *Galicja i jej dziedzictw*o, vol. 2, 86–88.

Tarnavs´kyi, Fylymon. *Spohady: Rodynna khronika Tarnavs´kykh iak prychynok do istorii tserkovnykh, sviashchenyts´kykh, pobutovykh, ekonomichnykh i politychnykh vidnosyn u Halychyni v druhii polovyni XIX storichchia i v pershii dekadi XX storichchia*, compiled and edited by Dr. Anatol´ Mariia Bazylevych and Roman Ivan Danylevych. Toronto: Dobra knyzhka, 1981.

Taylor, A. J. *Bismarck: The Man and the Statesman*. New York: Vintage, 1967.

Terlets´kyi, Ostap. *Halyts´ko-rus´ke pysmenstvo 1848–1865 rr. na tli tohochasnykh suspil´no-politychnykh zmahan´ halyts´ko-rus´koi inteligentsii*. Lviv: Vyd. red. Literaturno-naukovoho visnyka, 1903.

———. "Zhadka pro zhytie Volodymyra Navrotskoho." In *Tvory Volodymyra Navrotskoho vydane posmertne z portretom i zhytiepysom. Zakhodom Etnohrafychno-statystychnoho kruzhka*, vol. 1, xiv. Lviv, 1884.

Thomas, William I., and Florian Znaniecki. "A Polish Peasant Family." In *Peasants and Peasant Societies: Selected Readings*, edited by Theodor Shanin. Baltimore: Penguin, 1971.

Thomson, Francis J. *The Reception of Byzantine Culture in Medieval Russia*. Aldershot, UK: Ashgate, 1999.

Todorova, Maria. *Imagining the Balkans*. New York: Oxford University Press, 1997.

Tołstaja, Swietłana N. "Ojczyzna w ludowej tradycji słowianskiej." In Bartmiński, *Pojęcie ojczyzny*, 17–22.

Torzhestvennyi Literaturno-muzykal´nyi vecher, posviashchennyi pamiati I. G. Naumovicha v 100 letniuiu godovshchinu so dnia rozhdeniia 26.1.1826–26.1.1926. Programma. Lviv, 1926.

Trehubova, Antonina. "Deshcho z zhyttia Ol´hy Frankovoi." In *Za sto lit: Materiialy z hromads´koho i literaturnoho zhyttia Ukrainy XIX i pochatkiv XX stolittia*, bk. 5. Kyiv and Kharkiv: Derzhavne vydavnytstvo Ukrainy, 1930.

Treugutt, Stefan. "Geniusz." In *Słownik literatury polskiej XIX wieku*, 318–21.

Triinyk, I. I. *Slovnyk ukrains´kykh imen*. Kyiv: Vyd-vo "Dovira," 2005.

Trofymuk, Myroslav. "Natsional´na svidomist´ cherez pryzmu zhyttia i tvorchosti Andriia Chaikovs´koho." In Chaikovs´kyi, *Spohady*, vol. 3, 332–38.

Trush, Ivan. "Z moikh spomyniv pro Franka." *Dzvin* 3 (2003): 124

Trylovs´kyi, Kyrylo. *Z moho zhyttia*. Toronto: Takson, 1999.

Turii, Oleh, ed. *Holovna Rus´ka Rada (1848–1851): Protokoly zasidan´ i knyhy korespondentsii*. Lviv: In-t istorii tserkvy Ukrains´koho Katolyts´koho Universytetu, 2002.

Turii, O. Iu. "Hreko-katolyts´ka tserkva v suspil´no-politychnomu zhytti Halychyny, 1848–1867." Candidate of Historical Sciences dissertation, Lviv, 1994.

Tvardovs'kyi, Omelian. "Nahuievychi—selo Ivana Franka." In *Drohobychchyna—zemlia Ivana Franka*, vol. 1, edited by Luka Lutsiv. Vol. 25 of *Ukrains'kyi arkhiv*. New York: Naukove tovarystvo im. Shevchenka, 1973.

———. "Vasyl' Franko rozpovidaie pro svoho stryika Ivana Franka." In *Drohobychchyna—zemlia Ivana Franka*, vol. 2, edited by Luka Lutsiv. Vol. 32 of *Ukrains'kyi arkhiv*. New York: Naukove tovarystvo im. Shevchenka, 1978.

Tykholoz, Bohdan. "Ivan Franko-filosof (Do kharakterystyky styliu ta evoliutsii myslennia)." *Suchasnist'* 12 (2002): 115.

Tyrowicz, Marian. "Kostecki, Platon." *Polski Słownik Biograficzny*, vol. 14, 240-41. Cracow: Polska Akademia Umiejętności, 1968-69.

The Ukrainian Poets, 1189–1962. Translated by C. H. Andrusyshen and Watson Kirkconnell. Toronto: Published for the Ukrainian Canadian Committee by University of Toronto Press, 1963.

"Ukrains'ki pisni-himny: Istoriia ta rodovid." *Ternopil'* 1 (1992): 24.

Unowsky, Daniel. "'Our Gratitude Has No Limit': Polish Nationalism, Dynastic Patriotism, and the 1880 Imperial Inspection tour of Galicia." *Austrian History Yearbook* 34 (2003): 148-49.

Ustrzycki, Mirosław. *Ziemianie Polscy na Kresach 1864–1914: Świat wartości i postaw*. Cracow: Wydawnictwo Arcana, 2006.

Ustyianovych, K. N. *Pys'ma*, vol. 1: *Poemy ystorychni*. Lviv: Tovarystvo im. Shevchenka, 1875.

Ustyianovych, Kornylo. *M. F. Raevskii i rossiiskii panslavizm. Spomynky z perezhytoho i peredumanoho*. Lviv: Nakladom K. Bednarskoho, 1884.

Vakar, Nicholas. *Belorussia: The Making of a Nation: A Case Study*. Cambridge, MA: Harvard University Press, 1956.

Vavrik, V. R. *Narodnaia slovesnost' i seliane-poety*. Lviv, 1929.

Velykyi Zhovten' i hromadianska viina na Ukraini: entsyklopedychnyi dovidnyk, edited by I. F. Kuras et al. Kyiv: Holov. red URE, 1987.

Verves, H. D. "Ivan Franko u robitnychii hazeti 'Praca.'" In *Ivan Franko iak istoryk*, edited by I. O. Hurzhii, M. Kalenchenko et al. Kyiv: Vyd-vo Akademii nauk URSR, 1956.

Vinograd, Yeshayahu. *Otsar ha-sefer ha-Ivri: reshimat ha-sefarim she-nidpesu be-ot Ivrit me-reshit ha-defus ha-Ivri bi-shenat 229 (1469) ad shenat 623 (1863)*. 2 vols. Jerusalem: ha-Makhon le-bibliyografyah memuḥshevet, 1993.

Vitchyzna: Zbirnyk vyslovliuvan' diiachiv rosiis'koi ta ukrains'koi kul'tury pro Vitchyznu. Kyiv: Derzh. vyd-vo khudozh. lit-ry, 1953.

Vityk, Semen. "V chasy Ivana Franka." *Kultura i pobut*, 16 May 1926, 3.

Volchko-Kul'chyts'kyi, Ivan. *Istoriia sela Kul'chyts' i sela Draho-Sasiv (700-littia sela i 1000-littia rodu)*. Drohobych: Vydavnycha firma Vidrodzhennia, 1995.

von Hagen, Mark. "The Dilemmas of Ukrainian Independence and Statehood, 1917–1921." *Harriman Institute Forum* 7, no. 5 (January 1994): 7–11.

von Reden, Alexander Sixtus, and Josef Schweikhard. *Eros unter Doppeladler. Eine Sittengeschichte Altösterreichs*. Vienna: Ueberreuter, 1993.

von Smolka, Stanisław [Stanislaus]. *Die Reussische Welt: Historisch-politische Studien*. Vienna: Zentral-verlagsbüro des Obersten polnischen Nationalkomittees, 1916.

Vozniak, Mykhailo. "Zhurnal´ni plany Franka v rr. 1884–1886." *Ukraina* 3 (1927): 30.

———. *Iv. Belei i Ol. Konys´kyi: Do zv´iazkiv Halychyny z Naddniprianshchynoiu v 80 rr. XIX v.* Lviv, 1928.

———, ed. *Materialy dlia kul´turnoi i hromads´koi istorii Zakhidnoi Ukrainy*, vol. 1: *Lystuvannia I. Franka i M. Drahomanova*. Kyiv: Drukarnia Vseukrains´koi Akademii nauk, 1928. [=*Vseukrains´ka Akademiia nauk. Komisiia Zakhidnoi Ukrainy. Zbirnyk istorychno-filolohichnoho viddilu* 52.]

———. *Iak diishlo do pershoho zhinochoho almanakha*. Lviv, 1937.

———. "Iz strakhu pered zhyttievoiu nezabezpechenistiu. Koly rozkhodylys´ Ivan Franko i Ol´ha Bilyns´ka." *Nazustrich* 11 (83), 1 June 1937.

———. "Nimets´ka dopovid´ Franka dlia shveda pro Ukrainu." *Lvivs´ki visti*, 18 June 1942.

———. "Franko iak doslidnyk i istoryk ukrains´koi literatury." *Ukrains´ka literatura* 3 (1945).

———. "Lysty Ivana Franka do Klymentyny Popovych." In Ivan Franko, *Statti i materialy* 3 (1952): 54–66.

Vushko, Iryna. "Evoliutsiia chytats´kykh interesiv l´viv'ian u druhii polovyni XIX st. Za danymy pro diial´nist´ Biblioteky Ossolins´kykh." *Ukraina moderna* 8 (2003): 127–41.

Walicki, Andrzej. *Poland between East and West: The Controversies over Self-Definition and Modernization in Partitioned Poland*. Cambridge, MA: Harvard Ukrainian Research Institute, 1994.

Wandruszka, Adam, and Peter Urbanitsch, eds. *Die Habsburgermonarchie 1848–1918*, vol. 3: *Die Völker des Reiches*, pt. 1. Vienna: Verlag der Osterreichischen Akademie der Wissenschaften, 1980.

Wapiński, Roman. *Polska i małe ojczyzny Polaków: Z dziejów kształtowania się świadomości narodowej w XIX i XX wieku po wybuchu II wojny światowej*. Wrocław: Zakład Narodowy im. Ossolińskich, 1994.

Weeks, Theodore R. "Polish 'Progressive Anti-Semitism,' 1905–1914." *East European Jewish Affairs* 25, no. 2 (1995): 49–67.

Wehler, Hans-Ulrich. *Die Gegenwart als Geschichte. Essays*. Munich: C. H. Beck, 1995.

Weintraub, Wiktor. "Poeta." In *Słownik literatury polskiej XIX wieku*, 711–15.

Wendland, Anna. *Die Russophilen in Galizien:Ukrainische Konservative zwischen Österreich und Russland, 1848–1915*. Vienna: Verlag der Österreichischen Akademie der Wissenschaften, 2001.

Wiegandt, Ewa. *Austria Felix, czyli o micie Galicji w polskiej prozie współczesnej*. Poznań: UAM, 1998.

Wilcher, Asher. "Ivan Franko and Theodor Herzl: To the Genesis of Franko's 'Mojsej.'" *Harvard Ukrainian Studies* 6 (1982): 233–43.

Willey, Basil. *Nineteenth Century Studies: Coleridge to Matthew Arnold.* New York: Columbia University Press, 1964.

Windakiewicz, E. *Das Erdöl und Erdwachs in Galizien.* Vienna, 1875.

Wisnowski, S. "Listy Amerykanina z Galicyi." *Gazeta Polska,* 28 December 1877.

Wistrich, Robert S. "The Jews and Nationality Conflicts in the Habsburg Lands." *Nationalities Papers* 22, no. 1 (Spring 1994).

Wolff, Larry. "Inventing Galicia: Messianic Josephinism and the Recasting of Partitioned Poland." *Slavic Review* 63, no. 4 (Winter 2004): 818–40.

Worobec, Christine D. "Temptress or Virgin? The Precarious Sexual Position of Women in Postemancipation Ukrainian Peasant Society." *Slavic Review* 49, no. 2 (Summer 1990): 227–28.

Wróbel, Piotr. "The Jews of Galicia under Austrian-Polish Rule, 1869–1918." *Austrian History Yearbook* 25 (1994): 97–138.

Wyka, K. "Warunki i przebieg rozwoju kultury polskiej w drugiej połowie XIX w." In *Historia Polski.* Edited by Żanna Kormanowa and Irena Pietrzak-Pawłowska, vol. 3, pt. 1: *1850 / 1864–1900.* Warsaw: Polska Akademia Nauk, Instytut Historii, 1967.

Wyka, Kazimierz. "Gruszecki, Artur." *Polski Słownik Biograficzny,* vol. 9, 59–61. Cracow: Polska Akademia Umiejętności, 1960–61.

Wynn, Charters. *Workers, Strikes, and Pogroms: The Donbass-Dnepr Bend in Late Imperial Russia, 1870–1905.* Princeton, NJ: Princeton University Press, 1992.

Z. B. W. "M. Dragomanow, Nakanunie nowych smut (Genewa, 1886)." [Review.] *Przegląd społeczny* 2 (1887): 155.

Zabushko, Oksana. *Filosofii ukrainskoji idei ta ievropeiskyi kontekst.* 2nd ed. Kyiv: Fakt, 2006.

Zakhara, Ihor. "Pozytyvizm u sotsiialnii filosofii Ivana Franka." In *Ivan Franko—pysmennyk, myslytel, hromadianyn.* Materialy Mizhnarodnoi naukovoi konferentsii. Lviv, 1998.

Zaks, Zofia. "Walka dyplomatyczna o naftę wschodniogalicyjską, 1918–1923." *Z dziejów stosunków polsko-radzieckich: Studia i materialy* 4 (1969): 37–60.

Zamorski, Krzysztof. "Zasadnicze linie przemian demograficznych Galicji w drugiej połowie XIX wieku i na początku XX wieku." In *Galicja i jej dziedzictwo,* vol. 2, 2.

Zawadski, Władysław. *Pamiętniki życia literackiego w Galicji,* edited by Antoni Knot. Cracow: Wydawn. Literackie, 1961.

Zayarnyuk, Andriy. "Framing the Ukrainian peasantry in Habsburg Galicia: 1846–1914 (with a focus on the Sambir area)." Ph.D. dissertation, University of Alberta, 2003.

———. "Ruski patrioty v Halytskomu seli 1860–1870-ykh rokiv: sviatoiurtsi, obriadovtsi, paternalisty i populisty (Na prykladi Sambirskoi okolytsi)." *Ukraina moderna* 8 (2003): 113.

———. "The Dobrivliany Affair of 1886: A Nodal Approach to Consciousness Formation." Accessed at http://www.univie.ac.at/spacesofidentity/_Vol_4_3/_HTML/Zayarnyuk.html.

Zborowski, Mark, and Elizabeth Herzog. *Life Is with People: The Culture of the Shtetl.* New York: Schocken, 1962.

Żechowski, Zbigniew A. *Socjologia Bolesława Limanowskiego.* Poznan: UAM, 1964.

Zhdanovych, O. "Velykyi i blyz´kyi." In *Nezhasnyi ohon´ viry: zbirnyk na poshanu polkovnyka Andriia Mel´nyka, holovy Provodu Ukrains´kykh Nationalistiv.* Paris, 1974.

Zhuk, Sergei I. *Russia's Lost Reformation: Peasants, Millennialism, and Radical Sects in Southern Russia and Ukraine, 1830-1917.* Washington, DC: Woodrow Wilson Center Press; Baltimore: Johns Hopkins University Press, 2004.

Zhytets´kyi, Ihnat. "Kyivska Hromada za 60-tykh rokiv." *Ukraina* 1 (1928): 95-96.

Zięba, Andrzej A. "'Gente Rutheni, Natione Poloni': Z problematyki kształtowania się Ukraińskiej świadomości narodowej w Galicji." In *Prace Komisji Wschodnioeuropejskiej Polskiej Akademji Umiejętności,* vol. 2, 61-77. Cracow: Nakł. Polskiej Akademii Umiejętności, 1995.

Zientara, Benedykt. *Świt narodów europejskich: Powstawanie świadomości narodowej na obszarze Europy postkarolińskiej.* Warsaw: Państ. Instytut Wydawniczy, 1985.

Zv'iazky Ivana Franka z chekhamy ta slovakamy, compiled by M. Molnar and M. Mundiak. Bratislava: Slovats´ke vyd-vo khudozh. lit-ry, 1957.

Zweig, Stefan. *The World of Yesterday: An Autobiography.* New York: Viking, 1943.

Żychowski, Marian. *Bolesław Limanowski, 1835-1935.* Warsaw: Książka i Wiedza, 1971.

Zyga, Aleksander. "Monat, Henryk." In *Polski Słownik Biograficzny,* vol. 21. Cracow: Polska Akademia Umiejętności, 1976.

Zyga, Aleksander. "Pisarstwo polskie o początkach przemysłu naftowego." In *Krosno: studia z dziejów i regionu,* vol. 3, edited by Stanisław Cynarski. Rzeszów: Krajowa Agencja Wydawnicza, 1995.

Index

Names

Locations

Other

CPSIA information can be obtained
at www.ICGtesting.com
Printed in the USA
BVHW040849121119
563577BV00004B/121/P

9 781618 119681